THE CHICANO HERITAGE

This is a volume in the Arno Press collection

THE CHICANO HERITAGE

Advisory Editor
Carlos E. Cortés

Editorial Board
Rodolfo Acuña
Juan Gómez-Quiñones
George F. Rivera, Jr.

*See last pages of this volume
for a complete list of titles.*

AN ECONOMIC AND SOCIAL HISTORY OF MEXICAN CALIFORNIA 1822-1846

Volume I:
Chiefly Economic

Jessie Davies Francis

ARNO PRESS
A New York Times Company
New York — 1976

Editorial Supervision: LESLIE PARR

First publication in book form,
1976 by Arno Press Inc.

THE CHICANO HERITAGE
ISBN for complete set: 0-405-09480-9
See last pages of this volume for titles.

Manufactured in the United States of America

Publisher's Note: This book has been reprinted
from the best available copy. Page 270 was
missing from the original book and is not
included here.

Library of Congress Cataloging in Publication Data

Francis, Jessie Hughes Davies.
    An economic and social history of Mexican California, 1822-1846 : volume I, Chiefly economic.

    (The Chicano heritage)
    Originally presented as the author's thesis, University of California, 1935.
    1.   Mexican Americans--California--History. 2. California--History--To 1846. 3. California--Economic conditions. I. Title. II. Series.
F870.M5F72   1976   309.1'794'03   76-1238
ISBN 0-405-09502-3

AN ECONOMIC AND SOCIAL HISTORY OF MEXICAN CALIFORNIA
(1822—1846)

Volume I: Chiefly Economic

Jessie Davies Francis

ACKNOWLEDGMENTS

Words are inadequate means to acknowledge debts of the spirit. Yet silence would be a still poorer return. I therefore take this opportunity to express my sincere gratitude to all those whose inspiration and encouragement have helped to make this thesis possible. It would be a pleasure to call by name many who have had part in shaping my tastes and guiding my energies. There is room, however, to mention only those whose influence has borne most directly on the present undertaking.

Professor Herbert Eugene Bolton of the University of California is the dean of that group. His instruction, encouragement and friendly advice have been liberally available since I took my first course with him a dozen years ago. He, more than any other, has pushed out my historical horizon, so that eras and localities studied for their own sakes have fallen into suitable perspective and proportion with relation to the whole historical panorama.

Professor Owen C. Coy of the University of Southern California and the California State Historical Association is another tutor and friend of as long standing. To my association with him I owe much of my research technique as well as a grounding in fields of California history into which I probably would not have delved independently.

Although personal contacts with Professors Charles Edward Chapman and Herbert Ingram Priestley of the University of California have been less close, I have been continuously a beneficiary of their scholarship, through their books. I am glad to express to them here my appreciation of blessings which they have unknowingly showered on me for a decade and more.

Most deeply and personally realized is my debt to my father, to whose example and precept I owe impulses toward discovery and ideals of intellectual integrity; and to my husband, whose generous and happy comradeship have smoothed all the way.

Jessie Davies Francis
Jessie Davies Francis

AN ECONOMIC AND SOCIAL HISTORY OF MEXICAN CALIFORNIA

(1822--1846)

Volume I: Chiefly Economic

CONTENTS

Acknowledgments

Frontispiece: California, a Territory and Department
    of Mexico, 1822--1848 (Map)

Foreword

Synopsis of Chapters

List of Tables

Notice to Readers

Chapter I: Mexico, a Foster-Mother with Good Intentions

Chapter II: "God, Give Us Men!"

Chapter III: " -- and Money!"

Chapter IV: Arms and Alarms

Chapter V: "Fomento de California"

Bibliography (with Annotations on the Unpublished Sources
    and on Individual Periodical Items)

Prospectus: An Economic and Social History of Mexican
    California (1822--1846), Volume II: Chiefly Social

AN ECONOMIC AND SOCIAL HISTORY OF MEXICAN CALIFORNIA
(1822--1846)

Volume 1: Chiefly Economic

SYNOPSIS OF CHAPTERS

                pp.

Chapter I (Introductory): Mexico, a Foster-Mother with Good Intentions..........

1. The Birth and Heritage of a Nation. 1-- 9
2. The Good Intentions............... 9-- 22
3. The Junta de Fomento de Californias 23-- 51
4. Mexico's Handicaps................ 52-- 66
5. Mexico's Failures and California's Disillusionment................ 66-- 77

Chapter II: "God, Give Us Men!"

6. Off to a Poor Start............... 78-- 83
7. Mexico Takes Over................. 83-- 87
8. Convicts, Vagabonds and Foundlings. 87-- 90
9. Vain Protests and Antagonisms..... 91-- 94
10. Remarks in Extenuation............ 95-- 97
11. The Island Domain................. 97-- 98
12. The Northern Frontier............. 98--103

AN ECONOMIC AND SOCIAL HISTORY OF MEXICAN CALIFORNIA

(1822--1846)

Volume I: Chiefly Economic

SYNOPSIS OF CHAPTERS (Continued)

Pp.

13. The Great Colony................. 104--119
14. Progress on the Northern Frontier. 119--125
15. Foreign Colonization............. 125--140
16. Ten Thousand Irishmen............ 141--149
17. Wanted: Assorted Foreigners!..... 149--152
18. Peopling California with Cali-
    fornians..................... 152--166
19. The Forgotten Men................ 166--168

Chapter III: " -- and Money!"

20. From Royal Wardship to Republican
    Responsibilities.............. 169--181
21. The Tyranny of Taxes............. 181--207
22. Public Finance in the Pueblos.... 207--208
23. Mother Church's Share............ 208--212
24. Tidying up the Treasury Department 213--219
25. Untangling the Customs Administra-
    tion......................... 220--232
26. Foreign Trade Regulations........ 232--264

AN ECONOMIC AND SOCIAL HISTORY OF MEXICAN CALIFORNIA

(1822--1846)

Volume I: Chiefly Economic

SYNOPSIS OF CHAPTERS (Continued)

		Pp.
27.	Laws without Teeth...................	265--281
28.	Los Contrabandistas................	281--289
29.	Starting with Empty Pockets.........	289--294
30.	The Territorial Purse................	294--311
31.	Making Ends Meet....................	311--325
32.	The Californios Had All the Answers..	325--336

Chapter IV: Arms and Alarms

		Pp.
33.	Cholos.............................	337--344
34.	"Starvation and Nakedness"...........	344--354
35.	Breakdown of the Presidial Organization...........................	354--364
36.	Decline of Buildings and Armaments...	364--371
37.	Aspirations and Actualities..........	371--377
38.	The Missions and the Military........	378--380
39.	National Ranches....................	381--385
40.	The Sons of the Country and the Presidios........................	385--389
41.	The Californians Favored a Big Army..	389--403

AN ECONOMIC AND SOCIAL HISTORY OF MEXICAN CALIFORNIA
(1822--1846)
Volume I: Chiefly Economic

SYNOPSIS OF CHAPTERS (Continued)

		Pp.
42.	Citizen Soldiers......................	404--410
43.	Citizen Subsidization of the Army.....	411--415
44.	A Californian Navy -- Envisioned......	416--419
45.	"Indians!".............................	419--438
46.	The Vecinos as Indian Campaigners.....	438--442
47.	Projects and Problems of Indian Defense..............................	442--447

Chapter V: Fomento de California

48.	"Paralysis" under Spain and Mexico....	448--457
49.	The Dons were Promoters...............	458--461
50.	The Californians Lacked Land!.........	462--478
51.	Land, Ho!.............................	478--483
52.	Real Estates that were not Real Estates...............................	483--493
53.	The Clutch of the Dead Hand...........	493--501
54.	"Falta de Brazos, Falta de Manos!"....	501--505
55.	Slavery...............................	505--509

AN ECONOMIC AND SOCIAL HISTORY OF MEXICAN CALIFORNIA
(1822--1846)
Volume I: Chiefly Economic

SYNOPSIS OF CHAPTERS (Continued)

		Pp.
56.	The Splendid Forties................	509--518
57.	Hides and Tallow.....................	518--538
58.	Horses, Mules and Cattle.............	538--544
59.	Caballeros -- of the Plow............	545--561
60.	Vines and Wines......................	562--568
61.	The Middle Age of Agriculture........	568--577
62.	Profits from Ocean and River.........	577--601
63.	Mining before 1848...................	602--628
64.	Making by Hand.......................	628--643
65.	Who'll Buy?..........................	643--663
66.	Aspirations toward Sea Power.........	664--713
67.	Purchasing Power and Volume of Trade...	713--733
68.	Dons of the Counter and Counting-House	733--741
69.	Promotion of the Northern Frontier...	741--752
70.	Conclusions: Arcadians at Work.......	752--761

LIST OF TABLES

Table		Page
I.	De Razón Population, Hispano-Californian and Foreign, 1810--1848	153
II.	Estimated Immigration from Mexico, 1822--1848	156
III.	Estimated Hispano-Californian Natural Increase, 1820--1848	157
IV.	Estimated Hispano-Californian Birth Rate, 1820--1848	162
V.	Birth Rates, 1930 -- For Comparison	164
VI.	Birth Rates, 1886 -- For Comparison	165
VII.	Los Angeles Pueblo Account Sheet, 1833--1840	208
VIII.	Territorial Revenues, 1823--1846	298
IX.	Emergency Reductions in the Territorial Civil Budget, 1844	317

LIST OF TABLES (Continued)

Table   Page

X. Military Salary List and Payments on Account, 1820--1830...............348

XI. Decrease of Presidial Forces, 1821--1841..........................357

XII. Distribution of San Diego Presidial Forces, 1828, *ca.*....................359

XIII. Territorial Ordinance and Artillerymen, 1841..........................370

XIV. Estimated Annual Value of Hide-Tallow Exportation, 1826--1847..............535

XV. Import-Export Values and Ration, 1840--1841 (after Duflot de Mofras)..724

XVI. Estimated Import-Export Business, 1843--1845..........................731

GRAPH

Estimated Import-Export Trade, 1823--1845....732

FOREWORD: THE ARCADIAN MYTH

The conventional pictures of California as an Arcadia of the '20s and '30s or a pageant of the "splendid idle forties" are charming, but superficial and static. No picture -- unless cinematographic -- can present more than one aspect of its subject; and that lacks the dimension of depth.

Regarding the Arcadian concept, one feels at first the need of a mental stereoscope to transport one into the midst of the scene by the magic of perspective. But the more earnestly one gazes at a stereoscopic view, the more pronounced becomes one's impression of suspended animation within the line of vision and of fascinating activities and outlooks just behind some pictorial obstruction to the view or just beyond the limits of the picture. One finds it unsatisfying to have penetrated *into* the scene only, and becomes obsessed with the idea of exploring behind it and all around it.

In the case of "Arcadian" California, the way in and about lies open. Quite properly, the rule for getting through the looking-glass, so to speak, reverses an established maxim. He who reads may run. For reading the first-hand accounts of the activities and hopes, the perplexities and preoccupations of the first Californians, one speedily passes into a land and a society no less vital for being reconstructed out of materials a century old.

For a time the still-life picture of "Arcadia" lingers vaguely, like a scenic backdrop against which the drama of young California is played. But the drama, not the backdrop, has become the cynosure. Presently the "Arcadia" is lost sight of altogether, like the painting on a wall behind which one has penetrated. In the hinterland of the looking-glass, as a matter of fact, one finds points of view diametrically opposed to tradition's "Arcadian" standpoint.

One looks about on a lonely land -- half military, half missionary frontier -- peopled with a handful of elderly Spaniards and younger Spanish creoles of quality, a scattering of ragamuffin troops and convict "settlers" (chiefly mixed bloods), some thousands of more or less civilized Indians under the regimentation of a few padres, and a swarm of gentile aborigines constituting an ever present menace and a frequent scourge. It is a land which has suffered extremely; a land forgotten by Spain, neglected by Mexico, unprepared to work out its own salvation and destined to easy conquest by men of alien birth, religion and temperament.

But none of that is to concede that California under Mexico was resigned to her fate -- or oblivious of it. Probably no outlanders anywhere have concerned themselves more ardently with their political and material destinies than did the Californians (<u>de razon</u>) of 1822--46. They recognized themselves as men of a transition period, and after a false dawn of hope out of

Mexico bent to the task of lifting themselves by their own bootstraps from the morass of handicaps in which events had set them down.

They cried out to Mexico and to each other against the difficulties that beset them -- the _males de California_: lack of population and defenses against intrusive foreigners and savages, of roads and mails and land transport, of schools and an organic law, of a naval squadron and a merchant marine, of an unhampered agriculture and industry and trade, and -- first, last and always -- of funds and _brazos_ to provide the barest elements of all or any of these.

Dip into the records where one will, one cannot turn many pages without finding one's self in the midst of anxious efforts, becoming desperate as the dangers close in with the years, to remedy the _males_ and _fomentar_ the development of California. Sometimes it is a Mexican Congress decreeing great projects (generally unsubsidized) for _el territorio más precioso_; sometimes it is a Mexican governor conferring with the territorial *diputación* on *cosas mas importantes* for the salvation of the department; most often it is one of the great or of the lesser Californians expounding, exhorting, pleading for *remedios indispensables*.

Every phase of their need and their danger was dilated upon, times without number. So far from being men unaware or apathetic, they were men struggling against the nightmare of helplessness before a menace closing inexorably about them. Indeed, their habit of pelting each other with letters crammed with plans for the rescue of the country and flaunting the spirited cliche' "*Diós y Libertad!*" is more suggestive of the first French Republicans than of placidly dallying Arcadians.

Their activities were not confined to theorizing and mutual admonition. In so far as circumstances could be forced to permit, the *Californios* were practical statesmen.

Nor were their failures ignominious and culpable, as has usually been represented. Even when culpable, they were explicable in the light of conditions.

The *dons* have sometimes -- to their profound disparagement, of course -- been contrasted with the admirable and efficient Pilgrim Fathers. For half a hundred reasons the comparison is invalid. The Californians of 1822--46 were not, primarily, voluntary pioneers. They were creoles who had been born into a system of colonial dependence and minute regulation entirely foreign to English practise; or they were -- and in the larger proportion -- human dregs: mixed bloods and *presidarios* conscripted in Mexico by force of arms for deportation as Californian *habitantes*.

The best of them looked back to the tradition of the *caballero* for whom military or other official preferment was the great desideratum. A few of the older men had attained to some such distinctive experience under Spain. Mexico barred them from public affairs, for fear of loyalist intrigues. Sudden responsibility therefore descended upon the young creoles, whom the

Spanish system had excluded from all but petty officialdom. So they were at once covetous of political advancement and untrained for it.

That situation entailed contentiousness, inefficiency and often political bad faith; and was aggravated by their peculiarly involved and all-inclusive family relationships. Intermarriage of Californian women with the interloping foreigners further complicated matters and reduced the country's chances of preserving herself as a department of Mexico or a self-determined nación.

Perhaps if the Californians had been allowed even a little time in which to grow up they might have worked out their salvation. But time for growing has been oddly brief in the various stages of California's history. She was a Spanish outpost only fifty years; a far province of Mexico only half that time; and scarcely was the ink dry on the documents which made her a possession of the United States before the discovery of gold threw her, still embryonic, into political and social problems as complex as any adult state has ever been called on to face.

Not the span of a single generation intervened between California's declaration of allegiance to Mexico and her conquest by the United States; and throughout that time the forces militating against her were in steady motion. For her *males* had all raised their heads in Spanish times: her over-regulation, her under-population quantitative and qualitative, her Indian problem, her mission problem, her foreign problem. For a dozen years she besought exigently the aid and protection which were her due as a Mexican territory. Then, perceiving Mexico overwhelmed with domestic and foreign difficulties, she tried her hand at home rule beginning in 1836. By 1841 it was obvious to her shrewdest leaders, though inadmissible publicly, that little hope remained of staving off *los gringos*, more particularly *los Yanquis*.

The Californians of the middle period were like boys locked in a laboratory to work out the formulas and methods of government by experimentation -- and given no time in which to experiment. With all our modern political and social *savoir-faire* it took us a decade and a half to make up our minds about prohibition, and that experiment is still only in its second, consequential, stage. By that comparison, the generally accepted sweeping indictment of "Arcadian" California for ineptitude seems as absurdly out of scale as, measured by the mass of recorded evidence, it is incorrect in detail. Unquestionably the distortion, partly inadvertent and careless, has also been, from the beginning, partly a tendency of "manifest destiny" to justify itself in so far as possible on the "backward peoples" ground.

The Italo-Ethiopian situation today, deriving from similar motive and pretext, has aroused the indignant challenge of western civilization. Yet the tribesmen of Abyssinia are incomparably lower in the cultural scale than were the Californians. Perhaps the western world has grown more conscientious. Perhaps it is merely more articulate and organized

for interference. Of course the powers leading
the League resistance have large national interests
at stake.

The present undertaking is no attempt to ink
out shortcomings deplored by the Californians themselves. Those shall be set down duly. But they
will be balanced with a fair statement of efforts,
of circumstances extenuating errors, and of conditions predetermining failure.

Once upon a time some California tourist --
wasn't it Vancouver? -- threw off the phrase "Spanish Arcadia." It was a convenient stamp for recording a hasty impression: so convenient, in fact,
that it was adopted as the text of a chapter in
California history, which in turn became expanded
into an entire interpretation embracing a subsequent
era.

The falsity of the Arcadian concept as misapplied has been borne in on the present writer innu-
merable times during fifteen years' interest in
California history, a dozen of which have permitted
more or less regular recourse to original sources in
the Bancroft Library and other great collections.

New side-lights here, new flashes of illumination there, have shed, in the aggregate, a flood-light of revelation dissipating most of the Arcadian features, like shadows, and making plain many long obscured aspects of the Mexican-Californian scene.

To undertake to reinterpret an era, however, is no small responsibility. The present study has therefore been entered upon cautiously, and worked out in sober spirit, with full realization that it runs directly counter to the large body of crystallized and recognized opinion. The writer has attempted, with utmost conscientiousness, to compile the facts -- as many facts as possible. Every relevant lead has been followed up. Nothing has been suppressed and nothing glossed over.

To be sure, the investigation has been limited to Bancroft Library manuscripts. Other sources, particularly the Mexican archives, would doubtless yield a wealth of additional information. That it would be chiefly corroborative information, however, seems entirely probable in view of the unanimity of the testimony afforded by the Bancroft materials.

If, therefore, the case for the territorials is stated strongly, it is because the entire body of uncovered evidence bears it out.

The Arcadian verdict, here appealed, was not of Bancroft's pronouncement. His *History of California* summarizes for the defense at most points where he commits himself. But, "My conception of the province of history," he once wrote, "is a clear and concise statement of facts . . . . . leaving the reader to make his own deductions and form his own opinions."[1] As Bancroft presented a tremendous aggregation of facts, closely condensed and arranged for the most part chronologically, deeper study of his findings is frequently necessary to the formation of sound deductions and valid opinions than the average reader realizes or is disposed to make.

It is no derogation of Bancroft's great achievement to add that time and again his need to compress led to the imbedding of significant items in close-packed paragraphs -- particularly in footnotes -- like precious stones in a matrix. Easily overlooked or unrecognized in that form, such informational gems must be freed from the surrounding mass, developed into their many-faceted significance and placed in suitable settings, if their light is

---
[1] MS fragment in Bancroft Library

to shine forth.

Among two pages of foot-note items, for example, crowded into his local annals for Los Angeles in the 1830s, Bancroft makes reference to a petition of citizens for the establishment of a new *campo santo*, the old one having become, through years of use, a menace to public health. The favorable action of the *ayuntamiento* is noted. "But," concludes Bancroft's brief note, "nothing was accomplished for five years."

On the face of it, this bit supports the charges of pusillanimity so commonly made against the Californians. The documents behind it, however, tell a quite contrary story of five years' persistent endeavor: of the raising of a citizen subscription fund for defraying the expenses involved; of legal and political red tape patiently untangled; of the sturdy stand of laymen against ecclesiastical insistence on prerogative -- which insistence was the obstruction to the realization of the project.[2]

In its general implications, this single small item of pueblo history points half a dozen factors

---
[2] See *post*, pp. 209-211.

xvi

CHAPTER I (INTRODUCTORY):   MEXICO, A FOSTER-MOTHER
              WITH GOOD INTENTIONS

1. The Birth and Heritage of a Nation..pp. 1-- 9
2. The Good Intentions..................... 9--22
3. The *Junta de Fomento de Californias*.... 23--51
4. Mexico's Handicaps...................... 52--66
5. Mexico's Failures and California's
        Disillusionment................... 66--77

NOTICE TO READERS

__Sources and Translations:__ Most of the original sources drawn on in the preparation of this thesis are manuscripts of the Bancroft Collection in the University of California. Since they are preponderantly Spanish, direct quotations are given in translation. Care has been taken throughout to conform the English renderings as closely as possible not only to the letter and intent of the Spanish originals, but to the emotional coloring as well.

__Pesos and Dollars:__ As it was the practice of Bancroft and indeed the frequent use of the Californians themselves to indicate __pesos__ by the dollar sign, the two designations are used interchangeably throughout this thesis. Whenever possible, the symbol employed in the original document has been retained.

__References to Chapters VI—XI, inclusive:__ As the present thesis comprises the first volume of a two-volume study projected as a whole, references are made occasionally to chapters VI—XI, which comprise __An Economic and Social History of California, Volume II: Mainly Social.__ For this reason, a prospectus of the second volume, now in course of writing, is appended to this thesis.

which he investigated. His histories are like guidebooks to the extensive regions and times which he explored. His inspiration points the way to countless lesser and particularized investigations by countless minor explorers.

It has been under Bancroft's inspiration and with the travel facilities which he afforded that the present writer has journeyed back into the California of a century ago, to resurvey its much publicized "Arcadian" features. The reconnaissance has been a labor of love and adventure. The personal reward has been an immensely augmented appreciation of the people so long and so generally underrated as "Arcadians."

Carlos María Bustamante dedicated his Nuevo Bernal Diaz to "La sombra generosa" of General Antonio León. A similar salute seems in order here, and is heartily extended, to las sombras generosas de los primeros Californios.

of importance directly refuting the Arcadian temper of the people and revealing cogent reasons for their backwardness. Here was the old dead-lock between lay and ecclesiastical authority. Here was an example of the petty tyranny of the church organization of the time. Here were illustrated certain handicaps of the political system: for in the first place, the laws of Spain and Mexico had to be searched for authority, and in the second, the departmental assembly had to go into the matter. Quite probably the issue was taken still further, and somewhere in Mexico's archives is filed the complete serial story that grew out of the desire of the little Los Angeles community for a new burying ground.

Bancroft's purpose was not to serialize, but to synopsize. He conceived and accomplished an unparalleled feat of collection, digestion and summarization of data. It is part of the imperishable glory of his work that it is not exhaustive but practically inexhaustible.

His library comes perhaps as close as man may encompass to re-creation of the epochs and the peoples

CHAPTER I (INTRODUCTORY): MEXICO, A FOSTER-MOTHER
WITH GOOD INTENTIONS

1. The Birth and Heritage of a Nation

In 1821, a nation was born, out of long and bitter travail. Infant-like, it was weak and inarticulate and had all the lessons of co-ordination to learn. Infant-like, it was at the mercy of such strong hands as might lay hold of it. It had inherited, moreover, certain peculiar disabilities which its sons were not to fling off for generations to come.

That its territorial heritage was dominion surpassed in extent only by that of Russia and that of China[1] was part of its misfortune. Spain and the Spanish Bourbons had fretted over the problems of administration and defense which new-born Mexico was at once, and entirely without preparation, called upon to assume.

Unlike her lusty young neighbor, the United States of America, Mexico had no tradition of self-rule, and no homogeneity. The English forebears of the Atlantic

---

[1] W. H. Bishop, Old Mexico, p. 291.

freemen had been learning the lessons of governance since Magna Carta, and had passed down a vast system of political science and practice by which the Americans profited incalculably. This heritage, along with their pioneering and practically homogeneous racial stock, gave the United States a long start toward political, economic and social stability.

Mexico's case was in utter contrast. From "Aztec times,"[2] and for centuries earlier, her history had been that of suppression of weak by stronger and alien elements. The so-called Aztec empire was the typical barbarian device, maintained by force, for the exploitation of tributaries restive and tribally unrelated. The Spanish conquest, rapid and wide, imposed the encomienda system of forced gang-labor; and the conquistadores, finding the tierra caliente ideal for sugar culture, promptly introduced negroes and a negro problem into the already complex racial picture. Before 1575, blacks outnumbered the whites in nearly every bishopric of New Spain.[3]

Whereas British occupation in the new world had proceeded by a repeated thrusting of the Indians out of the

---

[2] Beginning in the fourteenth century.

[3] Herbert Ingram Priestley, The Mexican Nation, p. 126.

path of advance, across frontier after frontier, Spain attempted a policy of assimilation. Indeed, the Spaniards, like the French, displayed a capacity for intermixture with the barbarians in striking contrast with British aloofness. Yet no racial cohesion or national consciousness resulted. This lack of solidarity explains the collapse of numerous projects for Mexican independence, dating from the very days of Cortez;[4] as well as Mexico's failure up to the present time to achieve political and economic stability.

Spanish social custom placed the hurdles in the way of Mexican folk-consciousness, by segregating the people of New Spain into a score of categories based on blood-mixture. Not only were the offspring of white and Indian parents designated as *mestizos*, and the offspring of white and negro parents as *mulattos*, says Priestley; "the offspring of a *mestizo* and a Spanish woman was known as a *castizo*; the offspring of a mulatto and a Spanish woman was called a *morisco*. .... The *salta atrás* was one born in a white family but having the dark complexion which indicated that somewhere in his ancestry there was a strain of negro blood. The *chino* .... was the offspring of the 'throw back' and an Indian woman, that is to say,

---

[4] Priestley, *Mex. Nation*, p. 124.

that he had somewhere a streak of negro blood. ....
Other curious racial admixtures were those known as
lobos (wolves), zambos, and coyotes. .... the social
distinctions described by these [last] designations were
gradually eliminated, the lower group of society coming
to be known generally as los pardos y demás castas --
the dark ones and other castes."[5]

    Manuel Castañares, California's delegate to the
Mexican Congress of 1844--45, wrote feelingly of the deplorable lot of the submerged masses: "They live
wretchedly, labor for mere existence, often in mines
whose gold enriches a master almost always a foreigner.
They make up the conscripted legions of the caudillos.
They have many more needs than the Indians, and their
life in sophisticated centers breeds in them greater
propensities for vice and crime. They fill the prisons
and their blood stains the gallows. They compose the
terrible masses in the great centers of population ....
Yet when educated .. they are capable of great deeds and
noble achievements .... The number of their illustrious
is few, but so is their opportunity for education, to
which they have little access -- to speak plainly, none.
Only let enough schools be opened, let them be educated,

---

[5] Mex. Nation, p. 125.

and we shall soon have a civilized and rich population; for ... they are intelligent, more aggressive than the aborigines, have the advantage of the language .... We in authority must elevate them from their submerged state."[6]

Besides the mixed bloods, there were the creoles -- Mexican-born children of Spanish-born parents. It might be supposed that at least between these two groups no line was drawn. On the contrary, in political opportunity and significance, even in business, the creoles were but a step higher than the suppressed and exploited sons of confusion. It was Spain's jealous policy to designate only Peninsulars for political and military preferment. The theory is said to have been current, even among the fathers of creoles, that the sunny skies of New Spain had a deteriorating effect on those born beneath them, incapacitating for responsibility.

However influential that superstition may have been, Spain had reason shrewdly to suspect that under her mercantilistic exploitation even the first generation of colonials might perceive the gulf between their interests

---
[6] May 16, 1845, Castañares to M. G. Vallejo, in Vallejo Doc., MS, vol. 12, #141, pp. 1--3. Don Manuel speaks of this class as criollos, but evidently has especially in mind the mixed bloods.

and hers, and might serve her less well in serving themselves better. At any rate, she barred creoles from participation in any but municipal politics; and as under her administrative system the municipalities had neither initiative nor influence, few men of Mexican birth had opportunity to learn the science of government in that only effective school, experience. Not until the close of the eighteenth century, moreover, when her territorial claims were too vast, and pressure against her too great for Peninsular forces to cope with, did she risk the creation of a colonial army, by which a military career at least of sorts was opened to creoles.

Even Mexico's final struggle for independence, though it was inaugurated by an Indian rabble under the patriot-priest Hidalgo, and carried forward by creoles and _mestizos_, did not triumph through the united strength of the oppressed. Instead, when Spain's radical cóŕtes of 1820 forced Ferdinand VII into at least a pretense of liberalism, clerical-official-aristocratic New Spain, which had always supported the monarchy, sprang to protect its privileges by the extreme but only practical means: the assertion of independence. It was actually with troops of the crown, whose command he had secured from the viceroy under pretense of defending Mexico City against the rebels, that Iturbide moved into the field, negotiated his understanding with the insurrectionist Guerrero, and evolved the Plan de Iguala, proclaimed February 24, 1821, and providing a working agreement under which the mutually antagonistic classes of New Spain could co-operate to be rid of the Spanish yoke.[7]

The Plan, followed by the Treaty of Córdoba signed by the viceroy August 24, 1821, provided for a crowned head to rule Mexico. Iturbide was acclaimed regent until a monarch should be found. Mexico was a nation -- at least nominally. She began to take stock of her domain and essay her sovereignty.

Agustín Fernandez de San Vicente, canon of the Durango Cathedral, was sent to the Californias to feel out their attitude, foment the spirit of independence, secure their adherence to Mexico and start the new machinery of constitutional government working.[8] The mission of the canónigo prospered. On the presumption of mutual interest and fellowship, California took the oath of allegiance to the Mexican empire in April, 1822.[9]

Unhappily, Iturbide's was not the selfless patriotism of an Hidalgo or a Morelos; and he quickly made his way

---

[7] Priestley, Mex. Nation, pp. 244--47, passim.
[8] Bancroft, California, vol. 2, pp. 455--56.
[9] Ibid., p. 451.

from control of the regency to the throne as Emperor Agustín I. His assumption of the imperial mantle aggravated liberal fears of strongly centralized government. For a time after his downfall, anarchy reigned from Texas to Yucatán.[10] So that ubiquitous evil genius of Mexico, Santa Anna, was given his first opportunity to execute a *coup de force.* He seized the moment to declare for a republic.

Then the perplexed constitution-makers had to choose between a strong central government -- such as Mexico needed but had good reason to distrust -- and a federal type modeled after that of the United States. Fear and jealousy for local rights and preferments decided the issue, and Mexico's republican Constitution of 1824, like the *Acta Constitutiva* which had preceded it, was modeled in the main on the Constitution of the United States. To make matters worse, of the Spanish employees who had acquired political expertness in posts of importance, scarcely any wished to take part in the new order.[11]

Most unfortunately, the Mexican people had the entire long way to travel along the road of self-government

---

[10] *México a través de los Siglos,* Vicente Riva Palacio, ed., vol. 4, pp. 97--99.

[11] *Ibid.,* p. 24.

-- a road whose end they do not yet clearly see. Naturally, they were as far from the capacity to administer remote frontier dependencies still in the formative stage.

2. The Good Intentions

Nevertheless, and although the constitution of 1824, accepted by Alta California early the next year, made no provision for territorial governments, President Victoria and the Congreso projected a vigorous administration of the territories.[12] Agricultural, industrial and commercial development, expansion and defense against foreign aggression and exploitation were the policies contemplated. A new world power was in the making, whose most distant possessions, even were to be raised to greatness.

In the zero hour before the Spanish-American colonies wrenched themselves free, California had been pointed out as Spain's weakest part, capable of being developed into a member of great strength. Writing in 1830, Carlos María Bustamante, the lawyer-writer destined to a long public career in the nation about to emerge, had urged the protection and development of the northern Pacific province, the encouragement of agriculture and stock-raising there, the subsidization by the crown of the fur industry and of

---

[12] The two Californias, Colima and New Mexico.

a California-China trade, the inauguration of a coastwise commerce so that foreigners might be fended off. He reminded of the various means of promotion, including colonization, projected "in times less agitated than these"; and pleaded for free trade and a liberal administration, without which success could not be anticipated.[13]

In 1821, under the short-lived Regency, a statistical report of the Mexican empire was prepared by Tadeo Ortiz de Ayala. This official document urged the political and economic organization of the territories, their fortification and colonization, with special attention to sparsely settled regions. Threatened on all sides by foreigners, without a fleet, Mexico must tranquillize and develop her empire. Such steps were *esencialmente necesario* in the two Californias, New Mexico and the oriental and occidental provinces comprising part of the "monstrous and vast" intendancies of Potosí, Durango and Sonora. Ortiz denounced the state of abandonment in which those provinces lay, and cried the menace of the Americans, Russians and English not only to the undeveloped territories but to the entire empire. If the Mexican government failed to take prompt and adequate measures, the

---

[13] C. M. Bustamante, *Medidas para la Pacificación de la America Mexicana*, MS, vol. 1, pp. 142--56.

Americans would quickly spread north and west from Louisiana and Missouri, absorbing New Mexico and the country beyond the Rockies and pushing on up the Columbia River to the coast, eventually enclosing the Mexican empire from the Atlantic to the Pacific, and becoming masters of the trade of the northwest and that of China and India.

He called attention to the presence of the Russians in California -- perhaps under some secret agreement with Spain -- only thirty leagues from magnificent San Francisco Bay; in California, one of the most important and choice regions of the empire by virtue of its situation, climate, fertility, abundance of rich productions and excellent ports suited to the Mexico-Lima-China trade and that of the Philippines -- yet exposed, lacking colonies and defenses, courts of justice, political organization, a commercial company to profit from the abundance of otter and various other furs, fine pearls and the valuable Halistis or Monterey shell (the currency used in the fur-trade with the Indians). Settlement must be promoted by the planting of penal colonies. Trade must be fomented -- free trade. Communications must be opened between California, New Mexico and Sonora. Occupation by colonization must be made to extend to Missouri, and California must be linked to the country of the Otomitas and the provinces of the east coast, whither it could send its products by the Rio Bravo del Norte via steamboats. All this in 1821![14]

It was characteristic of the progressive spirit prevailing that the first governor sent by Mexico to the Californias -- Lieutenant-Colonel José María Echeandía -- had been director of a college of engineering.[15] Promptly on completing the voyage from San Blas to San Diego,[16] he dispatched his aide-de-camp, Alférez Romualdo Pacheco (also an engineer) to the Colorado River, to join Captain José Romero in an exploration for

---

[14] T. Ortiz de Ayala, *Resumen de la Estadística del Imperio Mexicano*. The report is dated October 10, 1821. Pages 95--100 are devoted to California. The *Otomitas* were the Otomís, a hunting tribe of the high regions and forests north and northwest of the Valley of Mexico. The Rio Bravo del Norte was the Rio Grande. It is to be noted that Ortiz de Ayala was considerably better informed as to the nearness of the Russian advance than common for his time. See *post*, p. 28.

[15] Ignacio del Valle, *Lo Pasado*, MS, p. 1. Angustias de la Guerra Ord, *Ocurrencias*, MS, pp. 42--43. Bancroft, *Calif.*, vol. 3, p. 8. Echeandía was governor from some time in November, 1825 to January 31, 1831, for his first term; and a second time -- by force of intrigue, from November 6, 1831 to January 14, 1833.

[16] He had stopped off at Loreto to organize Baja California.

overland routes which should bind the frontier territories to the Mexican states.[17] Romero's explorations continued through several years and were the subject of at least seventy-five official communications.[18]

On February 2, 1826, Echeandía, addressing to the Minister of War what seems to have been his final report on the opening of the Paso de los Yumas (from Tucson to San Diego), emphasizes the importance attached by the supreme government and in his own judgment to the maintenance of this line of communication. Only by its means could the Californias be organized and fomented, he declared. He reported the stationing of an *escolta* on the route (apparently near Gila Junction) and gave assurance that his best efforts had been devoted to pushing the work forward.[19]

---

[17] Following the Garcés and Anza expeditions (1768--1776), the Spaniards had attempted to maintain permanent communication by land with the northwestern provinces; and to that end had established settlements in the vicinity of Yuma, in 1779--80. Indian ferocity obliterated those beginnings within a year, after which the sea continued to be the main highway between the old and the new regions of New Spain.

[18] Bancroft, *Calif.*, vol. 2, pp. 507--9.

[19] *St. Pap., Sac.*, MS, vol. 19, pp. 24--26.

The fortification of San Gorgonio Pass was also attempted at this time, but doomed by the heavy snows to abandonment.[20] In 1826, an order went out from the director general of artillery for a topographical plan of every fortified place in the territory, so that the government might know the advantages of those Californian antemurales de la defensa de la República.[21] Though without practical results, these essays indicate the early republican zeal for consolidation.

More effective to that end was Mexico's maintenance, until nearly 1850, of the line of presidios planted by Spain from the western coast to the Gulf of Mexico, in accordance with the Reglamento of 1772.[22]

One of the earliest activities of Canónigo Fernandez in the north was a personal investigation of Fort Ross; for it had been feared that Spain would cede the Californias to Russia or to France in return for military reinforcement against

---

[20] Bancroft, Calif., vol. 2, p. 509.

[21] Ibid., p. 674, n. 43.

[22] Reglamento e instrucción para los presidios que se han de formar en la linea de frontera de la Nueva España. Resuelto por el Rey Nuestro Señor en cédula de 10 de Septiembre de 1772. A few changes in locations were made under Mexico. H. R. Wagner, Spanish Southwest, #159d.

the Spanish liberals. The <u>comisionado</u> ordered the abandonment of the settlement within six months, failing which, he threatened, it would be forcibly evacuated.[23]

American encroachments had also caused apprehension, and part of the responsibility laid on Fernandez by the Iturbide government had been to discover just how great the foreign menace was. Foreign interest in the territory was generally discouraged by the circulation of tidings of complete rapport between Mexico and California. Propaganda to that effect was ordered to be spread by every homeward-bound English and American vessel.[24]

As for the territorials themselves, they were artfully encouraged to loyalty by intimations that their adherence was matter of fact and matter of course. An early official communication attributed to them, suggestively, a disposition to maintain order and the established sovereignty without coercion: "'They have always shown a strong attachment to the supreme powers, and given constant [sic] evidence with ardent fidelity that they are, and glory in being, excellent Mexicans; and their estimable gefe político Argüello answers in his latest communications for good order and strict administration of justice, even in their present [transitional] condition.'"[25]

---

[23] Bancroft, <u>Calif.</u>, vol. 2, pp. 463--65, 482--3; I. B. Richman, <u>Calif. under Spain and Mexico</u>, p. 230.

[24] Bancroft <u>op. cit.</u>, p. 515; Richman, <u>op. cit.</u>, p. 231.

[25] Bancroft, <u>op. cit.</u>, vol. 3, pp. 6--7, n. 7.

That bland expression of confidence tactfully ignored the recalcitrance of the missionaries, the reluctance of the older Californios for Mexican domination, the more or less active opposition of some of the younger, and the indifference of the majority. As a matter of fact, the frontier provinces had been a source of worry to Mexico throughout the revolutionary period and so continued under the regency and empire.

All through the revolution, Alta California had remained loyal to Spain; and despite certain propagandist efforts of the insurgents, had been roused to neither enthusiasm nor interest in the struggle for independence. Only one phase of the war had come close to her -- the hard times which it entailed. For eleven years she had been cut off from her Spanish subsidies. The result had been, not a business depression such as war precipitates in our industrial era, but dearth of many near-essentials of life.

Save at the missions -- which also suffered[26] -- deprivation was universal, protest on every tongue. Not

---

[26] It had devolved on them to provide for the troops, in the emergency. In return for presidial drafts on the Spanish treasury -- which were never honored -- the padres supplied agricultural products and foreign goods received in exchange for their hides and tallow. They considered the dissipation of their profits a hardship, particularly since the coast trade was flourishing as never before. C. E. Chapman, A History of California: the Spanish Period, pp. 380--91.

disaffection from Spain nor a passion for independence motivated California's Mexican allegiance; but a weariness of things as they were, an unreasoned craving, on the part of the lay population,[27] for a "new deal." Supply -- of goods and money -- was the crying need of the isolated young province; and Mexico, should she prove willing and able to purvey, might collect her profits in loyalty.

The new government was not aware of its psychological moment, yet it intended well, and actually sent an early shipment of goods, with some money.[28] But much more was needed. As early as 1816, Governor Sola had represented the presidios as falling to ruin, and declared -- though doubtless hyperbolically -- that "the good troops of California" were "entirely naked, and their families likewise."[29]

Neither Iturbide nor the Victoria government had any idea of relying on those pathetic colonial veterans of Spain, nor on diplomacy, wholly, to unite the northwestern frontier to Mexico. Under the regency it was

---

[27] Mission policy was royalistic, because of the republic's advocacy of secularization.
[28] Bancroft, *Calif.*, vol. 3, p. 14.
[29] Richman, *Spain and Mexico*, p. 215.

at first intended to send an army of occupation of one hundred and fifty troops.[30] Echeandía was escorted by a company of forty infantrymen permanently assigned to California. A troop of artillery went north at about the same time, under Lieutenant Miguel Gonzalez who, by elevation to captaincy, became ranking officer and therefore commandant at Monterey. At least one other detachment of infantry embarked for the California presidial service in the first few months of the republic.[31]

No record of their number is available; but the evidence seems clear that in all something like a hundred Mexican troops, at least, were moved to the northern frontier at this time. Inconsiderable as such a show of force would appear today, it was bound to make an impression in a territory garrisoned by only a few hundred men and officers most of whom had long lacked the equipment and the spirit for effectiveness.[32]

The fact that money for the army payrolls actually went forward with or before the troops of the republic is evidence that Mexico was not only in earnest, but keyed up, momentarily, to an unusual pitch of efficiency. One

---

[30] Richman, Spain and Mexico, p. 231.
[31] Bancroft, Calif., vol. 3, pp. 13--15.
[32] On the territory's presidial strength, see post, chap. IV, secs. 34--41.

great oversight was made, none-the-less. Although
Spain's Californian troops had transferred their allegiance to the new government, and were expected to remain
in service, no appropriation was made for their wages!
The nearest approach to such a step was a reminder to Congress, by the Minister of War in his report, of the past
service and present needs of the soldiers of the old organization.

Mexico could have taken no more effective measure to
secure the fidelity of her territorial subjects than
prompt remuneration of the old presidial forces for service
from the time of their acceptance of the new regime. Yet,
although Governor Sola's complaints of the destitution of
the troops due to arrears in pay continued through 1824,
the only result was an unofficial communication from
Gervasio Argüello, the habilitado general in Guadalajara,
stating that no aid could be hoped for from the treasury.[33]

Echeandía had been in the upper territory barely a
month before he perceived the urgency of succoring the
colonial army. On September 1, 1825, he ordered that
the regulars be advanced three months' pay; although perhaps, as Bancroft suggests,[34] he was merely making a

---

[33] Bancroft, Calif., vol. 2, pp. 514--15.

[34] Op. cit., vol. 3, pp. 14--15. Depart. Rec., MS, vol. 2, p. 2; vol. 1, p. 105.

liberal gesture for popularity's sake, since he must have realized that compliance with his order was impossible.

In her zeal for the effective fiscal administration of Alta California, Mexico did, however, send a <u>comisario subalterno de hacienda,</u> or deputy commissioner of finances, Don José María Herrera. He reached Monterey in July 1825.[35] Responsible directly to the <u>comisario general de occidente</u> at Arizpe, Herrera was largely independent of Governor Echeandía. Since he was sometimes unable to accept the gubernatorial judgment (as in the case of the presidial salary advance), administrative harmony was far from complete. The purpose was served, however, of checking the governor and entrenching the central power.

One of the most considerable tasks deputed to Canónigo Fernandez was the political organization of the territory. The governor, of course, was to be provided from Mexico. Already, in the spring of 1822, the regency had invited California to elect a <u>diputado</u> to the Mexican <u>Congreso,</u> and that had been done, the honor going to popular Sola.[36]

---

[35] Bancroft, <u>Calif.,</u> vol. 3, pp. 14--15.

[36] <u>Ibid.,</u> vol. 2, pp. 453, 455. Don Pablo Vicente de Sola, who had begun his rule in 1815, was California's last Spanish governor, and was continuing in office until his successor could arrive. The territorial <u>diputado</u> had no vote, since California lacked a population of 40,000. (Bancroft, <u>Calif.,</u> vol. 3, p. 2.)

Probably along with the instruction for the congressional election was sent, or assumed, authorization for the election of a territorial diputación[37] as provided for in Spain's liberal Constitution of 1812, not yet abrogated. But no such organization had been proceeded with in California. Fernandez made it his business to inquire why. Sola's explanations sifted down chiefly to the assumed unfitness of Californians for self-government. To this the comisionado countered that there must be a diputación if it had to be composed of Indians, and that the art of self-government could best be learned by practice.

Accordingly, the congressional electors presently met again at Monterey and selected five vocales or diputación members, and two suplentes or alternates. A secretary was also named. The governor would serve as ex-officio president.[38] Bancroft could not discover the

---

[37] "Legislature," generally -- but loosely -- translated; in function comparable with a British governor's council, i.e., of advisory rather than legislative capacity.

[38] Bancroft, Calif., vol. 2, pp. 462--63.

full details of how the electors were chosen.[39] He did, however, find instructions for the Indians at each mission to choose an *elector de partido* through their native *alcaldes* and *regidores,* "with the padres' advice." Thus, he points out, the neophytes found a voice (though the electoral machinery must have all but drowned it out) in California's first general elections.[40]

Fernandez saw to it that the municipal, as well as the territorial, civil organization was completed. The pueblos had always had *ayuntamientos* composed of one or two *regidores* each; but the highest local authority had resided in the governor's *comisionado.* This office, partaking of martial rule, was now to be abolished; and Los Angeles and San José were to have their municipal staffs increased by a *síndico* or counsellor and a secretary each.[41]

---

[39] *Partido* (district) electors designated five provincial electors, who were augmented by the ad interim governor and three army officers "holding seats by what authority I know not . . . . Instructions for the presidios and pueblos I have not found, neither are any records extant of the local elections." Bancroft, *Calif.,* vol. 2, p. 454.
[40] *Ibid.*
[41] *Ibid.*, pp. 461, 462.

3. **Junta de Fomento de Californias**

Mexico did not stop with providing troops, financial and civil administrators for the Californias. A governmental commission was set up, much in the modern fashion, to inquire into the condition of the territory[42] and to make recommendations for its development.

This Junta de Fomento de Californias, which functioned for several years -- probably at least a decade -- numbered ten members. The personnel changed frequently, and had included twenty-one by 1827.[43] Prominent among them was the

---

[42] The two Californias were administered as one military and political unit until the middle of 1839, when Baja California was attached to the comandancia general of Sonora and was assigned its own governor. Bancroft, Calif., vol. 3, p. 34.

[43] The following persons signed documents emanating from the Junta during 1825--27 (see infra, n. 45): Juan José Espinosa de los Monteros, Licenciado Carlos María de Bustamante, Pablo Vicente de Sola, Tomás Suria, Tomás Salgado, Licenciado Mariano Dominguez, José Mariano Almanza, Manuel Gonzalez de Ibarra, José Ignacio Ormaechea, Francisco de Paula Tamariz, Ignacio de Cubas, Mariano Bonilla, Francisco Cortina, Francisco Fagoaga, Alejo García Conde, Servando Mier, Isidro Icaza, Diego García Conde, Pedro Lionisio Cárdenas, Juan Francisco Azcarate and Crecencio Suarez.

member from California, Don Pablo Vicente de Sola. Bancroft is inclined to disparage his part in the activities of the *Junta*; but his whole attitude toward Don Pablo is perhaps a little prejudiced. Vallejo and Alvarado are emphatic as to Sola's leadership; and the reports of the *Junta* embody policy after policy which the ex-governor had consistently espoused.[44]

The recommendations of the Junta, set forth in a remarkable series of documents published in 1827,[45] bore on

---

[44] Bancroft, *Calif.*, vol. 3, pp. 3; 5, n. 3. M. G. Vallejo, *Historia de California*, MS, vol. 1, pp. 299--300. J. B. Alvarado, *Historia de California*, MS, vol. 1, pp. 122--23, 233--36.

[45] *México, Junta de Fomento de Californias. Colección de los principales trabajos en que se ha ocupado la Junta nombrada para meditar y proponer al Supremo Gobierno el progreso de la cultura y civilización de los territorios de la Alta y de la Baja California.* The Bancroft Library contains a copy of this rare work. Mr. Robert E. Cowan of Los Angeles also has one. A notice on the title page of the first item of the collection reads: "*Este documento y los que subsecuentamente se imprimirán sobre dichos territorios se encontraron entre los papeles de la testamentaría del Exmo. Sr. D. José Mariano Almanza.*" The contents of the *Colección* are therefore mere casuals from a larger file of evidence of the *Junta's* activity. Search in the Mexican archives would doubtless reveal valuable additional items.

every phase of defense and promotion. There was a
dictamen relative to the duties of the governor;[46] a
scheme for subjecting the missions to civil control; a
reglamento for foreign settlers; a plan de colonización
for Mexican nationals and a bill for the administrative
reorganization of Alta and Baja California. Most enterprising of all, there was a plan político-mercantil for
the development of the Californias.[47]

None of those projects was enacted just as submitted
by the Junta, but many of the policies advocated were incorporated in subsequent legislation. That fact, the protracted activity of the commission and the volume of its
correspondence and reports still preserved in the Mexican
Archives[48] indicate a lively sentiment for promotion.

---

[46] This is the more interesting for the fact that at least in the Bancroft collection the governor's instructions themselves are not available.

[47] Bancroft, Calif., vol. 3, p. 3, n. 2 lists the contents of the Colección.

[48] Bancroft says (loc. cit.) that the Junta was dissolved in 1827 -- as is indicated by the final document of the printed Colección of that year. Apparently, however, the body was not a special but a standing committee, or else it was revived from time to time; for Herbert Eugene Bolton, Guide to .... Archives of Mexico, p. 328, not only gives indices of documents of 1824--26, but cites (pp. 337--38) two legajos covering the years 1321--31. Additional records mentioned in various contemporary writings noted by Bancroft (Calif., vol. 3, p. 34, n. 5) were apparently lost or destroyed, along with so much other valuable documentary material, in the several vicissitudes to which the Mexican archives were subjected in their early years. (See Bolton, op. cit., pp. 8--11).

Indeed, it was largely over-enthusiasm which led the early republic beyond its depth and brought to failure undertakings which, pursued on a modest scale, might have borne some fruits. The conclusion seems inescapable that political inexperience and poverty, not lack of interest or realization that the territory was worth developing, lost California to Mexico. No other one of the Mexican possessions more urgently required systematization of government, defense, etc., than California, the Junta declared,[49] after bewailing the long delay in the development of that territory due to the deflection of the conquistadores to less propitious regions by the lust for power and a stake in more remote fields of exploitation.

A survey of the proposals of this first development board of California, with some reference to their attempted incorporation in Mexican policy, will throw light on the aspirations of the new republic for its territories.

The dictamen concerning the governor's instructions is the first item in the Colección of Junta reports.[50] Alta California especially, destined to importance by its frontier position and its variety of natural wealth, was recommended to the governor's attention. Emphasis was laid on the need

---

[49] Colección, Item 5 (Iniciativa, Voto Final), p. 40.
[50] There are eight items in all.

to gather precise information regarding the country, its inhabitants and resources. The governor should make it his first duty to investigate those matters.

The Mexicans had a passion for gathering statistics, and repeated orders went out, through the years, for the collection of data for the basing of puissant and sagacious policies -- which somehow never matured into action. They did, indeed, need Californian data at this stage. The first item in the Coleccion lists their sources of information: the Noticia of 1757, of Miguel Venegas (actually prepared by Andrés Marcos Burriel), and earlier accounts; the Historia Universal, of 1788; the narrative of the voyage of the vessels "Sutil" and "Mexicana" in 1792, printed in 1802; Humboldt's Ensayo Politico sobre la Nueva España, 1818; and Ponchet's Diccionario Universal de la Geografia Comerciante, printed in the year 7 of the French Republic.

They had no idea, as Bancroft remarks,[51] of the quantities of first-hand information available in the form of missionary and other official records. In so far as they were familiar with ecclesiastical reports, they showed themselves openly suspicious of the accuracy of those sources. Yet they realized and deplored as a handicap in their undertaking the

---

Calif., vol. 3, p. 4.

"vagueness, ignorance or brevity" of the accounts at their command.[52] They asked that the governor familiarize himself with the works which they listed, and bring those up to date, enlarging on them and correcting them in his statistical report.[53]

Considering their lack of information, it is not strange that the "fomentors" had an impressionistic rather than a precise idea of Californian geography. Bancroft remarks[54] a confusion of the two Californias; and a report of January 1835 mentions "the Russians, who, having extended their rule to the northernmost limits of Asia on the South Sea, might advance within our limits."[55] By 1827 sufficient data had been compiled to render the Junta's knowledge -- and alarm -- more definite regarding "Russia, that political colonist which, having mastered the confines of Europe and a part of Asia, has now taken possession down to the port of Bodega, distant less than one degree from that of San Francisco," and is encroaching on Mexican commerce and perhaps inciting the Indians to hostility.[56]

---

[52] Colección, Item 5 (Iniciativa, Voto Final), pp. 35, 43.
[53] Ibid., Item 1 (Dictamen), pp. 4--5.
[54] Calif., vol. 3, p. 4.
[55] Colección, Item 1 (Dictamen), pp. 14--15.
[56] Ibid., Item 5 (Iniciativa, Voto Final), p. 40.

The **Junta** felt the mission and Indian problems to require the greatest circumspection for the moment; but the end in view was the adoption and vigorous enforcement of laws placing the ecclesiastical establishments under civil jurisdiction, reclaiming from church control the resources and wealth of the territory, and extending civil rights and liberties to the neophytes as rapidly as feasible.[57]

Meanwhile, Canónigo Fernandez elicited from the padres "a full report on each mission, with particular reference to geography, lands, and natural resources, ... being perhaps the most complete descriptive document extant on the subject." Population, livestock,

---

[57] The *dictamen*, so far as it relates to Indian policy, is incidentally quoted by Manuel Castañares in an address of March 30, 1844 to the *Congreso*, included in Castañares, *Colección de Documentos*, pp. 13, 14, 50. Don Manuel was California's representative in Mexico during 1844 and 1845. His devoted efforts and his policies are discussed *post, passim.*

crops, mines, fisheries, geography and needs for defence were the seven heads under which the information was organized.[58]

Such Indians as seemed so adapted might, with the consent of the governor and the padres, take their share of mission property and become pueblo residents, or -- always under supervision -- live elsewhere, by themselves or in any decent households. The missions were commended to the watchfulness of the diputación; and the Indians were definitely to be prepared for a normal place in society. The lash was declared abolished in favor of a "stick applied to the clothed back," or of stocks, shackles, etc., all "gently applied"; and the padres must exert themselves beyond their past effort in the instruction of the Indians. The latter, including the neophytes, were to share the civil obligation of all good citizens to help resist invasion in case of need.[59]

---

[58] Bancroft, Calif., vol. 2, p. 460. The resultant document yielded a wealth of material for Bancroft's various chapters on "Local Annals." He cites it as Misiones, Cuaderno de Estado, 1823, MS -- a radical abbreviation of the original lengthy title which incorporated the names of all the missions.

[59] Bancroft, op. cit., pp. 461--62.

In this connection it is interesting that Minister of Relations Lúcas Alamán, in his report of November 8, 1823 to Congress, declared: "If the mission system can be considered best suited to draw savages from their wild life, it can do no more than inculcate the first principles of civilization, it cannot lead men to highest social development. Nothing is better to accomplish this than to bind individuals to society by the powerful bond of property. The government believes, therefore, that the distribution of lands to the converted Indians, lending them from the mission fund the means for cultivation . . . . would give a great impulse to that important province of California.."

In the same report he proposed the formation of a Board of Philanthropy for California similar to Mexico's Board of Health, to be supported from mission funds and to cope with the greatest urgencies and institute reforms.[60]

In the *dictamen*, the *Junta* referred to all the points on which it had attempted to prevent missionary interference in temporalities; and looked toward secularization, at least partial, to be instituted as soon as possible. Indicating that the philosophical ideas which had had and were still to have such momentous effect in stimulating republicanism

---

[60] México, Memoria de Relaciones, 1823, pp. 30--34.

throughout the world were fermenting in Mexico also, the <u>Junta</u> protested against the mission system as having subjected the neophytes to obligations without their previous consent by means of a free social pact.[61]

The pressure toward secularization, typical as it was to be of Mexican policy, originated under Spain. In 1814--15, a <u>teniente de navio</u>, Francisco de Paula Tamariz, presented a <u>memoria</u> to the king and viceroy, denouncing the Alta California mission system as a sacerdotal monopoly, and urging energetic secular development of "<u>el país más fértil y sano de los comprendidos en las costas de Oriente del reino de Nueva España</u>."[62]

---

[61] <u>Colección, Item 1 (Dictamen)</u>, pp. 7--10.

[62] "<u>Memoria que presenta al Rey . . . . sobre mejorar el sistema de gobierno de la Alta California</u>," in "<u>Archivo y Biblioteca de la Secretaría de Hacienda, Colección de documentos históricos</u>," vol. 2: <u>Las Misiones de California</u>, pp. 87--111. Official correspondence concerning the <u>memoria</u>, in <u>ibid.</u>, pp. 111--17. Tamariz claimed to have spent several years in California, and was well informed as to the resources of the province; but the writer has so far failed to find any record of his presence in the north, or, indeed, any biographical data relative to this intensely interesting figure save such as may be gleaned from his efforts to promote California. Possibly his sojourn was in Baja California; or he may have visited the upper province repeatedly, on Spanish vessels, and chosen to look on his frequent stays there as residence.

He submitted a comprehensive scheme to that end, with such effect that the king ordered a *junta* of five to seven persons of practical and business knowledge, and familiar with the country, to consider his proposals. This *Primera Junta de la California*, as it came to be known, was, according to Richman,[63] convened by Viceroy Apodaca in July of 1817, and having consulted, advised His Majesty to demand -- though with circumspection -- why, after forty years, the missions had not been secularized in accordance with the Laws of the Indies. Vigorous opposition of the clergy seems to have nipped the movement in the bud.[64]

The early promotion of the Californias by Tamariz is recorded here because he became a republican and a member -- the most energetic and inspired member -- of the Mexican *Junta de Californias*. The *Junta* set up by President Victoria's government was organized after the Secretary of War and Navy had informed himself on Tamariz's earlier memorial; and the recommendations of 1814--15 are reembodied in the Colección of 1837. Whether some of the Tamariz projects in the earlier period were more or less original, or voiced a considerable body of opinion, cannot

---

[63] *Spain and Mexico*, p. 239.
[64] Tamariz, "Memoria," in op. cit., pp. 119--254.

be decided here. The significance of this quondam royalist naval officer for the present subject consists in his linking of Spanish and Mexican policies in direct continuity. When it is remembered that Spain had been actively developing her northern frontier up to the time of the Mexican revolution, this wholesale adoption of Spanish policy by the new régime has striking force.

Colonization of the northern regions by immigration from Mexico was an essential feature of both the Spanish and Mexican development programs. Tamariz had given it full consideration in his memorial to king and viceroy;[65] the republican Congress of 1824 had voted a general <u>Decreto . . . . sobre Colonización</u>, August 18, 1824 (to be supplemented by a <u>Reglamento para la Colonización</u> of November 21, 1828 and slightly modified by a law of April 6, 1830); and the <u>Junta de Fomento</u> submitted its <u>Plan de Colonización Estrangera in April</u> 1825, and its <u>Plan de Colonización de Nacionales</u> in May.[66]

Tamariz had advocated the peopling of the frontier from Sonora and San Blas; the <u>Congreso</u> and <u>Junta</u> contemplated joint settlement by nationals and aliens, but

---

[65] "Memoria," pp. 90--92; 105.

[66] <u>Colección</u>, Items 3, 4. The laws of 1824, 1828 and 1830 are discussed <u>post</u>, secs. 7, 15.

provided for the safeguarding of Mexican interests and rights, the limitation of land grants, and discrimination in favor of Mexican citizens in land distributions.

Tamariz had lamented the fact that only the seacoast had been occupied. The Congreso limited colonization, unless with approval of the supreme executive power, to areas ten leagues or more inland. It undertook to check foreign encroachment by prohibiting, unless by supreme executive favor, settlement within twenty leagues of the boundary of a foreign nation. All land grants, moreover, were to lapse unless the grantees maintained residence within the republic. The Junta plans included included occupation of the coast islands, which areas should also be studied diligently. An exact "corographic map" of California was necessary, showing its interior features, not yet known as were the exterior shores and islands, depicted in the map of Vizcaíno of 1602 and in the subsequent map, based on Vizcaíno, of José Antonio Alzate. Subsidies were to be furnished Mexican pioneers, and regulations were to control foreign settlers.[67]

Those policies were partially embodied in the general law of November 1828, regulating colonization of Mexican territory. Save for minor amendments, that act remained

---

[67] Colección, Item 1 (Dictamen), p. 6.

in force throughout the Mexican period. Two of its stipulations were that grants to families or private individuals should be valid only with the consent of the territorial diputación, or of the supreme government in cases of appeal; and that the consent of both the diputación and the supreme government should be required to validate grants to contractors for groups of settlers.[68] In other words, republican Mexico, while lacking the manpower to carry on the Spanish tradition of exclusiveness, very definitely intended to regulate and control the influx of settlers, whether foreign or Mexican, into the territories.

The gravest consideration of governor, president and congress was directed by the Junta toward foreign relations.[69] The Russian and American intrusions were particularly to be resisted. Although the forty-second parallel as Mexico's northern boundary was still in question, any passing of that line by alien interlopers was to be prevented at all hazards.

----

[68] H. W. Halleck, "Report on Land Titles," App. #5, pp. 141-- (U. S. House Exec. Doc. #17, 31st Cong., 1st Sess.); Bancroft, Calif., vol. 3, pp. 34--35.

[69] Colección, Item 1 (Dictamen), pp. 13--15.

For the adequate protection of the northern coast, a naval force was an urgent necessity. Since the time of Philip V it had been recognized that California must possess some sort of _marina_ -- if only for the sake of her domestic prosperity; for the recommended fomentation of export of California's fruits and products could not be achieved without sea power, which was needed as well for coast-guard duty and defense, in the absence of a sufficient land force to cover the territory. The _mezquino departamento de marina_ established in the Californias by the _reglamento_ of 1779 must be placed on a footing that would make it worthy of the name and capable of some effect.

It seemed no mad dream, in view of California's geographical position, and her extent, equal to that of England,[70] to look upon her as destined to confer on the Mexican republic sea power equal to that of Britain's. "At least we must -- as Don Lucas Alamán, the Minister of Relations, said in his _memoria_ to the second sovereign constituent congress, begin to regard the vast and fertile peninsula of the Californias with a new interest. The

---

[70] The _Junta_ greatly underestimated California's size, or greatly overestimated that of "England," even if it meant, here, the British Isles!

attention of the Congress and government should be fastened on the rich commerce of which that peninsula ought one day to be the center . . . . and on the aid which it is capable of lending to the achievement of a national marine."[71]

Time and again this need of frontier defense, by sea and by land, was stressed: in the reports of the Junta on different subjects, on the floor of the Congreso and in official communications from California. In 1827, at the instigation of Diputado Sola, the President recommended to Congress the establishment of a California coast-guard of two war frigates, two brigantines and two corvettes. This armada should not only serve as a defense against aggression, but should patrol the mouths of the rivers and put a stop to the activities of interloping fur-traders. At the same time, also on Sola's recommendation according to Alvarado,[72] the President supported a proposition for the transfer of the San Blas naval station and shipyard to Monterey.

This, again, was an oft-discussed project dating back to the Spanish era. Bancroft cites[73] a document of

---

[71] Colección, Item 1 (Dictamen), pp. 15--16.

[72] J. B. Alvarado, Historia de Calif., MS, vol. 1, pp. 233--36.

[73] Calif., vol. 1, p. 604. The document is Salazar, Condición Actual de California, 1796, MS, pp. 73--82.

the eighteenth century, recommending the transfer to Monterey or San Francisco, and claiming as advantages of such a change that wages and food would be cheaper than at San Blas, while California's industries would be developed.

Tamariz, in his <u>memoria</u> of 1815 to the king, had also put forward that suggestion,[74] on the grounds that southern California produced everything needed save iron; a saving of 340,000 <u>pesos</u> a year could be effected by the transfer; the San Blas population, composed chiefly of artisans, if moved to California would prove able and willing colonizers; the completed ships could clear from California for San Blas, Acapulco and Guayaquil laden with such products as Mexico would otherwise have to import from Lima and Chili; and the resulting impulse to trade would attract entrepreneurs of those Mexican ports and of Tepic to commercial ventures in Alta California.

The same requirements of a naval squadron for California and the transfer of the San Blas shipyards to Monterey, together with projects for a maritime base at San Francisco, a military governorship and a <u>comisario</u>

---

[74] Pp. 92, 105. In the same connection he refers to an accompanying memorial enlarging on his reasons for urging the transfer.

de guerra, strengthened land defenses and the establishment of a military academy were urged in the *iniciativa de ley* or draft of an organic law for California presented by the Junta.[75] (Bancroft found no evidence that this or any general organic law for the territories was ever enacted.)[76] The colonization law of April 1830 authorized the reservation or condemnation of lands for the erection of fortifications.[77]

Defense, expansion, colonization -- all were preliminary to agricultural, industrial and commercial development, projects for which reached their climax in the *plan político-mercantil para el más pronto fomento de las Californias*, enthusiastically elaborated by the *Junta de Fomento*. The heart and soul of that politico-mercantile scheme was the proposed *Compañía Asiatico-Mexicana, Protectora del Fomento de la Península de Californias*.

Again Tamariz seems to have been a leading spirit. As chairman or secretary of the committee, he signed a number of the documents in the file. Associated with him were ex-Governor Sola, Mariano Bonilla and Juan Espinosa de los Monteros.[78]

---

[75] *Colección*, Item 5; Bancroft, *Calif.*, vol. 3, pp. 35--36.

[76] *Calif.*, vol. 3, p. 35.

[77] Halleck, "Report," pp. 121--22.

[78] Vallejo, *Hist. de Calif.*, vol. 1, p. 299.

Unfortunately, much of the record of this subcommittee's work seems to have been lost or scattered, although a portion is preserved in the Mexican central archives. It seems safe to assume, however, that the Tamariz recommendations of 1814--15 to the king and viceroy were more or less completely incorporated in the program of the <u>Junta.</u> At that time he had proposed active prosecution of the fur trade, mining and agriculture; the establishment of work dépôts of various sorts -- fisheries, tanneries, flour mills, cloth mills, etc; and of course the transference of the shipyard from San Blas to Monterey. A lively import and export trade, borne in California bottoms, would result from such coordinated utilization of the region's unparalleled resources.[79]

Ambitious as had been the projects of Tamariz for the region which he considered the most precious of New Spain, he and the other enthusiasts of Mexico's <u>Junta de Fomento</u> went further. The Asiatic-Mexican Company which they conceived was to transform lonely Monterey into a great maritime and commercial center, and render California strong enough not only to resist foreign aggression, but to appropriate to herself the Pacific trade

---

[79] "Memoria," pp. 89, 91--92, 102, 104--5.

for which England and the United States were contending. A prospectus and proposed *reglamento* of the company round out the *Colección* of 1827.[80]

The corporation was to enjoy the immediate protection of the supreme government for twenty years; and despite the partially political motive of its founding, was to concern itself with mercantile affairs solely.[81]

A capitalization of 4,000,000 *pesos* was contemplated, the stock to be divided into 2,000 shares rated at 2,000 *pesos* par. The central government would assume fifty shares, and the people of the nation -- states, bishops, monasteries, public bodies and employees of all classes, even those of small salaries -- were urged to support the great undertaking, for the good of all.[82]

---

[80] Item 8. General Vallejo diligently copied into his *Hist. de Calif.* MS, vol. 1, pp. 300--317, the proposed sixty-four articles of incorporation and regulation. He used, says Bancroft (*Calif.*, vol. 3, p. 6, n. 6) an original formerly in the possession of David Spence. The company is also mentioned in Castañares, *Col. de Doc.*, p. 50. Bancroft (*loc. cit.*) assigns a few lines only to the great mercantile project.

[81] *Junta de Fomento, Colección*, Item 8, p. 9, Art. 1

[82] *Ibid.*, Art. 3; p. 19, Art. 49.

Although Mexican citizens were to be given preference as purchasers for four months after the inception of the company, foreigners were thereafter to be eligible as shareholders. In case of war with powers of which stockowners were or had been subjects, the proprietorship of their shares was to be regarded as inviolable and protected under international law, and the stock would be disposable by them as they wished. At the death of foreign stockholders, their rights should pass to their respective heirs, in accordance with the laws of the countries of which they were natives.[83] [In other words, the promoters fully realized the need of capital to float their projects, and while guarding against foreign domination strove to attract foreign investment.]

Since the chief object of the company was the prosperity of the Californias and their inhabitants, and since the government desired them to have a direct interest in the company as well as in its developmental projects, fifty shares were to be reserved for six years, at the end of which time they were to be available for purchase by Californian corporations, religious organizations, natives and other residents,[84] who by then, it was supposed, would be in a position to buy.

---

[83] *Junta de Fomento, Colección,* Item 8, pp. 20--22, Arts. 55, 56, 51, 52.

[84] *Ibid.*, p. 20, Art. 50.

The percentage of profit to shareholders was to be decided upon after the general sale of stock.[85]

The President of the United States of Mexico, or his proxy, was to conduct the first meeting of the company, at which a board of seven directors should be elected for their commercial experience, skill and probity. Thereafter the President should withdraw, leaving the management of the company in the hands of its directorial board.[86] [While the corporation, therefore, was to owe its existence and privileges to the supreme government, it was not to be under official surveillance too closely for efficiency and initiative to have scope.[87]]

The ships of the organization were to fly a standard bearing the arms of the Mexican Republic and the initials "C. A. M."[88]

The company was to export chiefly all the products and manufactures of Alta and Baja California and of (su

---

[85] Junta de Fomento, Colección, Item 8, pp. 21--22, Art. 56.

[86] Ibid., pp. 22--23, Arts. 58, 59.

[87] A number of articles, of course, were devoted to the internal organization and administration of the company and to provisions for its effective working, stability and solvency. They are not of interest here.

[88] Colección, Item 8, p. 10, Art. 31.

continente) Sonora and Sinaloa, since the principal object of the enterprise was the promotion of that precious peninsula; and also, if space allowed, products of the adjoining states of Galisco, Durango, Chihuahua, New Mexico and those of the Pacific Ocean were to be carried.[89]

Exports were to be duty-free, including exported foreign goods such as the company might wish to handle speculatively. Money, as well as merchandise, would have to be exported for the China trade, and as well as merchandise should go duty-free.[90]

The port of Monterey, headquarters of this commerce, should be declared a free port. Asiatic wares and produce deposited there should be exempt from all taxes, maritime and internal, and if sold there should be duty-free; but should be subject to a storage fee of 4% of invoice value, which amount should be applied to the building up of the peninsula. Goods of the company entered through the usual Pacific ports should pay the usual duties, less 25%

---

[89] *Junta de Fomento, Colección*, Item 8, pp. 11—12, Art. 12.

[90] *Ibid.*, p. 12, Arts. 13, 14.

remitted in recognition of the company's services to the government and the 4% storage fee.[91]

The arrival and contents of cargoes from Asia should be given prompt and wide publicity throughout the states of the Republic and those of South America; as should full lists of prices, which should be fixed in accordance with the principles of equity.[92]

For the good of the commerce, the greatest care was to be exerted to avoid any offense to Asiatic nationals or any discord with them. Besides the Asiatic traffic, trade was to be conducted along the Californian and southern Pacific coasts and among the adjacent islands; in which business, however, the company was to enjoy no special privileges. Special pains must be taken to export the most profitable commodities and import the most useful.[93]

---

[91] *Junta de Fomento, Colección*, Item 3, pp. 12--13, 13, Arts. 15, 16, 46, 17. The 4% charge on warehouse deposits for reshipment was an obvious attempt to wrest from Honolulu its title of dépôt and clearing-house of the Pacific trade -- a title which had been won and was retained throughout the period by virtue of the extremely low import duty of 5%. W. H. Davis, *Seventy-five Years in California*, p. 104.

[92] *Ibid.*, p. 13, Art. 13.

[93] *Ibid.*, p. 14, Arts. 32, 33, 24.

All shipyards, warehouses and offices of the company should be established close to Monterey and other ports, harbors and roadsteads of the Californias, Sonora and Sinaloa.[94]

The company's administrative and maritime officials were to enjoy the same privileges and exemptions as did the officers of the national armada; and were to engage in no other service.[95]

Natives and denizens of the Californias, Sonora and the United States of Mexico were to be given preference as officers and seamen. While foreigners found competent and of good faith were not to be excluded, the company was to make sure that at least half its maritime personnel were sons of America.[96]

Old and skilled officers of the armada were to be encouraged in the company's service by special recognition.[97]

Of equal importance with the export and import trade as objects of the corporation's activities should be the

---

[94] Junta de Fomento, Colección, Item 8, p. 15, Art. 27.
[95] Ibid., Art. 28.
[96] Ibid., Art. 29. Whether "America" was used in the sense of Hispanic-America or of Mexican America is a question.
[97] Ibid., pp. 15--16, Art. 30.

gathering of furs, fishing, whaling, sealing, pearl- and shell-fishing, all those industries being true branches of commerce and so interrelated that the prosecution of each was favorable to that of each other.[98]

The company was to enjoy a monopoly of those industries, which were as valuable as they were exclusively the nation's own.[99]

Reimbursement of fisherman in all those branches on a percentage basis, rather than by a meagre pittance of day-wages, would be to the company's best interests. [Here was a very modern touch, indeed, of profit-sharing!] The fisheries, as a sort of training school, would help to build up the nation's maritime efficiency. Californians and Sonoreños were to be given preference for all posts in the fisheries.[100]

The company's fisheries and storage plants were to be afforded free police protection.[101]

---

[98] *Junta de Fomento, Colección*, Item 3, p. 10, Art. 32; pp. 17--18, Art. 41.

[99] *Ibid.*, p. 10, Art. 33.

[100] *Ibid.*, Arts. 34, 35.

[101] *Ibid.*, pp. 16--17, Art. 36.

All materials purchased for the construction of boats for the pearl fisheries or for the prosecution of that industry should be duty-free. Deep-sea, coastal and river fisheries of all sorts should enjoy exemption from taxes on their catches. Similar exemptions should extend to the products of Californian agriculture and industry as carried on by the company, since its prosperity was bound up with that of the peninsula.[102]

Fishing of all sorts affording only seasonal and insufficient support for families, fishermen were to be utilized by the company in the making of sailcloth and in similar services to the merchant marine.[103]

In return for its many privileges, the company was to promote and subsidize colonization, by recruiting families, artisans and master workmen of all sorts, and transporting them with their implements of trade and agriculture to the frontier ports.[104]

---

[102] *Junta de Fomento, Colección*, Item 8, p. 17, Arts. 38, 39; p. 18, Art. 42.

[103] *Ibid.*, p. 17, Art. 40.

[104] *Ibid.*, p. 18, Art. 44.

It was also to aid in the suppression of contraband trade, prejudicial to its interests as well as to those of the nation, by supplying extra ships for the coast-guard service when needed.[105]

The scheme, for all its refreshing scope and verve, was not original. For centuries, European mercantile monopolies of one kind and another had served the ends of empire. Very possibly the project of the "C. A. M.," as its promoters fondly called it, was more or less inspired by the example of certain Spanish companies of a hundred years earlier. Such were the Caracas Company and the Santo Domingo Company, which, founded on the erection of the viceroyalty of Nueva Granada in 1739, had helped to hold off Dutch smugglers.[106]

The very modelling of the project on tested precedents showed a disposition toward practicality. Bancroft's criticism was that the Junta devised its "liberal and enthusiastic measures without the slightest idea as to where the money to give them effect was to come from."[107] This is too sweeping a statement. The stockholders were to initiate the great program. Once under way, however, it was to be self-liquidating.

---

[105] Junta de Fomento, Colección, Item 8, pp. 18--19, Art. 45.

[106] Priestley, Mex. Nation, p. 181.

[107] Calif., vol. 3, p. 5, n. 3.

The transplantation of the San Blas _apostadero de marina_ to Monterey was to serve the triple purpose of economy in ship-building, settlement, and development of the frontier territory. Colonization was to be subsidized from the profits of the "C. A. M." and from the mission surplus as well. Warehouse charges on stored "C. A. M." imports were to be applied to the erection of public buildings. Foreign capital was to be attracted to an enterprise which should serve largely to ward off foreign encroachment. Long established devices of paternalism and protection were to foster colonization, agriculture, industry and trade; and each phase of development was to contribute to each other phase in a great comprehensive and interlocking system.

Certainly the whole inspiring program was plausible enough to captivate the imagination of President, Cabinet and Congress -- all in expansive mood. But there its progress ended. As Alvarado expressed it, with something of Hibernian force, the program "died without being born."[108]

---

[108] _Hist. de Calif._, MS, vol. 1. p. 234.

4. Mexico's Handicaps

The causes of mortality were not far to seek. The
Congreso of 1824 was of a magnificently enterprising
temper. Without hesitation it voted "dockyards, literary
institutes, museums, pensions, cathedrals, water carnivals
(juegos de aguas), arsenals, warships, libraries and a
thousand other items," -- in mood resembling the debonair
munificence of our own "new deal" administrators -- when it
could scarcely pay the soldiers on which its political life
depended. As Don Mariano Estrada expressed it to Don Ignacio Vallejo, the liberal-minded republicans " 'wished to
wear velvet and couldn't buy calico.' "[110]

Direct material aid, such as California desperately
needed, they were in no position to provide. Very early
the captains of the republic faced the necessity of
balancing a budget which listed heavily to the liability
side. The decision of the government to suspend payment
on the public debt until equilibrium could be restored in
the national ledgers gave rise to widespread disaffection.
As time went on, fiscal involvements became hopelessly
intricate, methods of raising funds flagrantly irregular,
and the importunities of creditors, foreign and domestic,

---

[109] Alvarado, Hist. de Calif., MS, p. 235.

became ominous, while financial depression balked every Mexican aspiration.

Little attempt has been made at demilitarization after the establishment of constitutional government. Instead, generals were given administrative powers. The result was probably to aggravate the reactionism of the privileged classes, especially of the old Spanish residents. A campaign of expulsion of the latter led to a counter-revolution directed from Cuba, in 1829.

Victoria's attempt at coalition government resulted in administrative factionalism and dead-lock. As a matter of fact, the Constitution of 1824 allowed too much political participation to a people uneducated in democracy; and exposed to all the hazards of an experimental federalism a country which had known only centralism, royalism and traditionalism.

The secular-clerical issue introduced elements of dissension which presently had to be suppressed by force of arms. Political opportunism made capital of popular confusion; and with Santa Anna to give initial momentum, political agitation set in motion that sequence of corrupt elections, cuartelazos and farcical constitutionalism which has continued to mark Mexico's fluctuations between administrative impotence and caudillismo. It was Santa Anna who had given the first blow to the throne of

Iturbide; and beginning with the fall of that very temporary monarch, the history of Mexico, says Alamán,[110] might properly be called the history of the revolutions of Santa Anna.

The latter contrived various machinations in connection with the presidential campaign of 1828; made himself dictator in 1833; in 1834 dissolved Congreso, diputaciones and ayuntamientos, and deposed governors, filling the vacancies with his adherents. The military-clerical opposition secured the upper hand for a time, from 1835; and in a sort of unconstitutional constitutional convention drafted the Siete Leyes of 1836, which became for the time being Mexico's organic law.

The new constitution had the merits of restoring centralism to the divided nation and checking the use of the illiterate and indigent population as political pawns, by limiting suffrage on an income basis. For the rest, it was an elaborate and unique mechanism for the paralysis of government; for its originators, anticipating the return of Santa Anna to power, had spared no effort to check the executive -- and the administrative and judicial branches as well, since they expected those departments to be more or less under his influence.

---

110   Lucas Alamán, Historia de México, vol. 5, pp. 686, 689.

Most inept, and provocative of widespread public resentment, was the *Poder Conservador*, or Conserving Power of five members, created to "maintain an equilibrium between the executive, legislative and judicial branches . . . . secure the enforcement of the laws," and, by what clairvoyance was not **indicated,** on special occasions to interpret the "will of the nation."

Under the Constitution of 1836, says Priestley, "the Departments had no liberties, the legislative branch no initiative, the judiciary no independence; but the worst feature of all was that of subjecting the Chief Executive to the Poder Conservador . . . . which might depose him, suspend Congress, annul laws, or reverse judicial sentences. It was responsible only to Deity, which it barely recognized." Moreover, as might have been expected, it "exercised its privileged position to thwart the very interests it was supposed to promote."[111]

As might equally have been expected, attempts to deprive the *Poder Conservador* of some of its prerogatives, and finally to abolish it, were futile. To make matters

---

[111] *Mexican Nation*, pp. 266--74, *passim*; 293.

worse, centralist President Bustamante, who had mounted to office on a reform platform, proved reactionary.[112] So the radicals resorted to force; Santa Anna, as usual, joined the fracas, and as usual, by measures direct and indirect, eventually had things his own way. His *Junta* of Notables in 1843 foisted on Mexico its third constitution in twenty years -- the *Bases Orgánicas de la República Mexicana* -- characterized by Priestley as "a most cynical attack on popular rights under an assumption of the form

---

[112] Priestley, while giving Bustamante credit for rather unusual administrative powers, declares him an opportunist of the first water, and his government a pure military despotism. *Mex. Nation*, pp. 292, 267--68. Bancroft found much to commend in Bustamante -- his "frank character, unselfish and honorable record . . . . He was a brave soldier, however, rather than a statesman, somewhat slow of reflection, vacillating, and devoid of moral energy," and "with undefined **ideas and** scanty means he had started upon the experimental course, trusting to fortune and bad advisers and neglecting the lessons taught by experience." *Hist. Mex.*, vol. 5, pp. 235--36.

of democracy. . . . . Here was the apogee of personalistic centralism. . . . . Graft lost all vestiges of refinement. Huge sums expended in pleasures led to demands upon the people for still greater sums to be expended, it was alleged, upon preparations for resistance to the United States, France, and England . . . ." But the dictator's exploitation of his countrymen was so flagrant as to arouse "more than a suspicion of his intention to do nothing . . ."[113]

Civil strife over the presidency followed, with no fewer than three "chief executives" in the field; and then war broke out between the United States and Mexico. Yet even during that crisis, Santa Anna, having returned from exile and changed his political coat again, resumed his career of intrigue. He and other opportunistic promoters of discord kept Mexico prey to faction for another decade. Not till the desperate struggles led by Juarez did the Mexican people find their feet at last on the path -- though but at its entrance -- to modern statehood.[114]

It is not surprising that antagonism to such manipulations as the country had suffered for the personal gratification, in large part, of a few unscrupulous militarists, reached widespread secessionist proportions. It had been

---

[113] Priestley, Mex. Nation, pp. 293--96.
[114] Ibid., pp. 296--98.

doubtful, indeed, for some time after independence, if the northern states would remain in the Mexican federation; in 1829, Jalisco and its neighbors, and in 1833 the nine north-central states, had strained at the leash of their allegiance; and the imposition of the Seven Laws produced a revival of what Priestley neatly phrases "the centrifugal spirit," with San Luís Potosí and Sonora ready, in 1837, to become members of a projected mountain Republic of Sierra Madre.[115]

California, of course, had shared in the unrest of 1836, tentatively declaring herself in that year a "free and sovereign state," but reverting to a sort of home rule basis when Mexico sanctioned the attempt at self-government -- being scarcely in a position to do otherwise. New Mexico, too, entertained ideas of independence or of throwing in her lot with Texas, in 1837 and again in 1841. Practically to the time of the Mexican War, in fact, secession and threats of secession, overt and covert, harassed Mexico.

Texas, however, was the case most momentous for Mexico -- and for California. The Texas crisis was already piling up as the New Mexican nation reached something like working order. California was potentially in danger; but Texas was imminently so. Both were frontier departments, flung out as

---

[115] Mex. Nation, p. 292.

buffers against the pressure of foreign encroachment; but the Texas frontier was the older, the more traversed and the more debated. Mexico's attention was bound to be distracted from California so long as she had her Texas problem; and she had that problem until, through her inability to solve it and her refusal to compromise with it, she lost, not only Texas, but considerably more than half her original area, including California.

It was in 1821 that Moses Austin secured his grant and privileges as an *emprendedor* of colonization; so Mexico may be said to have been born with the Texan doom upon her. Probably within a mere matter of months, Mexican officials realized that despite the fraternal benevolence with which the United States had looked on the new republic's struggle for liberty, the Yankee and the Hispanic elements were not readily assimilable. Moreover, it was soon obvious that the live-and-let-live spirit of the Monroe Doctrine was not the spirit of the Yankees in Texas.

But it was one thing to perceive the set of the tide, and another to roll back the flood. The substitution of a reactionary for a liberal policy would have precipitated disaster -- did, as a matter of fact, when eventually resorted to. As it was, wave upon wave, with startling rapidity from the outset, the crisis on the northeastern frontier mounted. There were administrative troubles, naturally. Even the Mexicans could understand, perhaps, the desire of Yankee-dominated Texas for a political organization of its own, separate from that of Coahuila with which it was being administered. Enlightened Mexicans, too, could sympathize with the Yankee demand for prerogatives of self-rule utterly incompatible with dictatorship by Santa Anna or centralism according to the Seven Laws. Yet Yankee arrogance and disregard for Mexican authority were not promising foundations on which to set up a Yankee-administered Mexican state. And there were other matters for anxiety.

Almost at once had come the Fredonian Rebellion -- a first straw in the wind of Mexican border turbulence; and almost simultaneously came overtures from the United States for the purchase of the area between the Sabine River and the Rio Grande -- clear indication of the trend of American territorial ambitions. As early as January 1830, Mexican authorities best qualified to know were convinced that "'{the United States will carry out their project of possessing Texas at the first opportunity, which opportunity will be as soon as they think we are torn by civil strife.'"[116]

---
[116] Jan. 6, 1830, Lt. Tarnava to Min. of War, citing opinion of General Téran, comandante general of the Eastern States, in close touch with Texan affairs. Quoted in translation by Howren, "Causes and Origin of the Decree of April 6, 1830," in Southwestern Historical Quarterly, vol. 16, p. 383.

For more than two years past, General Téran had been urging plans for the effective occupation and defense of the frontier regions of Texas-Coahuila. Vigorously supported in his efforts by President Bustamante (who had been his predecessor as comandante general of the Eastern States) and by clear-sighted Minister of Relations Lúcas Alamán, he had secured full congressional co-operation in the matter of allotments of men and money.[117] But not Congress, nor any other power in Mexico, could actually provide those two essentials of empire.

At the close of 1829, the republic had for the protection tection of all its Eastern States, 650 so-called effectives. Of those, but 400 were available for duty in the interior; and they had to be spread over Tamaulipas as well as Texas. The seacoast was thus unguarded but for 100 men in Tampico supplemented by a fever-ridden newcomer-detachment of 150, which "'should be at the rear, becoming acclimated in Victoria; for to station it at once in Tampico will be to lose those still surviving. It has 150 men reported as fit for duty, but the truth is, all are sick.'"[118]

---

[117] Howren, Southwestern Hist. Quarterly, vol. 16, pp. 391--94, 399--401, 404--5.

[118] Nov. 14, 1829, Téran to Min. of War, quoted in translation by Howren, op. cit., pp. 401--2.

There was not even a mobile force equipped for sudden marches to a threatened point; and it must be remembered that in addition to the foreign threat there was the ever-present Indian menace. Yet things were to become worse. Priestley states[119] that in August 1832 the soil of Texas was without Mexican soldiers.

A letter of Téran, of June 30, 1828, to President Victoria, vividly describes the Texas situation. Already, he says, the ratio of foreigners to Mexicans is as ten to one; and the Mexican population is of the lowest class, while the political administration is rudimentary and helpless.

"The [American] colonists murmur against the political disorganization of the frontier and the Mexicans complain of the superiority and better education of the colonists . . . . Every officer of the federal government has immense districts under his jurisdiction . . . . The whole population here is a mixture of strange and incoherent parts, without parallel in our federation: numerous tribes of Indians, now at peace, but armed and at any moment ready for war . . . .; colonists of another people, more progressive and better informed than the Mexican inhabitants, but also more shrewd and unruly; among these foreigners are fugitives from justice, honorable laborers, vagabonds and criminals, but honorable and dishonorable alike travel with their political

---
[119] Mex. Nation, p. 283.

constitutions in their pockets, demanding the privileges, authority and officers which such a constitution guarantees. The most of them have slaves, and these slaves are beginning to learn the favorable intent of the Mexican law toward their unfortunate condition and are becoming restless under their yokes.'"[120]

It will be seen that Mexico's illusions about the Yankees in Texas -- if she had ever had any -- were short-lived indeed. It was realized, too, that if Texas were taken, a like fate would be suffered by "'Chihuahua, New Mexico and part of Sonora, they being exposed to and half surrounded by our dangerous neighbors, who would be at the doors of our richest states.'"[121] Texas, then, not California, was from the start the ailing child of Mexico and the focal point of her jealous apprehensions.

----

[120] Quoted in translation by Howren, Southwestern Historical Quarterly, vol. 16, pp. 395, 397--98. In addition to the fact that republican Mexico naturally had its face set against slavery, men like Téran and Alamán realized clearly that to allow the fastening of the slave system on Texas would be to open up a new promised land to the southern expansionists of the United States.

[121] Jan. 6, 1830, Lt. Tarnava to Min. of War, quoted in translation by Howren, op. cit., p. 407.

This fact alone accounts for much of her insufficiency --
despite her initial zeal -- as foster-mother to California.
But she had, as well, a thousand other pressing worries.

As for anything like adequate port defenses, a coast-
guard, or even regular communications by sea between various parts of the republic, those existed only in the fervid
projects of military and other authorities in a position to
know but powerless to do.

Efforts had been made to create a navy and merchant
marine. In 1823 the War Department had reported to Congress the following elements of sea power: a brigantine in
need of careening, a schooner ready for launching (echarse
al agua), two seaworthy vessels in port at San Blas, a
schooner at Vera Cruz, and a customs department at Campeche
-- "not sufficient to be considered even the basis of a
navy." It was proposed to buy a frigate and eight corvettes
from the United States; and one craft was actually purchased,
which, renamed the "Iguala," became the first war-ship of
the Mexican navy.[122]

As late as 1852, however, leading Mexicans complained
that all efforts to form a navy had been fruitless, the
country lacking even a merchant marine, a necessary element

---

[122] México a través de los Siglos, vol. 4, pp. 59, 71--72.

for the existence of a navy.[123] And it must not be forgotten that smuggling had been rampant along the entire seaboard from Spanish times; that various filibustering expeditions had signposted paths to invasion; and that armed aggression by foreign powers, on one or another pretext, loomed early on the horizon.

Mexico, indeed, had had more than half her dominions wrested from her before she was well past what would have been the age of majority for a man; and nations mature less rapidly than men -- especially nations born, like Mexico, with no birthright of social coherence, economic stability and political *savoir-faire.*

For the Mexican nation did not spring into full self-realization and self-direction with the creation of Agustín's empire, nor with the establishment of the Republic. Iturbide, Santa Anna, Bustamante -- they were not Mexico, but accidents to Mexico, from which she had to recover before she could assert herself. Meantime, she had her potential statesmen, honest, forward-looking and zealous -- but with all the lessons of practical politics to learn.

---

[123] *México a través de los Siglos,* vol. 4, pp. 45--46. California's own efforts for naval and coast-guard defense are discussed *post,* chap. IV, sec. 44; for the creation of a merchant marine, chap. V, sec. 66.

As early as 1821, said Alamán (and he was in a position to know), there were not lacking "wise and honorable men who, by their probity, talent and prestige, not only ameliorated or reduced our troubles of state (males publicos), but furnished sound principles for healthy social organization; but men of this class were not able to secure efficacious results, for political developments had not given them the knowledge, nor did events as yet work out" to such an end. [124]

5. Mexico's Failures and California's Disillusionment

Perhaps it would have been better for the Californians had the republic possessed fewer men of a calibre to inspire hope for the future. Despite their sincerity and zeal, those forerunners of an administrative vigor which Mexico has not yet attained beguiled the department into wasting precious years in subordination and neglect; and those were the critical years in Hispano-California's history.

It is not absolutely beyond the realm of possibility that a Californian republic -- especially if under the

---

[124] Hist. de Mex., vol. 4, pp. 45--46.

protection of a strong power -- might have survived.[125] It is even probable that a California independent of Mexico and therefore untouched by the Texas catastrophe would early and eagerly have sought affiliation with the United States; for even hampered by her Mexican allegiance, she proved an apt subject for the "peaceful penetration" policy of which Thomas Larkin was the chief administrant. So she might have been spared years of deprivation and anxiety, and all the vicissitudes of conquest.

But Mexico seemed always on the verge of tendering salvation. As late as 1844--45, Manuel Castañares, then

---

[125] The United States was for some time in no position to enforce the Monroe Doctrine; and what has been called the "Polk Doctrine," reiterating and amending the earlier pronouncement, and amounting to "a contingent declaration of war" in the event of any sort of European interference on the North American continent, was not made public until just before the war with Mexico -- i.e., on December 2, 1845; although secret instructions of similar tenor, directed specifically against British or French intervention in California, were directed a few weeks earlier to Secretary of State Buchanan. (Eugene Irving McCormac, James K. Polk, pp. 692--94.)

California's Congressman, received such prompt and cordial official responses to appeals on behalf of his Department that action seemed _finally_ assured. In a lengthy report on California's _males_ and proposed remedies, submitted September 1, 1844 (probably to the Minister of Relations), he closed with the statement that he would continue to work faithfully and assiduously, as in the past, to promote the interests of his constituents, devoting himself to that end "with all the more pleasure in that the disposition which the Supreme Government has manifested to me in this regard is beyond measure favorable to my Department."[126]

A few days later he rendered heartfelt thanks to the government, and particularly to the president, for aid promised California.[127]

Early in 1845, he acknowledged to General José M. Tornel, just retired from the Ministry of War, "the attention which you gave unfailingly to my pleas, and the resolution and ardor which you showed for ameliorating the **forlorn condition of California** . . . . My Department would be in a different situation if you had not withdrawn from the Ministry."[128]

---

[126] _Col. de Doc._, p. 51.
[127] _Ibid._, pp. 52--53.
[128] _Ibid._, p. 5.

At the same time, Ministers Cuevas and García Conde were exerting themselves in California's interest. In their reports of March 1845, says Bancroft,[129] both alluded to the Department's lamentable condition. They regarded its defense as of the highest importance, recognized the real causes of recent political disturbances there, regretted past neglect on Mexico's part and announced the purpose of the government to avert the consequences of that neglect by prompt action. García Conde foretold measures to assure the integrity of the precious department; and Cuevas looked forward to the sending of men, money and armaments, together with "'a new chief [to replace deposed Micheltorena], who by his wise conduct may be able to conjure the evils with which California is threatened.'"[130]

It was too late for even conjury, probably, to avert the *males* closing down on California, but something might have been accomplished by the sending of "wise chiefs" -- a succession of them -- earlier. The *Junta de Fomento de Californias* had in 1837 vigorously urged the appointment of Francisco de Paula Tamariz as governor of California, expatiating on "his distinguished merit in all relating to the welfare of Californias. His knowledge and advice

---

[129] Calif., vol. 4, pp. 525--26.
[130] Ibid., vol. 4, p. 526.

have been the soul of all the Junta's efforts . . . .
Whatever progress has been made by the Junta is owing to
his zeal, and for twenty years he has been the most fervid
agent of the welfare of those territories, sparing no
labor or effort. The Junta would like to see him sent to
the Californias to establish the purposes of the sovereign
Congress and at the same time receive the just reward of
his labors."[131]

The final word of this particular Junta (which seems
to have dissolved in 1827, though its work was apparently
resumed later by a new committee under the same name) was
a plea -- though indirect -- for the appointment of Tamariz.
"If such a person is sent, the Junta will have fulfilled its
duties in so far as lies within its ability."[132]

What an opportunity was lost there! Tamariz, royal
naval officer turned republican (and become, it seems, a
comisario-general) might have done much for the region
which he so fervently promoted throughout his career. He
seems to have been such a man as would have exchanged his
Mexican governorship for the presidency of a free California,
if no other way had offered to fulfill his vision of frontier development.

----

[131] Colección, Item 5, pp. 3--4, 42, 43.
[132] Ibid.

But he dropped from sight -- one of history's untimely discards; and Mexico sent reactionary **V**ictoria to succeed Echeandía, precipitating the political disorders that racked California till Figueroa's advent in 1833.[133]

The metropolis, in fact, wasted nearly all its opportunities to assign able chiefs to the northwestern frontier. Figueroa -- the outstanding exception -- had been an "out" whose elimination from local politics had been urgently desired by apprehensive "ins." A political prisoner, he had been "too popular a man to be shot and too dangerous to be allowed to remain in Mexico." His appointment to California was in the nature of an exile.[134]

In large part, it was inferior specimens, of the "carpet-bag" variety, who were sent to fill the posts in the Department. Cárlos Carrillo said[135] that Mexico was

---

[133] Echeandía governed from November 1825 to January 31, 1831; Victoria's rule of January 31, 1831 to December 6, 1831 was ended by revolt; after which the Echeandía-Pico-Zamorano claims filled the interim to January 14, 1833; then Figueroa took office, to remain till his death on September 29, 1835.

[134] Bancroft, Calif., vol. 3, pp. 234--35, n. 23.

[135] Guerra Doc., MS, vol. 4, p. 243.

full of eager aspirants to office in California, where they hoped to emerge from the poverty of their lot in Mexico to the exalted station of viceroys. Naturally the official ineptitude and meretricious ambitions of such ~~political~~ spoils-gatherers made for inefficiency, conspiracy and strife in the territory.

Similarly, the colonists sent, and the soldiers -- who were intended to become colonists at the expiration of their military service -- were frequently the very dregs of Mexican society. Here again was cause of violent resentment on the part of the Californians, and of disorders of various sorts. Moreover, failure properly to equip and provide for soldiers and settlers left them a burden on the already impoverished population.

As for the ever urged and ever promised financial aid, Mexico seems never fully to have realized that California, at the time of independence, had been eking out a mere subsistence on borrowed money[136] for a decade. Some slight relief, as has been mentioned, was sent -- at the very first; though with no conception of the extent of the need. Nor was the worthy gesture followed up. Financial administrator Herrera promptly ran into difficulties which he was powerless to overcome. Criticized for inefficiency, he could only enter the pathetic and incontrovertible plea that creditors were many and resources small.[137]

---

[136] Obtained from the missions.

[137] Guerra Doc., MS, vol. 6, pp. 148--49; Bancroft, Calif., vol. 3, p. 15, n. 28.

Resources, in fact, consisted solely of such customs revenues as could be collected without coast-guard, navy, adequate port defenses or a properly organized and trained customs administration; and the civil and military expense accounts far exceeded this income.

Lower California, moreover, was from time to time administered as a part of California, either politically or for military purposes or both, thus seriously dividing the attention of the gefes políticos y militares. As late as Micheltorena's term, when crisis impended, the peninsula -- at the moment attached to the comandancia general of Sonora y Sinaloa -- was again assigned to the California governor for military, as well as political, administration.[138] As has been mentioned,[139] the conduct of California's financial affairs was subject to supervision from Arizpe, in Sonora; and the various higher courts were in Sonora and Sinaloa -- at distances immense for those days.[140]

Mexico was trying to do too much, with too little effective wealth and man-power, and too little political poise.

----

[138] Vallejo, Hist. de Calif., MS, vol. 4, p. 270; Bancroft, Calif., vol. 4, pp. 286, n. 16; 287, n. 17.

[139] Ante, p. 20.

[140] June 25, 1829, J. M. Echeandía to Min. of Justice, in Depart. Rec., MS, vol. 7, p. 23; Bancroft, Calif., vol. 2, p. 677, n. 47.

Yet with the psychology of the under-dog, she jealously refused to yield ground. Repeatedly, from 1835 to 1845, offers were tendered by the United States for the purchase of part of the troublesome northern regions. In 1844, Secretary of State Calhoun tried, through a secret agent, to break the Texas boundary dead-lock by the purchase, for ten million dollars, of certain Mexican territory: that lying north of a line drawn from midway between San Francisco and Monterey due east to the Rio Grande, and down that river to the Gulf.[141] But, unprepared as she was, Mexico preferred war.

Meantime, through more than a score of years, California had hoped for a strong man to rise to the supreme power. Vallejo thought that Bustamante might be that man. Those two corresponded with considerable frequency; their relations were cordial and they exchanged gifts. On April 25, 1840, two very reassuring letters were addressed to Vallejo from Mexico: one from Bustamante himself, and another from the trader Virmond -- who was very close to affairs -- bolstering up Don Guadalupe's faith in Bustamante's intention and ability to aid California.[142]

At the close of 1845, even, Vallejo found cause to rejoice in the fact of Bustamante's return to the republic,

---

[141] Bancroft, *Calif.*, vol. 4, p. 450, n. 17.
[142] *Vallejo Doc.*, MS, vol. 9, #122, #123.

foreseeing in that happy event benefit for the Department of California. As for Bustamante's greatly appreciated letter, every word of that was "a ray of patriotism"; Don Anastasio had always shown a notable predilection for California, and with joy Vallejo perceived that this remote country had recovered its most constant and powerful protector.[143]

But no man or group of men strong enough to find the way out for California and for the republic could emerge from the conditions which gripped Mexico prior to 1846 and for a decade longer. As Vallejo reflected in retrospect, events rendered impossible realization of the early republican ambitions for the development of the territory, though "homage is due the perspicacity" of the promoters. There was no doubt in his mind that it was "the continual revolutions which without cessation and without mercy racked unfortunate Mexico during the first fifty years of her political existence" which had prevented California from being enabled to occupy, from 1836, "the first rank among Pacific centers of commerce . . . ."[144]

---

[143] Nov. 22, 1845, Vallejo to Bustamante, in *Vallejo Doc.*, MS, vol. 12, #157, pp. 1, 7. (There are two copies of this document, a 10-page draft or blotter copy, and a 14-page "clean" version without corrections or interpolations. The draft, written in Victor Prudon's small, neat hand, is the more legible, and the citation here is to that copy.)

[144] *Hist. de Calif.*, MS., vol. 1, p. 317

"Fifty years later," was Alvarado's sad comment on the abortive projects of the Junta de Californias, "in the hands of energetic men backed by coin, some of these plans might have proved successful."[145]

It is interesting to speculate as to what Mexico might have done with California had Porfirio Diaz, just preceding whose ascendancy Vallejo and Alvarado wrote, made his appearance in the first scene of the Mexican drama. But in the '20s and '30s and '40s the time was not yet ripe for the "fomentation" of California, at least by the republic. Nor were the Californios blind to that fact. They saw only too early and clearly their foster-mother's insufficiencies.

Vallejo might in 1845 welcome back Bustamante as a benefactor; but for years he had been hammering Mexico with a barrage of bitter complaints of California's desperation and disillusionment. For years he and Alvarado and other sons and adopted sons of the country had sought to develop a California for Californians. They had experimented with self-rule from 1836 to 1843. They had been considering the various possibilities of a foreign protectorate.

Mexico's neglected children of the northern frontier continued to importune her, it is true, till the war-cloud

---
[145] Hist. de Calif., MS, vol. 1, p.236.

burst. But they also sought other means of salvation and development. They struggled desperately to help themselves, and they looked more and more to the _estrangeros_ for promotive aid and tutelage not otherwise to be had.

It has long been the fashion to condemn them as do-nothings who sold their birthright to the traders for commodities which they should themselves have produced. How exaggerated those charges are, it will be the purpose of the succeeding chapters to set forth. For, while Mexico and her unfulfilled good intentions will not be lost sight of, our point of view now shifts to California and her efforts at self-help, despite her handicaps of inexperience, lack of every practical means, and exposure to the mercy of powerful and ambitious neighbors. It is the purpose now to analyze the Department's problems, recall her struggles and discover the reasons for her failure. For our story concerns primarily not Mexico, but California.

CHAPTER II: "GOD, GIVE US MEN!"

6. Off to a Poor Start........................pages 78-- 83
7. Mexico Takes Over............................. 83-- 87
8. Convicts, Vagabonds and Foundlings............ 87-- 90
9. Vain Protests and Antagonisms................. 91-- 94
10. Remarks in Extenuation........................ 95-- 97
11. The Island Domain............................. 97-- 98
12. The Northern Frontier......................... 98--103
13. The Great Colony..............................104--119
14. Progress on the Northern Frontier.............119--125
15. Foreign Colonization..........................125--140
16. Ten Thousand Irishmen.........................141--149
17. Wanted: Assorted Foreigners!..................149--152
18. Peopling California with Californians.........152--166
19. The Forgotten Men.............................166--168

CHAPTER II: "GOD, GIVE US MEN!"

6. Off to a Poor Start

That nation which would become a colonial power, and that colony which would thrive, must be blessed qualitatively and quantitatively with men. Mexico was not, California was still less, so blest.

The territory's population *de razon* in 1820, estimated by Bancroft[1] on the basis of numerous *padrones* and other local records, was 3,270 souls. This figure would include the soldiery, numbering about 700 just then, though much fewer before and after,[2] and two score padres, reckoning the usual two for each mission as yet established. The remainder -- 2,500 in round numbers -- would represent California's lay and civilian population.

Had all been supermen, they would have had to succumb, through numerical weakness alone, to the forces already operating against them. But these were not supermen. Very few of them were even selected men. The majority were illiterate mixed bloods -- dregs drawn from that submerged and variegated society on whose deplorable condition in Mexico Congressman Castañares has already been quoted.[3]

---
[1] *Calif.*, vol. 2, p. 653.
[2] See *post*, p. 357, Table XI.
[3] *Ante*, pp. 4--5.

California's paucity of human effectives, like Mexico's, was a heritage from Spain. Spanish California had been taken and held with even greater economy of man-power than had Mexico. Not force of arms, but spiritual conquest by fewer than half a hundred brown-robed Franciscans, had won the northwesternmost Spanish province.

The crown had attempted to people and develop the region, to the point, at least, where it could support its small quota of soldiers -- never as many as one per linear mile. But Spain being unable to spare the men from the European scene, the burden of human supply had been shifted to Mexico; and Mexico had few to spare save undesirables.

The Spanish pueblos -- San José founded in 1777 with 66 or 68 settlers, Los Angeles in 1781 with 44, and Branciforte in 1796 with 17 -- were poor essays at colonization.

Efforts had been made to improve the calibre of the populace. Subsidies had been offered. Homesteading opportunities with tax exemption for eight years had been extended to veterans of the Napoleonic wars and of the antirevolutionary expeditions to Hispanic America. Unpropertied civilians had been baited with lottery chances on small home sites. Provincial women of respectable background and character had been urged to migrate to the northern frontier.[4] All such

---

[4]Bancroft, Calif., vol. 1, p. 605. J. D. Francis, "Los Angeles, Area 4 Square Leagues, Population 44," Calif. Hist. Nugget, vol. 3, pp. 65--71; idem, "San José was Modern 150 Years ago," op. cit., pp. 114--20.

enterprises had failed, however, For while to persons of initiative and ambition the outposts of empire are often the signposts of opportunity, Spain's absolutism and commercial exclusiveness gave to her frontiers the character of fences, the more confining for the savage remoteness of the regions enclosed.

The best of the troops were incomparably better pioneer stock than the civilians of early California, and veterans and inválidos, with their wives and children, gradually built up civil settlements around the presidios or helped to swell the pueblo rolls. Indeed, in 1806 Governor Arrillaga advised the viceroy that if it were not for the inválidos the pueblos would amount to nothing.[5] But Spanish autocracy, characteristically defeating its own ends, required of its officers and men-at-arms official authorization -- from Spain, not from local or Mexican superiors -- before marriage could be contracted. Applications and correspondence regarding such applications catch the eye from time to time as one runs through documents of the period.

Even when a soldier's petition to marry was granted, it might be only after years of waiting. Luis Antonio Argüello requested permission to make Rafaela Sal his wife in 1800, but did not receive the desired authorization until 1807 --

---

[5] Bancroft, Calif., vol. 2, p. 168.

and then it was conditioned on La Sal's renunciation of all claims on the Montepio Fund unless Don Luis should be killed in battle. In tribute to the steadfastness of both lovers, it is to be noted that they had not changed their minds during their seven years' wait.[6]

Forbes attributed the regulation of soldier-marriages to the deliberate intent of limiting the number of soldiers' descendants, in the interests of the mission system. So "it could easily be managed that as many marriages were permitted as were desired, and no more. This fully accounts for the very scanty number of free colonists that exists in California."[7]

Forbes was well-informed and in a position to know whereof he spoke in most matters relating to Alta California. His theory in this case does not tally, however, with the fact that many of the soldiers were sent to the province accompanied by their wives and families, so that the garrisons might become at once nuclei of settlement. Yet inconsistencies of policy are not without precedent in most governments.

Official after official recognized the need of a Spanish-Californian population. Revilla Gigedo, in a letter of 1793, favored the settlement of Spanish families at the missions.

---

[6] Bancroft, Calif., vol. 3, p. 11, n. 22.
[7] Alexander Forbes, Alta Calif., p. 132.

Costansó', in a report of 1794, declared that the first thing to be thought of was to people the country. "'Presidios to support missions are well enough for a time, but there seems to be no end of them. . . . . Californians understand this and clamor for industrious citizens.'" Borica was an earnest advocate of colonization. In 1795, he sought to promote soldier-settler marriages, and even discouraged the enlistment of settlers' sons in the presidial companies, in an effort to boost the civil census. In 1797, he issued orders requiring retired soldiers to live in the pueblos. He also instituted a "drive" for marriageable women as settlers; but despite the support of the viceroy seems to have failed in his purpose.

Fathers Señan and Salazar pointed out and Governor Borica recognized the fundamental deterrents to Spain's colonization of California: the low grade of settlers introduced, the lack of a market for their produce and of a reliable system of purveyance of needed commodities.[8]

Until the wars of independence, however, despite the urgencies of crown officers and padres and the "clamor" raised by the few better-class lay residents of the province, no change in policy was effected. After 1810 the sending of colonists ceased entirely. Indeed, for some years before,

---

[8] Bancroft, *Calif.*, vol. 1, pp. 602--5.

efforts in that direction had been relaxed, Governor Arrillaga considering the region without particular advantage or promise of development.[9] So under Spain California's census list increased chiefly by the offspring of soldiers and of a few ignominious settlers, and such wives as they had either brought with them or found for themselves among the Indians.

7. Mexico Takes Over

Mexico entered enthusiastically into projects for the effective colonization of her territories and interior states. Halleck mentions[10] a series of colonization laws promulgated as early as April 11, 1823, although these were suspended almost immediately, and probably never had effect.[11]

As has been mentioned, the Junta de Californias, having devoted earnest attention to the subject of colonization, submitted in May 1825 its plan for the settlement of California by Mexican nationals, and in April of the same year its plan for colonization by foreigners,[12] which recommendations, though not adopted as a whole, were

---

[9] Bancroft, Calif., vol. 2, p. 169.

[10] "Report," p. 120.

[11] Bancroft, Calif., vol. 2, p. 662, says: "I have not seen the law referred to." (I do not find these laws in Dublan y Lozano. The Arrillaga compilation, of course, was not inaugurated for another fifteen years. Its resume' of preceding legislation extends back only to 1828, and is fragmentary. J.D.F.)

[12] Colección. Items #3, #4.

partially incorporated in subsequent legislation. That legislation, however, was designed for all the territories, while the <u>Junta's</u> proposals, being directed at the promotion of California specifically, included certain special inducements for Mexican nationals to settle in that territory. As these provisions seem never to have attained legal status, they are resumed here briefly:

In addition to grants of land, expenses of the journey to the colony were to be paid.

Farmers were to be furnished with livestock and tools, and with rations and a small cash subsidy over a three-year period.

Non-agricultural settlers were to be supplied with the tools of their trades, a house-lot per family, and a year's rations.

The expense of this subsidization was to be defrayed from capital believed to have accumulated at the missions.

Meantime, a decree of August 18, 1824, issued by the constituent congress, had made general provision for territorial colonization; and a series of regulations published under date of November 21, 1828, incorporating many of the <u>Junta's</u> recommendations of 1825, limited and defined the decree of 1824. Halleck found the 1824, and the 1828, laws still in force in July 1846; with a statute of April 6, 1830 somewhat modifying them.[13]

The law of 1824[14] made the following specifications:

Preference in land distribution was to be given Mexican citizens. (Art. 9).

No grantee residing out of the republic could retain lands acquired therein under this law. (Art. 15).

Lands within ten leagues of the coast could not be colonized without approval of the supreme executive power. (Art. 4). (This limitation was motivated by the desire to extend territorial occupation inland.)

---

[13] "Report," p. 121. The laws of 1824, 1828 and 1830 will be considered in this chapter in their bearing, first on the promotion of colonization by Mexican nationals (sec. 7), and later on foreign colonization (sec. 15). Their special effects in the matter of the distribution of land to nationals will be treated in chap. V, secs. 50, 51, 52; and in that of land grants to foreigners, in chap. VIII.

[14] Manuel Dublán y José María Lozano, Legislación Mexicana, vol. 1, pp. 712--13. Text and translation in Gustavus Schmidt, Civil Laws of Spain and Mexico, pp. 340--45. Translations in Halleck, "Report," App. #4, pp. 139--40; Alfred Wheeler, Land Titles, pp. 7--8; John W. Dwinelle, Colonial Hist. of San Francisco, Add. #12, pp. 23--24. Bancroft, Calif., vol. 2, p. 516, n. 8, gives the substance of the 16 articles.

By the regulations of 1828,[15] the governor was empowered to make grants, at his discretion, after due investigation and formality and with the approval of the <u>diputación</u>, to individual petitioners or families; the decision resting with the supreme government if the <u>diputación</u> withheld approval. (Arts. 1--6).

Grants to <u>empresarios</u> were all subject to the approval of the supreme government; and no such grant would be considered unless the <u>empresario</u> contracted to bring in at least twelve families. (Arts. 7, 10).

If an <u>empresario</u> failed to fulfill his part of the contract, his grant would become invalid, but the governor might revalidate it in proportion to the degree of fulfillment. (Art. 11).

New settlements were to be established with all possible regularity and in accordance with the existing laws. (Art. 13).

The minimum of irrigable land assignable to one person was to be 200 <u>varas</u> square; of agricultural land, 800 <u>varas</u> square; of grazing land, 1,200 <u>varas</u> square; and house-lots were to be of the usual 100 <u>varas.</u> (Arts. 14, 15).

Areas between colonized lands might be granted to those proprietors of contiguous holdings who had cultivated their grants with the greatest application and who had not received the maximum legal allotment; or to their children. (Art. 16).

---

[15] Translations in Halleck's "Report," App. #5, pp. 141--42; Wheeler, <u>Land Titles</u>, pp. 8--9; Dwinelle, <u>Colon. Hist. S.F.</u>, Add. #14, pp. 25--26. Bancroft, <u>Calif.</u>, vol. 3, pp. 34--36 gives the gist. (I do not find this law in Dublán y Lozano. J.D.F.)

The law of April 6, 1830[16] had no special bearing on colonization by nationals. It will be considered presently (sec. 15) in its connection with colonization by foreigners and with national defense.

8. Convicts, Vagabonds and Foundlings.

Had Mexico been able to produce pioneer material as adequate as her colonization laws, all might have been well. But lacking that surplus of vigorous and enterprising manpower requisite to possession of the earth, she resorted to impressment of the unwilling -- and unfit. From the ranks of the most abject, not excluding the vagabond and criminal orders, she seized her reluctant guardians of empire -- adopting for herself what had been an old Spanish custom with regard to the peopling of the territories.

For it had perhaps been Governor Fages, Bancroft thought, who initiated this plague of wretches in California. During the last decade of the eighteenth century the commutation of Mexican convict sentences to exile in California had become a fixed policy of the crown. The heads of Branciforte's nine original families were vagabonds and criminals (though superior to the other pueblo founders in being at least

---

[16] Dublán y Lozano, Legislación Mex., vol. 1, pp. 238--40.
Translation in Halleck, "Report," pp. 121--22. Bancroft apparently did not have access to this law except through Halleck's "Report" (see Calif., vol. 3, p. 35, n. 7).

nominally of Spanish blood). Other groups were sent from time to time -- to labor with shackled feet, for rations; or to learn and teach trades, or serve out their sentences as soldiers; and of course to become permanent settlers.

The opening of the new century had been inaugurated for California by the arrival of nineteen foundlings (nine of them girls of marriageable age) sent from Mexico by Spain. These, far more promising than the convict and vagabond material, were distributed -- like puppies, one of them later recorded,-[17] among respectable families in the different presidios. The boys developed into robust men, and most of the girls became wives and, undoubtedly, mothers.

Had foundlings alone been consigned to the province, results might have been beneficial -- for most of these young waifs had had the benefit of institutional care and training. But the practise of sending *presidarios* persisted, though under the last years of the Spanish régime the vigorous protests of governor and commandants seem to have had some temporary effect in checking the evil.[18]

---

[17] A. Lorenzana, Memorias de 'La Beata', MS, p. 1. "La Beata," as she came to be called, was one of those who justified her existence by faithful and valuable, though humble, service as handmaid and nurse in missions and private families, in the San Diego district.

[18] Bancroft, Calif., vol. 1, pp. 169, 604--5.

The wars of independence afforded a further breathing spell. Then Mexico resumed the vicious practise where Spain had left off. The most enlightened of the new statesmen — leaders like Ortiz de Ayala and Alamán — looked on colonization by means of criminals as a practical and generally beneficial measure. Such a policy, said Alamán, could be expected not only to develop the territories, but to make of the criminals "farmers useful to the nation, good fathers, good neighbors, and finally good citizens."[19]

By the deportation of convicts, therefore, Mexico inaugurated her attempt to occupy California. Along with her first officials and troops she sent eighteen convicts, under guard of a small body of infantry. "With few exceptions," says Bancroft, "the newcomers, whether officers, soldiers or convicts, were Mexicans of a class by no means desirable as citizens." He adds a few personalities which indicate that these *presidarios* were no mere political prisoners.

Their number included, for example, Vicente Gomez, reputed a fiend in human form, torturer as well as killer; and several of his companions, of whom one was such an inveterate thief that he is said once to have robbed his own *monte* bank at Santa Bárbara, "to keep in practise." This man was lynched in 1860 for cattle-stealing. Gomez and others

---

[19] Ortiz de Ayala, *Resumen*, p. 3; Alamán, *Mem. Relac.*, 1823, p. 33.

met violent deaths. Some became ordinary thieves and vagabonds. A few became respectable; while two -- Solís and Ávila, the latter having murders as well as robberies to his account -- won new notoriety in the revolt of 1829.[20]

In April of that same year, the Secretary of Justice circularized the judges of Mexico, urging them to sentence their prisoners to California instead of to Vera Cruz -- for reasons of public utility and welfare as they bore on the occupation, improvement and special development of Alta California.

Further regulations were issued from time to time thereafter, and in accordance with the Law of April 6, 1830, announcement was made that the government would transport to California the families of such convicts as might so desire.[21] In 1829--30, close to 150 criminals arrived in the territory. Bancroft was able to assemble public and private archives listing the names, places, dates and crimes of very many of these exiles to the "northern Botany Bay."[22]

---

[20] Bancroft, Calif., vol. 3, pp. 15--16.

[21] Basilio José Arrillaga, Recopilación, 1829, pp. 67--69; 260--70; Dublán y Lozana, Legislación Mex., vol. 1, p. 239, Art. 5; Mex., Mem. Justicia, 1830, p. 19.

[22] Calif., vol. 3, pp. 47--49.

9. Vain Protests and Antagonisms

The residents of California were naturally outraged by such a visitation and the prospect of its continuance. At a mass-meeting in Monterey, "all those who could read and write" signed a solemn negation of Mexico's prerogative to infest the territory's incipient population with criminals, and petitioned the gefe político for relief. Echeandía deplored the situation, apologizing for his government on the ground that it was unaware that decent and cultivated families existed in the territory.[23]

He also addressed a prompt protest to the war office, declaring[24] that the sending of criminals would result in disorder and corruption in the Californias and would antagonize the respectable residents. He asserted California's utter inability to confine, guard or even feed the prisoners, explaining that those already in the territory had had to be allowed at large in order to earn their livings. Only the most dangerous could be kept imprisoned, and those but temporarily, for lack of jails and soldiers. The lives and property of the citizens were in danger. He besought the Minister of War to take up the matter with the President of the Republic, requesting that no more criminals be sent and that those already in the country be taken elsewhere.

---

[23] Vallejo, Hist. de Calif., MS, vol. 2, pp. 70--73.
[24] Sept. 18, 1829, Dept. Rec., MS, vol. 7, pp. 38--40.

Bancroft[25] characterized this protest as rather feeble, inasmuch as the governor included in his plea a request that only "useful" convicts be sent. The whole tenor of Echeandía's communication, however, as of the diputación's, is urgent. The exception made by the governor was in favor of "desirable" prisoners such as deserters from the cavalry forces. It will be realized that under Mexican methods of impressment, many unfortunates might find themselves in the army through no volition of their own, and might justifiably seek escape at the earliest opportunity. Cases even of mass desertion are common enough in the records, and there is reason to believe that many of those apprehended for such disaffection should be considered as no more than political prisoners or, at worst, vagabonds.

In April 1830, California's diputado in Mexico, Maitorena, seems to have added his protest against the sending of convicts.[26] In May, leading citizens again met in Monterey, drew up new resolutions and appointed a committee to exhort the governor to return convicts whence they came, in the vessels that brought them.[27]

The diputación, meeting in August, adopted resolutions for forwarding to Mexico, strongly opposing the deportation of more convicts and urging the withdrawal as soon as possible of those already sent. Probably realizing, however, the futility of the latter hope, they approved a plan suggested

---
[25] Calif., Vol. 3, pp. 47--48.
[26] Ibid., p. 48, n. 34.
[27] Depart. St. Pap., S. José, MS, vol. 5, pp. 34--35.

by Echeandía for the establishment of a public workshop for such <u>presidarios</u> then in the country as had trades. These might thus become self-supporting, instead of a drain on the treasury, and the products of their hands be useful. In future, the <u>diputación</u> implored, let the supreme government send only good and useful families such as would be an addition to the population and an asset in the development of the country.[28]

Despite all this counter-agitation by the <u>Californios,</u> and the governor's approval and concurrence, the influx from Mexico's criminal courts and prisons continued for years.

In February 1830, some 80 <u>presidarios</u> arrived from Acapulco. Refused permission to land at San Diego, they were transported to Santa Bárbara in March. There they were equally unwelcome, and discussion as to how to be rid of them emanated from all sides. Finally, late in April (until which time perhaps all remained on shipboard), 30 of the most disreputable, and probably many more, Bancroft surmised, were sent to Santa Cruz Island with a supply of cattle and grain, tools and fish-hooks, to eke out an existence. (This was in line with the suggestion of the <u>Junta de Californias</u> that the coast islands be settled, one of them as a penal colony.) The remainder of the wandering pariahs were allotted to the service

---

[28] <u>Leg. Rec.</u>, MS, vol. 1, pp. 158--61.

of private employers of the Santa Bárbara and Los Angeles regions.[29]

The convicts, wrote Mrs. Ord[30] (whose father, Captain Guerra, took eight or ten into his own employ, furnishing them with clothing and exhorting them to good conduct), had arrived "naked and in a very filthy condition." A fire on the island soon destroyed their settlement there, and no relief being sent, the wretches built rafts and succeeded in making shore at Carpintería and points along the Rincón. In July, their ranks were increased by 50 new arrivals from Mexico.[31]

As a matter of fact, most of these people developed into tolerable citizens and left respectable descendants. But that happy ending could not be foreseen at the time, and the Californios continued to resent vociferously having their land reduced to a penal colony. Study of many personal narratives leaves no room for doubt that much of that antipathy of Californians for Mexicans which was to trouble the territory for the entire period traced to this unwise policy of the supreme government, initiated at the outset of and continued through the régime.

---

[29] Bancroft, Calif., vol. 3, p. 48.
[30] Ocurrencias, MS, pp. 25--27.
[31] Bancroft, op. cit., p. 49.

10. Remarks in Extenuation

Nevertheless, some allowance must be made for the new and inexperienced metropolis. She began the struggle for her own existence under the handicap of social afflictions which had been festering for more than two centuries. Crime and disorder had been aggravated by years of political and military turmoil. The lower orders of the population were numerically preponderant, the administrators without sufficient strength or institutional facilities for law enforcement. Deportation, along with prison-ships and dungeons, was at the time commonly resorted to by nations better situated to control their criminals at home. Jeremy Bentham had just begun, Charles Dickens and Victor Hugo not yet taken up, the crusade for prison reform; and that wave of humanitarianism which was soon to sweep the civilized world did not get well under way until after Mexico's sovereignty over California had ended.

Moreover, Mexican statesmen were not oblivious and not careless of the human values at stake. In a report rendered in 1830 on the crime situation, the Minister of Justice lamented the country's lack of prisons and the unsanitary condition of those in existence. Prisons should command the attention of all governments, especially of representative governments, such as Mexico's, which boasted of its paternal and philanthropic spirit. Yet Mexican prisons were at variance with what should

be the principle of such institutions, being unhealthful
and serving only to oppress, demoralize and harden, instead
of leading from vicious ways; and those whose offenses were
light were thrown in with confirmed criminals, for lack of
means of segregation.

This official was deeply concerned with the penal situation in the territories -- most of all in the Californias,
since *presidarios* from all the states were being sent there;
and it was as a constructive measure that the proposal to
unite wives and families with deported convicts was made.
For reform was the end in view, whereas only further immorality
and the increase of undesirables could be expected from separating men from their families or reducing them to a position
in which they could not support wives.[32]

Mexico, in short, recognized and endeavored to ameliorate
the evils of the deportation system. But the problem was one
of many too overwhelming for her to solve. California herself seems to have countenanced banishment -- for Mexico's
reasons -- when the prisoner was her own and sent elsewhere.
The case is recorded of one Murrillo sentenced in 1835 in
a California court to ten years in Texas.[33] Californians
knew only too well the effects of such procedure. But --
what to do?

---

[32] Mex., Mem. Justicia, 1830, pp. 1, 18--19.

[33] Bancroft, *Calif.*, vol. 3, p. 674, n. 5, "1835."

Meanwhile the forlorn attempt at expanding and consolidating occupation of the territory with the unsuitable materials available went on.

11. The Island Domain

One of California's vulnerable features was her island domain. Originally, the territorial governments were prohibited from making grants of land on bay and coast islands without express authorization from Mexico. But the matter seems to have been under advisement in the '30s,[34] and in 1838 the governor was instructed to "proceed with activity and prudence, in conjunction with the departmental junta," to make coast island grants to Mexican citizens desiring them. The specified purpose of this authorization was not only to settle the islands, but to prevent foreigners from occupying them to the detriment of Mexican commerce and fisheries.[35]

----

[34] Depart. St. Pap., MS, vol. 4, p. 137. This is a mere index entry, giving no details, of a supreme government order dated July 20, 1836, bearing on the colonization of Californian islands.

[35] Halleck, "Report," pp. 121, 143, App. #7. Bancroft, Calif., vol. 3, p. 575. The order recommended that precedence be given Cárlos and Antonio Carrillo, who were to have exclusive possession of one island, in recognition of patriotic services. Some years later, Don Cárlos did secure claim to the island of Santa Rosa.

However, success did not attend the project of insular buffer colonies. In 1845, Congressman Castañares was still promoting occupation of the islands as a necessary countermove to foreign encroachment. He extolled their salubrity and fertile soil; their combination of all the requisites for successful colonization; and the good water, construction woods and safe, commodious harbors of Santa Catalina and Santa Cruz, especially. "At present, so far from being profitable to the Department, they are a menace, serving only as hideouts for foreign contrabandistas."[36]

12. The Northern Frontier

Perhaps the obviously more desirable features of mainland real estate diverted Californians of a hundred years ago from seaward expansion. Perhaps mere physical inability to be in two places at once was a sufficient deterrent. For they were faced with the immediate need to settle and hold the vast northern frontier against Russian, American, English and, quite possibly, French interlopers.

It will be remembered that although Mexico had only an approximate knowledge of what she was inheriting from Spain in the Californias, being in doubt as to whether the northern boundary was the forty-second or the forty-ninth parallel or still a matter of negotiation, she was determined to make

---

[36] Col. de Doc., p. 24.

good the maximum claim. Canónigo Fernandez had made a reconnaissance of Fort Ross one of his first concerns as Iturbide's <u>comisionado</u> to California; and he had served on the Russians an ultimatum to the effect that, failing voluntary evacuation within six months, they would be forcibly ejected from the territory.

The <u>Junta de Fomento de Californias</u>, in 1825, solemnly called attention to the emptiness of the stretch of country between Mexico's uncertain northern limit of empire and the northernmost presidio at San Francisco; and of the regions on up to the Columbia River. All this territory, they warned, was open to such as might take advantage of the situation and, perhaps with the aid of the unreduced tribes of the vicinity, might plant establishments there. (As yet they were not aware of the Russian posts long established at Bodega and Ross.)[37]

Part of the responsibility placed on the first Mexican governor was to extend settlement against the Russians and other intruders. But this Echeandía found it impossible to accomplish.

In June, 1827, he received orders from the home government to establish a fort in the vicinity of San Rafael or San Francisco Solano. This would serve the double purpose of a check to the Russians and protection for prospective

---

[37] <u>Colección</u>, Item #1 <u>(Dictamen)</u>, pp. 13--14.

settlers against the hostile gentiles of the region. The missions were to assist with laborers, implements and food. Echeandía reported himself without the means to carry out this instruction; but declared that he would endeavor to construct quarters for a military guard near San Rafael. He did order Romualdo Pacheco to select a suitable site for the garrison, "which is the last I hear of the matter," wrote Bancroft.[38]

By way of extending settlement, Echeandía made a grant of land in 1831. "Inasmuch as it is of supreme importance to the security and integrity of the national territory that the region between the Mission of San Rafael and the Russian establishment of Bodega be populated, by way of forming a frontier against any further encroachment by the Russians . . . . I grant to . . . Rafael Gomez the . lands known as Santa Rosa . . . ."[39]

The grantee seems never to have occupied the tract -- whether for lack of confirmation of title or other reason does not appear.[40]

Diputado Carrillo kept before Congress the menace of the Russians, to whom he attributed warlike propensities;

---

[38] Calif., vol. 3, pp. 114--15.

[39] Depart. St. Pap., Ben., Mil., MS, vol. 71, pp. 7--8.

[40] Bancroft, op. cit., p. 721, n. 20.

and Mexico seems never to have wavered in her desire -- ineffective though it was -- to maintain her sovereignty to the forty-second parallel. Figueroa's instructions[41] stressed this object, enjoining him to further colonization in every way possible, though with prudence and circumspection and in accordance with the laws. The northern frontier, especially, must be occupied as a stay against the Russians and the North Americans. Veterans and others were to be aided in establishing themselves on the land.

Figueroa entrusted to Alférez M. G. Vallejo the exploration for a suitable site and the opening up of lands to settlers; called on the missionaries to facilitate the enterprise as need might direct; and commandeered the services of the convict laborers attached to private ranchos for the building of a fort. But the prefect of the northern missions, though regarding the project with approbation, declared that the missionaries were in no position to help; "and so far as I can learn," wrote Bancroft in finis to this as to other such undertakings, "nothing was accomplished" before the end of 1833.[42]

----

[41] May 17, 1832, Ortiz Monasterio to Figueroa, in Sup. Govt. St. Pap., Dec. & Despatches, MS, vol. 8, pp. 35--36.

[42] St. Pap., Miss. & Colon., MS, vol. 2, pp. 299--308; Bancroft, Calif., vol. 3, p. 247.

Vallejo, meantime, at the governor's orders, had gained entrée to Bodega and Ross on what purported to be a friendly visit in the interests of trade, but was actually also a tour of the keenest inspection to determine the strength of the Russians. He had then attempted to plant settlements at Petaluma and further north in the Santa Rosa Valley. Ten families, aggregating some 50 persons, were assigned to the first location, and an unspecified small number to the second; whereupon the padre of San Francisco Solano claimed as mission property the hitherto unoccupied sites. He sought to give color to his claim by sending to Petaluma a band of horses, in charge of several wranglers who were to build living quarters for themselves; and, to Santa Rosa, a few hogs and two neophyte swineherds.

Neither the governor nor the alférez, however, was to be routed by hogs and horses. During the months that followed, Figueroa continued to agitate the plan for the northern foundations, discussing the matter with the <u>diputación,</u> and sentencing at least one criminal to serve out his term "at the new establishment about to be founded at Santa Rosa." In May 1834, he granted the <u>rancho</u> of Petaluma to Vallejo, thus virtually quieting the mission claim (though Vallejo's subsequent title, confirmed by the United States, rested on a re-grant by Micheltorena).

Vallejo had already made good his claim to occupation of the site by having several of the settlers whom he had recruited remain at the disputed location and put in crops, including ten bushels of wheat for himself.

As for the more northerly establishment, apparently the handful of settlers and the swineherds of Solano dwelt there in peaceful community for a period. On learning that a band of colonists from Mexico (the Híjar and Padrés company) would soon arrive in California, Figueroa personally examined the Santa Rosa region in the fall of 1834 (including Ross in his survey), with a view to satisfying himself as to the most advantageous frontier location for the expected increment of population. The result was his confirmation of Vallejo's choice of settlement in the Santa Rosa Valley, which he renamed Santa Anna y Farías after Mexico's president and vice-president.

The Santa Rosa -- or Santa Anna y Farías -- project, however, seems to have been abandoned some time in 1835, because of the hostility of the Indians.[43] As for the new contingent of Mexican colonists, it was destined never to occupy the Santa Rosa site, nor indeed to settle anywhere as a unit, although Californian preparations for its organization included the authorization by the diputación of the full complement of pueblo civil officials.[44]

[43] Bancroft, Calif., vol. 3, pp. 254--57; vol. 4, p. 161.
[44] Leg. Rec., MS, vol. 2, p. 206.

13. The Great Colony

The Híjar and Padrés colony marks the climax of Mexico's attempts at populating California. In the ramifications of its history and personalities it touched practically every salient problem with which the territory was afflicted -- sufficient explanation of the storm of controversy which broke over it. Despite the discredit which still attaches to the project and its leaders in the minds of many casual readers of history, there seems no ground for criticism more serious than that some loose ends were left in the organization of the undertaking. Following Bancroft's compilation of the known facts,[45] we shall here briefly consider the enterprise in its colonizing aspects, referring to it from time to time again as we discuss other phases of Mexican Californian efforts and failures to hold the territory.

José María Padrés was a Mexican of Puebla, who had served in Loreto as lieutenant of engineers and secretary of the commanding general, acting as commandant and <u>sub-gefe político</u> after Echeandía's departure for California in 1825.

---

[45] Calif., vol. 3, pp. 259--91.

In 1830, Padrés came to California with the rank of lieutenant-colonel and the appointment of *ayudante inspector* of troops, which office placed him second to the governor in military authority. The next year he added the inspectorship of customs to his responsibilities, and also served as *fiscal* in the trial of a notorious criminal case (the Rubio affair).

Close to Echeandía and evidently high in his favor, Padrés shared other than professional and official interests with his chief. Both men were republicans of the better class, imbued with the progressive ideas which inspired such Mexicans. Padrés was by his record the more energetic of the two, and was probably the more advanced thinker. He was apparently the instigator of Echeandía's secularization decree, in which connection he drew on himself the wrath of Echeandía's reactionary successor, Victoria, and was ordered back to Mexico in 1831.[46]

He went, says Bancroft,[47] pledged to an ardent Californian following to return fully empowered to effect the reforms which he advocated. For a year or so his hands were tied, politically, in Mexico, since he was at odds with the administration, and the Californian Congressman, Carlos Carrillo, was a staunch supporter of the mission system. Nevertheless, Padrés

---

[46] Bancroft, *Calif.*, vol. 4, p. 765.
[47] *Ibid.*, vol. 3, p. 259.

did not bide his time idly, but devoted himself to promoting California as a field for settlement and enterprise. In Mexico City, at this time, Bancroft concluded, "Californian affairs were attracting perhaps more attention than ever before, largely due to the influence of José María Padrés . . . ."[48]

When Padrés succeeded in enlisting the cooperation of the wealthy and worthy José María Híjar, in addition to many others, plans for leading a colony to the northern territory crystallized rapidly. Free transportation and modest subsidies of cash, rations, livestock and implements, all in the nature of advances, repayable when the colonists should be self-supporting, were offered as inducements to emigration.

Then, in the spring of 1833, the political sun began to shine again. Gomez Farías, personally and politically attached to Padrés and perhaps already in sympathy with the California development project, became, first, vice-president, and then, on one of Santa Anna's characteristic "retirements," acting president of the republic. At about the same time came word from California that Governor Figueroa sought to be released from office by reason of ill health. Padrés, still retaining his title of ayudante inspector, would by such a release of the governor automatically

---

[48] Bancroft, Calif., vol. 3, p. 259.

become gefe militar of the territory. At this happy
juncture, moreover, conservative Congressman Carrillo was
succeeded by Juan Bandini, "one of Padrés's northern disci-
ples," who entered promptly and actively into the furtherance
of the Híjar and Padrés enterprise.

From then on, events moved rapidly. Híjar was appointed
gefe politico of California, to succeed Figueroa on the
latter's retirement; and director of colonization of the
projected new settlements. Padrés, already prospective gefe
militar, was given the additional title of sub-director of
colonization.

In large part through the influence of the now powerful
combination of Californian promoters, the secularization
law of August 17, and the supplementary decree of November 26,
1833, were passed.[49] These two measures called for immediate
secularization of the missions of the two Californias, to be
effected by such means as would assure settlement; and the use
of the Pious Fund revenues in the manner best calculated to
facilitate the success of "the commission and families now
in this capital bound for that territory."

---

[49] Decree of Aug. 17, 1833, in Arrillaga, Recopilación,
1833 (Aug. -- Dec.), pp. 19--21; translation in Halleck,
"Report," pp. 135, 148--49. Decree of Nov. 26, 1833, in
Arrillaga, op. cit., pp. 311--12.

The instructions to Colonization Director Híjar, based on the new secularization statutes, authorized him to occupy at once all mission properties. Transportation and the usual subsidies to desirous colonists were provided for; the selection of favorable sites for settlement was prescribed, frontier locations to be occupied as soon as possible; town plans were specified and the granting of house-lots and farming lands in full ownership was authorized; the distribution of mission livestock and the disposal of moveable mission property and its proceeds were regulated; while the customary regular reports of progress, conditions and needs were stipulated.[50]

The colony leaders did not rely solely on mission and Pious Fund resources, however. In partnership with other men of substance, they organized a commercial company which, by means of a fleet of trading vessels to be acquired gradually, was to provide means for the exchange of Californian produce for commodities needed in the territory. This Compañía Cosmopolitana gives indication of the farsighted and comprehensive nature of the colony's development project.

------

[50] Nov. 4, 1834, "Ynstrucciones a que deberá arreglar su conducta Don José Mª Híjar, Gefe Político de la Alta California y Director de la Colonisación de esta y de la Baja," in St. Pap., Miss. & Colon., MS, vol. 2, pp. 270--73. Bancroft gives a synopsis in Calif., vol. 3, p. 273, n. 5.

"Of course it was only by some such commercial scheme," comments Bancroft, "that the empresarios could legitimately hope for profit beyond the salaries of a few officials; and it is very certain that a patriotic desire to develop the resources of California was not their sole motive."[51]

Neither was a corresponding desire the sole motive of the Pilgrim Fathers, nor of the American builders of the far west. The typical pioneer is not primarily and sheerly a patriot. He is a "rugged individualist," with eyes fixed resolutely on his own advantage. The Hijar and Padrés colony is no more to be disparaged on the score of private interests than the Massachusetts Bay Colony or any of the other American colonies, earlier or later; and its motives seem to have partaken in as large a degree as any others of patriotism and idealism. The point is that here were capital and enterprise firmly uniting a considerable band of individuals in the project of wresting a livelihood and more from an as yet unutilized country, and of setting up an enlightened society in a comparative wilderness. The Compañía Cosmopolitana lifts the project of the colony from the realm of the visionary, where under the circumstances it might otherwise be relegated, to a sound business basis.

---

[51] *Calif.*, vol. 3, p. 263.

Launched thus auspiciously, the enterprise attracted more than 250 persons, according to Bancroft; nearly 300, according to Forbes.[52] Ninety-nine men, fifty-five women and fifty children were beneficiaries of the proffered subsidy. The expedition, quite in the manner of the American immigration of the plains, took up its march with the men on horseback, the women and children in covered wagons.

Not only in its size was this group unparalleled in the annals of Mexican-Californian colonization. Qualitatively, also, it was unique. It included men of education and property, many of whom became valuable residents and leaders of their adopted communities.[53]

It was strikingly free of the element of rabble which

---

[52] Bancroft, *Calif.*, vol.3, p. 262; Forbes, *Alta Calif.*, p. 142.

[53] Bancroft, *op. cit.*, p. 263, n. 43, lists some of these: Ignacio Coronel and family, Agustín Olvera, José Ábrego, Victor Prudon, Francisco Guerrero, Jesús Noé, Mariano Bonilla, Zenon Fernandez, August Janssens, Florencio Serrano, José María Covarrubias, José de la Rosa, Gumesindo Flores, Francisco Castillo Negrete, Francisco Ocampo, Nicanor Estrada, Juan N. Ayala, Simon O'Donojú, and Charles Baric.

marred practically all the other efforts of Mexico --
and of Spain -- at the civil settlement of California; and
it included a great variety of professional men, tradesmen
and artisans in addition to a few farmers, each adult male
apparently belonging to one or another of those categories.[54]

It has become customary, in fact, to attribute impracticality to such an array of non-agricultural pioneers. Forbes
remarks that they were "of every class except that which
would have been useful -- artisans and idlers [the mathematician and musician, perhaps, being assigned to the latter
category], but not a single farmer . . . . . "   Salvador
Vallejo declared of the colonists, "we had everything else
except hardy pioneers represented"; and of their callings,
"useful trades indeed in large cities where good taste

---

[54] Bancroft, Calif., vol. 3, p. 263, n. 41, gives the vocational make-up of the colony: 19 farmers [whom Forbes overlooked], 11 painters, 12 seamstresses, 8 carpenters, 8 tailors, 4 shoemakers, 5 tinners, 5 silversmiths, 3 hatters, 3 physicians, 2 barbers, 2 saddlers, 2 blacksmiths, 2 printers, 2 goldsmiths, and also a mathematician, a gardener, a surgeon, a machinist, a ribbon-maker, a rebozo-maker, a midwife, a distiller, a candy-maker, a vermicelli maker, a navigator, a founder, a pork-man, a musician, a vintager, an apothecary, a boatman and a carriage maker, besides 6 teachers and the officers.

prevails, but worse than useless in California, a land then not yet fully redeemed from the grasp of the 'gentiles' . . . ."[55] But Forbes was not disinterested; and Salvador Vallejo had personal and political grievances against the colony.

Bancroft, while surmising that "such farm laborers as as could have been obtained from the Mexican provinces would not have done so well for themselves or California," agrees that "the number of artisans was somewhat too predominant over that of the agriculturists."[56]

These criticisms seem to call for some refutation. One of the recognized drawbacks to California's development to that time had been the lack of a market for agricultural produce already or potentially in excess of consumption needs. On the other hand, just such commodities and services as the Híjar and Padrés colony had to offer were definitely and explicitly needed. The make-up of the group suggests careful consideration of exactly what type of population the territory needed, in the light of Padrés and Bandini's first-hand knowledge of conditions there. Even Forbes's objection to "goldsmiths proceeding to a country where no gold or silver existed"[57] loses force with a little consideration; for the existence of those precious metals in California was known,[58] and in any case the use of coins for fashioning

---

[55] Forbes, *Alta Calif.*, p. 142; S. Vallejo, *Notas Hist.*, MS, pp. 44—45.

[56] *Calif.*, vol. 3, p. 263.

[57] *Alta Calif.*, p. 142.

[58] See *post*, sec. 63.

buttons, saddle- and bridle-decorations and other ornaments was no unheard of device.

But far more serious attacks than mere charges of impracticality awaited the ambitious colony in California. Conservatives in both Mexico and California regarded the whole project as a conspiracy for the looting of the missions. There is no evidence of any such intent, was Bancroft's conclusion, though he concedes that the powers granted the empresarios by the government were so large that perhaps they would have been abused had opportunity allowed.[59]

It should be remembered that the whole spirit of that republicanism of which Hijar and Padrés and their associates were worthy protagonists was opposed to human exploitation. Their very demand for secularization was partly a protest against the holding of the Indians in wardship; was in keeping with the laws regarding the missions; and was fulfilled by legal and honorable means.

Secularization as generally understood and legally prescribed did not mean the turning loose of hordes of pauperized Indians to prey on a small and defenceless populace. Not to that end had church and government labored to attract the gentile multitudes from the wilderness to the

---

[59] Calif., vol. 3, pp. 264--65.

centers of civilization; but to the end of raising the
Indians to the status of enlightened and useful citizens,
endowed with the land, livestock and implements necessary
to self-maintenance. In the absence of any abrogation or
challenge of the existing secularization laws, and of
any evidence of bad faith in the history of the colony or
its leaders, it seems only logical to conclude that no
subversion of the established ethic and order was intended.

An examination of Hijar's instructions bears out the
theory of inherent recognition of the Indians' rights to
their proportionate share of the proceeds of secularization.
There is no reason to believe that the reference in Article
11[60] to the distribution of the moveable property of the
missions meant other than distribution among the neophytes
according to the secularization laws. Article 7[61] seems
to make specific recognition of the policy of establishing

---

[60] "The moveable property of the missions having been distributed, one-half of what is left shall be sold to the best advantage." Instructions, in St. Pap., Miss. & Colon., MS, vol. 2, pp. 272--73.

[61] "Native settlers shall be mixed with the Mexicans, but no town shall be inhabited by Indians exclusively." Op. cit., pp. 271--72.

the emancipated neophytes as citizens, on the same basis -- at least in theory -- as the Mexican colonists;-and such was Bancroft's interpretation.[62]

The indications seem clear that whatever bad faith was shown in connection with the Hijar and Padrés colony was on the part of its political opponents, of whom there were many with motives pure or otherwise, in both Mexico and California. Naturally the padres looked on any secularization scheme as premature and pernicious. The Californians generally had learned, during the past decade, to distrust most manifestations of Mexico in California.

Moreover, a generation of young republicans, inspired by prevailing ideas of self-rule, was maturing in the territory. Many of these young men had been fired to action by magnetic Padrés himself. They were beginning to feel their power for political self-determination. On the very verge, in fact, of declaring for home rule, they looked on Mexico's auspicious but tardy attempt at exploitation of their territory as an infringement of their own rights.

There **had long** been a recognition of the fact that on many counts the mission-presidio system militated against civil development. Complaint was rife that the missions had usurped all the bestlands. Now the mission monopoly was to be shattered -- in the interests, argued the Californians, of

---

[62] Calif., vol. 3, p.345.

Mexican outsiders. The resentment was the keener for the fact that, although the partial secularization already effected under Echeandía and Figueroa was being administered by Californians, Hijar and Padrés proposed -- or were believed to propose -- distributing all such authority among their own people.

To make matters worse, the colony came under the auspices of the Santa Anna--Gomez Farías administration; and California was looking askance at the unpredictable Santa Anna, fearing some antirepublican intervention on his part.

But Santa Anna and Gomez Farías were also at odds, the president suspecting the acting president of utilizing California as a base of operations from which to restore himself to power when overthrown in Mexico; or at least as a choice new field to cultivate in self-interest. Florencio Serrano thought that certain circumstances indicated an intention on the part of the colony leaders to declare California independent of Mexico in certain contingencies; but Antonio Coronel was never able to trace the rumors of political plots to any reliable source.[63]

Both Serrano and Coronel were members of the colony and credible witnesses. The political instability and dissension which racked Mexico and involved California bred plots and

---

[63] Bancroft, *Calif.*, vol. 3, p. 264, n. 44.

suspicions of plots, the latter as dangerous to national effectiveness as the former.

From Mexico itself came the quietus of the great colony project. Santa Anna again ensconced himself in the presidential chair, and thrusting aside the vice-president and his policies, hurried a special courier overland with a countermand of Híjar's appointment as _gefe político_. As for the claim of Padrés to the military command, that was automatically voided by Figueroa's retention of the governorship.[64]

The _diputación_, in consultation with the governor (who lacked official instructions save those countermanding Híjar's authority) gave careful consideration as to how the colony might be provided for. The result was a _bando_ of October 21, 1834, recognizing Híjar as colony director subject to the territorial government, but denying him any authority, in his reduced capacity to secularize missions, receive mission property or occupy lands. Until other instructions should be received from Mexico, the secularization situation was to remain _in statu quo_. All possible aid was to be afforded the colonists.

"The course decided upon," says Bancroft, "was an eminently just and proper one."[65]

---

[64] Forbes, _Alta Calif._, p. 144; Bancroft, _Calif._, vol. 3, pp. 270--71.

[65] _Calif._, vol. 3, pp. 274--76, 278.

Padrés, given his choice between the title of <u>ayudante</u> <u>inspector</u> and that of subdirector of colonization, chose the latter. As the inspector's title would have given him far greater official and personal prestige, his choice seems to have been a disinterested one.

Plans now went forward to establish the immigrants on the northern frontier, and during the winter of 1834--35 the majority were assembled at San Francisco Solano. By spring, however, it had become clear that means were not available to subsidize so large a colony until it could become self-maintaining.[66] Accordingly the governor, overriding considerable objection, disbanded the colony, ordering its members to disperse to separate locations of their own choosing.

For at least a year, various communities rendered aid to the newcomers so favoring them. Vallejo, impelled, as he later wrote, by neighborly charity, gave shelter to sixty "of those unfortunates," gradually, out of his own means and without subsequent claim for reimbursement, establishing them

----

[66] Híjar's estimate of the expense had been $45,000 per year. (Bancroft, Calif., vol. 3, p. 279, n. 14). He had, of course, been counting on mission and Pious Fund resources.

"on their own hearths."[67] Gradually more than 200 of the colonists merged into the territorial population,[68] constituting, after all, the most valuable single contribution made by Mexico to the peopling of California.

As for the leaders themselves, their titles and prerogatives were suspended by the governor, and along with several of their followers they were returned to Mexico to answer for alleged participation in the much over-emphasized Apalátegui revolt of March 1835.[69] Bancroft's conclusion, after consideration of the very voluminous records of that episode, was that while one member of the colony was probably involved, "there is no evidence to connect either the colony or its directors with the movement in any way."[70]

14. Progress on the Northern Frontier

Efforts for occupation of the northern frontier continued. In June, Figueroa instructed Vallejo to lay out a town, garrison and colonize it, keeping the Mexican population always in excess of the foreign. Perhaps because Vallejo was kept in the vicinity of Mission San Francisco

---

[67] Vallejo Doc., MS, vol. 12, #304, pp. 4--5.
[68] Bancroft, Calif., vol. 3, pp. 279--80.
[69] See post, chap. VI.
[70] Calif., vol. 3, pp. 285--86.

Solano by his duties there as commissioner of secularization, that vicinity, instead of the earlier site of Santa Rosa, was selected for the new pueblo.

Unable to afford much support other than moral, Figueroa appealed to the diputación for "hearty co-operation," and exhorted Vallejo to carry the project through -- even at the personal sacrifice of helping to finance it -- for the honor of the national government and the sake of posthumous fame![71]

The appeal was not in vain, as the subsequent history of Vallejo and the northern frontier testifies. The young officer promptly laid out the town of Sonoma and established there a number of families, some Californian and some drawn from the ranks of the Hijar and Padrés colony. With a small military force,[72] he nevertheless succeeded, chiefly through alliance with the powerful Suisun chief Solano, in securing a remarkable control over the gentile tribes of the interior.[73]

Contemporaneously with the establishment of Sonoma, a small settlement sprang up at Yerba Buena, between Mission

------

[71] Leg. Rec., MS, vol. 2, p. 48; June 24, 1835, Figueroa to Vallejo, in Vallejo Doc., MS, vol. 3, #59.

[72] This included the San Francisco presidial company -- or rather its remnant -- transferred to Sonoma at this time because its presence was needed at the new settlement and the peninsular fort was almost in ruins. See post, pp. 363, 367.

[73] See post, pp. 431--34.

Dolores and the practically abandoned San Francisco presidio.[74]

Until the American occupation, Vallejo continued as chief guardian and builder of the northern frontier. He was more than pioneer, more than *empresario.* He was statesman, soldier, promoter, financier and agriculturist -- all in signal degree. At first it was difficult to attract settlers, even by the offer of every aid. The region was isolated from the rest of the territory by "an immense lake." (Elsewhere he calls this portion of San Francisco Bay "the Gulf of Sonoma.") The Indians were so savage that his first concern had had to be "a continual campaign" against them -- until he was able to enlist their friendship and labor.

At his own expense, he brought in settlers and started them with livestock. By 1839, he had the satisfaction of recording extraordinary progress. Twenty families had been established. He had accepted for himself the obligation to keep them supplied with every aid promised and necessary to maintain the buffer settlement against the invading Indians.[75]

Soon afterward, he was able to report that without expense to the national treasury, the desires of the Supreme

---

[74] Bancroft, *Calif.,* vol. 3, pp. 707--8, n. 6.

[75] Vallejo, *Órdenes,* #6.

Government for northern settlement had been realized. Twenty-five families were actually located, and others were coming to occupy lands in the interior which he, as director of colonization,[76] had allotted them. The garrison itself, and the soldiers' families, were helping in the work of occupying the land. Vallejo was subsidizing them in order that they might establish themselves as agriculturists, when veterans.[77]

He offered inducements for artisans from the southern part of the territory, and for others, to settle in the north. A letter of 1839, from Pablo de la Guerra, asks if Don Guadalupe wishes sent up by Fitch's vessel, along with the tanners, carpenters and blacksmiths for whom he had asked, ten to twelve Indians very adept at tile-making. "They are of excellent character, good Christians -- and anxious to go as they have heard that you treat every one very well, give lands, cattle, etc."

----

[76] A title conferred by Figueroa, along with that of "Commander of the Northern Line." In the latter capacity, Vallejo had authority southward to Santa Inés.

[77] May 10, 1839, Vallejo to Min. of War, in Vallejo Doc., MS, vol. 7, #28.

[78] Jan. 4, 1839, Pablo de la Guerra to Vallejo, in Vallejo, Correspond. hist., MS, p. 49.

Gradually knowledge of the northern frontier spread and interest in it grew, thanks to the efforts of its promoters. In 1841 Osio wrote to Vallejo that several families were en route to the northern settlement -- useful, honorable and industrious people to augment the population and foment agriculture and various other needed industries. Osio himself was "sighing for Point Reyes," which he hoped to secure for his own. He had bought two hundred heifers, and was making arrangements to purchase others.

Don Antonio had also persuaded his brother-in-law to come up from arid Lower California, to settle in the fertile San Francisco region. As a special attraction, Osio had assured him that on the bay he could be both farmer and sailor. So the brother-in-law had come to California and had started to look at the land talked of; and he had brought inquiries from six farming families of his acquaintance back in Baja California, who wanted to go to the northern country if they could get lands there. They knew dairying -- how to get much milk and make good cheese. "Among them is an American with a Californian family, who is a good blacksmith and carpenter, has a boat and a capital of 14,000 pesos." Osio asked Vallejo to advise which locations would be best for these families.[79]

---

[79] Jan. 27, 1841, Antonio M. Osio to Vallejo, in Vallejo Doc., MS, vol. 10, #53.

When in 1842 Victor Castro asked for a grant in the Nicasio region, the site selected was adjoined on two sides by occupied lands.[80] By this time, men of prominence, some already well established to the south, were acquiring holdings in the Sonoma district. In 1843, Captain of Cavalry Don Juan Castañeda submitted his petition; and in 1844, Pablo de la Guerra, "Juan" Cooper and Alvarado himself were apparently all personally interested in the Nicasio title, although just what the situation was is not clear from the data at hand.[81] Meanwhile, Vallejo had been planning to push the area of settlement toward the Russian establishments.[82] When the Russians abandoned California two years later, both he and Alvarado urged the establishment of a colony and garrison at Ross. These pleas evoked only an aggravating set of instructions for taking over and administering what the Supreme Government evidently surmised to be a flourishing settlement

---

[80] May 4, 1842, José de los Santos Berreysa [sic] to Vallejo, in *Vallejo Doc.*, MS, vol. 11, #214. A 1-page inaccurate copy follows the 3-page original.

[81] May 24, 1843, Vallejo to Micheltorena, in *Vallejo Doc.*, MS, vol. 12, #108; Bancroft, *Calif.*, vol. 4, p. 672, n. 12.

[82] May 10, 1838, Vallejo to Min. of War, in *Vallejo Doc.*, MS, vol. 7, #28.

left behind by the abdicating Russians.[83]

Repeatedly the commander and colonizer of the northern line appealed for aid in carrying the increasingly heavy burden of the work to which his personal and financial sacrifices had given such initial momentum. The assistance, as will be seen, was never forthcoming; nor were the commercial concessions which he sought in the interests of his colonists.[84]

15. Foreign Colonization

Writing in Mexico in the middle 1830s, Alexander Forbes,[85] the Scotch business partner in Tepic of Great Britain's consul-general, commented on the problem of California's colonization: " . . . . nothing can be expected of emigration from other Mexican states, which are themselves but too thinly populated, and whose inhabitants are but ill fitted for such a country as California." Therefore, he argued, foreign colonization under wise laws offered the best solution.[86]

Mexico had reached Forbes's conclusion more than a decade earlier; and despite the lesson of Texas, was driven by her poverty of man-power to risk the experiment in

---

[83] Bancroft, Calif., vol. 4, pp. 177--78; post, p. 389.
[84] See post, sec. 69.
[85] Not James Alexander Forbes, Britain's Scotch vice-consul in California from 1842.
[86] Alta Calif., pp. 148--49.

California likewise. Indeed, all the territories had been opened to foreign colonization by the laws of 1824 and 1828.

But even before the passage of the 1830 modifications, efforts were made to counteract the evils of foreign settlement by discretion in the application of the existing laws. The Texas experience had been demonstrating the rapidity with which the wilderness could be made to flourish when opened to the human stream. "'In three hundred years,'" quotes Howren, "'Spain had managed to people Texas with some four thousand souls, while in one decade, 1820--1830, under the new colonization scheme, the civilized population increased to five times that number, of whom the English-speaking inhabitants were in a great majority.'"[87]

Since the English-speaking inhabitants were proving so unassimilable and aggressive, Mexican statesmen were attracted by the idea of European -- even Asiatic -- immigration. Teran, in 1830, urged the establishment of Swiss and German colonists in Texas as an antidote to the Yankee evil.[88] The principle of divide and rule seems to have been the inspiration here.

---

[87] Southwestern Hist. Quarterly, vol. 16, p. 380; quoting in translation from the transcript of a letter by Teran, in the Austin Collection, University of Texas.
[88] Ibid., p. 409.

Alamán believed that foreign colonies, "which perhaps might be Asiatic," would give a great impulse to Californian development.[89]

It becomes pertinent here to examine the colonization laws as they bore on the promotion and regulation of foreign immigration.

The Law of 1824[90] promised security in person and property to foreigners settling in Mexican territory and conforming to Mexican laws. (Art. 1).

Lands within twenty leagues of the boundary of a foreign nation, or within ten leagues of the coast, could not be colonized without approval of the supreme executive power. (Art. 4).

No taxes might be imposed on foreign newcomers for the space of four years after the publication of the law. (Art. 6).

Before 1840, the national Congress could not prohibit the entry of foreigners to colonize, unless compelled to do so for strong reasons in individual cases. (Art. 7).

The government was to take precautionary measures for the security of the federation. (Art. 8).

---

[89] Mem. Rel., 1823, p. 33.

[90] See ante, p. 85, n. 14. Bancroft (Calif., vol. 2, p. 516, n. 8) gives the term of tax-exemption as five years -- a typographical slip.

Mexican citizens were to be preferred in the distribution of lands. (Art. 9).

Limits of land allotments (to both foreigners and nationals) were specified. (Art. 12).

Colonists (both foreign and Mexican) were restrained from transferring their possessions in mortmain. (Art. 13).

Contracts entered into with *empresarios* of colonization were guaranteed. (Art. 14).

No non-resident of the republic might retain lands granted under these laws. (Art. 15).

"The provisions of the act were certainly liberal and wise, if not, as Tuthill says, 'so liberal as to excite wonder what hidden motive suggested its wiser provisions,'" comments Bancroft.[91]

Halleck found the restrictions of the Law of 1824 fully recognized, although the ability to enforce them was another matter.[93]

The regulations of November 21, 1828[94] made no distinctions

---

[91] *Calif.*, vol. 2, p. 516.

[92] (No foot-note 92).

[93] "Report," pp. 121, 119--23, *passim.*

[94] See *ante*, p. 86, n. 15.

between foreigners and nationals, merely outlining the
routine for application for and granting of lands.[95]

Meanwhile, in January 1827, notwithstanding the
laws of 1824, notice was served that the governor would
grant no lands to foreigners.[96] Bancroft found that the
regulations of November 1828 were apparently not published
in California for nearly a year.[97] In February 1830, in
connection with the applications of Abel Stearns and
other foreign residents of California, Alamán sent
Echeandía instructions to make grants from the public lands
to such applicants as could comply with all the requirements,
being careful, however, that Russians and Americans be kept
in a minority and be given central locations.[98]

On April 6, 1830 was promulgated the famous law abrogating foreign colonization privileges.[99] This decree, declares Howren, was "the fruit of Terán's importunities, Bustamante's support and Alamán's zeal." It incorporated all of Terán's recommendations, and went further.[100]

---

[95] See ante, p. 86.

[96] Depart. St. Pap., S. José, MS, vol. 5, p. 12.

[97] Calif., vol. 2, pp. 662--63.

[98] Sup. Govt. St. Pap., MS, vol. 6, p. 4; Bancroft, Calif., vol. 3, p. 179.

[99] See ante, p. 87, n. 16.

[100] Southwestern Hist. Quarterly, vol. 16, pp. 406, 421.

Not only was Article 7 -- the most liberal and only remarkable provision -- of the 1824 law repealed; foreigners of adjacent countries were prohibited from colonizing the frontiers. (Art. 11).

The reverberations set up by Texan resentment of this article and the one calling for enforcement of the existing slave laws (Art. 3) soon penetrated to California, and eventually gave rise to a series of acrimonious protests from United States Minister to Mexico Waddy Thompson, as well as to a deal of loud-voiced alarm over the "persecuted" and perilous condition of Americans on Mexican soil.[101] Thus did Mexico learn, all too quickly and thoroughly, the disadvantages of trying to recede from a liberal policy.

It does not appear, however, that she had erred greatly, or that more caution in the beginning would have profited her in the end. Even the *empresario* system might have worked out if discreetly entered into with other than Yankee contractors. As a matter of fact, neither that feature of Mexico's colonization program nor the European immigration phase was ever put to the test in California, though projects of both types came up for consideration from time to time.

Probably the most serious defect in the new republic's colonization theory was her naive expectation that by endowing aliens with land and exempting them from taxes, she could summarily transmute them into good Mexicans and Catholics.

----

[101] "U. S. Govt. Doc.," 28th Cong., 1st Sess., *Sen. Doc.* #390 (ser. #436), pp. 1--16; and *see post*, chap. VIII.

A set of undated naturalization regulations compiled by Schmidt[102] and attributed by Bancroft "probably to 1828," their general purport being circulated by Echeandía on June 4, 1829,[103] includes the provision that "colonists come to populate colonizable lands shall be considered as naturalized after passage of one year from the time of their settlement." (Art. 14).

Certainly there was justice in the notion that allegiance should be returned for land and opportunity. The error of expecting any such rule to hold was one of psychology rather than of logic.

From an examination of colonization efforts in Mexican California, two facts emerge strikingly. First, Mexico never lost sight of her purpose in resorting to foreign colonization: the establishment of buffer populations on frontiers, or of developmental settlements in less exposed areas which she lacked the man-power to defend and exploit. Second, until Micheltorena's time (near the collapse of the Mexican régime in California, so too late to matter practically), California's executives seem to have been discreet in the matter of land grants to foreigners, adhering to the supreme government's policy of conservatism on that score.

---

[102] *Civil Law of Spain and Mex.*, App. #7, pp. 352--59.
[103] *Calif.*, vol. 3, p. 179. On the general subject of regulation of foreigners, and on land grants to foreigners, see *post*, chap. VIII.

Under Echeandía, as we have seen, land distribution and colonization were barely started.

Figueroa's instructions provided that colonization be furthered in every way possible, including foreign immigration; but "with prudence and circumspection and in accordance with the laws." Warning was made against a certain foreign element already established in the territory, which was a source of embarrassment to the government. Not more than one-third of the families settled were to be Russians or from the "Estados Unidos del Norte." Especially to be encouraged was the Sonoma colony project of Henry Virmond. Efforts must be made to extend occupation to the forty-second parallel and to consolidate it by the stationing of garrisons and the establishment of veterans and others as agriculturists.[104]

Figueroa endeavored to comply with these instructions

---

[104] Sus. Govt. St. Pap., Leg. & Desp., vol. 8, pp. 35--36. Virmond was a German merchant long established in Acapulco an married to a Mexican woman. He did considerable business in California, was well known to the padres, military and official leaders in both the territory and the metropolis, and was extremely influential and active in politics, though indirectly. He visited California in 1828--30, but of his Sonoma project nothing more is known, according to Bancroft. (Calif., vol. 3, p. 398, vol. 5, p. 764.) Duflot de Mofras (Exploration, vol. 1, p. 508) calls Virmond of French origin.

in the spirit and to the letter, stressing their points in his orders of 1835 to Vallejo for the development of the northern frontier. The Mexican population, he warned, must be kept in excess of the foreign, and the granting of lands was to impede, not to facilitate foreign encroachment.[105]

Certain special problems of infiltration faced Figueroa and his successors. For one thing, an element extraneous though largely of nominal Mexican nationality, and scarcely more welcome in the territory than foreign undesirables, was penetrating from the direction of New Mexico. For years, rovers from that region, regularly visiting California under color of exchanging textiles and other Mexican and New Mexican products for livestock, conducted actually a lively business in horse and cattle raids and general thieving. These invaders came in force, and were of a variety of origins from Indian to white, including or even led by the more desperate type of "mountain man" from the western United States and Canada. Californians considered these *Chaguanosos*[106] no less a vexation than hostile Indians, and discouraged their settlement in the country. Nevertheless, occasional stragglers insisted on staying.

---

[105] St. Pap., Miss. & Colon., MS, vol. 2, pp. 406--8.

[106] Apparently "Shawnees," says Bancroft (*Calif.*, vol. 4, p. 77). The name was applied loosely, the bands so designated sometimes numbering more whites than Indians.

Political uncertainties in New Mexico, as well as inferior opportunities, attracted others -- more desirable -- from that region. True to expressed principle, Californian authorities sought to allocate such immigrants to the outskirts of settlement. In 1841, a colony under Lorenzo Trujillo settled in the San Bernardino region, having obtained from Juan Bandini a portion of the Jurupa rancho. The location seems to have proved unsatisfactory.[107]

In 1845, José A. García, for himself and thirty-three others, asked for a grant of all the San Gabriel Mission lands; and Santiago Martinez deposed that, not being able to remain in the San Bernardino region, he and twenty families for whom he spoke requested the site of "La Savonería" (La Jabonera) near Los Angeles.[108] Although García's petition was at first rejected, both these efforts were eventually successful, according to Bancroft.[109]

From about the middle '30s to the close of the period, various immigrant colonies of the *empresario* type were proposed by Americans and Europeans. Though none of these materialized, their projection helped to swell indications that California was already the cynosure of *miras ambiciosas* from a number of directions.

---

[107] Bancroft, *Calif.*, vol. 4, p. 638, n. 14, "1845."
[108] *Leg. Rec.*, MS, vol. 4, pp. 50, 112.
[109] *Calif.*, vol. 4, p. 638, n. 15. (He gives *Leg. Rec.*, MS, vol. 4, pp. 23--24 as authority, which appears to be a mis-citation.) Undoubtedly the Jurupa location was too exposed to gentile attack. On California's Indian scourge *see post*, secs. 45--47.

As early as 1834, the Yankee schoolmaster and prophet of far western greatness, Hall J. Kelley, travelled to Oregon by way of Mexico and the Pacific coast. Although his first concern was the stimulation of American settlement in the northwest, he made as complete a reconnaissance of the two Californias as time and circumstances permitted; and in person or by letter laid before Mexican leaders, including President Santa Anna and Governor Figueroa, a proposition to settle California when he had initiated his Oregon enterprise.

A map of the Sacramento Valley and an excellent description of the country published by Congress five years later were the only tangible results of Kelley's enthusiasm for California;[110] and while Figueroa assured the eastern expansionist of his approval and interest, it seems highly likely that in neither Mexico nor California could any such occupation as Kelley proposed have been countenanced. Sentiment in metropolis and territory was already definitely anti-Yankee. Figueroa was under urgent instructions to limit and control colonization from "the United States of the North"; and himself repeatedly warned Mexico of the aggressiveness of immigrants from that quarter. Considered in this light and in that of the governor's well

---

[110] Bancroft, *Calif.*, vol. 3, pp. 409--11.

known indirectness, his cordiality to Kelley may reasonably be ascribed to tact; particularly as all assurances of cooperation were neutralized by his expressed and actual inability to authorize or help finance the prospective _empresario's_ plan.

In 1839, Sutter requested an _empresario's_ grant; but although cordially received by Governor Alvarado, was persuaded that his colony was too small to justify such a grant and method.[111]

Throughout the Alvarado-Vallejo régime, the greatest emphasis was placed by both _gefes_ as well as by Mexico on the need to check American and Russian encroachment. To that end, European immigration was earnestly agitated. In 1837, the president of the republic had announced a scheme with the two-fold aim of attracting colonists from abroad and absolving the nation from the heavy foreign debt which she found herself unable to repay in cash. One hundred million acres of land, more or less, in California and other north Mexican regions, were to be set aside for paying the debt directly and for securing bonds to be used in payment.[112]

This proposal stimulated the considerable hopes entertained by certain private individuals and business concerns

---

[111] Bancroft, _Calif._, vol. 4, p. 128.

[112] _Ibid._, pp. 99, n. 49, end; 382.

for the promotion of English interests in California. A correspondence of 1843--44, between W. E. P. Hartnell and Robert C. Wyllie throws light on the aspirations of one such group.[113]

Wyllie, active on the committee formed to look after the interests of English holders of Mexican bonds, wrote on August 10, 1843 from Tepic, and again on November 5, from Mexico City, to Hartnell, long a resident of Monterey and a naturalized Mexican citizen. The letters went into the matter of Mexican finances and included a questionnaire of twenty-four heads, with sub-heads, relative to Californian lands -- how held, what portion was populated and what portion available, where the mines were located, what site Hartnell believed most desirable for settlement, etc. -- and products, trade, and state of public order.

The last point was particularly inquired into as the rulers of Great Britain would "give no protection whatever to British subjects settling in California as citizens of Mexico, nor do they wish to see it in any other hands but those of Mexico. I know this to be the fact," affirmed Wyllie, "and that Commodore Jones' apprehension was a perfect bugbear."[114]

---
[113] Bancroft, Calif., vol. 4, pp. 451--52.
[114] Vallejo Doc., MS, vol. 33, #s 349, 369.

Hartnell, having taken up the matter with Micheltorena, replied to Wyllie that although no instructions whatever had been received in California touching the exchange of bonds for land, His Excellency had promised everything possible to facilitate a colony grant. "The governor told me plainly that he wished very much that settlers would come out from Europe so that all vacant lands should not be given to Americans, and he even hinted that he should like to take a share in the speculation himself, as he has always professed himself particularly favorable to the English."[115]

In a reply of November 13, 1844, from Honolulu, Wyllie referred to American expansionist ambitions, and pointed out that if the United States should make war on Mexico, only Great Britain could save California; in which case, "nothing could justify her interference so much as previous grants of land, under the Mexican government to British subjects." Therefore Hartnell was urged to "be ready to grasp all you can for me and for yourself." Of course, if the grants could be obtained free, that would be better than paying for them in deferred bonds.[116]

Having returned to England, Wyllie published an

---

[115] *P. Pico Doc.*, MS, vol. 1, #85.
[116] *Vallejo Doc.*, MS, vol. 34, #72.

exhaustive report on Mexican finances, with a documentary appendix, for the benefit of "traders, emigrants, and bondholders." One of the documents reproduced was a proposal from Alexander Forbes, author of *Alta California,* for wide powers and policies to be lodged in a prospective California colony and trading company. Forbes justified his project of the company on the ground that he did not believe that colonization in any Hispano-American country could be successful otherwise; and by calling attention to American designs as evidenced by the Jones affair, to the doubtless similarly ambitious plans of France, and to the likelihood that "'if there be not adopted, and that soon, a prudent scheme of colonization, the Californias will cease to be a province of Mexico.'"[117]

Also appended to Wyllie's published report was a letter of October 10, 1843, from Wyllie to Bocanegra, setting forth "'the great advantages to be derived by the Mexican republic by the colonization of her public lands.'" The system recommended," resumes Bancroft, "was similar to that of the United States; and the benefits were to come not only from

---

[117] Bancroft, *Calif.,* vol. 4, pp. 383--84, citing (n. 5) Wyllie, *México, Noticia sobre su Hacienda Pública bajo el Gobierno Español y después de la Independencia.* (Mexico, 1845). Bancroft adds that he has not seen the original edition, probably published in 1844, in London.

the payment of public debts, and the development of the country's industries, but, in the case of the northern frontier departments, from the security acquired against the foreign aggression to which they were especially exposed. True, there was a prejudice against foreign colonization, well founded on the 'ingratitude and treason of the Texan colonists'; but the latter were much influenced by the fact that they came from an adjoining nation, by the arts of land speculators, and by the 'notorious project' of a part of the American congress to annex the territory with a view to the extension of slavery; while 'a colony of Europeans, subjects of monarchical governments, being in circumstances diametrically opposite, would adhere spontaneously and in gratitude to the Mexican government.'"[118]

Hudson's Bay Company officials, too, recognized in California a great field for exploitation, and according to Larkin[119] applied for a large grant of land.

The British government's clearly defined policy of "hands off" was, however, discouraging to such aspirations;[120] and as the American expansionist tide approached flood in California, the British ebbed.

---

[118] Bancroft, Calif., vol. 4, pp. 383--84.

[119] June 30, 1844, Larkin to Sec. of State, in Official Corresp., MS, vol. 3, pp. 6--7.

[120] This restraint is intimated, incidental to a discussion of England's prescience in the matter of the American advance Californiawards, in F. L. Paxson, "England and Mexico, 1824--25," in "Univ. of Colo. Studies," vol. 3, #3; reprinted from the Quarterly of the Texas State Historical Association, vol. 9, pp. 138--41.

16. Ten Thousand Irishmen

Nevertheless, one more colonization project was urged on Mexico by subjects of Britain. This was the largely conceived plan of a London promoting organization -- represented in Mexico and California by the Irish priest Eugene McNamara -- to establish ten thousand Irish Catholics in California.[121]

In letters of 1845, addressed to the President of Mexico, McNamara outlined his proposition and his triple motive. He projected -- with the Archbishop of Mexico -- colonies on San Francisco Bay, in the Monterey vicinity and at Santa Barbara. "By this means, the entire coast . . . . would be completely secured against the invasions and pillages of foreigners."

For his aims were not only "to advance the cause of Catholicism" and "to contribute to the happiness of my countrymen"; but "to put an obstacle in the way of further usurpations on the part of an irreligious and anti-Catholic nation." If his plan were not allowed to go into effect, he played on Mexico's well known apprehensions, "your

---

[121] The history of this enterprise may be traced broadly in copies of the correspondence bearing on it, printed in "U. S. Govt. Doc.," 30th Cong., 1st Sess., Sen. Rep. #75; supplemented by Leg. Rec., MS, vol. 4, pp. 363--68. Bancroft, Calif., vol. 5, pp. 215--21 resumes concisely.

Excellency may be assured that before another year the Californias will form a part of the American nation."[122]

McNamara's persuasions were of similar truth and cogency to those of Wyllie and Forbes. His application received the generally favorable consideration of two Mexican administrations, "though of course there was no thought of granting coast lands, or least of all at the ports mentioned by the priest; and though there were not wanting those in Mexico who believed Irish settlers more likely to side with the Yankees than the Mexicans."[123]

The Amigo del Pueblo of October 25, 1845 demanded: "'Todavía no se conoce que todo él que habla el idioma inglés ha de tener más simpatías hacia los rapaces Yankees que hacia nosotros?'" And McNamara told Larkin that although President Herrera had approved the scheme, the new president objected that the Irish would join the Americans, and declared that he wanted no English-speaking colonists.

The outcome of protracted negotiations in Mexico seems

---

[123] "U. S. Govt. Doc.," 30th Cong., 1st Sess., Sen. Rep. #75, pp. 19--20; 77--79. The latter citation is to the Spanish version, the former to the English. Bancroft says (Calif., vol. 5, p. 216, n. 26) of these undated documents whose source is not indicated: "There is no reason to doubt their authenticity."

[123] Bancroft, Calif., vol. 5, p. 216.

to have been "some encouragement but no positive promises from the government," with a recommendation that McNamara "go to California, select lands suitable for his purpose and submit his project in regular form to the departmental authorities."[124]

On July 1, 1846, McNamara, at Santa Barbara, formally submitted to Governor Pico his plan to bring 2,000 families or 10,000 souls to the territory; and solicited ownership of "the land selected between the river San Joaquin, from its source to its mouth, and the Sierra Nevada, the limits being the river Cosumne [sic] on the north, and on the south, the extremity of the Tulares, in the neighborhood of San Gabriel."[125]

Pico referred the petition, with his provisional approval of the project and the tract chosen, to the departmental assembly on July 4, 1846. Apparently he had had conversation with McNamara in which he had attempted to pin the Irishman down to specific promises instead of lofty numerical generalities; for he spoke now of 317 families. The grant to be made must conform with the twenty-leagues-from-the-boundary provision of the colonization law; and with all other Mexican legal specifications.

---

[124] Bancroft, *Calif.*, vol. 5, pp. 216--17.
[125] "U. S. Govt. Doc.," 30th Cong., 1st Sess., *Sen. Rep.* #75, pp. 22--23.

(This would of course make confirmation of the grant by the supreme government a requisite.) The governor put forward as the reason for making the grant the defense and development of California and the preservation of its integrity, as well as the propagation of the faith.

On July 6, the assembly, having heard the petition and the governor's approval, referred the matter to committee (of Argüello and Bandini); and on July 7, recommended that the grant be made, in agreement with the sentiments expressed by Pico and with certain stipulations of its own:

1) The lands granted should be of definite extent, with intervening reservations of good extent and quality interspersed for government purposes.

2) The tract should lie on the far side of the San Joaquín River, between the tulares and the Sierra Nevada, and across the Río de las Animas.

3) Any residents of the Department, or others legally permitted therein, were to be able to join said population; and to enjoy all the usual privileges of the respective municipalities which they might join.

4) Colony lands might never be voluntarily alienated to any foreign government or other dominion, under any pretext, without consent of the Mexican nation and previous knowledge of the departmental government.

5) The amount of lands ceded was to be in proportion to the number of souls actually arriving; the balance to be

145

reserved for a suitable number of years in case the balance of the promised number should come.

6), 7) Taxes should be suspended and the free entry of necessary goods for the establishment of the colony should be permitted for a period of years, in order to facilitate settlement and place it on a sound basis.[126]

In making the grant, which he seems to have done promptly, Pico fixed substantially the terms proposed by the assembly, specifying however that the tract was to lie wholly in the interior, twenty leagues from the coast; that each of the 3,000 [not 2,000, as proposed earlier] families was to have one league if the tract was large enough to permit, otherwise less; and that the government should reserve to itself any portion remaining unoccupied after the distribution.[127]

---

[126] "U. S. Govt. Doc.," 30th Cong., 1st Sess., Sen. Rep. #75, pp. 23--25; Leg. Rec., MS, vol. 4, pp. 363--68; Bancroft, Calif., vol. 5, pp. 217--18.

[127] "U. S. Govt. Doc.," loc. cit.; Bancroft, op. cit., p. 219.

Pico's grant to McNamara bore the date of July 4, 1846 -- being obviously one of the fraudulently antedated California grants. The assembly's authorization, voted on July 7th, could not have reached Pico until July 12th or 13th -- after the American occupation of the 7th.[128] Had the document been properly dated, the title would of course have been invalidated by the conquest. But a grant dated before the assembly's authorization was in any circumstances as undeniably void; and of course there had been no time -- apart from any other consideration -- for confirmation by the supreme government. The pre-dating device was a forlorn one, resorted to in the hope of saving what might be saved from Yankee seizure. As Larkin advised McNamara, moreover, the governor had no authority to confer more than eleven leagues in a single deed.

The grant seems never to have reached the stage of confirmation in Mexico, though it was approved by the Colonization Committee of Congress. Finally, no attempt seems ever to have been made to secure recognition of the title in California, although McNamara has been quoted as writing, in September 1846, to J. A. Forbes, British vice-consul at Monterey: "'I am also very desirous of doing something about that grant of land. I will give the Yankees as much annoyance as I possibly can in the matter."[129]

---

[128] Bancroft, *Calif.*, vol. 5, p. 219.

[129] "U. S. Govt. Doc.," 30th Cong., 1st Sess., *Sen. Rep. #75*, pp. 23--25; Bancroft, *Calif.*, vol. 5, pp. 219--20.

For a variety of reasons, therefore, the McNamara scheme, ambitious as it was, had no permanent significance, except in so far as its history illustrates Mexico's inclination (tempered by her apprehensions of foreigners generally and of English-speaking foreigners in particular) to utilize European colonists; and her determination to deal with them cautiously.

Undoubtedly a land-grabbing scheme looking to rapid appreciation in values following the long anticipated American seizure of California, the proposition was framed around features especially appealing to the Hispano-Americans: the religious coloring, the anti-Yankee bias and the large-scale occupation (perhaps never actually intended) of territory which Mexico had so long struggled vainly to populate. Despite these shrewd appeals to the susceptibilities and ambitions of the country, however, the McNamara project failed to sweep away at a stroke the fears and defensive policies fundamental to Mexicans and Californians alike.

Bancroft's summing up of the situation seems so just and so apropos as to justify quotation here *in extenso:*
". . . . when the speculating presbítero arrived in California, where colonization on a large scale had always been a popular idea, with all his special inducements of opposition to the Yankee invaders and lobos metodistas, he found the

authorities by no means in a hurry to disregard the laws and put him in possession of the whole department. He obtained little more than any presumably responsible man might have obtained in ordinary circumstances -- the concession of an immense tract of land, valueless then and nearly so for many years later, away from the coast, inhabited by gentile tribes, of extent in proportion to the actual number of colonists sent to occupy it, with title not transferable -- hampered, in fact, by all the legal conditions. The chance for speculation on a grand scale was not very apparent. It may be doubted that the London company would have cared for the grant even had their clerical agent not been obliged to tell them that it was fraudulently antedated. At any rate it would have been sold at a low figure to some Yankee speculator during the subsequent years of litigation."[130]

Finally, it seems logical to infer that the grant was partly in the nature of a vehement though futile gesture on the part of Pico and the Assembly against the Yankees; and was motivated, as well, by the wish if not the hope that concessions to the London company, and the importation (though but prospective) of thousands of British subjects, might persuade the so far disinterested British government

----

[130] Bancroft, *Calif.*, vol. 5, pp. 220--21.

149

to extend her protection to California. For no well informed Mexican or Californian doubted that the Damocles' sword of American aggression which had so long hung over Mexico and her territories was at the instant of falling.

California's leading citizens were in the midst of schemes for a European protectorate, and England had already been sounded out on the subject, with discouraging result.[131] Undoubtedly Pico (who had long favored England) and the Assembly looked on the McNamara colony as a possible though uncertain lever for prying the weight of England into a position of resistance to the otherwise irresistible momentum of American expansion.

17. Wanted: Assorted Foreigners!

As for settlements of non-English-speaking Europeans, they never materialized. In 1845, Castañares was vainly attempting to arrange the immigration of a colony of Spaniards to whom, on behalf of the Californians, he assured not only a cordial welcome but every aid to becoming established. The exasperated Congressman declared that this project, cordially backed by the Chief

---
[131] See post, chap. IX.

of the War Department, General José Gomez de la Cortina, would have been far advanced if the Minister of Relations had taken the necessary action in accordance with his promise.[132]

Simultaneously, General Vallejo was desperately urging counter-colonization against the North Americans, in the shape of a numerous and heterogeneous importation of "Germans, French, Swiss, Poles, etc., of a moral and religious sort, with capital, or useful trade, health, activity and capacity -- all to be positively certified to by a commissioner of colonization to be named by the government. Such a colony might even be drawn from the United States, which has many citizens of the countries mentioned."[133]

That suggestion was not impractical. During the decade in which Vallejo wrote (1840--50), 1,713,251 immigrants poured into the United States from the old world.[134] By their labor, skilled and unskilled, they contributed tremendously to the upbuilding and expansion of eastern North America. Orderly, law-abiding, industrious, they

---

[132] Castañares, Col. de Doc., pp. 7--8.
[133] Nov. 22, 1845, Vallejo to Bustamante, in Vallejo Doc., MS, vol. 12, #157, pp. 8--10, Prudon draft.
[134] Lippincott, Econ. Develop. of the U. S., p. 137.

151

showed themselves willing, for benefits received, to
fulfil the obligations of loyal citizens of the country
of their adoption -- of, presumably, any country of their
adoption. There seemed no reason why immigrants of that
type might not be assimilated easily in fairly large
numbers in California; particularly if enough nationalities were represented to prevent alien solidarity against
the hijos del país. By seeking such prospective settlers
among the foreigners already on the North American continent but not yet rooted in the United States, an enormous
saving of time and promotion money and effort might have
been effected.

The foreign-born in California in 1845 represented
less than 10% of the de razon population.[135] Corresponding figures for that year for the United States are not
at hand; but in 1860, the Middle Atlantic states had a
foreign-born population of 20.8% -- morethan twice as
high as the percentage of foreigners in California in
1845. The Pacific states of the United States, in 1860,
counted 34.9 foreign-born to every 100 natives; the New
England states, 15; the Eastern North Central states,
17.3; the Western North Central, 16; the Mountain states,
13.8. Only in southern United States, where the peculiar
conditions almost precluded any attraction of foreign
----

[135] See infra, Table I.

immigration, was the alien element relatively smaller than in the California of 1845.[136]

18. Peopling California with Californians

Statistics of the population *de razon* for the Mexican period[137] reveal that, despite the anxiety of the Californians for a considerable European immigration as an aid against Yankee aggressiveness, dependence was by no means entirely or primarily on the hoped-for alien influx. The following table illustrates this:

---

[136] Lippincott, Econ. Develop. of the U.S., p. 135.
[137] Figures for the neophyte population will be considered in chap. VIII.

TABLE I

De Razón Population,

Hispano-Californian and Foreign, 1810--48[138]

Year	Population de Razon	Foreign Population	Hispano-Cal'n Population	Hispano-Cal'n Increase
1810	2,130	---	2,130	
1820	3,270	12	3,258	1,128
1830	4,250	150[a]	4,100[s]	842
1840	5,960[b]	380[a]	5,580[s,b]	1,480
1845	7,300[c]	680[a]	6,620[s,c]	1,040
1848	14,000	6,500[d]	7,500	880

Probable increase of 1845--55,
based on 1845--48 increase.........2,933

[s] Smallpox: apparently in 1821; in 1828--29, 1838 and 1844. See post, pp. 160--62.

[a] Included many naturalized and married to Californians.

[b] Bancroft (Calif., vol. 3, p. 699) gives a population de razon of 5,780; the foreign population as 380, "more than half of the number probably being included in the preceding figures." For the present purpose, therefore, 200 foreigners are considered as included in Bancroft's figure 5,780; and the remaining 180 have been added to give the total de razon population in 1840. Correspondingly, from Bancroft's figure of 5,780 de razón, the

[138] Bancroft, Calif., vol. 2, pp. 158, 653--54; vol. 3, pp. 168, n. 36, 699; vol. 4, pp. 73--74, 588, 649, 651, n. 1; vol. 5, pp. 524--25, 643.

200 foreigners which he included have been subtracted, here, to give the Hispano-Californian population for 1840.

c

Bancroft's figure (*Calif.*, vol. 4, p. 649) for the population de razón is 6,900; for the foreign (male) population, 680, "of which number I suppose that somewhat less than half should be included in the figures given above." As he refers, in the same context, to "nearly 400 foreigners, newly arrived and unsettled, or at least beyond the reach of Mexican registers," it is clear that his "somewhat less than half" of the 680 foreigners included in the 6,900 meant the difference between the 680 and the 400, or 280. For the present purpose, therefore, 280 foreigners are considered as included in Bancroft's figure of 6,900; and the remaining 400 have been added to give the total population de razon in 1845. Correspondingly, from Bancroft's figure of 6,900 de razón, the 280 foreigners whom he included have been subtracted, here, to give the Hispano-Californian population for 1840.

George L. Rives, (U. S. and Mex., 1821--48, vol. 2, p. 22), citing the Bancroft source used here, gives

the Mexican population (here called Hispano-
Californian) as 8,280 in 1845. But he has subtracted the entire foreign population of 680 from
Bancroft's de razon figure of 6,900, making no allowance for the 400 of the foreign population who,
according to Bancroft, should be considered as
additional to the 6,900. The Hispano-Californian
population estimate of Rives for 1845 is therefore
probably a little too low.

d Bancroft (Calif., vol. 5, pp. 524--25, 643) includes half-breed children in this figure, which he
reached by deducting 280 known deaths and departures
from the 4,200 foreign males of known identity, and
allowing for a 2,580 increase of unknowns, females
and half-breed children. His estimate is liberal
since, in addition to the inclusion of the children,
he makes no deduction for "at least twice as many" as
280 foreign males "of whose later presence there is
no definite record."

The fluctuation in rate of the Hispano-Californian increase was doubtless in part at least the result of the
recurrent smallpox epidemics. Yet in 1845--48, despite a
severe epidemic, the rate of increase took an upward trend

which, if it may be used as an index to the increase from 1845--55, resulted in the striking population increment, for that decade, of 2,933.

The Hispano-Californian portion of the population is here seen to have doubled itself in the 29 years or scant generation intervening between 1820 and 1848, the increase being 4,242, or 1.3 plus per cent.

A comparatively small portion of this increase represented immigration from Mexico. The influx from that source seems not greatly to have exceeded -- if, indeed, it reached -- 1,500. The following tabulation gives Bancroft's figures for soldiers, colonists and convicts of known number, and makes liberal allowance for additional convicts, officials and all others:

TABLE II

Estimated Immigration from Mexico, 1822--48[139]

Soldiers, including soldier-convicts	with Echeandía	100
	" Figueroa	75
	" Micheltorena	350
Híjar and Padrés Colony		350
Presidarios of known numbers		298
Liberal allowance for all others		427
		1,500

[139] See ante, p. 18; post, pp. 338--40; ante, pp. 110, 89, 90, 93, 94.

In the light of these figures, it appears that the rise in population was due principally to natural increase. While adequate statistics of births and deaths during the Mexican period are lacking, an estimate of average natural increase may be roughed out on the basis of the figures at hand:

TABLE III

Hispano-Californian Natural Increase, 1820—48[140]
(Estimated)

Hispano-Cal'n population:	Hispano-Cal'n population:
1848.................7,500	1820.................3,258
1820.................3,358	1830.................4,100
Increase in 29 years....4,242	1840.................5,580
Mexican immigration.....1,500	1848.................7,500
Natural Increase in	20,438
29 years........2,743	Mexican immigration.....1,000[a]
	19,438
Average natural increase per year........94.55+	Average Cal'n population of period (¼ x 19,438).4,859.5

Estimated Average Natural Increase Rate: approximately 19.45+/M

[a] The preponderant part of the Mexican immigration did not merge with the population de razon and become a factor in its increase. The 250 Híjar and Padrés colonists did become such a factor, as did some of the officials. Of the cholos and presidarios, a few brought wives from Mexico; and probably a good many

---

[140] See ante, p. 153, Table I; p. 156, Table II.

others married or at least became the fathers of children in California. Their consorts, however, seem to have been neophyte women, for the most part, and their increase was in all probability classed as neophyte population, rather than <u>de razón</u>. In computing the birth rate <u>de razón</u>, therefore, 500 of the Mexican immigrants of the <u>cholo</u> class are here deducted. This still leaves a doubtless over-liberal allowance for Mexican immigration which did become a factor in the increase of the <u>de razón</u> population.

Natural increase represents, of course, the difference between births and deaths. For lack of adequate vital statistics for Mexican California, no positive assertions can be made as to either the death rate or the birth rate. However, it is possible to arrive at theoretical minima well within the bounds of probability and doubtless far too low. It would be unquestionably safe, for instance, to assume a death rate of 10 per thousand. Speaking of present-day conditions in the United States, Walter F. Willcox asserts that "any group which has an average proportion of young and of elderly members i.e., [as contrasted with a typical army group, for example] is almost sure to have a death rate above 10.[1]

---

141 W. F. Willcox, <u>Intro. to Vital Statistics</u>, p. 17.

This statistical authority supplies figures on the crude death rate for the United States (given by geographical divisions) which yield an average of 10.4 plus deaths to every thousand in rural areas, and 13.4 plus per thousand in urban areas.

World Almanac figures[142] on deaths in the United States during the years 1915--32 inclusive show an average rate for the entire country of 13.64 per thousand.

Death rates of today, however, despite the appalling factor of traffic casualties, afford too low a norm for application to the California of a century ago. Most of the tremendous strides in medicine, surgery, sanitation and disease control are the product of the last generation and a half.

United States death rates for an early period are lacking, official collection of mortality statistics in this country dating only from 1900.[143] A table for 1886, however, published by the United States Public Health Service, brings us closer to our period, though it is modern enough to keep our theorizing distinctly on the conservative side; and affords figures for sixteen European countries, Australia and New Zealand, the then death registration area of the United States, and Connecticut,

---
[142] P. 373.
[143] Willcox, Intro. to Vital Statistics, p. 16.

Massachusetts and Michigan.[144] These data yield a general average of 21.13 per thousand.

That figure can undoubtedly be accepted as a safely conservative theoretical death rate for Mexican California, and is still probably very low, particularly in view of the known high infant mortality and the fact that smallpox epidemics raged in the territory at least three times, probably four, during the period under consideration.

In 1821, 54 persons at Monterey were vaccinated by the Russians.[145] Pattie claimed to have secured his release from prison in San Diego in 1828 by agreeing to inoculate Californians de razón and neophytes against smallpox. According to his own doubtless rhetorical estimate, he immunized 22,000 persons throughout the length of the territory. "Strangely enough," Bancroft comments, "there is no record in the archives respecting the ravages of smallpox in this year or Pattie's professional tour; yet his statement is confirmed by the fact that the statistical tables show an extraordinary number of deaths this year among the Indians of all the

---

[144] John W. Trask, Vital Statistics, p. 64, Table 8. The rate for the United States death registration area is for the year 1880.

[145] Bancroft, Calif., vol. 3, p. 168, n. 38

northern missions." He says further that early in 1829 vaccine was brought to the territory by a Russian vessel, and W. A. Richardson was employed to vaccinate at the missions.[146]

In the late '30s, Vallejo circularized all parts of California, urging vaccination, cleanliness, temperance, etc., as defences against smallpox, from which the Indians on the northern frontier were dying by thousands.[147]

It cannot be supposed that the population de razón was unaffected by such ravages. We simply do not have compiled figures on such matters comparable with the data on neophyte births and deaths tabulated in the mission records. Valuable information on vital statistics for the gente de razón would probably reward research in the registers kept by the padres in connection with their parochial duties.

Some fragments of information for 1844 do, indeed, seem to refer to smallpox precautions and losses among the population de razon. In that year, the Monterey *ayuntamiento* found it necessary to establish a pest-house; and the New York dentist Streeter vaccinated 300 persons in Larkin's house. Although Bancroft found no record in the archives, again

---

[146] Calif., vol. 3, pp. 167--69, passim.
[147] Ibid., vol. 4, pp. 73--74.

personal testimony establishes the fact of the epidemic. According to Bidwell, 80 died of the disease in that outbreak.[148]

Assuming, therefore, as seems fully justified, the figure 21.13 plus per thousand as a probable average death rate for Mexican California, and combining it with our our natural increase rate of 19.45 plus per thousand, it becomes possible to compute a probable average birth rate for the period:

TABLE IV
Estimated Hispano-Californian Birth Rate, 1820--48[149]

Estimated Hispano-Cal'n average death rate	21.13[a]
" " " " nat'l incr'se rate	19.45
" " " " birth rate	40.59

[a] Decrease of the Hispano-Californian population by emigration was probably not an important factor, and has not been considered here. To allow for such an additional natural decrease in the population would of course automatically raise the probable birth rate. The aim, however, is to be thoroughly conservative in this estimate.

It becomes of interest to compare the figure arrived at for California with other birth rates. Although in the United States, birth records as indicated in census reports are to be

---

[148] Bancroft, *Calif.*, vol. 4, p. 651, n. 1
[149] See ante, pp. 158--60; 157, Table III.

found intermittently from 1850, it was not until 1915 that a continuous federal record based on registration of births was started.[150] The rate for 1930 -- 18.89 per thousand[151] -- is not without interest for our purpose, representing as it does a period of depression in many respects comparable with California's destitute years under Mexico!

Similarly, world birth rate figures for 1930 (in so far as they are available) invite comparison:

---

[150] Willcox, *Intro. to Vital Statistics*, p. 55.
[151] *Ibid.*, p. 79.

TABLE V
Birth Rates, 1930 -- for Comparison[152]

England and Wales..............16.3
Scotland......................19.6
Ireland (North)...............20.8
Irish Free State..............19.8
Australia.....................19.9
New Zealand...................18.8
Canada........................23.9
Union of South Africa.........26.6 (white)
United States.................18.9
Germany.......................17.5
France........................18.0
Italy.........................26.7
Denmark.......................18.7
Sweden........................15.4
Austria.......................16.8
Hungary.......................25.4
Belgium.......................18.7

These figures yield an average birth rate for the depression year 1930 of 20.1 plus per thousand.

---

[152] Joseph *Whitaker's Almanac,* p. 588, "Comparative Table of Vital Statistics."

United States Assistant Surgeon-General Trask has made available birth rate figures of 1886, for sixteen European countries, Australia and New Zealand, Connecticut, Massachusetts and Michigan:

TABLE VI
Birth Rates, 1886 -- for Comparison[153]

Australian Commonwealth	35.4
Austria	38.3
Denmark	32.4
England and Wales	32.8
Finland	35.3
France	23.9
German Empire	37.0
Hungary	45.6
Ireland	23.2
Italy	37.0
Netherlands	34.6
New Zealand	33.1
Norway	31.2
Roumania	42.2
Scotland	32.9
Servia	42.0
Spain	36.7
Sweden	29.8
Connecticut	22.3
Massachusetts	25.4
Michigan	21.3

[153] Vital Statistics, p. 26, Table 3.

This table yields an average of 32.96 plus per thousand. The fact that the figures for Michigan and Connecticut include still-births indicates a slightly lower average birth rate and a lower actual minimum birth rate than indicated in the table.

On the basis of these figures, California's conservatively estimated birth rate of 40.59 per thousand places the _hijos del país_ well forward in the ranks of the world's producers of man-power.

19. The Forgotten Men

Unlike the Atlantic colonists, whose numbers were continually augmented by excess or dissatisfied man-power from Europe, the _Californios_ dwelt isolated and almost without reinforcement. They were Mexico's forgotten men. Their territory was no land of promise, but a remote frontier, reputedly dreary and semi-barbaric; commonly confused with desolate Baja California; and held in general repugnance, even dread, as a region of exile and penalty.

Unlike the Atlantic colonists, the Hispano-Californians lacked the numerical strength to drive from their vicinity the tens of thousands of hostile Indians who harassed them constantly.[154] Unlike the Atlantic colonists, they were handicapped by thousands of half-gentled primitives in their

---

[154] See _post_, chap. IV, secs. 45, 46, 47.

very midst, who constituted a heavy burden at best, and a menace or scourge in revolt.

Unlike the Atlantic colonies, California lay directly in the path of one of the world's most aggressive nations, whose conviction and watchword was its "manifest destiny" to possess the entire breadth of the continent. Other dangers threatened or seemed to threaten, from time to time; but the double menace of Indians and Yankees never abated.

Within the "closing circle of peril" as they themselves were accustomed to call it, and denied effective recruitment from Mexico, the sons and adopted sons of the country undertook to build up, by self-multiplication, their capacity for defense and development. The supreme government's apparent hope that California might populate itself found some justification in the territory's ever mounting human crop. In connection with a census of the Mexican Republic, Alamán noted, in 1832, that the Californians propagated "*en extremo*, that householder being rare who stops at having 5 or 6 children, and those being infinite who have exceeded 12 to 20."[155]

In a letter of 1828, Juan Bandini made a similar but more conservative comment, his statement carrying the greater weight

---
[155] Depart. St. Pap., MS, vol. 16, p. 1.

of the actual resident: " . . . . in the limited time of fifty years this generation has been formed; fecundity is extreme, often more than 10 and 12 children, rarely as few as 5--6." Most of the whites, he added, came from a small number of families.[156]

Nor is it to be assumed that this exuberant fruitfulness was purely instinctive. The need of facilitating marriage and the raising of families had been openly recognized at least from the close of the eighteenth century, when Borica made his efforts to that end.[157] The territorial government was never in a position to offer baby bounties. But the young men of California married early, and were so encouraged by their parents partly, said William Heath Davis, "because they desired to have the sparsely settled country populated as rapidly as possible.[158]

It was an ambitious attempt to father a nation, and attended with remarkable success so far as time allowed. But a nearly empty country cannot be populated, even by the most earnest and prolific breeders of men, in a single generation.

---

[156] Nov. (?) 3, 1828, Juan Bandini to Eustaquio Barron, in Bandini Doc., MS, #8, pp. 17--18. On intermarriages between the few families that formed the original Hispano-Californian stock, see post, chap. X.

[157] See ante, p. 82.

[158] Seventy-five Years, p. 160.

CHAPTER III: " -- AND MONEY!"

20.	From Royal Wardship to Republican Responsibilities................ pp.	169--181
21.	The Tyranny of Taxes..............	181--207
22.	Public Finance in the Pueblos......	207--208
23.	Mother Church's Share.............	208--213
24.	Tidying up the Treasury Department.	213--219
25.	Untangling the Customs Administration............................	220--232
26.	Foreign Trade Regulations..........	232--264
27.	Laws without Teeth................	265--281
28.	*Los Contrabandistas*...............	28I--289
29.	Starting with Empty Pockets........	289--294
30.	The Territorial Purse.............	294--311
31.	Making Ends Meet..................	311--325
32.	The *Californios* Had All the Answers	325--336

CHAPTER III: " -- AND MONEY!"

20. From Royal Wardship to Republican Responsibilities

California's lack of financial resource lay even less in her power to remedy than did her lack of men. Spain had kept her in a state of wardship -- neglected, practically abandoned, it is true, for more than a score of years; yet never promoted to that legal majority which could have enabled her to make her way toward financial independence. The young Mexican nation, with its own way all to make, was in no position to discharge obligations of guardianship, much less of subsidy. Therefore when California -- with little choice in the matter -- submitted to the new state, she found herself suddenly confronted with the problem of self-support.

Under Spain, she had suffered from over-regulation, exclusionism and exploitation; but, at least for a time and partially, her material needs had been provided for. Each year, the royal mother, until her own financial **stringency** prevented, had drawn on the royal purse -- latterly in the amount of some 80,000 pesos[1] -- for California's anticipated expenses of the ensuing twelve months. Each year, until the system broke down, California's ship had come in -- a royal galleon laden with supplies and a little spending money.

---

[1] Bancroft, Calif., vol. 1, p. 629.

Under Mexico, most of the old disabilities remained in force, but without the compensation of the *memorias* which had rendered the Spanish discipline tolerable.

Yet Mexico, as we have seen, intended well. Congress interested itself in the northwestern territory for years, as the existence and exertions of the *Junta de Fometo de Californias* indicate.[2] There was even more reason in the territories than in the states, the Minister of Relations declared,[3] to provide for the salaries of the *jefes politicos* and the secretaries. Enlightened Mexicans like Híjar and Padrés, Ábrego and Coronel, Bandini, Herrera and Castillo Negrete gave themselves and their means to the development of the waiting land. But despite her republican fervor, Mexico was unable to clear at a barrier between the old system and modernity. Against that barrier bound the barrier her hopes for California and California's hopes of her were shattered.

Much has been made of the oppressiveness of imperial Spain's fiscal and commercial systems; of the impossibility of colonial progress under the mercantilistic yoke. And much has been made of the Californians' Arcadian freedom from financial exactions and vexations under Mexico.

----

[2] See *ante*, pp. 23--51.
[3] Mex., Mem. Relac., 1827, p. 36.

"Unburdened by taxes of any kind," declared Kotzebue, "and in possession of as much land as they choose to cultivate, they live free from care on the rich produce of their fields and herds."[4] Except for the reference to the produce of fields and herds, that statement is diametrically opposed to fact.

Even so generally reliable a witness as Sir James Douglas wrote: "No direct taxes whatever are levied on the inhabitants of California not engaged in trade . . . Merchants have to pay a Municipal duty of one dollar monthly; and a Municipal charge is made on all spirituous liquors landed from vessels of $1 per gallon. There are no other local taxes whatever."[5] Both his first and his last assertions are untrue.

Kotzebue's statement appeared in 1824, at the beginning of Mexico's rule of California; Douglas wrote in 1841, toward the close of the period. Both were in the main well-informed and intelligent observers. Moreover, their comments on the point in question were typical of the conclusions drawn by pre-conquest visitors. Naturally, therefore, tax-free beatitude became a duly incorporated tenet of the doctrine of "Arcadian" California.

The fact is that under Mexico the Californians carried

----

[4] Otto V. Kotzebue, *New Voyage*, vol. 2, p. 101.
[5] James Douglas, *Voyage*, 2, p. 91.

categorically the same direct and indirect tax burdens that they had carried under Spain; and under Mexico those burdens were consistently heavier.

The clues -- indeed, the clear evidences -- lie open in Bancroft's footnotes, in the irrefutable form of fragments of accounts of various dates, showing types and amounts of assessments for both territorial and local purposes; and in national and territorial tax enactments and regulations. That the levies oppressed all classes, directly or indirectly or both, is indicated by protests and appeals from officials, settlers, missionaries and even neophytes.

In July 1822, Governor Sola granted petitioning **pobladores** of San José a year's exemption -- in consideration of crop failures following drouth -- from the tax of 33% on the tallow of cattle and deer.[6]

In the fall of 1824, padres and neophytes submitted to Governor Argüello a plea for relief from taxation; and in December of that year, Padre Presidente Sarría protested to demands of the territorial government for mission supplies that most of the missions, after paying the various taxes, duties and forced loans, could barely clothe their

---

[6] July 6, 1822, Sola to Comisionado Luis Peralta, in St. Pap., Sac. MS, vol. 6, p. 49.

neophytes, etc.[7]

In 1826, Padre Duran protested to Herrera against furnishing the diezmo of cattle branded for the national rancho, since the mission had already delivered a much larger consignment than the year's tithing.[8]

In 1827, farmers of San José, again afflicted by crop losses, offered cash at the rate of 2 pesos a fanega in place of the usual tithe of grain.[9]

In the '30s, Vallejo and Alvarado voiced California's demand for relief from high tariff evils, urging free trade, a tax on productive property, and a small but dependable subsidy to tide the territory over the anticipated period of revenue adjustment. In the '30s and '40s, Vallejo persistently pleaded for exemption of the pioneers of the northern frontier, especially, from the crushing weight of indirect taxes paid on essential imports; and Congressmen Carrillo and Castillero urged application of Pious Fund proceeds to the support and general upbuilding of the territory. In 1844-45, Congressman Castañares made repeated appeals for "a combination of revenues" and special legislation freeing the

---

[7] Leg. Rec., MS, vol. 1, pp. 35--36; Bancroft, Calif., vol. 2, pp. 521, 517--18.

[8] Bancroft, Calif., vol. 3, p. 88, n. 4.

[9] S--é. 5, 1827, Mariano Duarte to Echeandía, in Leg. St. Pap., Ben., Pref. y Juzg., MS, vol. 6, p. 45.

territorio naciente from destructive tariff impositions.

To these constructive efforts at the reorganization of the fiscal and commercial systems, more detailed attention will be given later.[10] The immediate purpose is to consider the territory's sources of revenue, giving special attention to the tax situation both before and after the change of régime, in support of the statement made above that the tax nuisance was more acute under Mexico than under Spain.

Spain had proceeded on the theory that all that California produced belonged to the crown, which in turn was responsible for the maintenance of the colony. Accordingly, year after year the royal treasury had advanced tens of thousands of *pesos* for supplies, which were furnished the provincials at cost except that from 1790-94 half the regular duties seem to have been collected -- on national goods, of course, all foreign goods being prohibited; and that under Sola, all exports and imports save articles for church or missionary use were dutiable, although the tariff was apparently modified to meet Californian conditions.[11] During the Spanish régime, therefore, California suffered not too severely from customs imposts.

---

[10] See *post*, secs. 31, 32.
[11] Bancroft, *Calif.*, vol. 1, pp. 624-25; vol. 2, p. 419.

The severity of the *alcabalas*, or sales taxes, was also tempered. Between 1787 and 1792, and between 1794 and 1804 -- for fifteen years in all -- the province was entirely free from those levies. Between 1792 and 1794, only half the regular rates were exacted.

The ecclesiastical tithe of all products became transmuted into a civil due as a result of its sale by the Bishop of Sonora to the royal treasury, at a 5% discount, and its subsequent administration by treasury officials or by the highest cash bidders for the prerogative of farming it. Settlers of less than five years' establishment in the country, and the missions, were exempt from the tithe.

Spain's most considerable revenue from California -- "as in all other Spanish provinces where no rich mines were worked" -- came from the tobacco monopoly. This netted an approximate average of 6,000 *pesos* a year, in 1791--1800; in the next decade, 7,000 *pesos*.[12] Other commodities en *estanco* were gunpowder and playing cards, after 1807; and salt.[13]

Postal revenues, which averaged around 700 *pesos* annually in 1791-1800, and 400 *pesos* in 1801--10; sales of cattle from the *rancho del rey*; supplies produced in the country, including salt; and doubtless a few miscellaneous

---

12 Bancroft, *Calif.*, vol. 1, p. 633; vol. 2, pp. 186--87.

13 *Ibid.*, vol. 2, p. 187, n. 28.

taxes, as on stamped paper, slaughterings and inheritances, of which, however, there is almost no record, round out the picture of California's financial returns to Spain.14 Certain other dues were collected, in the form of deductions from soldiers' pay -- but for benefit purposes: for the fondo de retención, from which veterans were supplied with a sort of nest-egg, on taking up civilian life; for the fondo de inválidos or pension fund; and for the fondo de montepio (in the case of officers), for widows' pensions.15

Then, under Mexico, the territory was opened to foreign trade, all the evils incidental to the high tariff system in its most aggravated and aggravating form were fastened on California. For Mexico depended on the territorial import and export duties for the bulk of territorial maintenance. To that end, all the old devices were employed to squeeze out the highest possible percentage.

Besides high import and export dues, of which more than one might be imposed on a commodity, ad valorem taxes in the form of internación and avería (transportation) duties were exacted; as well as tonnage and anchorage, wharfage and storage charges; the payment of a license to carry on

---

14 Bancroft, Calif., vol. 1, p. 633; vol. 2, pp. 186--87.
15 Ibid., vol. 1, p. 694, n. 3.

the retail trade and of a guard when the customs regulations required one.[16] In addition, "voluntary contributions" were requisitioned from time to time of masters or supercargoes of vessels, for the improvement of port facilities; as when in 1833 Mexico ordered that 10 pesos 4 reales be collected from each whaler, for pier building.[17]

Besides the indirect taxes paid in the form of import and export duties, the Californians paid a retail sales tax on imports. In 1843, for example, a "consumption tax" of 20% of the 25% import duty was charged on flour, salmon and butter. The consumption tax on liquors ran very high.[18]

---

16 In Echandía's time, the anchorage tax was 10 pesos for each vessel, and the tonnage rate was 2 pesos 4 reales per torelada. The internación duty was 15% and the avería duty 2½%. With the 25% import duty then being charged in California, the duties were thus 42½% -- exclusive of anchorage, tonnage, etc. Bancroft, Calif., vol. 3, p. 117. In 1846, 1/2 real was charged for wharfage and 1 real for storage in the custom-house of each large bale. At about the same time, the retail trading license was 50 pesos monthly. Bancroft, Calif., vol. 4, p. 555; vol. 3, p. 117; T. O. Larkin, Official Corresp., MS, vol. 2, p. 99.

17 Bancroft, Calif., vol. 3, p. 369, n. 8.

18 Ibid., vol. 4, p. 376, n. 16.

Davis at one time estimated that the combined import duties under Mexico amounted to 80%--100% of invoice values; and later declared, and repeated, that they averaged 100%.[19] Forbes placed the figure as high as 150%--200%.[20] Bancroft found that from 1836--40, duty collections amounted generally to 100%, as was also the case in 1841.[21] During at least part of this time, Mexican tariff law called for a 100% duty on glass, etc. and a 125% initial import duty on cotton goods, with additional charges totalling a 20¢ levy on 6¢ cloth.[22] But the Californians had their own system of tariff abatement, by which they escaped the most intolerable levies.

The effective administration of the system would have necessitated a civil and enforcement list utterly beyond the capacity of California or of Mexico to support. Indeed, it is doubtful whether full effect could have been achieved, given every facility. As it was, while the goose that laid the golden eggs was not actually killed by the demands on its productivity, at least it learned to lay its eggs, as often as opportunity could be seized, in the laps of the contrabandistas.

---

[19] Seventy-five Years, pp. 46, 105, 106--7.
[20] Alta Calif., p. 302.
[21] Calif., vol. 4, pp. 80, 209--10.
[22] Arrillaga, Recopilación, 1837, Law of Feb. 17, p. 86; post, pp. 279, 660, 716.

Frequent fluctuations in tariff schedules were inherent in the system; for as it was never possible to please everyone, of course, the rates were continually revised. When the government needed extra funds, moreover, tariff rates shot up: as in April 1843, when a 20% increase in import duties was ordered "during the war in Texas and Yucatan."[23] Illicit commerce combined with tariff adjustment to make the customs revenues a variable quantity; and at most successful, they were wholly inadequate.

Mexico attempted to make up the deficit, not by such treasury advances as Spain had made, but almost entirely by extracting as much more as possible from the people of California. The time-worn economic contrivances of an earlier age were all ready to hand, never having gone out of use: the government monopolies; forced and "voluntary" loans; contributions and special assessments; civil tithes; stamped paper tax; certain fines; deductions and suspensions of pay for benefits never received or for the relief of impecunious government. Mexico found them all to her purpose, and resorted as well to the ever useful device of debt repudiation. Finally, there was the postal

---

[23] Bancroft, *Calif.*, vol. 4, pp. 376--77, n. 16.

revenue (extremely small); the product of the national ranchos and ~~of~~ That the territorial fur fishery.[24]

It is true that assessments for national purposes, although enacted, were not enforced against California. But the very threat of enforcement must have added to the harassment of long impoverishment. It is true that the yield from levies for territorial and local purposes, with the exception of the customs, was not large. But the country was on the mere threshold of productivity and of a money economy.[25] The very insufficiency of the system to provide for the territorial needs must have rendered it the more obnoxious.

As for any subsidization of the struggling territory by the supreme government, this seems to have been limited to the $22,000 and the $22,397 in supplies sent in 1825; possibly one or two small amounts sent later; and a few drafts on the national treasury, which in one way or another foreign or resident traders were induced to accept from territorial officials as security for loans or in payment for goods supplied. For the rest, there were good intentions: $12,000 ordered sent through the Comisaría of the West, in 1825; a decree of November 1827, on a future

---

[24] See post, sec. 39; pp. 583--88.
[25] See post, sec. 29; chap. V.

loan, part of which was to go to pay the troops of California; a congressional decree of 1828 by which the Californias were to have $140,940; a request of 1830--31 from the Secretary of the Treasury to Congress for $131,440 for the cavalry companies and $5,890 for mail transport; an order of 1842 for payment of $8,000 per month to aid in the maintenance of Micheltorena's troops; and possibly a few other magnanimous gestures. The sum total, in actual remittances, was -- practically nothing at all.[26]

21. The Tyranny of Taxes

Detailed consideration of customs and other levies goes beyond the present purpose. However, a rapid scanning of certain revenue items of special interest for one reason or another will make it clear that, so far from basking in the immunity attributed to them, the Californians under Mexico were a tax-ridden people, beset at every turn by one or another sort of exaction or retention. A chronological series of relevant items, rather than topical treatment, seems best designed to convey an idea of the persistent and protean manifestations of California's tax evil. Levies for territorial purposes will be considered first; then local impositions.

----

[26] Bancroft, Calif., vol. 3, pp. 57--59; vol. 2, p. 671, n. 39; vol. 4, p. 287.

In 1822, in addition to import and tonnage charges, an export duty of 6% payable by the seller and 6% by the buyer obtained. In June, the missions and other producers were called upon to advance all duties, plus 6% to 12% on all sales of produce. This forced loan was to be repaid in the [unusual] event of the arrival of the "usual" supplies from Mexico.[27]

An imperial decree of December assessed California in the amount of 11,139 pesos for 1823, toward meeting a 6,000,000 peso deficit in the national budget. The sum was to be raised by a national subsidy tax of 4 reales per year per person of either sex between 14 and 60 years of age, inclusive; and a consumer's tax amounting to 10% of the annual rent of the residence of each family (or, just possibly, since the wording of the transcript is obscure, to 10% of four times the rent of the residents). It is interesting that Alta California's population for purposes of this tax was estimated at 20,871![28]

The Plan de Gobierno of 1824 listed among the sources of territorial revenue: tonnage charges on foreign vessels;

---

[27] Bancroft cites (Calif., vol. 2, p. 473) various documents on this "loan," in which the tax is variously referred to as 6% and 12%.

[28] Su... Govt. St. Pap., ..., vol. 1, pp. 1--2; ante, p. 153, Table I.

import duties; 6% from foreigners on exports, 12% from sellers on exports; 10% on all cattle branded, on crops, wine and brandy; and authorized the Junta to devise other means of income if needed. The lay citizens might pay the tithe in kind; the missions must pay in cash.[29] Such a tithe in a pastoral and agricultural land is comparable to an income tax in a country with a more highly organized economy. The tithe paid by the mission at San Francisco was approximately 3,400 pesos in 1824, and again in 1828.[30] Forbes had the idea that the missions were exempted from the payment of tithes.[31] There seems to be plenty of evidence to the contrary.

From 1820 to 1825, the deductions from soldiers' pay at Monterey, for the Montepio and Inválidos funds, ranged between 450 pesos and 650 pesos annually.[32] This compulsory insurance premium must have been yielded up regretfully by officers and men unable to collect pay long in arrears, and with no prospect of the retirement or widows' pensions ever materializing.

------

[29] Plan de Gobierno, Title III, Art. 2, in Guerra Doc., MS, vol. 7, pp. 134--40.
Resumed in Bancroft, Calif., vol. 2, p. 512, n. 2.
[30] Bancroft, Calif., vol. 2, p. 672, n. 39.
[31] Alta Calif., p. 302.
[32] Bancroft, Calif., vol. 2, p. 610, n. 5.

In October 1824, the Junta General resolved to make clear to the population the fact that the tenth of crops and of stock increase provided for as a tax for territorial purposes in the plan de Gobierno (Title III, Art. 9) had nothing to do with the ecclesiastical tithe, as some citizens believed.

A few days later, the Junta repealed, as of January 1, 1825, the two taxes of 12% and 6% on coin exports; but replaced them by a 25% tax on coin exported on foreign vessels. This was probably an attempt to minimize in so far as possible the burden of the coin tax as borne by the Californians. In 1835, a 2% derecho de circulación was charged on money sent from California to San Blas.[33]

At about the same time, the Junta removed the tax on exports, as of January 1, 1825 -- probably partly in response to that autumn's petition of padres and neophytes for tax relief, and partly to encourage the exportation of territorial produce.[34]

The federal treasury in 1825 held California debtor for tobacco received during the first eight months of the year amounting to 23,863 pesos. In the fall of 1826, notice was given that 100,000 pesos' worth more was to be shipped into

---

[33] Bancroft, Calif., vol. 3, p. 369, n. 8, end.

[34] Leg. Rec., MS, vol. 1, pp. 35--39, passim.

the territory, and that none must be introduced from other sources. It is not to be supposed that this plenteous supply -- many times the quantity sent by Spain -- was in answer to demand. The population had increased by probably less than 2,000, including women and children. In 1827-28, moreover, the soldiers, forced to buy at 12 reales, were glad to sell at 4 -- so bad was the quality.[35]

In 1826, Echeandia decreed that the missions, like the citizens, might pay the tenth of produce and of stock increase in kind; but he also urged on the Ministry of War the desirability of levying another tithe -- evidently in cash -- on the missions, some of which, he was informed, were hoarding from 70,000 to 100,000 pesos.[36]

At the end of June of that year, advice was received in California to the effect that Mexico would pay all drafts presented within six months -- of the preceding January 1. All others were to be outlawed.[37] This practical repudiation had the effect of taxing away all debts outstanding from Mexico to California and Californians. Owing to the variety and amount of such debts, the

----

[35] Bancroft, Calif., vol. 2, p. 672, n. 39, passim.
[36] Ibid., vol. 3, p. 88, n. 2.
[37] Ibid.

consternation caused by receipt of the decree must have been almost universal -- although, in the nature of things, the obligations would doubtless have remained unpaid, decree or no decree.

The custom in California with regard to Mexican drafts had been and continued to be their endorsement over to foreigners, Mexican traders and travellers as negotiable paper or security for loans, the recipients always finding it possible to dispose of the orders in Mexico, to <u>agiotistas</u>, or bill brokers, with political affiliations, who knew the secret of extracting funds from the public treasury. Of course, this system subjected drafts to heavy discount -- 60% to 80% -- which, borne by the original holders, had all the effect of a direct tax.[38]

On December 27, and again on December 30, 1826, orders arrived from the supreme government commandeering for the national treasury half the territorial revenues.[39] In 1827, the diputación gave careful attention to the need of providing support for public education, and

------

[38] Alvarado, <u>Hist. de Calif.</u>, MS, vol. 5, p. 47. The <u>agiotistas</u>, according to Alvarado, shared their profits with officials of the national treasury department.

[39] Dept. St. Pap., Ben., Mil., MS, vol. 1, p. 72--73, 89--91.

although the municipalities continued to carry their share
of responsibility for the primary schools, an elaborate
reglamento worked out by the <u>vocales</u> allocated the proceeds of a liquor tax to that purpose. The schedule
fixed was $5 per barrel of 160 quarts for native brandy,
and $2.50 for native wine, in the Monterey and San Francisco
jurisdictions; $10 and $15, respectively, in the south;
and $20 and $10 per barrel respectively on foreign brandy
and wine. All buyers and producing retailers were subject
to this tax. This <u>Reglamento de Contribuciones sobre
Licores</u> was published in the form of a governor's
decree on July 12th. On August 6th, it was supplemented
by an announcement by <u>Comisario Subalterno</u> of Finances
Herrera that by superior orders a duty of 80% on foreign
liquors and 70% on foreign wines was to be exacted, besides
the 15% <u>internación</u> tax.[40]

A law of 1828 designated one-eighth of the customs
receipts for payment of the foreign debt.[41] In 1845, as
much as two-thirds of the proceeds were ordered to be remitted
to Mexico[42] -- although as a matter of fact probably no
part of them was ever so sacrificed.

----

[40] Bancroft, <u>Calif.</u>, vol. 3, p. 187.
[41] <u>Ibid.</u>, vol. 3, p. 672, n. 39, ll. 7--8.
[42] <u>Dpt. Rec.</u>, MS, vol. 4, pp. 262--65.

To ard the end of the '20s, California's destitution commanded some indulgence by the supreme taring power. In 1828, probably in response to a petition of 1827, the *internación* levy (an import tax) was reduced to 10%.[43]

In 1829--30, by presidential order, the soldiers of California were exempted from certain discounts on pay which seem to have been in force till then.[44]

At about the same time, a tax of 5% and 10% was levied on incomes in all Mexican territory; but the assessment was not collected in California.[45]

On August 17, 1829, a forced loan and salary discounts were imposed on California with other territories.[46] The troops of California were exempted from contributing, however, through discounts on their pay, to a fund decreed on September 14th for the war against Spain.[47]

Throughout the decade 1821--30, numerous orders, says Bancroft,[48] required the payment of tithes. Statistics are

---

[43] Bancroft, *Calif.*, vol. 3, p. 132.
[44] *Ibid.*, vol. 2, p. 672, n. 39.
[45] *Ibid.*
[46] *Ibid.*, vol. 3, p. 46, n. 27.
[47] *Ibid.*
[48] *Ibid.*, vol. 2, p. 672, n. 39.

lacking, for the amounts so paid; but protests and relevant correspondence indicate that the civil tithe was by no means a dead letter. A law of October 1833 abolished this form of taxation as an obligation; but although most citizens took advantage of the exemption, certain officials who realized the public need of revenue, assigned to the territorial account their claims on the government for back pay, thus effecting a compromise between their convictions of civic obligation and their natural desire for tax relief.

The abolition of 1833 did not end the tithing system. Like the income tax today, it was too obvious a method of raising revenue to be renounced. A series of orders running from May to August, 1839, bore on a tithe for the establishment of a mail route between the two Californias. Ranches of less than five years' establishment were apparently exempted, as was traditional. In August of that year, we find a tithe collector being appointed in San Diego; and in 1840, one in Los Angeles.[49]

Figueroa's opening speech to the diputación in 1834 contains an excellent example of those informal levies imposed by moral suasion on officials whose sense of public responsibility moved them to comply. The supreme government

---

[49] Bancroft, Calif., vol. 4, p. 100, n. 63; vol. 3, p. 617, n. 10, "Items of Revenue and Finance"; p. 637, n. 4, "1840."

had ordered the establishment of a strong garrison for the protection of the northern frontier. Figueroa was determined to see the project accomplished. Lacking funds, however, he threw the burden of the undertaking on the _diputación_; and he urged on Vallejo the utmost co-operation, at personal cost, to be compensated by posthumous glory. In other words, Figueroa's eloquent appeal was in effect an extraordinary tax levy on such volunteers as could be induced to bear for patriotic considerations the expenses of a territorial undertaking, means for which were not otherwise available.

Vallejo's remarkable response to this call, which put him to an expense of many thousands of _pesos_, is the outstanding illustration of the fact that the forthright contribution, like the politely termed "loan" type of tax was a highly practical revenue device in California. Time and again it afforded the only means of getting necessary things done; and time and again the open-handed territorials either responded to a call or volunteered support for projects for the general welfare.

When in April 1822, the _junta_ which decided for adherence to Mexico was informed that California was invited to send a territorial _diputado_ to the new _Cortes_, it was voluntarily decided to elect such a delegate at once, and to provide for his first year's salary (set at 4,000 _pesos_) by voluntary subscriptions if possible, otherwise by a pro rata tax. The governor issued a great appeal for a _donativo_ gracioso, failing which a *contribución forzosa* would be resorted to; and Sarría circularized the padres, all of whom, Bancroft tells us, promised *más o' menos*. If a military man should be elected to Congress, his salary as *diputado* was to be decreased by the amount of his soldier's salary. The members of the *junta* showed their ambition for the practical independence of the new territory -- and for economy -- by agreeing among themselves to petition Mexico for exemption from representation in Congress in future.[50]

Alvarado had personally to assume a share of the public expenses, in 1838, in order to preserve his government: "Funds have been completely exhausted. . . . For any indispensable expenditures I must make very great sacrifices."[51]

The next year, we find Vallejo proffering 8,000 to 10,000 *pesos* "out of his own pocket" to the Department Treasurer, for the payment of soldiers, since public funds were lacking.[52]

---

[50] Bancroft, *Calif.*, vol. 2, pp. 453--54.

[51] Aug. 18, 1838, Alvarado to M. G. Vallejo, in *Vallejo Doc.*, MS, vol. 5, #145, p. 5

[52] July 10, 1839, M. G. Vallejo to Depart. Treasurer, in *Vallejo Doc.*, MS, vol. 6, #147. (The original document is unnumbered, and with dozens of other unnumbered originals is bound in with a corresponding sheaf of copies numbered 4 -- 156. This sheaf just precedes original document #3, which is followed by original document #157. The confusion is the greater as the sheaf of copies looks like a single document, #4.)

In 1841, the *juez de paz* of San Jose and the sub-prefect of the district advanced money for an Indian expedition.[53]

Examples might be multiplied, but it need only be added here that in 1840 Douglas remarked on the discrepancy between governmental revenues and costs, and noted that "the persons in office must scrape together [the balance] the best way they can . . . ."[54]

In 1842, Alvarado resorted to a suspension of pay of the members of the *Junta Departamental*, although Bancroft doubts that this measure increased the public funds, "as it does not clearly appear that the salaries had ever been paid at all." The salaries of all civil employees, save special exceptions directly specified by the governor, were likewise to be held in abeyance.[55]

In 1843, the problem of underwriting the governor's salary -- or enough of it to provide for his support -- was met by the voluntary contributions of public-spirited citizens.[56] At about that time, too, we find army officers billeted with civilian families.[57]

----

[53] See post, p. 413.
[54] Journal, MS, p. 78.
[55] Bancroft, *Calif.*, vol. 4, pp. 295--96.
[56] Ibid., p. 351.
[57] Ibid., p. 355.

For the burden of making ends meet was not confined to the highly placed. When need arose, the general citizenry was called upon as a matter of course. In 1840, every owner of two horses, in the San Diego district, was requested to furnish one for an Indian expedition.[58] Of course, the horse might be returned; but it might be killed or disabled or stampeded by the Indians. Even failing any such casualty, the return of the animal could by no means be taken for granted. In 1843, citizens of Monterey complained to the authorities that the expeditions sent against the Indians had generally failed to return the horses and saddles furnished by the *rancheros*.[59]

The obligation of citizens to support necessary enterprises for which governmental funds were lacking, as thoroughly understood and accepted. In 1840, when the Indian situation demanded the stationing of an *escolta* at Pacheco's ranch, the *rancheros* were invited to share the expense. When, in that year, Alvarado found it necessary to order a mobile force of forty men to patrol the Monterey district against the wild Indians and other marauders, the defenders had to be billetted on the people of the countryside.[60]

---

[58] Bancroft, *Calif.*, vol. 4, p. 65.
[59] *Ibid.*, pp. 361--62.
[60] Dept. St. Pap., S. José, MS, vol. 5, pp. 58--60.

In April 1843, when an armed force found it necessary to operate for two months against the gentiles in the Sierra, José Castro advanced 300 pesos for expenses, on the somewhat doubtful chance of getting it repaid later -- a chance which does not appear to have materialized. In December, citizens of San José, petitioning the governor for a permanent detachment of troops, volunteered to contribute to its support.[61]

The establishment of a presidio in the Tulares was projected in 1843 -- expenses to be defrayed by contribution.[62] On the northern frontier, that year, Vallejo obtained donations of 3,063 pesos in cash, plus grain, cattle, building materials and labor, from a mass-meeting called to subscribe loans for maintaining the garrison and meeting other public obligations.[63]

In 1843, also, with the soldiers existing on half a real a day, the officers on one-fifth of their salaries, and all back pay suspended until further instructions, Micheltorena urged that creditors, as well as soldiers and officers, must submit to sacrifices. Here was the moratorium idea, resorted to nowadays. A few weeks later, employees on the civil list were placed on one-third their stated salaries, **battalion** officer

---

[61] Bancroft, Calif., vol. 4, p. 362, n. 27.
[62] Ibid., p. 409.
[63] Vallejo Doc., MS, vol. 11, #412.

on one-fourth -- their general, however, receiving nothing.
Even the Supreme Court judges had to accept a two-thirds cut.
In 1844, in his *Bando Económico*, the governor suspended the
entire salaries of various civil and military officials.[64]

When, in 1844, a high school at Monterey was projected
for the territory, contributions were sought for its establishment, and 900 *pesos* a year for three years was subscribed.[65]

All these impositions, direct and indirect, were for
territorial or national needs.[66] Local revenues had also to
be procured, of course. To Figueroa's time, the chief reliance for that purpose seems to have been taxes on retail
trade,[67] along with fines for minor offenses, and the liquor
tax of the *Reglamento* of 1827 for support of the public schools.
The ancient custom of the *peaje* -- the obligation of citizens
to work at or supply labor for road and bridge repair also
survived. Community enterprises not provided for by
these means had to be financed by subscription.

Temporary stoppage, for one reason or another, of any of
these sources of supply, precipitated local crises -- as when,

---

[64] Bancroft, *Calif.*, vol. 4, pp. 361, n. 1; 358.

[65] *Ibid.*, pp. 402--3. Schools in the other municipalities were supported out of local funds.

[66] For data on territorial revenues, see *post*, **sec. 30**.

[67] June 20, 1828, Echeandía to *Teniente* Ignacio Martinez, in *Dept. Rec.*, MS, vol. 6, p. 58.

in 1832, the refusal of a high official to pay the excise
tax on several barrels of brandy in his possession caused
a "strike" of liquor merchants against the liquor sales
tax, and the public schools had to be closed till funds
should flow again with good cheer.[68]

In addition to meeting its strictly local responsibilities, each pueblo was expected to contribute toward the expenses of the *diputación*: that is, toward provision for its meetings, and the payment of its secretary. Perhaps occasionally, though certainly not often, the condition of a local treasury permitted some modest compliance with that obligation. In December of 1833, the San José *ayuntamiento* voted to send its surplus funds to swell the territorial treasury, though how large a surplus -- if any -- was found to exist after the balancing of the accounts, does not appear.[69] We do know that in January, 1834, Figueroa was forced to borrow 300 *pesos* to fit up a room for the *diputación*.[70] Once in a while, some momentarily affluent pueblo might contribute to special territorial needs -- as when in September 1834, the Los Angeles *ayuntamiento* sent a contribution to Monterey for powder

---

[68] Bancroft, *Calif.*, vol. 3, p. 379.

[69] *Ibid.*, p. 729, n. 25, "1833."

[70] *Ibid.*, p. 379.

and flints.[71]

Provinces of municipal [...] and [...] kept officials in continual perplexity. Frequent deliberations on the matter, by the *ayuntamientos* and the *diputación*, resulted, in August 1834, in the publication by Figueroa of a *Plan de Propios y Arbitrios para Fondos Municipales de los Ayuntamietos [sic] de la Alta California*.[72] As this *bando* remained in effect with small variation in rates until the conquest, its provisions are resumed here:

Arts. 1 and 2 ordered the survey of the *ejidos* (commons) and *propios* (other properties) of each pueblo, and their rental or auctioning off in small lots in emphyteusis (perpetual or protracted lease).

Art. 3 established grantees' fees of 6 *pesos* 2 *reales* per front *vara* on town building-lots of the usual 100 *varas* square, and 2 *reales* per front *vara* on smaller lots and on the excess frontage of larger lots.

Arts. 4 and 5 set a tax of 12 *reales* for the granting and registering of cattle brands.

Art. 6 specified that 1/2 *real* per head should be

---

71 Bancroft, *Calif.*, vol. 3, p. 365, n. 4, "1834."

72 "Earliest Printing," #4; There is a poor translation in Dwinelle, *Colonial Hist.*, Add. Ald, pp. 29--30. Bancroft gives the gist in *Calif.*, vol. 3, p. 369, n. 21.

charged on cattle and sheep, and 2 _reales_ on hogs slaughtered for market.

Art. 7 provided for license fees of 1 _peso_ per month on drygoods shops, 4 _reales_ per month on grocery stores, _cantinas_ and other retail establishments.

Art. 8 ordered a charge of 1 _real_ for each weight and measure guaranteed by the inspector (_ejecutor_).

Art. 9 imposed a tax of 2 _pesos_ the performance on theatrical productions and puppet shows.

Art. 10 set the billiard room license at 1 _peso_ per month.

Art. 11 established fees for the landing of goods at the five ports (San Pedro being included) as follows: for each parcel landed from national vessels, 1/2 _real_; for each parcel landed from foreign vessels, 1 _real_.

Art. 12 fixed a special tonnage tax of 2 _reales_ per _tonelada_ on foreign vessels, "in behalf of the treasury of the diputación."

Art. 13 assessed hunters 4 _reales_ on each otter and beaver skin taken.

Art. 14 allotted to the municipal funds fines imposed by _alcalde_ or _jefe_ for minor offences.

Arts. 15 and 16 revised liquor taxes on national wines and spirits downwards: to 3 _pesos_ on brandy, 2 _pesos_ on Angélica, and 12 _reales_ per barrel on wine; the foreign brandy and gin tax being set at 1 peso per gallon, and that on wine and beer at 4 reales per gallon.

Art. 17 called for voluntary contributions for wharf-building from all vessels anchoring at Monterey.

Art. 18 set a 3-peso tax on auction sales.

Arts. 19--21 were concerned with provisions for the execution of the law.

An unusually complete local financial account, containing numerous entries showing conformance to the bando, was published by Lwinelle in 1863.[73] Many fragmentary accounts and a variety of correspondence assembled by Bancroft afford ample documentary evidence that the taxes and rates specified in the Plan de Propios _ Arbitrios were collected by municipal authorities through the remaining years of Mexican rule.

A few odds and ends from the Bancroft sources and digests seem sufficient confirmation here:

In 1844, the first juez of Sonoma wrote to the second alcalde, asking him to proceed with the collection from the shops of that pueblo of the usual fixed taxes for the months of January, February and March of the

---

[73] Colonial List., Add. #54, pp. 75--81. The account is that of "Don Juan" Fuller, sindico of San Francisco, and is for the years 1839--42.

current year, giving receipts and holding until further
orders the amounts collected.[74]

An exchange of letters took place in the same year
between José de la Rosa and his wife Doña María Dolores,
of the Híjar and Padrés colony, who had gone into the
retail wine and liquor business in California. Don José,
temporarily in Monterey, wrote in reply to certain questions of his wife keeping shop back in Sonora. She had
written that she was paying a 3-peso tax each month, and
also a 12-real tax. She had been paying too much, her
husband advised her:

"They collect 3 pesos in Monterey; but no 12 real
tax -- instead, one of 4 reales, and this only if there
is a bar. If no bar, the consumers' tax, or derecho de
introducción alone is required. . . . . You have only to
pay the tax for introducing the brandy into your house,
and you do not have to pay the 12 reales . . . . for
you maintain no public bar . . . . Immediately on receipt
of your letter I went to the general's house, and . . . .
took up with him the matter of these abuses which occur
so often. The rates established in this capital are:
18 pesos for foreign brandy, 3 pesos for native

------

[74] March 14, 1844, J. P. Leese to 2nd Alcalde, in Vallejo
Doc., MS, vol. 12, 216.

brandy, 12 reales for wine and other liquors."[75]

Even the upward revision of the rates set by the Plan de Propios y Arbitrios evidently resorted to at times and places did not always suffice to meet local expenses. In such cases, special levies were made. Thus, in 1822, when San Jose needed a prison and casa real, word went forth that one-third of the tallow taken from cattle and deer must be contributed for the purpose by the people of the community.[76]

The fine was an important and convenient source of local income. Pueblo receipts for Los Angeles for January to September, 1833, for example, show that of a total of $977, $448 came from fines.[77] A variety of police regulations (prohibiting standing on streets during mass, requiring lights before houses and shops, and the like), afforded opportunity -- like certain minor traffic regulations and other city ordinances today -- for replenishing exhausted municipal coffers in the name of public order. In at least one case on record, the tables were turned on the penalizing power. In 1844, the governor himself had fixed a municipal fine for failure of the citizens to keep lights before their

---

[75] Aug. 8, 1844, Jose de la Rosa to wife, in Vallejo Doc., vol. 12, #76.

[76] Bancroft, Calif., vol. 2, p. 604, n. 44, "1822"; and see ante, p. 172.

[77] Bancroft, Calif., vol. 3, p. 635, n. 4.

houses. José María Castañares -- apparently as a prank, since he was friendly with Micheltorena and one of his political supporters -- put out His Excellency's own light, and reported its absence to the <u>alcalde</u>. The governor duly paid to that official the amount of the fine -- 5 <u>pesos</u>.[78]

Fines on officials for negligence or complaisance had the merit, besides their exemplary effect, of running rather higher than fines for a mere infringement of a regulation. Thus, in 1839, the justices of Monterey were fined 20 <u>pesos</u> by the governor for permitting the game of bagatelle to be played on holy days.[79] A little later, the <u>alcalde</u> of Los Angeles paid a like penalty for permitting card-playing in a tavern on Sunday.[80] In 1839, too, each member of the Los Angeles <u>ayuntamiento</u> was fined 10 <u>pesos</u> for countenancing a memorial of citizens in connection with a political "tumult" over the location of the flag. The twenty citizens who signed the memorial were fined only 5 <u>pesos</u> each.[81]

Fines for non-attendance of officials at political meetings were also in vogue. On one occasion in San José

---

[78] Bancroft, <u>Calif.</u>, vol. 4, n. 1, "1844," end.
[79] <u>Ibid.</u>, vol. 3, p. 675, n. 5, "1839."
[80] <u>Ibid.</u>, p. 639, n. 5, "1839."
[81] <u>Ibid.</u>, pp. 588--89.

such absentees were assessed 2 reals each. In 1834, the
diputación upheld the Los Angeles ayuntamiento in its
refusal to remit a fine on one of its members for non-
attendance, even though he had pleaded ill health as an
excuse. Unexcused absence from Los Angeles council
meetings in 1845 involved a penalty of 5 pesos.[82]

Taxes on wood seem to have taken the two forms of
fines for illegal extraction, and sales taxes. In 1834,
the military commandant of San Francisco advised the
diputación that strangers within his jurisdiction were
cutting timber and destroying the forests. He asked for
a revision of the reglamento of August 17, 1830 setting
penalties for the extraction of wood.[83] At about the
same time, a tax of 1 peso per vara of thickness was being
imposed by the ayuntamiento of Branciforte on every tree
felled.[84] The Monterey ayuntamiento had been devoting
much attention to the same subject. Early in 1845, it
appointed a committee to draw up a tariff on wood and
timber, and on January 31st the rates were set. Again on
August 10th the matter came up, this time in the form of

[82] Bancroft, Calif., vol. 3, p. 731, n. 25, "1832"; 635,
n. 4, "1832"; vol. 4, p. 634, n. 12.
[83] Los. Rec., MS, vol. 7, pp. 68--69.
[84] Bancroft, Calif., vol. 3, p. 696, n. 17.

a 10% sales tax.⁸⁵ In Santa Cruz, again, in 1844, lumbermen were called upon for a 5% tax; but there was trouble about the amount and the collection. In August, the governor ordered the *alcalde* to stop the saw-mills unless the tax should be paid.⁸⁶

One *peso* per pelt was being collected on otter skins, by order of the Branciforte *ayuntamiento*, in 1834, just before the *Plan de Propios y Arbitrios* of August 6 set the rate at 4 *reales*.⁸⁷

On salt which the Russians and other foreigners were allowed to take from the *salinas* in the '20s and '30s, a duty was charged, although its collection was not always successful.⁸⁸

In 1839, at San Diego, a tax was imposed on the hide-salting establishments of foreigners, as had been done in 1834.⁸⁹ In 1845, the Los Angeles *ayuntamiento* considered augmenting its revenues by "a small contribution" from salt

---

85 *Dopt., Actas del Ayunt.*, in "Ashley Doc.," MS, pp. 59, 60--61.

86 Bancroft, *Calif.*, vol. 4, p. 654, n. 10. It is of interest in this connection that most of the sawyers in this vicinity were foreigners.

87 *Leg. Rec.*, MS, vol. 2, p. 62.

88 Bancroft, *Calif.*, vol. 2, p. 649, n. 38; vol. 3, pp. 374-75. The duty was 4 *reales* per *cental* in 1827-28.

89 *Ibid.*, vol. 3, p. 617, n. 10, "1839," end.

and pitchers.[90]

The next of supplies for the Monterey boys' school concerned the ayuntamiento, at about the same time. The committee on public instruction was authorized to "invite" the residents of the town to "contribute voluntarily each as much as possible." At least two members of the ayuntamiento seem to have responded on the spot: Regidor Joaquín Gomez offered two planks for the construction of seats or desks, and enough paper to enable two boys to learn to write, the written sheets to be returned to him;[91] and Regidor Hartnell made a similar offer plus a bottle of ink, making the same stipulation that Gomez had made regarding the return of the paper.[92]

Contributions had also been sought for a girls' school for Monterey, in 1835, Alvarado being appointed to solicit them; and for support of four prisoners at work on a

---

[90] L. A. Arch., AC, vol. 5, p. 295.

[91] Doubtless to be smoked up, since the paper commonly used for writing purposes was cigarette paper. Since the sheets were of foolscap size, they might also be useful for wrapping small articles. According to Bancroft (Calif., vol. 2, p. 671, n. 37), writing paper, in 1821-30, cost anywhere from $4.25 to $16 per ream.

[92] Jan. 24, 1836, Mont., Actas del Ayunt., in "Ashley Doc.," MS, pp. 58--59.

casa consistorial.⁹³

Despite the stringency of 1843, the Junta Económica spoke for the support of schools throughout the territory by means of contributions from the citizens.⁹⁴ Micheltorena's Bando Económico echoed that resolution, calling particularly on the fathers of families for the support of the primary schools in the various pueblos. Alumni of the Monterey school were asked to provide an escribanía (desk) for the teacher.⁹⁵

Early in 1844, the Los Angeles ayuntamiento recommended to the Departmental Assembly the assessment of a monthly tax on each padre de familia, to help support the primary school. At this same session, two other means of swelling the insufficient municipal income were reported out of committee and recommended to be given general effect by the Assembly. Half the municipal commons were to be placed under cultivation, on a rental basis; and a tax was to be collected from vineyardists.⁹⁶

Although these were but recommendations to the Assembly, a document of the next year indicates that they -- or a part

---

93 Bancroft, Calif., vol. 3, p. 674, n. 5, "1835"; 617, n. 10, "Mar. 19th."

94 Ibid., vol. 4, p. 397.

95 Dept. St. Pap., Ang., MS, vol. 10, pp. 34--35.

96 L. A. Arch., MS, vol. 5, pp. 287--91; and see post, pp. 333--35.

of them -- were given force by that body. In May 1846, we find the residents of Santa Bárbara appealing for the exemption of vine-grape growers from the taxes imposed on them. The petition came up for its second reading on June 3rd.[97]

22. Public Finance in the Pueblos

In the nature of things, local incomes could not run into many figures. Most of the imposts were in amounts unproductive of substantial revenue, yet nonetheless resented as nuisance taxes and undoubtedly evaded as consistently as possible. A record of 1828, showing total receipts and expenditures for the six districts except San José and San Francisco,[98] indicates how little the localities had to work with:

Receipts.......3,388 pesos
Expenditures...1,637 "
Balance........1,751 pesos

The impression of rudimentary finance is borne out by a summary of Los Angeles income and expenditures for the 1830s in so far as Bancroft was able to glean the items from hundreds of

---

[97] Leg. Rec., MS, vol. 4, pp. 344--45.
[98] Bancroft, Calif., vol. ., p. 672, n. 39, enl. The six districts ould be those depending on the four presidial towns and the two larger pueblos. Branciforte was administered with San José.

scattered references.[99]

Table VII
Los Angeles Pueblo Account Sheet, 1833--40

Year	Receipts	Disbursements
1833 (Jan.--Sept.)	977 pesos	923 pesos
1834	919	936
1835	530	583
1836	644	518
1837	381	460
1838	337	334
1839	739	no record
1840	567	517

Generally speaking, it may be concluded that the municipal revenues like those of the territory, were so derived as to impose hardship if properly enforced, resentment and chronic insufficiency whether enforced or not.[100]

23. Mother Church's Share

Although not to be confused with civil obligations, the exactions of the church cannot be ignored in a consideration of early California's public economy. Under Spain, church and state worked hand in hand. Under Mexico, despite republican determination to restrict the church to the spiritual

----

[99] Calif., vol. 3, pp. 635--37, n. 4.
[100] On California's efforts to secure a reconstitution of her sources of revenue, see post, **sec. 32.**

sphere, Catholicism remained the state religion, and the Californians continued to take their faith seriously. Under those conditions, church demands were persistent, and more or less severe as they were more or less successful.

As we have seen, in the Spanish period the sale of the ecclesiastical tithe to the secular authorities metamorphized it into a civil tax. Throughout the Spanish and early Mexican periods, the missionaries seem to have felt as the last straw of an overwhelming load of responsibilities the parochial duties which they were called upon to perform for the _gente de razon_; and they were generally disposed to exact as much as possible for their services. The result was a series of nuisance taxes, sometimes paid, sometimes not.

An altercation which dragged on through five years, holding up an urgent public health project, affords illustration of the disposition of the church authorities to levy tribute when and as they could; of the conflict between civil and ecclesiastical jurisdictions; and of the hesitance of the good Catholics of California to oppose their spiritual fathers too drastically. Bancroft tells the first part of the story. In 1839, citizens of Los Angeles petitioned the _ayuntamiento_ on the state of the town cemetery, which, having been in use since 1822, had become totally inadequate to the pueblo's needs, and was endangering the health of the community. The petitioners asked that a proper site be selected, and that the *ayuntamiento* and priest take up the matter of transferring remains from the old *campo santo* to the new.

The *ayuntamiento* acted promptly, to the end that a new cemetery was ordered established at the cost of the petitioners and with the co-operation of other citizens. Bancroft thus resumes the incident of the petition and council action, finishing with the comment that "nothing was accomplished for five years."[101] The entire story, however, is to be found among the Coronel manuscripts, where nearly a score of closely written pages are devoted to the telling.

The gist of the matter is that the ecclesiastical authorities took issue over the question of burial fees. The *ayuntamiento* maintained that no such charges should be made, at least for the interment of Angelinos, since the community would bear the cost of establishing and maintaining the cemetery. The ecclesiastics took the stand that with the blessing which would consecrate the ground, the place would become church property, and a

---

[101] Bancroft, *Calif.*, vol. 3, p. 632, n. 1, "1839."

charge for burial services could become a church prerogative.

After much searching of the law, Spanish and Mexican, evidence was uncovered to the effect that the establishment of cemeteries pertained to the civil authority. Nevertheless, and although the public health was considered in danger, and private funds had been contributed for the abatement of the menace, the *ayuntamiento* hesitated to enter into definite opposition to the church authorities on so delicate a question. Finally, the *ayuntamiento* assumed direction of the new *campo santo*, but referred the complications of the situation to the Departmental Assembly. What the issue was remains unwritten, perhaps unrecorded, history.[102]

After secularization, Bishop García Diego, inspired with great plans for the church in California, and handicapped by the universal absence of funds, sought to enforce collection of the ecclesiastical tithe throughout the territory. In the Santa Bárbara region he seems to have had fair success. For the rest, his zeal was apparently ineffective. The law left the matter to individual conscience, and Micheltorena made clear the impossibility of lending the secular arm to enforcement, although, says

---

[102] Coronel Doc., MS, p. 92--110.

Bancroft, he "ingeniously contrived to put his refusal in the shape of a zealous plea in favor of church prerogatives."

The Californians, however, particularly of the north, had little inclination to submit to a new and considerable drain on their frequently tapped resources. For a time the territory rang with controversy. Vallejo made flat refusal to pay, or to recognize the right of the bishop to exact, a diezmo of his property to be spent on '"impracticable and profitless episcopal schemes'" -- although he had heavily supported the Sonoma church for years, and was ready to continue to give liberally for religious purposes.

According to Alvarado, Padre Quijas preached very pointedly at Vallejo on this score; but Don Guadalupe was too much of a potentate for more drastic measures to be used against him. Others were less secure. Many lived from hour to hour in fear of excommunication by the bishop. From Don José Sanchez--that upright and valorous soldier who had pioneered in California from 1791, sharing in more than a score of Indian campaigns and explorations--the consolations of his religion were withheld on his deathbed, because of his refusal to pay the church tithe; and for a time at least his body was denied Christian burial.[103]

-----

[103] Bancroft, Calif., vol. 4, pp. 372--74.

24. Tidying up the Treasury Department

In the administration of her fiscal system, as in the sources to which she looked for revenue, Mexico followed the general lines laid down by Spain. Under the old régime, the management of all branches of the revenue had been in the hands of the <u>habilitados</u>, or army paymsters. Despite their general honesty, says Bancroft, their want of skill kept the accounts always in confusion. In 1793, the forwarding of supplies was suspended until the accounts could be adjusted. It was not until 1795, moreover, that final orders were issued for the settling of the old accounts of the expeditions of 1769--74.[104] Mexico, therefore, took over a system which had been a makeshift to begin with, and which had already deteriorated badly when she began her struggle with it.

Collection was on a commission basis, under Spain; and during the larger part of the '20s, at least, under Mexico. Spain paid from 5 to 8%; Mexico, apparently, not more than 5% as a rule, sometimes as little as 3%, although there was an occasional exception.[105]

In 1799, Spain had named the <u>habilitado-general</u> at Monterey administrator-general of the Californian revenues,

---

[104] Bancroft, <u>Calif.</u>, vol. 1, pp. 631, 633--34; vol. 3, p. 59.

[105] <u>Ibid.</u>, vol. 1, p. 633; vol. 2, pp. 473, 672, n. 39, 521, n. 18.

giving him, however, very little authority over the other revenue collectors. In 1824, Mexico conferred a similar title and jurisdiction on Chief Paymaster José M. Estrada, making him responsible to the diputación;[106] and the junta which had drawn up the Plan de Gobierno attempted some regulation of fiscal details. From now on, apparently, the habilitados collected only at the presidios, the síndicos performing that function in the pueblos and their outlying regions. Three per cent of the local proceeds was paid to the local collectors; 3% of all collections to Estrada.[107]

Subsequently the duties of tax-collector were sometimes assigned to such citizens as were willing to undertake the labor for the small profit it promised, or to alcaldes--whether on commission or as a matter of official routine is not certain. Thus, in 1840, Pio Pico accepted appointment as collector of tithes in the Los Angeles district, at a 4% commission; and in 1844, the second alcalde of Sonoma was charged with collecting the monthly license fees of shopkeepers.[108]

Improved financial management was one of the most

---

[106] Bancroft, Calif., vol. 1, pp. 633-34; vol. 3, p. 59.
[107] Dept. St. Pap., San José, MS, vol. 4, pp. 14--15; Leg. Rec., MS, vol. 1, pp. 21--3.
[108] Bancroft, Calif., vol. 3, p. 637, n. 4, "1840"; Vallejo Doc., MS, vol. 12, 16.

urgent features of the reform program for California consistently pressed on the supreme government by Echeandía throughout his administration.[109] Presumably among those who seconded his efforts was Gervasio Argüello, California's *habilitado-general,* stationed at Guadalajara; but the records are non-committal on this point. At any rate, the ancient forms, at least, continued in use, though apparently, says Bancroft, "mainly for show, ... since of the fragmentary accounts extant many are wholly unintelligible, and some certainly deal with amounts and payments that were purely imaginary."[110]

Nevertheless, Mexico did attempt, at the beginning, to set California's finances in good running order. In 1825, she placed J. M. Herrera in charge, officially independent of the *gefe politico* and responsible directly to the *comisario-general* of finances of Sonora-Sinaloa.

For political and personal reasons, Herrera was able to command neither the cordial co-operation of his subordinates, the *habilitados,* nor the friendship of the governor. Although he seems to have been able and intelligent, and Bancroft failed to find any proof of irregularity or unfaithfulness in his official conduct, Echeandía ordered a

----

109 Bancroft, *Calif.,* vol. 3, p. 53.
110 *Ibid.,* vol. 2, p. 671.

secret investigation of his administration, in 1827, and presently hurled charges of embezzlement, although no shortage was indicated. Of the ensuing quarrel, the only features relevant here are that the governor ordered the sub-comisario to restore to the habilitados all their former powers (which had included disbursement, a function taken over by Herrera); that the sub-comisario tendered his resignation, in reply; and that general supervision of the financial administration devolved on the gefe político for the next couple of years. The handling of the revenues continued to be managed by the habilitados as of old, under immediate supervision of Chief Paymaster Estrada and then of Paymaster Vallejo.[111]

At the end of 1828, Echeandía appointed a young Mexican, Manuel Jimeno Casarín, acting comisario or administrator of revenues, "his position," says Bancroft, being similar to that held by Estrada before the coming of Herrera" -- that is, he had little authority, and did not control disbursements. J. M. Bandini was appointed subordinate comisario, for the San Diego district. In 1829, Antonio María Osio replaced Jimeno for a time, but no change was made in the system, which was for all practical purposes the same at the end of the decade as it had been when Mexico took over.

---

[111] Bancroft, Calif., vol. 3, pp. 59--6.

The effort at reform had produced only temporary
disruption, increased confusion, and, undoubtedly, lapses
in the records. Indeed, Figueroa subsequently made the
charge -- although its accuracy seems unlikely -- that no
accounts had been rendered by Herrera and his successors.[112]

Osio, Jimeno and Bandini were all able men. They
"are mentioned as comisarios during 1830, without much
regard to chronology," says Bancroft, " . . . . though there
is inextricable confusion, not only in dates, but in the
offices of comisario, administrador and contador."[113]

The confusion continued throughout the next several
years -- in the records and most probably in fact. Victoria's arbitrariness caused the resignation in 1832
of Bandini, who seems to have been for the preceding two or three years acting *comisario principal*
ad interim. Don Juan declared that he had been "prevented
by many circumstances" from organizing his department.

From the time of his resignation to 1834, his successors under Victoria, Echeandía, Zamorano and Figueroa
followed on each other's heels too closely for any possibility of progress in organization or coherence in regulation. Confusion was worse confounded at this period by

---

[112] Bancroft, *Calif.*, vol. 3, pp. 65, 118, 125.
[113] Ibid., p. 86.

uncertainty as to whether California belonged to the comisaría of Sinaloa or (as was the case) that of Sonora, orders and complaints regarding the territory emanating from both.

The later years of Figueroa's rule and the return of J. M. Herrera from Mexico to resume his former position brought pause to the senseless scramble of revenue officers. At about the same time, Mexico planned to send a visitador to restore order in the treasury department -- though nothing resulted.[114]

With Alvarado's accession to power, following the revolution of 1836, the revenue department was stabilized and simplified. Although the records are not quite unanimous, Bancroft's conclusion was that a single official -- the faithful and competent W. E. P. Hartnell -- with the title of recaudador or tax-collector, administered treasury and customs departments through 1837, on a commission basis (5%). In 1838, the two branches of revenue administration were again separated. An army man headed the treasury department for something over a year, though almost nothing is known of him. Thereafter José A. Abrego had charge, until the conquest.[115]

----

114 Bancroft, Calif., vol. 3, pp. 375--80, passim.
115 Ibid., vol. 4, p. 97, n. 44.

The first years of his administration are a blank in the records. But his unblemished reputation for integrity and ability give reason to believe that he did what could be done in such troubled and impecunious times to inject efficiency into the country's financial affairs. Documentary evidence becomes available in 1839--40. By that time, something of order and system had been introduced into the keeping of accounts, Bancroft observes, and the revenues were largely increased.[116] In 1843, we find Alvarado recommending Abrego to the Minister of the Interior for appointment to the post of jefe de hacienda;[117] and a letter from the governor to José Castro further commends his fiscal management.[118]

Abrego remained in the treasurership after Micheltorena's assumption of office and during the subsequent reorganization of the receptoría or revenue department. He offered his resignation in 1845, when in Pico's governorship the attempt was made to transfer the capital to Los Angeles; but General Castro refused to allow the change, and Don José María carried on into 1846.[119]

---

116 See post, pp. 298--99, Table VIII.
117 Bancroft, Calif., vol. 4, pp. 96-99, passim.
118 1840, (no mo., no da.), Alvarado to José Castro, in Depart. St. Pap., MS, vol. 11, p. 14.
119 Bancroft, Calif., vol. 4, pp. 674--75, 556--58, passim; vol. 5, p. 570.

28. Untangling the Customs Administration

For the sake of clarity, the organization and personnel of the customs branch of the revenue department is given separate consideration here, although there was much administrative overlapping with the treasury department, and although confusion sometimes blurs the record.

Under Spain, customs, like other fiscal business, had been handled by presidial officers. Herrera, of course, was able to effect no more in the customs than in the treasury department. A <u>contador</u> was appointed in 1827, after which things ran along on the usual basis until, at the end of the next year, Echeandía appointed Osio and Bandini <u>comisarios subalternos</u>, each with "something very like a customhouse" under his charge, at Monterey and San Diego respectively.[120]

The Mexican Jimeno Casarín soon superseded Osio at Monterey, and in 1829 was named <u>contador</u> -- whether acting in the two capacities or only the latter is not clear. The same year saw the appointment of Rafael Gonzales -- still in Mexico -- as <u>administrador</u> of customs.[121] After that, through 1830, "inextricable

----
120 Bancroft, <u>Calif.</u>, vol. 3, pp. 67, 136.
121 <u>Ibid.</u>, p. 136, n. 47.

confusion" in dates and titles was noted by Bancroft in the records.[122]

A plan of organization for the Monterey custom-house, however, drawn up in 1830, is extant and of interest. It provided for an administrator, with duties of *comisario*, at 1,000 *pesos* a year; a *contador*, with duties of *vista*, at 800 *pesos*; a commandant of the guard, with duties of *alcaide* at 800 *pesos*; a *guarda* and clerk at 400 *pesos*; a servant at 144 *pesos*; a *patron* and two sailors at 144 and 96 *pesos* respectively.[123]

The combination of the duties of customs officer and treasury official, and of more than one customs post, typifies the lack of sharp differentiation in administrative functions which was an effect partly of medieval tradition and partly of the need to economize. From the same causes, it sometimes happened that an official was given jurisdiction over both maritime and frontier customs -- as in the early 1830s, when Antonio María Osio, as *receptor* at Los Angeles, had to watch over both the port of San Pedro and the inland trade with Sonora.[124]

Remuneration in the customs service might be at a fixed salary, or -- far more reliably -- on a commission

---

[122] Bancroft, Calif., vol. 3, p. 86.

[123] Dept. St. Pap., MS, vol. 2, pp. 155--56. Bancroft, Calif., vol. 3, p. 86, n. 51 has *alcalde* for *alcaide* -- a typographical slip.

[124] Ibid., p. 377.

basis. In 1839, receptor Francisco Guerrero of San Francisco was allowed 25% of his collection.[125]

Forbes observed[126] that "some order" was introduced into the collection of duties following Echeandía's appointments. On Victoria's accession, however, early in 1831, followed friction and changes in the personnel. Rafael Gonzalez, the recently named administrator of customs, had not arrived in California from Mexico; and his duties were being performed at Monterey by Joaquín Gomez, on Victoria's arrival. Osio was in San Francisco temporarily, as contador and perhaps sub-comisario of the treasury department, under the slightly higher authority of Bandini of San Diego.

Victoria refused to concede any but local authority to Bandini; eliminated Osio from the service; and regarded Joaquín Gomez as sub-comisario. J. M. Padrés, on whom Echeandía had conferred the post of visitador of customs just before relinquishing the governorship to Victoria, and who apparently performed his duties of inspectorship for a part of 1831, was summarily returned to Mexico by Victoria before the end of the year.

Bandini's resignation came some time in 1832. In the

----

[125] Bancroft, Calif., vol. 3, p. 700, n. 3.
[126] Alta Calif., p. 300.

fall of that year, Zamorano appointed José Mariano Estrada to supersede <u>sub-comisario</u> Joaquín Gomez at Monterey, the latter having resigned under fire. Estrada's duties presumably combined treasury and customs business, as those of Gomez had done.

In 1833, Figueroa arrived to take over the governorship, bringing Rafael Gonzalez to fill the post of <u>administrador</u> of customs to which he had been appointed in 1829. Gonzalez had charge from January, 1833 to July, 1834, when he turned over his office to Angel Ramirez; and also performed Estrada's treasury department duties between Don José's resignation in May 1833 and the return from Mexico of J. M. Herrera, in October 1834, to resume his former position of departmental commissioner of revenues. In 1834, too, Bandini re-entered the service as <u>visitador de aduanas</u>.

Don Juan, however, had returned to California with the Hijar and Padrés colony. As we have seen,[127] the claims of officialdom presented by the colony leaders were regarded with suspicion and resentment in California. Bandini's case was no exception. Ramirez refused to let the new inspector inspect the Monterey custom-house, and instructed his subordinates at the other ports to follow his example, until specific instructions on the point of the authenticity of Don Juan's appointment could be received from the Director

---

[127] <u>Ante</u>, pp. 113--17.

de Rentas in Mexico. Whether or not any such order was
ever received, Bandini was soon eliminated from the picture
by involvement in a smuggling scandal which resulted in
his suspension from office, and the confiscation of the
contraband goods which he had introduced and of 700 pesos
due him from the territorial treasury.

Concurrently with all these changes of heads of departments, numerous appointments and replacements of
subordinates took place at the various ports.[128] With it
all, San Francisco was without any customs officer in
1836--38, although W. A. Richardson was captain of the port
for a part of that time.[129]

These kaleidoscopic transformations of department
personnel would have nullified the most efficient system of
revenue collection and administration ever devised. Figueroa
deplored the havoc worked on organization and records by
the rapid succession of officials,[130] and made frequent
recommendations for reform. Yet nothing seems to have been
accomplished during his administration -- probably for the
two reasons that he could do little without authorization of
the supreme government, which was not forthcoming; and that

---

[128] Bancroft, Calif., vol. 4, p. 765; vol. 3, pp. 370--72, 375--77, passim.

[129] Ibid., vol. 3, p. 700, n. 3.

[130] Ibid., p. 377, n. 18.

the clash between the ambitious Mexicans in California and the hijos del país had first to work itself out.

Even before selecting a governor, however, the "Constituent Congress of the free and sovereign state of Alta California" in 1836 reorganized the revenue department. All the old customs offices were at that time suppressed, and a collector at a salary of 1,000 pesos, aided by a clerk at 365 pesos, was placed in charge of all revenues.[131] W. E. P. Hartnell, as we have seen, was named recaudador in accordance with this decree.[132]

Almost simultaneously with this attempt of the Californians at centralizing the revenue control and reducing revenue costs, Mexico was evolving an elaborate decree regulating customs administration throughout the republic.[133] Among other specifications, it set up the following staff and salary schedule for the Monterey custom-house:

---

[131] Castro Decreto #3, in "Earliest Printing," #27.
[132] Bancroft, Calif., vol. 3, p. 274, n. 34.
[133] Arrillaga, Recopilación, 1837, Decree of Feb. 17, pp. 86--120.

Administrator	3,000	pesos
Accountant (Contador)	2,000	"
First Official	1,500	"
Second "	1,000	"
Clerk	500	"
Chief Warden (Alcaide)	1,500	"
Commandant	2,000	"
Wardens (Celadores), 4 @ 800 pesos	3,200	"
Coxswain (Patron)	400	"
Sailors, 4 @ 260 pesos	1,040	"
Grand Total	16,140	pesos

This document devoted a great deal of space to detailing the obligations of employees and penalties for dereliction of duty from various causes ranging from deliberate dishonesty to incompetence. Gambling and drunkenness were made causes for discharge. Elaborate regulations were laid down regarding the meticulous keeping of employees' attendance records. Absences were punishable by docking or, if they became flagrant, by discharge. Salary contributions toward pension benefits for widows, mothers and children were required; and for retirement annuities which, after 30 years' service, were to consist of full pay up to 6,000 pesos a year! Ten years' service would entitle to one-third of salary; fifteen years', to half-pay; and 20 years', to two-thirds.

On May 10, the highest-salaried officer specified in the decree of February 17th was appointed. He resigned a few weeks later, however, without coming to California.[134] Of course the expansive prescriptions of the decree as to personnel and salaries never had effect.

Despite the general ineptitude of her Californian fiscal policies, Mexico was nevertheless at this time devoting earnest effort to reorganization of the customs administration throughout the republic. The statute of February 17, 1837 established five custom-house classifications and provided for the erection of frontier customhouses along the northern boundary: at Nacogdoches in Texas, Taos in New Mexico, San Cárlos and Paso del Norte in Chihuahua, and San Francisco in Alta California. As settlement pushed closer to the frontiers and to the public highways, the supreme government was to be kept informed, to the end that the custom-houses might be pushed forward to the new centers of population.[135]

The same decree provided for the services of *interventores* to observe, help regulate and collect data for use in later legislation to be based on fuller knowledge of revenue conditions throughout the republic. It was followed up in 1838

---

[134] Bancroft, Calif., vol. 4, p. 96, n. 40.

[135] Arrillaga, Recopilación, 1837, Decree of Feb. 17, pp. 86--98.

with a circular broadcast by the Inspector General of Customs and Accounting, setting forth his administrative difficulties and calling for information and co-operation.

His first effort had been an attempt to find out the number and constitution of the existing customs establishments--a thing absolutely unknown, since under the federal system the treasury department of each state had been administered individually, and the direction-general of finances had knowledge only of the District of Mexico, the territories and maritime customs. His inquiries, however, although addressed to all the principal and known offices, had met with lack of co-operation, for reasons political and deliberate as well as because of distance, the ignorance of most of the employees, negligence and deception; and so great delay had been caused in ascertaining the facts. At length, on May 1, 1838, as accurate a compilation of such information as possible had been issued for the enlightenment of employees, who were exhorted to study and know the law and apply it intelligently. Specific causes of difficulty were cited, with the laws to cover. Reference was made to twenty-four circulars previously issued to date by the <u>Inspector-General</u>.[136]

Here is evident a noble attempt at systematization and regulation. The circular of May 1, 1838, however, did not benefit California, since it had been compiled "for all

----

[136] Arrillaga, <u>Recopilación, 1838</u>, pp. 144--95.

except the two Californias, New Mexico and Texas, which are disturbed by revolution." In any case, it was probably of slight importance to California. Its issuance, with the circumstances which called it forth and the difficulties which beset its preparation, are mentioned here as a sidelight on the administrative confusion with which inexperienced Mexico was wrestling, and the ease with which Californian -- or other -- customs officials might be deceived by spurious claims of entry in some distant part of the republic.

Whether in conformance with instruction from Mexico, or because the local situation required it, the two branches of California's revenue administration were separated again in 1838. Early in that year, Antonio María Osio was again sworn into the customs service, as *administrador*. He gave bond in the amount of 4,000 *pesos*.

For the next several years, Don Antonio served "much to the satisfaction of all concerned, being regarded by merchants and masters of vessels as not only a competent official, but a courteous gentleman," comments Bancroft. His only subordinate was Pablo de la Guerra, who served as first official and *vista* from 1838. Don Pablo furnished 2,000 *pesos!* bond.[137]

---

[137] Bancroft, *Calif.*, vol. 4, p. 97. Several subordinate officials were added to the staff, on paper, by appointment in Mexico, but never came to claim their posts.

From now on, in the customs department as in the treasury branch, began a marked access of harmony, efficiency and revenue, despite the sectional struggles of 1836--38.[138] In 1839, Alvarado, deploring the state of the public treasury resulting from previous "lack of just and proper administration, in distribution as well as in collection," ordered that "in future, no funds received in the offices of the department be used for any other purpose than indispensable expenses, the balance to be remitted to the sub-comisario [Ábrego]."[139] A year later, in commending the good management of California's fiscal affairs under this separation of the receiving and disbursing functions, the governor divided the credit between Customs Administrator Osio and Treasurer Ábrego.[140]

Mexico might well have been satisfied to leave the departmental finances in such good hands. Instead, she sent Manuel Castañares to Monterey to replace Osio. Like Ábrego, Osio and Pablo de la Guerra, Castañares was capable,

---

[138] Bancroft, Calif., vol. 4, p. 99; and see post, pp. 298--99, Table VIII.

[139] Jan. 4, 1839, Alvarado to Admin. of Customs, in Dept. St. Pap., Ben., MS, vol. 3, p. 17; Osio, Hist. de Calif., MS, p. 397.

[140] 1840, (no mo., no da.), Alvarado to José Castro, in Dept. St. Pap., MS, vol. 11, p. 14.

and became popular. His advent, as it happened, did not greatly affect the customs department, in any case; for he became secretary of the prefecture, shortly after his arrival, and Osio was left in undisturbed control of the *aduanas* until the fall of 1842, when Castañares finally assumed formal charge. Other activities called for Don Manuel's attention, however, through most of 1843; and in 1844--45, he represented California in the Mexican Congress. His duties of administrator of customs, therefore, were for the most part performed by Contador Pablo de la Guerra.[141]

In 1845, Alvarado himself -- than whom there was no more able man in California, and none of whose official records seems ever to have been marred by dishonesty -- was made customs administrator. Responsibility soon reverted to de la Guerra, however, as Alvarado resigned after a few weeks to do other government service. Thereafter, Guerra, and finally Hartnell again, administered the customs branch.[142] Even the subordinate personnel at the various ports changed comparatively little, during this period, and was of generally worthy character and ability.

---

[141] Bancroft, Calif., vol. 4, p. 31, n. 54; vol. 2, p. 748; vol. 4, pp. 210-11, 341, 377, 431.

[142] Ibid., vol. 4, pp. 556, 569.

Osio, Hartnell, de la Guerra managing the customs, with Castañares and Alvarado barely breaking the continuity; and Ábrego handling treasury affairs: here were men of fidelity and capacity, in a bare decade bringing order and solidarity into what had been California's most confused and hopeless governmental branch. The financial progress made during their incumbencies augured well for the decade to follow.[143] But no decade was to follow for the Californios.

26. Foreign Trade Regulations

Mexico dared not abandon the fiscal system which she had inherited from the old régime. It was the only system she knew, and theoretically it combined the two virtues of producing revenue and protecting home industry. It was short-sighted of her not to recognize as decisive refutation of the high tariff theory the plague of contraband trade which beset all her coasts. It was still more short-sighted not to include within her conception of home industry the interests of her outlying domains. Mexico, in fact, had not had time to grow up to her extensive republican responsibilities. She still thought provincially.

California, on the other hand, had still less to gain from exploitation by Mexico than she had had by Spain;

---

[143] See post, pp. 298--99, Table VIII.

and she had suffered too grievously not to know the
fallacies and afflictions of the fiscal system which
circumstances had foisted on her. The history of
trade regulation in the period under consideration
reduces to the fundamental formula of struggle between Mexico adhering to the ancient theories and California striving for liberalization.

Even before the oath of allegiance to Mexico had
been taken -- when Spain's control was but relaxed --
all mandates for the exclusion of foreign trade were
ignored in California, although -- for the need was great
and no other succor at hand -- duties were collected:
25% on imports and 12%, divided equally between buyer and
seller, on exports. As a matter of fact, one of Mexico's
first legislative concerns was the removal of some of the
restrictions on foreign trade; but it was some time before
these were known in California.[144]

The *Plan de Gobierno* promulgated by Argüello's *junta*
of 1824, and nominally California's organic law until the
oath of allegiance to the Republic was taken early in 1825,
incorporated in its specifications of revenue sources: [145]

---

[144] Bancroft, Calif., vol. 2, p. 473.

[145] Title III, Art. 2, in "Earliest Printing," #4.

1   Tonnage on foreign vessels as in last
        Mexican tariff
2   25% on sales of goods imported on foreign
        craft, after deducting 12.5% "as before"
3   10% on imports by Mexican vessels
4   6% from foreigners on exports
5   12% from sellers on exports

Bancroft, in his résumé of the Plan,[146] questions the phrasing in provision 2, "after deducting 12.5% as before," indicating that the allusion is not clear. There seems no reason to doubt, however, that the reference is to the suspension, under Spain, of half the regular duties.[147] To be sure, no duties on foreign-borne goods were charged, under Spain, since such goods were denied entry. Spanish transport, however, had now become, by political metamorphosis, foreign. The practise of continuing to halve import charges on Spanish goods and extending the rebate to all foreign-borne goods undoubtedly commended itself to the Californians on general principles.

As for the export tax on produce, the *junta* removed that entirely, effective January 1825.[148]

Detailed resumption of tariff changes in California lies outside the scope of the present study. The general

----

[146] Bancroft, *Calif.*, vol. 2, p. 512, n. 2, Title III, Art.
[147] See *ante*, p. 174.
[148] *Leg. Rec.*, MS, vol. 1, pp. 35--39.

statement is beyond question justifiable, however, and will be borne out in subsequent discussion, that the <u>hijos del país</u> did not share Mexico's faith in the high and inclusive schedules nor, for the most part, in prohibitions. There is no room to doubt that, had any other source of revenue been available, California would have declared emphatically for free trade with a few minor qualifications designed to protect and foster native industry and commerce, and deemed advisable because the country was "<u>absolutamente naciente.</u>"

Echeandía interfered in matters commercial only to the extent of confining all trade to the four presidial ports. This decree, however, imposed a handicap on the trade activities of both missionaries and citizens in other localities. Accordingly, an exception was soon made of the port of San Pedro, to accommodate the people of Los Angeles; and permits to trade at such wayports as Santa Cruz, San Luis Obispo, Refugio and San Juan Capistrano were issued by the governor to the masters of vessels, with little question except in cases of special suspicion.[149]

Had Mexico seen fit to let well enough alone, California might have worried along on her then basis, carrying indirect taxes of only 25% on foreign imports (the 12.5% deduction indicated in the <u>Plan de Gobierno</u> was not allowed by Mexico),

---

[149] Bancroft, <u>Calif.</u>, vol. 3, pp. 29, 117.

10% on Mexican imports, and tonnage charges; and being not too restricted in her port activities to allow of some industrial and commercial progress. In June 1826, however, Herrera transmitted orders from the <u>Comisaría-General</u> in Sonora prohibiting all vessels from loading or unloading in any port other than Monterey. Herrera's apologies went out with his issuance of the order, and his assurance that he had protested against it as ruinous to territorial commerce. But he could only obey orders.

Echeandía interposed his discretionary powers to countermand the order provisionally. At this juncture, however, an <u>internación</u> duty of 15% and an <u>averiá</u> duty of 2½% were added to the 25% import duty, making a total of 42½%, besides tonnage at 2 <u>pesos</u> 4 <u>reales</u> per <u>tonelada</u>, and a 10-<u>peso</u> anchorage tax.[150]

Naturally the Californians -- consumers, producers and traders -- raised their voices against such impositions. They demanded the unrestricted access of foreign vessels to all ports and embarcaderos, the subdivision of cargoes for convenience in transportation and sale, and the reduction of duties to the original 25% at most -- <u>internación, avería</u> and tonnage dues all to be abolished.

In 1827, the <u>diputación</u> took it upon itself to decree the legality of these prerogatives and remissions and of the

---

[150] Bancroft, <u>Calif.</u>, vol. 3, p. 117.

coasting trade -- subject to approval of the supreme government. In a gesture of compromise, the *internación* tax was recommended to be retained on goods carried inland more than four leagues. For all practical purposes, this was equivalent to its abolition. National products, except gold and silver, were declared free of export duty. The missions were asked to provide bonds for the suspended charges, pending Mexico's decision.[151]

Mexico seems to have relented, briefly, in the matter of the closed ports; for before the action of the *diputación*, she issued permission for foreign vessels to touch at Santa Cruz, San Luis Obispo, Purísima, Refugio and San Juan Capistrano.[152]

Almost at once, however, all embarcaderos except San Pedro were again ordered closed. Echeandía gave out this regulation, by order of the supreme government, in January 1828; and in so far as possible it was enforced. In July, San Pedro was also closed; Monterey and Loreto were declared the only ports open to foreign commerce save when necessity demanded the use of one of the presidial ports; and the coasting trade was confined to Mexican bottoms.[153]

---

[151] Bancroft, *Calif.*, vol. 3, pp. 125-26.
[152] *Ibid.*, p. 127.
[153] *Ibid.*, p. 131.

Regulations were still further tightened in September, when the presidial ports of San Francisco and Santa Barbara were closed provisionally, except that empty vessels might call there for produce (other than breeding-cattle)[154], and that such vessels might carry lumber from Monterey to Santa Barbara. In November, Echeandía requested through the Minister of War the full and formal reopening of San Diego to foreign commerce; and, says Bancroft,[155] there is no evidence that the order closing San Francisco and Santa Barbara was obeyed in 1828.

The very flagrant and insolent contraband operations, with insult to Mexican officials and soldiery, by Captains John Bradshaw of the "Franklin" and John Lawlor of the "Karimoko," together with an access of contraband activity generally (provoked by the partial enforcement of the Mexican regulations) apparently induced a reaction in Governor Echeandía. In 1829 he showed a disposition to enforce the orders of 1828, limiting foreign trade to Monterey and, provisionally, San Diego. At other ports it was allowed only "by special license and under strict precautions; that is, in a few instances a trader might carry goods duly examined and listed at Monterey or San Diego to other ports for sale by paying the

---

[154] Honey was also excepted.

[155] Bancroft, *Calif.*, vol. 3, p. 132.

expense of a guard to remain on board and watch each transaction."[156]

Although a treaty between Mexico and England, putting the vessels of the two nations on equal terms with regard to duties, was forwarded from San Blas in July of this year, Bancroft found no evidence that the document had any effect in California.[157]

On the statute books, at least, the territory was now pretty tightly closed to foreign commerce. The situation was aggravated by the advent of Governor Victoria, full of zeal, ignorant of Californian conditions and intent on strict enforcement. He promptly declared Monterey the sole port of entry for foreign goods; insisted on the exclusion of prohibited goods and on the discontinuance of the retail trade by foreign vessels; and attempted to force the payment of all duties in cash, contrary to previous practise which had been to accept duties in kind when the traders could not pay all in coin.

Bandini, then in charge of the *comisaría*, resented Victoria's interference, asserting that the governor had no authority in revenue matters, and maintaining that California's peculiar circumstances and necessities justified latitude in enforcing the revenue laws, this being, tacitly sanctioned

---

[156] Bancroft, *Calif.*, vol. 3, p. 136.
[157] Ibid.

by the supreme authority. Needless to say, the rest of California's officialdom, and the population, overwhelmingly supported Bandini in his stand.

Victoria's order does not appear to have had any real effect, comments Bancroft, "though for the next several years the law requiring each vessel to come first to Monterey for a settlement of duties was more strictly enforced than before." Mexican vessels from foreign ports, laden with foreign goods, were subject to the same requirement, in these respects, as foreign vessels. The coasting trade in foreign bottoms, however, continued.[158]

Figueroa perceived the impracticability of strict compliance with the revenue laws, and joined his forces with those of the Californians in urging reforms. His views are clearly expressed in a letter written when he had been in the territory but a few months: he disapproved of export duties (<u>derechos de extracción</u>) and regarded the sales taxes (<u>derechos de alcabala</u>) as oppressive. The supreme government should be consulted on the reorganization of the customs branch; on the establishment of a border customs department (<u>aduana terrestre</u>); on the provision of means of collecting duties; and on the peculiar

---

[158] Bancroft, Calif., vol. 3, pp. 367-68; 369, n. 8. Feb. 1833, Admin. of Customs Gonzalez to Figueroa, in <u>Dept. St. Pap., Ben., C.-H&., </u>MS, vol. 2, p. 17.

circumstances of the country.[159]

Yet no changes seem to have been effected during Figueroa's administration. Bandini was in Congress, for part of that time (1833), urging that San Diego and San Francisco be opened to foreign commerce and that Monterey, Santa Barbara and San Pedro be constituted minor ports for the coasting trade in national vessels. He failed in both these aims, however, and Monterey remained the only *puerto habilitado.*

In 1834, Figueroa made a comprehensive report to the supreme government on the condition and past history of the foreign trade, incorporating recommendations that San Francisco, Santa Barbara, San Pedro and San Diego be declared open to the coasting trade, which should be allowed to continue for five years more; and that the full complement of employees be maintained at the Monterey custom-house.[160]

Nothing came of this; and with Chico's governorship the pendulum swung the other way once more. On May 11, 1836, the new executive published a *bando* regulating commerce

---

[159] June 5, 1833, Figueroa to Admin. of Customs Gonzalez, in *Dept. St. Pap., Ben., C.-Hse.*, MS, vol. 2, pp. 23--24.

[160] Nov. 28, 1834, Figueroa, *Cosas Financieras,* MS, in *Dept. St. Pap.,* MS, vol. 3, pp. 191--204.

in accordance with the letter and spirit of the Mexican laws. It was his purpose to rid the territory of its great obstacle to commercial advancement -- the wardship in which it was kept by the foreign monopolists. He cherished the lively desire to protect national maritime enterprise and the growing fortunes of the Californian merchants, and to promote national commerce within the department, "placing those who engage in it in an advantageous position so as to expedite and stimulate commercial activity."

He therefore declared retail trade on foreign vessels in the ports and roadsteads of California "absolutely prohibited"; required every foreign ship, immediately on arrival, to land and declare its cargo at Monterey; stipulated, perhaps for emphasis, that no foreign ship might open a store on board while trading in the territory; limited foreign vessels to wholesale trade, and defined wholesale trade that there might be no pleas of misunderstanding; prohibited all foreign vessels from touching at any port on the coast where there was no <u>receptor</u>, except in case of necessity and after advance notice to the custom-house, from which it would take on board an attache to act as <u>receptor;</u> stipulated the need to obtain permits and return waybills; and stated penalties for non-conformance. Six months of grace were allowed vessels trading along the coast at the time of the issuance of the bando.[161]

Chico's incumbency, however, did not last through the six months' indulgence period. The Californians took matters into their own hands in November; and on December 9th, the Constituent Congress issued its Decree No. 9,[162] reducing duties by 60%, cutting tonnage dues to 8 reales per tonelada, and restoring to foreign vessels the right to conduct coast trade under government permit. This was done in appreciation of the aid rendered by foreigners to the cause of freedom, the decree asserted; as well as in consideration of the incalculable advantages to the state of protecting commerce, etc.

Inherent in the policy, of course, was the aim of eliminating a portion of the indirect tax load, through the reduction of prices; and that of diverting as much contraband trade as possible to legitimate channels.

Alvarado declared later that the decree fulfilled its purposes: "One of the first acts of the Congress of the State of California when it resolved upon its conditional separation from the Republic of Mexico was to issue a law opening the ports and creeks of the state to foreign trade and reducing considerably the duties; our purpose . . . . was to prove to the foreigners that we favored them, and to diminish somewhat the incentives to contraband trade . . . .

---

[161] Chico's Bando of May 11, 1836, in "Earliest Printing," #13.

[162] "Earliest Printing," #33.

The result proved that we had not been mistaken."[163]

Wilkes declared[164] that the duties were doubled again before more than two vessels had benefitted by the reduction, because the customs receipts proved insufficient and the new government feared to tax the people and the missionaries too openly. Whether right or not in declaring Decree No. 9 a failure, he of course stated the dilemma which confronted California and would confront her as long as the old fiscal system survived: she might have a high tariff on paper, with little legitimate trade; or she might have a fair volume of legitimate trade on the basis of a low tariff schedule. The particular hopelessness of this particular dilemma was that, on whichever horn the territory might be impaled, the revenues would be insufficient.

The Californians, having had the doubtful advantage of being tossed, first on one horn then on the other, to an eminence affording wide observation, realized full well that salvation lay only in total release. That they intended, from the first, to seek such release, is apparent in the wording of Decree No. 9: " . . . . for the present, and until

----

[163] Alvarado, Hist. de Calif., MS, vol. 3, pp. 183--84. Bautista's reference to the opening of the creeks, al with the ports, is interesting and suggestive. See p pp. 710--13. 747.

[164] Charles Wilkes, Narrative of U. S. Exploring Expediti vol. 5, p. 180.

the state treasury system can be regulated . . . ."[165] The general direction of the contemplated regulation was, as will be seen, away from dependence on the tariff for revenue, and away from the elevating of prices and the choking off of licit trade, toward liberalization and modernization.[166]

In contrast with <u>Decreto</u> 9 of California's Constituent Congress are the almost simultaneous Mexican enactments regulating the territory's commerce -- or attempting to regulate it, for actually no notice was taken by the provisionally "free and sovereign state" of these new emanations of authority from the far south:

Monterey, alone, was to remain open to foreign commerce and the coasting trade. San Diego and San Francisco were to be open to the coasting trade only. The duties on raw goods and manufactures of wool, hair, feathers and skin were to be 50%; those on delftware, crystal and glass, 10%; and those on cotton, 125%. The prohibited list was to include, besides certain spirituous liquors: starch, sugar, rice, raw cotton, indigo, copper and brass wire of all sizes; leather boots and half-boots, men's and women's; buttons stamped with [foreign] national or Spanish arms; coffee; iron nails

---

165 "Earliest Printing," #33.
166 See <u>post</u>, sec. 32; pp. 744--51.

of all sizes; household copperware; worked tortoise-shell and horn; buckles of all sorts; tin ore (<u>estaño en greña</u>); coarse and fine cloth; flour; cotton thread and yarn; soap; children's toys of all sorts and materials; hog-fat; molasses (miel de caña) wood of all classes save for ships' masts and yards and round timber; parchment; cotton and silk <u>rebozos</u>; readymade clothing of all sorts, inner and outer including ecclesiastical vestments, and excepting only kerchiefs of all sizes, gloves, hats and stockings; common salt; wool and cotton blankets, <u>serapes</u> and **corbetores**(?)tobacco in leaf and cigarettes; wheat and all sorts of grains, leguminous plants and vegetables except, in special cases, — corn; hog products including pork--salt, cured or seasoned; shoes.[167]

The designation of Monterey as the only open port and of San Francisco and San Diego as the only <u>puertos de cabotage</u> was re-enacted in Mexico in 1838.[168]

Widely as Mexico and California differed on the tariff, they were agreed that a native retail trade could never be built up so long as foreigners controlled the business of <u>escala y cabotage.</u> Mexico had attempted to choke off the foreign traders from the start, in mercantilistic style.

---

[167] Arrillaga, Recopilación, 1837, pp. 86--87; 157--59.
[168] Ibid., 1838, p. 187.

California had felt the need of the goods available only in the floating bazaars. As has been said, Figueroa, perceiving the reasonableness of this demand, had recommended in 1834 that all ports be opened to the foreign coasting trade for another five years; and the Constituent Congress had put such commerce temporarily on a legitimate basis, for expediency's sake.[169]

It is idle talk to say that the territory should have operated her own merchandising business from the start. She could not emerge over-night from the state of economic inactivity to which Spain had confined her.[170] Industrial and commercial independence could be built up only with time and arduous effort. The *hijos del país* hoped urgently for the first and supplied the second means of development. So rapid was the progress thus brought about that Figueroa's faith in the country's capacity to create her own commerce within half a decade proved well founded. Here was a "Five-Year Plan" that worked! For by 1839 the time was deemed ripe for a first move toward loosening the grip of the strangers who were mulcting the country.

Toward the close of that year, the Administrator of Customs, by order of Governor Alvarado, began advising

---

[169] See *ante*, pp. 241, 243.

[170] On this phase of California's problems and efforts, see *post*, Chap. V,

foreign merchants that the laws limiting the retail coasting trade to national vessels were about to be enforced to the letter.[171] In January 1840, the governor's order to that effect was circulated to officials throughout the territory.[172] In February, the matter was taken up in the Junta: the retail coasting trade, in the hands of foreigners, afforded limitless opportunities for contraband; hurt the territory's internal commerce and demanded a coast-guard force such as the public treasury was unable to provide. Violent reversion to law enforcement would seriously impair the interests of the foreign traders; but they had been notified that in future they must limit themselves to a wholesale business. They ought to co-operate. The Junta, in drafting a new set of trade regulations, must try to serve the country's interests and at the same time produce as practical a code as possible.[173]

In December 1840, Alvarado notified the supreme government of his intention, which he discussed in its various aspects. He reiterated his oft-repeated complaint against the foreign retail monoply and the contraband evil; also against the increasing numbers of foreign crew deserters. Retail

[171] Oct. 31, 1839, Admin. of Customs to shipmasters and shippers, in Dept. St. Pap., Ben., MS, vol. 3, pp. 6--7
[172] Bancroft, Calif., vol. 4, p. 93.
[173] Feb. 16, 1840, Leg. Rec., MS, vol. 3, pp. 51--53.

trade, contraband, deserters, all could be put under
control within a few years. True, the Boston men might
stop coming to California for a time. "In the first two
or three years, undoubtedly, the public treasury will
suffer great shortages . . . . but if the Supreme Government
will aid the Department with an annual subsidy for a short
period, I am certain that the departmental treasury will
become self-supporting . . . . and the country will make a
great step forward toward prosperity."[174]

The Californians were ready to make a stand for their
commercial salvation. They had pointed out to Mexico the
one thing needed to make the experiment a success. In
January 1841, Alvarado published the order prohibiting
the retail coasting trade to foreigners, and to that end
requiring the discharge of all cargoes and payment of all
duties at Monterey. At the same time, foreign sugar, salt
and timber were declared contraband, as by the Mexican
revenue laws. Vessels at the moment plying the coast were
allowed time to dispose of their cargoes. This order was
presently given legality by Mexican approval;[175] but not
practicality by Mexican subsidy

---

[174] Dec. 12, 1840, Alvarado to Min. of Interior; quoted, Feb. 13, 1841, by Min. of War for Vallejo's information(!) in *Savage Doc.*, MS, vol. 4, #329.

[175] Bancroft, *Calif.*, vol. 4, p. 206.

A correspondent of Larkin's made prophetic comment on the new regulation: it would "unquestionably be carried into effect until the poverty of the government compels them to alter it."[176]

Bancroft gives the sequel: "In July the Boston ship *Tasso* and a schooner arrived at Monterey, and on hearing that they could not engage in the coasting trade, at once prepared to depart without discharging their cargoes. This threat, involving a prospective loss of about $20,000 in duties, brought the government to terms, and the vessels were allowed to trade as before. There is no record that the privilege was formally extended to other vessels; but neither does it appear that there was any further attempt to enforce the edict; and the reopening of the Californian ports was announced in Honolulu."[177]

Thereafter, through 1842, Bancroft found "no evidence of the slightest effort to prevent the coasting trade by foreign vessels, nor of any other changes in the method of trade"; though neither trade nor visits to other ports was allowed except on permit secured at Monterey.[178]

---

[176] Jan. 29, 1841, Estabrook to Larkin, in Lark. Doc., MS, vol. 1, p. 122.

[177] Bancroft, Calif., vol. 4, p. 207.

[178] Ibid., p. 340.

As we have seen, the Alvarado administration had not been blind to the hazards of its bold gesture. It was commonly recognized in the territory that revenue from other than maritime trade sources must be forthcoming before the country could proceed on a sound working basis. Carrillo, Alvarado, Vallejo, Castañares, and others had repeatedly petitioned Mexico for "a small but dependable subsidy" to tide over the exigencies of initial development and fiscal reorganization.

It was part of Vallejo's very comprehensive scheme for the regeneration of the revenue system and the generation of a thriving territorial commerce that the custom-house should be transferred to San Francisco, where thanks to natural strategical advantages and to the adequate presidial force which he also urged for that point, enforcement of the revenue laws would be facilitated. With the retail coasting trade abolished, it would be practicable to establish at San Francisco -- as it was not, under the old system, at Monterey -- a great and single receiving center for the foreign wholesale trade, and a distributing point ideal in its water and land approaches, for a territorially operated retail trade. Of course subsidization of the treasury was "necessary formerly and now more than ever."[179]

---

[179] M. G. Vallejo, Exposición, (no place, no date. 21 pp.) Probably printed on the hand-press at Sonoma about 1837.

On details of this scheme, see post, sec. 32; pp. 459--61; 744--50.

Perhaps it as in the hope -- forlorn though that must have been -- of forcing Mexico's hand in the matter of the subsidy that the prohibition of 1841 was voiced. Perhaps it was deemed advisable in any case to remind the ever more closely encroaching foreigners of the rights and ambitions cherished by the sons of the country; to serve notice that those rights and ambitions had not been renounced in favor of aliens, but constituted the goal toward which the territorials were striving. At least the serving of such notice -- successful or not -- could do no harm.

The futility of the struggle toward fiscal and commercial self-determination was emphasized when, in response to a Mexican decree of 1843 prohibiting retail trade by foreigners throughout the republic, the United States Government protested in strong terms through Minister Waddy Thompson that such action was "an open infraction of the treaty between the two countries." Bocanegra, protesting, sustained his side of a protracted diplomatic controversy,[180] but no attempt was made to enforce the decree in California.

----

[180] "U. S. Govt. Doc.," 28th Cong. 1st Sess., Sen. Doc. #390 (ser. #436), pp. 16, 17--19. The treaty in question was that of April 5, 1831, of Amity, Commerce and Navigation, negotiated for the United States by Anthony Butler, and for Mexico

Nevertheless, Larkin advised American traders to prepare, with a view to collecting damages, certified inventories of goods which they might be restrained

----

by Lucas Alamán and Raphael Mangino, and in force in its entirety or with modification until Nov. 30, 1881 when terminated by the United States.

A careful reading of this treaty indicates no violation on the part of Mexico in her attempt to exclude the "Boston men" from the retail coasting trade in California. The compact was in the nature of a "favored nations" agreement, and contains the express stipulation that all rights accorded under it were "subject always to the laws, usages and statutes of the two countries respectively"; and the specific acknowledgment: "The liberty to enter and discharge the vessels of both nations of which this article treats shall not be understood to authorize the coasting trade, which is permitted to national vessels only."

The protocol of a conference held on Sept. 7, 1831 by the three plenipotentiaries who had drafted the treaty contains the additional

from retailing.[181]

----

agreement (result of a refusal on the part of the Mexican Congress to accept certain doubtful wording in the original document): "After free and mature deliberation, the undersigned parties have agreed that the construction to be given . . . . shall in no matter restrain the power possessed by each nation respectively of regulating sales by retail of goods, wares and merchandise within the respective states and territories." There followed considerably more to similar and positive effect. (*Treaties, Conventions, between the U. S. A. and other Powers, 1776--1909.* Compiled by William M. Malloy. Vol. 2, pp. 1085--99; especially pp. 1086, 1098--99.

[181] Bancroft, *Calif.*, vol. 4, p. 428.

Meantime, after making declaration and payment of duties at Monterey, the foreign sea-traders continued to ply the coasts of California, selling at wholesale or retail as suited them. All ports and embarcaderos remained open to this trade at this time, despite Mexican laws to the contrary.

Unsubsidized, California simply could not relinquish her customs income, depleted though it was by the inroads of the contrabandistas. The very volume of illicit trade drove her to the expediency of favoring foreign-borne commerce even to the prejudice of Mexican carriers. In 1843, Micheltorena declared his intention to prohibit the introduction of foreign goods by Mexican vessels, except on payment of the same duties exacted from foreigners; and in 1844, he placed this resolve in effect.[182]

This apparent about-face in the matter of the floating retail trade indicates no inconsistency on the part of the territorials, and no bad faith with Mexico. It was a desperate stroke for self-preservation. Legal abolitions

---

[182] Ibid., pp. 428--29.

of the foreign monopoly had failed of practical effect --
as they had probably been expected to fail. Mexican neglect
to provide the financial aid which would have enabled California
to throw off the twin incubi of foreign commercial monopoly and
dependence on the customs for revenue had left the territory
for the time inextricably in statu quo. Mexican tariff and
port regulations had inflicted heavy losses on both the Californians and the foreign traders. The contrabandistas had
been reaping the profits; and Mexican traders, under color of
legality, had shared in the illicit business which drained the
country more effectively than did legitimate -- or illegitimate
but officially countenanced -- foreign trade which paid duties.

The Mexican traders, indeed, had proved more evasive
of regulations and more rapacious than the foreigners. Only
the latter paid duties and supplied cheap goods, complained
Customs Administrator Gonzalez in 1833. "The national vessels
just oppress the people, for their goods are dear, extremely
dear (caros, carísimos)." Mexican shippers consigned under
custom-house permits of Mexican ports, indicating that they
had paid their duties there, "which is pernicious, for as
there are no coast-guard vessels, they [the Mexican traders]
buy and sell on the strength of those passes, and never pay
a real of duty."[183]

----

[183] May 31, 1833, Gonzalez to Director-General of Revenues
in Dept. St. Pap., Ben., C.-Hse., MS, vol. 2, pp. 14--

No duties and excessively high prices were bad enough. But presently the national merchants changed their system. Instead of taking advantage of the high price-levels induced by the heavy duties on foreign-borne commerce to charge correspondingly for Mexican goods, they began introducing foreign goods duty-free, on the pretext of having nationalized them by paying all duties in Mexico; and undersold the foreign traders, who had either to dispose of their cargoes for less than cost, transportation and entry, or be forced out of legitimate business. The resultant threat of the "Boston men" to abandon the coast brought California -- without other income -- to the very brink of destitution so far as public funds were concerned.

Even Micheltorena, fresh from Mexico, could not fail to appreciate the territory's predicament. In the extremity, he took the measure which Bancroft calls "one of self-defence justified by circumstances -- perhaps not beyond the scope of his 'extraordinary power.'" Larkin read into the ruling the aim of procuring the payment of duties in California rather than in Mexico. Certainly the revenue increment would have been welcome; and the territorials resented strongly enough the exploitation which forced them to pay -- even at the reduced prices -- an indirect tax which went into Mexico's pockets.[184]

---

[184] Bancroft, *Calif.*, vol. 3, p. 369, n. 8; vol. 4, pp. 375--76, 428--29.

Indeed, the period closes on a note of retaliation, with an incident justifying Larkin's comment, although it occurred in the Pico-Castro administration. In the case of one vessel, the valuably laden Star of the West, says Bancroft,[185] it was planned to "nationalize" foreign goods in California by the collection of nominal duties, and re-ship to Mazatlan for free entry. To the territorial treasury, the duties would be sheer profit; to the trader (John Parrott), they would permit a large saving over the regular charges otherwise payable at Mazatlán. Loss of the vessel and cargo nipped this hopeful project in the bud, however.

Early in 1845, Pico revoked Micheltorena's decree prohibiting the introduction of foreign goods nationalized in Mexico; and called for strict compliance with Mexican laws on the coasting trade. To the latter mandate "no attention was paid," Bancroft remarks. Pico also revoked the regulations which Micheltorena had placed on trade by whalers.[186] In March 1846, Don Pio declared -- over the protest of the customs administration at Monterey -- that the tax of 600 pesos a year on each foreign vessel was abolished.[187]

---

[185] Bancroft, Calif., vol. 4, pp. 555, 568.
[186] Ibid., vol. 4, p. 555.
[187] Ibid., vol. 5, p. 570.

The records for these last years of Mexican rule are meagre; yet the motivation of Pico's policies seems clear enough, in the light of what is definitely known of the country's fiscal and commercial circumstances and ambitions. Micheltorena's encouragement of the coasting trade, as has been pointed out, was a desperate expedient to stave off territorial bankruptcy, and was at cross-purposes with the fundamental aims -- common to officialdom amd citizenry alike -- of escaping from the tariff-for-revenue system and promoting territorially controlled industry and commerce. Naturally, the concessions forced from Micheltorena's administration by its responsibility to raise revenue had been unpopular with the countrymen generally. They would have liked a solvent public treasury, to be sure. But still more urgent was their desire for personal solvency. They wanted relief from the high cost of living within the law; and they wanted scope for their enterprise, and markets for their produce -- for they had become entrepreneurs and producers, in the score of years just closing.[188]

Pico thought to develop a new source of revenue to augment, and accordingly to render the country less dependent on, the customs intake. This was the sale or lease

---

[188] See post, Chap. V.

of mission estates.[139] The project failed, but Pico could not foresee that it would when he undertook to abolish foreign retail trade monopoly, removed the prohibition on cheap "nationalized" goods introduced via Mexico, and re-restored full scope to the commercially-minded whalers.

To round out and clarify the picture, an understanding of the importance of the whalers to the people of the country is necessary. Beginning, undoubtedly, with the relaxation of Spanish surveillance during the wars of independence, whale-ships -- chiefly American and British -- had begun putting in at Californian ports to barter for supplies.[190] Soon a brisk trade was plying between the whalers and the *rancheros*. According to Customs Administrator Gonzales, in 1833, "some years as many as 60 whalers used to come, and it is safe to say they left not less than 35,000 to 40,000 *pesos* in cash . . . . Now, when they do not come, there is a great poverty."[191] Bancroft counted 15 whalers -- "more than usual" -- in the fleet of 1844.[192]

Legally, the whalers were limited to the volume of trade incidental to their resupply. Actually, they purveyed

---

[189] See *post*, Chap. VII.
[190] Bancroft, *Calif.*, vol. 2, pp. 473-74.
[191] Feb. 15, 1833, Gonzalez to Director-General of Reven in *Dept. St. Pap., Ben., C.-Hse.*, MS, vol. 2, p. 8.
[192] *Calif.*, vol. 4, p. 43?.

ever larger consignments of desiderata.

To the countrymen, trade with the whalers offered two potent advantages over trade with the merchantmen. The whalers, being bent, theoretically, merely on barter for food, were at first allowed to introduce their offerings duty-free, or at most were required to pay a small port charge (10 to 20 *pesos*) and sales percentage.[193] This enabled them to offer more attractive prices than could the regular traders; more attractive, even, than could the *contrabandistas*, since there was no risk of confiscation or fine and since the nature of the trade did not involve the heavy expenses incident to the regular trade.[194]

More important, and increasingly so as the territorials profited by their new opportunities under Mexico to develop the country, was the fact that whereas the merchantmen were interested in carrying away only hides and tallow, the demand of the whalers was for the diversified products which the Californians were eager to produce and market in quantity.[195]

It followed that the whaler trade rapidly outgrew its original character and legal volume. The readiness of the

---

[193] Larkin, *Official Corresp.*, MS, vol. 2, p. 100.
[194] See *post*, ¶¶523--25.
[195] See *post*, pp. 559--60, 650--53, 656--62.

Nantucketers and the British blubber-hunters to practise merchandising on the side, and of the hijos del país to meet all offers, soon opened up a new branch of contraband activity which levied heavy losses of duties on the treasury and of customers on the merchantmen.

Regulations had gradually to be tightened. In 1822, each whaler was required to pay 10 pesos 4 reales, probably as an anchorage fee.[196] In 1824, tonnage dues were required of them.[197]

Later they were exempted from both tonnage and anchorage charges, because of the country's need of them as an outlet for Californian production. Not only were they hailed with welcome. Special courtesies were shown them by way of attraction to various ports. In 1832, Zamorano approved exempting them from all charges, as their purchases of supplies were directly beneficial to the farm population.[198]

Revenue officials understood as well as rancheros the value of the whaler trade to the country. In 1833, the customs administrator complained to the Director-General of Revenues that heavy tonnage dues had driven this trade to

----

[196] Bancroft, Calif., vol. 2, p. 473.
[197] Leg. Rec., MS, vol. 1, p. 28.
[198] Oct. 26, 1832, Zamorano to S. F. Comandante, in Valle Doc., vol. 1, #327.

the Sandwich Islands, to the great injury of California. He asked for congressional permission to collect tonnage from the whalers at the rate of no more than one *real* per *tonelada*, and to devote the proceeds to constructing a custom-house and a mole.[199]

As time went on, however, and abuses of privilege became more and more flagrant, the customs administration became restive. In 1841, goods introduced by whalers were declared dutiable, and were limited in value to 500 *pesos!* worth per vessel. Anchorage and tonnage dues, however, were still abated.[200]

By 1843, the whaleship trade had become a serious menace to the continuance of legitimate, revenue-producing ocean commerce. The privilege of trading was therefore withdrawn from the whalers.[201]

The next year -- so emphatic had been the protests of the *rancheros* -- the ban was lifted; but a 30-*peso* trading license-fee was imposed, with the obligations to anchor where ordered and to receive revenue guards on board ship, like the regular trading craft. Sales were limited to an amount on which the duties would be not in excess of 400 *pesos* per vessel.

---

[199] Feb. 15, 1833, Gonzales to Director-General of Revenues, in *Dept. St. Pap., Ben., C.-Hse.,* MS, vol. 2, p. 8.
[200] Bancroft, *Calif.,* vol. 4, p. 209.
[201] *Ibid.,* p. 376.

In Pico's administration, the limitation on the volume of trade was removed. Goods to any amount might be sold -- subject to the regular duties -- in exchange for produce. The 30-peso tax was suspended -- whether in all cases or just in the San Francisco Bay area is not clear -- and either the whalers themselves or their launches might penetrate to any part of San Francisco Bay.[202] The explicit policy was that whalers should be treated well, so that they would be attracted to Californian ports.[203]

Larkin's comment on this liberalization was: "The Californians are determined to exchange their produce with whalers for domestics, etc., their own way."[204]

In the light of the value of the whaler market to the rancheros, and of the general opposition to protecting high-priced, hide-and-tallow-obsessed foreign merchant shippers, Pico's letting down of the bars to the whalers, along with his restoration of the Mexican trade in "nationalized" foreign goods and his abandonment of the expedient of favoring the Boston monopolists fits perfectly into the pattern of California's struggle toward economic regeneration.

---

202   Bancroft, Calif., vol. 4, p. 555.
203   Ibid., p, 620, n. 2, "1845".
204   Sept. 29, 1845, Larkin to Sec. of State Buchanan, in Lark. Official Corresp., MS, vol. 2, #26, p. 28.

27. Laws without Teeth

The difficulty of reconciling the immediate need of revenue from the customs with the country's primary interests was not the only vexation with which the territorial government struggled. Even had circumstances permitted the achievement of a nice legal balance between the conflicting elements, difficulties of enforcement would still have loomed insuperably. Most of these difficulties have been suggested incidentally in the preceding pages.

There was the chronic condition of administrative upheaval incident to the internal friction and shiftings of personnel obtaining until 1836. There were the perplexities and misunderstandings and practical impossibilities inherent in the constant reshaping of the laws by distant administrations antagonistic to each other and concerned, at best, with the interests of the metropolis rather than those of the territories. There were the confusions and blunders unavoidable in a system of charges subject to frequent alteration and administered for the most part by inexpert persons lacking clear instructions and adequate accounting forms.

There was the handicap of insufficient staffs with a combination of duties and of jurisdictions; and that of insufficient equipment for the performance of duties.

In the notorious case of Captain John Bradshaw's flouting of the customs officials at San Diego in 1828, Governor Echeandía was forced to apply to the foreign visitor Duhaut-Cilly for a boat to put a guard on the offending craft. Unable to refuse this courtesy, the Frenchman nevertheless interposed delays, and warned Bradshaw, who cut the "Franklin's" cable and ran her out of port, "the officers and crew shouting their derision of the Mexican flag as they passed the fort."[205]

In 1833, Administrator Gonzalez of Monterey complained of lack of a suitable pier and buildings, boats, furniture, scales, etc., for want of which two-thirds of the revenue was being lost.[206]

In 1841, it was with obvious triumph that Alférez Prado Mesa, commandant at San Francisco, reported to Vallejo the acquisition of a boat at that garrison. The feat seems to have been accomplished by seizure, although the point is not clear. (The faithful Juan Prado Mesa being a near-illiterate, his chirography, orthography and rhetoric are obscure.) Whatever the method of attainment, the elation implicit in the painstakingly scrawled note is unmistakeable: "The boat . . . . is now in my power and is a

---

[205] Bancroft, Calif., vol. 3, pp. 133--34.
[206] Ibid., p. 377, n. 18.

little damaged but will be serviceable enough and we don't have to take off our hats to any one we shouldn't when a packetboat undertakes to pass, as heretofore."[207] It is to be hoped that the San Francisco presidial launch did good execution; but it could scarcely have served all the purposes of law enforcement.

Captain of the Port José de la Guerra of Santa Barbara had been less fortunate than the San Francisco commandant. In 1839, he reported that although he had sought diligently to purchase a launch, in accordance with Vallejo's order, he had had no success -- there was no boat to be had.[208]

The inadequacy of the presidial defences to enforce respect of the law and of the flag is discussed elsewhere.[209] Of revenue cutters or naval monitors there were none, although the need had been urged upon the supreme government from Echeandía's time. In 1826, he pleaded for a coast-guard vessel, as of prime necessity.[210] Soon afterward he supported the petition of the *diputación* for one or two gunboats,

---

[207] Nov. 30, 1841, Prado Mesa to *Comandante General*, in *Vallejo Doc.*, MS, vol. 10, #368.

[208] Sept. 10, 1839, José de la Guerra to Vallejo, in *Vallejo Doc.*, MS, vol. 8, #91

[209] *See post*, Chap. IV.

[210] April 22, 1826, Echeandía to Min. of War, in *St. Pap., Sac.*, MS, vol. 19, p. 29.

and a naval station at San Francisco.[211] In 1828, he urged again the sending of a warship, as he had asked "numerous times."[212]

A decade went by, during which California's importunities continued but with no results out of Mexico. Years later, writing of the contraband problem in 1836, Alvarado regretted: "We had no coast-guard vessels."[213] He and Vallejo did their best to make up the lack of sea power, for both defense and commerce. ~~Their~~ Plans and efforts on that score are discussed later.[214] They were not successful.

Meantime, the seafaring *estrangeros* had the territory at their mercy, as they and the territory knew. If the officers in charge of a vessel refused to pay tonnage or port dues or the full amount of duties, the revenue men had little chance of doing anything about it. Nor were such refusals uncommon. In 1840, to cite a single example, the American brig "Joseph Peabody" declined to pay tonnage.[215] Port officials were often forced to compromise on the amount of the duties to be paid, and on other regulations, as

---

[211] Bancroft, *Calif.*, vol. 3, p. 126, n. 26.
[212] Oct. 20, 1828, Echeandía to Min. of War, in *St. Pap., Sac.*, MS, vol. 10, p. 40.
[213] *Hist. de Calif.*, MS, vol. 3, pp. 183--84.
[214] *Post*, sec. 44, sec. 66.

[215] Bancroft, *Calif.*, vol. 4, p. 104, n. 54.

the price of collecting anything at all;[216] and as in the case of the "Tasso;" a restrictive measure might be nullified by threat of the traders to withdraw entirely.[217] Here was contraband by *tour de force.*

As for preventing surreptitious trading without the law, the Californians were utterly without the means. They could do little other than place guards on board vessels under suspicion, and hope -- forlornly -- for the best.[218]

Another obstacle to consistent enforcement of the revenue laws must be mentioned. The foreign traders, whether from shrewdness or insufficiency of capital, commonly presented themselves at the ports of entry without funds enough to cover the duties to which they were liable. Consequently the customs collectors had been forced into the practise of accepting payment in kind instead of in coin. The theory was that only choice goods were so acceptable, and at a discount of 25% on current prices.[219] There were no means of insisting on either condition. The traders undoubtedly did not turn their choice stock in trade over to the revenue men; and they managed to effect an indirect reduction in their duties by setting up their price schedules to exorbitant levels.

---

[216] Bancroft, *Calif.*, vol. 3, p. 368; Osio,

[217] Bancroft, *Op. cit.*, vol. 4, pp. 206--7.
[218] See *post*, sec. 28.
[219] Douglas, *Journal*, MS, p. 90.

viewed the mounting prices with alarm, and as a result considered the I. O. U. of any one of themselves of more value than a draft issued by this office, though with all legal formalities."[221]

The Alvarado administration, without going to Chico's profitless extreme of attempting to exact all customs in cash, tried to mitigate these evils by requiring a stated portion of duties to be so paid, as follows:[222]

Amount of Duties	Cash Requirement
Up to 3,000 pesos	Full amount
From 3,000 -- 6,000	2/3 "
" 6,000 -- 12,000	1/2 "
" 13,000 pesos up	1/3 "

Osio recommended further that tonnage duties be met with spot cash; and that the customs department reserve the prerogative of refusing goods for duties if the prices were not suitable, and of requiring instead produce of the country at current rates. He also suggested that when the

---

[221] April 9, 1839, Osio to Alvarado, in Dept. St. Pap., Ben. C-Hse., MS, vol. 5, pp. 12--13.

[222] April 8, 1839, Alvarado decree, in Dept. St. Pap., Ben., MS, vol. 3, p. 21. Osio gives the scale a little differently in his Hist. de Calif., MS, pp. 402--4; but agrees with Alvarado's figures in his letter of April 9, 1839 to the governor, cited above.

duties of any Boston vessel reached 6,000 pesos, terms might be allowed in order to make feasible collection of the required portion in cash. Two installments might be arranged: the first due 40 days from the date of appraisal, the second in 80 days.[223]

Evidently the requirement of coin for tonnage dues recommended by Osio was instituted.[224] It appears, too, that the installment plan was adopted; for a few months later, Abrego allowed terms to the brigantine "Corsario."[225] This was done "in view of the great scarcity of coin," probably in preference to accepting payment in goods.

To be sure, all this was not putting teeth into the laws; but California was too young to have cut her teeth. She could only issue regulations designed to persuade to and facilitate compliance with regulations already on the books.

The spectacle of a government powerless to enforce a body of unpopular law became a thoroughly familiar one in the United States during the prohibition era, even though, in contrast to California's predicament, we had at our command every resource and modern aid to enforcement. It must

---

[223] April 9, 1839, Osio to Alvarado, loc. cit.
[224] Pinto Doc., MS, vol. 1, p. 244.
[225] Aug. 21, 1839, Abrego in Dept. St. Pap., Ben., vol. 3, p. 4.

be remembered, too, that the United States did not inherit the prohibition problem full-blown and fastened on the country, from an earlier régime, as California did her smuggling evils; and that repeal of the provocative restrictions offered Uncle Sam a way out which was barred to the Californians. Prohibition, moreover, imposed no such general economic hardship and restraint as did California's revenue laws.

In one respect, however, the circumstances were similar: the people of each country, decrying the unjustifiability of the law, sympathized and trafficked with the law-breakers. It was almost universal popular conspiracy which thwarted Uncle Sam's best efforts to make prohibition a reality; and which, alone, would have defeated the Californian government in its war on smuggling, had all the handicaps already mentioned been non-existent.

There was another side to the story of the laws' failure. Despite earnest attempts to enforce regulations when such enforcement was in the territorial interest -- either of the treasury or of the *rancheros* -- there were numerous occasions when execution would have been prejudicial to those interests. So patent and serious was this divergence between the law and the welfare of the country that conscientious officials, from late Spanish times on, ventured to ignore or expressly set aside the harmful ordinances. If no reprimand and reaffirmation of the law was forthcoming from Mexico, they customarily claimed the government's "tacit sanction" of their intervention.

Bandini used this thoroughly established justification in his controversy with literal-minded Victoria,[226] and Osio, whose honesty and zeal were proverbial throughout California, was as uncompromisingly convinced of the need to compromise: "Necessity forced the infringement of certain fiscal laws," he declared, "and this required a certain interference with the administration of the customs department. The governor-general, by not reproving this did not challenge, but by his silence confirmed [it]."[227]

On another occasion, Don Antonio reported matter-of-factly to Alvarado that in the case of foreign effects prohibited by law, but whose admission was a necessity, a fixed duty of not less than 40% would be collected.[228]

Smuggling was a natural corollary of the mercantilistic system. Spain's dominions in the new world had suffered under both evils, from the seventeenth century. The brief

---
[226] Bancroft, Calif., vol. 3, pp. 367--68.
[227] Osio, Hist. de Calif., MS, p. 401.
[228] Jan. 31, 1839, Osio to Alvarado, in Dept. St. Pap., Ben. C.-House, MS, vol. 5, p. 4.

experiment in modified free trade attempted toward the close o the eighteenth century, under the reforming influence of the great Galvez, roused the colonials to a keener zest for economic liberty, not to be quenched when the monetary demands of the European wars put an end to the adventure in commercial liberalism.[229]

The occupation of Alta California had been effected by Galvez; and while she was still too isolated and undeveloped to benefit by the free trade tentative,[230] the best of her soldier and settler pioneers undoubtedly looked forward to new opportunities for individual initiative on the frontier established under such promising auspices. Naturally enough, disappointment revived all the old tendencies toward the evasion of exploitatory regulations. Despite infrequency of opportunities, contraband trade became firmly established in Upper California during the first decade of the nineteenth century.

An estimate of 1805, by Captain Shaler of the "Lelia Byrd," set at $25,000 the amount of contraband goods left annually in the province by American smugglers at that time. The Russians, in 1806, sold nearly $5,000 worth of goods legally outlawed though disposed of with the approval of the governor.[231]

---

[229] Priestley, Mex. Nation, pp. 178--79.
[230] Bancroft, Calif., vol. 1, p. 458.
[231] Ibid., vol. 2, p. 183.

Of conditions toward the beginning of the Mexican period, Bancroft says: "At first in spite of Spanish laws all the ports were open to foreign vessels; and even later, under imperial and republican rule, restrictions were largely disregarded by the authorities . . . ."[232]

On the imperative nature of the public exigency demanding such official indulgence, Governor Figueroa wrote in 1834, in his report on California's commerce and revenues:

"About 1819, due to dire distress of the general public, as well as the soldiers, in need of all sorts of necessities of life, Governor Sola' [sic] opened the ports to foreign commerce -- about the time when the trade of the Sandwich Islands was developing." Having recapitulated the evils of the maritime trade laws and the difficulties confronting his own efforts at reform, Don José confessed that "to enforce the regulations literally would be to place the people under the hardship of not being able to secure the necessities and of losing their sole market . . . ."[233]

Alvarado declared: ". . . . it is well known that we Californians did not consider the foreign contrabandistas criminals, for the heavy duties which the Mexican government

---

[232] Calif., vol. 2, p. 670.

[233] Nov. 28, 1834, Figueroa to Sec. of Finances, "Report on the Commerce and Revenues of California," in Dept. St. Pap., MS, vol. 3, pp. 192--99.

imposed on all commodities imported from abroad were sufficient inducement for the contraband enterprises." Officials who lent themselves to illicit trade were considered culpable, "since such officials had obligated themselves to fulfill the duties of their office."[234] Such official lapses, however, had to be covert and motivated by the desire for personal gain, to be frowned on. Express or tacit suspension of oppressive regulations, for the public welfare, were hailed with general appreciation.

Under such conditions, "smuggling again became prevalent and profitable."[235] After 1836, the state of affairs was aggravated, for "civil war had paralyzed all industries, especially agriculture," wrote Vallejo; and blamed Alvarado for having consented -- in return for official recognition as governor, so Don Guadalupe claimed -- to the re-imposition of the Mexican port regulations and charges, which "were the most powerful incentive to smuggling enterprises."[236]

On the participation of all classes in the illicit commerce, Vallejo wrote elsewhere: "It is notorious that

---

[234] Alvarado, Hist. de Calif., MS, vol. 3, pp. 165--66.
[235] Bancroft, Calif., vol. 2, pp. 521--22.
[236] Vallejo, Hist. de Calif., MS, vol. 4, pp. 6--7.

in 1836 all the padres, all the merchants, all the sailors, all the <u>rancheros</u> and even the public employees except those of the customs department engaged in contraband; for the excessive duties levied by the Mexican government authorized us (<u>nos autorizaban</u>) to resort to this method . . . ."[237]

In times of special economic stress, popular resentment of commercial over-regulation and over-taxation approached the truculent. Administrator Gonzalez wrote in 1833 that attempts of the revenue officers to enforce the laws were handicapped not only by lack of resources, but by the disapproval of the people; and as for the soldiers, if they got no relief they might easily seize control of the department and, further, seize the authorities -- perhaps kill them -- for withholding needed supplies.[238]

It is obvious that no conviction of guilt worried the Californians on the score of their extra-legal business operations. They were merely exercising their prerogatives as free men to preserve life and to refuse tribute. The Mexican regulations were not of their making, not by their consent and not for their benefit. They were -- despite the territory's lone representative in Congress -- victims of taxation without representation. Not only were the prices resulting

---

[237] Vallejo <u>Hist. de Calif.</u>, MS, vol. 3, p. 194.

[238] May 31, 1833, Gonzalez to Director-General of Revenues, in Dept. t. Pap., Ben., C.-House, MS, vol. 2, p. 15.

from the excessive and multifarious charges on imports ruinous, and the effect of export taxes on a new country struggling for its earliest development and its first markets paralyzing; but the Mexican tariff was designed specifically for the protection of Mexican productions, and was frequently highly prejudicial to territorial interests. Cloth, for example, being among Mexican products, was highly protected. So the Californians, who imported all but coarse mission weaves, paid 20¢ a yard in duties on material worth 6¢ a yard.[239]

The fact that the Mexican traders generally took advantage of the situation to hold their prices up to the prices on heavily dutiable foreign goods intensified the economic burden and the resentment of the territorials.[240]

Finally, the lists of prohibited goods included many items of which California stood in particular need, and which for one reason or another she was unable or unready to provide from her own resources. Generally those desiderata were manufactured goods. Occasionally, however, the importation of raw materials seems to have been undertaken with a view to manufacturing commodities otherwise obtainable only at very excessive cost.

---

[239] Larkin to Rogers, in
p.1 of letter. On Mexico's prohibition of cloth manufacture in California, see post, pp. 630--31.
[240] Bancroft, Calif., vol. 3, p. 369, n. 8, "1833."

Cotton was one of the raw stuffs that, if available in quantity, would have enabled the Californians to scale down their expenses considerably. But cotton was a principal crop of important regions of Mexico; and cotton cloth was one of Mexico's most jealously protected manufactures. At one time the supreme government went so far as to require the burning of all foreign raw cotton in the territories -- an order which went quite disregarded in California.[241]

Other territories shared California's handicap and resentment on this account. In 1845, united action was initiated to secure alleviation, and the supreme government was actually moved to consider the matter. At that time the secretary of the national Chamber of Deputies submitted to the Californian Assembly, for its opinion, certain bills proposed by the assemblies of Jalisco and Puebla relative to the suspension of the law prohibiting the introduction of foreign raw cotton (algodon en rama) into the republic.[242]

----

[241] Bancroft, Calif., vol.

[242] July 11, 1845, Leg. Rec., MS, vol. 4, p. 92. It will be remembered that both Puebla and Jalisco had been noted for their great textile manufacturing centers since the eighteenth century. Fisher, Viceregal Adminis., pp. 112--13.

It was past the eleventh hour, however. The period was closing -- a period of which it can only be said that in the matter of indirect taxes the sons of the country found themselves, without recourse, between the upper and the nether millstones.

28. Los Contrabandistas

The methods of foreign contrabandistas, like those of the modern bootleggers, were various and devious, and altered to meet changing conditions. Many isolated points on the coast were utilized as trading rendezvous and as places of secret deposit. Especially frequeted for such purposes were the Refugio coast, above Santa Barbara, and San Pedro where, year after year, in his warehouse on the sands, "Don" Abel Stearns operated a contraband clearing-house.[243]

Catalina and the Channel Islands were ideally located for contraband purposes. The principal portion of a valuable cargo could be deposited, after which the vessel could put in at Monterey, pay duties on the remnant and receive in return its permit to trade along the coast. For the next couple of years it would then be free to sell, replenishing with goods as frequently as business demanded, with no one the wiser.

---

[243] Bancroft, Calif., vol. 3, p. 375; vol. 4, p. 95.

At least as early as 1833, the Californians recognized the need to fortify the Santa Cruz region (of the mainland);[244] and they were still urging that project on Mexico at the close of the period, together with the proposition -- also urged from the '30s -- that the islands along the coast be settled, since they served no purpose but that of smugglers' resorts.[245]

Sometimes stocks were renewed at sea, by transshipment from supply vessels which never approached the California coast. "Constant and long experience have shown," wrote Vallejo, "that it is impossible to prevent contraband trade under circumstances where foreign vessels are allowed to touch at will, before and after appraisal, at Santa Barbara, San Francisco and other coast points. Due to transshipments at sea, and unloading of the most valuable parts of their cargoes in unfrequented places prior to passing the customs, they don't declare half their consignments and don't pay half the imposts due. Perhaps not a vessel anchors in harbor that cannot reasonably be said to be in ballast; and declared cargoes are of minor value, generally comprising empty reed boxes, palm mats from the Sandwich Islands, brooms and thousands of fire

----

[244] Bancroft, Calif., vol. 3, p. 694, n. 16, "1833."
[245] Castañares, Col. de Doc., pp. 41--42; and see ante, pp. 97--98.

crackers from China, or similar things, with a few exceptions. They pass the customs, then pick up their hidden contraband and proceed to trade where they please, with entire liberty."246

Due to the notorious inadequacy of the military and enforcement branches, a considerable volume of smuggling was carried on under the very shadows of the presidios, either surreptitiously or, as has been mentioned elsewhere, in blatant defiance of the law and the military. The presidial port of Santa Bárbara was described as a hotbed of smuggling in 1833.247

Vessels did not hesitate to enter any port or roadstead, even when it was legally closed, since one or another pretext of needing water or wood or supplies or repair could always be invoked to give color of justification to their presence. In the course of their stay, considerable quantities of goods which had never been in Monterey could be transferred to Californian ownership.

Osio thought to meet this situation by the requirement that such vessels take a revenue guard on board. Since their officers, although thoroughly informed that Monterey was the only port of entry, and that they should put in there

---

246 Vallejo, Exposición, pp. 7--9.
247 Bancroft, Calif., vol. 3, p. 652, n. 3, "1833."

first, insisted on touching previously at other ports, "in future when they do so they are to take on board a guard whom they are to pay 50 pesos."[248]

It did not take the traders long, however, to learn to hoodwink or bribe the guards. Indeed, Californian officialdom did not long deceive itself that the guard device or any other of its attempts at revenue law enforcement was effective. "In an attempt to check these pernicious abuses, means have been adopted which seemed suitable, and lately, in each of the vessels plying the coast, a guard has been placed to prevent all crooked work; but this measure offers little hope of success, for it is no difficult matter to undermine, in a manner not susceptible of investigation, the good faith of a single individual." Thus Vallejo, on the guard precaution.[249]

W. H. Davis, recalling his supercargo days, has described the secret landing of a $20,000 cargo under cover of darkness during the presence of the guard. Eleven hundred dollars' worth of goods was left on board as a sop to the customs appraiser. In this instance, the guard was bribed,[250] although in some cases he might merely be

----

[248] July 22, 1839, Osio to Comandante of Santa Bárbara, in Guerra Doc., MS, vol. 6, p. 24.

[249] Exposición, p. 9.

[250] Bancroft, Calif., vol. 4, p. 375.

duped by clever work on the part of the officers and crew of the guarded vessels.

Sometimes the guard arrived too late to prevent mischief. With all the watchfulness and diligence in the world, that might easily happen, under the circumstances. A vessel might slip landward at night and in the dark of the moon, take buyers or receivers aboard by pre-arrangement, and turn over a large part of its cargo before ever the customs officials could be aware of its arrival.

To obviate such eventualities, a law of 1838 forbade any person to precede the customs guard aboard a newly arrived vessel. The penalty for a first offense was 10 pesos; that for a second offense, 20 pesos; " and finally that of a rebel."[251] At the same time or subsequently, a heavier penalty was charged to the account of the vessel receiving any one aboard in advance of the revenue officer. In 1842, the Administrator of Customs at Monterey notified the supercargo of the frigate "Barnstable" that he had incurred a fine of 300 pesos for breach of this law.[252]

Despite all efforts to make the customs guard system effective, however, Bancroft gathered that during the last years of the period the taking on of such an officer -- as

----

[251] Bancroft, Calif., vol. ?, p. ?, n. 20.

[252] July 7, 1842, Dept. St. Pap., Ben., MS, vol. 3, p. 13.

a blind, merely -- had supplanted to a great extent, on the part of the supercargoes, the earlier trick of landing goods in out-of-the-way places for reloading after the form of entry had been gone through, with a vestigial cargo, at Monterey.[253]

With or without a guard, moreover, it was always possible to present fictitious invoices representing the value of the goods entered at perhaps a quarter of actual selling price.[254]

Mention has already been made of the fact that the whalers shared the general flair for dealing outside the law. Not only did they sell on their own accounts far more than the legal limit imposed on them, and evade regulations in restraint of their commercial activities when such regulations became necessary to the retention of legitimate business; they also lent their services and facilities as confederates of other contrabandistas.[255]

Toward the close of the period, the whalers, coming in greater numbers than ever before, were a source of much trouble to the revenue men. Sauzalito became a regular resort of theirs. They claimed its wood and water as the

---

[253] Calif., vol. 4, p. 375.
[254] Davis, Seventy-five Years, pp. 106--7.
[255] Bancroft, op. cit., p. 376.

attractions, but it was generally understood that there were exceptional facilities there for illicit trade, since Captain of the Port "Don Guillermo" A. Richardson, who resided at Sauzalito, was indulgent toward trade peccadillos. (His duties were not those of a revenue officer, but of a recorder, rather, of marine arrivals, sailings, cargoes, etc.) In 1844, during a long controversy between the revenue officers and the masters of whalers and other craft frequenting Sauzalito, Richardson sided with the law breakers.[256]

Unquestionably the lighters, of which seven were by this time plying the inland waters and the bays -- particularly that of San Francisco -- played their part in the exchange of undeclared imports for country produce loaded at the embarcaderos of the ranchers. In 1844, licenses were required for the operation of such small craft -- though whether vessels were forced to employ such registered lighters rather than their own boats does not clearly appear, says Bancroft.[257]

The Russians, too, came in for a part of the sub rosa barter with the rancheros, though their contraband activities seem to have been comparatively limited.[258] Territorial official indulgence permitted that "as the smaller vessels

------

[256] Bancroft, Calif., vol. 4, pp. 429, 675.
[257] Ibid., pp. 430, n. 16; 569--70.
[258] Ibid., vol. 3, p. 368.

of the neighboring Russians cannot make the run to Monterey as easily as larger vessels, they may trade without so doing." Naturally, they were expected to comply with the other legal requirements including the payment of duties, non-compliance involving discontinuance of trade privileges and possible confiscation of merchandise.[259]

It is of course as impossible to make any definite estimate of the volume of California's contraband trade as it is to gauge that of the American bootleg business during prohibition days. A few speculations and comments, made at the time or based by Bancroft on his search of thousands of relevant documents, are not without interest, however. Of such recorded customs receipts as he found for 1826, Bancroft concluded: "If the total of $13,000 were doubled, it is evident that the amount would be but a small part of the percentage due on imports."[260]

Vallejo recalled[261] that in the late '30s the customs brought in "nothing of any account," due to the revival of smuggling on a flourishing scale. This reference seems to relate to the years -- blank today, so far as records go --

----

[259] Aug. 21, 1834, Admin. of Customs to Receptor of San Francisco, in Dept. St. Pap., Ben., C.-House, MS, vol. 2, p. 3.
[260] Calif., vol. 3, pp. 117--18.
[261] Hist. de Calif., MS, vol. 4, p. 6.

1836--38; that is, the period during and just following the revolution.

Bancroft's estimate for the three years of 1836--40 for which he found records was that goods entered unlawfully must have been at least equal to the average of $70,000 a year introduced legally.[262] For 1841, he concluded that contraband cargoes were "certainly not less than half the amounts [apparently totalling $101,150] entered at the custom-house."[263]

Of the trade in 1843, Bancroft's surmise was: "I think there can be no doubt that three fourths of the year's importations paid no duties, the amounts entered at Monterey being, as a rule, absurdly small."[264] On the basis of the known custom-house receipts for that year, this would make the figure for contraband trade at least $156,000.[265]

29. Starting with Empty Pockets

Among the handicaps from which the territory suffered was extreme shortage of currency. Little money had ever been sent into the country. Spain had furnished by the

---

[262] *Calif.*, vol. 4, p. 30.
[263] *Ibid.*, p. 210.
[264] *Ibid.*, pp. 375, 378.
[265] See *post.*, p. 299, Table VIII.

supply ships the salaries of the governor and one or two other officers, with a small amount for the soldiers. An order of 1794 called for the payment in coin of all balances due the presidial companies, one-fourth of the amount to be in small change; "but I find no evidence that anything of the kind was ever done," says Bancroft.[266] In 1808, the **tribunal de cuentas** decided that no coin need be sent to California for the purchase of supplies, as loans could be made from the padres, repayable at San Blas.[267]

For all practical purposes, California therefore lived on a barter basis, as a Spanish colony. Mexico, which had long been drained of both precious metals and coin by the exports of the first to Spain and the exhaustion of the second in foreign trade,[268] was never able to send any considerable sums to California. The shortage continued through the '20s, '30s and '40s, being mitigated only as the traders brought coin into the territory. As we have seen, however, they did not bring even enough to pay their duties. The effect was "detrimental to the treasury and to the national trade, and has put money out of circulation." Accordingly, as has been mentioned, the meeting of tonnage charges

----

[266] **Calif.**, vol. 1, p. 630.
[267] **Ibid.**, vol. 2, p. 185, n. 20.
[268] Lillian Estelle Fisher, "Commercial Conditions in Mexico" (paper read before Southwestern Social Science Ass'n., Dallas, Texas, Mar. 26, 1932), p. 161

and of a certain percentage of the customs in coin had to be insisted upon by decree; and an installment plan was worked out to facilitate ~~money~~ cash payments.[269]

Mexico had tried to conserve the territory's cash supply -- and more particularly, undoubtedly, add to her own -- by levying an export tax on coin. In 1822, this was only 3.5%, apparently.[270] In 1835, a 2% derecho de circulación was imposed on currency sent from California to San Blas.[271] In 1840, the supreme government insisted that the free exportation of money was forbidden to passengers as well as to vessels.[272]

Sometimes, as in the case of other commodities, more than one charge was imposed. The Junta de Gobierno repealed a 12% and a 6% Mexican tax on coin in 1825, replacing them by a 25% duty on currency extracted from the province by a foreigner on a foreign vessel.[273] This arrangement -- had it survived -- would have greatly reduced the hardships

---

[269] April 8, 1839, Alvarado to Osio, in Dept. St. Pap., Ben., MS, vol. 3, p. 21; April 9, 1839, Osio to Alvarado, in Dept. St. Pap., Ben., C.-House, MS, vol. 5, pp. 12--13; Pinto Doc., MS, vol. 1, p. 244.
[270] Bancroft, Calif., vol. 2, p. 473, n. 43
[271] Ibid., vol. 3, p. 369, n. 8.
[272] Ibid., vol. 4, p. 94, n. 33.
[273] Leg. Rec., MS, vol. 1, pp. 38--39.

worked by Mexico's tribute exactions, and could have served far better the territorial need to protect its circulation. The legislation of the Junta de Gobierno, however, was one of the many Californian efforts destined for the discard by Mexico.

Cash continued a rarity. "Money is extremely scarce," wrote Bandini in 1828. "Barter prevails."[274]

Of the years just following, José Sepúlveda recalled: "There was scarcely any money here in '33--'35."[275]

"There is absolutely no copper money in circulation in my department," wrote Vallejo in 1839; and a day or so later: "There is no silver in California." He hoped that the deficiency could be overcome through the efforts of California's diputado, the Congress, Bustamante and Virmond.[276]

In 1842, Victor Prudon, Vallejo's secretary and commissioner to Mexico, charged with urging on the supreme

---

274 Nov. (?) 3, 1828, J. M. Bandini to "Don Eustaquio" Barron, in Bandini Doc., MS, unnumbered document, p. 14. (This 31-page letter is bound between documents #8 6 and 11. No. 6 follows #7, the order being: 7, 6, document cited here, 11.)

275 San Diego Arch., MS, "Misc. Pap., 1830--43, Los Angeles," p. 13.

276 Nov. 29, 1839, Vallejo to Sec. of War, in Vallejo Doc., MS, vol. 8, #327; Dec. 1, 1839, Vallejo to Virmond, in Vallejo Doc., MS, vol. 8, #335, p. 2.

government important Californian reforms, had to take his travelling expenses in the form o 500 pesos in cash and 1,000 pesos' worth of cloth.[277] Bancroft suspected a possible obstructionist trick, here, on the part of political opponents; but the device was sufficiently matter of course to be plausible at the time.

Hartnell gave an interesting estimate in 1844: "The amount of circulation in California I should think does not exceed about 60 or 70 thousand dollars."[278]

Besides prevailing scarcity, great heterogeneity obtained in the Californian currency. In 1826, the ship "Waverly" took away Spanish dollars and guilders.[279] Davis relates that "the coin generally used by the merchants was Spanish and Mexican doubloons (gold); also American gold coin. Silver money of Mexican, Peruvian and United States coin was likewise in circulation. I never saw in California any of the paper money in use in the East."[280]

Such a cosmopolitan currency must have given rise to many abuses. The territorials could not possibly keep abreast of fluctuations in exchange; and could not always be familiar with the intrinsic value of all coins current.

----

[277] Bancroft, Calif., vol. 4, p. 282, n. 2.
[278] Pico Doc., MS, vol. 1, #37, p. 1.
[279] Bancroft, Calif., vol. 3, p. 149, n. 69, "Waverley."
[280] Seventy-five Years, p. 159.

Of course, being scarce, money commanded a high rate of interest -- 2% per month in 1844, according to Hartnell.[281] Moreover, business had to be conducted on an installment or a barter basis, or even, due to the peculiarities of the hide and tallow trade, a combination of both.[282]

An unstable currency, barter and credit, trade monopoly and high tariff: none knew better than the Californians the disadvantages to which all these conditions subjected them at the will of the traders. The latter had the upper hand, for not only must the territorials have manufactured goods; they must have markets for their own productions.

Every son and daughter of the country knew that much of the import and export levy on the foreign trade was promptly reclaimed by that trade in the form of exorbitant prices. Every enterprising Californian felt the handicap of this steady drainage of the country's capital, and this undervaluation of the country's goods. But there was no alternative. Bit by bit, one step backward to two steps forward, must be the progress toward economic independence.

30. The Territorial Purse

In 1830, Echeandía commented, in a letter to the Comisario-General of Finances, that commerce, carried on by

----

[281] P. Pic. Doc., MS, vol. 1, #87, p. 1.

[282] See post, sec. 57.

the peculiar system "'authorized by force of circumstances'" in
California, yielded barely two-fifths of the territory's
expenses; while mission contributions, by dint of constant
requisitions and annoyances, yielded not more than one-fifth
of the deficit.[283]

"Theoretically " adds Bancroft, "the national treasury
should have paid the territorial expenses and received the
net product of the territorial revenue; but practically,
the territory was left to pay its own expenses, nominally
about $130,000 a year . . . ."[234]

The budget of 1831, in fact, seems to have called for
approximately 131,000 pesos. Revenues for the year were,
in round numbers, 32,000 pesos[235] -- some 20,000 pesos
under Echeandía's estimated two-fifths.

The chronic insufficiency was of course paralyzing to
the business of government. When duties were collected,
there were always many more claims on them than they could
possibly be stretched to cover. Only the most urgent debts
or fresh expenditures could be considered. The irregularity
of income, resulting from its source in the customs, added to
embarrassment. For perhaps months at a time, the treasury

---

[283] Bancroft, Calif., vol. 3, p. 58, n. 3.
[284] Ibid., p. 58.
[285] Ibid., p. 379, n. 20.

would be empty or practically so; and there was no way of knowing when a vessel (willing to pay duties) might arrive to mitigate the destitution. As lat as April 25, Micheltorena's financial report for the year 1843 read:[286]

    "Entradas.............000 pesos

    "Salidas..............000 "

    "Existencias..................4 reales"

Yet the situation was not hopeless. There is reason to believe that, given autonomy and a few years, the Californians would have mastered their abstruse mathematical problems. They worked for the solution from every angle: from that of producing, by means of improved organization and management, a larger yield from the system fastened on them; from that of cutting expenses; and from that of evolving an entirely new system of state financing in the modern manner. At this point we shall consider their success in rendering more efficient the antiquated system under which they labored. Their efforts to throw off the old system, and meanwhile to cut expenses at whatever sacrifice, will b discussed presently.[287]

The reorganization of the fiscal administration following the revolution of 1836, together with the country's

---

    286 Bancroft, Calif., vol. 4, p. 35.

    287 See post, secs 32, 31.

ever increasing productiveness and purchasing power,[288] resulted in comparative stabilization of the revenues, which showed as well a definite upward swing.[289] "From the year 1838 on," wrote Osio, "the customs receipts mounted to as much as 70,000 pesos, taking one year with another." He added, with gratification, that the frontier army having been diminished by a third, the revenues were sufficient to cover its needs.[290]

As a matter of fact, the figure 70,000 pesos was an understatement. The average for the final seven years (1839--45) of the era was almost 86,000 pesos a year.[291] As for the 1836--40 period, Bancroft concluded that "for the three years for which alone records are extant, the average of total revenue from duties was $70,000 but the figures for 1837--8, if known, would probably reduce that average below $60,000."[292]

With the genius of the *Californios* for getting along on little, the outlook for their maintaining a balanced budget would have been bright had Mexico imposed no new

---

[288] See *post*, Chap. V.
[289] Bancroft, *Calif.*, vol. 4, p. 99.
[290] *Hist. de Calif.*, MS, p. 401.
[291] See *infra*, Table VIII
[292] Bancroft, *Calif.*, vol. 4, p. 80.

burdens on them and, particularly, had their aim of abolishing the customs-for-revenue system been attainable.

Unfortunately, fiscal records for the 1820s and most of the 1830s are too fragmentary to allow of year-by-year comparison with figures for the rest of the period, which are apparently complete and reliable. However, a tabulated résumé of known data affords some interesting general indications. (When no comment is made as to the records, the figures are practically complete.)

Table VIII
Territorial Revenues, 1823--46[293]

Year	Receipts	Comment on Records
1823	17,538--24,038 pesos	Not clear, and perhaps incomplete
1824	8,000	Perhaps incomplete
1825	11,036	" "
1826	13,500	Very complete
1827	14,000	"Virtually no records at all"
1828	24,503[a]-40,000	Meager and contradictory
1829	119,708[b]	"More meager than ever"
1831	32,000	
Je, 1833-- Je, 1834	50,109	Somewhat less incomplete than in previous years
1835	about 50,000	"Comparatively complete"

[293] 1823, Bancroft, Calif., vol. 2, pp. 492--93; 1824, ibid., p. 521; 1825, ibid., vol. 3, p. 29, n. 52; 1826, ibid., pp. 117-18; 1827, ibid., p. 125; 1828, ibid., vol. 2, p. 672,

1835--6	44,649ᵃ --56,741ᶜ pesos	Complete but conflicting
1836	about 60,000	Incomplete
	Hartnell-Larkin figures / Bancroft figures	
1839	85,613 / 85,628	Figures probably close to accuracy
1840	72,308 / 72,372	
1841	101,150 / about 100,000	
1842	73,729 / 74,000	
1843	52,000 / 52,504	
1844	78,739 / 76,625	
1845	138,370 or 142,309 / about 140,000	

Annual average
1839--45   85,985   85,875
1846 (to April)   26,826

[a] Echeandía's figure for "total receipts in 1828."
[b] See discussion, infra.
[c] About 30,000 pesos belong to 1836.

---

n. 39. and vol. 3, p. 131; 1829, ibid., pp. 135-36, n. 47; 1831, ibid., p. 379, n. 20; 1833-34, ibid., p. 366, n. 5; 1835, ibid., pp. 366--67; 1835--36, ibid., vol. 4, p. 84, n. 9; 1836, ibid., p. 84; 1839, ibid., p. 93; 1839, 1840, ibid., pp. 95, 99; 1839--45, Hartnell, in Pico Doc., MS, vol. 1, #85, p. 1, and Larkin, Official Corresp., MS, vol. 2, p. 111; 1841, Bancroft, Calif., vol. 4, pp. 209-10, n. 11; 1842; ibid., p. 339, n. 17, ¶2;
1843, ibid., p. 377, n. 16, "Financial Items"; 1844, ibid., p. 432; 1845, ibid., p. 560; 1846,

Due to the fragmentary character of its earlier items, this table affords no basis for hard and fast specific conclusions. Yet, examined in the light of known conditions, it is not entirely non-committal.

Before any inferences can be drawn, however, comment on the figures for 1828 and 1829 is necessary. The

----

ibid., vol. 5, p. 570, n. 28.

It has been thought worth while to include the Hartnell and Larkin statements for 1839-- April, 1846 because although Bancroft sometimes used their figures exactly or in round number form, he occasionally varied slightly, due to discrepancies in the many documents under his investigation. Hartnell and Larkin seem to have had access to the same source -- possibly Larkin used Hartnell's figures, although he carries the record further. Both were well informed men and close to the fountainhead of revenue information, particularly Hartnell, of course, who was in charge of the department just after the revolution, served again in the customs branch in 1843, and in 1844 was no less than "first officer, inspector, interpreter and acting administrator of customs" at Monterey. He continued in the service to and after the conquest. (Bancroft, Calif., vol. 3, p. 777). As de la Guerra's son-in-law, moreover,

latter amount stands out strikingly, and in view of the known incompleteness of the records suggests itself at first glance as perhaps a truer index to the run of customs receipts than are the very much smaller amounts for the preceding years of the decade. But this implication is not borne out by the later -- and more nearly complete -- amounts up to 1836.

Oddly enough, too, not only are the 1829 revenue accounts characterized by Bancroft as "more meager than ever," but of the 119,708 *pesos*, 117,267 *pesos* purported to have been collected at San Diego alone; and amounts for Monterey -- the principal port of entry -- are wholly lacking in the customs record. Yet the duties of the Boston ship "Brookline," which put in at Monterey this year, were $31,000, according to a letter of her supercargo. Further investigation reveals that San Diego receipts were only 2,000 *pesos* up to June 1, and only 826 *pesos* in August.[294] This leaves a difference of 114,441 *pesos* to be made up in only five months' time -- an average of 22,888 *pesos* per month -- at San Diego alone. Such freak fortune seems too good to have been true, even though San Diego was the only port besides Monterey open to foreign trade in 1829.[295]

----

he was in touch with revenue affairs practically throughout the Mexican period.

[294] Bancroft, *Calif.*, vol. 3, p. 135, n. 47.
[295] *Ibid.*, p. 136.

The question naturally occurs: was the trading fleet of 1829 phenomenally large? Reference to the marine list of 1825--30, for whose compilation Bancroft combed more than a thousand sources, reveals the contrary. He found only 23 names for 1829, plus 4 doubtful ones. One of the 23 was built in California, that year; 11 were arrivals of 1828, engaged in trading along the coast; and at least 2 or 3, perhaps half a dozen, were whaleships exempt from duties and probably from tonnage and anchorage charges at the time. So at the utmost, only 8 or 9 vessels of 1829, plus the 4 doubtful listings, were customs possibilities.

Of these, the American ship "Brookline" (376 or 417 T.) is known to have paid 31,000 pesos -- at Monterey; and the American "Volunteer" (a bark of 126 or 226 T.) paid 4,054 pesos -- at San Francisco. It becomes of interest to glance at the remaining craft as potential producers of 116,267 pesos plus the collections not included in the "more meager than ever" record, remembering that the lesser traders paid anywhere from one thousand to several thousand pesos; and the great floating emporia from Boston -- of 300 tons and up -- supplied the bulk of the territory's income, paying from 25,000 pesos to an occasional 50,000 pesos or so.

As, for lack of full information, it is impossible

to segregate more than 2 or 3 whaling vessels from the general list, the following catalog perhaps includes 1 or 2 of the non-revenue-producing whalers:[296]

    4 doubtful English listings, mentioned in a single list, with no details

    1 Russian brig of 202 T., which paid only 1,216 pesos in duties in 1828

    2 or possibly 3 Mexican schooners -- 1 under 200 T. and possibly 1 under 100 T.

    2 Hawaiian brigs under 200 T. and 1 unidentified Hawaiian brig

    3 or possibly 4 American vessels of the smaller class (about 200 T. to less than 100 T.), of which one is known to have paid, on three previous entries during the decade, 49 pesos, 232 pesos and 93 pesos, respectively

    1 English vessel of 201 or 301 T., known to have paid, on three previous entries during the decade, 2,185 pesos, 2,199 pesos and 858 pesos, respectively

    3, possibly, but probably 2, American ships of more than 300 T. burden

---

[296] Bancroft, Calif., vol. 3, p. 135, n. 46; pp. 145--49, n. 69, passim.

This is not a promising bag of tricks from which to conjure 117,267 pesos plus the unknown but major quantity of Monterey's intake -- even if each vessel declared its full cargo. Customs receipts of course included export with import duties; but both classes of income were limited by the cargo capacities of the trading vessels. It took 20 traders, and 7 whalers paying duties up to 500 pesos each, to make up the 100,000 pesos collected in 1841.[297] Even in 1828, 14 vessels out of a fleet of 36 seem to have contributed to the year's customs proceeds,[298] which Echeandía reported as 24,503 pesos.[299]

The governor's figure is probably accurate. Bancroft mentions, however, "a few meager items of revenue" bringing the 1828 total to 40,000 pesos. It is noteworthy that of this amount, San Diego, again, appears as having taken in the preponderant part, 34,000 pesos -- more than the governor's report of receipts for the entire year. Yet San Diego was less, rather than more, important as a consuming and producing center than the other ports.

Finally, the usual governmental poverty does not appear to have been lightened in 1828--29 and 1829--30, although the indicated customs receipts for the latter year should have

---

[297] Bancroft, Calif., vol. 4, pp. 209--10.
[298] Ibid., vol. 3, p. 131.
[299] See ante, pp. 298--99, Table VIII.

covered practically all current expenses. We have Echeandía's estimate of yearly expenses, in 1829, as 123,000 pesos, along with his complaint of 1830 to the commissioner-general of finances that commerce yielded barely two-fifths of the territory's expenses.[300] That indicates a total income of something under 50,000 pesos at just about the time when San Diego appears to have collected 117,000 pesos.

Most probably it was this San Diego record of 1829[301] which prompted Bancroft to remark that "of the fragmentary accounts extant [for the early period] . . . . some certainly deal with amounts and payments that were purely imaginary."[302]

It is not asserted offhand that the 1829 San Diego record is apocryphal. Yet it is so extremely questionable that neither can it be accepted summarily as authentic. A number of possible explanations of its impressive proportions spring to mind. Inexpert book-keeping may have resulted in snowballing in the posting of receipts. Quite probably -- since Bandini of San Diego was at the time ranking customs officer -- figures for the entire territory are included, though not identified; and quite possibly a little

---

[300] See ante, p. 298, Table VIII.

[301] Dept. St. Pap., Ben., C.-House, MS, vol. 1, passim.
[302] Bancroft, Calif., vol. 2, p. 671.

creative imagination affected the accounting. Bandini's passion to have San Diego declared a regular port of entry, on a par with or in preference to Monterey, was a leading motive in his political career. Although undoubtedly above suspicion in his handling of public funds, he was enough of a political sophist to be capable, perhaps, of evolving a customs record which might sooner or later be held up in justification of San Diego's claims over Monterey.

These are speculations, merely. It would be interesting to trace through the records for possible hidden light on the 1829 San Diego collections but the investigation lies outside present bounds, which preclude, also, too wide an excursion into the field of speculation. The question must remain for the present a nice little problem inviting some detective willing to train his powers of investigation and logic on a century-old suspicious document. Meantime, the figure for 1829 is of too doubtful reliability to justify inclusion on an equal footing with the other data for 1823--36, and we can only leave it aside in present reckonings.

This eclecticism is in accordance with Bancroft's own judgment. He summarized the figures for 1821--30 with the generalization that duties amounted to "from $10,000 to $30,000 annually . . . ."[303] Nevertheless, in attempting

---

[303] Bancroft, Calif., vol. 2, p. 670.

to arrive at some gauge of customs receipts before 1836, e shall retain here the somewhat doubtfully high figure of $40,000 for 1828, since our aim is to make the estimate so liberal as to give its comparison with the figures for the period after 1836 unquestionable validity for our purpose of rather broad generalization.

And now for the comparison and the generalization: Apropos of the range of $10,000 to $30,000 annually which Bancroft found indicated in the customs records through the '20s, he commented that "despite contraband entries the receipts must have been I think three times as large as the amounts mentioned."[304] A tripling of the amounts for all the 1820s recorded (except 1829), using always the highest figure supplied,[305] yields a total of 332,000 pesos in round numbers, or 56,000 pesos a year as a round average.

Looking next at the figures for 1831-36, inclusive, and adding 50%[306] -- to compensate for incompleteness in the

---

[304] Bancroft, Calif., vol. 2, p. 670.
[305] See ante, p. 298, Table VIII.
[306] This is probably a more than ample allowance, since the records available for these years are far more complete than are those for the preceding years. See "Comment" column, Table VIII.

records -- to the amounts for all but 1835, which is based on "comparatively complete" reports, we arrive at a round average of 58,000 pesos.

Combined with the average of 56,000 pesos for the recorded years preceding 1831, this sum gives us a hypothetical annual average for the recorded years up to and including 1836 (though exclusive of 1829) of 57,000 pesos.

This figure is possibly a good deal too high. Forbes, generalizing on the financial state of the country, in 1831, declared without qualification or remark as to an exceptional falling-off of receipts at the time that "the net amount of revenue does not exceed 32,000 dollars."[307] More positively indicative is Echeandía's implied specification of a revenue below 50,000 pesos at the close of the period;[308] and his surmise of 1827 that with certain administrative changes government income might be made to aggregate 30,000 to 40,000 pesos per year.[309]

Our hypothetical figure, whether too high or too low, is not set up as a positive and final index; but it is derived from a liberal interpretation of existing records

---

[307] Alta Calif., p. 307. The book was not published till several years later.

[308] See ante, p. 305.

[309] Oct. 28, 1827, Echeandía to Comisario General de Sonora, in Dept. Rec., MS, vol. 5, p. 139. Bancroft, (Calif., vol. 3, p. 65, n. 10) gives the above

and known conditions, and is undoubtedly accurate enough to serve the only purpose for which it is intended -- that of a straw in the wind to indicate the financial drift of the close of the Mexican period. The average for those last years -- nearly $6,000 pesos -- is sufficiently larger than the tentative 57,000 pesos average of the preceding decade and a half to justify the conclusion that California's revenue had been very materially increasing during the seven years preceding the conquest.

Some such increase, indeed, might have been predicated on the increased consumer-demand and the cry for production outlet signalizing the development of the country's resources through these years.[310] But the wide prevalence of the tradition that the territory was but marking time or actually losing ground during the "splendid idle forties" and the "Arcadian" thirties makes desirable the gathering and fitting together of various phases of evidence which, when assembled, reveal the true picture in its coherence and completeness.

The access in the country's financial strength was not, it is true, sufficient to disperse from her door all the wolves of want that had been littered there. Yet aided by

----

rendering of the phrase in the original document: "ascenderan anualm^{te} desde 30 hta. 40 mil p^{s}."

[310] See post, Chap. V.

drastic economies, it did materially lessen the odds against the Californios. Again, without dogmatic assertion, the general tendency can be observed.

From the beginning, and continuously to 1839, receipts were hopelessly inadequate for expenses. The Mexican theory, retained in vogue after 1836, was that the civil and military branches should share equally in the revenues, the expenses of collection being, however, a first lien.[311] In practise, available revenues at any given time might be sufficient only to pay the customs employees something on account. Thus, in June 1831, San Diego receipts of 389 *pesos* were all paid out to employees.[312] Or a balance for distribution might be too small to share between civil and military. On such occasions, the group presenting the most urgent case -- or that nearest the distributing arm and heart -- would receive the benefit.

This hit-or-miss method of revenue disbursement was of course productive of discord. Partiality toward certain branches of the public service, or certain groups in certain branches, was charged first by one and then by another disappointed aspirant for something on account.

Animosities developed between officials weighted down with responsibilities but light of funds. Vallejo and Castro

---

[311] Osio, *Hist. de Calif.*, MS, p. 397.

[312] Bancroft, *Calif.*, vol. 3, p. 617.

believed that the country's salvation demanded the allocation of more than half the revenues to the support of the army; and that in any case more than the legal quota was being diverted to the uses of the civil service. The bitterly necessitous condition of all the departments of government, and the consciousness of crisis impending over the territory intensified these resentments far beyond the normal of political rivalry. On this score Vallejo and Alvarado, Vallejo and Ábrego, Pico and Castro and Pico and Ábrego waged vehement controversies.[313]

In 1844, the army men triumphed to the degree that the ratio of military to civilian receipts was as 8 to 7, while the budgetary allotments assigned more than three times as much to the army as to the civil list. In 1845, the army rated two-thirds of the total revenue, except that debts accrued from the recent political upheaval were to be paid de preferencia, direct from the custom-house, with a view to restoring government credit.[314]

31. Making Ends Meet

Despite the budget-defeating exigencies of the hand-to-mouth existence imposed by dependence on the customs

---

[313] Bancroft, Calif., vol. 4, pp. 99--100.

[314] Micheltorena, Bando Económico, MS, in Dept. St. Pap., Ang., MS, vol. 10, pp 32--41; Bancroft, Calif., vol. 4, pp. 432, 559--60.

for the country's revenue, rigid economies of a type rarely practised in any commonwealth, together with the order introduced into the collecting and distributing branches after the revolution of 1836, soon produced notably salutary effect. In 1839, with an obvious lift of the spirit, Alvarado wrote to Vallejo: "I think that the military and all other expenses will be paid this year and we will have a considerable balance."[315] Nor was his optimism overweening.

As soon as the disorders incident to the revolution had subsided, Ábrego had worked out a budget of 96,000 pesos per year.[316] This was more than 25% below the 131,000 peso schedule which had obtained before 1836.[317] Beginning at the same time, it will be remembered, customs receipts rose to an average of more than 85,000 pesos per year. On the basis of these figures, the yearly deficit would have been only 11,000 pesos -- an utterly insignificant sum which could at any time be made up by voluntary contribution.

Indeed, it was in this very year of 1839 that Vallejo wrote to Ábrego: "From the advices that you have sent ~~this~~

---

[315] May 10, 1839, Alvarado to Vallejo, in Vallejo Doc., MS, vol. 7, #32, p. 2.

[316] Vallejo Doc., MS, vol. 7, #406.

[317] Forbes, Alta Calif., pp. 306--7; Bancroft, Calif., vol. 3, pp. 58; 379, n. 20.

this *comandancia general*, it is evident that there are not sufficient funds at your command to pay the troops and departmental employees, consequently the *comandante general* will assist at once out of his own pocket to the extent of 8000 or 10000 *pesos*."[318]

To be sure, the deficit for 1844 was twice 11,000 *pesos*; and the years 1840, 1842 and especially 1843 imposed still greater stringency. But an occasional resort to suspend salaries would have tided over such temporary crises, and would have inflicted no novel hardship; while financial stabilization would have been effected by the imposing surpluses of 1841 and, particularly, 1845.

Solvency seemed just around the corner.

The Californians, left to themselves, would probably have turned that corner; for with the release of private initiative and industry -- suppressed under Spain -- the country had entered upon an era of rapid development.[319]

But the Californians were not left to themselves. In 1842 came Micheltorena, with his "Batallón Fijo de Californias" of between 300 and 400 hungry cholos.[320] True,

---

[318] July 10, 1839, M. G. Vallejo to Department Treasurer, in *Vallejo Doc.*, MS, vol. 6, #147. On the location of this document, see *ante*, p. 191, n. 52.

[319] See *post*, chap. V.

[320] See *post*, pp. 339--44.

the new governor was the proud bearer of drafts on the national treasury for 8,000 pesos per month for the support of that batallón. But there is no evidence that any one of those drafts was ever honored by the government, although a few thousand pesos were realized on them from sales to speculators.[321] The order for remissions may even have been countermanded by Mexico.[322] One of the many variations on the general theme song of territorial subsidization which Diputado Castañares dinned into the ears of Congress and the Cabinet in 1844--45 was a spirited appeal for payment, "sin escusa ni pretesto alguno," of the 8,000 pesos per month designated for the support of the military.[323]

The new emergency completely upset the comparative balance between revenues and expenses achieved by the Californian government. To Micheltorena's credit be it said that he joined his personal endeavors and sacrifices to those of the hijos del país in an effort to restore financial equilibrium.

He had arrived at San Diego on August 25, 1842; but did not take the oath of civil office until the last day

---

[321] See ante, p. 186, and post, p. 321.
[322] Bancroft, Calif., vol. 4, p. 402, n. 2.
[323] Castañares, Col. de Doc., pp. 13--19; 38--39.

of the year.[324] One of Alvarado's last acts before turning over the governorship had been to suspend the pay of all civil employees.[325] One of Micheltorena's first official concerns was to enjoin the strictest economy in all quarters. Not only soldiers and officers, but creditors must sacrifice. In March, he ordered Ábrego to suspend all back pay until further instructions; and placed current salary payments on the following basis:

    Military and civil employees, generally.......1/3 pay
    Officers of the battalion (Batallón Fijo).....1/4 "
    General of the battalion..(Micheltorena)...... 0 "
    Judges of the Superior Court..................1/3 "

Alvarado was assigned 1,300 pesos, de preferencia, on account of back salary.[326]

As luck would have it, 1843 was the year of the lowest revenue in the entire period 1839--46.[327] Moreover, no vessels made entry during the first quarter of the year. It was as of April 25 of this year that Micheltorena made his sad accounting of the treasury: "Entradas, 000 pesos; salidas, 000 pesos; existencias, 4 reales."[328]

---

[324] Bancroft, Calif., vol. 4, pp. 290, 295, 350.
[325] Ibid., p. 341.
[326] Ibid., p. 351, n. 1.
[327] See ante, p. 299, Table VIII.
[328] Bancroft, Calif., vol. 4, pp. 350-- 51; and ante, p. 296.

In October, a junta of officials was summoned to the governor's house to wrestle anew with the old problem of ways and means. This was no perfunctory gathering. Sixteen anxious men representing the Department's entire official family rallied to the call.[329] In the course of the next few days, a 20,000-peso reduction in the civil budget was worked out. Micheltorena promised to meet this economy with a corresponding cut in military expenses.

The results of the paring operations of governor and junta are presented here in tabular form, as completely and accurately as the documents permit. The figures are deemed interesting for the light they throw on general salary levels, as well as on the extent of the budgetary

----

[329] Those present were: General José M. Micheltorena; colonels M. G. Vallejo and J. B. Alvarado; lieutenant-colonels Rafael Tellez and José Castro; captains Juan Abella and Francisco Noriega; chief of artillery Captain Mariano Silva; captain of the port Pedro Narvaez; Commandant of presidial company Captain Nicanor Estrada; governor's secretary Manuel Jimeno; president of the tribunal Juan Malarín; prefect of the first district Ramon Estrada administrator of customs Manuel Castañares; customs appraiser Pablo de la Guerra; treasurer José Abrego; and chief customs warden Rafael Gonzalez. Bancroft, Calif., vol. 4, p. 357, n. 14.

pruning.

Table IX

Emergency Reductions in the Territorial Civil Budget, 1844[330]

Officer	Old Salary	Salary Recommended by Junta Económica	Salary Fixed in Banco Económico
Governor	5,000 pesos	no recommendation	no salary
Governor's sec'y	1,500--2,500	1,200 pesos	1,500 pesos
" clerk	600	500	No clerk
5 Justices at 4,000 pesos	20,000	(5 at 1,200): 6,000	(2 at 1,200): 2,400
Sec'y of Tribunal	1,500	1,200	1,200
Clerk "	480	No clerk	No clerk
4 Prefects at 2,000 pesos	8,000	no prefects	No prefects
4 Sec'ties of Prefectures at 700 pesos	2,800	" sec'ties	No sec'ties
4 Sub-prefects at 375 pesos	1,500	" sub-prefects	" sub-prefects

330 Junta Consultativa y Económica en Monterey, Octubre de 1843, MS,

Principal of Monterey School	1,200	1,200	1,200
Teacher, Monterey	1,000	Had resigned; not replaced	Eliminated
Mayors and Justices of the Peace (number unknown)	360 each	Only their fees as judges of first instance	Only fees
Finance Commissioner	1,200 to 1,500 (2% of distributions)	To be replaced by treasurer at 1,000--1,500 pesos salary	Salaried treasurer at 1,000 pesos
Customs Administrator	3,000	3,000	3,000
Appraiser or Chief Clerk of Customs	1,500	1,500 (but his additional pay as interpreter to be cut 50%)	1,500 (but his interpreter's pay to be cut 50%)
Head Customs Warden	1,800	No recommendation	1,800
Customs Wardens 4 at 700 pesos	2,800	" "	(2 at 700 pesos) 1,400

in Vallejo Doc., MS, vol. 11, #464; vol. 14, #124. (Vallejo was secretary of the Junta.) Some of the documents are in duplicate, but it is hard to know whether or not the record is complete.

318

Owing to several unknown quantities indicated in this tabulation, it is not possible to give totals.331 However, the recommendations of the *Junta Consultativa* are on record as having called for a 20,000-*peso* reduction in the civil list.

Micheltorena adopted these recommendations with further revision downward, so that something over 34,000 *pesos* was trimmed off.

He undertook like drastic treatment of the military list. The salaries of all militia officers were to cease, and those functionaries were to be given instead -- thanks. The 40 *pesos* per month hitherto paid for clerical services for the *comandante general* were to be disallowed, only the pay due the secretary's military rank to continue. Remuneration for surgical attendance was similarly discontinued.

Micheltorena, *Bando Económico, 1 de Enero, 1844,* MS, in *Dept. St. Pap., Ang.,* MS, vol. 10, pp. 34--41. Bancroft's beautifully concise summary of the labors of the *junta,* and of Micheltorena's *Bando* are given in *Calif.,* vol. 4, pp. 357--58.

[331] There may also be some slight error in figures here, as the records are fragmentary and perhaps further confused by copyists' errors.

All other military officers, including the <u>comandante general</u>, were placed on half-pay with rations.

The final saving on the military budget seems to have been 15,042 <u>pesos</u>.

Altogether, these grim slashings chopped practically 50,000 <u>pesos</u> off the Micheltorena budget, which was thereby reduced to just over 132,000 <u>pesos</u> per year. The new schedule became effective January 1, 1844 as announced in the governor's <u>Bando Económico</u>.

Cut to the quick as the costs of government had been, still further operation was necessary for financial survival. An additional 12,000 <u>pesos</u> was therefore lopped off the military arm, making a total cut of more than 34% and narrowing the budget down to 120,000 <u>pesos</u>.[332]

Customs receipts that year were only about 77,000 <u>pesos</u> -- not a hopelessly inadequate revenue for purposes of Abrego's 96,000-<u>peso</u> pre-Micheltorena budget; but seriously short of meeting the needs of the new administration with its "army" of hungry <u>cholos</u>.[333]

----

[332] Bancroft, <u>Calif.</u>, vol. 4, p. 401. Bancroft summarizes the details slightly differently, using round numbers; but arrives at the same result: a $120,000 budget.

[333] See <u>ante</u>, p. 298, Table VIII; pp. 312--14.

In December, Ábrego, Andrés Pico and Thomas O. Larkin sailed for Mazatlan, "the business of the former two, and probably of the last as well," says Bancroft, "being to obtain funds on Micheltorena's orders for the amount of $8000 per month that had been assigned him . . . ." There is no record of their negotiations.[334] However, according to Vallejo,[335] Pico and Ábrego succeeded in selling 18,000 pesos' worth of the paper for 10,000 pesos in cash.

In 1845, another emissary -- Captain J. M. Flores -- was dispatched to the capital to seek aid, "but with results that are altogether unknown," says Bancroft.[336] Severe as had been the overturn in the fiscal plans of the Californians, and heavy as was the resultant financial distress, Bancroft has this to say of the year 1844: "two Boston ships early in the year paid $58,000 in duties, more than two thirds of the total revenues of the year; $2,000 in money was obtained from Vallejo in payment, together with provisions supplied the year before, for the Soscol rancho; additional aid was obtained from the trader Limantour; and probably also from Thomas O. Larkin. So that the financial

---

[334] Bancroft, Calif., vol. 4, pp. 401--2.
[335] Hist. de Calif., MS, vol. 4, pp. 382--83.
[336] Calif., vol. 4, p. 402.

troubles of 1844, excepting perhaps those at the end of the year, resulting from extraordinary events to be noticed later, were not altogether insuperable after all."[337]

Nor did Micheltorena rule in such utter destitution as his accounting of April 1843[338] portended. A balance sheet of 1845[339] indicates that more than 200,000 pesos were received and distributed during his term of something over two years.

If there were any doubt that the arrival of the cholo army was the factor which upset the practical financial equilibrium achieved by the Californians in the years just preceding, this statement of disbursements under Micheltorena's administration would banish it. The largest single allotment from the departmental funds was that of 127,000 pesos for the batallón. The presidial companies came next, with 13,000 pesos; then the artillery, with 11,000 pesos. At the foot of the list were the inválidos, among whom were distributed 36 pesos. (These faithful citizens, however, were doubtless living in sufficient comfort off their ranches and truck gardens.)

----

337 Calif., vol. 4, p. 402.
338 Ante, p. 296.
339 April 1, 1845, Departmental Treasury Account, in Larkin Doc., MS, vol. 3, #98.

The sun of governmental prosperity looked forth in 1845, when customs receipts reached the new peak of 140,000 pesos. The civil budget that year seems to have called for 56,000 pesos, including 14,000 pesos as the cost of collection and distribution. Officers' salaries amounted to 34,000 pesos.[340] A balance of 50,000 pesos therefore remained for the partial payment of soldiers and of something on account of debts, and, possibly, the laying by of that glorious prodigy -- a nest-egg.

Even the debt situation was not hopeless. What might be called th active debt -- that is, the debt incurred in the past two to three years -- was about 159,000 pesos. According to Larkin,[341] who had one of the largest claims, the amounts were:

```
Vallejo (special accounts)............17,474 pesos
Larkin...............................12,750
20 other private persons.............32,401
28 civil employees (salary accounts)..32,000
50 military officers including
     Vallejo (salary accounts)........45,000
Soldiers (salary accounts)...........19,000
                                    158,625 pesos
```

---

[340] Bancroft, Calif., vol. 4, pp. 560--61; and ante, p. 299, **Table VIII**.

[341] Official Corresp., MS, vol. 2, pp. 112--16.

In other words, the Californians were for the most part in debt to themselves. They had always shown a peculiarly sweet reasonableness in the trying matter of back salaries and old claims. This disposaition grew with the improvement in their private fortunes made possible by new opportunities in the land.[342] There is every reason to believe that if liquidation was delayed, the greater part of the debts of 1845 would have been written off the books by consent of the creditors -- as had frequently been done before.

The conclusion seems inescapable that, even handicapped as it was, the country would have worked out its financial salvation within a few years. The <u>hijos del país</u> had attacked their problems intelligently and resolutely. They had spared no effort or sacrifice. The volume of their trade, increasing with the growth in their productivity and buying power, was yielding ever higher revenues.

Perhaps the Recording Angel has somewhere filed, along with his tomes on What Has Been, sheafs of jottings on What Might Have Been. If so, it would be worth while to glimpse the pages devoted to the California that Might Have Been, of the years subsequent to 1845.

---

[342] See <u>post</u>, chap. V.

Lacking access to any such source, we can only note the final items of the mundane record at hand. Receipts from customs between January 1 and the April before the long-dreaded war broke were 26,826 pesos; disbursements were 32,566 pesos (including 11,552 pesos for extraordinary expenses); and on May 1, 1846, the treasury held a balance of 10,835 pesos.[343]

32. The Californios Had All the Answers

A very little research into the territory's fiscal situation reveals that the men of the country knew all the answers to their problems. Had circumstances permitted, they would have lost no time in transmuting those answers into reforms. But sheer physical weakness prevented the provisionally "free and sovereign state of California" from continuing free and sovereign. Once back under Mexican domination, her only recourse was to clamor insistently for alleviating action by the supreme government.

And clamor insistently she did. It is doubtful if the trained economists of today could point out the inherent fallacies and failures of California's fiscal system of a hundred years ago more accurately and comprehensively than did the territorials of the time. It is entirely outside the realm of probability that the economists of today would

---

[343] Dept. St. Pap., MS, vol. 13, pp. 16--17. The extraordinary expenses were for armaments and war supplies, ocean-freight on the same and the

be moved to anything like their vehemence in the matter

That vehemence had for its objective no half-way measures -- though immediate urgencies came in for a continual share of attention. What the people of California most earnestly demanded was the abrogation of the entire tariff-for-revenue system and substitution of a moderate tariff, at worst; at best, of free trade with some protective features, and property taxes.

The project of free trade for California was agitated in one quarter or another throughout the Mexican period. Even before the wars of independence had ended -- as early as 1820 -- Carlos María Bustamante, writing then as a monarchist, had urged that free trade could work the magic of raising cities in deserts. Human nature demanded property, liberty and security in return for labor. It was "absolutely necessary that the settlers be permitted to build up their private interests, which [opportunity] alone makes attractive any project or enterprise."344

---

costs of the voyage of the commissioner sent to secure them; and for 100 horses purchased from M. G. Vallejo -- undoubtedly as mounts for his soldiers.

344 <u>Medidas.</u>, MS, vol. 1, p. 156; and <u>see ante,</u> pp. 9--10.

In his statistical report of the Mexican empire, prepared under the regency, Tadeo Ortiz de Ayala similarly urged free trade as essential to the development of California.[345]

In California, Vallejo seems to have been the most consistent champion of tariff abolition, particularly as indispensable at San Francisco and Bodega for the development of the northern frontier, although he recommended it also for the territory in general. It would be tautologous to resume here all his correspondence at hand bearing on this subject. It seems sufficient to cite three letters of the spring of 1839, in which he pleaded with the President of the Republic, the Minister of War and the influential man of affairs Virmond to support the project of exempting from duties for ten years the cargoes of all vessels touching only at San Francisco. If this proposition could be given reality, the northern frontier, so long the subject of deep concern, could be populated without the expenditure of a *real* by the government, and the San Francisco Bay region, so tremendously important and on which all foreigners cast covetous eyes, could so be saved to the nation.[346]

----

[345] See *ante*, pp. 10--12, **passim.**

[346] March 10, 1839, Vallejo to Bustamante, in **Vallejo Doc.**, MS, vol. 7, #37; May 10, 1839, Vallejo to Min. of War, in **op. cit.**, #28; May 11, 1839, Vallejo to Virmond, in **op. cit.**, #60.

The appeal to Bustamante brought forth, several months later, the cordial agreement of that reassuring individual to "take up with the national Congress the privilege of duty-free import requested, asking it not only for the inhabitants of the frontier, but for all those of the Californian peninsula; for all are entitled to the paternal solicitude of the government."[347]

In 1845, the departmental assembly sought approval by the supreme government of a recommendation that duties on foreign goods be reduced at least 10%; that no class of goods be prohibited; and that national goods be entirely free.[348]

Until the sweeping reforms contemplated in California -- or such of them as Mexico would countenance -- had had time to become reliably productive, the country would of course have to be helped out with an allowance.[349] Vallejo, Alvarado, Castañares, Carrillo and others all made clear that the desired changes could not be ventured without such assistance. Therein lay the rub. For Mexico would not undertake to supply the subsidy.

----

[347] August 6, 1839, Bustamante to Vallejo, in *Vallejo Doc.*, MS, vol. 8, #11.

[348] July 16, 18, 1845, in *Leg. Rec.*, MS, vol. 4, pp. 94--95.

[349] See *ante*, pp. 248--49, 251.

To be sure, Mexico's own financial history had been unhappy; her stress -- public and private -- was severe. In 1831, bankruptcies were so prevalent, especially among nationals and aliens engaged in foreign trade, that Congress took action to check the rapid succession of "robberies under legal title."[350]

The government could not meet its most routine and fundamental obligations. "They make use of the war to claim that there is no money, but even when there was no war I was able to get nothing out of them, and now less," wrote Congressman Carrillo with solecistic emphasis; and, a little later: ". . . . for more than two months, no pay, for no money . . . . no means of paying a real."[351]

To multiply such illustrations of the supreme government's impecuniosity almost indefinitely, as might be done, would serve no purpose. There is no question that Mexico was unable to subsidize California. And there is no question that -- prize, as she was, to which foreign pioneers and foreign governments aspired -- California must have subsidy to maintain her organization for defense, until revenue reforms could be made productive.

----

[350] Oct. 6, 1831, C. Carrillo to J. de la Guerra, Carta #6, in Guerra Doc., MS, vol. 4, pp. 218--19.

[351] Oct. 12, 1831, Carrillo to de la Guerra, Carta #7, in op. cit., p. 222; Apr. 14, 1832, Carrillo to Guerra, Carta #12, in op. cit., p. 239.

One resource the territory did have -- rightfully her own -- which might have been utilized: the Pious Fund. Carrillo made earnest prayer for the utilization of part o the income from that endowment to tide the territory over its first difficult years of development.[352] Under Gomez Farías, the proceeds of the Fund were actually placed at the disposal of the Híjar and Padrés Colony. Santa Anna, however, foiled all such plans.[353] Bishop García Diego was promised Pious Fund aid in his religious labors for California's gente de razon; but that too, came to nothing,[354] as did the attempts of the departmental junta and diputado Andrés Castillero, in 1839--40, to collect revenues from Pious Fund estates for the payment of territorial expenses.[355] After all, California received no benefit from that source while under Mexican domination.

Many legal, moral and religious considerations clustered around the subject of Pious Fund distribution; and as will be shown later,[352] the trust had been maladministered and misapplied. Whether the wreck might have been made to support

---

352 See post, chap. VII.
353 See ante, pp. 107--8. 117.
354 Bancroft, Calif., vol. 4, p. 372.
355 Ibid., vol. 3, p. 590.

California while she reorganized her entire economy is a question probably unanswerable today. Mexico did not try to answer it in the '30s and '40s.

Throughout those years, the appeals for radical tariff revision, tax reform and temporary subsidy continued. The need of assistance would not last long. Granted relief from her present unfortunate position, the Department would within a few years produce sufficient to meet all her own needs, urged Alvarado.[356]

Reference to these subjects must be recurrent, in various connections; but two documents of the '40s set forth the Californian argument so concisely that they are included here in part, in translation.

The first is an excerpt from the congressional papers of California's *diputado* to Congress in 1844--45, Manuel Castañares: "California being still a colony, and needing development in all branches, it lacks that combination of revenues which other Departments enjoy, and needs the protection of the supreme government as yet, rather than the establishment of any sort of imposts. . . . . California requires exceptional legislation because of its lack of money, industry, population, its nascent commerce, its absence

---

[356] Dec. 12, 1840, Alvarado to Min. of Int., quoted Feb. 13, 1841, by Min. of War to Vallejo, in *Savage Doc.*, MS, vol. 4, #329.

of relations with adjacent Departments and its isolation from the rest of the Republic .... It should have some control over maritime duties. It is still and will be for some time a colony. It needs a tariff that will not be prohibitive or provocative of contraband, though when need arises to protect the department's artefacts, protective rules can be set for special cases."[357]

A letter from Vallejo to Bustamante argues further: "California has no source of revenue other than that of the customs. These are very inadequate and are causing the ruin of the country while they enrich the trading companies whose vessels ply this coast. Blaming the duties, which in fact are exorbitant, they raise prices scandalously, even on goods of the first necessity .... So it results that the system of high tariff, whether or not it is advantageous to the rest of the Republic, is ruinous for this department. What we need is a special tariff for California, or, better, none. This last proposition may seem reckless, at first glance, but when you consider this country, in its infancy, without industries of any sort, very poor in coin, though rich in fertility, and populated almost entirely by laborers, you will agree that the only way to carry on without frequent and considerable remittances

----

[357] Col. de Doc., pp. 29--30, 25--27.

from the national treasury . . . . is to levy a direct tax on productive property, based on the Department's budgetary needs. Thus, and with some subsidies from the national treasury remitted regularly, governmental income would be certain, and not haphazard as is the customs revenue. Salaries could be paid punctually, money would circulate, there would be an active commerce and export of farm products, and commodities would be easily purchased without ruining the consumers as today. Permit me to recommend this matter particularly to your attention . . . ."[358]

Back in the eighteenth century, Spain had experimented with a property tax in New Spain. But that had been directed at the Indians, who till then had been forced to render tribute; and the quality of the lands assigned, together with the natural indolence of the tribesmen, had foreordained failure.[359]

In California, no tax had ever been assessed on property according to its value.[360] It does not appear from available data that Mexico gave any consideration to recommendations of such a tax; nor could the territorials legally reconstitute their revenue system on such a basis, on their own

---

[358] Nov. 22, 1845, Vallejo Doc., vol. 12, #157, pp. 3--5, Prudon draft.

[359] Priestley, Mex. Nation, p. 75

[360] Bancroft, Calif., vol. 3, p. 380.

initiative. It is interesting, however, that projects to establish what would have been practically a property tax under the existing law, for municipal revenue, were essayed by the Californians for at least a dozen years before the conquest. This impost was to take the form of an annual ground-rent, assessable on small farms to be laid out or already being operated on town commons and other suburban lands. Provision for the survey of such rental properties and their letting for short terms or on protracted or perpetual lease were the subject of the first two articles of the Plan de Propios y Arbitrios of 1834.[361]

Ancient law assigned four leagues' extent to each pueblo. The lands surrounding the areas of actual settlement were used as common pasture; for purposes of revenue -- as, for instance, the sale of wood; or for such other disposition as the ayuntamiento might choose to make. Sometimes use of portions of pueblo lands was extended to citizens; as when, in 1842, the juez and sub-prefect of San Jose' were authorized to license honest and industrious pobladores to cultivate suburban fields.[362] Sometimes provisional grants of pueblo tracts were made.[363] The Plan of 1834 included provision for a considerable grantees' tax.[364] It does not appear,

---

[361] See ante, p. 197.
[362] San Jose' Arch., MS, vol. 2, pp. 47--48.
[363] Bancroft, Calif., vol. 3, pp. 708--9, n. 6.
[364] See ante, p. 197, Art. 3. This fee seems to have been payable only at the time of allotment, not annually.

however, that in California public holdings were extensively developed as rental properties.

The reason is perhaps not far to seek. Grants of regular home sites with patches of land for subsistence farming had at first supplied the needs of the settlers. Coincidentally with the development of markets for surplus produce, mission and frontier tracts began to be opened up for occupation. It was from those outlying lands that the great Mexican grants were carved. As California had not yet developed a middle class of any proportions, there seem to have been few renters to occupy the more modest suburban properties, the subsistence homesteads with which the <u>pobladores</u> were regularly endowed continuing to meet the needs and opportunities of the humbler population.[365]

Endowment whether with wide estates or with the small home and farm sites, except under certain conditions not obtaining in California, conferred on the grantee neither full title nor control.[366] Technically, only the usufruct

---

[365] The writer makes no claim to the last word on these matters. The subjects are almost untouched, inviting investigation.

[366] Land grants and the land laws are discussed <u>post</u>, secs. 50--53.

of the land was his. Therefore, the project to place on a rental basis lands which were virtually as much the occupants' as the regular grants were the grantees', came close to the property tax idea, and, once established, would have paved the way for a territorial tax on land grants outside pueblo bounds.

The establishment of rates for the use of pueblo lands was recommended anew in 1845 by the Los Angeles ayuntamiento, for the action of the diputación.[367]

This need for the town council to submit its proposals for raising local revenues to the departmental assembly, which in turn had "powers so minute and limited" that it could "not do much for the communities"[368] affords a good example of the governmental paralysis which kept California inert.[369] She had not the power to direct her destiny as she knew it must be directed if she was to survive. She could only struggle against the disabilities that prostrated her, and cry ceaselessly -- to Mexico and to herself: "The first thing necessary is to create funds and population -- all else is impracticable theory."[370]

---

[367] L. A. Arch., MS, vol. 5, pp. 289--90; Bancroft, Calif., vol. 4, p. 643, n. 12; ante, p. 206.

[368] Castañares, Col. de Doc., p. 26.

[369] On the territory's political handicaps and efforts see post, Chap. VI.

[370] Jan. 20, 1838 (1837?), Vallejo to Alvarado, in Vallejo, Ordenes, #3.

CHAPTER IV: ARMS AND ALARMS

33. <u>Cholos</u>..................................pp. 337--344
34. "Starvation and Nakedness"............ 344--354
35. Breakdown of the Presidial Organization........................ 354--364
36. Decline of Buildings and Armaments.... 364--371
37. Aspirations and Actualities........... 371--377
38. The Missions and the Military......... 378--380
39. National Ranches...................... 381--385
40. The Sons of the Country and the Presidios........................ 385--389
41. The Californians Favored a Big Army... 389--403
42. Citizen Soldiers...................... 404--410
43. Citizen Subsidization of the Army..... 411--415
44. A Californian Navy -- Envisioned...... 416--419
45. "Indians!"............................ 419--438
46. The <u>Vecinos</u> as Indian-Campaigners..... 438--442
47. Projects and Problems of Indian Defense........................... 442--447

CHAPTER IV: Arms and Alarms[1]

Severe limitation in her attempts at defense of her domain was one of the most direct consequences of Mexico's human and financial dearth. Her expeditionary forces made a poor showing, qualitatively as well as numerically. Even the officers whom she sent to California were less uniformly of that sturdy and patient reliability which seems to have characterized Spain's colonial officialdom.

As for the rank and file, they derived, notoriously, from los de abajo, ranging the entire gamut of the blood spectrum and of human wretchedness. Although they included very many criminals, they were by no means all of that class. For the greater part, however, they were utterly unsuited to their dual rôles of soldiers and pioneers. Inability of the government to feed and clothe them decently, let alone to provide them with the equipment of their superimposed callings, fostered in them discontent and turbulence,

---

[1] Owing to the quantity of statistical materials used in this chapter, Bancroft is a constantly recurring authority almost throughout. The purpose of the chapter, however, is not to present new material, so much as to assemble and interpret data copiously scattered through Bancroft's pages.

and a natural propensity to forage for subsistence not otherwise to be assured.

The trouble began in Echeandía's time, many of his soldiers sharing the stigma and frailties which handicapped the civilian settlers (other than those of the Híjar and Padrés Colony) introduced by Mexico.[2]

It does not appear that Victoria, who had been stationed in Lower California as comandante principal for several years before becoming governor of California,[3] brought any military reinforcements other than, undoubtedly, a small personal escort.

With Figueroa, in 1832, came some 75 officers and men. Bancroft says that the soldiers were "cholos" of a not very desirable class . . . . but lately released from prison and pardoned for revolutionary attempts."[4]

---

[2] Bancroft, Calif., vol. 3, p. 15.

[3] Ibid., p. 181.

[4] Ibid., p. 236. The term cholo, in American provincial Spanish, meant the offspring of a Spanish father and Indian mother; but according to Bancroft (Calif., vol. 2, p. 255, n. 14) was never used in California except in an offensive sense, with reference to character rather than to race. It was applied only to "riff-raff" that came from Mexico.

Gutierrez, whom Figueroa, on relinquishing the joint command in 1835, named gefe militar, received that appointment by reason of being the ranking military officer in California, where he had been stationed from the time of Figueroa's own advent. His assumption of office meant no influx of new troops.[5]

Nor does Chico seem to have brought any considerable defense increment, although he came from Mexico as the appointee of the new centralist government of 1835.[6]

Micheltorena, however, who relieved Alvarado and Vallejo in 1842, headed a battalion which, after various vicissitudes, probably reached California some 300 strong, and was augmented later by 40 or 50 apprehended deserters.

Having projected the sending of as many as 1,000 to 1,500 troops, Mexico finally concentrated on raising 500, of whom 200 were to be regular soldiers, and 300, convicts. Since criminals could not legally be recruited into the army, Santa Anna's order for the impressment of the 300 from Mexican prisons eschewed reference to the military career designed for them. Instead, it specified, euphemistically, that part or all of the sentences of those deported might be commuted in recognition of good conduct

---

[5] Bancroft, Calif., vol. 3, pp. 298--99, 414.
[6] Ibid., pp. 420--21.

on the journey to the territory or of "services which they might render." The implication was probably clear enough to all concerned, doubtless the service referred to consisting, says Bancroft, "of an engagement to enlist as soon as a pardon had freed them from all taint of criminality! At any rate, they were soldiers when they landed in California."[7]

Of the 300 prospective subjects of this dubious clemency only some 150 were actually obtained, or else the balance deserted before sailing time. At Guadalajara, Micheltorena was to secure from General Paredes, commanding in Jalisco, the 200 regular soldiers destined for California service. Paredes, concludes Bancroft, "took advantage of the opportunity to get rid of all the useless and unmanageable men in his army, filling up the number with a forced levy of recruits from the farms near Guadalajara."

Thus was composed the Battalón Fijo de Californias. But not all reached California. "Many succeeded in escaping on the road and at San Blas and Mazatlan . . . . I suppose there were about three hundred who finally sailed from Mazatlan, though there is no accurate record of the number extant; and there were forty or fifty of the deserters who were arrested and sent to California two years later."[8]

----

[7] Bancroft, Calif., vol. 4, pp. 287--88.
[8] Bancroft, Calif., vol. 4, pp. 288--89.

Arrived in the territory, Micheltorena gave several weeks to organizing and drilling his battalion. "It was long before any considerable portion could be trusted with weapons; but from the first the battalion showed marked proficiency in foraging for supplies by night. Moreover, on overhauling the munitions it was found that the bullets as a rule would not fit the muskets, and had to be remelted. Financial obstacles were also encountered from the start, making it difficult to support the troops sent to protect the country."[9]

Accordingly, Micheltorena's *cholos*, as they came to be generally referred to, entered upon that career of hen-coop and kitchen raiding for which they were chiefly to be remembered, and which in large measure incited the Californians to their revolt of 1845.

Such was the nature of the reinforcements sent by Mexico to bolster up the failing presidial organization in its arduous duty of holding the *territorio más precioso* against an increasingly interested world. Small wonder that throughout the Mexican régime the sons and particularly the daughters of the country looked with apprehension on

---

[9] *Ibid.*, p. 290.

their "protectors" de la otra banda. Complaints like that of San Diego in 1836 that, during the absence of the townsmen on an expedition against the Indians, the soldiers committed thefts and outrages, were typical.[10] The visitation of Micheltorena's cholos was the long-drawn-out and emphatic climax to a situation dating from Mexico's taking over of California.[11]

The consequence, had it not been for the war with the United States, would doubtless have been the republic's loss of the territory by secession. In the months just preceding the conquest, the Californios were giving vigorous consideration to the question of their political future. Larkin reported confidentially to his superiors at Washington in 1844 that the natives feared the cholos more than foreign invasion; and that Micheltorena, in case of war, could depend only on his 250 Mexican troops to follow him, the 150 Californian soldiers and the 1,000 citizens available as militia not being disposed to fight for a government in which they took very little interest.[12]

---

[10] Bancroft, Calif., vol. 4, p. 67.

[11] Alvarado(Hist. de Calif., MS, vol. 3, pp. 11, 12) traced animosities arising from the cholo plague back to the arrival of the San Blas Company following the Bouchard invasion. (See post, pp. 355--57).

[12] Aug. 18, 1844, Larkin to Sec. of State, in Larkin, Official Corresp., MS, vol. 2, p. 8.

Commenting on the cholos, Bancroft remarks that they were not as bad as painted by the Californians [who regarded them as desperate characters], nor as might have been expected -- despite their pilferings of "poultry and other edibles, as well as of other miscellaneous articles that could be utilized in barracks." They were bad enough, however, "to become an intolerable nuisance to all citizens whose houses, stores or ranchos were within reach." But he doubts "if any soldiers could be restrained by any discipline -- certainly not by Mexican discipline -- from such excesses, when not paid and very inadequately fed and clothed. As Micehltorena wrote to the government, it was hard to shoot a hungry, unpaid soldier for pilfering food; and there was, moreover, no little danger, if severe measures were resorted to, of transforming the convict batallon into an armed band of roving marauders, with the lives of the Californians largely at their mercy."

The unfortunate governor and commander, therefore, "listened patiently to complaints; paid for all losses so long as he had any money . . . .; and not only chided offenders, but often had them arrested and flogged, always retaining, however, the friendship and respect of all, and thus a certain control over them which it would have been dangerous to lose . . . . It is true enough that Micheltorena was an easy-going, indolent officer; and it is possible that a more energetic man might have managed the matter better, though difficult to say exactly how."[13]

34. "Starvation and Nakedness"

A little cash would doubtless have quieted most of the restless spirits of the conscript and convict army. But a little cash was the hardest thing in the world to elicit from Mexico. Nor were the *cholos* the only sufferers.

It will be remembered that the presidial companies had sustained a decade of abandonment by Spain, during the wars of independence. Indeed, shortages of pay dated back more than another decade. In 1794, $12,000 was owing the Santa Bárbara Company. Not until 1795, were the final orders issued for the settling of the old accounts of the first expeditions -- of 1769--74. "Many soldiers were now dead and their descendants scattered," says Bancroft. "Whenever the sum due was large, the heirs were to be sought; otherwise the money was to be spent in masses for the souls of the dead pioneers. In 1797 Borica in the north and Arrillaga at Loreto were still at work on the accounts of the past decade." In 1801, the governor doubted that a

---

[13] Bancroft, *Calif.*, vol. 4, pp. 365--67, *passim*.

settlement would ever be reached.[14]

The pleas of acting governor Sola, and Echeandía's intercession, within a month of his arrival in California, in behalf of the long-deprived colonial army, were without practical result.[15] Yet throughout the period, the desperate condition of the army and the inadequacy of armaments and fortifications were pressed on the attention of the supreme authorities in countless appeals from Mexican and Californian officials and private individuals.

Bancroft's gleanings, from many sources, of California's defense needs throughout Mexico's rule, make a gloomy record.

In 1826, Echeandía complained that only the officers who had come with him were being paid, to the great discontent of the rest; and two petitions from the soldiers set forth that they were getting la ración, nada más, as in years past, despite promises of the government.

In 1827, the comisaría had no funds with which to supply blankets. There was great lack of food and money, and no possibility of a loan. Echeandía met this emergency by personally lending $600. Toward the end of the year, the national government decreed a loan, of which part was to go to California for relief. The decree seems to have been the end of the matter.

---

[14] Ibid., vol. 1, p. 631.
[15] See ante, pp. 19--20.

In 1823, the troops were reported to be naked, in great want and unable to collect any part of their dues; and the governor advised the comandante general that no supplies had been sent from Mexico for a considerable time.[16]

At Monterey, that year, a large part of the cavalry, joined by the mission escoltas, struck for their pay and marched out of the presidio, taking their weapons. J. J. Vallejo said[17] that these soldiers were pitiably destitute; and Amador agreed, adding that some deserted in order to seek a livelihood en los campos.[18] Echeandía ordered their commandant to try them in court martial, but if he could not master them, to offer pardon; and reported to the Minister of War that he hoped by the aid of the artillery lately arrived to prevent further disorders of the sort, but that he needed officers.[19]

At San Diego, too, the garrison made protest against hunger and nakedness, and asked for something on account of back pay. The commanding officer, Lieutenant Argüello, attempted to put five spokesmen in irons. The troops,

---

[16] Bancroft, Calif., vol. 3, pp. 56--57, n. 1.
[17] J. J. Vallejo, Reminiscencias históricas, MS, pp. 15--16.
[18] J. M. Amador, Memorias, MS, pp. 86--87.
[19] Bancroft, Calif., vol. 3, pp. 66--67.

however, demanded that he release them, whereupon the five took their plea to the general. He promised justice; but the only result of the affair seems to have been the transference of the articulate ones to other presidios.[20] If this seems like harsh and faithless treatment, it must be remembered that the officers were faced with the serious problem of maintaining discipline, and that their promises of succor, as the soldiers well knew, were contingent on Mexico's response to their desperate, continuous pleas.

In San Francisco, too, the year 1828 seems to have been marked by insubordination, although the records give no particulars.

In 1829, when protesting that there were no means of feeding the convicts being sent to California, Echeandía declared that it was impossible, even, to feed the garrisons.[21]

That was the year of the Solís revolt, which, starting at Monterey as a demonstration by destitute soldiers, was first put down and then -- renewed and extended northward to San Francisco and southward to Santa Bárbara -- took on the appearance of a full-fledged Californian rebellion

----

[20] Bancroft, *Calif.*, vol. 2, p. 549, n. 17.
[21] Sept. 18, 1829, Echeandía to Min. of War, in *Dept. Rec.*, MS, vol. 7, pp. 38--40.

against all *de la otra banda.* During and after the revolt, Echeandía continued his appeals to the Minister of War for men and money --with no more success than before.[22]

The extent of Mexico's delinquency toward her troops is indicated in even the fragments of the *habilitados'* accounts for those years which are available. In 1825, $50,148 was owing the artillery company, alone, since 1822. But payments to all the troops for the years 1820--27 totalled only $50,894. At about that time (1827--30), the various army payrolls and the various payments on account were, in round numbers, as follows:[23]

Table X

Military Salary List and Payments on Account, 1820--30

Unit	Monthly Salary List, 1827--30	Yearly Salary List, 1827--30
Artillery	$ 725	$ 8,700
San Blas Company	460	5,520
Mazatecan "	850	10,200
4 Presidial Companies, $1500 each	6,000	72,000
	$8,035	$96,420

Total Payments, 1820--27...$50,894
Average annual payments,
 1820--27 (7 years).......$ 7,271

---

[22] Bancroft, *Calif.*, vol. 3, pp. 67--84, *passim*; and see *post*, chap. VI.

[23] Bancroft, *Calif.*, vol. 2, p. 672, n. 39, citing from various accounts.

That is to say, at a time when the army's wage budget totalled more than $96,000 a year, the army managed to collect an average of about $7,200 a year -- or 7½% of its due: less than its regular monthly payroll.

The wonder is that more officers and men did not follow the example of the lieutenant who in 1841 employed an attorney to collect for him $1,335 -- back pay for four years and ten months -- from the territorial treasury.[24] Doubtless the futility of any such effort is a principal explanation of the lack of evidence of numerous such proceedings.

As for the officers and men on the retired list, it is recorded as of December 1833 that they had not been paid for many years. At about the same time, it was ruled that army officers might have certificates with which to negotiate for their pay.[25]

The San Francisco presidio mutinied again, in 1833, joined by the Santa Clara *escolta*. The grievance was chiefly lack of food and clothing. "No force seems to have been used," Bancroft concluded, but "by irregular and unmilitary methods" the soldiers sought to be rid of their *comandante*, Vallejo, to whom they attributed the blame for their privations. Although Vallejo demanded severe penalties for this

---

[24] Bancroft, Calif., vol. 4, p. 198, n. 18.
[25] Ibid., vol. 3, p. 379, n. 20.

breach of discipline and loyalty, the members of the court martial were satisfied to order the transfer of the eight ringleaders to other presidios,[26] as had been done before in at least one similar case. In view of their extremity and hopelessness, it speaks highly for the troops that they were not more vindictive in their demonstrations.

For, so far from improving, matters went from bad to worse. Throughout 1834, complaints of destitution in the army came in frequently, especially from the south.[27] In the spring of that year, Alférez Juan Salazar of San Diego could not go to Monterey for lack of a shirt and jacket, having only a poor cloak to cover the frightful condition of his trousers. If the forthright simplicity of that report provokes a smile today, poor Salazar doubtless saw nothing humorous in his plight. This is the more likely as he was not a common soldier, with small dignity to uphold, but _alférez, habilitado,_ and more often than any other during the decade (1831--40) is named as acting commandant.[28]

The next year, Commander General Gutierrez complained

---

[26] Bancroft, _Calif._, vol. 3, p. 248.
[27] _Ibid._, pp. 258--59.
[28] _Ibid._, pp. 609--10.

to Governor Castro that the troops were getting not even half-rations.[29]

In 1836, a year of severe Indian ravages in the south, complaints from San Diego were "frequent and loud" that the army could afford no protection, for lack of weapons, supplies and pay.[30] The soldiers themselves, the San Luís Rey detachment along with them, struck for cash or provisions.[31] The Los Angeles *ayuntamiento* resolved that the troops which had been asked for and which had arrived should go to San Gabriel as there was no food for them. But presently the squad at San Gabriel refused to serve longer without clothing; and their commanding officer, lacking means for their maintenance, applied for permission to place them on furlough so that they might earn their own livings.[32]

In 1837, over $30,000 was due the San Francisco Company in back pay.[33]

In 1839, Captain Guerra petitioned for $12,000 of back pay[34] -- doubtless in the hope of collecting a fraction of that amount.

----

[29] Bancroft, *Calif.*, vol. 3, p. 379, n. 20.
[30] *Ibid.*, vol. 4, p. 67.
[31] *Ibid.*, vol. 3, p. 483.
[32] *Ibid.*, pp. 631, n. 1, "1836"; 636, n. 4, "1836."
[33] *Ibid.*, p. 701, n. 4, "1837."
[34] *Ibid.*, p. 584, n. 9.

In the spring of 1841, Guerra, called upon to send troops from Santa Barbara to Los Angeles for duty, had to let them go "barefooted and badly equipped". By midsummer, his successor in command found it necessary to order the retirement of the soldiers from service to earn their own livelihoods. (Ten men were retained, as a prison guard, at the request of the juez.)[35]

This method of feeding an army was a common resort of California's harassed officialdom. Sometimes leave was granted for definite periods -- as in 1828, when eight men of the Monterey Company were given three months in which to pick up some earnings.[36] Sometimes the release amounted to a temporary discharge, or "provisional retirement," the men being subject to call when needed.[37]

When official authorization was withheld, the hungry troops frequently went absent without leave to forage for themselves. In 1839, the San Luis Rey escolta of eight men of the San Diego unit quit the service -- informally and against orders -- to seek a living. At the company headquarters in San Diego, only one soldier remained. That was the year of which Vallejo recorded on August 7th that

---

[35] Bancroft, Calif., vol. 4, p. 641, n. 19.
[36] Ibid., vol. 3, p. 57, n. 1.
[37] Ibid., vol. 2., p. 709.

"'not a cent's worth of anything,'" had been received for the artillery; and of which Bancroft remarks: "Military correspondence is devoted almost exclusively to complaints of destitution."[38]

In 1843, Micheltorena reported that his men were living on half a real (6¼¢) a day [presumably apiece]; and that his officers were receiving only one-fifth of their pay.[39] In view of the commissioned men's financial stringency, it may be surmised that the Mexican custom -- "not known in California before this time, I think," says Bancroft[40] -- of billeting officers with civilian families, inflicted an onerous obligation on the householders, and aggravated their sense of grievance against those de la otra banda.

In 1845, Congressman Castañares wrote to the Minister of Relations of Micheltorena's plight in December, 1844: "He had in his command 195 men destitute of all supplies, with arms of various calibres, with 4 rounds of cartridges to the man, with 30 pesos as his only means of purchasing provisions for his men and some 20 officers, confined in the port of Monterey, and without anyone to give him credit for so much as a pound of meat."[41] The italics are Don

---

[38] Bancroft, Calif., vol. 3, p. 592, n. 28; ibid., pp. 609-10

[39] Ibid., vol. 4, p. 351.

[40] Ibid., p. 355.

[41] March 24, 1845, Castañares to Min. of Rel., in Col. de Doc., p. 65.

Manuel's.

Volumes might be filled with details of the privations of the troops and the impoverishment of their officers; and with appeals from various quarters for governmental relief. Such intensive consideration goes beyond the present purpose. It is sufficient to note here that Vallejo did not exaggerate when, toward the close of the period, he wrote to Bustamante that his "incessant prayer" to the government had been for troops and money, "but the first without the second is vicious, and only by means of the two can California emerge from the circle of peril which is closing round her."[42]

Don Guadalupe's appeals to Mexico, although the most consistently vigorous and unremitting, as was natural in view of his large and protracted military responsibilities, were matched over shorter periods by those of every governor and congressman, and, on numerous occasions, by those of the diputación and asamblea. In short, no effort seems to have been spared in California to bring to the attention of the home government the desperate need of and for troops.

35. Breakdown of the Presidial Organization

The year 1820 was a peak year of army strength in California. During the preceding ten years, the rosters

---

[42] Nov. 22, 1845, M. G. Vallejo to Bustamante, in Vallejo Doc., MS, vol. 12, #157, p. 8, Prudon draft.

listed an almost unvarying 410 officers and men, including those on active service, <u>inválidos</u> and veterans. Spain's annual expense for this force was $89,000 -- "an expense," says Bancroft, "rendered much less burdensome by the fact that it was never paid." There was also a militia artillery company, several times called into service, which numbered 82 men in 1816 but had fallen off to 64 in 1819.[43]

The Bouchard scare in 1818 startled Viceroy Apodaca into dispatching to California's aid in the summer of 1819 two shiploads of troops and munitions. The reinforcements took the form of an infantry company from San Blas and a company of cavalry from Mazatlan, each approximately 100 strong. These two units came to be known as the two auxiliary companies, since for several years they retained identity apart from the regular presidial companies. In 1820 arrived a further reinforcement of 15 or 20 artillerymen.

Although continuing as nominally separate entities for a time, the San Blas recruits and the Mazatecos were

---

[43] Bancroft, <u>Calif.</u>, vol. 2, pp. 422--23.

were within a few weeks of arrival distributed pretty evenly among the four presidios, which were accordingly increased by about 50 men each.[44]

The Mazatlan cavalry, commanded by Captain Pablo de la Portilla, was "composed of a good class of men," Bancroft discovered, "who subsequently gave no grounds for complaint." In contrast, the San Blas infantrymen, under command of Captain José Antonio Navarrete, were, except for their officers, "emphatically a bad lot," chiefly recruited by press gangs from the lépero class in Nueva Galicia. They were "altogether ignorant of military discipline or the use of arms." Before the end of 1820, sixteen of the number were returned to San Blas because of insubordination.[45] These were the cholos to whom Alvarado traced[46] the beginnings of the Californian-Mexican antipathy which was to become so marked and so consequential.

The new vicious element, augmented by more of the ilk brought by Echeandía, Figueroa and Micheltorena, could not help but undermine the effectiveness of the Presidial organization, especially as the cholos presently outnumbered the

----

[44] Bancroft, Calif., vol. 2, pp. 252--55.
[45] Ibid.
[46] Hist. de Calif., MS, vol.   , pp. 11--12.

"old reliables." The dissolution of the standing army was practically completed by the absolute necessity of allowing the troops liberty in which to support themselves.

Although the available data, fragmentary and occasional, does not lend itself to uniformity of presentation, the following tabulation may help to make clear the breakdown of California's presidial organization during the years 1821--41:[47]

Table XI

Decrease of Presidial Forces, 1821--41

	1821	1831	1841
Presidial Companies (Cavalry)	410	220	100 (Sonoma, Monterey and Santa Barbara)
Mazatecos (Cavalry)	100	50 (from 1828 considered infantry)	"Has been for many years dispersed" so that soldiers might be self supporting
San Blas Company (Infantry)	100	40	From 1841 merged with presidial companies
Artillery (including Militia)	100	40 (exclusive of militia)	24
Invalidos and Veterans	Included above	60	Included above
	710	410	124

The above table calls for some analysis, lest it be interpreted wrongly. The figures indicate, not the force

---

[47] 1821: Bancroft, Calif., vol. 2, pp. 189--90; 422--23; 675. 1831: Ibid., pp. 672--73; 675. 1841: Ibid.,

on active service, but the regulars in service plus the reserve corps of veterans and *inválidos* subject to call in emergency, and the artillery militia. It is not possible, always, to isolate the various elements, due to incomplete data. In 1831, however, the *inválidos* are listed separately, as 60 -- reducing the number actually on duty to 350, which is again, quite possibly, too high, as Bancroft supplemented faulty records with a liberal estimate of the strength of the two auxiliary companies.

It must also be remembered that although army statistics are grouped around the four original presidios and, after the mid-'30s, Sonoma, there was no such massing of the troops at those five points as the bare statement of company numbers seems to indicate. Each presidio had to share its men with the missions and civil settlements in its district, for whose protection it was responsible.

The few hundred troops had to cover, in other words, not five points, but twenty-five or more. As will be seen,[48] the Indian danger alone made it imperative that each of those points have what protection could be afforded;

---

p. 675; vol. 3, p. 592, n. 28; vol. 4, pp. 197--98.

[48] *Post*, secs. 45, 46, 47.

while foreign intrusion had to be met along six hundred miles of coastline; from the Columbia; and at eastern approaches ranging from Yuma to the overland routes into the Sacramento country. The resultant dissipation of an "army" inconsiderable enough in its full strength, limited the force at any given point to a mere escolta or squad.

In 1830, for example, the San Diego presidial roster showed 120 men. But of those, 15 were inválidos, about half of whom were not even in barracks, but made their homes at the pueblo; and about half the remaining force was detailed to guard duty at the missions of the district. We have the actual figures of distribution for an unspecified year a little earlier:[49]

Table XII

Distribution of San Diego Presidial Forces, 1828, ca.

Presidio	35
Mission San Diego	5
" San Juan Capistrano	6
" San Luís Rey	8
" San Gabriel	11
Total on active service	65

The number of inválidos on reserve is not indicated.

Although the presidio was abandoned some time in the '30s, the buildings lying in ruins by 1839, a last trace of the old presidial organization at San Diego remains in a

---

49   Bancroft, Calif., vol. 2, p. 544.

report of 1842 referring to a total force of 14 men without arms or ammunition. In that same year, there was nothing to prevent Captain Phelps of the hide-drogher "Alert" from spiking the guns of the fort (which were undoubtedly "out of service" in any case), on hearing that Jones had taken Monterey. "After 1842," says Bancroft, "there is nothing in the records on company, officers, or military finance except an occasional complaint that there were neither soldiers nor arms for defense."[50]

Thanks to the patriotic devotion of Captain José de la Guerra y Noriega, for nearly thirty years (from 1815) commandant at Santa Bárbara, the presidial organization at that point was maintained as effectively as possible. In 1830, Bancroft estimates, about 80 men were quartered at the presidio, while about 20 were on detached duty. But of the 80, about a dozen were invalidos, and about 20 were engaged in earning their livings, for lack of rations and pay.[51]

Till about the middle '30s, Captain Guerra managed to retain a nominal roster of 30 to 40 rank and file, with half a dozen artillerymen and as many Mazatecos; and some 15 or 20 inválidos appear on the payrolls. Thereafter, the force was about half as large. "But in both periods more

---

[50] Calif., vol. 4, pp. 320; 617--18.
[51] Ibid., vol. 2, pp. 572--73.

than half the men were not actually serving as soldiers . . . ."[52] In other words, the active force numbered not much more than a score, during the first half of the decade, and hardly more than a dozen during the second half.

In 1841 and 1842, the inválidos had to be counted to make up a total of 10 to 15 actually at the presidio, though the rolls still showed 34 to 48 rank and file. Early in the second year of the decade, Captain Guerra, past sixty and worn out by the unequal struggle for military preparedness, retired after a service of nearly forty-five years. Two or three months later, his successor in command of the post was forced to dismiss all but 10 of the soldiers, to support themselves.[53]

Of the 120 enrolled in the Monterey presidial company in 1830, 20 were inválidos and 40 or more were detailed about at missions, pueblos and ranchos in need of protection,[54] leaving about 60 effectives at headquarters.

During the next decade, the company varied very greatly, ranging from 20 to 50, including inválidos, in the old presidial organization; an artillery force of 4 men, generally; and an infantry detachment of about 25;

---
[52] Bancroft, Calif., vol. 3, p. 651.
[53] Bancroft, Calif., vol. 4, pp. 640--41.
[54] Ibid., vol. 2, p. 609.

at most, therefore, 79, including <u>inválidos</u> and the <u>escoltas</u> on detached duty.[55]

During 1841--45, the regular cavalry force was listed at anywhere from 20 to 58, although an official report of 1842 gives only 9 cavalrymen available. These were of course augmented -- or overwhelmed -- by Micheltorena's battalion of <u>cholos</u>, originally 300 strong. Although the presidio had disappeared, a <u>castillo</u> or fort was maintained, mounting 3 or 4 effective guns and manned by a dozen artillerymen, more or less. Bancroft found the records too confused and fragmentary to permit further analysis.[56]

At San Francisco, in 1821--30, the effective military force seems to have been about 45, with 25 more on <u>escolta</u> duty, and about 7 <u>inválidos</u> living at San José.[57]

During the next five years, about 10 to 18 cavalrymen remained at the presidio, with about 8 artillerymen; while the <u>escoltas</u> at missions Santa Clara, San José, San Rafael and San Francisco Solano accounted for 15 to 20 more men. Six or 8 <u>inválidos</u> helped to lengthen out the roster.

---

[55] <u>Ibid.</u>, vol. 3, p. 671.
[56] <u>Calif.</u>, vol. 4, pp. 652--56.
[57] <u>Ibid.</u>, vol. 2, pp. 584--86.

In 1835, the presidio on the peninsula was practically abandoned, only 2 or 3 men under an __alférez__ remaining until 1836, the rest of the company being transferred to Sonoma. In 1837, "San Francisco was [for a time] abandoned by the regular soldiers, but for an occasional visit by an inspecting officer; and the mission __escoltas__ were also recalled."[58]

A little later, however, Vallejo succeeded in reestablishing there 9 or 10 soldiers of the Sonoma Company, with an __alférez__ and a sergeant. Visitors' reports rarely agreed with the rosters as to the presence of more than 2 or 3 at any one time, reports Bancroft;[59] which is doubtless explained by the fact that the missing soldiers were off on the business of earning their livings.

The Sonoma Company, organized about 1835, had been built up to about 50 men by 1840, and was maintained at that strength probably to the time of its disbandment by Vallejo in 1844.[60]

But little can be added here in the way of regular army statistics, except to say that in 1841 -- a year in which California's imminent subjugation was pretty

---

[58] Bancroft, __Calif.__, vol. 3, pp. 700--2.

[59] __Ibid.__, vol. 4, p. 67.

[60] __Ibid.__, vol. 3, p. 702; vol. 4, pp. 677--78.

definitely indicated -- the three remaining presidial companies (at Sonoma, Monterey and Santa Bárbara) mustered only about 100 cavalrymen (including inválidos) and 24 artillerymen.[61]

Presidial history throughout the Mexican period indicates, in retrospect, but the continuance of a quantitative and qualitative deterioration which was already well under way in the first years of the nineteenth century. The early cavalry organizations had broken down by Echeandia's time, wrote Osio. ". . . . the greater portion of the soldiers who were entitled to be called distinguidos by reason of their honorable records (honradez) had disappeared from the ranks, and the replacements were a vicious and abandoned set (hombres perdidos, llenos de vicios); nor did they own their own horses and accoutrements, like the old timers, who presented at reviews eight service horses (caballos de lista) of their own, and could even present twenty-five or more."[62]

36. Decline of Buildings and Armaments

The melancholy business remains of noting the steady decline of fortifications and armaments. This collapse might of course be left to inference, in view of the

---

[61] Bancroft, Calif., vol. 4, pp. 197--98.
[62] Osio, Hist. de Calif., MS, pp. 120--21.

shortage of men and money. But some intimation of the extent of the calamity is germane to a consideration of the ineffectuality of California's resistance to invasion, military and "peaceful."

Adobe defense works are none too durable. Storm and earthquake work havoc with them. Even under favorable circumstances, disintegration is fairly rapid, unless repairs are kept up. Repair work calls for man-power, and for the means to support that man-power while it labors non-productively. The work of ruin had therefore already well advanced when Mexico inherited the territory; for Spain's decline and California's isolation during the wars of independence had produced that dearth of men and means which was to remain the rule until a nation superlatively blest with those resources should take over the country.

As early as 1824, the <u>diputación</u> was agonizing over the deplorable condition of the forts at Monterey and San Diego. Other means of repair lacking, it was decided to appoint a competent person at each pueblo and presidio to watch for and report to the governor vagabond, lazy and idle persons, who would then be set to work on the defenses at a cost of only half a <u>real</u> per day for rations. If sufficient labor could not be recruited promptly by that device, the missionaries were to be asked for Indian workmen.63

In 1826, a commission composed of Captain Portilla, Domingo Carrillo and Lieutenant Romualdo Pacheco reported the San Diego presidial buildings in "a lamentably ruinous condition." Repairs would cost at least $40,000. The fort at Point Guijarros, though hardly in better case, might be put in repair for only $10,000.64

In 1827, a series of earthquake shocks damaged buildings in the Santa Barbara military reservation.65 At about the same time, Captain Beechey visited the Monterey and San Francisco presidios. He made the interesting comparison: "The [Monterey] presidio is in better condition than that of San Francisco, still as a place of defense it is quite useless."66

In 1829, Echeandía wrote despairingly to the Minister of War: "In Alta California there is no presidio, for the four [places] which bear the name are were squares of adobe huts, in ruins, where with their families are quartered the reserve troop, without any defense of ditches, stockades,

---
63 Leg. Rec., MS, vol.1, pp. 23--24.
64 Bancroft, Calif., vol. 2, p. 547.
65 Ibid., p. 574.
66 F.W.Beechey, Narrative, vol. 2, pp. 85--86.

walls, batteries, advantageous situation, water supply, wood, food, ..." And there was no money with which to pay artisans or buy materials to correct those deficiencies.[67]

The San Diego presido was abandoned during the early or middle '30s. By 1839, according to Vallejo, not a building was left.[68]

About 1835, the ruinous condition of the San Francisco presidio was reason, along with the need of its garrison at Sonoma, for its evacuation. As early as 1834, Vallejo had reported that rains had almost destroyed the fort and reduced the other buildings to wreckage. He demanded immediate aid to save the war materials, and received authority to act and make estimates. Later, he suggested that the buildings be sold to the soldiers on account of back pay, or to others for livestock for the national ranches; and was authorized to make such disposition of the buildings, reserving barracks.[69]

In 1839, he applied to the Minister of War for means to repair the fortifications, describing the unprotected condition of the region and warning of the danger of

---

[67] Sept. 18, 1829, Echeandía to Min. of War, in Dept. Rec., MS, vol. 7, pp. 38--40.

[68] Bancroft, Calif., vol. 3, p. 610.

[69] Ibid., p. 701, n. 4.

foreign encroachment.[70]

Through the late '30s he also importuned the supreme government for permission to fortify Angel Island, making that, instead of the less strategical San Francisco site, the main defense of the region. Permission -- though no more substantial encouragement -- to carry out this project was actually given by Mexico in December, 1839.[71]

At Monterey, the original presidio had disappeared by the early 1840s, but was soon replaced by a fort and simple battery mounting 3 guns.[72]

When in 1842, Commodor Jones called for the surrender of Monterey, Captain Mariano Silva, the officer commanding at the presidio, could only advise Alvarado that the fortifications were "of no consequence, as everybody knows."[73]

As for armament, it was for the most part obsolete and defective, and generally insufficient for even a vestigial army; though as this declined toward the

----

[70] Bancroft, *Calif.*, vol. 3, p. 583, n. 9.
[71] *Vallejo Doc.*, MS, vol. 6, #217, p. 3; *Dept. Rec.*, MS, vol. 3, p. 3.
[72] Bancroft, *Calif.*, vol. 4, p. 652, n. 1.
[73] *Ibid.*, p. 307.

vanishing point, there were occasionally more guns
than men. In 1841, for example, the territory's 24
artillerymen presided over 43 cannon, not to mention
17 useless pieces.[74]

Lacking supply from Mexico, the commandants were
from time to time reduced to outfitting their men with
such weapons as could be borrowed -- apparently from
civilian residents. Thus in 1836, the officer in charge
at San Diego succeeded in borrowing 3 guns; and in 1839,
4 firearms and pikes (the latter loan being evidently
for the San Luís escolta, as the garrison proper had
already dissolved).[75]

In 1830, although the total armament in Californian
presidios consisted of 54 cannon of brass and iron, ranging between 3 and 24 pounds' calibre, only 1 brass
4-pounder of all the scrap-heap was fit for service.[76]

Despite the monotonous regularity and emphasis of
the appeals to Mexico which poured out of California from
beginning to end of the period, arms and ammunition were
no more obtainable than men, commissary and money. In
1841, the chief of artillery at Monterey, reporting to

----

[74] Bancroft, Calif., vol. 4, p. 198.
[75] Ibid., vol. 3, p. 610, n. 2.
[76] Ibid., vol. 2, p. 67, n. 40, end.

the war ministry, listed, "besides useless guns and
miscellaneous war material, the following ordinance
and artillerymen in California.[77]

Table XIII

Territorial Ordinance and Artillerymen, 1841

Presidio	Armament	Artillerymen
Monterey	18 guns	1 Captain 1 Sergeant 2 Corporals 1 Drummer 7 Privates
San Francisco	6	1 Man
Sonoma	7	5 Men
Santa Bárbara	3	6 "
San Diego	9	1 Man
	43 guns	25 (Officers and Men)

This equipment of 43 guns, manned by 20 soldiers and
3 non-commissioned officers, with (at Monterey) a captain
and a drummer for good measure, constituted California's
first line of defense against foreign invasion from the sea.

Even had ordinance been plentiful, ammunition was not.
Repeatedly, in time of need -- against Indian and foreign
aggression alike -- the Californians were rendered helpless
by their lack of powder and ball to give effect to such
guns as they had available for such troops as they could
mobilize. The deficiency was too extreme to allow

---

[77] May 12, 1841, Report of Mariano Silva, in **Vallejo Doc.**, MS, vol. 10, #125.

dissembling. Like Rezánov in Spanish times, Kotzebue, in 1824, had to supply the powder for the presidial salute of courtesy;[78] and in July 1846, when Sloat, hesitant on the verge of calling for California's capitulation, offered to salute the Mexican flag, the honor had to be declined by the local authorities, since they lacked means of returning the salvo.[79]

37. Aspirations and Actualities

In striking contrast to the actualities, was Mexico's ambitious program of Californian defense, reiterated time and again by diverse administrations. "Claims unsustained by effective force are vain and contemptible even in the eyes of friendly powers. So vigilance and caution must be supported with force, either sea-power or the fortification of some point along the coast suitable for the protection and defense of our possessions," pronounced the Junta de Fomento de Californias impressively, in 1825.[80]

---

[78] Bancroft, Calif., vol. 2, p. 522.

[79] "U. S. Govt. Doc.," 30th Cong., 1st Sess., Sen. Report #75, (ser. #512), pp. 40--41, "Deposition of John R. Wilson, Midshipman, U. S. N.," who affirmed that the presidio could not return the salute "eith r from want of powder or guns, I do not recollect which." [It might well have been both!]

[80] Colección, Item #1 (Dictamen), p. 14.

In its Iniciativa de Ley,[81] the Junta went into specifications. There should be a comisario of war in each of the two territories (Alta and Baja California), who should review the troops every two months, and report on their condition to the gefe militar, who should report to the President of the Republic through the Minister of War. Each of the two territories should have a military academy, to which should repair twice a week for instruction such officers as were not on active service at the moment. The batteries at San Francisco, Monterey, Santa Barbara and San Diego should be put into the most effective state of defense.

The closeness to San Francisco of the Russian establishment at Bodega (the Junta's information had been greatly augmented by 1827) demanded some maritime force for coast-guard duty, to protect the shores, the fisheries and the marine fur industry; also to facilitate retail trade between San Francisco and Mazatlan, and commerce with Peru and other South American ports, as well as with Asia. The San Blas shipyards (apostadero) should be transferred to Monterey. Meantime, no delay should be suffered in providing a small fleet of gunboats and war vessels to ply the California coast constantly, guarding ports and islands and protecting the coast trade.

---

[81] Op. cit., Item #5 (Iniciativa), pp. 20--24.

San Francisco and Monterey should be the bases of this sea force. The ships could be constructed in San Francisco, the iron and sailcloth, with five or six construction workers, to be sent from Mazatlan. Other requirements of shipbuilding could be met in San Francisco itself. Two frigates, two brigantines and two war schooners should be put in service; and Alta California should have a comandante de marina, with a subordinate to administer the department in Baja California, each of those officials to have an aide.

The resourceful Junta even had in mind a "soldiers of the sea" branch of the military service, deeming it "very useful to the nation to have sailors in the southern region, in case of a hostile invasion [by land]". In cases of naval attack the [projected] merchant marine could meet the emergency.

When Echeandía visited San Francisco for the first time, his enthusiasm was unbounded. He declared that Mexico had no realization of what she had acquired; and spent days on plans for fortifying the region -- "castles in the air," mourned Vallejo[82] in subsequent disillusionment.

Through the years, not only did Mexican officials in California join the hijos del país in prayers for military preparedness; the home government itself voiced policies

---

[82] Hist. de Calif., MS, vol. 2, p. 69.

and orders for supporting, reforming, and reinforcing the
military organization. In 1827, a decree relative to a
future loan stipulated that part of the proceeds should
go to pay the troops of California and other states.

In 1828, national law required that each of the 6
territorial presidial companies maintain a strength of 76
men and 4 officers. For the support of each company,
$22,740 was to be allowed; and for effective martial administration, an ayudante inspector should be assigned.

After the usual hiatus between law enactment and effect,
Lieutenant-Colonel José María Padrés (later of the great
colony) arrived from Loreto in the summer of 1830, as
General Echeandía's second in command, charged with the
inspectorship. Padrés was California's first ayudante
inspector since Spanish Captain Soler had held that post
in 1781--88; and was also her last. In 1830, too, the
Secretary of the Treasury asked congressional authorization
to expend $131,440 for the 6 companies of Californian
cavalry -- a slash of $5,000 from the 1828 budget of
$136,440.[83]

Financial stringency interfered more and more with
defense projects. In 1832, the Minister of Relations advised
the governor that want of resources had prevented the

----

[83] Bancroft, Calif., vol. 2, pp. 672--74; vol. 3, p. 46.

organization of a military post on the Lower California
frontier. Nevertheless, the Minister stressed the necessity
of augmenting the wretchedly equipped small force at the
time stationed thirty leagues below San Diego.[84]

Through the years of economic depression, this
recognition of "indispensable necessities," which had nevertheless to be dispensed with, continued to mark official
communications; and Mexico maintained her show of optimism,
while in the territory discouragement became more and more
severe, and disillusionment more bitter.

In 1838, Virmond, the German merchant of Acapulco and
Mexico, replied to one of Vallejo's anguished communications
that the commissioners sent by the Californians to solicit
aid had been very well received by the government; that the
President had wanted to send at once all needed supplies,
armaments and money; the uniforms and arms had been ready
for some time; but Mexico's own problems [the French blockade
because of unpaid claims] had rendered this impossible,
for lack of means. The blockade had left the government so
entirely without resources that a forced loan on city and
rural properties and on commerce had had to be

----

[84] May 17, 1832, Alaman to Figueroa, in *Sup. Govt. State Pap.*, MS, vol. 5, pp. 7--8.

resorted to.[85]

Surprisingly enough, the good intentions thus reported by the politically knowing Virmond were given some effect when, six months or so later the commissioner Castillero returned to California with a veritable "plenitude of supplies": 598 coats, 477 pairs of pants, 297 shirts, 298 stocks, 289 pairs of shoes, 200 cloaks, 400 caps and casques, 400 *maletas* (knapsacks), 200 *chabrases*, (?) 100 muskets, 200 carbines, 99 sabres 49 lances, 4 trumpets, 3000 flints, 15,580 cartridges.[86]

It was doubtless the war with France, itself, which had given rise to such zeal on the part of Mexico in behalf of her exposed Pacific territory. Bancroft counted over forty communications regarding this alarm, including of course orders for the strenthening of the coast defenses.[87]

In 1840, the reorganization of the Californian artillery was ordered, and Captain Silva was appointed to the chief command and renovation of that branch of the service.[88]

Mexico accomplished little or nothing in the way of

----

[85] June 20, 1838, Virmond to Vallejo, in *Vallejo Doc.*, MS, vol. 5, #97, pp. 5--6.

[86] Bancroft, *Calif.*, vol. 3, p. 583, n. 9.

[87] *Calif.*, vol. 3, pp. 592--93.

[88] *Ibid.*, vol. 4, p. 198, n. 9.

military reform, however, like his constructive essays too frequently got no further than intent, or were, at best, very imperfectly executed. To ard the close of the period, Congressman Castañares was still imploring on behalf of his constituents "600 or 800 infantry and cavalrymen, the latter being the most important . . . . This force should be composed of chosen veterans, temperate men with trades and families, and should come completely equipped." Moreover, he demanded that the Minister of Relations make effective "sin escusa ni pretesto alguno" the order for the 8,000 pesos per month for the payment of the Batallón Fijo, which had not been honored by the Customs Department at Mazatlan!

"The fortunes of the native Californians are in their infancy . . . . and if the troops are obliged to live at the expense of the country, they will destroy those incipient fortunes in a very few months, and the government will never be able to repair that evil."[89] In view of the desperate straits in which he himself described the territory as being, it seems likely that the diputado's use of the future tense, rather than the past, was a diplomatic device.

---

[89] Castañares, Col. de Doc., p. 10.

38. The Missions and the Military

It was natural that, despite friction recurring chiefly from what the padres considered the bad influence of the soldiers on the neophytes, Mexico should look to the missions for military subsidy. Under the Spanish system, troops and missionaries had been mutually sustaining, in fact though not in theory. Under the Republic, the trend was decidedly toward applying mission resources to general development and humanitarian purposes.

But monopolists are notably conservative; and the padres, however disinterested personally, were no exception to the rule. That aid which had been rendered more or less as a matter of course (though not without grumbling) to the troops of Spain, came hard when Mexico demanded it. Indeed, it would have been strange had the padres eagerly nourished a republicanism from which they had nothing to hope but the nullification of their labors and the supplanting of their system.

The disposition to withhold aid grew with the essays at secularization, and as emancipation of the neophytes proceeded, was attended more and more by inability to comply.

In 1825, Padre Duran told Lieutenant Martinez of San Francisco that he could send no more supplies to the troop, and that it would be best to discharge the soldiers if there were no rations for them. Padre Viader pleaded that his mission of Santa Clara had to buy wheat for its neophytes, while the pueblo had plenty of grain to sell the presidio; and a little later, upbraiding Liuetenant Martinez for not paying for blankets, he declared: "'My friend, we have reached the point of <u>date et dabitur vobis.</u>'"

At San Diego, where the soldiers suffered great privation, the padres seem to have helped all they could. But Captain Guerra of Santa Bárbara had a sharp controversy with Padre Ibarra of San Fernando, "trying to prove," says Bancroft, "that the furnishing of supplies was by no means a special favor to the troops, but an ordinary duty of the missions . . . ."

In Mexico, the guardian urged payment of something on account of the unpaid drafts long outstanding and totalling $259,151; and assured Alaman that matters in California were critical, the Indians being disgusted at having to labor for the support of the padres, the government and the troops, as well as o themselves.[90]

The Indians would naturally feel such resentment; and indeed it appears from time to time in connection with

------

[90] Bancroft, <u>Calif.</u>, vol. 3, pp. 20--21; 38, n. 4.

various neophyte protests and revolts.

Nevertheless, appeals to the missions on behalf of the needy military were frequent, especially in the south. In March, 1839, the mission at San Diego was held responsible for the support of the families of soldiers absent on service (apparently the San Luís Rey escolta).[91]

José Fernandez, writing from thirty years' experience as soldier and civil official in Hispano-California, declared that "if it had not been for the missionaries, who supplied all sorts of necessities of life to the presidios, California would have reverted to the Indians, for the soldiers at various times wanted to go to Sonora to escape" their Californian hardships.[92]

The padres frequently supplied as well, over a period of years, neophyte labor and the tools for repairing fortifications, since it was impossible for the insufficient army to keep up the presidial buildings and guard missions, pueblos and ranchos, fight Indians and support itself.

By the middle '30s, however, the common response of padres and comisionados to pleas for mission and ex-mission aid was that it was absolutely impossible to help, since they could barely feed and clothe the Indians remaining in their charge.[93]

---

[91] Bancroft, Calif., vol. 3, pp. 258--59; 624, n. 17, "1839."

[92] José Fernandez, Cosas de Calif., MS, p. 27.

[93] Bancroft, Calif., vol. 3, p. 351.

39. National Ranches

To the natural query, "Why could not the army live off the country, as did the missions?" the answer is that the army made the attempt. The ranchos del rey, run in connection with the presidios during the Spanish era, were continued as ranchos nacionales under Mexico. Santa Bárbara Presidio's San Julian Ranch was "a prosperous institution down to 1826 at least. It not only kept the troops supplied with meat and paid its expenses, but furnished $350 to buy an organ for the chapel, and left a cash balance of $940, besides 2,221 head of cattle."[94]

The Purísima Ranch of San Diego Presidio had 250 head of cattle in 1828, and 25 horses. It supplied meat and mounts for the troops, says Bancroft; "but we have no statistics and no information save an occasional complaint that the cattle are almost exhausted and should be replenished from the missions. All tithes of cattle were added to this rancho."[95]

At about this time, an attempt was made to extend and re-invigorate the national ranch system. In 1826, Hartnell

---

[94] Bancroft, Calif., vol. 2, p. 574. The habilitado's report on the rancho from 1817--26 is included in Guerra Doc., MS, vol. 3, pp. 52--53.

[95] Calif., vol. 2, pp. 546--47.

of Monterey -- a good Anglo-California, though as yet
unnaturalized -- loaned 264 head of cattle to the
commissary department, doubtless to stock a presidial
ranch. The loan had not been repaid in 1839.[96] In 1833--34,
plans went forward for the creation of ranches for Monterey
and San Francisco presidos. Lists were drawn up of livestock and implements to be loaned by the missions for six
years. In 1834--35, property of the sort and for the
purpose, in the amount of $1,513, was received from Mission
Soledad for Monterey. Two provisional grantees of land
were ordered by the governor to vacate in the presidial
favor; and controversy waged between the Monterey *ayuntamiento* and the company commanders over other lands, part
of which the council had already conferred on a citizen.[97]

Vallejo collected tithes amounting to 170 head of
cattle for the San Francisco Company's ranch; and the
governor called on the missions for further livestock contributions. Vallejo asked and received permission to sell
some of the ruined presidial buildings in exchange for
animals for the ranch. In the fall of 1835, he sent 600
cattle and some horses by the Indian chief Carquínez to
the frontier rancho, from which no profit could be expected,

---

[96] Bancroft, *Calif.*, vol. 3, p. 57, n. 1.
[97] *Ibid.*, p. 672, n. 4.

however, for two years.[98]

A letter of his is preserved in which he ordered his brother and subordinate officer, Comandante of San José J. J. Vallejo, to plant fields for the maintenance of a military force to be raised and established there as soon as possible, there being no other means of supporting them. If possible, a surplus of crops should be grown, to assist other units.[99]

In January 1842, arrangements were made to buy Rancho San José from Abrego, and stock it with cattle for the Monterey Company.[100]

The same difficulties stood in the way of the success of the national ranches as of the army itself, however -- lack of man-power and of capital. It takes men to run stock-ranches and farms. In those days, it took additional men to guard the stock and fields against the inroads of Indians. Hence it was not so simple a thing as might seem at first glance to support an army off the land.

----

[98] Bancroft, Calif., vol. 3, p. 701, n. 4, passim.
[99] Nov. 18, 1841, M. G. Vallejo to J. J. Vallejo, in Vallejo Doc., MS, vol. 10, #352.
[100] Bancroft, Calif., vol. 4, p. 652, n. 1, "Military Affairs . . . Jan., 1842."

A letter of Vallejo's written in 1841, throws further light on conditions. He complains that the government, in the hands of inexpert persons, has exhausted every means of support, even to the point of not respecting the properties of the presidial company, and disposing of them without the <u>comandancia general's</u> knowledge. The only practical means of subsistence for the garrisons under the circumstances is for each company to hold land enough to support the cattle and horses and produce the food necessary for that company's cavalry supply and subsistence. Therefore he asks the return of the company lands, or for others. The lands of the various army units having been grante to private individuals, the ruin of the garrisons is threatened, or, in some cases, has actually occurred.

On that frontier with whose protection and colonization he is especially charged, he has set apart the Rancho Soscol, and stocked it himself, for the maintenance of the troops and their mounts; but he fears that it will meet, any day, the fate of the other national ranchos. He asks that it be granted as a garrison ranch. If that is impossible, he hopes that it may be granted him in payment of the arrears of his salary from 1824--37, when he served from cadet to <u>teniente;</u> of the 9,000 <u>pesos</u> which he has spent on the fine barracks of the frontier troops; and of all the expenditures which he has made out of his own pocket to provision the garrison for six years, at a cost of about

1,000 pesos a year, without any drain on the public treasury; also of the expenses to which he has been put in purchasing and mounting the artillery -- 7 pieces in first class condition for service.[101]

40. The Sons of the Country and the Presidios

It has appeared, incidentally thus far, that the hijos del país concerned themselves earnestly with shoring up their weak defences. Their efforts, as apart from Mexico's deserve consideration.

Mention has been made of the constantly and vigorously reiterated demands for subsidies and reinforcements from the supreme government, which are an outstanding feature of the documentary record of the period. But even in the first flush of hope in a new régime, the Californians did not merely clamor for the benefits of the anticipated "new deal." While awaiting the time when the settlement of Mexico's political differences should permit national attention to territorial government, Argüello's Junta of 1824 incorporated in its Plan de Gobierno provision that the Monterey presidial company should consist of 80 men and officers, and each of the

---

[101] Jan. 1, 1841, Vallejo to Min. of War, in Vallejo Doc., MS, vol. 10, pp. 1--4. (There is also a copy of this document a little more legible than the original, slightly out of place, in a sheaf of copies bound in between the original documents #1 and #4.)

others of 70, the artillery to continue as before.[102]

We found the *diputación* exercising itself in January 1824, over the deplorable condition of the forts at Monterey and San Diego, and devising such scanty means as circumstances permitted for effecting repairs.[103]

This anxiety for the preservation of the presidial works continued throughout the period. Although in the north it became necessary, in 1835--36, to merge the San Francisco garrison with the *caballería permanente de la frontera* at Sonoma, Vallejo never abandoned hope of reestablishing a force at San Francisco; but chief of his plans for the protection of that region was the re-location of the major fortifications. "The Island of Los Angeles [Angel Island] is beyond doubt the best place for the purpose. It has wood and water close at hand, absolutely commands the entrance to the Bay and is the key to the inner gulf.[104]

In 1839, the Comandante of the North actually received permission from Mexico to proceed with his Angel Island project. What appears to be a draft or copy of an official notification to the departmental government,

---

102 Bancroft, *Calif.*, vol. 2, p. 512, n. 2.

103 *Ante*, pp. 365--66.

104 Feb. 6, 1839, Vallejo to Min. of War, in *Vallejo Doc.*, MS, vol. 6, #217, p. 3.

under date of December 5th of that year -- though without
superscription or signature -- stipulates that "the principal fort of the port of San Francisco is to be established on Angel Island";[105] and in 1840 we find Vallejo
calling on the governor for aid in connection with the
stationing of a San Francisco company.[106] Both projects
were defeated by the usual insuperable difficulties.

Nevertheless, Vallejo continued not only his solicitations for enough aid to permit the work of self-help to
go forward, but, as well, his personal subsidization of
the territory's defences. In February 1839 -- as on
numerous other occasions -- he called to the attention
of the war ministry the ruinous state of all the presidios,
and advised that he had used every available resource,
including some of his own, to fortify the northern frontier.[107]

Other Californian leaders, notably Captain Guerra,
supported the _comandante_ in these efforts. The attitude
of the Santa Bárbara commandant is indicated in an appeal
of 1841, to the governor, stressing the necessity of

---

[105] _Dept. Rec._, MS, vol. 10, p. 33.

[106] Bancroft, _Calif._, vol. 3, pp. 701--2, n. 4.

[107] Feb. 6, 1839, Vallejo to Min. of War, in _Vallejo Doc._, MS, vol. 6, #217, pp. 1--2.

ncreasing the presidial organization.[108]

General Castro, who shared Vallejo's distrust of Sutter, aspired to build a government fortress on the Sacramento. Larkin believed that Don José had "no funds and but little energy to do so."[109] At least the first shortcoming was a certainty. Of energy, judging by his long and creditable performance as soldier and public official in a great variety of capacities, not to mention his activities as rancher and fur hunter,[110] Castro seems to have had more than Larkin was willing to credit him with. Bancroft's estimate was that "he had much energy."[111] Larkin's derogation may be attributed in some degree to the exigencies of the cause he was serving.

Governor Alvarado, finding it impossible to further the progress of presidial reinforcement to any marked extent, and finding the demands of the civil budget too immediate and imperative to permit of increased military expenditures, was sometimes forced to disappoint Vallejo, Guerra and other army leaders in the matter of military

[108] Feb. 7, 1841, J. de la Guerra to Alvarado, in Guerra Doc., MS, vol. 6, pp. 13--14.

[109] Official Corresp., MS, vol. 2, p. 109.

[110] See post, pp. 656--57, 591--92.

[111] Calif., vol. 2, p. 752.

appropriations. Vallejo, particularly, became bitterly critical of the governor on this score. Nevertheless, Don Bautista's lack of co-operation seems to have traced to administration poverty.

In a letter of 1839, he exhorted Vallejo to continue urging a military establishment on the northern frontier, promising, himself, to lose no opportunity to support the recommendation.[112] Upon the evacuation of Fort Ross by the Russians, he championed a program of garrisoning that point with 40 to 50 men, to preserve the integrity of that frontier.[113] But in 1844, Castañares bewailed[114] the fact that the Mexican government had taken no steps to occupy Ross. The Russian artillery had been acquired by Sutter; and the establishment of "Don Estevan" Smith, at Bodega, was affording a foothold to other foreigners.

41. The Californians Favored a Big Army

The Plan de Gobierno issued in January 1824 by the Junta which Governor Argüello called to determine what course California should follow in the uncertain days

---

[112] June 5, 1839, Alvarado to Vallejo, in Fernandez, Cosas de Calif., MS, pp. 89--90.

[113] Jan. 11, 1842, Alvarado to Min. of Relations, in Dept. Rec., MS, vol. 13, p. 10.

[114] Col. de Doc., pp. 48--49.

following Mexican independence, included in its provisions, as has already been mentioned,[115] the requirement that the regular army forces at the presidios be maintained at a strength of 70 men and officers per company, except for Monterey, which should keep 80 enrolled; and that the artillery be continued "as before". This latter provision would doubtless mean a regular artillery muster-roll of some 35 to 40 men, since the 1810--20 average of 15 or so had been reinforced in 1820 by Apodaca with 15 or 20 from Mexico.[116] The Californians, therefore, contemplated maintaining a regular army strength of about 330.

Low as that figure appears at first glance, it actually represented a very high percentage of the territory's total man-power, as appears from a brief exercise in population statistics supplied by Bancroft:[117]

Total population, gente de razon, 1830....4,250
"   "   "   "   " , 1820.....3,270
Increase for decade 1820--30......... 980
Estimated increase for half-decade........ 490
" de razon population, 1824.......3,760

---

[115] Ante, pp. 385--86.
[116] Bancroft, Calif., vol. 2, pp. 189--90, 422; ante, p. 355.
[117] Calif., vol. 2, pp. 653--54; ante, p. 153.

Estimating one out of every five of these 3,760 persons de razon considered to be living in the territory in 1824, a male of military age -- and probably this is too liberal an estimate -- a total potential military muster of 552 men is indicated. A standing army of 330 would therefore mean the absorption into the military service of approximately 60% of the adult males of the territory, leaving only 40% to support the men-at-arms and the minor and female population, develop the resources of the nearly empty country and build up its trade. These figures, moreover, make no allowance for aged men or adult males otherwise incapacitated for bearing arms. The projected military-civilian ratio set by the Junta de Gobierno seems the more remarkable in view of the fact that a considerable portion of the energies and time of the 40% civilian element was expected to be devoted to militia service, as will appear presently.

In the light of these considerations, it appears that the Californians of 1824 voluntarily committed themselves to an almost staggering "big army" program, in their determination to defend the country at all costs against hostile invasion. That they had the courage of their convictions seems evident in the surprising uniformity with which they participated, as officers or enlisted men, in regular army service. There is almost a monotony in the frequency of the designation of "soldier" or of officer of one or another grade recorded by Bancroft of the men of this period, in his "Pioneer Register."

They had undertaken, however, tasks too heavy for their strength. The younger generation did not mature rapidly enough to afford needed replacements as the older troops died off or were retired, and at the same time to develop the country to the point of supporting more than half its men in non-productive pursuits. Had the territory been a "going concern" agriculturally, industrially and commercially, the ordeal would have been severe enough. But everything had as yet to be started; for under Spain, California had been no more than a military-missionary province, the few attempts to populate and develop it having failed signally.

What the Californians hoped for in 1824 was, of course, that as faithful followers of the new star rising in Mexico, they would find ways and means to that self-realization denied them under Spain's ascendancy. A little lightening of baleful influences, a little favoring circumstance, would have given them a fighting chance to master their destiny; and they were willing to fight -- did fight as a matter of course, with the habitual patient courage of men long trained in adversity.

As the promise of Mexico vanced, that habit of struggle against unequal odds kept California's leaders doggedly at their self-imposed tasks of defence and development. Calls for recruits from within the territory were circulated from time to time,[118] and upon the inauguration of the "home rule" experiment, Vallejo instituted an organized and persistent drive for the restoration of the presidial forces to their old-time strength and quality, pointing out that unless that goal should be attained, the country's ruin was certain.

In the first weeks of 1837, he issued circulars to all the presidial comandantes.[119] He called to their attention the fact that the presidial troops had always been those to maintain public order and keep the gentile Indians pacified; that those troops had fallen away in number, and -- due to the incursion of a vicious element from Mexico -- in quality. Therefore it was necessary

---

[118] Bancroft, Calif., vol. 2, p. 673.

[119] These orders, printed and bound into a little unpaged book under the title Órdenes de la Comandancia General, 1837--9, comprise one of of the earliest examples of Californian press-work.

to reorganize and reinforce them in so far as possible. The replacements must be youths worthy of the title of defenders of their country.

The San Francisco recruits should be sent to the northern frontier for training, and until they could report there must be kept on duty at the old presidio under the commanding officer's immediate supervision.[120]

In a notice addressed to the alcalde constitucional of the Pueblo of Alvarado [San José], the comandante general declared that not only the public welfare and the security of the state, but the very existence of the pueblo demanded the reorganization of the presidial companies. Since their decline, robberies of stock, murder and other crimes had flourished. Therefore, the alcalde was ordered to seek the aid of men up to the number of 30, to guarantee the security and tranquillity of the region; and the comandante was sending a recruiting officer to take charge of the work.[121]

To Alvarado, Vallejo wrote that the present moment of [political] tranquillity was the time when the government must act for the reorganization of the presidial companies, which were so lacking in both men and equipment that gentiles and neophytes were out of control and perpetrating murders

---

120 Vallejo, Órdenes, #1.
121 Ibid., #2

and robberies in civilized communities. That the companies might be recruited to at least half-strength, and the country halted on the path to ruin, the governor was asked to send the necessary orders for recruiting to the ayuntamientos.[122]

Success seems to have been greatest at San José [de Alvarado] and San Juan [Bautista] [de Castro]. In these vicinities about 60 youths were enlisted within four or five months, and sent to Sonoma for military training. Salvador Vallejo was dispatched to Ross for arms and clothing for them.[123]

At Sonoma, too, an infantry company was organized, of about 25 selected Indians enrolled under Spanish names. The cavalry company was increased to something over 40 men.[124]

Both General Vallejo, however, and his brother Salvador, Captain of the Sonoma post, emphasized the imperative need of greater strength. Handicapped severely by the usual financial lack, they blamed the administration at Monterey for withholding support. To their importunities for increased army personnel and support, Guerra added his.[125]

In June 1839, the general addressed an exhortatory

---

122 Vallejo, Órdenes, #5.
123 Idem, Hist. de Calif., MS, vol. 3, p. 246.
124 Bancroft, Calif., vol. 3, p. 722, n. 20, "1839."
125 Ibid., vol. 4, p. 641, n. 19.

letter to the governor, again begging for assistance in the prompt rebuilding of the regular companies. "This is the only hope of saving the country. The Indians are not the only enemies among us. Others inspire to disorder, and glory in seeing us inert, without a permanent force to guard and protect . . . ."

At the same time Vallejo urged on Alvarado the stationing of garrisons in all the ex-missions, each of which should maintain its own force. He finished this plea with an earnest argument for a democratically composed army of high moral calibre: "The permanent presidial companies, made up of worthy men, without distinctions, and with neither rich nor poor excused, are the salvation of the country. This was the rule of our fathers, and by it they were enabled to bear with honor and brilliance the arms confided to them. Moreover, the military calling was as open to the son of an honest laborer as to that of the most distinguished person. If that was the policy in those times, which knew nothing of equality, why is it not so today when all men glory in being equal."[126]

The general felt keenly the disrepute into which the respected old presidial forces had been brought by the infusion of the vicious elements recruited in Mexico.[127]

---

126 Vallejo, Órdenes, #7.
127 Idem, Hist. de Calif., MS, vol. 3, p. 244.

In 1839, in a letter to Alvarado, he declared flatly that he would not accept criminals into the army. There followed a series of complaints of the low grade of men being sent him -- vagabonds whom the municipal authorities sought to be rid of and who were entirely unsuited to be soldiers. One such batch of recruits, whose members proved to be physically unfit or grossly immoral, he ordered returned to Los Angeles, whence they had come.[128]

Nevertheless, such was the shortage of men and the need of them to develop the country, that the army continued to serve as a dumping-ground for undesirables. In 1843, the sub-prefect of the San José district called on the juez to supply 20 young men "whose immoralities and other characteristics suit them to soldiering."[129]

Through these years, Vallejo was seeking to build up the morale of the army by creating classes of cadets to be sent to military college in Mexico. Having obtained permission from the supreme government to carry out this project, in November 1839 he ordered each of the presidial commanders to find two young men eligible for such careers. Letters of December, from the commandants at San Diego and Santa Bárbara, reported no success to date in finding

---

[128] Bancroft, Calif., vol. 3, p. 591, n. 26.
[129] Ibid., vol. 4, p. 686, n. 22, "Military Items."

available youths of the necessary physical and other qualifications.[130] Whether any practical results ensued from these endeavors does not appear in the records at hand.

Possibly modesty kept Captain de la Guerra of Santa Bárbara from selecting one or both candidates from his district from among his own sons. Perhaps there was at the moment none of age and free to go. Perhaps he feared for them, in Mexico -- because of his Spanish birth -- some such rebuff as he had received when he journeyed to the national capital in 1827 to represent California in Congress, and was refused his seat, as well as deprived of his military command for a time.[131]

The grand old man of Santa Bárbara, however, whose devotion to the service can scarcely be considered less profound than Vallejo's own, though his lower rank gave him less scope, had no doubt of the acceptability of his sons for duty in California. Indeed, one -- José Antonio -- had already earned a rank equal to his father's, and sometimes took his father's place as *comandante* at Santa Bárbara, besides filling various other functions as soldier, civilian official and rancher.[132]

----

130 *Vallejo Doc.*, MS, vol. 8, #388, #389.
131 Bancroft, Vol. 3, pp. 33--34; vol. 2, pp. 671--72.
132 *Ibid.*, vol. 3, p. 768.

A paragraph of a letter from Alvarado to Vallejo, written early in 1837, gives further evidence of the patriotism of the Guerras: "Don José [de la Guerra y] Noriega asked that five minor sons be made drummer-boys, and Pablito a soldier," the brief reference runs. But, adds the governor, affording a side-light on the ever present need of men to perform the variety of tasks necessary for the country's development, "I don't want to use Pablo for that -- I have other service for him."[133]

It was this insufficiency of men to keep civilian functions going that made conscription impracticable in California. Theoretically, all men of military age and capable of bearing arms were subject to draft under Mexico as they had been under Spain. In practise, however, impressment was the final recourse. When, in 1824, Governor Argüello issued a call for 25 recruits from Los Angeles and Santa Bárbara, his order of preference was for volunteers if possible, otherwise available vagrants; with unmarried men to be drawn by lot as a last resort.[134]

Vallejo, in his zeal for the country's defense, would have invoked the draft law. This issue was one of the

---

[133] Mar. 9, 1837, Alvarado to Vallejo, in *Vallejo Doc.*, MS, vol. 4, #212, p. 8.

[134] Bancroft, *Calif.*, vol. 2, p. 673, n. 41.

causes of disagreement which arose between him and Alvarado in the late '30s and the '40s. Worry over the aggressiveness of the Missourians and other Yanquis badgered him, and he believed a conscript army the only practical means of staving off the "North Americans."[135] In 1839 and thereafter, he demanded the governor's compliance with a national decree requiring the presidial companies to be filled by conscription.

Alvarado promised to place the draft order in effect when instructions should arrive from Mexico; but protested that he had no authority under the provisions of the law without express instructions.[136] The controversy went on for years.

Undoubtedly, the <u>comandante general</u> vainly attempted to elicit the required instructions from Mexico; and undoubtedly, the governor's demurral was only technically on account of their lack. The one thought chiefly in terms of civilian, the other in terms of military progress. Each recognized that in view of the country's paucity of man-power one phase of development must be sacrificed at least temporarily to the other.

----

[135] Nov. 17, 1841, Vallejo to Alvarado, in <u>Vallejo Doc.</u>, MS, vol. 10, #349.

[136] Bancroft, Calif., vol. 3, p. 591, n. 26.

The governor looked on the application of _la ley que trata de sorteos_ as an actual threat to the peace of the department, under the circumstances. "Such a step, taken with reference to the small population of this department, comprised of laborers forced to work for the mere maintenance of themselves and their families, would cause a disruption of the public peace such as must be prevented at all costs."[137] The militia, therefore, he reasoned, would have to bear the brunt of defense, supplementing the regular army as needed.

The _comandante general_, while laboring to build up the militia as well as the regular army, looked on the civilian auxiliaries as emergency forces, and in no case as safe a reliance as the _soldados permanentes._ "The country's civil forces are of different political opinions; and most of them are farm workers, without other source of maintenance than their personal labor. If they abandon this at sowing time, either indigence remains to them or the government must maintain them and their families. And discipline is necessary, in time of active warfare. Certainly a civil force should be maintained always in a proper state of defense; but not to the prejudice of the

---

[137] Jan. 11, 1842, Alvarado to Min. of Rel., in Dept. Rec., MS, vol. 13, p. 12.

regular companies."[138]

Alvarado gave what support he could to Vallejo's efforts, ordering the municipalities to furnish recruits. He was, says Bancroft, "less enthusiastic in the matter [than Vallejo], but whatever his desires, he could barely find funds to support the few men already in arms."[139] Through the relevant correspondence of the time, the familiar refrain runs dolefully: "No men, no money!"

In the nature of things, Vallejo's efforts were foredoomed to failure -- or to that partial success which cannot fend off failure. The Californians were patriotic. They were courageous. But they had to eat or starve. In the army, men starved or came close to starving. In the army, self-respecting men turned into ragamuffins like the shirtless, coatless and nearly trouserless Salazar of San Diego;[140] while their families suffered want. Despite all efforts to restore the service to its pristine vigor and repute, a military career had come to mean no career at all.

Meantime, all California awaited development. Opportunities unknown in Spanish times were open, under, however great handicaps, to Mexican citizens. What more

----

[138] June 10, 1839, Vallejo to Alvarado, in Vallejo Órdenes, #7.

[139] Calif., vol. 3, p. 583.

[140] See ante, p. 350.

natural than that the generation which, had it been numerous enough, might have furnished the recruits of the '30s and '40s, should look to the land -- and the sea -- for their careers?[141] Here was scope for service as patriotic as any. If it should be ignored, the *estrangeros* would soon possess the country, soldiers or no soldiers. Besides, not unless her resources and trade were developed could California support even a small army.

So the prestige of the military profession waned. Rare as were conscription levies in the territory, Davis wrote[142] that one of the reasons for early marriage among the Californians was the desire to escape the draft -- for married men were not called, being left to care for their families.

The documents seem to throw no light on this point; but even if draft-dodging became fairly prevalent so far as regular army service was concerned, the evidence seems to indicate that militiamen, both married and single, enlisted as a matter of course, and rode forth readily to meet Indian trouble or such other emergency as arose.

----

141 See *post*, chap. V.
142 *Seventy-five Years*, pp. 160--61.

42. Citizen **Soldiers**

The participation of the citizens in auxiliary military duty was a natural frontier device, as indeed it has always been in societies lacking the means to maintain adequate standing armies. In California it traced back to provincial times. An artillery militia company of 70 men, required to devote two hours to drill each Sunday, had been organized in 1805, in accordance with a recommendation of Arrillaga.[143] This force had increased to 82, in 1816, and had been several times called into active service. In 1819, it numbered 64.[144]

California's own Plan de Gobierno of 1824 provided that all men from 18 to 50 years old should be enlisted to form companies (militia) of infantry or cavalry, and the militia artillery companies should be kept full and "in a good state of instruction."[145]

In 1828, the Spanish regulations for the artillery militia were given circulation; and the next year Echeandía reported that the citizen soldiers were as thoroughly organized as possible, in 5 companies; though it had cost

---
143 Bancroft, Calif., vol. 2, pp. 30--31.
144 Ibid., pp. 422--23; ante, p. 355.
145 Ibid., p. 512, n. 2, Title II, Art. 2.

great labor to teach the rules to the 500 available men.[146]

In May, 1834, the diputación discussed matters relating to the artillery militia.[147] Other references to the militia--artillery and other branches -- occur from time to time in the records, through this period, though revealing little or nothing of the status of that arm of the service. We know that squads of citizens rode often against the Indians; but how formally or officially they were organized does not appear.

Bancroft suggests that "probably there was in reality no such organization beyond the general understanding that the citizens of each district were to hold themselves in readiness for service in case of emergency."[148]

This inference seems borne out by documentary evidence tending to show activity in 1835--36 and later toward formal militia organization. In June of 1835, San Diego was called on to furnish its quota of artillery militia.[149] In February 1837, Governor Gutierrez forwarded to the alcalde of San Diego advice of a decree re-establishing los cuerpos

---

[146] Bancroft, Calif., vol. 2, p. 675, n. 44.
[147] Leg. Rec., MS, vol. 2, p. 69.
[148] Calif., vol. 2, p. 674.
[149] Ibid., vol. 3, p. 610, n. 2.

de la milicia local.[150]

When the Californians took the government into their own hands in 1836, one of the first acts of the *diputación* was to order the formation of militia companies, on the basis of a census of all males of the "free and sovereign state of California" between the ages of 15 and 50. The order went out as Decree No. 4 of the so-called "Castro Decrees," or "Decrees of the *Diputación*," being among those issued by Castro as president of the legislature in the interval between the surrender of Gutierrez on November 5th and the selection of Alvarado as ad interim governor on December 7th.

The requirement was for the furnishing, by the *ayuntamientos*, of a census of all males between 15 and 50; the enumeration to be ready within eight days, at latest, from publication of the decree. From these lists, the rosters of the companies of militia (cavalry) were to be made out at Monterey, the officers in each case to be named in consultation with two commissioners

---

150 San Diego Arch., MS, #82. This document is bound in upside down -- like many others in this collection, which is very badly confused in arrangement and numbering, the sequence in great part running from back to front. No. 82 (also marked, in pencil, #16) is included in the "Documents, 1836" section.

from each municipality. The organization of an infantry company of riflemen was also authorized.151

The highest militia commissions were bestowed on Alvarado and Castro, as Colonel and Lieutenant-Colonel, respectively -- ranks, as Bancroft points out, that in Spanish times could have been attained only after long service. A few days earlier, Vallejo, at the time commanding the northern line with the rank of lieutenant, had assumed the post of <u>comandante general</u> of the forces of California; and in order that his army grade might correspond better with his new responsibilities, he was commissioned a colonel of [regular] cavalry in December, in accordance with a vote of the Constituent Congress.152

From this time forward, the militia service seems to have been maintained actively; and when (at once) the commander-in-chief of the army began his campaign for the restoration of the presidial forces, he made the more effective organization of the militia a part of his objective. As early as January 12, 1337 -- only six weeks after assuming his enlarged responsibilities -- he was able to report to the governor that three companies

---

151 <u>Castro Decree #4</u>, in "Earliest Printing," #28.
152 Bancroft, <u>Calif.</u>, vol. 3, pp. 471--74.

of approximately 80 men each had been organized at San Francisco and [San José de] Alvarado, and one of 30 at Sonoma. All, he added, were enthusiastic in the cause.[153]

These companies seem to have been fully and competently officered, the one at San Francisco, for example, being captained by the experienced regular army man Francisco Sanchez, and counting 2 lieutenants and 2 alféreces, with 3 sergeants, 6 corporals and 72 privates -- a total of 86.[154]

Although, due to the wide scattering of the population when land became available to the citizens, regular drill was probably not always feasible, the census lists were apparently kept up faithfully to the end of the period, and bodies of militia were called into active service from time to time as needed. A document of June 1842, for instance, states that there were only 5 men (3 of them foreigners) at San Diego, the rest being absent on their ranches. But 71 citizens (exclusive of foreigners) able to perform militia service were listed for the district in 1844; in 1845, 53 such men were reported; and in 1846, 73, the upper age limit at that time

---

153 Bancroft, Calif., vol. 3, p. 511, n. 56.
154 Ibid., p. 701, n. 4, "1837."

being, not 50, but 60 years, the lower limit remaining at 15.[155]

Bancroft found no definite reports on military affairs at Santa Bárbara after 1843, and militia records seem to be entirely lacking for the years just before and after that date.[156] There is no reason to believe, however, that the citizen-soldier arrangement which prevailed elsewhere through the department was allowed to lapse in the Santa Bárbara district. Militia regulations were issued by the departmental government and the commandant general for all of California; and the Barbareños had always done their share, under Captain Guerra's leadership, to maintain the country's defences.

Although the records for Monterey for this period are confused and fragmentary, several allusions to the militia occur. In 1841, an auxiliary company of 4 to 19 men was headed by Captain Santiago Estrada, once presidial commandant. In 1844, a cavalry company of *defensores de la patria* mustered 32 men and was budgeted at $600 a month; while San Juan maintained a similar company.[157]

A San Francisco roster of *defensores* of 1844--45 names 46 soldiers including corporals and sergeants, with a

---

[155] Bancroft, Calif., vol. 4, p. 618, n. 1, ¶ 2.
[156] Ibid., p. 640.
[157] Ibid., p. 652, n. 1, "Military Affairs", *passim*; pp. 655--56.

captain, a lieutenant and 2 *alféreces* -- 50 in all.[158]

Sonoma, at that time, had 59 citizens enrolled as liable for militia duty. (Twelve were foreigners, and 6, Indians.)[159]

It was in 1844 that Larkin made his reference to 1,000 citizens available as militiamen; and in 1846 he wrote that in a popular cause Pico and Castro could bring into the field 800 or 1,000 men to serve for a month without pay -- some of them for a longer period whether paid or not; and that 300 to 400 could be raised for the purpose of aiding Mexico to expel "the emigration."[160]

In 1845, the total Hispano-Californian *de razon* population was 6,620.[161] Thus it appears that one person in every six or seven was considered on call for militia duty, or -- allowing for females, minors, the aged and incapacitated -- probably every physically fit male between 15 and 60 not in the regular army.

---

[158] Bancroft, *Calif.*, vol. 4, p. 667, n. 12, "Military Affairs;" pp. 673--74.

[159] *Ibid.*, pp. 677--78.

[160] Larkin, *Official Corresp.*, MS, vol. 2, pp. 8, 96.

[161] *See ante*, p. 153, Table I.

43. Citizen Subsidization of the Army

The militia branch of the service must be considered as almost wholly a citizen-supported, as well as a citizen-manned, project. Various orders or authorizations for militia organization or retention in service came out of Mexico: in 1839, 1841, 1842 and 1845;[162] but it does not appear that much, if any, assistance came from that source for the purpose.

When in 1845, Vallejo begged Bustamante's aid in "the creation of a body of militia of the country,"[163] it was not further authorization which he sought, but support of an enterprise long established and long considered a matter of course, which nevertheless was severely handicapped on the score of equipment and supply.

Citizen subsidization of the government, direct and indirect, had come to be a tradition in California. The soldiers aided indirectly, as we have had copious evidence, by serving over long periods for a fraction of their pay or none at all, and going at times almost destitute of food and clothing, not to mention armaments. Soldiers and

---

[162] Bancroft, Calif., vol. 3, p. 583; vol. 4, pp. 198, n. 20, 288, n. 20, 602.

[163] Nov. 22, 1845, Vallejo to Bustamante, in Vallejo Doc., MS, vol. 12, #157, p. 9, Prudon draft.

citizens alike, who possessed the means, aided directly with loans or gifts of supplies and money. Such volunteer assistance became the more common and necessary, of course, as the decline of the mission system reduced the subsidizing potentialities of the missions to the vanishing point.

The shortages in the military budget, which had already assumed startling proportions before the close of the eighteenth century, became, in the years that followed, an almost total deficit. The annual expense to the Spanish government of $89,000 for the support of the presidial forces during 1811--20, says Bancroft, was "rendered much less burdensome by the fact that it was never paid." [164]

Governor Argüello's purchase, with borrowed money, of the vessel "Rover," in 1823[165] was motivated largely by a determination to secure supplies for the army if he had to send half-way round the world for them. When Captain Cooper brought the "Rover" back from China, a few months later, laden with cloth, blankets, rice and other means of feeding and clothing the wretched troops, captain and cargo received a welcome not to be described, said J. J. Vallejo.[166]

---

[164] *Calif.*, vol. 2, p. 422.
[165] See *post*, pp. 671--79, **passim**.
[166] *Reminiscencias*, MS, pp. 15--16.

In 1839, in a series of letters to the supreme government, Vallejo called attention to the fact that the defence, as well as the settlement, of the northern frontier had been financed chiefly by himself; and begged the Minister of War to call the matter to the attention of the President, so that other arrangements might be made, as his resources were nearly exhausted.[167]

Nevertheless, he continued to provide. Six of the ten guns of the Sonoma artillery company, with all their appurtenances, were his gift.[168]

Two months after applying to the war department to relieve him of the financial burdens which he had been carrying for the government, he tendered to the Department treasurer his offer, already noted,[169] of an 8,000 to 10,000 peso contribution from his own pocket to make up army payroll insufficiencies.

In 1841, the juez de paz of San José alluded to money advanced by himself and the sub-prefect for an Indian expedition,[170]

It was in the same year that Vallejo advised the

----
[167] Vallejo Doc., MS, vol. 7, #s 26--28.
[168] Bancroft, Calif., vol. 3, p. 722, n. 20, "1839."
[169] Ante, p. 191.
[170] Bancroft, Calif., vol. 4, p. 686, n. 22, "Military Items."

Minister of War that he had been supporting the Sonoma garrison at an expense of about 1,000 pesos per month, besides mounting 7 guns; and asked for the Soscol rancho for the support of the company, or else for himself on account of the 4,000 pesos due him for salary in 1824--37 and of the 9,000 pesos which the barracks had cost him.[171]

In offering his resignation from the post of comandante general in 1841, he sent the government a statement with vouchers of the sums owing for garrison support. His agent, Virmond, informed him that there was no probability of his claim being allowed, much less paid. Others with valid claims, adds Bancroft, fared likewise.[172]

Eighteen months later, in June 1843, Vallejo presided over a meeting called in Sonoma to devise means for maintaining the garrison, as well as for other public needs. Again, he gave liberally himself. By way of evidence of community participation, we have the original subscription sheet, with its signatures and the "crosses" of those who could not write, showing that 31 vecinos subscribed $3,063 in cash, besides grain, cattle, building materials and labor.[173]

----

[171] See ante, pp. 384--85.
[172] Calif., vol. 4, p. 285.
[173] Vallejo Doc., MS, vol. 11, #412.

Bancroft's population estimate for the Sonoma jurisdiction -- that is, for all territory north of the Bay -- in 1845 (two years after this subscription) was "probably about 300," exclusive of foreigners in the Sacramento Valley and newly arrived and roving immigrants of the Sonoma and Napa valleys.[174] The average citizen volunteer cash subsidy of June 1843 was therefore well over $10. The actual individual contribution of course averaged much higher, since only 31 persons attended the meeting. This attendance itself, however, was a high average for a widely scattered community of 300 souls, of whom the majority were poor and unlanded, while all were pioneers and none of more than nine years' establishment in the region.

When Micheltorena's cholos were threatened with privation despite their pilfering exploits, Vallejo proposed, at a meeting of the junta, that the batallón be sent to Sonoma, where it could be fed from the surplus of beef and grain from his own Petaluma and his brother Salvador's Napa ranchos -- though he warned that he could give no money to any soldier except those few who had for years been in his service.[175]

---

[174] Calif., vol. 4, p. 677.

[175] Vallejo, Hist. de Calif., MS, vol. 4, p. 382.

44. A Californian Navy -- Envisioned

Characteristically, the Californians did not let the heavy burden of the army smother their hope of eventually building up a small coast-guard and naval force. Throughout the Mexican régime they continued to reiterate their need of a few vessels along the coast.

Echeandía was quick to recognize the justice of their demand, and made increasingly earnest pleas to the supreme government on that, as on other scores.[176] He pointed out that a coast-guard was needed not only to enforce the revenue laws, but to protect the fur fisheries of the two Californias from unlawful inroads.[177] Reporting on the Russian intrusions, he declared, in March 1827, that an armed vessel was greatly needed to protect the coast from Cape San Lucas to the forty-second parallel. A reply of June promised a man-of-war -- which did not materialize.[178]

In August 1827, the *diputación*, through the governor, appealed to the supreme authorities for a naval station at San Francisco, as well as one or two gunboats.[179]

----

[176] Bancroft, *Calif.*, vol. 3, p. 53.

[177] April 22, 1826, Echeandía to Min. of War, in *St. Pap. Sac.*, MS, vol. 19, p. 29.

[178] Bancroft, *Calif.*, vol. 2, p. 649.

[179] *Dept. Rec.*, MS, vol. 5, pp. 128--29.

In 1828, Echeandía reiterated his plea, made "numerous times," for a warship.[180]

The Alvarado-Vallejo administration made earnest efforts to develop a navy, and even a force of fighting marines. Fear of punitive or reactionary interference from centralist Mexico seems to have been an added spur at this time, to the old ambition. "Don Federico" Becher, supercargo of the Mexican vessels "Leonor" and "Catalina" along the coast early in 1837, being suspected of centralist activities threatening California's autonomy, had his ships, goods and credits seized at San Francisco by Vallejo's orders. The intention of the Californian authorities was to confiscate the vessels, along with the goods and credits, all to be used in the country's defense should Becher's guilt be proved.[181]

In March 1837, Alvarado wrote to Vallejo that he had attempted to buy the brigantine "Bolivar" from Señor [Alpheus B.] Thompson, payment to be made in hides and tallow, and the collection of duties on Thompson's cargo to be held in abeyance until the "Bolivar" had been paid for. The offer, however, had been rejected, the American

---

[180] Oct. 10, 1828, Echeandía to Min of War, in St. Pap. Sac., MS, vol. 10, p. 40.

[181] Jan. 12, 1837, Vallejo to Alvarado, in Vallejo Doc., MS, vol. 4, #56; Jan. 20, 1837, Vallejo to José Castro, in ibid., #57.

having at the moment no other vessel on the coast with which to collect his return cargo nor distribute his present load. But the brigantine "Diana" was expected shortly from the Islands. On its arrival, Thompson might do business.

Of Thompson's refusal to sell, the governor wrote: "This was a great blow to me, for I recognize the need of arming two good brigantines . . . . Mexico has neither money, supplies, nor sailors; and here, while we lack the first, we have the rest; and so far as I can see, with our resources we can do much more than they in the matter of a navy."

Besides being useful in watching possible movements of Mexico against California, the desired vessels would check contraband activities along the coast, would afford a practical naval school for the youth of the country, would obviate the necessity of paying freight for moving troops, and would afford means of deporting undesirables from the country . . . . Some of the missions were in a position to supply means for buying the vessels. Such a fleet would promote confidence in and respect for the government among natives and foreigners -- a thing impossible without adequate means of defense.

Alvarado awaited only Vallejo's advice and opinion

before sending urgent orders to Santa Clara and San José to collect produce in as great amount and as rapidly as possible, and at the cost of some sacrifice if necessary . . . .

"We do not lack sailors. You know that from **Figueroa's** time we have had marine registries (*matrículas de mar*), chiefly in Monterey where Captain Cooper and other pilots and sailors are located, all married and with families established in the country [that is to say, these men had become *Californios*]. We have more than enough sailors to make up the crews of two and even more **vessels**; and we have our own native soldiers whom we shall **accustom** to the sea, for which some of them show an **inclination**.

"When I divulged here in Santa Bárbara my idea of buying the brigantine, all the young fellows wanted to enlist on her."[182]

Who can say that, allowed a generation or so of immunity from foreign aggression, the Californians might not have progressed far in the development of a system of defense by land and by sea?

45. "Indians!"

Not alone encroachment from without hampered the growth of the country and kept it in a state of perpetual

---

[182] March 9, 1837, Alvarado to Vallejo, in **Vallejo Doc.,** MS, vol. 4, #212, pp. 3--8.

anxiety. To the end of the Mexican régime, and on into the American period, the Indians were a serious and continuous affliction throughout the territory.

The tradition of California's inoffensive "Digger" Indians has become fixed, effacing recollection of the fierce tribes of the Colorado and the Tulares, the Sierra and lake country, and of the treacherous renegade neophytes. Yet never a year went by without its raids and depredations and occasional murders.

On the basis of many official and personal records, Bancroft has compiled some enlightening though highly compressed data on this subject. It is possible, by culling the more significant bits from his annals of Indian hostilities, to piece together a rough picture of a phase of life in "Spanish Arcadia" that has rarely been recalled.

There was, for example, the revolt of southern neophytes in 1824, involving three missions on a large scale and others to a less degree. The occasion was the flogging of a neophyte; but the underlying cause seems to have been widespread discontent with the mission-presidio system as it worked out in the lean years following the suspension of the memorias.

At Santa Inés, where the revolt broke out, a large part of the mission buildings was burned. At Purísima, four white men and seven Indians, apparently, were killed.

Bancroft gives a graphic account of the progress of the uprising. "Masters now of the situation locally, reinforced from Santa Inés and perhaps to a slight extent from other missions, the rebels [of Purísima] began to prepare for defence by drilling, erecting palisade fortifications, cutting loop-holes in the adobe walls of the church and other buildings, mounting one or two old rusty cannon hitherto used chiefly to make a noise on días de fiesta, sending messages of exhortation to gentiles and neophytes, and taking every precaution that native ingenuity could devise."

The insurrection spread to Mission Santa Bárbara, where four of Captain Guerra's men were wounded. After incurring several casualties, the Barbareñ neophytes fled to the hills, and thence to the Tulares, taking all the mission property -- save church effects -- that they could carry. Stragglers were killed by the troops, and native rancherías sacked. But neither punitive measures nor negotiations pacified the renegades.

The governor sent a hundred men from Monterey to co-operate with Captain Guerra. This detachment, reaching Purísima without having united with Guerra's forces, joined the battle with the neophytes, who, "now said to have been about four hundred strong, returned the fire from cannon, swivel-guns and muskets, to say nothing of the clouds of arrows." Fortunately for the Californios, the guns were ineffectively handled. After two and a half hours of combat, the rebels attempted flight. They were checked by the cavalry. In the extremity they begged for the intercession of Padre Rodriguez, who had the firing stopped.

Three Californians had been wounded, one mortally. Sixteen Indians had been killed, and a large number suffered wounds. Seven were condemned to death and shot before the end of the month. Four more were sentenced to ten years of presidio and perpetual exile from the territory; and eight others, to eight years of presidio in California.[184]

Meanwhile, the Santa Barbara neophytes remained in the Tulares, where, Padre Ordaz wrote the governor, a Russian was instructing them in the use of firearms. The Indians of San Fernando had also run away, presumably to join the rest; and those of San Buenaventura and San Gabriel showed alarming signs of revolt, the padre added; though as no mass movement resulted, Bancroft concluded that that danger had been exaggerated.

----

[184] Bancroft, Calif., vol. 2, pp. 530--32.

Guerra fought two indecisive engagements, during which three civilians with the soldiers were wounded. Then a promise of pardon sent by Padre Ripoll and followed up by a force of one hundred and thirty Californians persuaded the fugitives to surrender. The revolt, which had broken out on February 21, 1824, was thus ended in June, though as late as October 1826 a dispatch to the Minister of War indicated that not all the refugees had yet surrendered; and the mission report for 1827--28 also implies that some were still abroad.[184a]

In 1824, also, the tribes of Marin and Quintin gave trouble along the northern Contra Costa. A forty-five day campaign in the north, and miscellaneous minor hostilities chiefly on the Lower California frontier are recorded; and, by way of good news, the capture and execution of the San Francisco renegade neophyte Pomponio, whose career of depredation had continued through several years.[185]

Two considerable battles were fought in 1826 in the San Diego region by Lieutenant Ibarra. Although he lost several men of his Mazatlan squadron, he killed twenty-eight of the Indians in one encounter and eighteen in the other -- official proof being given by the remission of the ears of the slain (in pairs).[186]

[184a] Bancroft, *Calif.*, vol. 2, pp. 532--37.
[185] *Ibid.*, pp. 537--38.
[186] *Ibid.*, p. 549; vol. 3, p. 109.

As effective or more so was the revenge wreaked by Alférez Sanchez, in the same year, on the Cosumnes of the San Joaquín Valley. His week's campaign, though it ended in a forced retreat, netted about forty Indians killed and as many captured,[187] It was his <u>Journal</u> of this expedition that Sanchez declared "written with gunpowder on the battlefield," according to Beechey.[188]

Alférez Sanchez also commanded two movements of 1829 against Estanislao, the chief who, after having been educated and having served as <u>alcalde</u> at Mission San José, reverted to savagery in 1827 or '28. This Indian, with one Ciprisno, became the leader of a band of renegade neophytes and gentiles. His retreat was in the San Joaquín Valley, where Stanislaus River and County perpetuate his name. In addition to his raiding activities, he was believed responsible for attempts to instigate a general rising of neophytes. By arrogance and a parade of defiance, moreover, he aggravated the Californians' resentment against him.

In the spring of 1829, Sanchez led forty soldiers of San Francisco, with San José <u>vecino</u> and Indian reinforcements, in a bitter two day battle. Insufficiency of ammunition,

---

[187] Bancroft, <u>Calif.</u>, vol. 3, p. 109.
[188] F. W. Beechey, <u>Narrative</u>, vol. 2, p. 27.

and the damaged condition of the swivel-gun which had
been taken into the action with high hopes of good
effect, caused Sanchez to abandon the field. He had
lost two soldiers killed and eight wounded, besides
one Indian ally killed and ten wounded.

Another *entrada* was immediately undertaken. This
time Alférez M. G. Vallejo of Monterey was associated
with Sanchez. The young subaltern was just back from
an engagement in the Tulares, in which he had accounted
for forty-eight Indians slain, without casualty in the
Californian ranks -- a remarkable showing for a twenty-
one-year-old officer new to Indian fighting and numbering
only thirty-five men in his command.

The Sanchez-Vallejo expedition against Estanislao
counted one hundred and seven men. Again battle was
waged desperately for two days, the Indians refusing to
surrender and the Californians pursuing relentlessly
and burning away the woods in which the savages took
cover. But, again for lack of ammunition, the white men
were forced to yield the advantage so painfully won, and
leave the field to the enemy.[189]

The San Diego district was kept apprehensive,
through the spring and early summer of 1833, by rumors of

---

[189] Bancroft, *Calif.*, vol. 3, pp. 110--14, **passim.**

a projected rising of neophytes and gentiles to seize mission property. There was reason for belief that invitations to participate had been sent to the different missions, and that El Cajón was the rendevous from which the attack was to be made. It is not clear how serious the mischief brewing was; but a small force seized the ringleaders at Cajón, and the unrest seems to have subsided for the time in that area.

Several expeditions from San José into the interior valleys afforded Indian news for the balance of the year, however; and during 1834 all the southern missions -- especially San Gabriel -- suffered. In October, the San Bernardino Rancho of San Gabriel Mission was raided, Padre Esténega being held prisoner for a time. In December, the ranch was attacked again, the buildings were looted and burned and several persons killed, wounded or captured. The excitement continued through January and February. The leading spirits in the disorders were ex-neophytes of San Gabriel, according to refugee reports.

At about the same time, friendly Indians warned Serrano to leave Temescal, as Colorado River Indians were to attack the Angeles district.

In 1836, Vallejo appears to have joined forces with Chief Solano to reduce the troublesome Yolos of the northern

437

interior; and planned (but seems not to have effected) an expedition against the Indians of the Tulares, who as usual were keeping San José and the surrounding region more or less continually disturbed.

In this year, too, the frontier settlement of Santa Anna y Farías, which Figueroa and more especially Vallejo had been at such pains to establish in 1834, was abandoned because of the insecurity of its location in savage gentile country.[190]

The years 1836, '37 and '39 brought repeated diaster to the San Diego district at the hands of the Indians. The scourge was so severe that it was decided to establish a garrison at Santa Isabel; but that proved impossible of accomplishment with the means at hand. So the harassment continued. "Again and again," Bancroft gleaned from the records, "the frontier ranchos were plundered until most of them had to be abandoned; and the town itself was often thought to be in danger, with neither soldiers, arms nor supplies for effectual defense."[191]

Among the sufferers were Juan Bandini and his family, reduced to poverty and serious want by the sacking of

---

[190] Bancroft, Calif., vol. 3, pp. 358--61; 630--31, n. 1, "1834"; 257.

[191] Ibid., vol. 4, p. 67; vol. 3, p. 615.

their Tecate Rancho.[192]

Several persons were massacred at Rancho Jamul, at about this time, and two girls carried into captivity from which they never returned. (These victims -- all workers on the ranch -- may have been Indians, though Bancroft found them spoken of in several accounts as white.) A punitive expedition which pursued the attackers into the mountains was defeated, with many wounded.

In 1839--40, "few if any of the ranchos [of the San Diego district] escaped plunder, most of them being entirely abandoned at different times."[193]

A plot to destroy San Diego and its inhabitants was discovered at about this time. The homes of the townspeople were to be opened to the enemy by conspiring Indian servants. Fortunately, the plan leaked out and was frustrated by the summary arrest and execution of several of the faithless employees.

Of San Diego's plight, Bancroft says: "Notwithstanding the fragmentary nature of the records, it is evident that in all these years the frontier ranchos were continually ravaged by Indians, and that there was no security for

---

[192] Bancroft, Calif., vol. 2, p. 709; vol. 4, p. 69, n. 60.

[193] Ibid., vol. 3, p. 614, n. 3, "1839--40."

either life or property. The condition of this more than any other part of California resembled that of the Apache frontier in Sonora and Chihuahua, though the loss of life was much less."[194]

Central California was almost as heavily afflicted, the San José region being particularly exposed to the onslaughts of marauders sweeping down upon the coast through the passes from the interior valleys. Gentile and ex-neophyte horse-thieves, abetted by treacherous mission Indians and often incited by foreign rangers of the wilderness, murdered, burned, raped and looted. Soldier and citizen operations against these destroyers were an ever prominent feature of the life of the time.

The year 1839 was marked by an access of depredations which evoked even more than the usual punitive activity. An expedition led by Captains Buelna and Estrada to the Kings River region in June, resulted in the taking of seventy-seven prisoners, chiefly women and children -- which suggests considerable killing of the men, remarks Bancroft. Alférez Prado Mesa also did effective execution in a summer *entrada*; but in December, a band of pillagers which he had pursued to the Stanislaus country turned on him in a surprise attack, killing three of his citizen

---

[194] Calif., vol. 4, pp. 67--70, *passim*.

volunteers and wounding him and six of his soldiers.

The central Californians met the ever mounting number and severity of the Indian forays by a determined and at least temporarily successful big offensive on several fronts in 1840. In these operations, J. J. Vallejo defended the southern settlements of the district, and Lieutenant Martinez, materially aided by John Marsh and other Americans, did good service in the Mount Diablo vicinity.[195]

In June of 1843, citizens of the Monterey district complained to Micheltorena of the long series of ravages which they had sustained, and declared that if protection were not afforded they would soon be compelled to abandon their ranchos, as no *majordomos* could be found to take charge of them, so great was the insecurity of life. The Indians invaded the very towns, on their looting expeditions.[196]

The depredations centering about Los Angeles and on up to the Santa Margarita divide were so largely inspired and conducted by foreign plunderers that, says Bancroft, they hardly belong to the topic of Indian affairs at all.

The Chaguanosos, indeed, did not limit themselves to thieving expeditions under cover of trading. Soldiers of

---

[195] Bancroft, *Calif.*, vol. 4, pp. 74--76.
[196] *Ibid.*, p. 361.

431

fortune of the most unscrupulous type, they threw themselves into any enterprise that promised profit. On occasion, they constituted themselves political partisans and even defenders of public security, aiding the abajeños against both northern opponents and hostile Indians;". . . but they allowed nothing to interfere long or seriously with their regular business of stealing horses, in the prosecution of which they employed gentiles and neophytes." In April 1840, they ran off 1,200 horses from San Luís Obispo alone. One of several pursuing parties drew close enough to perceive that more Americans than Indians were concerned in this rustling operation.

The case had been similar in a raid of 1837, wherein two Indian defenders had been killed.[197]

Only on the northern frontier was comparative security maintained -- and that precariously, subject to disruption by the conjunction of unfavorable circumstances. Toward the end of 1842, Vallejo warned Micheltorena of the isolation of his frontier and of his inability, through lack of men and means, to meet a combined attack of **indios joaquineros** and those of the Sacramento, with the "Missourians" on one side and the Sotoyomis on the other.[198]

---

[197] Bancroft, Calif., vol. 4, pp. 75--77.
[198] Oct. 15, 1842, Vallejo to Micheltorena, in Vallejo Doc., MS, vol. 11, #283, p. 3.

Nevertheless, the young commander defended the back country of the northern Contra Costa with remarkable success. His domination of the long and hazardous front was accomplished by indefatigable zeal; a well drilled body of troops maintained practically at his own expense; an organized armed citizenry; a sagaciously developed system of Indian alliances, based on specific treaty agreements and cemented by friendship with the powerful Suisun chief Solano; and a policy of absolute equity, beneficent or stern according to the situation, in dealing with friendly and hostile savages alike.

Even Solano, important to the Californians as his good-will was, learned that he could not with impunity violate treaty promises to Vallejo and to other tribes. When in 1838 the Suisun chieftain lent himself to the capture of Indian children to be sold to the whites as servants, Vallejo had him seized and imprisoned, and caused all the children to be restored to their families.[199]

One of the drawbacks to the Indian-alliance policy was that it frequently involved warfare on behalf of one or other of the friendly tribes. Yet Vallejo never failed, apparently, to fulfill his obligations in that respect. Indeed, it seems very unlikely that, without such alliance

---

[199] See post, pp. 506--7.

and compliance, the northern frontier could have been held against the numerous and warlike hordes of the north bay region. For it must be remembered that the **linea del norte** extended south to Santa Inés, comprising therefore a territory almost hopelessly vast for the means of defense at its commanding officer's disposal.

Through the years of his commandancy of the northern line, Don Guadalupe's life was in one of its aspects a protracted Indian campaign. Nor did the gentile scourge, neophyte apostasy and the perfidy of renegade white interlopers constitute the full tax on his vigilance. Forced to resort to the enlistment of Indian troops, he sometimes had to cope with disaffection within their ranks.

In 1840, such a rising assumed dangerous proportions, the native infantry attacking the cavalry and, on being repulsed, deserting to the gentiles. The combined enemy were defeated with much loss by Californian soldiers and Indian allies under Solano. Nine of the deserters and two of the non-treaty chiefs who had harbored them were executed.

Although above suspicion of bloodthirstiness, Vallejo never hesitated to make stern reprisals in the interest of public security. In this case, summary retribution was the more urgent since he had reason to believe that the renegades had enlisted the co-operation of Sacramento tribes.[200]

Another direction which Indian control had sometimes to take was that of restraining neophytes from unprovoked raids on gentiles, which were undertaken for the purpose of securing women or animals, or, sometimes perhaps, in sheer reversion to savagery. In 1840, for example, San José Mission Indians visiting around Sutter's Fort committed outrages on Indians employed there. A number of captures and ten public executions was the immediate retaliation, conducted by Sutter with decision and courage; but the affair was not finally settled until Californian forces had ridden several times into the valley to rescue gentiles still held, and to apprehend guilty mission Indians still at large.[201]

From 1839 on, Vallejo, in his repression of the trans-bay tribes, had the doubtful benefit of Sutter's domination in the Sacramento Valley. The Swiss was in his way as successful in dealing with the Indians as was Vallejo. Unlike the latter, however, he was motivated in all his dealings not by aspiration for California's immediate and ultimate advantage, but first, last and always, by personal interest.

That disposition was reflected in his Indian policy despite its many wise and liberal features. Like Vallejo,

---

[200] Bancroft, Calif., vol. 4, pp. 70--77, passim; vol. 3, p. 723, n. 20, "1840."
[201] Ibid., vol. 4, pp. 137--38.

he entrenched himself largely by means of alliances. Unlike Vallejo, he based his Indian relations on considerations of profit, often to the detriment of equity. If he did not actually receive stolen stock from the tribesmen, he sometimes found it to his advantage to look leniently on their horse-theiving propensities, even, says Bancroft, affording some protection indirectly to those who respected his own animals.[202]

Still more subversive of the principles which Vallejo sought to inculcate in gentiles and mission Indians alike was the Swiss entrepreneur's inclusion, in his concerns, of the seizure and sale of Indian children and the sale of adult Indian labor.[203] Certain of the *Californios*, as we shall see,[204] were not loath to avail themselves of those commodities, either as provided by Sutter and others or as secured by individual effort.

Despite his obvious shortcomings as a frontier reinforcement, however, Sutter did for a time serve as a buffer against the Indians, in so far justifying the administration's concession to him of the Sacramento grant. In 1842, Alvarado was enthusiastic over his initiative and achievement,

---

[202] Bancroft, *Calif.*, vol. 4, pp. 64, 132.
[203] *Ibid.*, pp. 138, 544.
[204] *Post*, sec. 55.

attributing to him a large measure of credit for the pacification of the gentiles of the north.[205]

The *Californios,* inured to the Indian situation, seem to have accepted its hazards and challenge with remarkable sang-froid. William Heath Davis observed[206] that they seemed to consider a few of themselves match for any number of Indians. It will be seen later[207] that for reasons beyond the control of aspirants to land, few private grants were made until the last decade before the conquest -- the original Spanish estates almost certainly numbering well under a score, and the Mexican grants, with a very few exceptions, coming chiefly after the middle '30s and in greatest number in the '40s. However, in the early days and later when land could be had, grantees did not hesitate to establish themselves and their families, with only a few servants (generally Indian), in isolated locations close to the gentile country.

Almost any site a little removed from the coast and the settlements was perilous enough; but there are numerous examples of *haciendas* on the very fringe of savagery. Out

---

[205] Jan. 11, 1842, Alvarado to Min. of Relations, in Dept..Rec., MS, vol. 13, pp. 10--12.

[206] *Seventy-five Years,* p.

[207] Chap. V, sec. 50, 51.

from San Diego in the Yuma country, and elsewhere on the desert's fringe; deep in the San Bernardino wilds; in the exposed little valleys of the central coast range; along the southern Contra Costa and north of the Bay, men like the Picos and Argüellos and Carrillos; the Lugos and Yorbas; Pacheco and the Alvisos; Moraga and Martinez and the Vallejos, risked their lives and property.

But, too few in number to distribute themselves over the entire length and breadth of their territory, unaugmented from Mexico, and intruded upon by foreigners, the men of California had no recourse save to employ the strangers in their midst, in so far as possible, as aids to occupation and defense. For that specific reason, grants were made to foreigners: to Michael White in consideration of his keeping the Cajón Pass closed; to Yount and Mark West and Stephen Smith as buffers along the northern frontier; to Marsh and Sutter as guardians of the great interior stretches.

"When I first went into the Valley," wrote Sutter, my nearest neighbors were a hundred and more miles away. There was Dr. Marsh at Monte Diablo, and Yount at Napa valley. In other words there was not a single settler in either the Sacramento or the San Joaquin vallies when I went in there." [208]

---

[208] *Personal Reminiscences*, MS, pp. 62--63.

It is not to be inferred that, having established their *estrangero* settlers on the Indian threshold, the *Californios* abandoned further responsibility. In the face of the common danger, sons of the country and foreign interlopers rode into action side by side, as appears throughout the records of Indian warfare. Alvarado went so far as to charge the Commander of the North with failure to give Sutter all the aid he deserved[209] -- an accusation without apparent foundation. Gladly as Vallejo would have seen Sutter evicted from the too strategical and too independent location on the Sacramento, he seems to have treated the Swiss with meticulous fairness. From time to time, as occasion demanded, he furnished needed assistance against the Indians, and in 1840, a year of decided turbulence on the northern frontier, he circumvented a plot against New Helvetia.[210]

46. The *Vecinos* as Indian Campaigners

In the struggle with the barbarians, the sorely taxed military were supplemented by citizen auxiliaries. Indeed, it seems likely that a large part of the time which the

---

[209] Jan. 11, 1842, Alvarado to Min. of Rel., in Dept. Rec., MS, vol. 13, pp. 10--12.

[210] Bancroft, *Calif.*, vol. 4, p. 137, n. 30.

picturesque "Arcadian" caballeros spent in the saddle was devoted to fighting Indians.

Nor did the vecinos always leave it to the soldados to initiate action. So ready were they to pursue and avenge that in 1834 the governor from time to time issued orders prohibiting citizen sorties after horse-theives except in company with the troops.[211] This regulation was intended largely to check the impulses of certain rancheros toward securing laborers by strong-arm methods under cover of punitive steps. Against such practises Figueroa found it necessary to issue strict orders.[212]

From the Californians' point of view, there was doubtless a certain justice in making that particular sort of reprisal for assaults on their haciendas and herds, and the murder or capture of their working people. In 1836, a proposition of Don Silvestre Portilla to subdue the San Diego Indians at his own expense, if allowed to keep prisoners as servants, was approved by the ayuntamiento on the ground that the Indians were outlaws.[213]

----

[211] Jan. 21, 1834, Dept. St. Pap. San José, MS, vol. 4, p. 143.

[212] Jan. 24, 1835, Ibid., pp. 164--65.

[213] Bancroft, Calif., vol. 4, pp. 67--68.

Either the enterprise failed or it was never actually launched, however; for the next year an Indian crisis in the same locality caused the forces enlisted against Alvarado to defer their political objective and engage the more malignant foe.[214]

Adequate military force being unavailable, various efforts at extraordinary means of Indian control were resorted to. In May 1836, Chico ordered the formation of local <u>cuerpos de seguridad y policía</u>, at about the same time declaring to the <u>diputación</u> that the constant thefts of horses and cattle constituted one of California's greatest evils. A law of December 29, 1835, newly arrived from Mexico, brought such malefactors within the ordinary military jurisdiction.[215]

From the late '30s on, many references occur in the documents to a militia and citizen patrols maintained against the Indians. In the San José district were formed two companies of militia, each of 44 men rank and file, "most of the vecinos enrolling themselves." This particular organization seems to have dissolved in 1840.[216] But

---

[214] Bancroft, <u>Calif.</u>, vol. 3, p. 614, n1 8, "1837."
[215] <u>Ibid.</u>, p. 424.
[216] <u>Ibid.</u>, p. 732, n. 26; vol. 4, p. 76.

there is reference, in the records of 1841, to a "temporary auxiliary company" for Indian service. A general order of February 16, 1841, issued in Mexico, called this body into existence; and a document of September of that year indicates the cessation of its activities.[217]

Obviously these Indian-fighting militia companies organized from time to time when need arose. There was no particular necessity of permanent units of the sort, as the men were always ready to ride forth at an alarm, and were kept in good training, without drill, by the exigencies of the Indian situation itself.

A bando of 1840[218] contains Governor Alvarado's regulations for a "mobile patrol" of 20 men to defend the Monterey district against wild Indians and other marauders. The force was to operate in two sections. It was constantly to cover threatened points, protect all individuals demanding protection, and pursue and arrest pillagers. Wild Indians were not to be allowed through the lines (of settlement) without passports. Except when their presence was demanded for defense, the patrols were not to remain longer than two days at any one ranch. The defenders would

---

217 Bancroft, Calif., vol. 4, p. 198.
218 Dept. St. Pap., San José, MS, vol. 5, pp. 58--60.

have to rely on the ranchers for supplies, but would be paid from the appropriation of 254 pesos a month from the public treasury. Changes or reforms in the organization of the patrols would be considered after three months' experience.

47. Projects and Problems of Indian Defense

The year 1841 was sufficiently quiet to lull the governor into a belief -- undoubtedly fathered by hope-- that the Indian situation was under control; but Vallejo continued to urge improved defenses, and declared, the next year, that unless military reinforcements could be secured, the gentiles would overrun the department.[219] That his judgment was better than Alvarado's on this point, time showed.

In 1843, Micheltorena ordered a detachment of soldiers to be stationed at the Pacheco rancho ("the rancheros being invited to share in the expense"). José Castro kept an armed force in the Sierras for two months -- and hoped for a 300-peso appropriation with which to pay for it. Citizens of San José petitioned the governor for a permanent escolta, for the support of which they were willing to contribute.[220]

----

219 Bancroft, Calif., vol. 4, pp. 196--97, 338.
220 Ibid., p. 362, n. 27.

The next spring, the establishment of a presidio somewhere in the Tulares was undertaken. Contributions were to be solicited for the defraying of expenses, and apparently materialized to the extent of 429 pesos, for a treasury statement of 1845 shows that amount disbursed for the Tulares establishment.[221] Castro was in the San Joaquin Valley on that business when recalled to the settlements by the outbreak of revolt in November.[222]

In 1845, the alcalde of Santa Cruz proposed sending 25 men against the gentiles every two weeks.[223]

The wild Indian problem was one of Pico's first concerns on assuming the governorship. By way of innovation, he tried letting a contract for the control of the tribes of the north. Captain Gantt, Dr. Marsh and others of the estrangero campaigners whom Sutter had marshalled to Micheltorena's standard in 1844--45 offered to perform the service at their own expense, in return for 500 cattle and half of all the livestock which they might recover. This instance of foreign enterprise seems to have come to nothing --in accordance with the prediction of failure by Sutter, who declared that the men were unwilling to accompany the leaders on the service contracted for. This was a handicap

---

[221] Larkin Doc., MS, vol. 3, 498.
[222] Bancroft, Calif., vol. 4, p. 409.
[223] Ibid., p. 664, n. 10.

from which Californian expeditions seem generally not to have suffered.

In the south, Pico planned a large movement of volunteer Indian-fighters from all the towns of the region. Preparations continued for nearly two months. The force, says Bancroft,[224] was to march from San Fernando on June 15th; but the documentary record ends about a week before that date.-- negative evidence, perhaps, of another abortive effort.

During the spring of 1846 and on into the summer, the old agitation for a presidio in the Cajón, against the Mojave Indians, was renewed. Isaac Williams offered to fortify the pass if allowed to introduce $25,000 worth of goods duty-free. It is not clear how his proposition was received; but one of the last pieces of business taken up by the departmental assembly was this matter of closing the Cajon against the wild transmontane tribes.[225]

It has not been attempted here to do more than indicate the severity of the barbarian scourge which the Californians were called upon to withstand. "The constant depredations of renegade neophytes, in alliance with gentile

---

[224] Calif., vol. 4, pp. 543--44.
[225] Ibid., vol. 5, p. 37, n. 11.

bands, and instigated by New Mexican vagabond traders and foreign hunters, kept the country in a state of chronic disquietude . . . . , being the most serious obstacle to progress and prosperity," declares Bancroft. "Murders of gente de razon were of comparatively rare occurrence, but in other respects the scourge was similar to that of the Apache ravages in Sonora and Chihuahua. Over a large extent of country the Indians lived mainly on the flesh of stolen horses, and cattle were killed for their hides when money to buy liquor could not be less laboriously obtained by the sale of other stolen articles. The presence of the neophytes and their intimate relations with other inhabitants doubtless tended to prevent general attacks and bloody massacres, as any plot was sure to be revealed by somebody; but they also rendered it wellnigh impossible to break up the complicated and destructive system of robbery."[226]

Estimates of the numbers of the wild tribes of California vary widely, and are, in the nature of the case, largely speculative. Salvador Vallejo, whose basis for judgment was perhaps as complete as any, estimated the gentiles at upwards of 740,000. He reckoned 60,000, his

----

[226] Calif., vol. 3, p. 361.

brother Guadalupe, 70,000, deaths among the tribesmen, resulting from the ravages of smallpox in the 1830s.[227]

Partially offsetting this Malthusian gain to civilization was the introduction of firearms among the savage population, on an increasingly large scale during and after the 1830s. Fur traders and other wilderness rovers exchanged arms for pelts and horses over a long period. Shortly before the conquest, the system seems to have found a wider application. "It is to be feared that the American emigrants from Oregon are beginning to spread firearms among the wild Indians in exchange for horses and cattle," complained Congressman Castañares; "and that the Indians rob the ranchos to supply the needs of the foreigners."[228]

The Indian problem, of course, was a formidable one. No system of defences, however well conceived and financed, no offensive, however ambitious and effective, could quiet the savage hordes that milled everywhere about California -- as the United States army itself discovered, just

---

[227] S. Vallejo, Notas hist., MS, p. 45; Bancroft, Calif. vol. 4, pp. 73--74. The disease was thought to have been brought into California by way of Fort Ross.

[228] Col. de Doc., p. 31.

following the conquest.[229] Only the slow wearing process of years of campaigning, or substantially extended occupation, could push back the barbarian frontier. These processes the *Californios* were effecting patiently and with good heart.

To the overwhelming numbers of the Indians, their few thousands opposed a resolute front, making up in courage what they lacked in numerical strength. A people of remarkable fecundity, moreover, they would, in a not too remote future, have multiplied to the point of actually possessing the earth which they had inherited.

But for them there was no future. The conquest was upon them.

---

[229] See *post*, *chap.* 11.

CHAPTER V: FOMENTO DE CALIFORNIA

48. "Paralysis" under Spain and
    Mexico..........................pp. 448--457
49. The Dons were Promoters............ 458--461
50. The Californians Lacked Land!...... 462--478
51. Land, Ho!.......................... 478--483
52. Real Estates that were not Real
    Estates............................ 483--493
53. The Clutch of the Dead Hand........ 493--501
54. "Falta de Brazos, Falta de Manos!".. 501--505
55. Slavery............................ 505--509
56. The Splendid Forties............... 509--518
57. Hides and Tallow................... 518--538
58. Horses, Mules and Cattle........... 538--544
59. Caballeros -- of the Plow.......... 545--561
60. Vines and Wines.................... 563--568
61. The Middle Age of Agriculture...... 568--577
62. Profits from Ocean and River....... 577--601
63. Mining before 1848................. 602--628

CHAPTER V: **FOMENTO DE CALIFORNIA** (Continued)

64. Making by Hand.........................pp. 628--643
65. Who'll Buy?............................   643--663
66. Aspirations toward Sea Power..........   664--713
67. Purchasing Power and Volume of Trade..   713--733
68. **Dons** of the Counter and Counting-House 733--741
69. Promotion of the Northern Frontier....   741--752
70. Conclusions: Arcadians at Work........   752--761

CHAPTER V: FOMENTO DE CALIFORNIA

48. "Paralysis" under Spain and Mexico

The tradition of California's utter indifference to self-development until after her Americanization has been for so long so solidly established that any mere statement to the contrary evokes amused and patronizing disagreement. Yet ample facts to substantiate such a contrary statement have long lain close to the surface in the placers of Bancroft's *History of California* and in the deeper though readily accessible mines of the information of the Bancroft Library.

Volumes might be written on the various phases of efforts to promote California before 1846. For purposes of the present undertaking, the entire subject, despite its ramifications and voluminousness, must be treated summarily in a single chapter. Here, therefore, it will be possible only to indicate broadly that, despite the impossibility of making any start under Spanish mercantilism, ecclesiasticism and autocracy, and despite the handicaps against which she labored as a Mexican territory, California had entered upon a phase of vigorous development before ever the *estrangeros* became a power in the country; and stood on the threshold of economic regeneration a decade before the conquest.

What the foreign interlopers mistook for the decadence of the Spanish flowering were actually the tentatives and unfoldings of a native Californian industrial and commercial burgeoning. Of agriculture, manufacture, trade -- except as conducted by the missionaries -- the country had practically none before the middle 1820s, very little before the '30s. When she did come into her opportunity -- of a generation's scant extent -- her every step was impeded by inherited disabilities only slowly and painfully to be eradicated: lack of men and money and means of self-defense; excessive regulation -- in the interests of the metropolis; commercial exploitation by Mexico, foreign monopolists and **contrabandistas**, alike; inexperience and isolation; and all the problems and pitfalls incidental to the emancipation of a culturally inferior but numerically preponderant people, and the reconstruction of the country's social, political and industrial economy along entirely new lines.

As Spanish provincials, the Californians (except for the missionaries) had had practically no opportunity to pursue even agricultural and pastoral occupations beyond a mere subsistence level. Those industries had been confined to a few worked-out discards from the army, and a scattering of low-grade mixed bloods whom over-regulation would have prevented from using initiative had they had any. Of trade there had been none, save an exploitatory and sometimes prohibited barter with the supply ships, until at the close of the period the foreign <u>contrabandistas</u> enclosed California in the grip which, for generations past, they had maintained on the rest of Hispano-America.

The time was not without its prophets of opportunity. There was Cancelada, who in 1811 incorporated in his <u>Ruina de la Nueva España</u> an indictment of Spain's stupid waste of Californian potentialities. He declared that in 1808 or thereabout a single American ship had introduced into the province manufactured goods which, supplied by Mexico, would have netted $300,000; and that in six months of 1809, 11,105 packages of provincial produce and $4,187 in money had been carried abroad!

There were Carlos María Bustamante and Tadeo Ortiz de Ayala, whose exhortations to Californian development and trade, on the even of Mexican independence, have already been mentioned.[2] And there were many others.

----

[1] Bancroft, <u>Calif.</u>, vol. 2, p. 194, n. 18.
[2] <u>Ante</u>, pp. 9--12.

Yet as a matter of fact, despite the opportunities so perceived and urged, serious obstacles impeded the growth of legitimate trade in the California of the eighteenth and early nineteenth centuries. "Spanish manufacturers had always been handicapped by the wealth of the Indies, since the huge gold supply . . . . caused prices to rise" to the advantage of more cheaply produced foreign goods, remarks Fisher.[3] The consequence to Mexico (feeder of the Spanish gold supply), was an exactly opposite condition -- scarcity of money -- producing an identical result -- high prices.

Spain and the foreign traders drained off New Spain's mineral wealth, leaving her merchants to carry on business in the early nineteenth century largely with foreign capital, at a price. According to the Bishop of Michoacan, only about one in twenty of the merchants of Mexico operated with their own funds. The others paid 5% on borrowings, or conducted business on credit at a penalty of 15%. Of invested capital, only 5% was in the form of money in circulation.[4] With currency in such demand, Mexico sold for all she could get. California -- in far greater financial distress -- must get all she could for what she spent.

Most urgently, California must develop her own latent

---

[3] Commercial Conditions in Mexico, p. 145.
[4] Ibid., p. 160.

resources. That was not possible during her enforced unproductiveness as a military-ecclesiastical frontier of Spain. It was exceedingly difficult under her handicaps as a territory of Mexico and a field for exploitation by foreigners with every initial advantage. Yet, as we shall see, the Californians of the middle period, fired with realization of the country's possibilities and with the craving for economic independence, cherished vigorous ambitions for the fomento de California; and made progress toward the realization of those ambitions beyond what was to have been expected of them or of far more experienced and aggressive and financially advantaged entrepreneurs.

Writing in the early '30s of California's attractiveness as a field for development by Britons, Forbes stipulated: "But all this presupposes great reform to be made in the character of the Mexican government and its agents; for it must be admitted that, at present, British emigrants would not find themselves much at ease under the control of the local authorities in any district of the republic. Nothing can be more different from the non-interference with private enterprise and private conduct which characterizes the British policy, than the meddling and vexatious interference of the military and civil authorities, which mixes in all the business of life in present Spanish-American countries, and which is thought necessary to enforce the infinity of laws and regulations enacted for the guidance of the citizens in the most minute affairs."5

Nevertheless, in spite of conditions daunting to John Bull, the _dons_ of California worked their way toward a place in the economic sun.

To be sure, Mexico evinced as good intentions toward this aspect of the territory's welfare as toward so many others. The _Junta de Fomento de Californas_ recommended "generous exemption of the settlers from tithes and land and sea duties (except on fish, pearls and furs) for six years" from date of immigration; and suspension, for the same period, of the tax of a fifth "on metals extracted and mines and placers that may be discovered and worked." After the expiration of the indicated term, only maritime duties were to be imposed, that trade might be fomented. This second stage of exemption was to continue until the government should decide that there was no further need for it. Retail trade should be limited to nationals, to whom also, as an incentive, certain immunities should be granted. Pearl, otter, whale and seal fisheries should be promoted. Sardines,

---

5 _Alta Calif._, pp. 324--25.

herring, salmon and other edible fish should be dried or pickled. A _junta_ of trade and agriculture should be appointed by the governors of the two Californias until promotive organizations (_sociedades patrióticas_) could be formed.[6]

Orders to and reports of the governors whom she sent amply evidence Mexico's desire to promote territorial productiveness and trade. Bancroft did not find the supreme government's original instructions to Echeandía, but there is no reason to doubt that they were in the spirit and along the lines of the recommendations made by the forward-looking _Junta de Fomento_, which had been created for the express purpose of investigating conditions in the territory and suggesting policies for its governance.[7]

Although Victoria was but nine months in office, he found time -- and that early in his incumbency -- to report on and make recommendations concerning California's industrial condition.[8]

Figueroa was instructed to follow the directions which had been issued to Echeandía; and was specifically ordered to further by all means possible the fomentation

----

[6] _Junta de Fomento, Colección_, Item #5 (_Iniciativa de Ley_), pp. 24--26.

[7] See _ante_, sec. 3.

[8] Bancroft, Calif., vol. 3, p. 186.

and prosperity of California. He was to promote the
export of surplus products, including furs, field crops
and tallow; and to induce the missions to build small
vessels that the coast trade might be facilitated. He
was to proceed with land distribution to Mexicans and
Indians and -- with discretion -- to foreign colonists;
to see that promising Indian youths were sent to Mexico
at the expense of the richest missions, to learn to be
teachers of trades; and was to render full statistics
on the possibilities of development of California and
her islands, and on her industries.[9]

As has been indicated,[10] Figueroa had been in the
territory but a few months when he went on record as
opposed to export duties and oppressive sales taxes,
and in favor of the reformation of the customs administration on the basis of the country's peculiar circumstances. In 1834, in his report to the supreme government on financial and commercial conditions, he
pointed out existing business evils and asked for reform of the harmful system of laws which could not

----

[9] May 7, 1832, Ortiz Monasterio, *Instrucciones generales* . . . . *al General Don José Figueroa, 1832,* MS, in *Sup. Govt. St. Pap., Decrees & Despatches,* MS, vol. 8, pp. 32--39, *passim.*

[10] *Ante,* pp. 240--41.

possibly be enforced.

Micheltorena's instructions enjoined him not only to protect agriculture, commerce and all the country's industries, and by all means at his command to encourage internal improvements and colonization, but even to foster the development of art.[11]

Despite so much eloquent fervor on the part of Mexico and her officials in California, however, inept laws and regulations continued to hamper progress, and with urgent and bitter protests the Californians continued to lament the consequent "total paralysis" of the country.

Meanwhile, alien speculators had seized the opportunities offered by the peculiar combination of circumstances to foist on the land a monopoly which was almost from the start too strong to be broken. Where Spain had employed mercantilism and Mexico the tariff, the foreign traders brought to bear the most powerful of economic weapons -- the boycott. They could not anticipate the term still to be inspired by Irish Captain Boycott's troubles of the 1880s; but their mastery of the method

---

[11] Feb. 11, 1842, Micheltorena, *Instrucciones que recibió* . . . ., in Vallejo, *Hist. de Calif.*, MS, vol. 4, pp. 268--72.

was none the less efficacious. They refused to trade except in certain commodities and on certain conditions. When those commodities were refused or those conditions not met, they sailed away or -- with compelling effect -- threatened to sail away without doing business (contraband excepted).[12]

The whole history of Mexican California's foreign trade is a history of the constraint of territorial resources and industry to the service of foreign interests. Begg and Company of Peru, through their Californian representatives McCullough and Hartnell, sought control of commerce by exclusive contract with the government, specifying wanted goods and prices.[13] Their competitors relied on direct action as a means to monopoly. In every case, however, the interest of the *estrangeros* was limited to a very few commodities. As the men of the country, without means to seek out buyers, were forced to deal with such customers as could be encouraged to keep coming to them, the direction of their productive enterprise was very largely determined abroad.[14]

---

[12] See ~~post, pp. 650-55;~~ ante, pp. 249--50, 263, 269.

[13] Bancroft, *Calif.*, vol. 2, pp. 475--77.

[14] For further discussion of the export specialties insisted on by the foreign traders, see post, pp. 650--55.

49. The Dons Were Promoters

Efforts for the reduction or abolition of crushing duties, and the suspension of trade prohibitions, have been mentioned earlier,[15] as has been Alvarado's abortive attempt to wrest the retail coasting-trade from the hands of foreigners. Don Bautista also urged development of "the infant branch of agriculture . . . . the most necessary and important branch of industry in the department and that most deserving of governmental protection"; and the determined building up of the territory's "nascent commerce." Elsewhere, in connection with his campaign for governmental subsidy as an aid in casting off the foreign monopolists, he declared that thus the great objective would be attained, namely, the promotion of the infant national commerce and of a merchant marine and land transport.[16]

A document of 1837 addressed by Vallejo to Alvarado throws further light on the promotive keenness of the sons of the country. Don Guadalupe begins on the note of contrast between the territory's public and private resources:

---

[15] Ante, sec. 32; pp. 247--50.

[16] Leg. Rec., MS, vol. 3, pp. 49, 50; Dec. 12, 1840, Alvarado to Min. of Int., quoted, Feb. 13, 1841, by Min. of War to Vallejo, in Savage Doc., MS, vol. 4, #329.

"If the public treasury in Alta California were sufficient to the need, this precious land would present to the world a happy aspect of fortune, with wealth proportioned to its population. . . ."

Having stated, then, the need to prohibit the retail coast trade to foreigners, and having recommended the transference of the custom-house from Monterey to San Francisco because of the latter point's greater defensibility as a port of entry, he discusses the advantages offered by the great bay for water-borne commerce with the interior, by way of "the brimful rivers of Sacramento, San Joaquín and Jesús María [Feather], navigable for more than 100 leagues; and others of little less merit and utility."

The region is also ideal as a center of distribution by land transport; for "all the population of the country, save for a very few points, connect by wagon road with the San Francisco shore; and the Californians have all the necessities for purveying, though till now held inoperative. Moreover, and particularly, granted the necessary exemptions from taxes to permit them to ply the coasts, the sons of the country would share their private embarcaderos with each other, to their own profit and that of national trade; and the coast trade and the overland carrying trade would stimulate each other, the inhabitants reaping the value of the freights and cargoes, and the treasury being greatly enriched."17

In 1841, in an intensely earnest letter to the Minister of War, the general asked for a protective tariff, a prohibited import list based on Californian, not on Mexican needs, and the elimination of foreigners from the coasting-trade, so that territorial production of both raw materials and manufactures might become profitable, and a territorial land transport might develop. The fruits and crops of all climes could be grown in California, particularly the grape, tobacco, olives, cotton, hemp. Yet, "we have to buy Catalán brandy, wines of all kinds, Virginia tobacco, oil from Marseilles, cloth from Boston, manufactures of all sorts, including the commonest articles such as brooms from the Sandwich Islands."

If existing law were enforced, the home vineyards and olive-groves would assume new value and attract more _empresarios_. With no imported English boots and American cloth, shoes and textiles of local manufacture would be sold. Moreover, the foreign vessels would be obliged to consign their goods to a retailer who, even should he be a foreigner, would be established (_radicado_) in the department. Then the coasting-trade could be undertaken by nationals, as

---

17 Vallejo, Exposición, pp. 2, 4, 10, 17--18.

could overland transport. There would be new opportunities for enterprise in the country and of the country; and many allied branches of industry would develop along with them.[18]

The views of Alvarado and Vallejo are of special significance because they embody the policies behind which the country aligned itself. That the two leaders were not lone prophets crying in the wilderness is proved beyond question by fragments from the pens of lesser men, preserved in ample quantity. Carlos Carrillo, for example, foresaw unlimited possibilities in promotion of the country with Pious Fund subsidy; and Manuel Castañares kept his fellow congressmen "Californiados" with his vivid exhortations to territorial fomento in every sphere from mining to whaling.[19] In the following pages, some of those lesser witnesses will be quoted, in evidence of the progressive spirit that possessed the people, and of the general realization of the handicaps to which the territory owed its retardment.

---

[18] Dec. 13, 1841, Vallejo to Min. of War, in Vallejo Doc., MS, vol. 10, #385, pp. 3--5.

[19] C. A. Carrillo, Exposición dirigida a la Camara de Diputados . . . ; C. M. Bustamante, Nuevo Bernal Diaz, vol. 1, p. 48; Castañares, Col. de Doc.,

50. The Californians Lacked Land!

Some of the handicaps from which California's Hispanic pioneers suffered were experienced, though in less degree and under time conditions permitting surmountal, by the continent's Atlantic settlers. One obstacle to self-help, however, placed the Pacific colonists peculiarly and grievously apart. Whereas Atlantic occupation and expansion were, broadly speaking, effects of free land or, at worst, cheap land, the Hispano-Californians were throughout most of their separate history an unlanded people.

That statement is of course sharply at variance with the popular notion of princely "Spanish grants" obtained for the asking. Few people are aware that the number of Spanish grants was practically negligible. Fewer still realize the corollary fact that since most of the grants were made in the Mexican period -- and then not till the '30s and particularly the '40s -- the Californians in 1846 were barely beginning to profit from their stake in the land.

Finally, those persons who glibly talk -- and publish -- of the failure of the indolent _dons_ to develop their vast estates are silent on the point that under Spain and Mexico, titles to land conveyed not ownership, but were usufruct; and that subject to withdrawal at the will of the crown or the supreme government or the local authorities. Such withdrawals, moreover, were common enough even in cases of fields under cultivation. The most enterprising American today would hesitate to invest much of his money or labor or time in cultivating soil to which he could have no title of ownership and of which even his right of use was tentative.

The history of land tenure under Spain and Mexico has been resumed by Bancroft briefly and in scattered bits, as necessitated by the comprehensive and basically chronological plan of his *History of California* -- but none the less plainly. Beginning with Spanish times, he points out that absolute title to all the province was vested in the crown. "No individual ownership of lands, but only usufructuary titles of various grades, existed . . . ." The aborigines held first claim to use of the royal lands for subsistence, according to the theory. As they emerged from savagery to civilized status, their needs could be supplied from more limited areas than would support them on wild game alone. So a land surplus became available for royal allotment. On this, after mission and presidial needs, the traditional four square leagues per pueblo constituted a first claim. House lots and small farms were assignable to settlers by the municipal authorities.

"These titles," continues Bancroft, "were the nearest approach to absolute ownership in California under Spain; but the lands were forfeited by abandonment, failure to cultivate, and non-compliance with certain conditions. They could not be alienated; and one instance is recorded of lands being taken for hemp culture from a settler [of San José or Los Angeles], who was given others in their place."

There remained the crown's surplus lands not occupied by missions and mission Indians, presidios and pueblos. As early as 1784, Governor Fages advised the <u>comandante general</u> that private individuals were applying to him for ranchos; that he had given written permission to several persons to occupy temporarily the lands they desired; and that he wished instructions in the matter. In 1786 he received authorization to grant tracts not exceeding three leagues, always beyond the four-league limits of the existing pueblos, without invasion of the domains of missions or <u>rancherías</u>, and on certain conditions including the building of a stone house on each rancho and the keeping of at least 2,000 head of stock.

However, adds Bancroft, "there is no evidence that any documents were ever given in place of the temporary permits, or that the few provisional grants subsequently made differed in any way from those permits." That the grantee therefore possessed no title to the land was conclusively demonstrated in the case of Rancho Los Nietos, granted to Manuel Nieto in 1784, occupied by him until 1804 and by his children thereafter; yet eventually denied to the heirs by United States Supreme Court decision confirming that of the Land Commission, on the ground that the permit issued by Fages precluded presumption of title.[20]

Presidios and missions were of course expected to develop into pueblos. As such, they would have the disposal of their municipal four square leagues; and the inference seems to have been that grants might be made in anticipation of the pueblo status. As might be expected, however, the padres did not favor distribution of land in the mission vicinities, even to or through neophytes. "In 1790," says Bancroft, " a pensioned corporal, Cayuelas, who had married a neophyte of San Luis Obispo, asked in the name of his wife for lands at Santa Margarita belonging to that mission; but the grant was opposed, probably with success, by the friars, on the ground that the land was needed for the community, to which the neophyte in question had rendered no service."

In a similar case of 1775, the governor had made a

---

[20] Bancroft, *Calif.*, vol. 1, pp. 607--9.

grant on application of the soldier-husband of a neophyte of San Carlos; but the land had been abandoned, for reasons unspecified. These are the only two instances which Bancroft found recorded of land requested in the names of neophytes before 1800. "In fact, only twenty-four neophyte women had married gente de razon since 1769."[21]

The case of the presidos and pueblos was in contrast. There was land in demand. But although in 1791 the presidial commandants were authorized by General Nava to grant lots and fields within the prescribed four square leagues to soldiers and settlers desiring them, there is "no clear evidence that any such grants were made."

In 1793, Arrillaga reported to the viceroy that no lands had been assigned by his predecessors under the authorization of 1786 to Fages, and that because of this failure and of the ultimate right of the natives to the best sites, he felt it best to refrain from land distribution until further orders, although he was constantly asked for ranchos and believed the granting would be good for the country. Early the next year, apparently while awaiting instructions, he permitted several persons to settle provisionally on the Monterey River, within three to five leagues of the presidio.

---

21 Bancroft, *Calif.*, vol. 1, p. 610.

In 1795, Arrillaga retired from the acting governorship on the arrival of Diego Borica to succeed Romeu. The new governor reported to the viceroy on the land situation. He did not know why his predecessors had failed to make grants, but he himself was opposed to such concessions. "It would be difficult to tell what lands the missions really needed," Bancroft paraphrases, "since new converts were constantly made. Troubles between the owners of ranchos and rancheria Indians would lead to excesses and war; the animals of the settlers would do injury to the food supply of the gentiles; the rancheros would be far removed from spiritual care and from judicial supervision; and finally the province had already livestock enough, there being no export. So he proposed that no ranchos should be granted for the present, but that settlers of good character should be allowed to establish themselves provisionally on the land asked for near a mission or pueblo, to be granted them later if it should prove best."

As a matter of fact, Bancroft pursues the subject, several ranchos already existed under those conditions. Even those provisional concessions, however, were frowned upon by Borica, and in some cases withdrawn or modified. "In 1796 a part of the land which Fages had allowed Nieto to occupy was taken from him, on the claim of San Gabriel

Mission that it was needed by the natives. In 1797 the Encino Rancho, held by Francisco Reyes, was taken from him, and both land and buildings appropriated by the new mission of San Fernando." Borica did give some sort of confirmation to Verdugo's title to San Rafael, "but we know nothing of its nature."

At the turn of the century, then, a scant generation before Mexico took over the territory and two very scant generations before the American conquest, California had reached the following stage of occupation and development: "eighteen missions and four presidios, each without settlers, but each intended to become a pueblo, and each entitled to four square leagues of land for distribution to settlers in houselots and sowing lands, or for other pueblo uses; three pueblos of Spaniards already established, entitled also to four leagues . . inhabited by over one hundred settlers, each of whom held about four acres of land still subject to conditions and not to be alienated or hypothecated; and finally twenty or thirty men raising cattle on ranchos which they occupied temporarily by permission of the authorities, without any legal title . . . ."[22]

The next two decades brought little change in system or methods of land distribution, and evidently few additions

---

[22] Bancroft, *Calif.*, vol. 1, pp. 610--12.

to the list of grantees. So far as can be known, reports Bancroft, absolutely no lands were in private possession around either San Diego or San Francisco. At San José, the grantee José Maria Larios sold his land and the house he had built on it to the Mission; whereupon Arrillaga (then governor by appointment) declared the transaction invalid, since Larios had possessed only the usufruct of the land. Six ranches seem to have been in (provisional) private possession in the Monterey region, Buenavista being the only one mentioned in the annals of 1800--10. In 1803, Arrillaga declined to eject the occupants of this rancho at the instigation of the missionaries of San Carlos, who declared that the mission needed the lands. In the same year, Mariano Castro returned from a visit to Mexico bringing viceregal license to occupy La Brea, near San Juan Bautista.

"It seems to have been the plan to form a kind of settlement at La Brea, six persons having agreed as early as 1801 to settle there. The friars protested against the grant, refused to remove their cattle, and so successfully urged their claims that before the end of the decade Castro had to give up for years all hope of possessing La Brea. It became necessary to find another desirable site, and accordingly in May 1807 Castro asked for the rancho of Salsipuedes, near the place since known as Watsonville, which had hitherto been used by the government for the pasturage of presidio horses. Of the result of this application we know nothing beyond the fact that in July Commandant Estudillo made inquiries with a view to learn if the concession would be in any way detrimental to Branciforte, and that the friars of Santa Cruz had something to say in defence of the mission claim to the property in question."

Bancroft assumed that "some if not all" of the six ranchos originally granted in the Monterey region were abandoned before 1810. In the Santa Bárbara and Los Angeles districts, "all the ranches of the last decade were still occupied . . . .," as were probably half a dozen others. At least two applications for ranchos had been refused; and in this connection "the friars expressed very freely their ideas respecting rancheros in general. Their presence was detrimental to the success of missionary effort; they led an idle, vagabond life, often left their farms and wives in charge of gentiles, and set a bad example, rarely coming to hear mass or missing a fandango. The Indians found it hard to understand why they should be flogged for not attending religious services neglected with impunity by the Spaniards; therefore Indians who were brought up among Christians were always hardest to convert. The rancheros, the friars claimed, did not accumulate property, nor add in any respect to the prosperity of the country."

The decade closes with an order forbidding commandants of presidios to own ranchos for the raising of livestock. Only a few milch cows and sheep were to be permitted them.[23]

In 1813, the Spanish Córtes decreed the reduction of public lands in the peninsula and the provinces to private ownership. The purposes of this act were first, expressly but doubtless incidentally, to promote the welfare of the pueblos, agriculture and industry; and second, and particularly, to meet "the desperate necessities resulting to the Spanish government from the attempt of Napoleon to place his brother upon the throne of Spain, and from the civil war to which it gave rise," says Dwinelle.[24] It is intersting that lands granted under this act were to be confirmed in fee simple after four years, though not subject to entail or transfer into mortmain. But the decree remained inoperative in

----

[23] Bancroft, *Calif*, vol. 2, pp. 170--72.
[24] *Colonial Hist.*, p. 39, sec. 52.

California, and perhaps unknown, says Bancroft, who found no copy in the provincial archives.

The Californian land situation, indeed, seems to have suffered greater inactivity than ever. The existence of private ranches is still not indicated in the far south; and in the far north, although it is known that beginnings of agriculture and stockraising were made in the East Bay region, the only recorded grant is that to Peralta in 1820. It is likely that one or two pieces of land were newly occupied during the decade 1811--20, and that some of the old ones were abandoned; but in these last years of Spanish control the changes were few, and the system remained monotonously in statu quo.

The padres still opposed the granting of private ranchos and kept up here and there a minor local quarrel with the occupants of such. To some extent ranchos of neophytes had been formed in connection with the missions; but this practise was not encouraged, because the neophytes' chief object was found to be removal as far as possible from the watchfulness of the missionaries, Bancroft sums up the situation. In 1820, Prefect of missionaries Payeras mentioned thirty-eight ranchos in the province; "but," comments Bancroft, "this doubtless includes

473

the farms cultivated by neophytes living at the missions as well as those occupied by Spanish rancheros."25

Mexico seethed with republican progressiveness when she took over the territory. The church was among the outworn institutions to be cast off in favor of the new order. No longer was ecclesiastical monopoly to crowd out secular and private enterprise. "The subject of secularizing the missions was deemed a most important one in these years by all secular authorities, and it derived most of its importance from the extent and value of the mission lands," says Bancroft. "On the distribution and occupation of territorial lands by actual settlers the future propserity of the country was understood to depend . . ."[26]

Nevertheless, neither secularization nor land distribution could be entered upon blindly or accomplished overnight. Careful survey must be made, all change must be well considered. So Canónigo Fernandez was sent by the regency to compile, among other reports, his weighty account of the state of the missions; and to order that no lands be distributed until regulations had been issued.[27]

---
[25] *Calif.*, vol. 2, pp. 414--15, 342, 375.
[26] *Ibid.*, p. 662.
[27] *Ante*, pp. 7, 29--30.

Halleck speaks of such a body of laws dated April 11, 1823 -- in the interim between the empire and the republic -- but says that they were almost immediately suspended and that "it is believed no grants of land were made under them in Upper California."[28]

Bancroft confirms Halleck's opinion of the inoperativeness in California of the laws of 1823, which, moreover, he did not find in the Californian archives or elsewhere.[29]

The Californians had evidently hoped for prompt allotments, for the subject was taken up in 1823 by the diputación which, however, had no power to act.[30]

The colonization law of August 18, 1824, as has been related elsewhere, gave mere general authorization for land distribution; and it was not until the complementary regulations of November 21, 1828 were adopted that the way was actually opened for applications and grants to be made.[31] Even then, "it seems to have been nearly a year before the last regulations were published

---

[28] Report, p. 120.
[29] Calif., vol. 2, p. 661; ante, p. 83, n. 11.
[30] Leg. Rec., MS, vol. 1, pp. 31--32.
[31] See ante, pp. 84--86.

in California," says Bancroft. At the same time it was decided that mission lands were not to be distributed, due to the great difficulties involved and Mexico's disposition to refrain from injustice to either friars or neophytes.[32]

Meanwhile, Echeandía's instructions had been to bend every effort to acquire precise information regarding the territory, and, pending the outcome, to refrain from any assignment of lands.[33]

In view of all these circumstances, the Californians began the decade of the '30s still a practically landless people. In 1828 Bandini had declared that stockraising by the whites was hampered by lack of land.[34] Bancroft found that by 1830 only forty-six ranchos had been granted to private individuals since the Spanish governor Fages had first been authorized to make a beginning of land distribution in the 1780s! Of the tracts in private possession, more than half had been conferred after 1820, "though only one or two under the regulations of 1828, and only one, so far as clearly appears, with the direct approval of the

----

[32] Calif., vol. 2, pp. 662--63.
[33] Ibid., vol. 3, p. 4.
[34] Nov. (?) 3, 1828, Bandini to Barron, in **Bandini Doc.**, MS, pp. 16--17.

diputacion." The distribution by presidial districts was: San Diego, 6; Santa Bárbara, 14; Monterey, 16; San Francisco, 10.[35]

In other words, Mexican land distribution had not yet gotten under way. A few ranchos were held on the strength of the old Spanish provisional grants; and a few others (probably the majority), having been acquired in the interregnum between Spanish and Mexican domination, rested upon still more precarious claims. Of the entire number, only sixteen were eventually confirmed by the United States Land Commission on the ground of the original concessions. That the American adjusters were not more exacting than the Mexican authority is evidenced by Echeandía's refusal, in 1829, to issue written titles to lands granted by his predecessors.

Even at this stage, "nothing like absolute ownership of land by individuals was yet recognized by the government . . . ."[36]

So much for ranchos. As to home sites and subsistence farms within pueblo limits, Beechey stated[37] that the privilege of pueblo land allotments formerly extended to retired soldiers was being withheld, "and the applicants have been allowed only to possess the land and feed their cattle upon

---

[35] Bancroft, *Calif.*, vol. 2, p. 663.

[36] *Ibid.*, pp. 663--65.

[37] *Narrative*, vol. 2, p. 11.

it until it shall please the government to turn them off."
At least in San Diego, probably generally, the practise
was to confer house-lots verbally. Thus in 1849--50,
Santiago Argüello, Juan Bandini and José Antonio Estudillo,
all of San Diego, petitioned for titles to their residence
sites, where they had built and had lived since "the old days"
when "it was not customary to give title," and when "this
type of grant was asked and made verbally."[38] The first
written title to a San Diego town lot seems to have been
issued in 1838.[39]

With the regulations for land distribution at last in
hand, the sons of the country seemed on the verge of securing their long craved share of the country. But Echeandía
was replaced by the martinet Victoria, whose well meant but
reactionary efforts at strong government provoked a political
situation scarcely conducive to the asking or granting of
favors by either side. The ejection of the unpopular gefe
at the close of 1831 aroused apprehension in Mexico, with
a disposition to deal sternly with the supposedly turbulent
territorials; and in 1832 Diputado Cárlos Carrillo wrote
disgustedly from Mexico that the distribution of lands, along
with other projects for which he had been

---

[38] "Location of Bandini, Estudillo and Argüello lots in the Pueblo of San Diego," in San Diego Arch., MS, #8. Post, p. 486.
[39] Bancroft, Calif., vol. 3, p. 612.

laboring, had "all gone to the devil."[40]

51. Land, Ho!

Not until Figueroa's advent in 1833 were conditions in the territory stable enough to permit the land question to become again a live issue. Fortunately, the new governor was liberal minded in the matter. Moreover, he was bent on opening up the northern frontier, and offered lands in that region to settlers. Finally, like Echeandía, he favored secularization; and in a move to anticipate Híjar and Padrés, and backed by the <u>diputación</u>, he took steps to effect the break-up of the mission system.[41]

Híjar's instructions, incidentally, contained authorization for the granting of farm lands to colonists in full ownership.[42] Of course, he had no opportunity to fulfill the promise of those instructions.[43]

Nevertheless, at long last, the lands of California were to begin to pass into private ownership! At the first subsequent term of the <u>diputación</u> -- that of 1834 -- "grants of public lands made by the new governor in accordance with

---

[40] 1832, no mo., no day, C. Carrillo to J. de la Guerra (Letter #9), in <u>Guerra Doc.</u>, MS, vol. 4, p. 231.

[41] Bancroft, <u>Calif.</u>, vol. 3, pp. 340--44; <u>post</u>, chap. VII

[42] See <u>ante</u>, pp. 107--8.

[43] See <u>ante</u>, p. 117.

the laws were presented for investigation and approval at nearly every session."[44]

Naturally the process continued through Alvarado's administration. "I have been distributing lands," wrote Don Bautista in 1837, "at which these old fellows are very gratified, saying that since Borica's time it has been impossible for them to get any."[45]

By 1840, something like 270 ranches had been assigned and were occupied. Of these, 21 were in the San Diego district, 39 around Los Angeles, 26 in the Santa Barbara region, nearly 100 in the vicinity of Monterey, and about 80 in the San Francisco Bay environs.[46]

This decade, as has been noted,[47] was a period of severe and almost incessant Indian depredations in the San Diego district. Most of the private ranchos had to be abandoned temporarily at one time or another. The small farmers of the presidial pueblo made no attempt to live on or near their fields and pastures scattered over

----

[44] Bancroft, Calif., vol. 3, pp. 251--52.
[45] March 9, 1837, Alvarado to Vallejo, in Vallejo Doc., MS, vol. 4, #212, p. 8.
[46] Bancroft, Calif., vol. 3, pp. 611-12, n. 7; 633--34, n. 3; 655--56, n. 5; 676--79, n. 6; 611--13, n. 15.
[47] Ante, pp. 425--29.

the municipal lands. Instead, they camped in <u>enramadas</u> or temporary shelters at those sites, for the working season. Nor did they hold any property rights in the lands which they cultivated, beyond the generally recognized convention that the man who utilized a field one year had a prior claim to do so the next[48] -- always provided the government did not see fit to designate it for other uses.

New grants made in the last half-decade before the conquest totalled about 320 ranchos plus a great many small lots.[49] The distribution was roughly: San Diego, 30; Los Angeles, 30; Santa Bárbara, 30; Monterey, 70; San Francisco, 160. Of the 160-odd northern Californian ranch concessions, about one-half were grants of 1844; and nearly one-third were refused confirmation by the United States.[50]

The high rate of distribution and the high percentage of invalid claims for these five years trace of course to the Micheltorena and Pico land policies. In the case of Micheltorena, gifts of land were used as bribes, in the revolution of 1844--45, for the support of resident aliens; and the hard-pressed governor went so far as practically to

---

[48] Bancroft, <u>Calif.</u>, vol. 3, pp. 611--12.

[49] <u>Ibid.</u>, vol. 4, pp. 620--21, n. 2; 634--35, n. 13; 642--43, n. 22; 655--56, n. 1; 670--74, n. 12; 626, n. 7; 667--68.

[50] <u>Ibid.</u>, p. 675.

delegate Sutter authority to distribute patronage in the form of Sacramento Valley lands in return for foreign armed support.[51] Quite apart from the question of legality of the power so vested in Sutter, grants to non-citizens of Mexico were of course invalid.[51a] Bancroft found, moreover, that Micheltorena apparently took a very discreditable part in the forged Limantour titles to much of the San Francisco area.[52]

Because of the rate at which he disposed of the public domain, Pico has long been decried as an unscrupulous land-grabber, bent on partitioning as great a domain as possible to His own friends. There is extremely little to be said for the logic or justice of such allegations. The Californians had waited more than half a century for their stake in the land. The endowment of private citizens with land was the surest -- the only -- way to develop the territory. Moreover, conquest by force of alien arms was obviously about to climax the long imposed and speedily accelerating process of absorption by alien infiltration. The Bear Flag turbulence supplied an

---

[51] Bancroft, *Calif.*, vol. 4, p. 478.
[51a] See *ante*, pp. 129--30.
[52] *Ibid.*, pp. 714, 740. These matters properly belong to the subject of land grants to foreigners, to be discussed *post*, chap. VIII.

added spur to action. Why should not a Californian governor, with the lands at long last available, give them to the men and the native sons of the men who had served the country through so many vicissitudes? Surely no other group of men had a better right to share in the ownership of California!

As to the claim that Pico favored his personal friends, Bancroft remarks: "It was by no means discreditable to him, that before his power was gone he was disposed to distribute the public land among his friends, so long as he acted legally."[53] It is of course always those with access to the "ins" who secure political advantage; and the "outs" of course always burn with righteous indignation until, taking their turn at being the "ins," they enjoy all the prerogatives of that status. Any administration, in any time and place, may be counted on not to bestow its favors on the oppostition.

The other prevalent criticism of Pico as a grantor -- namely, that he was party to the antedating of assignments made after the American occupation -- is probably true enough, although on this score Bancroft has to say: "My study of land litigation leads me to hesitate in condemning or exonerating any official or citizen, native or pioneer, on charges originating in that most unfathomable

---

[53] Calif., vol. 5, p. 277.

pool of corruption.[54] It should also be remembered that the Californians saw no justice in the seizure of their country by *estrangeros*, and that, unable to prevent the disaster by force, they must have felt justified in attempting to mitigate it by guile.

52. Real Estates That Were Not Real Estates

As has been indicated, private ownership of land in the sense of clear and outright individual title did not exist in California before the conquest. A grant on the northern frontier, made by Echeandía in 1831 as an inducement to settlement in the path of the Russian encroachment, is typical of many such documents scattered through the Bancroft manuscript collection. The site was assigned "provisionally" till the most excellent Diputación shall meet," and "with legal title (la posesión judicial) reserved."[55] It is interesting to speculate whether Anglo-

---

[54] Calif., vol. 4, p. 779, "Pico, Pio." The United States Government set July 7th, native, the date of Sloat's occupation of Monterey, as the chronologic limit of legitimate grants. On the evidence that Pico continued to grant lands (at least for the McNamara project) after that time, and subsequently lent himself to the falsification of the dates, see Bancroft, vol. 5, pp. 97, 218--19.

[55] Jan. 8, 1831, Echeandía to Rafael Gomez, Grant of Santa Rosa, in Dept. St. Pap., Ben., Mil., MS, vol. 71, pp. 7--8.

American expansion would have progressed as vigorously as it did, had the westard-looking Atlantic pioneers been permitted as little sense of proprietorship in the acres which they cleared and ploughed and defended against hostile Indians.

Foreign visitors to California were not all blind to the handicap of such equivocal and revocable titles. Both Duhaut-Cilly and Douglas commented adversely[56] on the system.

Mexican officials themselves complained of the resultant strangulation of progress. Alamán, speaking of the many claimants to land throughout the interior provinces, including California, deprecated the laws which made for such impracticality in matters of title.[57]

As early as 1827, Governor Echeandía sought to establish clear record, at least, of the few grants then in existence. In October of that year, he issued a bando for grantees to appear and give information as to their holdings and titles.[58] Again, in 1830, he summoned all

---

[56] A. Duhaut-Cilly, Viaggio, vol. 2, pp. 99, 120—21; Douglas, Journal, MS, p. 80.

[57] Mem. Relaciones, 1823, pp. 52—53.

[58] Oct. 24, 1827, Padre Prefect to missionaries, transmitting Echeandía's Bando of October 10, 1827, in Olvera Doc., MS, p. 1.

land-holders to present themselves and make such deposition.[59] The results, says Bancroft,[60] are unknown save that they probably account for certain new petitions and regrantings shown in the records.

Governor Figueroa made the land question one of the keynotes of his opening speech to the _diputación_ in May 1834.[61] He blamed the _mesquina política_ of the Spanish government and the inexperience of his Mexican predecessors in the governorship for persisting in the barbarous tradition of preventing the acquisition of virgin lands;[62] declared his own intention to distribute holdings, as was desired; and deplored the absence of safe titles. The declaration of the new governor's policy brought Don Cárlos Carrillo to his feet in an expression of appreciation and approbation of Don José's interest in the protection of titles, which former _gefes_ had neglected.[63]

---

59 July 15, 1830, Zamorano (Sec'y to the Governor), "_Alviso sobre terrenos,_" in _Dept. St. Pap., Ben., Mil._, MS, vol. 71, p. 3.

60 _Calif._, vol. 2, pp. 664--65.

61 _Leg. Rec._, MS, vol. 2, pp. 81--82.

62 The transcript reads: _de coatar la acquisición de terrenos caldios_ -- apparently a copyist's error for _de coartar . . . . terrenos baldios._ J.D.F.

These matters recur again and again in the records of diputación deliberations. In 1836, the subject of titles to town lands was agitated. It was complained that no one was protected by written deed; that such grants had been made verbally, at first by military commissioners and then by pueblo ayuntamientos. Boundaries were under dispute. Holders of town lots were asked to petition for regular titles.64

Halleck advises further that California's representative in Congress was instructed by the territorial junta of 1836 "to solicit from the general government an absolute confirmation of the grants of lands made in California under the colonization decree of August 18, 1824, and the regulations of November 21, 1828, releasing the proprietors from the restrictions contained" therein; and that again "in 1840 the territorial deputation [diputación] made a representation to the general government, asking that the law of colonization be extended so as to include lands lying within ten leagues of the coast of California, and that the grants already made by the territorial government within these limits be confirmed by Mexico. It is believed, however, that the

---

63 Leg. Rec., MS, vol. 2, pp. 82--83.
64 Bancroft, Calif., vol. 3, p. 634, n. 3.

however, that the general government never acted on this representation . . . ."[65]

The subject of private land grants within the proscribed ten leagues of the coast was a sore one with the Californians. Alvarado stated the situation spiritedly to the 1840 *junta*: Of late years a great many grants of land had been made, but most of them illegal, being situated within ten leagues of the coast in contravention of the law of August 18, 1824. These prohibited sites had been assigned because in the opinion of the various *gefes* and of the *diputacion* it would be exposing life and property to oblige the ranchers to settle in the interior of a defenceless country at the mercy of savage tribes which habitually wrought havoc and irreparable damage on the people of the country. For the sake of agriculture, the most vital activity in the department and that most deserving of protection, and of the livestock industry, ranches within the coastal strip should be legalized. Yet no petition had been sent to the supreme government on this point, he (incorrectly) declared; nor did he know that the supreme government was aware of conditions. The *junta* should therefore follow up the matter of securing legitimation of the grants in question.[66]

----

[65] Halleck, "Report," p. 121.
[66] Leg. Rec., MS, vol. 3, pp. 50--51.

Even in the case of lands legally open to private holding, retardments and difficulties of many sorts often intervened between the occupant and even such qualified title as Mexico was disposed to concede. To the traditional red tape and law's delays were added inadequate communication facilities and the "paralysis of affairs," as the exasperated Californians called it, resulting from the instability of Mexican officialdom and policies.

Again a case in point may be drawn from the northern frontier, which Mexico was so anxious to have occupied and developed. In 1843 the pioneer rancher Camilo Initia (?) wrote to Micheltorena that for six years he had occupied the lands known as Olompali; had there cattle, sheep and horses, a house, truckgarden, vineyard, etc.; but lacked a title deed. He had requested such a paper long ago, and in proof of claim had submitted his provisional deed (dueño de estilo) at that time; but he had been informed that it had since been extracted from the archives. He repeated his plea that title be granted him.[67]

The provisional nature of titles, as well as the vagueness of boundary specifications (to be discussed in a

----

[67] Oct. 22, 1843, Camilo Initia (?) to Governor, in Vallejo Doc., MS, vol. 11, #465.

moment), led to much confusion and disagreement as to
claims. Duhaut-Cilly, commenting on the resultant
entanglements and injustice, cited[68] a case of the 1820s,
of two litigants for a piece of property which, before
the question could be settled, was granted by the governor
to a third applicant.

In 1834, Simeon Castro and Trinidad Espinosa, who
had land allotments on the Rio Monterey under cultivation,
were ordered by the governor to vacate as soon as their
crops could be harvested, so that the national ranch,
which needed the land, might put it to use during the
current season.[69]

In 1835, the Monterey presidial company claimed as
horse-range the sites of San Francisquito and El Toro,
which the Monterey *ayuntamiento*, claiming as pueblo
lands, had granted to José Ramón Estrada.[70] This situation was sometimes reversed. In 1841 Vallejo complained[71]
to the Minister of War that the government, in the hands

---

[68] *Viaggio*, vol. 2, pp. 99, 120--21.

[69] Nov. 2, 1834, Figueroa to Emeterio Espinosa (in charge of *Rancho Nacional*, Monterey district), in *Dept. St. Pap., Ben., Commissary and Treasury*, MS, vol. 3, p. 14.

[70] Oct. 20, 1835, Zamorano to Gutierrez, in *Dept. St. Pap.*, MS, vol. 4, pp. 60--66.

[71] Jan. 1, 1841, Vallejo to Min. of War, in *Vallejo Doc.*, MS, vol. 10, #10, p. 1.

of inexpert persons, had exhausted every means of presidial support, even to the point of not respecting the presidial properties, but disposing of them without the foreknowledge of the comandante general.

One of the most pregnant sources of dispute regarding claims was of course the uncertainty of boundary definitions, due chiefly to lack of means for proper survey and marking. The Californians, from the first, urged greater care, expertness and precision in land allotment. Their very first representative in Congress -- Sola -- exerted consistent efforts to have the Californias surveyed and mapped by federal engineers. The missionaries, Don Pablo held, by misrepresentations and suppression of the truth, were largely responsible for official ignorance as to the extent and value of "the Peninsula". The whole country should be explored and opened up by colonization from Mexico. In the process of land distribution, care should be taken to intersperse the grants with sizeable government reservations.[72]

---

[72] Alvarado, Hist. de Calif., MS, vol. 1, pp. 222--23. The regulations of April 6, 1830 made provision for the desired reserves for fortifications and other government uses. Dublan y Lozano, Legislación Mex., vol. 1, p. 239, Art. 4.

However, the "floating grant" continued to be the type of Mexican, as of Spanish, land assignment. Indeed, even political and legal jurisdictions were of blurred outline, due to the impossibility of setting more than approximate bounds, in the absence of trained surveyors and necessary equipment. Thus the governor, when granting lands in the vicinity of the pueblos, had to do so "muy provisionalmente," declared Alvarado [73] to the diputación in 1840.

A letter from Vallejo to Chico clearly indicates full realization of the need to employ a competent surveyor to determine the boundaries of lands already assigned and those still open to colonization, so that confusion and complaint might be obviated in the present, order established for the future, and the way opened for actual occupation.[74]

Another letter from the military commander and director of colonization of the northern frontier to Alvarado stressed another of the points in the land program of the Californians. It was widely reported, wrote Vallejo, that certain persons had been selecting grants ostensibly for purposes of colonization, but actually with a view to

---

[73] Leg. Rec., MS, vol. 3, p. 50.

[74] July 19, 1836, Vallejo to Comandante General, in Vallejo Doc., MS, vol. 3, #125.

holding them for later sale. To avoid such speculative abuses, the greatest precaution must be observed in the making of grants, and the most rigid conditions must be written into the assignments. If the country was really to be occupied, the government must exert great foresight in this matter.[75]

Vallejo took all the precautions he urged. A typical Sonoma town lot conveyance by him[76] incorporates the condition that the site will be forfeit unless the grantee erects a house on it within one year. Time and again, in such deeds, a similar stipulation appears: in the case of house lots, a year or other reasonable time was allowed for the home building; in the case of lands for pasture or cultivation, they must be put to such use in good season.

The nature of the penalty -- that the grants might be retracted and conferred on other applicants -- is one of many indications of the general demand for land. At times an effort was made to compromise between the two evils of insecure titles and undeveloped regions. Thus, in 1833, Figueroa ordered that lands *del fondo* be granted by the

---

[75] May 27, 1837, Vallejo to Governor, in *Vallejo Doc.*, MS, vol. 4, #99.

[76] Jan. 4, 1837, Vallejo to Antonio Peña, in *Vallejo Doc.*, MS, vol. 4, #5.

municipal authorities to the most industrious citizens.
Sites already assigned must be cultivated, or the holders,
although not to be deprived of their claims, must be required to rent them.[77]

In 1841, in consideration of requests of various
citizens for lands for cultivation, Antonio Suñol, sub-
prefect of the San José district, requested permission
to assign sites. He and the local *juez* were jointly
authorized to proceed with distribution, among honest
and industrious citizens, of suburban lands to be placed
under cultivation. Neglect would entail loss of right
in the land. It must be understood that any new occupants
were eligible to no title to the properties -- which were
municipal estates -- but merely to the right of use.[78]

59. The Clutch of the Dead Hand

The holding of land in mortmain was the curse of
Spain, and despite early and repeated precautions became
that of Spanish America as well, says Priestley.[79] The
secular cross-section of *gente de razon* had always been
alive to that fact, having always suffered from it. Mexico

---

[77] Aug. 9, 1833, Gov. to Alcalde Pacheco (San José), in Dept. St. Pap., Ben., Pref. *y* Juzg., vol. 6, p. 13.

[78] Oct. 27, 1841, Antonio Suñol to *Juez de Paz*, in San José Arch., MS, vol. 2, pp. 47--48.

[79] Mex. Nation, p. 56.

always conceded, at least in theory, the rights of the Indians to their native soil, Bancroft remarks, but "the continued retention by Franciscan communities of all the best lands under the shallow pretence that the Indians were being fitted to enjoy their rights at some period in the distant future, was with much reason regarded as an absurd proposition. Argüello and others expressed these views very clearly in 1823."[80]

In connection with protests from the padres of San Gabriel that he had granted mission holdings to settlers, Argüello replied in what may be considered a typical expression of Californian opinion on this score: he had given the merited great consideration to all that the padres had written him as to their claim, but he could do no less for others of the country, among whom were many who had sacrificed their ease and youth defending the peace and soil of the province. Now they were denied the small reward of a share of the land which they had preserved. Yet clearly the peace, security and very existence of all the missions in the country depended on the territory's small number of useful settlers. Times had changed since the Franciscan Order had been given its wide domains. In the old days there was land in plenty and a scarcity of settlers; now there were many persons who

[80] *Calif.*, vol. 2, p. 662.

deserved consideration and participation in the benefits of the country and of its soil. Under present conditions, land allotments should be reduced in size, so that all might share. In view of doubts as to the justice of claims being made to areas now held by the missions, he had decided on the appointment of a commission to survey and determine the extent and location of properties of all the missions, so that, for the welfare of the country, allotments might be made to those soliciting them, and all disagreements and vexations obviated.[81]

The *diputación* earnestly took up the matter of land distribution in 1823; and went on record as favoring reduction in the size of holdings, both mission and private, to accord with the actual needs of the claimants. So resuolute was the temper of the legislature that Mission President and Prefect Sarría presented himself in person to defend the rights of the neophytes, individually and as communities. As will be remembered, California was at the moment in the anomalous position of having sworn adherence to Mexico (the regency) but having had little contact with the new régime save for a visit of Canónigo Fernandez in 1822. Under the circumstances, decisive action on a major issue by the *diputación* (empowered only under Argüello's plan of provisional government for the interregnum) would have

---

[81] Aug. 31, 1823, Argüello to padres of Mission San Gabriel, in *Depart. Rec.*, MS, vol. 1, pp. 35--38.

been premature. Accordingly, the land question, with others of recognized vital importance, was held open for consideration by the new state authorities.[82]

It will be remembered, too, that in 1834 the supreme government prohibited all distribution, pending investigation of the entire subject.[83] Nevertheless, the pressure of the Californians generally for landed property, and of the Mexicans and some of the Californians for secularization, was in no way abated. In 1826 Echeandía complained to the supreme government that the padres held and administered almost all the lands, labor, products and coin of the territory.[84] In October 1827, he requested a detailed report on the lands held by each mission, to be submitted within the calendar year.[85] "I find no such report in the records," remarks Bancroft, although "local reports for the next year did, in several instances, contain a list of mission ranchos."[86]

The scarcity of lands resulting from the mission monopoly was a serious one. The wild Indians who did not

---

[82] Leg. Rec., MS, vol. 1, pp. 31--32.
[83] Bancroft, Calif., vol. 2, pp. 662--63; and see ante, pp. 474--75.
[84] Dec. 6, 1826, Echeandía to Min. of Rel., in Depart. Rec., MS, vol. 5, pp. 132--33.
[85] Olvera Doc., MS, p. 1.
[86] Calif., vol. 3, p. 104.

hesitate to harry the coastal strip made stockraising in the interior not merely ruinous but at times impossible. In many places removed from the coast, moreover, lack of water was an obstacle to stockraising and agriculture alike.

In any event, what the Californians wanted was not mere subsistence farms, to which they were entitled in suburban areas even under Spanish regulation; but ample scope for agriculture and stockraising on a commercial scale. It would have been poor business indeed to plant such enterprises deep in savage territory and far removed from the only access to markets, the sea.

Nevertheless, through the '20s and early '30s, as we have seen, land distribution was kept almost at a standstill, and the missions maintained their long established monopoly little infringed. Meantime, secular resentment waxed hotter. The missions had seized upon practically all the lands in the territory, to the exclusion of private occupation, complained Bandini[87] in 1828. This allegation was supported on every hand by foreign as well as Mexican residents of the territory. Pueblo and presidial reserves, and the Indian menace, were likewise commonly remarked obstacles to land development.

---

[87] Bancroft, *Calif.*, vol. 3, pp. 104--5, n. 40.

A number of such statements were assembled and have been preserved among the Bancroft documents:[88]

"When I first came to the country (January 6, 1833)," deposed Samuel Carpenter, "the whole of the lands were pretty well occupied by the missions, except a few ranches."

"About 1833--35," corroborated Michael White, "most of the lands were occupied by the missions . . . ."

Pio Pico could not recollect the granting of any sites from '30 to '35. Of his own San Diego district he recalled: "The missions occupied a large portion; San Gabriel occupied San Bernardino, Chino, San Pascual, etc. It was necessary to go some distance to get lands -- to go beyond San Bernardino. There would be danger beyond San Bernardino from Indians . . . . There were no lands in San Diego, except you went into the mountains."

"Any person who had the means to occupy lands and some who had not could get lands in '31 and '36, by petitioning the governor," reads the statement of Abel Stearns. But the qualification is added: "The Pueblo of Los Angeles in community claimed a large portion"; and "the missions

---

[88] San Diego Arch., MS, "Miscellaneous Papers, 1830--43, L. A.," pp. 9--13, passim. (This material is badly confused in arrangement, some of it being on the reverse sides of pages, some of it upside down.)

from '31 to '34 occupied pretty much all the other lands lying on the coast."

This deponent remembered five or six grants by Figueroa, made in what was later the Los Angeles County area, from February 1833 to the latter part of 1835. "After Figueroa's death I think there were no grants until 1837. . . . . I asked for . . . . Chino and part of Guapa and San José -- I think eleven leagues." The application was not successful, due to the death of Figueroa. After secularization, the same statement continues, the country would have afforded fifty more such ranchos, besides those occupied.

Benjamin D. Wilson, who in 1842 purchased at $1,000 per league the Jurupa Rancho on which Riverside now stands, related that the location was then considered on the frontier, being in a wild country. "The Indians were very bad at that time. Bandini sold so as to protect the ranchos from Indians."

In his *Alta California*, published in 1835, Forbes reiterated: "The lands of California . . . . are almost exclusively in the hands of the missionaries, and consequently its agricultural operations are chiefly carried on by them."[89]

---

[89] P. 246.

Of the obstructions presented by the missionaries, even on the furthermost frontier, to Vallejo's efforts at colonization in the north, mention has already been made.[90] A sole case of voluntary relinquishment of a mission claim in favor of a private individual is indicated in the petition, made in 1823 by Francisco M. Castro, to the territorial assembly, for the three leagues of the San Pablo grant in the present Berkeley-Richmond area. The site, declared the petitioner, had been "formerly occupied by the Mission San Francisco," but had been "abandoned by said mission," and was being applied for "with the previous knowledge of its holy proprietors."[91]

That the Californians urgently desired land as a first step to enterprise is incontrovertibly evident everywhere in the record. They were willing to pioneer and to risk, if their land hunger might be appeased. Naturally, they wanted security of tenure. Indeed, the assurance of land "in ownership" would have been sufficient attraction to bring settlers all the way from Lower California to the northern frontier.[92]

---

[90] *Ante,* pp. 101--2.

[91] *Abstract of Title, Rancho San Pablo,* p. 7.

[92] Jan. 27, 1841, Osio to Vallejo, in *Vallejo Doc.,* MS, vol. 10, #53, pp. 2, 3.

"Ownership" the _dons_ never had. Such titles as they did possess dated, in the great preponderance of cases, from the decade immediately preceding the American conquest. The limitations of those titles were "not only onerous to the holders," wrote the American officer Halleck, in his report of 1849 on Californian land titles, "but contrary to the spirit of our laws. These onerous conditions should be removed by act of Congress."[93] In short, Uncle Sam, like John Bull's son Forbes, acknowledged the obstacles opposed to progress by California's land title defects.

Meanwhile the men of the territory, having vainly denounced the same impediments through decade after decade, and in spite of the brief duration of the qualified possession of the soil to which they finally succeeded, inaugurated, as we are about to observe, a remarkable production and commerce: an aggressive and conscious and effective _fomento de California._

54. "_Falta de Brazos, Falta de Manos!_"

Through the documentary record of territorial efforts at development runs, among other main themes, the oft-repeated refrain of "lack of hands." For California, like Mexico before her, suffered from an insufficient labor supply. To be sure, under the mission system in the province, as under the _encomienda_ and mission systems in Mexico, thousands

---

[93] "Report," p. 122.

of Indians had been regimented by a few padres and _encomenderos_ into pastoral, agricultural and industrial pursuits. But only constraint -- physical, spiritual or both -- kept the aborigines at such alien and uncongenial tasks; and even constraint could not make them efficient workmen, save for outstanding exceptions.

California's Mexican period, moreover, was the epoch of decline and abandonment of the mission system; of the removal of the constraint which had kept the neophytes at work and at least superficially compliant with the obligations of civilized society. As will be seen, secularization resulted not in the release of tens of thousands of _brazos_ to private enterprise; but in the dispersal and perversion of the territory's sole labor supply.[94]

After emancipation of the neophytes, California's population consisted, for all practical purposes, of just two classes: potential entrepreneurs -- such as the Vallejos and Castros, the Carrillos and Guerras, the Lugos and Picos, the Valles and Yorbas; and small farmers -- the private soldiers and settlers of Spain and Mexico, and their sons. The latter class was of course numerically preponderant -- so much so that Alvarado, opposing the enforcement of the draft law, described the country's man-power as "comprised of laborers forced to work for the mere maintenance of themselves and

---

[94] For a discussion of secularization and its consequences, _see post_, chap. VII.

their families."[95]

Even before secularization had gotten under way, Victoria had complained of the country's lack of labor other than that of Indians.[96]

Outrageous as the Californians considered Mexico's use of the territory as a penal colony, Captain Guerra made good the opportunity to take eight or ten of the presidarios of 1830 into his private employ, and other rancheros of the Santa Barbara and Los Angeles districts followed suit.[97]

In his opening speech to the diputacion on needs and prospects in 1840, Alvarado deplored as two major handicaps to the country's incipient development the shortage of men and the aggressions of the Indians: "Of late years a great many grants of land have been made to natives and foreigners, with great resultant progress in agriculture and stockraising. But due to insufficient population, there is a great dearth of defenders and of laborers; and the barbarity of the Indians has inflicted havoc and irreparable damage."[98]

---

[95] Jan. 11, 1842, Alvarado to Min. of Rel., in Depart. Rec., MS, vol. 13, p. 12.

[96] June 7, 1831, Victoria to Min. of Rel., in Depart. Rec., MS, vol. 9, p. 134.

[97] Ord, Ocurrencias, MS, pp. 25--27; and ante, pp. 93--94.

[98] Leg. Rec., MS, vol. 3, pp. 50--51.

The governor did not need to make the point that large numbers of ex-neophytes, instead of adjusting themselves to productive occupations outside the missions, habitually engaged with gentile Indians in the warfare against civilization. That fact was a commonplace to every Californian resident past infancy. Even before secularization, the association of renegade neophytes with wild tribesmen had complicated the country's Indian problem.[99] The increased demands on the missions for presidial support, in the years of Spain's decline and Mexico's need, had caused widespread resentment among the neophytes, whose forced labor produced the subsidies yet commanded scantier individual reward than in the good old days of prosperity. They preferred a savage life in the desert to one of slavery with insufficient food and clothing, Micheltorena observed.

Even among those ex-mission Indians who might have served proletarian purposes, demoralization resulted from the repeated changes of policy after the secularization experiment had been embarked upon. The continual transfer of Indians from missions to private service and back again was a great drawback to agriculture, as well as religion, concluded Micheltorena.[100]

A very definite correlation could probably be established between secularization and the marked access in number and violence of Indian depredations, particularly in the

---

[99] See ante, pp. 444--45.
[100] Bancroft, Calif., vol. 4, p. 370.

southern and middle districts, during the late '30s.[101] "Constant depredations of savages with ex-neophyte allies . . contributed to the work of ruin," wrote Bancroft,[102] who has recorded many examples in point.

The emancipated Indians, then, so far from meeting the country's need of brazos for fomento, became a new scourge upon the land, the bulk of their numbers constituting at best a class of parasites and petty criminals, at worst a horde of predaceous and revengeful destroyers.

55. Slavery

It is little to be wondered at, therefore, that under the two spurs of retaliation and need of manos, some of the Californians resorted to the age-old device of impressed labor. Theoretically, slavery was highly repugnant to the young Mexican nation, which looked back to the evils of the encomienda system and forward to the blessed social regeneration conjured up by republican idealism. The influence of missionary proselytism, however, helped to obscure the line between persuasion to Christian civilization and sterner persuasion or impressment. Thus so ardent a republican as Echeandía issued permission to settlers of San José, in 1826, to "induce" the gentiles of the Tulares to come into the settlements and work. He did, however, in 1829, censure the

----

[101] See ante, pp. 425--30.
[103] Calif., vol. 3, p. 693.

commandant at Monterey for permitting the distribution of captured Indians among the citizens, for servitude. Such Indians must be sent to the missions.[103]

Nevertheless, the disposition of the *rancheros* to augment their labor supply by seizure continued to manifest itself, and to find justification at times as a punitive measure. As has been mentioned, Figueroa strictly prohibited reprisal by enslavement; but in at least one case, in 1836, a local government voted to reward the reduction of surrounding tribes by private initiative and expense, with permission to the *empresario* of pacification to retain captured "outlaws" in his service.[104]

Vallejo, on the vague line between the savage hinterlands and the under-manned haciendas of fomento-minded frontier *rancheros*, had repeatedly to intervene in the cause of impressed and commercialized Indian labor. Thus, in 1836, he caused the arrest of the Castros of San Pablo and the release of several Indian children whom they had bought as servants.[105] In 1838, he brought his Indian ally Solano to book — or rather to the *calabozo* — for having engaged in a similar traffic; and secured the

---
[103] Bancroft, *Calif.*, vol. 2, p. 666, n. 27.
[104] *Ante*, p. 439.
[105] Bancroft, *op. cit.*, vol. 4, p. 71, n. 53.

restoration of some thirty little savages to their parents, from the captivity into which they had been sold round about San Francisco Bay.[106]

Through the '40s, he kept close check on the activities of Sutter, who was "from the first . . in the habit of seizing Indian children, who were retained as servants, or slaves, at his own establishment, or sent to his friends in different parts of the country."[107] Yet despite Don Guadalupe's vigilance, such was the demand for **brazos** that Sutter continued, throughout the period, to sell children and adult slaves "down the river" -- and up; while ranchers at least of the bay region continued to absorb the supply and even to conduct their own slave-hunts. As late as 1845, Californian frontiersmen made a sortie in the direction of Ross and captured 150 potential ranch-hands. A quarrel over the division of spoils brought the outrage to light and into the courts.[108]

It is not to be inferred, from the eagerness of the **Californios** to procure hands, that they were themselves averse to labor. The more one delves into the evidence, the more impressive are the indications that except for

---

[106] Bancroft, *Calif.*, vol. 4, p. 73; and **see ante**, p. 432.
[107] Bancroft, *Calif.*, vol. 4, p. 138, n. 31; and **see ante**, p. 435.
[108] Bancroft, *op. cit.*, p. 544.

the "submerged population" they were not only a hard-riding but a hard-working lot.

As has been said, however, the effectives of the country were divided into the two categories of subsistence farmers and large-scale operators. There was no inducement for the first class to leave their small farms and large families to labor for the second class, in competition with Indians whose compensation was about four _pesos_ per month.[109] On the other hand, big business could not be carried on without an adequate labor supply. Nor could the country as a whole be rapidly developed through the exertions of a small population of small farmers. For lack of time to allow the population to grow up to the country, a proletariat which would have enabled rapid development of industry and trade was definitely required; and was as definitely unavailable.

In the ordinary course of events, man-power and _fomento_ would have evolved gradually, each stimulating the other. But events did not follow an ordinary course in California. Despite the passage of years since 1769, there was literally no chance for such an evolution.

Nevertheless, and despite the handicaps enumerated and others to be enumerated, the decade before the American

---

[109] That wage prevailed in 1828. Bancroft, _Calif._, vol. 2, p. 666, n. 27.

conquest was one of remarkable economic development. The men of the country, long isolated and repressed, had come at last into opportunity, limited and hampered as that opportunity was. At the same time, they were pressed upon from every side by foreign competitors overwhelmingly at an advantage in resources and experience, and from countries which had already been transformed by agricultural and industrial and commercial "revolutions."

California was still in the pastoral stage, at the beginning of the Mexican era; and even that was an artificial development which had been imposed on semi-savages. Between the middle '30s and '40s, the mission system and the mission wealth disappeared; the men of the country secured a stake in the land; a new pastoral age was ushered in by private and lay initiative; and simultaneously, in the soil of territorial ambition and the heat of foreign aggressiveness and competition, Californian agriculture, industry and trade sprang into forced, magnificent bloom.

56. The Splendid Forties

Two fundamental misconceptions incorporated in the "Arcadian" theory are that the <u>Californios</u> inherited their character of stockranchers full-blown from Spain; and that they continued to confine themselves to that rôle through lack of initiative to do anything else. The fact is that the livestock industry as conducted on a large scale by lay ranchers did not -- could not -- have its beginning until a market was opened and the men of the country secured at least a tentative share of the land.

A few score of <u>pobladores</u> might graze their few hundreds of animals in the municipal pastures; but range cattle must have range -- and access to water. As has been noted, early California was monopolized by mission, presidial and pueblo reservations; Spain's land policy was a practical obstruction in the way of inland pioneering; and while Mexico's intentions were good, they took a dozen years to find effect.

During all that time, the Californians aspired vainly for scope for productive effort. When their opportunity came, it was so circumscribed that no other industry was so well adapted to all the conditions as was that of stockraising. If a rancher was forced to yield his claim on short notice, he could move his cattle on the hoof, with no harm done (provided he located suitable new range). Short of both capital and labor, and at all times subject to Indian forays, he could still make economic headway with his rapidly multiplying, free-running herds. Should markets fail, the flesh of his cattle could be dried in quantity for household consumption, the hides and tallow and by-products utilized in a hundred and one ways; and if a general _matanza_ had to be resorted to, the sacrifice would be less severe than in the case of a farmer compelled to destroy long tended, expensively grown crops.

As a matter of fact, as we shall presently see, the insatiable foreign demand for hides and tallow afforded the most reliable -- and tyrannical -- market of Mexican California, giving still further impetus to the livestock industry. That market and that industry (as a lay enterprise) originated in the '20s and reached impressive proportions in the '40s. Such a development, within a score of years, was not an effortless achievement, as the Arcadian theorists represent it. It was instead a triumph of released initiative and energy over conditions resulting from suppressive policies of nearly half a century's duration.

Under Spain, the various branches of the _rancho real_, at Monterey, San Francisco and San Diego, had furnished "a very large part" of the meat and "nearly all the cavalry horses" required by the presidios, thus seriously impairing almost the only market for the mission surplus. " . . . . but having founded the ranchos at a time when the missions had no livestock to sell, the government was not disposed to abandon them later; and indeed it was claimed that only by means of the rancho del rey and of the fixed tariffs of prices were the friars kept from maintaining an oppressive monopoly."[110] When, later, need arose to supplement the presidial ranch supply, money was lacking to make the "market" a paying one.

Here, then, was no incentive for the development of a grazing industry by the civilian population. The few ranches granted under Spain therefore stocked no great herds. More than that, the limitations already discussed stood in the way of general stockraising.

Even so, and despite the inroads of bears, wolves and Indians, cattle and especially horses were soon in excess of all demands, and depressed in value to four or five pesos a head. Only mules, having been raised in fewer numbers, found a ready market, and commanded as much as fifteen pesos each.

The eighteenth century closed definitely on the note of restriction of increase. In 1792, a yearly matanza of 200 cows was ordered. In 1794, three or four cows were the limit allowed in ownership to any soldier. At about the same time it was complained, incomprehensibly enough, that the royal herds had been "not much affected" (numerically) by the segregation of females. In 1795, the warning went out that ranch animals must not be allowed to increase.

----

[110] Bancroft, Calif., vol. 1, pp. 621--22.

In 1797, pobladores were restricted to possession of fifty head of large stock.[111]

From 1805--10, great matanzas of horned cattle and more especially of horses were resorted to, tens of thousands of beasts being disposed of. Throughout the subsequent decade, although no general slaughter seems to have been called for, various localities found it necessary to kill off excess stock which had been damaging crops and property, crowding needed grazing lands and even menacing human safety.[112]

With the opening of the country to foreign trade, under Mexico, an outlet was afforded for this embarrassment of wild riches. For some time, however -- whether through sheer inertia or because the extent of the market was not at first realized -- the new government continued a restrictive policy toward stockranching. As late as 1834, Figueroa voiced[113] in the diputación the dissatisfaction of the stockmen at the close limitations imposed on them.

The territory was even then on the verge of a new era, however: the era of horn and hoof, which was to inspire the

---

[111] Bancroft, Calif., vol. 1, pp. 622--23; vol. 2, p. 477, n.48.

[112] Ibid., vol. 2, pp. 182--83, 418.

[113] Leg. Rec., MS, vol. 2, p. 43.

appelation "splendid idle forties." The phrase is as picturesque with the "idle" deleted, and more truly descriptive of that boom period of stockranching.

For the fact that the Californians gave little attention to dairying, there is reason enough. Not only did the summer drouths which seared the accessible pasture and sucked rivers and water-holes dry make the raising of range cattle more practical for large enterprise; the consumer demand was not for dairy products, but for hides and tallow. There was no outlet for milk and butter, little for cheese. Davis tells us[114] that the Californians' own favorite cheese, made in the spring of the year, when the grass was green, had to be eaten on the day on which it was made. This asadera was regarded as a home delicacy, produced by the family cow and prepared by the señora or her servants.

Yet a little cheese suitable for export was made, and the possibilities of dairying were not ignored. In 1841, we find Osio writing enthusiastically to Vallejo of six families of prospective settlers for the northern frontier: "They know dairying -- how to get much milk and make good cheese."[115] In 1843 the territorial government schooner "California" listed 112 cheeses in her cargo for Mexico.[116]

---

[114] Seventy-five Years, p. 36.
[115] Jan. 27, 1841, Osio to Vallejo, in Vallejo Doc., MS, vol. 10, #53, p. 2.
[116] Bancroft, Calif., vol. 4, p. 563, n. 42, "California."

Forbes criticized the Californians for neglecting sheep culture, and speculated[117] as to whether Spain had discouraged that branch of industry, like others, in favor of Spanish enterprise. The explanation does not lie there; for Bancroft tells us[118] that in 1796—97 Borica endeavored to promote sheep-raising by the settlers, in the interest of the wool textile industry. At one time every *pobtador* was required to keep at least eleven sheep; and again it was ordered that the ratio of small and large stock should be as three to one.

Probably any cowman or sheepman today would be willing to hazard the guess that, under early California conditions of limited grazing lands, the close-cropping flocks, if run in considerable numbers, would quickly starve out cattle and horses.

Yet some sheep culture there was, not only in the mission pastures, but on private account. Ranchers of the San Francisco Bay area exported wool in 1837.[119] Davis

---

[117] *Alta Calif.*, p. 277.

[118] *Calif.*, vol. 1, pp. 621; 623, n. 45.

[119] Richardson, *Salidas de Buques, 1837—8*, MS, passim.

mentions[130] the fact that a part of José de la Guerra's immense wealth was in sheep; and in 1841 Governor Alvarado sold a flock of 1,100 to the Hudson's Bay Company, on government account, in one transaction.[121]

Reference has already been made to the frequency and severity of Indian inroads. On no form of enterprise, of course, did those assaults levy heavier toll than on the livestock industry; and at none were they more deliberately directed. The chief of a band of fifty Indian rustlers, who in 1838 attempted to stampede the horses at Sonoma with a band of tame animals, confessed, on being captured, that there were large droves of stolen horses on the Sacramento, in charge of the Moquelumnes.[122]

Castañares predicted[123] -- doubtless with undue pessimism -- that unless the barbarian incursions could be checked (and the *matanzas* regulated) the cattle industry would be wiped out.

Sutter wrote of the wild horses in the great central valleys, bred from stolen animals. "These rapidly increased

---

[130] Seventy-five Years, p. 239.

[131] Bancroft, Calif., vol. 4, p. 194, n. 6. These were apparently ex-mission animals. The missions, of course, had had large flocks.

[122] Ibid., p. 73.

[123] Col. de Doc., p. 24.

so that they become immense droves. They were not claimed by Indians. It was easier for the Indians when they wanted tame horses to steal them than to tame them. Later Americans and Californians went over there and lassoed them, catching what they wanted of them. They were . . . . caught and broken and used for breeding."[124]

Sutter refers here to the fact, also, that the Californians hunted elk and deer in the interior, for their hides and tallow; and Davis gives a description of the chase. Elk abounded by the thousands around upper San Francisco Bay, he tells us, and were killed "for their hides and tallow by the rancheros in considerable numbers, at the time they slaughtered their cattle. They would go out to the haunts of the elk, and capture them by the lasso . . . . and after killing the animals, secure the hides and tallow on the spot, leaving the carcasses. The tallow of the elk was superior to that of the bullock, whiter and firmer, and made better candles.

"This work was much more dangerous and exciting than the killing of cattle, and required the very best broken saddle horses and those most accustomed to the lasso, and also the best vaqueros, on account of the strength, agility, fleetness and fierceness of the elk . . ."[125]

----

[124] Sutter, *Personal Reminiscences*, MS, pp. 66--67.
[125] *Seventy-five Years*, p. 31.

Many of the rancheros won distinction by such exploits in the hunting-field; and even the less adventurous had to be men of strenuous industry to manage their great estates and to share personally -- as they did -- in the labor and skill required at rodeo and matanza.

57. Hides and Tallow

California's hide and tallow era began with Mexico's opening up of the land and of the ports. Under Spain, tallow had been shipped to Lima, along with some hides and a little grain and soap. But that traffic -- chiefly a mission monopoly -- was in no way comparable with the spectacular commerce of the '30s and '40s.[126]

In July 1822, to the gratification of Mission Prefect Payeras and Governor Sola, a three-year contract as of January 1, 1823 was concluded between the English firm of John Begg and Company, of Lima, and the missions. The contract was for an exclusive trade in so far as the Lima house could absorb territorial production. The governor attached the stipulation that pueblo and ranch output delivered at the waterfront be accepted on the same terms as mission produce.

Business was to be transacted through the new California branch of Begg and Company, to be known as McCulloch and Hartnell, W. E. P. Hartnell becoming the resident partner.

---

[126] Bancroft, Calif., vol. 3, pp. 419--20.

Begg and Company were to send at least one ship yearly to take on at each harbor and roadstead all hides offered and tallow to the amount of 25,000 *arrobas* (312 T.) in all. Payment was to be in cash or goods at the seller's wish. Thanks to the alertness of Payeras, who declared that "'the times had changed, and the day long passed when hides and tallow could be had for nothing,'" a sufficiently liberal scale of prices was agreed on, although, as Bancroft remarks, could the unlimited demand of the just then incipient Boston trade have been foreseen, a higher schedule would doubtless have been established.[127]

Begg and Company also offered, at first, a market for salt beef, and sent David Spence to oversee the work of a number of salters and coopers dispatched from Ireland and Scotland to start operations. The company had contracted to supply the Peruvian government with the **dried** meat. With Californian cattle available at four *pesos* a head or slightly more, a prosperous business was anticipated. The project seems to have been abandoned, however, when Peru proved an unpunctual debtor.[128]

Larger obstacles prevented the flowering of Begg and Company's brilliant enterprise for monopoly of the Californian

----

[127] Bancroft, *Calif.*, vol. 2, pp. 475--77.
[128] Ibid., pp. 477, n. 49; 518--19.

field -- although the English firm, through its McCulloch and Hartnell branch (known locally as "Macala y Arnel"), throve for some years. Almost simultaneously with Hartnell's coming, the Boston ship "Sachem" arrived, bringing a load of merchandise and supercargo and part-owner William Alden Gale.

A dozen years earlier, Gale had visited California on the fur-ship "Albatross," which had secured so many otter and seal skins of her crew's catching and by arrangement with the Russians that some of her water casks had had to be broken up, and her cables stowed on deck, to make room for the furry cargo. On that voyage, Gale had learned a great deal about California, besides acquiring wide first-hand knowledge of the Farallones and Channel Islands, the Sandwich Islands and China. Evidently he had been greatly impressed with the possibilities of trade between Boston and California, Mexico, South America and China; for his return in 1822 was the result of his persuasion of several Boston commercial houses to venture into the new field.

The "Sachem" put into port just too late to forestall the conclusion of the exclusive contract with Begg and Company. Therefore the securing of a return cargo at first proceeded slowly; but Gale offered half as much again for hides as the Begg contract stipulated, and a good price for tallow. So the "Sachem" was reloaded for the homeward voyage; and the Boston trade was born.[129]

At last, and for the first time, California had access to an unlimited market for at least her pastoral products. The assiduity with which she availed herself of it is evidenced by the heights of prosperity to which the ensuing hide and tallow boom swept both rancheros and traders. Before attempting to measure that prosperity, it will be well to consider briefly the nature of the traffic, taking into account its disadvantages along with its benefits.

The hides were demanded in ever increasing quantity by the leather manufacturers of eastern United States. Peru was the great market for tallow, which was converted into soap and candles and to the uses of the silver miners. Boston-bound vessels therefore exchanged their tallow for hides, with ships bound for Callao. As Manila had been the great clearing-house for Spain's American-Oriental trade, so Honolulu became the entrepôt of the American-Oriental commerce in hides and tallow.[130]

The trading reached its height in the slaughtering

---

[129] Bancroft, Calif., vol. 2, pp. 93--95; 475; 476--77, n. 48, passim.
[130] Larkin, Official Corresp., MS, vol. 2, p.100; Davis, Seventy-five Years, p. 154.

season of midsummer; but on a small sclae extended throughout the year. Writing of the San Francisco Bay area particularly, Davis said: "Even in winter, the dull season for trading, the fleet of small vessels owned in Yerba Buena was kept busy going to the different estuaries of the bay to collect hides that had accumulated during the winter months from cattle slaughtered for the use of the haciendas."[131]

Douglas has given us one of the most vivid firsthand descriptions of the traffic as conducted in California by the Boston men: "Two active supercargos acquainted with the language and country are placed in each vessel, who on the moment of their arrival in port, ride out into the country with their Books of Samples, and call from house to house, according to a list they carry . . . to display their samples, and procure orders for goods, which on their return to the ship they forward and receive payment in the killing season." Slaughter time "begins about the middle of June and lasts nearly 3 months, during which all the trading vessels are on the move and have their agents out in all directions selling goods and receiving payments."[132]

---

[131] Seventy-five Years, p.76.

[132] Journal, MS, pp. 82--83, 95.

Davis adds: "The supercargoes .... of course had occasion to visit all the settlements in the interior or along the coast to conduct their business with the people, and to travel back and forth and up and down the country."[133]

Here was an expensive mode of merchandising, with prices further elevated by the need to extend long-term credit. "The retail business in this country as at present conducted," remarked Douglas, ".... is unavoidably attended with a heavy expense in the shape of salaries, while the system of giving high credits, places the merchant in a state of great insecurity." The Hudson's Bay man, who was but an onlooker of the retail trade, proceeded to comment on the "baneful influence" of the credit system on the people of the country, conducive to overbuying which entailed "dishonest practises and improvident habits."[134] The picture which he invokes is highly suggestive of conditions resulting from the high-pressure installment selling so prevalent throughout the United States in the reckless years before 1929.

Davis, who was so to speak born and bred in the trade, asserts the absolute reliability of Californian buyers,

---
[133] *Seventy-five Years,* p. 58.
[134] *Journal,* MS, pp. 84--85.

and the safety of extending them credit for whatever goods they wanted[135] -- an endorsement in which "Don Guillermo" found himself unable to include the country's foreign residents.

The fact probably lies somewhere between the extremes of judgment of the disapproving Douglas and the notably benevolent-minded Davis. Yet, however dependable the Californians may have been as debtors, the need of protracted credit was bound to raise costs and prices. The traders commonly allowed the rancheros a year in which to pay.[136]

Large outlays of capital were tied up in cargoes, meanwhile, and in the vessels, which required one to two years to complete a trading voyage. Throughout that time, crews and agents had to be fed and paid. As Douglas noted, the travelling salesman method of purveying to buyers at a distance from the coast increased the overhead. Davis throws further light on this phase:

"In visiting down the coast they [the agents] usually went on the vessels, which had a fair wind most of the time going south; but on coming up there was commonly a head wind, which made the voyage tedious, and the supercargoes then took

---

[135] Seventy-five Years, p. 192.
[136] Dec. 1, 1839, Vallejo to Virmond, in Vallejo Doc., MS, vol. 8, #335.

to land and came up on horseback . . . . Some of the supercargoes of the vessels owned their horses, to the number of twelve or fifteen, and employed a vaquero continuously. When the supercargoes were at sea the vaqueros looked after these horses, and took them from point to point to meet the vessel when she would come into a certain port. When the supercargo landed he would find his horses there, and journey with them from place to place as his business required."[137]

Such royal progresses, so to speak, had to be paid for out of selling profits. Yankee notions of what constituted good business, and the barter basis of the trade, were additional rungs in the lofty price-ladder. Larkin reported that the Boston houses expected "about one hide to each Dollar invested in cargo, disbursements, wages, and value of vessel"; and Hartnell assured Wyllie that "a cargo of English goods, direct from home, would have an immense profit on the Invoice prices . . . ."[138]

Most compelling factor of all was the monopolistic hold of the American traders on the country. For the hide and tallow traffic was a monopoly from the beginning. By

---

[137] Davis, *Seventy-five Years*, pp. 58--59.

[138] Larkin, *Official Corresp.*, MS, vol. 2, p. 100; April (no day), 1844, Hartnell to Wyllie, in *Pio Pico Doc.*, MS, vol. 1, #85, p. 2.

sending aggressive itinerant retailers along with their wholesale consignments, the Yankees at once secured a mastery of the situation which no competitors were prepared to dispute. When the Hudson's Bay Company, arriving late in the field, contemplated large-scale commercial activity in California in the '40s, only a wholesale business was feasible. Chief Factor Douglas advised that limiting operations to the supply of country merchants with goods would "reduce the risk of loss and expenses generally." Of the retail trade he concluded: "We have no people competent to carry it on, and compete with the clever active men now engaged in it, who speak the language fluently, and know almost every person in California."[139]

The territorials were least of all in a position to maneuver the Yankees out of their strategic corner of the retail business. They were still struggling against the various handicaps which have been touched on in foregoing pages. In addition, the Boston men had speedily enmeshed the buyers of the country in a debtors' net. At worst, time to pay was the sine qua non of purchase; at best, the favor of credit commanded the return courtesy of continued patronage. So the supercargo who collected with one hand wrote up new time accounts with the other. California was

---

[139] *Journal*, MS, pp. 85--86.

learning the unhappy hidden implications of the formula: "Your credit is good."

Nevertheless, as has been mentioned before and as will be developed in the present connection a little later,[140] earnest though futile tentatives were made toward release from the foreign grip. Meantime, with all its drawbacks, the hide and tallow trade attained ever more striking proportions.

Although absence of complete official records precludes the possibility of anything like an exact statement of the volume of traffic between the hide-droghers and the stockmen, some figures compiled by William Heath Davis, while not of statistical value, indicate an enormous volume of business for the times and circumstances.

Born in "the Islands," where his father, a "Boston man," carried on trade with China and western America, Davis visited California several times as a boy, taking up residence at San Francisco in 1838 at the age of sixteen, when he became clerk and manager for the well-known trader Nathan Spear, his uncle. Later, "Don Guillermo" became associated with other leading merchants, as employee and partner; devoted himself to the business throughout the period under consideration and subsequently, married a

---

[140] See ante, sec. 26, passim; sec. 65, passim.

daughter of _ranchero_ and _juez_ José Joaquín Estudillo, and came to know commercial conditions from San Diego To Sonoma intimately.[141]

Davis first made an estimate of the hide-tallow trade covering the period from about 1826 to 1848 (or 1847). His figures were "gathered partly from actual knowledge of the cargoes taken by particular vessels, and partly estimated from the size of the vessels which loaded previous to my residence here; these vessels always taking full cargoes on their return to the Atlantic coast . . . ." The combined data, known and estimated, yielded a total for the score or so of years of 33 vessels and 1,068,000 hides; but at the time of making the calculation Davis considered it "probably an underestimate. The actual number of hides exported approximated one million and a quarter.[143]

Most vessels, according to his list, took anywhere from 10,000 to 60,000 hides; one took as few as 8,000; and perhaps 30,000 to 40,000 was about the average.[143] For broad reckoning, this appraisal of ladings tallies well enough with that of Larkin, who mentions 20,000 to 40,000 hides as average.[144] Larkin's statement was made more or

[141] Bancroft, _Calif._, vol. 2, pp. 776--77, 794.
[142] _Seventy-five Years_, pp. 255--57, 408.
[143] _Ibid._, list.
[144] _Official Corresp._, MS, vol. 2, p. 100.

less casually, in a general description of the Boston trade, while Davis aimed at precision.

Davis later revised his estimate, or rather supplemented it, in the light of a maritime list supplied him by James A. Forbes, British Vice-consul at Monterey. Unfortunately for the present purpose, which is to consider general territorial production as apart from missionary activity, this second set of figures covers the period 1800--47.[145]

However, for the first decade and a half of that period, commerce was almost negligible; and Bancroft tells us that although practically no obstacle was thrown in the way of free trade after 1816, "there is very slight evidence that any trade, even contraband, was carried on with foreign vessels except by the government" in the decade 1810--20.[146] Government commercial activity in those years, as we know, was greatly restricted by war conditions. Moreover, although "the Lima trade in Spanish vessels assumed considerable proportions, tallow being the chief article of export, ... the era of the hide-trade had not yet begun."[147] For the decade 1820--30, Bancroft found that only 9 or 10 traders came yearly before 1826.[148]

---

[145] Seventy-five Years, pp. 408--9.
[146] Calif., vol. 2, p. 419.
[147] Ibid.
[148] Ibid., p. 670.

That brings us close to the beginnings of secularization in 1830 (indeed, Echeandía's proclamation of partial emancipation was made in 1826) and to the dawn of the privately conducted stock-raising industry. After 1826, the traders indicated on the maritime lists mounted to 18 or 20 annually to 1830, and ranged between 20 and 30 each year subsequently up to 1846.[149] Obviously, therefore, the great bulk of the hide trade of 1800--47 was not with the missionaries, but with the rancheros.

It is to be noted, too, that resident foreigners played a negligible part in this phase of Californian development. In 1820, there were only 12 such residents of record; in 1830, only 150; and in 1840, 380. Of these, the majority were engaged in commerce or the trades. The immigration of 1841 and ensuing years swelled the total of registered and estimated aliens in the department to 680 by 1845; and of course the American occupation speedily ran the numbers into the thousands;[150] but the influx of the '40s was too roving and recent, and too far removed from the coastal strip to be a factor in coastal industry and commerce.

---

[149] Bancroft, Calif., vol. 3, pp. 363, 364, 365, 366; vol. 4, pp. 79, 95, 209--10, 339--40; 377--78, 432--33, 561--62.

[150] See ante, p. 153, Table I.

Of 600 arrivals of vessels in territorial ports indicated for the period by the Forbes list, Davis, in his supplemented estimate of the trade, uses only 200 as a basis of estimate, and figures on only 1,000 hides laden yearly by each of those 200. By this unimpeachably if not ultra-conservative approach, he arrives at the figure of 9,400,000 hides exported -- showing his earlier figure of 1,250,000 not excessive! He then cuts this total practically in half, in the further interests of conservatism, calling the estimate 5,000,000; but feels impelled to comment: "Probably my first figures of the revised estimate are the more correct of the two estimates."[151]

As for the tallow export, that figured to 2,500,000 *arrobas* (31,250 T.) on the basis of his original estimate of 1,250,000 hides exported in the period 1826--48, *ca.* Revising this figure in accordance with the Forbes marine list covering the period 1800--47, and again using his hide estimate as a basis, he calculated 18,800,000 *arrobas* (235,000 T.) of tallow; finally reducing that by nearly 50%, for caution's sake, to 10,000,000 *arrobas* (125,000 T.) of tallow.[152]

It should be added that his allowance of tallow

---

[151] *Seventy-five Years*, pp. 408--9.

[152] *Ibid.*, pp. 255--57; 408--9. The first estimate of tallow is given as 62,500,000 *arrobas* -- a typographical error for 2,500,000.

per hide was as conservative as all the rest of his reckoning.

" . . . . the killing season was when the cattle were the fattest, each bullock producing on an average three to four arrobas . . of tallow, besides the manteca reserved for home use. In the winter season, when cattle were killed for home consumption and for the use of the vessels, the tallow would average perhaps not over one arroba to the bullock. Taking the whole year through, I place the product of tallow, for export, at two arrobas for each animal killed . . . ."[153]

As the hide trade did not get under way until the middle '20s, and did not reach its heyday till the late '30s and especially the '40s, it is certainly safe to assume that twice as many hides were exported in the second half as in the first half of the forty-seven-year period (1800--47) for which Davis provided his figures. Taking what he believed the most nearly accurate of his estimates -- that of 9,400,000 hides and 18,800,000 arrobas of tallow -- and allowing one-third of those amounts for the first 26 years of the period, we have left a 22-year period in which 6,266,666 hides and 12,533,332 arrobas of tallow were exported: or an average annual export of 285,000 hides and 570,000 arrobas (7,125 T.) of tallow, in round numbers.

---

[153] Davis, Seventy-five Years, pp. 408--9.

Figuring an average Hispano-Californian population of 5,442 for the period 1826--47,[154] it appears that for every Californian -- man, woman and child -- in the department, 52 hides and 105 arrobas (1¼ T.) of tallow were exported each year during the splendid "idle" days of the rancheros.

As a matter of fact, the amounts were probably higher for the latter years of the period (though correspondingly lower in the earlier part), since the industry was so late getting under way. At the time of concluding the Begg contract, in 1822, Hugh McCulloch thought it would be possible to secure 25,000 to 30,000 hides a year; and in 1827 Duhaut-Cilly estimated the country's privately owned cattle at only 28,000 head -- though Bancroft comments, "there is no data for an accurate estimate, even the tithe and tax accounts being exceedingly fragmentary."[155]

----

[154] See ante, p. 153, Table I. The population is figured for present purposes as increased in 1826 by half the increase between 1820 and 1830; and in 1847, by two-thirds of the increase between 1845 and 1848.

[155] Bancroft, Calif., vol. 2, pp. 476, n. 48; 668, n. 32. Duhaut-Cilly, Viaggio, vol. 2, p. 145. The Frenchman calculated the mission herds as numbering 202,000, making a total of 230,000 head of horned cattle for the country.

It remains to determine the monetary value of the estimated hide and tallow traffic. The Begg contract set $1 per hide, large or small; but almost before the ink on that document could be sanded, Gale was offering $1.50.[156] Practically at once, the Boston men swung into keen rivalry. In 1844, Hartnell referred to hides as being worth $2 each; and at about the same time, Larkin mentioned them as bringing from $1 to $2 apiece.[157] The price of tallow in the Begg contract was $2 the *arroba*, with $3 offered for suet and $4 for lard.[158] Hartnell gave the rate as 12 *reales* ($1.50) the *arroba* for tallow, in 1844.[159] No doubt $1.50 per hide and the same price per *arroba* of tallow is near enough a general average for present purposes. At least it is not an over-allowance.

On that basis, then, and considering as tallow all fat exported, with no accounting made of the higher-priced

---

[156] Bancroft, *Calif.*, vol. 2, p. 476, n. 48.

[157] April (no day), 1844, Hartnell to Wyllie, in *Pio Pico Doc.*, MS vol. 1, #85, p. 2; Larkin, *Official Corresp.*, MS, vol. 2, p. 99.

[158] Bancroft, *loc. cit.*

[159] April (no day), 1844, Hartnell to Wyllie, in *loc. cit.*

suet and lard, the annual hide-tallow business of the territory for the years 1826--47 may be estimated in American money as follows:

Table XIV

Estimated Annual Value of Hide-Tallow Exportation, 1826--47

	No. of Hides	Amount of Tallow	Value of Hides	Value of Tallow	Total Value
Per capita	52	105 arr. (1¼ T.)	$78	$157.50	$235.50
Per representative family[a]	416	840 arr. (10½ T.)	624	1,260.00	1,884.00
For the territory	285,000	570,000 arr. (7,125 T.)	$427,500	$855,000.00	$1,282,500.00

[a] From what is known of the size of Californian families, it seems safe to assume eight members to a representative household.

That these figures are not excessive seems borne out by combined statistics from two other sources, both of the highest competence. The first of those is Larkin's generalization that owners of Boston ships expected "about one hide to each Dollar invested."[160] The second is Senator Dayton's quotation, in the United States Senate, from a letter of 1842 written by the *American* merchant Henry A. Peirce, of the statement

---

160 Official Corresp., MS, vol. 2, p. 100.

that the California hide and tallow trade employed "more than half a million of American capital."[161] Those two estimates, taken in conjunction, indicate a trade in excess of 500,000 hides yearly, which implies a Californian tallow export of 1,000,000 arrobas (125,000 tons), with a combined value of $2,250,000.

Whether one inclines to the Mofras-Larkin two million and a quarter or the Forbes-Davis million and a quarter estimate, the indication is of a striking enough commerce for the times and circumstances.[162]

---

[161] *Congressional Globe*, App., 28th Cong., 1st Sess., p. 226, col. 1.

[162] Larkin's estimate of 80,000 hides exported in 1846 by June 15th (*Official Corresp.*, HS, vol. 2, p. 94) suggests, at first glance, a probable 160,000 for twelve months. As there was no regularity in sailings, however, such an assumption would have no validity. Mofras (*Explor.*, vol. 1, p. 362) reported 100,000 hides shipped from San Pedro alone as early as 1834. His calculation for the territory for September 1840 -- September 1841 was 210,000 piastres in hides and 55,000 piastres in tallow (vol. 1, p. 500). Bancroft treats the piastre as equivalent to the dollar -- whether Mexican or American it is hard to tell, as he uses the dollar sign for both, as did the Californians. Webster's New International Dictionary identifies the piastre with the peso.

It is to be noted that no reckoning is included in the foregoing figures of various more or less important by-products of the hide-tallow trade, such as pickled beef, worth $4 a _cental_ (hundredweight) in 1823--26; horns, for which Gale paid $4 per hundred; horse-hair, cattle-hair and soap -- all in demand.[163]

Comparison of the volume of traffic in hides and tallow as estimated and summarized above, with figures supplied elsewhere[164] on the territory's export trade generally, reveals a wide discrepancy. This does not, however, invalidate either accounting. The general export estimates supplied later are figured on customs records and other indices to legitimate trade -- though a cautious allowance for contraband trade is made; while the hide-tallow computations are based -- and extremely conservatively -- on the numbers and capacities of trading vessels known to have carried away full cargoes. In other words, the figures on general export business deal with licit commerce primarily, whereas the hide-tallow accounting includes contraband ladings.

Accordingly, while it is here reiterated that the hide-tallow figures are offered not as statistics but as a rough indication of the importance of the trade; and while

---

[163] Bancroft, _Calif._, vol. 2, p. 476, n. 48.
[164] _Post_, p. 731, Table XVI.

the skeptic is invited to pare them as closely as he can think of reason for doing, the fact remains obvious that the Hispano-Californians of 1826--48 did a creditably thriving business, in this branch of trade alone, for a population (averaged for the period) less than that of Marysville or of Woodland today, of Martinez, Hayward, Pacific Grove, Culver City or Calexico; and half or less than half of San Leandro, Ventura, Santa Rosa, Vallejo or Whittier.[165]

As for soap, that important item of the cattle-products industry, Larkin thought that $10,000 worth must have been sent out of the country during the first 6½ months of 1846.[166] Salvador Vallejo declared[167] -- perhaps with exaggeration -- that when Frémont's men plundered his house and lands in 1846 he had $20,000 worth of soap ready for shipment.

58. Horses, Mules and Cattle

Nor does the hide-tallow and soap export alone indicate the size of the stock-raising industry. Horses, cattle and mules were sold overland both east and north; horses were shipped to Honolulu; and toward the end of the

---

[165] Comparisons from 15th Census of U. S.
[166] Official Corresp., MS, vol.2, p. 94.
[167] Notas hist., MS, p. 131.

period, a sort of glorified livery business, catering to foreign travellers, was cultivated by the smaller stockmen. This last enterprise was inspired by the influx of many aliens in the 1840s. Instead of selling cheap horses, certain **rancheros** of Los Angeles and especially of Santa Bárbara developed a specialty of fine mounts for hire. The animals — in charge of a **vaquero** — were rented out in small herds or **caponeras** of about 25 horses headed by a bell mare who was always, graphically supplies Davis, a **yegua pinta**.[168]

The Santa Fe trade in livestock -- particularly in mules -- seems to date from 1831, when William Wolfskill arrived in Los Angeles from New Mexico by way of the Green and Virgin rivers and the Cajón Pass, and David E. Jackson entered San Diego, from the same starting point, via Tucson and the Gila. Wolfskill's purpose was to trap; but Hayes, Warner and Widney declare[169] that they took back with them a string of mules whose size, fine appearance and cheapness "caused quite a sensation . . ., out of which sprang up a trade, carried on by means of 'caravans or pack animals . . . . which flourished for some ten or twelve years. These caravans reached California yearly . . . . They brought the woolen fabrics of New Mexico, and carried back mules, and silk, and other Chinese goods."[169]

---

[168] **Seventy-five Years**, pp. 36, 59.

[169] **Hist. Sketch of L. A.**, p. 18; Bancroft, **Calif.**, vol. 3, p. 395, n. 22.

Los Angeles was the point of arrival and the rendezvous for departure.

As early as September 1831, Jackson set out from Santa Fe with two men (J. J. Warner among them), specifically to purchase California mules for the Louisiana market. Almost simultaneously Ewing Young headed thirty men on the double quest of beaver and California horses and mules. By 1834, this commerce had assumed important proportions, one party of 125 traders arriving in February of that year, after mules.[170]

Mofras spoke[171] of the coming of the annual caravan to Los Angeles in November 1841, describing it as numbering about 200 New Mexicans and 60 Americans, besides a detached party of 40 others. They traded for four months throughout the territory, after which they departed with 2,000 bêtes chevalines. The French traveller may have exaggerated; for Bancroft, although noting the Mofras account elsewhere, states[172] only that the usual caravan came that autumn, to the number of about 36 men. The Niles' Register [173] reprints from the Evansville, Indiana, Journal a letter of July 29, 1841, from a member of the train,

---

[170] Bancroft, Calif., vol. 3, pp. 386--87, 395.
[171] Exploration, vol. 1, pp. 354--55.
[172] Calif., vol. 4, pp. 207--8.
[173] Dec. 4, 1841, vol. 61, p. 209, col. 1--3.

describing the departure from Santa Fe.

Mention has already been made[174] of the predaceous Chaguanoso element among these transmontane livestock-traders. One contemporary described them as being likely to steal what they could not buy; and as has been stated in the earlier connection, they were as willing to incite Indian raids as to deal in animals stolen on the tribesmen's own initiative. As for taxes on their transactions, they claimed exemption under a decree of 1830.[175]

Too little is known of the details of this trade for any venture at an estimate of its volume.

Similar mystery shrouds the overland horse and cattle export to Americans in the Oregon country and possibly to the Hudson's Bay Company; and indeed this trade may have been inconsiderable. In 1837, however, both the "Willamette Cattle Company" headed by Ewing Young and the Hudson's Bay Company represented by James Birnie attempted to purchase cattle for the northern establishments. Both offers were at first rejected by the Californian government, which feared to open the way for the estrangeros of the north to compete in the livestock industry. There is no evidence, says Bancroft, that the refusal to do business was reconsidered

---

[174] Ante, pp. 430--31.
[175] Bancroft, Calif., vol. 3, p. 396, n. 24.

in Birnie's case. Young, however, succeeded in obtaining a reversal of policy and purchased some 700 or 800 head from the government's ex-mission herds.

Deliberately, the wildest cattle were selected by the administrators, apparently to discourage the prospective stockmen of Oregon; but despite the vicissitudes of riding herd on the unruly animals through the little known intervening wilderness, the drovers eventually delivered at least 600 head in the Willamette Valley. Says Bancroft: "This is the first instance clearly recorded in which cattle were obtained in California for the north; though there are rumors that the Hudson's Bay Company had before driven a few from Ross . . . ."[176]

Since the extent of this trade -- if it was continued -- is not known, the subject would not have been introduced here save for the light it throws on Californian ambitions and apprehensions. A letter of Vallejo to Alvarado[177] discusses the pros and cons of the Young and Birnie propositions. Don Guadalupe considered the Columbia country and Alta California as belonging to the same great natural division, destined to comprise a single

---

[176] *Calif.*, vol. 4, pp. 85--87.

[177] March 18, 1837, in *Vallejo Doc.*, MS, vol. 4, #83.

nation. For that reason, there was something to be said for co-operating, even with aliens, to blaze a connecting route, promote one of the country's principal trade commodities and advance the region's development. It would be necessary, however, in so joining forces, to maintain government control of the traffic in all its aspects; to insure that all sales be made on government account for the present; and to take great precautions against abuses. One of the dangers to be guarded against was the developmnet of a northern rival in the stock industry.

Alvarado, though discussing the proposal in less detail, declined to entertain it, evidently through doubt of the government's ability to insist upon the safeguards urged by Vallejo. "I have concluded it best not to consent to this sort of petitions so long as the different branches of the country's administration remain unregulated . . . . "[178] -- a decision from which, as we have seen, he allowed himself to be persuaded.

----

[178] May 3, 1837, Alvarado to Vallejo, Vallejo Doc., MS, vol. 4, #236.

That the British company projected, at least, the development of a cattle industry threatening enough to Californian interests to justify the gravest apprehensions and utmost caution of the territorial authorities seems indicated in a letter of 1841 preserved in the Larkin correspondence. "The Hon. the Hudson's Bay Company are playing the Divel with the California cattle," advised the writer, Ethan Estabrook, "if not with California itself. They are preparing to purchase on a large scale. Capt Humphrey informs me that they want at least 100,000 cattle and ½ million of sheep if they can be had."[179]

In the export of horses to Honolulu, which began to flourish along with the Boston trade, in the '20s, a spirit of caution on the part of the Californian government was early in evidence. Thus, in 1832, the American brig "Bolivar" was permitted to load horses, but no mares.[180]

---

[179] Jan. 29, 1841, Estabrook to Larkin, in Larkin Doc., MS, vol. 1, #122, p. 2. Estabrook had been left at Monterey in 1840 as United States consular agent in charge of the Graham exile claims; but not being given government recognition, sailed from the territory in 1841. Bancroft, Calif., vol. 2, p. 792.
[180] Oct. 10, 1832, Zamorano to Acting Commandant-General, S.F., in Vallejo Doc., MS, vol. 1, #327, p. 1.

59. *Caballeros* -- of the Plow

Important as stockraising was and was considered in the Californian economy of a hundred years ago, it is profound though common error to conclude that no other line of endeavor occupied or attracted the *hijos del país.* Indeed, it will be shown presently that insistent demand of the customers, rather than lack of versatility of the *Californios*, was mainly responsible for the emphasis on the products of the range; and that the territorials resented their superimposed limitations and sought to fling them off.

Moreover, Spanish restrictions and Mexican delay in extending and safeguarding private ownership of land, along with lack of labor and of markets kept "dirt farming" in California close to the subsistence level until the late '30s and '40s. Although colonial agriculturists did not give implicit obedience to Spanish prohibitions in favor of Peninsular monopolists, husbandry could not flourish on any considerable scale sub rosa and in an atmosphere of repression.

"The Spanish court always viewed with suspicion," says Fisher, "American cultivation of the olive, the vine, the mulberry tree, hemp and flax. Royal orders came repeatedly after 1595 asking viceroys to prohibit the planting of vineyards. As late as the beginning of the nineteenth century the viceroy of New Spain was commanded to destroy the vines in the northern part of the country, where the wine industry flourished, because the merchants of Cadiz complained that their commerce in wines had decreased; happily this decree like many former ones was never put into effect. The prohibitive measures also applied to olive-growing and Humboldt stated that few of those trees existed in Mexico by the nineteenth century."[181]

In 1806, the governor of California urged the commandants to insist on obedience to the laws -- the stimulus to this exhortation being information received by His Excellency that Californian maize and cattle had been sold at Cape San Lucas and in the Sandwich Islands.[182]

In this tradition California's first settlers were reared. As pioneers on a new frontier, moreover, they were either pobladores, rigidly limited in production and even production goods; or soldiers under the still closer restrictions of military life. Only the missionaries had scope for enterprise. Mission monopoly was therefore inevitably the destiny of the province.

---

[181] *Viceregal Admin.*, pp. 110--11.
[182] Bancroft, *Calif.*, vol. 2, p. 184, n. 18.

Nevertheless, in so far as circumstances permitted, the sons of the country became, more and more, sons of the soil. Duhaut-Cilly, visiting Los Angeles in 1827, declared: "The environs of the village and the alluvial slopes . . . . seemed to me to be diligently cultivated. The principal crops consist of grain and grapes." He claimed to find the Angelinos particularly cheerful and debonair, quite in contrast with the presidial populations; and drew the conclusion: "It is so true that agriculture is, for the free man, the most copious fountain of happiness, and that on the contrary all is despondency and subjection under military regulation."[183]

Whether or not the French sea-trader expressed an articulate Californian point of view, the trend, at the time he wrote, was definitely from fort to field. Of San Diego in 1821—30, Bancroft observes, ". . . . both soldiers and invalids now cultivated to a considerable extent fertile spots in the vicinity of the presidios"; and of the territory generally, "The amount of agricultural products raised — chiefly for home consumption — at pueblos and ranchos must have been large in the aggregate."[184]

---

[183] A. Duhaut-Cilly, Viaggio intorno al globo, vol. 2, pp. 98—99.

[184] Calif., vol. 2, pp. 546, 667.

This tendency was encouraged by Mexican and Californian officials. Figueroa's opening address to the diputación in 1834 voiced the resentment of the Californians themselves against the mesquina política of Spain, which had "reduced agriculture to a nullity," and of the first Mexican governors, who had "kept it on the same basis." Spain's faults had been over-regulation and stupid ignorance, which multiplied human misery. The error of Figueroa's Mexican predecessors had been the inexperience which led them into conformance with the barbarous custom of restraining idle land from ownership. Later, to the same body, His Excellency lamented that lack of secure land titles discouraged agriculture.[185]

It was Vallejo's practice to put soldiers and their families at work on the land; and to set them up as farmers, even before their retirement, that they might become established agriculturists when veterans.[186] Micheltorena looked forward to the time when he could convert his soldiers into farmers.[187] Osio joyously announced the departure for the northern frontier of several hard-working families who would "foment agriculture" and various other needed industries; and the decision of his own brother-in-law to

---

[185] Leg. Rec., MS, vol. 2, pp. 43, 81--82.
[186] See ante, p. 122.
[187] Bancroft, Calif., vol. 4, p. 350.

come up from arid Lower California to settle in the fertile San Francisco region where he could be a farmer. There was land for all, very productive, exulted Don Antonio.[188]

Bandini looked, for the country's salvation, to its all-round agricultural development. The territory was capable of producing "grapes, olives, hemp, flax, cotton, and other such important crops," grapes offering the greatest scope for enterprise.[189]

Castañares urged California's agricultural opportunities on the Mexican Congress with all the virtuosity of a "lunch-and-lecture" man of today. Only lack of *manos* was holding the territory back agriculturally. With an adequate population, she could supply the needs of all the neighboring regions for wheat and other cereals. She was most certainly destined by her great range of climate to hold first place on the American continent as a producer of trade commodities in the greatest demand: of cotton, tobacco, sugar, coffee, flax and hemp; of grapes and many fruits and nuts so far imported from abroad by the Americas— such as almonds,

---

[188] Jan. 27, 1841, Osio to Vallejo, in VallejoDoc., MS, vol. 10, #53, *passim.*

[189] Aug. 9, 1839, Bandini to L. A. Ayuntamiento, in Leg. Rec., MS, vol. 3, pp. 45--46.

hazelnuts, etc.

So fertile was the soil of the territory, Don Manuel impressed on Congress, that wheat yielded 400- to 600-fold; corn, 1,000- to 1,200-fold; and beans, 500- to 700-fold. (Doubtless his abounding enthusiasm led him into extravagance here. Larkin wrote at about the same time that wheat produced from 40- to 50-fold under the most imperfect cultivation; while the Spanish padres had for many years obtained as much as 100-fold at some of the missions, and 180-fold had once been gathered near San José.)[190]

The grape grew abundantly and profitably in the territory, the gentleman from California enthused to his colleagues. The wines and *aguardiente* manufactured there, though made without the expert knowledge and the equipment of Europe, rivalled European liquors, in the judgment of competent persons.

Tests to see if cotton could be raised profitably had proved very gratifying, he expounded further; and the California crop was so superior to that of the Acapulcan coast that the attention of the textile manufacturers of Tepic had been strongly attracted. The soil of the territory was also adapted to the cultivation of flax and hemp. In Spanish times the Californian hemp-fields had supplied the tackle

---

[190] Official Corresp., MS, vol. 2, p. 96.

needs of the Pacific royal fleet; and the greater part of the linen cloth used in the old missions had been woven there from Alta Californian flax.[191]

The introduction of hemp culture in California had been an incident of Spain's flurry in liberalism toward the turn of the century. The industry had been initiated under government supervision in 1795 at San José. Ignacio Vallejo, father of illustrious Mariano Guadalupe, had been in charge. By 1800, the outlook for profit was so gratifying that an expert in the cultivation and preparation of hemp and flax -- Sergeant of Marines Joaquin Sanchez -- was sent from Mexico to oversee and promote the industry. By 1805 the culture had spread throughout the territory, and the *tribunal de cuentas* called the attention of the viceroy to its importance.

Till then, price-fixing had been left to the pursers of the transports, who were incompetent to decide the matter and set a maximum ($3.50 per *arroba*) which Sanchez protested was the minimum that would allow producers a profit. On the recommendation of the *tribunal de cuentas,* the determination of price was now referred to the governor's judgment; and a policy of accepting all hemp offered was adopted. With a new value of $4 the *arroba,* and an unlimited market, hemp

---

[191] Castañares, *Col. de Doc.,* pp. 23, 30.

sprang into immediate popularity with provincial growers. In 1810, 120,000 pounds (or, according to one report, 173,000 pounds) were exported; and a surplus of 98,750 pounds, for which cargo space could not be found, remained in storage.

The outbreak of the revolution put an end to this spurt of opportunity. The transports no longer came. Spanish dollars no longer rewarded endeavor. Arrillaga announced that the government had a sufficiency of the product on hand; and that thereafter farmers who chose to grow hemp must do so at their own risk or for their own use.[192]

That hemp growers were not entirely crushed even by this blow to enterprise nor by the decade of economic disaster which ensued is indicated by the fact that hemp was one of the commodities which the territory undertook to furnish under the Begg contract of 1822.[193] Yet the market seems not to have been adequate, for -- and despite some indications of a demand in Mexico in 1825 -- Echeandía reported to the Secretary of State in 1829 that the raising of flax and hemp, which grew well in the territory, had been abandoned for lack of export opportunities.[194]

---

[192] Bancroft, Calif., vol. 1, p. 619; vol. 2, pp. 177--78.

[193] Ibid., vol. 2, p. 476, n. 48.

[194] Ibid., p. 668, n. 31; May 19, 1829, Echeandía to Min. of State and Rel., in Depart. Rec., MS, vol. 7 pp. 15--16.

Flax culture, as a matter of fact, had not inspired the hopes that hemp had aroused. After experimentation, Sanchez had concluded, back in 1804, that the expense of growing and preparing the crop made it unprofitable for California.[195]

Grain offered better, though not glittering, prospects of reward. Before 1822, there had been little export of privately grown cereals. The beginnings of such a traffic had been foreshadowed in 1801, when the viceroy had authorized the shipment of 1,000 fanegas or more of Californian wheat to San Blas. Circularized as to the amounts they could furnish and at what price, pobladores and rancheros of the Los Angeles district responded with a tender of 2,270 fanegas (3,632 bushels) at $2.50. At least 24 individuals responded, with offers ranging from 40 to 300 fanegas.

"There is no record," says Bancroft, "that any shipment was made, and no reason is given for the failure of the project. This same year, however, the officers of the transports were ordered to take on board at San Blas only

---

[195] Bancroft, Calif., vol. 2, p. 179.

such supplies as were necessary for the voyage northward, in order that provisions for the return voyage might be bought in California; and accordingly . . . Captain Saavedra obtained supplies, chiefly of flour, for two vessels. The mills of San José were kept running day and night, but there seems to have been considerable difficulty in getting all that was required."[196]

It was scarcely to be expected that full cargoes of flour or even of grain would be readily available without notice in a country where there had hitherto been no incentive to do more than supply family needs, and where all land was public domain, subject to seizure at any time for government pruposes. It would be interesting to learn whether, under those conditions, the possibility of developing a grain trade with Mexico attracted any considerable number of citizens to risk the labor and capital required. But Bancroft found no reliable data on agriculture -- save as conducted at the missions -- for the balance of the period.[197]

During the Mexican régime, at least, corn was exported regularly to Acapulco,[198] and the Begg contract for Peruvian

---

[196] Bancroft, Calif., vol. 2, pp. 184--85.

[197] Ibid., p. 417.

[198] Duflot de Mofras, Exploration, vol. 1, p. 501.

supply included wheat, at $3 per *fanega*, among the products for export; although it could be accepted in large quantities only when the crop in Chile fell short.[199] However, these outlets were of course open to the mission growers, and it is impossible to draw any conclusion as to the bulk of private production and export. Moreover, as wheat became an increasingly important Mexican product, the Californian opportunity was probably never large.

The British posts on the Columbia River bought two shiploads of grain and other agricultural produce annually, from 1836--40.[200] But it was Russian America that became the territory's steadiest customer for wheat; and to the grain transports flying the double eagle special privileges were extended in encouragement of the trade. In the late '30s, two vessels (in ballast) a year were allowed to put into San Francisco Bay without prior call at Monterey, to load grain for Sitka.[201] Later a third vessel was added to the Russian cereal fleet.[202]

Bancroft found the grain imported from California for the Russian establishments in 1817--25, inclusive,

---

[199] Bancroft, Calif., vol. 2, p. 476, n. 48.
[200] Ibid., vol. 4, pp. 79--80.
[201] Depart. St. Pap., Ben., MS, vol. 3, p. 1; Depart. St. Pap., Ben., C.-House, MS, vol. 2, p. 3.
[202] Davis, Seventy-five Years, p. 22.

given by one Russian authority as 16,310 _fanegas_ (26,096 bushels) of wheat; 2,307 _fanegas_ (3,691 bushels) of barley; and 815 _arrobas_ (20,375 pounds) of flour. (In addition, there were 1,928 _fanegas_ (3,084 bushels) of pease and beans; besides 4,123 _arrobas_ (51½ tons) of tallow and lard, and 1,879 _arrobas_ (46,975 pounds) of dried meat.)[203]

No adequate statistics on California's grain export are at hand. Forbes figured the value of the 1831 crop at £17,256; but he included pease and beans with wheat, corn and barley, and counted in the mission production.[204] Larkin estimated the 1846 wheat export at 10,000 _fanegas_ (16,000 bushels) up to mid-June.[205] Prices seem to have remained pretty stable throughout the period, wheat and barley bringing $2, and corn $1.50 the _fanega._[206]

In addition to the grain exported, a very considerable quantity was converted into flour for territorial consumption. Each _hacienda_ had its single-horse-power grist mill operated by an Indian lad flourishing his cowhide whip. General Vallejo kept several such primitive contraptions busy at Petaluma. From about 1839, Nathan Spear ran a

---

[203] _Calif._, vol. 2, p. 636, n. 7.

[204] _Alta Calif._, pp. 259--60.

[205] _Official Corresp. MS_, vol. 2, p. 94.

[206] Forbes, _loc. cit._; W. M. Wood, _Wandering Sketches_, p. 228.

six-mule-power mill on present Clay Street in San Francisco, between Montgomery and Kearney Streets. Davis says that besides milling for himself, Spear ground for the grain farmers of the bay region, and so kept his mill "in full operation from the day it began grinding until 1845." Using twenty-four mules in four shifts, he turned out from "25 to 50 barrels of good flour a day. . . . . I have known Vallejo to have had five or six hundred fanegas of wheat at the mill at one time to be ground into flour. . . . . Spear owned several vessels which he used in his business. These carried grain and flour to and from the different embarcaderos around the bay. Salvador Vallejo and other tillers of the soil were patronizers . . . ."[207]

Of fruits and vegetables, olives and grapes, the territorials had an abundance for their needs and would have raised quantities for export, as we shall see,[208] had markets been available. Gardens, orchards, olive-groves and vineyards had flourished from the eighteenth century on. "Many varieties of fruit, including probably grapes, were introduced from the peninsula by the earliest

---

[207] Seventy-five Years, pp. 136--37. Davis says that Spear brought the mill machinery from Baltimore via Callao.

[208] Post, sec. 65; see also sec. 61, on other handicaps to agriculture.

expeditions between 1769 and 1773; nearly all the varieties were in a flourishing condition on a small scale before . . . 1784; and very few remained to be introduced after 1800." Governor Fages had as many as 200 fruit trees and vines in his garden in 1783--91.[209]

"Apples, pears, quinces and peaches are common all over California," wrote Larkin. "In parts of the country there are limes, oranges, almonds, figs and walnuts. Plums and cherries have not been introduced." Grapes of the very best quality flourished in abundance, those grown south of the thirty-fourth degree of latitude being the best.[210]

United States Pacific Fleet Surgeon Wood found "tolerable apples [they are no better today, such are climatic conditions], fine dried dates and figs grown in the country." He remarked on the excessive cost of the fruit -- 50¢ a pound;[211] but this was in all probability a "tourist price" directed especially at interloping and militant foreigners.

Olives had been grown in quantity, and olive oil pressed out, since mission days.[212] Castañares reported olives to be

---

[209] Bancroft, *Calif.*, vol. 1, p. 619.
[210] *Official Corresp.*, MS, vol. 2, p. 96.
[211] *Sketches*, p. 219.
[212] Bancroft, *op. cit.*, vol. 2, pp. 177, 668.

an important Californian product, in the '40s, the fruit of San Diego and the oil of San Luís rivalling those of Spain.[213]

Mention has been made of the prosperous and steadily increasing commerce in fresh food supply to the whaling fleet. Davis relates that in 1843, 1844 and 1845, thirty to forty whalers at a time lay anchored in San Francisco Bay, trading and taking on stores. His own business kept him moving about the region, from *hacienda* to *hacienda*; and he found the rancheros alert and anxious to cater to the demand for produce.

They "would ask me if I thought as many of the whalers would come another year as were there then. I told them I thought even more would come, as they had been encouraged by finding good supplies of vegetables, and would probably come again and advise other ships to come. They asked my advice as to what they should plant for sale to the ships another year. I told them to plant Irish potatoes, cabbage, pumpkins and onions, as those were the vegetables the vessels mainly depended upon.

"Among those who were most active and energetic in furnishing supplies of this kind, and interested in planting for the purpose, were Don Vicente Peralta, the Castros of

---

[213] *Col. de D c.* pp. 30--31.

San Pablo, Don Antonio María Peralta, Don Ygnacio Peralta, and Don José Joaquín Estudillo, all on the east side of the bay. The Californians, although mainly engaged in cattle raising, were fond of agriculture, and would have engaged in it extensively had there been any market for their products. When an opportunity presented itself, as in the case of supplying the whaleships, they availed themselves of it, and commenced planting."[214]

Saffron for dyeing seems to have been another commercial crop for at least a part of this period. Even sugarcane received at least experimental attention on the Pico ranch of Santa Margarita, where Davis observed stalks nearly as large as his arm;[215] and on the northern frontier Vallejo endeavored to establish a beet-sugar industry. Lacking the needed technical information, he employed the Frenchman Octave Custot to superintend large-scale operations at Petaluma; but the self-recommended expert "failed to produce any sugar except some cakes of an imported article remelted to keep the general in good courage."[216]

---

[214] Davis, *Seventy-five Years*, pp. 154--55. *See* also *post*, 656--57, 659--62.

[215] Bancroft, *Calif.*, vol. 2, p. 476, n. 48; Davis, *Seventy-five Years*, p. 285.

[216] Bancroft, *op. cit.*, p. 773.

Garden truck and other farm products were collected on behalf of the regular merchant ships by resident foreign traders, like Richardson of Yerba Buena and Sausalito. From the middle '30s he built up a large business in the distribution of country produce, keeping two or three small craft circulating about San Francisco Bay for this purpose.[217] Spear, Leese, Hinckley and others conducted a similar trade, as did several of the Californios.[218] In the early '40s, as many as seven lighters navigated California's inland waters.

Among the exports of 1837--38 of the San Francisco district recorded by Captain of the Port Richardson,[219] wheat, potatoes, flour, beans, squash and dried meat are listed along with cattle- and deer-hides, tallow and horns. His appraisal of exported produce for twenty-five sailings in ten months of 1837 is $75,711 -- $3,000 cargoes as average.

In 1843, the schooner "Susannah" carried to Mazatlan a cargo of potatoes which sold for $3,750; and the government schooner "California," on one of her south-bound trips for the same year, invoiced olives, dried fruit along with cheeses, hams and 127 casks of brandy, 6 barrels of pisco and 23 barrels of wine.[220]

---

[217] Bancroft, Calif., vol. 2, p. 709; vol. 5, p. 694. Davis, Seventy-five Years, p. 54.

[218] Bancroft, op. cit., vol. 5, p. 730; vol. 4, p. 710. Post, pp. 669--70; 711--12.

[219] Salidas de Buques, 1837--8, 40, pp. 23--31 and passim.

[220] Bancroft, op. cit., vol. 4, pp. 568--70; 563, n. 42, "California."

60. Vines and Wines

Viticulture was important from early times, and with the making of wines and <u>aguardiente</u> became increasingly so. As early as 1820, Prefect Payeras had taken occasion to protest against the prevalence of liquor manufacture, and to urge that the people might be better employed in other phases of industry.[221] In 1824, Kotzebue remarked[222] on the luxuriance and richness of the grapes of San José, although the best grape country was that south of Santa Bárbara. Wine and brandy appear as exports throughout the period, from the time of the Begg contract of 1822, which included them in its schedule, until Castañares declared that in 1843 approximately 2,000 barrels of various spirits had been exported.[223]

Indeed, by 1839, according to Vallejo, almost all vineyardists made <u>aguardiente</u>; so that political antagonists of Alvarado, seeking to bring about his downfall, proposed with mock seriousness a re-adoption of the liquor taxes

---

[221] <u>Ibid.</u>, p. 559, n. 3, "1820."
[222] <u>New Voyage</u>, vol. 2, p. 100.
[223] Bancroft, <u>op. cit.</u>, p. 476, n. 48; Castañares, <u>Col. de Doc.</u>, p. 23.

of 1823. For, explained Vallejo, these trouble-makers "knew well that any attempt to collect such taxes would raise a host of enemies and a storm not to be tranquillized . . . ."[224]

Liquor manufacture had as a matter of fact been a major and jealously cherished industry of California when Mexico took over the territory. The Plan de Gobierno of 1834, while including a 10% tax on wine and *aguardiente* as a revenue source, prohibited the importation of foreign liquors.[225] In the fall of that year, the diputacion reprimanded the governor for failure to enforce the ban on foreign brandy. Some of the members were for fining him for having allowed Spanish liquor into the country; but through doubt of their authority to do so, finally agreed to refer the matter to Mexico.[226]

The Plan de Gobierno was but temporarily in force -- until Mexican law could be ascertained and applied to the territory. Thereafter the prohibition of imported liquors had no force. In 1827, we find Bandini placing on record in the diputación a protest against the importation of brandy, and calling for its exclusion.[227] In the

---

[224] Hist. de Calif., MS, vol. 4, pp. 6--7.
[225] Title III, Art. 9, in Bancroft, Calif., vol. 3, p. 512, n. 2.
[226] Leg. Rec., MS, vol. 1, pp. 32--33.
[227] Ibid., p. 54.

same year, Captain Guerra, himself a vineyardist and distiller, complained that the profit was taken out of this branch of enterprise by "an impost almost in excess of the duties on foreign liquors. Moreover, the laws permit the introduction of foreign grape brandy, to the prejudice of our industry. If this cannot be prohibited entirely, at least let the foreign brandies be scrupulously limited to grape brandies as the law specifies; and let foreign liquors be taxed at a rate deemed suitable by the territorials; and let the tax on territorial liquors be modified." The good captain proceeded with true Spanish feeling for moralization, and not without bitterness, to descant on the thesis that "man wearies of profitless labor."[228]

Responsive to the widespread and emphatic demands thus voiced by Bandini and Guerra among others, the diputación drew up and adopted its elaborate liquor tax reglamento of the summer of 1827, already referred to.[229] Although -- since revenue was urgently necessary -- native wines and spirits had to pay their quota, ranging from $2.50 to $10 the barrel (160 quarts), the tax on imported liquors ranged from the maximum on the native brands up to $20 the barrel.

---

[228] Davis, Seventy-five Years, p. 240; Guerra Doc., MS, vol. 1, p. 2.

[229] Ante, pp. 186-87.

Almost immediately thereafter, financial administrator Herrera announced an impost by the supreme government of 80% and 70% on foreign liquors and wines, respectively, the 15% internación tax also to stand.[230] This seems to have been a temporary measure, however; for in July 1834, the diputación again took on itself the responsibility of voting a tax on imported spirituous liquors.[231]

In 1839 Bandini again championed the prohibition of fermented beverages from abroad. Most of the European and North American vessels took advantage of their opportunity to purvey such commodities, he complained, and the country's own production was being stifled as a consequence. This state of affairs should be ended, for the "sound and wise object of legislation is to give impulse to the welfare of the population represented." Certain portions of the republic lacked the vinelands necessary to provide for local consumption. California was capable -- as who could doubt? -- of supplying the entire nation with the juices of the grape, and of excelling all nations in her wine-grape production, if given government co-operation and protection. Even if foreign liquors might be obtained more cheaply, there was always the advantage, in

----

[230] Bancroft, Calif., vol. 3, p. 127, n. 27.
[231] Leg. Rec., MS, vol. 2, p. 181.

home industry, of development and of circulation of profits between growers and consumers. Therefore, Don Juan proposed, let the Junta Departamental suspend the importation of foreign grape liquors until the national Congress should approve or disapprove the prohibition bill being recommended to it.[232]

Evidently the supreme government withheld approval of any such ban, for in 1845 the asamblea again submitted to Mexico an iniciativa de ley prohibiting the introduction of foreign brandy and ordinary wines.[233]

Regardless of the supreme government's attitude on this score, the Californians would have found it as difficult actually to keep out prohibited liquors as they did to exclude other competitive foreign goods. Vallejo recorded[234] that the ships from Peru carried on an extensive illicit trade, selling spirits for less than the legal tax.

One of the last matters urged on the attention of the diputación in 1846 was a vineyardists' petition for abrogation

---

[232] Leg. Rec., MS, vol.3, pp. 44--45.

[233] Ibid., vol. 4, p. 40. No ban was asked of "liquors of the class of "mistelas" -- a Mexican version of the soft drink, made of wine diluted with water and flavored with sugar and cinnamon.

[234] Hist. de Calif., MS,

of taxes on the industry.[235] Despite all the handicaps under which viticulture and the wine and liquor trade seem to have labored, however, as many as one thousand barrels of brandy were reported by Larkin to have been shipped out of the country in the first six and a half months of 1846.[236]

As to the quality of these products, early visitors were not always complimentary. Duhaut-Cilly, in 1827, found them very inferior to the exquisite flavor of the grape, and opined that the fault was in the manufacture rather than in the quality of the soil.[237] Wood was more favorable in his appraisal of nearly twenty years later. He compared the red wine with a light port, and the white with still champagne.[238] At about the same time, Castañares made his claim that although the wines and brandies of the country were made without the expert knowledge and the equipment available in the European wineries, qualified persons adjudged them worthy to compete with the European product.

---

[235] *Leg. Rec.*, MS, vol. 4, pp. 344, 345.
[236] *Official Corresp.*, MS, vol. 2, p. 94.
[237] *Viaggio*, vol. 2, p. 98.
[238] *Sketches*, p. 219.
[239] *Col. de Doc.*, p. 23.

William Heath Davis, who bought territorial wines and liquors in large quantities for exportation, found them pleasant to drink and commercially "just as good as gold, and better, because there was a sure sale . . at a profit."[240]

61. The Middle Age of Agriculture

The **Californios**, then, were not limited in their interest as ranchers to the livestock industry. They made various tentatives and some marked advancement in diversified agriculture and allied branches. Every step of the way, however, was attended by difficulties.

Of the scarcity of land until well into the '30s, and the insecurity of land tenure, enough has been said. Shortage of labor for productive enterprise over and above self-maintenance remained a handicap throughout the period, Castañares naming it a prime factor of agricultural retardation in 1844.[241] The political commotions and preoccupations which characterized all these years were additional deterrents. Vallejo declared of the late '30s that civil war had paralyzed all industries, especially agriculture.[242]

It must be remembered, too, that whereas the United

---

[240] *Seventy-five Years*, pp. 287, 288, 293.
[241] *Col. de Doc.*, p. 23.
[242] *Hist. de Calif.*, MS, vol. 4, p. 6.

States, France, and especially England were enjoying the benefits of the agricultural "revolution," California had no share in those blessings during this era. Soil improvement and land reclamation, crop rotation, labor-saving devices, control of plant diseases and of pests-- all that is meant by scientific farming -- was the profoundly hidden secret of the future.

Nor does that fact imply congenital backwardness on the part of the territorials. Scientific husbandry is capitalistic husbandry, founded on surplus capital and labor, as well as on the application of experience and invention to problems of the soil. To not one of those production goods, material or otherwise, could California lay claim on her own account nor find free access. She was still in the middle age of agriculture, for the simple but ample reason that she had not had time to grow out of it.

Nor had the tremendous economic and social forces which were transforming much of the world around her yet impinged on her remote shores. The rise of the factory system, with its massing of non-agricultural populations to be fed; the piling up of capital demanding investment; the growth of the war markets of Europe; the soaring of prices on the wings of demand: all these lay below California's horizon.

It had been the pressure of expanding markets that set the agricultural "revolution" in motion; and that economic and social phenomenon was earliest notable and gained promptest momentum in the country where destiny first brought togethe r the impetus of demand and the mass of surplus capital and labor -- England. As for California, she was but an undeveloped and isolated frontier.

True, many of her inhabitants had advanced -- precociously, considering their limited opportunities -- to the stage of pioneer farming. But the elemental necessity of self-defense against a particularly insidious and persistent barbarian hostility still exacted much of their energy and attention.

Nor did the pioneer farmers of other times and places supply the world's needs. Like the Californians of the middle period, they profited by the preparatory work of the frontiersmen to plant small farms for their own sustenance, extending their enterprise cautiously, as they perceived, here and there, a commercial demand to be supplied. Not until it has provided for all its own subsistence needs, been linked by more or less adequate communication facilities to the markets of a less simply organized civilization, acquired, by slow growth and immigration, surpluses of labor and capital, with consequent capacities of demand and supply, can a raw settlement mature into a bustling emporium. Meantime, enterprise is restrained by the inability of the pioneering community to absorb surplus produce.[243] These are axioms generally left out of the reckoning when the case of Mexican California is under consideration.

Speaking of the westward movement in the United States, Lippincott remarks that the volume of production "increased so rapidly as to tax the consuming power of domestic markets. The difficulties in selling farm products were retarding factors at one time or another for every community, and it was not until relieved by a canal or a railroad that conditions began to improve." He quotes an editor of the old west: "'The farmer thinks it unnecessary to plant more grain than can be disposed of at home; thus part of his time passes in inactive languor; but once point to him a market where he may have

---

[243] To California's lack of men and capital, detailed consideration has been given in chaps. II and III. A special phase of the labor problem -- the failure of the mission communities to supply a proletariat -- willbe given further consideration in chap. VII. A section (#65) of the present chapter is devoted to the general subject of Californian markets; and one (#66) to that of Californian efforts toward a merchant marine.

a sure sale for his produce, and every nerve is exerted in the cause of industry.'"244

The Californians were no essentially different breed of men. Their industial and commercial shortcomings were not inherent, but circumstantial. They came into their first opportunity well after 1830. That they did not perform prodigies of accomplishment comparable to those, for example, of the American pioneers who at about the same time poured into the Canaan of the Ohio country, does not stamp them as men blind or indifferent to progress.

They were, rather, men without opportunity -- men without markets or accessibility to markets. Between them and the world of consumers stretched a wilderness of ocean on the one hand; and on the other, half a continent still regarded by the aggressive Yankees themselves as "the great American Desert," unconquered and unconquerable.

Here was no center of a great natural distributory system, such as linked the men of the Ohio country by radial streams to their entire periphery of markets -- east, south, and north. Instead, a few vessels owned and controlled chiefly by aliens served as carriers of such commodities as promoted alien enterprise, purchased at prices and under conditions dictated by alien interest. That the

---

244 Lippincott, Econ. Develop of the U.S., p. 150.

Californians aspired to increase and diversify their production, develop their own transport and attain to adequate consumer patronage availed them little. So they marked time, though not always patiently. They farmed in so far as there was incentive to farm, and by such methods as their scant experience and resources permitted.

A variety of pests afflicted them in those efforts, especially the chapulines, or locusts, worms and rodents -- the ardillas or ground squirrels, gophers and rats -- all of which had rapidly multiplied since mission fare had relieved the local Indians from dependence on them for food. Typical of the plaints of the time is the record in a mission document of 1823 that "'the threatening of the locust plague and the visitation of the worm have begun.'" As for the wild mustard, it "sometimes choked the crop and furnished a hiding-place for livestock." Diseases of blight or rust (commonly known as chahuistle, whether the result of fog or other weather effect or of worms at the roots) attacked the grains. Guerra reported that crops were rarely exempt from enfermedades y plagas.[245]

In addition, there was the factor of weather -- still

---

[245] Bancroft, Calif., vol. 2, pp. 177; 417; 493, n.20; 667. Guerra Doc., MS, vol. 1, p. 2.

omnipotent in farm destinies, despite all our science. The peculiarities of the Californian climate have given rise to considerable agricultural experiment in our own day, not all of it successful. There was still a long way to go along those lines in the 1830s and '40s. As for "unusual" weather, it seems to have been as common then as now, and as disastrous on occasion; while the system of forecasting and recording meteorological caprices, and the technique of crop protection, were rudimentary.

Weather reports had been kept "with tolerable regularity" from Spanish times; but Bancroft comments that "no such thing as a rain-gauge was known, and these reports are so vaguely worded as to convey no idea of the successive seasons which could be utilized in the generalizations of modern science."[246] Whether even those inadequate efforts were continued in the Mexican period on any systematic basis does not clearly appear.

While, moreover, in mission days irrigation works of considerable extent and engineering excellence had been built, there seems no reason to believe that this sort of development was prosecuted under Mexico, or, indeed, that systems inherited from Spain were kept in repair. "The territorial government did nothing for agricultural

---

[246] Bancroft, *Calif.*, vol. 2, p. 177.

development beyond issuing now and then a law against kindling fires in the fields," says Bancroft.[247] Certainly the paucity of resources and the lack of agricultural markets are partial explanation of this failure to "foment" husbandry, although many other of the factors and problems already touched on must also have figured.

Californian rancheros seem thus to have farmed opportunistically, thankful for harvests secured between drouth and flood, in much the same stoical spirit as moves the planters of the Mississippi bottomlands, to this day, to brave the whims of "ole man River" (even at the risk of life and all) to snatch at prosperity in the "good years."

The law of averages seems to have been in normal force, in the one case as in the other. Thus, 1822 and 1823 were years of drouth, and of such crop wastage that Señan found himself obliged to allow the faithful to eat meat, eggs, etc., due to the lack of corn and beans;[248] whereas 1824--25 was a winter of unprecedented rains, which destroyed not only crops but buildings, and altered the drainage map of the country. Nevertheless, crops for the year were the largest

---

[247] Calif., vol. 2, pp. 667--68.

[248] July 6, 1822, Sola to Luís Peralta, in St. Pap., Sac., MS, vol. 6, p. 49. Bancroft, Calif., vol. 2, p. 493, n. 20.

of the decade except for that of 1821, Bancroft discovered; (though what part larger sowings played in that circumstance is not evident). It seems likely that a very dry year followed: for a newspaper item of 1852, attributed to Salvio Pacheco, reported that between 1824 and 1826 hardly any rain fell.[249]

The precipitation was excessive again in 1827--28, flood conditions at least around Monterey being likened to those of 1824--25. Crops were so short in 1827 that the farmers offered to pay their grain tithes in money —scarce as that was -- at the rate of $2 per *fanega*.[250] The year 1829, in contrast, was one of unparalleled drouth. The fields dried up, and the total harvest was "the smallest from 1796 to 1834, and less than half the average for this decade . . . ."[251]

Without delving deeper into the weather annals of Mexican California, it seems sufficient to add that in 1841 drouth again worked havoc. Not only was the harvest ruined; plantings were abandoned as hopeless. That year, instead of shipping cereals to Acapulco, the territorials imported flour from San Blas and Guaymas.[252]

---

[249] Bancroft, *Calif.*, vol. 3, pp. 29--30.

[250] *Depart. St. Pap., Ben., Pref. y Juzg.*, MS, vol. 6, p. 45.

[251] Bancroft, *op. cit.*, p. 115.

[252] Duflot de Mofras, *Exploration*, vol. 1, p. 50.

That year, too, the tidal wave of Yankee immigration which was soon to inundate California began to break in force over the territory; and the new arrivals (not excluding some of official status, such as United States Naval Lieutenant Charles Wilkes) began the wholesale circulation "back east" of those mistaken strictures on the country and its people which created the widespread misconceptions never since radically revised.

63. Profits from Ocean and River

Another mistaken notion, as widely current, is that the possibilities of the fur catch and fur trade were entirely overlooked by the sons of the country. Yet the record is clear that under Spain, government and "privileged" monopoly debarred private enterprise, and that under Mexico, despite the continued discouragement of monopolistic and over-regulatory laws, the Californians pretty generally hunted and traded for skins, exported them and used them extensively in barter.

It was the possibilities offered by California's fur supply, and publicized in the English navigator James Cook's account of his voyage along the northwestern coast of America, that first turned Spain's attention to commercial development of the province. Government monopoly was of course the Spanish objective. A project of 1785 contemplated the exchange of Californian peltries, on government account, for Chinese quicksilver, greatly in demand for mining purposes and itself a government monopoly in Spanish dominions. A commissioner was dispatched from San Blas to set the new enterprise in motion.

Governor Fages undertook to collect 20,000 skins annually -- more, if occupation could be extended north of San Francisco. La Pérouse, at about that time investigating fur trade prospects in the interest of France, later declared in his published narrative that San Francisco alone furnished 10,000 otter skins annually, and that Spain could easily obtain as many as 50,000 within the province if China continued to absorb the supply at a good price.

However, one of the peculiarities of accounts -- contemporaneous and otherwise -- of the Pacific fur trade is their broad exaggeration. Unfortunately, Bancroft found only meagre records of the "take" of 1785 and following. Apparently, only 1,800 otter skins were secured in the first few months; while no more than 9,729 appear to have been shipped to Manila on the royal account up to 1790 -- and that represented Old California's contribution along with that Alta California. Meantime, expenses of administering the trade had run up to $87,699.

Meantime, too, the Philippine Company had petitioned for

exclusive privileges in the field; and the government had agreed to the proposition on condition that the company assume all expenses to date. This seems to have been considered unreasonable, for the Philippine corporation abandoned its efforts to secure the concession. Spain herself withdrew from the traffic in 1790, although the government seems to have bought a few skins during the next several years, despite the royal order to the contrary.

It might be supposed that private enterprise then had full scope, as indeed it did nominally. Duty-free export of otter skins, ordered by the viceroy in 1794, was a favoring circumstance. But, as the governor of California pointed out in a letter of 1795, the fact that the Philippine Company held a monopoly on the China trade nullified the privilege of taking otter in California. Excluded from the great fur emporium, the provincials had little incentive to collect skins until, as Spanish control relaxed, the American *contrabandistas* presented a new consumer demand.[253]

Some furry cargo did find its way to the Philippine market by way of Mexico, the missionaries sending small consignments to San Blas by the transports; but the necessity to share profits with perhaps several middlemen presented

---

[253] Bancroft, *Calif.*, vol. 1, pp. 438--42, *passim*.

an unattractive prospect for lay enterprise, which could not command the services of a host of wageless workers.

Indeed, the matter of price had been controversial from the outset. Basadre -- the royal commissioner -- had offered $2.50 to $10, according to size and color. The _audiencia_ had protested that this was too high a scale; that prices formerly had ranged between one _real_ and one _peso._ Missionary President Lasuen explained that such depressed values had been the result of abundant supply and no demand; and that if the missions were allowed to trade with China they could command still higher rates than those challenged. That the bleak outlook for profits cooled the interest of the padres, despite their advantage of neophyte labor, is evident from a circular of several years later, in which Lasuen advised accumulation of otter skins again, as better prices were promised in Mexico.[254]

Thereafter for the next several decades a more or less desultory collection and exportation of pelts was conducted by the friars. A mission report of 1822, recommending the employment of Alaskans to instruct the neophytes in the special skills of otter hunting, seems to indicate a quickened interest just as Mexico took over the territory.[255]

---

[254] Bancroft, _Calif._, vol. 1, pp. 439; 442; 626, n. 4.
[255] _Ibid._, vol. 2, p. 520, n. 16.

Davis relates that during the Mexican period the missionaries of the San Francisco Bay region secured large quantities of furs from the Indian trappers. He himself on one occasion in 1844 received from the padre in charge of San José several thousand dollars' worth of beaver and land-otter skins which had been collected by mission Indians on the Sacramento and San Joaquin rivers; and he recalled that in 1833, at Mission Dolores, "we went into the 'otter-room,' so-called, a large apartment in the upper story or attic of the building. From the rafters and additional light timbers which had been placed across the room were hung the otter skins which the Mission had collected and had on hand at that time; there being probably eighty to one hundred ready for sale, or exchange in trade. We got them all."[256]

The missions, then, through their command of cheap labor, had succeeded to the field relinquished by Spain's governmental and commercial monopolists. It will be enlightening to trace the fortunes of private enterprise to this point and beyond.

During the attempt to corner the industry for the crown, all but the padres -- acting as royal agents-- had been severely excluded from any participation in the

---

[256] Seventy-five Years, pp. 205--6.

fur trade. "Neophytes must relinquish to the friars all the skins in their possession; skins obtained from neophytes by soldiers or settlers were liable to confiscation, the informer receiving one third of their value; those legitimately obtained from gentiles must be sent at once to the nearest authorities; all trade by private persons was prohibited; and any skins reaching San Blas through other than the regular channel would be confiscated. The aim was to make the government . . . the sole purchaser, though peltries were to be received and forwarded by commanders of presidios" after the departure of the royal commissioner Basadre. Such were the viceregal commands. Governor Fages proceeded to issue enforcing orders -- at once and at intervals during the next several years, indicating that the injunction was not generally effective.

Not only private individuals, but the necessitous presidial companies seem to have grasped eagerly at the new opportunity for gainful occupation. In 1782, of 267 otter skins shipped on two vessels, "97 belonged to presidio of Monterey, 62 to Lieutenant Ortega . . . ." Again, in 1792, the Santa Bárbara Company tendered 59 skins. By this time the royal monopoly had been yielded, with salutary effect on the price standard; and the rewards of this little extra-military enterprise totalled $439 -- an average, per skin, of almost $7.50.[257]

With no further data at hand on fur history under Spain, it is impossible to hazard a guess as to how large exportation bulked for the rest of the period. That the attitude of Spanish officialdom did not grow more encouraging toward private initiative seems indicated in an incident of 1805, when Sergeant Sanchez, in charge of hemp culture, berated "'the stupidity and want of zeal of the settlers, one of whom wished to use his whole crop for making a net to catch otter, regardless of the royal needs.'"[258] The cessation of transport service which cut communications between the province and the peninsula during the wars of independence would in any case have put an end to this opening -- such as it was -- for enterprise.

Begg and Company swung the door ajar again in 1823, seeking "many skins of otter, bear, deer, fox, etc." and pledging themselves to accept private as well as mission offers.[259]

Within a year, however, the territorial authorities barred the way. It was the old story, only the authors being new. Ad interim Governor Luis Argüello signed a

---

[257] Bancroft, Calif., vol. 1, pp. 439; 441, n. 22, 23.

[258] Ibid., vol. 2, p. 177.

[259] Ibid., p. 476, n. 48.

contract taking the Russian American Fur Company into partnership with the territorial government, the Russians to hunt otter on shares in Californian waters, supplying ten Aleuts with <u>bidarkas.</u> California was to feed the Aleuts and would keep ten Indian apprentices on the hunt.[260]

This first contract ran for only four months, but was thereafter renewed several times. The <u>Junta de Gobierno</u> of January 1824, in fact, listed among the territorial revenues outlined in its <u>Plan</u> "the product of the otter-fishery lately established";[261] thus early indicating a disposition to extend the arrangement, which had then run about half its term.

Argüello was a native son. The <u>Junta</u> was composed not entirely of <u>hijos del país,</u> but certainly of progressives anxious to see the country "fomented." That they felt themselves obliged to apply the brake of the Russian contract to private initiative in the fur trade is one of the many instances in their history of the tyranny of poverty. The <u>Junta</u> was attempting to carry on the administration of the territory which Spain had abandoned and to whose financial rescue Mexico had not come. Revenue must

---

[260] <u>Bancroft, Calif.,</u> vol. 2, p. 494.

[261] <u>Plan de Gobierno,</u> 1824, Title III, Art. 8, in Bancroft, <u>op. cit.,</u> p. 513, n. 2.

be had, and sources were few. Russia had long sued for the privileges allowed by the new arrangement. She offered, moreover, one of the few markets open to territorial produce. The fur concession would be immediately profitable to the government and should consolidate the friendly commercial relations which so far had been hampered by Spanish policy. Finally, not even the ghost of Spanish protection hovered about California now; Mexico was an unknown quantity, but certainly not a formidable power; and California -- as the Californians were only too discouragingly aware -- was helpless to repel a Russian advance should the clash of interests bring things to such a pass.

The arguments pro were strong enough to impress both Sub-commissioner of Finances Herrera and Governor Echeandía with the expediency of the contractual relation, although these two, who could not work together without friction, bickered over the details of regulation. Repeated renewals seem to have continued the arrangement, therefore -- with minor modifications from time to time -- to 1830.[262]

The record is not complete on the profits of the Russo-Californian venture. Equal division of the catch seems to have been prescribed throughout most of the partnership.

---

[262] Bancroft, *Calif.*, vol. 2, pp. 520, 648, 650--51; vol. 3, p. 132; vol. 4, p. 160.

Douglas recorded[263] a statement to him by Alvarado that the Russians had always turned over half the proceeds of their hunt to the government. Fernandez has left a similar testimony, adding[264] that the Russians were to sell all their portion to Governor Argüello at $45 the skin, taking payment in wheat.

(An unsigned and undated contract[265] between Echeandía and Clebnicoff [sic] names one-third as California's portion of the current catch; and in 1825 the territory received only 161 of 468 skins. This departure from the equal division basis was explained by Klebnikof, according to Bancroft,[266] on the score that the Russians thus took compensation for "past delays." Apparently the delays were in renewing the contract, since this was the year when Echeandía and Herrera quarreled over terms. The circumstance throws further light on the Russian determination to have Californian skins in the face of Californian inability to resist.)

As the government could now compete in the open market, where the best skins were worth $60,[267] and as

---

[263] *Journal*, MS, p. 16.

[264] *Cosas de Calif.*, MS, pp. 25--26.

[265] In *St. Pap., Sac.*, MS, vol. 11, pp. 13--14.

[266] *Calif.*, vol. 2, p. 648.

[267] *Ibid.*, vol. 3, p. 374, n. 13.

the grain growers were anxious to extend their business, the Russian arrangement seems to have been on the whole very beneficial to California. The purchase of the vessel "Rover" by Governor Argüello in 1823 gave direct access to the great fur center of Canton.

On December 31, 1823, Ygnacio Martinez, reporting on the condition of the otter fishery, noted 324 skins obtained to date.[268] It is not clear whether this was the territorial share for the month for which the first contract had then run, or whether it included skins taken by Californians prior to the signing of the contract, and purchased by the Argüello administration on speculation. In view of the number, the latter seems the stronger probability.

A Russian record gives California's portion of the 1824 proceeds as 677, with 838 for the Russian share. The apparent deviation from the equal division principle in this case is probably accounted for by the fact that under the terms of this second contract -- as agreed in advance, with naive unlegality, in the first -- the Californians were to pay the wages of the Aleutian otter hunters. Bancroft found no Spanish record of the "take" under the 1824 contract.[269] However, the "Rover" departed on her first government voyage to China in February of that year, with 302 otter

---

[268] St. Pap., Sac., MS, vol. 13, p. 1.
[269] Calif., vol. 2, p. 494.

skins and 1,310 seal skins -- gathered chiefly under the Russian contract-- to be exchanged for articles needed by the troops; and on her trip of 1825--26, she sold furs at Canton to the amount of $7,000 -- which proceeds Argüello protested were too low.[270]

Within the thirteen months from the signing of the first agreement to the end of 1824, the partnership netted 1,500 skins for division.[271] A report of 1826,[272] in which Echeandía accounted to the supreme government for 154 skins delivered to him in November 1825, sets a value of 2,399 *pesos* 6 *reales* on the share -- the average of $16.50 per skin being far in excess of the best that Spain had ever permitted in the way of profit. Yet (doubtless for very politic reasons) the governor's evaluation was far below the Canton market level.

Gratifying as these conditions were for purposes of government finance, for the *pobladores* they meant just one more blow to initiative. In January 1824, the governor reprimanded the commandant at San Francisco for maintaining, with a partner, an otter fleet of eight canoes. "This is prohibited, as detrimental to the government catch. An immediate accounting of the number of skins taken is demanded,

---

[270] See *post*, pp. 671--679.
[271] Bancroft, *Calif.*, vol. 2, pp. 644--45.
[272] April 22, 1826, Echeandía to Min. of War, in *St. Pap., Sac.*, MS, vol. 19, pp. 28--29.

and the fleet of eight cayucos must desist from further fishing and disband, unless it is desired that it become an adjunct of the provincial fishery."[273]

In 1826, Echeandía complained to the Minister of War that the hijos del país, as well as foreigners, were catching fur along the coasts of the two Californias, without license. A reglamento and a coast-guard vessel were prime necessities.[274]

In 1831, Pacheco, at Santa Bárbara, evidently defending himself against charges, denied having permitted otter hunting within his jurisdiction.[275]

It was the unpopular Victoria who, in 1831, with characteristic insistence on enforcement of the law to the letter, refused to countenance further infraction of the orders excluding Russians from the territory. He had at first permitted a continuation of the arrangement, for the months of April and May 1831, exclusively, on condition that two-thirds of the crews be Californians; that San Francisco be the northernmost limit of hunting; and that duties

---

[273] Jan. 12, 1824, Argüello to Comandante of San Francisco Presidio, in Depart. Rec., MS, vol. 1, p. 76.

[274] Apr. 22, 1826, Echeandía to Min. of War, in St. Pap., Sac., MS, vol. 19, p. 29.

[275] Bancroft, Calif., vol. 3, p. 374, n. 13.

be paid on the Russian share of the catch;[276] but almost at once he rejected the urgencies of Khlebnikof (representing Wrangell, the new Governor of Russian America) for cotinuance of the fur partnership. The Aleut fishermen whom, along with their bidarkas, Wrangell had sent with Khlebnikof on the "Baikal," found themselves scheduled for a round trip on that vessel.[277]

In his report to the Minister of Relations on conditions in California on his arrival, Victoria called attention to the developmental possibilities of the otter, beaver and seal fisheries, and to their value as a source of revenue for the national and territorial treasuries.[278] In August 1831 he announced that beaver hunting would be free to Californians so long as they held no intercourse with foreigners and inflicted no abuse on gentiles;[279] and at about the same time Mexicans taking otter were relieved from the obligation to pay duties to the national treasury. The tax payable to the territorial exchequer seems to have

---

[276] Depart. Rec., MS, vol. 9, p. 94.

[277] Bancroft, Calif., vol. 4, p. 160.

[278] June 7, 1831, Victoria to Min. of Rel., "Informe General sobre Calif.," in Depart. Rec., MS, vol. 9, p. 135.

[279] Depart. Rec., MS, vol. 9, p. 41.

been from $1 to $3 per skin.[280]

A number of Spanish names appear in the records, at about this time, in connection with taxes on skins, licenses to take fur-bearing animals, etc. Among the otter hunters were Teodoro Gonzalez, J. B. Lopez, Joaquín Ortega, Ramon Estrada, Salvador Vallejo, José Castro and J. B. Alvarado.[281]

The last five, indeed, having organized themselves into the "California Fishing Company," operated a fleet of eighteen **bidarkas** which skimmed the waters of San Francisco Bay and vicinity in quest of otter and seal. For the canoes they had had to apply to the Russians, who supplied Kadiak crews as well. The fishing company also hired thirty Indians from Mission San José. Salvador Vallejo was superintendent. The eighteen-year-old **empresario**, who seems always to have had a zest for boats and boating, directed the fleet operations from his three-paddle **cayuco**. The catch was divided equally with the Russians.

Don Salvador recorded[282] that while seal and otter continued plentiful, the California Fishing Company flourished,

---

[280] Bancroft, Calif., vol. 3, p. 145, n. 68.

[281] Ibid.; Dept. St. Pap., MS, vol. 3, pp. 92--93; Salvador Vallejo, Notas Hist., MS, p. 36.

[282] Notas Hist., MS, p. 35.

and everyone engaged in it reaped good profits. Alvarado confirmed this statement, and added an explanation of the subsequent dissolution of the partnership. Having started on a shoestring, so to speak, the young entrepreneurs [most of whom were in their early twenties] had no means of sending their catch to China, and so were often forced to sell to the Russians, who did not pay what the pelts were worth. When the contract for supply of the bidarkas expired, moreover, the Russians withdrew boats and Kadiaks, "for they had no wish to help establish competitors."[283]

The foreign traders offered a market, of course; but one conducted on their own terms, which could be depended on not to favor the territorials. Nevertheless, through the 1830s and '40s, the fur traffic seems to have been an important phase of maritime commerce. "In 1831--32, etc., there was a considerable trade in otter skins," recalled Francisco X. Alvarado.[284] Beaver skins were among the exports of the port of San Francisco listed by Richardson[285] in the later '30s. Davis emphasized the importance of the pelt trade, and made many references to business transactions

---

[283] Alvarado, Hist. de Calif., MS, vol. 3, p. 8; vol. 2, pp. 39--40.

[284] S. D. Arch., MS, "Miscell. Papers, 1830--43, L.A.," p. 13.

[285] Salidas de Buques, 1837--8, MS, passim.

of his own, as of his father before him, in which fur figured largely.

From the experience of the elder Davis it is obvious that the discouragements of the Spanish system and the ensuing isolation of the province during the wars had not deterred the Californios from piling up a few sea otter skins against a sunny day. Davis, Senior made it a custom to put in at Refugio, that discreetly remote embarcadero of the Ortega rancho, where was done so much trading that never appeared in the customs records. To meet him there went "Many of the wealthier Californians . . . . and purchased from the vessel choice articles of merchandise, as also did the Padres. The captain did not take hides and tallow in payment, but the rancheros and the priests . . . . paid for their purchases in coin, or in sea otter skins, which were then plentiful."

The captain declared, runs the account in Seventy-five Years, "that my father's voyages . . . were very successful; and that on each voyage he realized about $25,000 profit, in Spanish doubloons and sea otter skins, from sales in California . . . ." In three voyages to California, the elder Davis "collected, in payment for goods sold, beside the money received, about 1,500 sea otter skins . . . ."

José de la Guerra of Santa Barbara did a cash business

in otter and other furs, over a long period of years, and gave that as partial explanation of the great wealth of coin which he was able to amass in the long course of California's economic depression.

The Boston ships loaded a great many pelts, as did vessels hailing from other ports, Davis also related.[286] Bancroft observed of the period 1831--35 that "hardly a vessel sailed without carrying away more or less skins, which all traders were eager to obtain."[287] Writing at the very end of the period, Larkin declared: "In former years considerable Fur was exported . . . . There is now some fur . . shipped . . . ." His estimate of the value of skins exported in 1846 up to mid-June was $20,000.[288]

Through all this time, the prices paid to the Californians were so far below the known value of the skins abroad that incentive must have been greatly dashed. Davis, the elder, had offered as much as $30 a pelt.[289] Larkin said[290] of the closing years of the period that prime sea otter skins for the Canton market were worth as

---

[286] Seventy-five Years, pp. 200--201, passim; 203, 240, 104, 148, 252.
[287] Calif., vol. 3, p. 374.
[288] Official Corresp. MS, vol. 2, pp. 100, 94.
[289] Davis, Seventy-five Years, p. 203.
[290] Official Corresp., MS, vol. 2, p. 100.

high as $40 apiece. Davis, Senior was said by his wife to have received from $80 to $100 the skin, in China.[291] This was possibly an exaggeration. Chamisso, who was a member of Kotzebue's Pacific expedition in 1816, about the time of Davis, Senior's operations, mentions $60 as an average at Canton.[292] Alfred Robinson spoke of the Chinese price for selected skins as $60 in the '30s.[293]

Here was an improved market condition over the days when Spain had quarreled about a price range of $2.50 to $10![294] Even the Russians had been willing, in 1824, to appraise their own share of the catch at $45 the skin for purposes of exchange for Californian grain.[295]

Even so cursory a survey as the present reveals quite a different situation from that total negligence and ignorance of the possibilities of the fur hunt and fur trade in California almost invariably attributed to the hijos del país. Their efforts to exclude alien interlopers from the field present a similarly contradictory version of

---

[291] Davis, Seventy-five Years, p. 301.
[292] Bancroft, Calif., vol. 2, p. 420.
[293] Ibid., vol. 3, p. 374, n. 13.
[294] See ante, p. 580.
[295] See ante, p. 586.

another phase of the subject.[296] The degree and variety of discouragements to which their enterprise was all along subjected is one more element generally omitted from the story. Those discouragements have already been touched on in so far as they related to humanly imposed restrictions. It remains to note certain natural limitations which still further explain why the Californians did not make as impressive a showing in the fur field as it has ever since been alleged they should have done.

In the first place, while the fur hunters ranged as far down as the Lower California coast, the greater portion of occupied California was too far south to produce skins of the best grade.[297] "Beaver and land-otter could not be profitably trapped farther south than the Tulare Valley," declared Sutter.[298]

Moreover, while Spanish policy still restrained territorial activity, the Yankees and Russians had worked the field intensively. As early as 1803--4, Joseph O'Cain and Jonathan Winship, from Boston on the sailer "O'Cain," had hunted otter on shares with the Russians, in Russian bidarkas

---

[296] See post, chaps. VIII, IX, passim.

[297] Bancroft, Calif., vol. 1, p. 442.

[298] Personal Reminiscences, MS, p. 66.

with Aleutian crews. The "O'Cain" was along the coast and at the Farallones again in 1806 with Winship and his brother Nathan commanding another Russian-American expedition; and in 1806--7, Captain Campbell conducted a similar hunt under similar auspices. In 1807, Swift led fifty Aleuts, and Jonathan Winship, fifty others; and in 1808--9, George Eyres had charge of a native band. Again in 1810, each of the Winships led a hunt.

It was at this time, as captain's clerk to Nathan Winship, that William Gale, the Boston trader of later years, made his acquaintance with California. This was the occasion when water casks on Gale's vessel had to be destroyed and cables piled on the open deck to make room for the excess of furs. On this voyage, moreover, three other companies of sealers and otter hunters were encountered.

These expeditions combed the waters of the mainland and of Catalina, the Channel Islands, the Farallones and the islands off the peninsula. In every case they were said to have netted more than 1,000 skins, while Jonathan Winship's catch was reported as 5,000 on one occasion and 5,400 on another.[299]

Some figures from Gale's log-book of the "Albatross" throw further light on the rape of the fur fisheries. For

---

[299] Bancroft, Calif., vol. 2, pp. 25--26, 39--40, 78--79, 82, 84--85, 92--95, passim.

the fourteen months between August 1810 and October 1, 1811, Gale recorded the "Albatross" party alone as having taken 73,402 seal at the Farallones, and secured 639 sea otter, besides 53 land otter, 243 beaver, and raccoon, wildcat, badger, fox, mink, squirrel, skunk, muskrat and mole, the estimated value of the whole at Canton prices being $157,397. Meanwhile, two of the other vessels hunting at the same time were said to have turned over as the Russian share of their catch a total of 4,216 sea otter skins. To the first mate of the "Albatross," on one of her earlier trips (1808--9) is attributed the statement that in two years at the Farallones the ship loaded 130,000 seal, besides many otter. In 1811, each of two vessels working on a share basis were believed to have yielded 700 otter as the Russian portion, and a third ship to have collected 900 skins for division.[300]

From 1812--40, the Russians themselves maintained a station at the Farallones, as well as at Ross. For half a dozen years they succeeded in taking 1,200 and 1,500 seal a year, "though Winship, Gale, Smith and other Americans had taken the cream of this natural wealth a few years earlier," remarks Bancroft. "After 1818 the seals diminished rapidly until only 200 or 300 a year could be caught, and the

---

[300] Bancroft, Calif., vol. 2, pp.94, n. 29; 95--96.

business was no longer profitable; but still a Russian with from six to ten Aleuts was kept at the station to kill sea-lions and gulls, collect eggs, and prepare the products of this industry for use at Ross and Sitka."[301]

Small wonder that when the territorials found themselves free to compete, in their private capacities, along in the 1830s, they found no shoals of seal and otter crowding about their bows, to be pulled aboard after a blow with a paddle! Even the Russian-Californian contracts were too late for big profits as profits had been reckoned during the era of unrestrained slaughter. As early as 1824, the commandant of San Francisco reported that a fleet of twenty cayucos had failed to find a single otter, and had returned to Bodega.[302]

The depletion of supply had become evident, in fact, a decade and a half earlier. From 1811--20, says Bancroft, "the Russians took a constantly and rapidly decreasing number of otter each year . . . ."[303] The Spaniards and Californios themselves, while all the time predicting the annihilation of their fur-bearing animals, had no way of knowing how close to fulfillment their prophesies had come.

---

[301] Bancroft, Calif., vol. 2, p. 633.
[302] Ibid., p. 520, n. 16.
[303] Ibid., p. 420.

Vallejo later declared that in 1812 the otter were so abundant that boatmen killed them with their oars, in passing through the sea-weed; and that the Russians took 10,000 a year for the next five years, and 5,000 annually thereafter to 1831.[304] This was hearsay on the part of Don Guadalupe. Choris and Chamisso, both with Kotzebue in 1816, agreed that the yearly catch ran around 2,000.[305]

The fact seems to be that both slaughter and supply were enormously over-estimated. The Russians never received an immense revenue from furs taken by their Ross colony, says Bancroft. "The post was profitable in this respect during but a very small part of its existence, if at all .... The catch on the New Albion coast ... never gave a large margin of profit; and even with the poaching and contract operations in and south of San Francisco Bay, it may be doubted if such a margin was kept up much later than 1820."

He proceeds to quote statistics from the Russian authorities, whence it appears that the average annual sea otter catch for the whole period was 144; that for the years 1812--23, 114; and that for 1824--34, 175! The highest "take" in all this span was given as 500 in 1825, with 475

---

[304] Bancroft, *Calif.*, vol. 2, p. 420, n. 17.
[305] Ibid., p. 635, n. 6.

in 1824, 287 in 1826 and 153 in 1815 as next best; while to 1828 and 1832, only one otter each is ascribed.

As for seal, none were taken at the Farallones after 1834, according to one of these accounts. The contract hunting between 1803 and 1812 is credited with having yielded 9,181 skins, as against a total of 3,287 for the period 1812--34.[306]

Meantime, ever since the overland entry of Jedediah Smith in 1826 and of Peter Skene Ogden two years later, trappers from the "United States of the North" and from the Columbia had been taking beaver from the streams of the interior. Efforts of the territorial government to check or regulate these inroads on their natural wealth were, as we shall see,[307] for the greater part foreordained to failure.

Statistics and estimates, as the conflicting statements just summarized indicate, leave much to be desired in the way of clarity, continuity and especially certainty. But they do seem to indicate clearly that the Californians never really had a chance at their own fur fisheries.

---

[306] Bancroft, *Calif.*, vol. 2, p. 634.
[307] *Post*, chaps. VIII, IX, *passim.*

63. Mining before 1848

In reviewing the subject of mines and mining in Mexican California, it is to be remembered that the great Mother Lode, on the clue to whose treasure Marshall stumbled in 1848, lies entirely in what was "gentile country" to the territorials. To be sure, they might have gone prospecting for the pot at the end of the rainbow, in good old _conquistador_ style. But there had already been too much of that sort of thing in Spanish-American history -- not all of it profitable, certainly not all of it beneficial to the populations of the metalliferous regions exploited.

In their desire for the _fomento de California,_ neither the Mexican government nor the men of the country thought in terms of ready-made fortunes. Their plans were for all-round development, inclusive of mining, of course, but with emphasis on effective occupation, agriculture, manufacture and trade. The search for earth's largess had already delayed too long the earning of earth's hire in vast areas adapted to cultivation and commerce. In their lust for conquest and enrichment the Spaniards had already lost too much time questing in remote regions, ignoring the immense wealth to be derived from the development of a country blessed in climate and in maritime and terrestrial possibilities including mineral wealth.[308]

That the presence of precious metals in California was well and widely known from missionary times is established beyond question by the frequency of evidence in the documents. As early as 1796, "there were several supposed discoveries of rich mineral deposits, including one of quicksilver in the black mud at Santa Bárbara," says Bancroft. "In fact, Father Salazar reported that the province was supposed to be very rich in metals, which were not developed for fear that foreigners would rush in . . . ."[309]

The Indians from a very early period had learned from the padres something of the value of gold, according to Davis, who speaks of six or seven thousand dollars' worth of the yellow metal gathered by California neophytes and sent in a fine silk purse to Rome as a gift to the Pope. Even the presence of gold in the Sacramento Valley was known to the padres, says Davis, and reported to him under pledge of secrecy by Father Muro of Mission San José, with later confirmation by Father Mercado of San Rafael, San Antonio and Santa Clara. "Don Guillermo" gives a circumstantial account of these confidences:

"Father Muro, while I was visiting him along in 1843 or 1844, ... mentioned to me his knowledge of the existence of gold in the Sacramento valley as a great secret,

[308] *Mexico, Junta de Fomento, Colección*, Item 5 (*Iniciativa, Voto Final*), p. 36.
[309] *Calif.*, vol. 1, p. 618.

requiring me to promise not to divulge it. I have never mentioned it to this day to anyone. Afterward, in conversation with Father Mercado, the same subject was gradually and cautiously broached, and he confided to me his knowledge of the existence of gold in the same locality. Both of the priests stated that their information was obtained from **Indians** . . . . After he had imparted the news of gold in the Sacramento valley, I would interrupt the discourse, and, for the sake of argument, suggest that it would be better to make the matter known to induce Americans and others to come here, urging that with their enterprise and skill, they would rapidly open and develop the country, **build towns** and engage in numberless undertakings which would tend to the enrichment and prosperity of the country, increase the value of lands, enhance the price of cattle, and benefit the people. He would answer that the immigration would be dangerous; that they would pour in by thousands and overrun the country; Protestants would swarm here, and the Catholic religion would be endangered; the work of the Missions would be interfered with, and as the Californians had no means of defense, no navy nor army, the Americans would soon obtain supreme control; that they would undoubtedly at some time come in force, and all this would happen; but if no inducements were offered, the change might not take place in his time."[310]

It may seem unlikely, as Bancroft implies,[311] that so enterprising a man as Davis would have kept this sort of secret without trying to realize on it. We are not called upon, however, to accept any such improbability. As a matter of fact, although his predilections were for the sea and trade, Davis did actually take a fling at prospecting, as he recorded in his memoirs published long after Bancroft's histories. The experience was not conducive to further essays of that nature.

The particular "lost mine" whose location he sought to learn from native initiates was in Lower California. His companions in the adventure were "three of the Argüellos." Davis relates that after penetrating well into the country, they sent for an Indian chief, who arrived only after a three-day interval. One after another the white men strove to extract from the Indian the secret of the mine's location; but no persuasion availed, and they were finally obliged to abandon the project, with no reward but the experience.

The Indian made clear his reasons for guarding his knowledge, saying that "more than seventy years ago, he was instructed by the Fathers of Santo Tomás never to divulge to any one, outside of the Church, the covered wealth of

---

[310] Davis, *Seventy-five Years*, pp. 222, 166.

[311] *Calif.*, vol. 4, p. 680, n. 18.

Lower California; if he did he would incur the wrath of God, and would die instantly."

"These early teachings of the Fathers," commented Davis, "were indelible in the minds of these Christianized Mission Indians, who were deeply impressed with the Church notions, of keeping the world ignorant of the whereabouts of this buried ore.

"It was well known to the early inhabitants of that part of the peninsula, that gold existed; and the priests handled plenty of it, through the Indians of the Missions. But the secret of the deposits was kept by the priests, as a matter of policy and from political and religious convictions; and by the Indians because of their superstitions."[312]

It is not to be supposed, however, that lay Spaniards and Mexicans were oblivious of the existence of precious metals in California. A part of the wealth of the Ortegas was derived from a silver mine discovered as early as 1800 by Ignacio, son of Captain José Francisco Ortega, founder of the colonial branch of the family. The site was only a league from San Juan Bautista, near the foot of Gabilán or Hawk's Peak, overlooking the Salinas — the height to which Fremont later gave publicity. Assay by a mining expert arrived on one of the royal transports in 1802 showed the ore

---

[312] Davis, *Seventy-five Years*, pp. 321—22.

rich in lead and silver, a small quantity of the stuff yielding, even with the imperfect apparatus available, six ounces of fine silver.[313]

True, in a report of 1806, Governor Arrillaga declared that no indications of precious metals had been found in California so far as explored.[314] But it is not difficult to find possible explanation of His Excellency's omission to mention the Ortega mine. The hard-driven old soldier, who was lieutenant-governor, governor ad interim or governor by appointment, of one or both Californias, from 1793 to his death in 1814, wrestled (expertly) with the tangled presidial accounts of both old and new California, led explorations and fought Indians in the Colorado country, besides conducting his routine gubernatorial duties with plodding efficiency; alternated his residence between Loreto and Monterey, during his two decades of officialdom; and was at the southern capital from 1794 to 1806.[315] Possibly the existence of the Ortega claim was a detail which temporarily escaped Don José's notice as he plowed through his report of 1806. Quite possibly, too, the beneficiaries of

---

[313] Bancroft, Calif., vol. 2, pp. 144--45; vol. 4, p. 760.
[314] Ibid., vol. 2, p. 176.
[315] Ibid., pp. 205, 703.

the mine, and other provincials with hopes of "striking it rich" on their own accounts, felt it in their best interests to dissimulate knowledge that might attract Spanish treasure-seekers to California in new quest of El Dorado, or Spanish treasury officials in old quest of the perquisites of crown and bureaucracy.

José de Jesús Pico recalled that with his boyhood companions he had been intrigued, toward the close of the Spanish régime, by certain mysterious experiments with quicksilver conducted secretly in the cuadro of Mission San Luís Obispo.

In 1818, Governor Sola made official report that most of the mountains of the province showed signs of ore; and spoke of silver extraction by smelting several years before -- probably alluding to operations at the Ortega mine. In 1820, though writing chiefly of Lower California, he advised García Conde (later prominent in Mexican officialdom) that mines were lying unworked for want of speculators.

Missionary reports of 1822 mentioned the Ortega deposits as the only ones yet found in California; but spoke of rumors and "'dreams'" of rocks veined with metal within five leagues of Puríma; of the operations (unsuccessful so far as known) of the prospector Pedro Posadas in the San Luís Rey district; and of declarations by travellers that the mountains around San Luis Obispo must contain metals. A fine specimen of quartz gold exhibited at the British Royal Institute in 1850 and identified as having been found in California about 1820 by a visiting English captain may have been the foundation for this latter assertion, suggests Bancroft.[316]

There is reason to believe, in view of the recollections of Pico, Davis and others, that the padres generally exercised a good deal of discretion in the statements which they gave out relative to precious metals in California. On at least one occasion, however, it served a missionary's purpose to report the existence of such treasure. In 1823, Padre Amorós of San Rafael asserted to Governor Argüello that the Russians had recently discovered a silver mine during an exploration inland from Bodega, and that therefore the Spaniards should make every exertion to explore and retain that region. "The fact," comments Bancroft, "that the padre wanted some men at the time for an expedition after converts and runaways may have had much influence on his opinion."[317] Yet in this connection the subsequently worked "Silverado" mine,[318] on the slope of Mount St. Helena which the Russians explored and named, springs naturally to mind.

---

[316] *Calif.*, vol. 2, pp. 417, 666.
[317] *Ibid.*, pp. 666--67.
[318] The site of one of Robert Louis Stevenson's temporary homes, and the setting of his *Silverado Squatters*.

610

In any event, the reason urged by the missionary for Spanish initiative north of San Francisco Bay, like other incidents just mentioned, is indication that California's mining possibilities were by no means entirely unreckoned at the time when Mexico assumed control of the territory. Subsequent developments show continued interest and some activity.

The *Junta de Fomento de Californias*, while stressing effective occupation and development of the territory, rather than mere exploitation of its mineral wealth, sought to foster the mining industry, along with colonization, by recommending a six-year suspension of the tax of a fifth on metals extracted from mines and placers that might be discovered and worked in California.[319]

The first party to explore the Sonoma region, that of July 1823, reported the presence of what was believed to be lime between Sonoma and Napa.[319a]

About 1825, a man named Romero discovered rich silver-bearing rock in the mountains back of Carmelo Valley, according to David Spence. Romero set off southward to secure laborers, but died on the way. His wife María and their children kept the secret of the mine and worked it themselves, selling an occasional

---

[319] *Colección*, Item 5 (*Iniciativa*), p. 25.

[319a] John Smith Flett (*Encyc. Brit.*, 11th ed., vol. 16, p. 698, col.1) tells of "great quantities of silver lead ore, which have yielded not a little gold," being obtained from lime-stones in Colorado; and of copper ores likewise found "in great quantity in Arizona in rocks of this kind."

small bar of silver mixed with lead to Captain Cooper and others.

In 1828, some gold dust was washed out at San Isidro in what was later San Diego County.[320]

The probability is that not only the padres, but laymen fortunate enough to have learned the sites of precious metals observed every precaution of secrecy. Even under present-day conditions of supply and operation, a tax on mining profits is a matter of no small concern. "It is considered a conservative estimate that a severance tax on gold would close one-third of all the gold mines now operating in California."[320a] How much more nearly fatal would have been the blow dealt by Mexico's needy treasury department under mining conditions of the pre-1848 epoch! No wonder little bruiting about of mining news was indulged in! Yet that some activity went on in scattered localities through these years seems definitely indicated, however scanty the details as to number, location and ownership of claims. At the wedding of Martina Castro to Governor Alvarado in 1839, the rings used were of California gold.[321]

---

[320] Bancroft, *Calif.*, vol. 2, pp. 666, n. 28; 667.

[320a] *S. F. Chronicle*, Oct. 18, 1935, editorial, p. 14, col. 1.

[321] Bancroft, op. cit., vol. 3, p. 593, n. 31. (The marriage took place by proxy, José Antonio Estrada substituting for the groom who absented himself to welcome and confer with Cyrille La Place, commander of the visiting French man-of-war "Artémise," (Bancroft, *Calif.*, vol. 3, p. 593.

Two years later, Alvarado sent a commission to the Mexican government, carrying three ounces of native gold with full information regarding its discovery, and asking that the supreme government send up a body of trained mineralogists to make a survey. He believed that the new-found placers lay along a spur of Mexico's own Sierra Madre, and should contain great mineral wealth. "The request brought no results," regretted Don Bautista, "for the reason that Mexico was in a condition of turmoil, as usual, through all these years."[322]

Either a series of placers was uncovered in quick succession in 1840--43, or there is an unusual confusion of dates and other details in the record. Davis, who may easily have been inaccurate as to the year, says that "the first discovery of gold in California to be made public was in 1840 in the valley of San Fernando, in the present county of Los Angeles. It was made by some Mexicans, from Sonora, who were passing through going north. They were familiar with the gold placers in their own country, had their attention attracted to the locality, and made the discovery."[323]

Alvarado places the first publicized discovery in 1841.[324] As he was governor at the time, and took the official action just mentioned, of calling for a Mexican survey, his version should be correct.

----

[322] Alvarado, *Primitivo Descubrimiento de Oro, 1841,* MS, pp. 5--6.

[323] *Seventy-five Years,* p. 159.

[324] Alvarado, op. cit., p. 1.

The Hayes-Warner-Widney account mentions June 1841, but adds that the discovery -- resulting from the pulling of wild onions -- was of "a pebble like some that Andrés Castillero had found before in the latter part of 1840 or the early part of 1841 and had declared to indicate the presence of gold."[324a]

Bancroft,[325] citing a letter of Manuel Requena to Eustace Barron, has it that "the first authenticated finding" was in March 1842.

Bandini gave the date as April 1842,[326] though he is himself on record as having staked claim to a *veta mineral* near the Yucaipa rancho in the San Bernardino region in 1841, as well as again in 1842.[327]

Hayes, Warner and Widney state that "the auriferous fields . . . . embraced the greater part of the country drained by the Santa Clara River, from a point some fifteen or twenty miles from its mouth to its sources, and easterly beyond them to Mount San Bernardino."[328]

According to Bancroft,[329] who follows the Requena version, the *placeres* were on the San Francisco rancho, formerly belonging to San Fernando Mission, but at the

---

[324a] *Hist. Sketch of L. A.*, p. 10.
[325] *Calif.*, vol. 4, pp. 296--97; 630, n. 11, "1842."
[326] *Hist. de Calif.*, MS, p. 42.
[327] *Calif.*, vol. 4, p. 297; 631, n. 11, "1842."
[328] *Hist. Sketch of L.A.*, pp. 10--11.
[329] *Calif.*, vol. 4, pp. 296--97.

time the property of the Valle family. Alvarado,[330] on the other hand, gave the Vaca rancho in the San Fernando Valley as the site of the first publicized find. Quite possibly these were two separate placers along the same vein, and the first discovery was kept as quiet as possible for reasons of prudence.

Similar uncertainty clouds the identity of the original discoverer. Abel Stearns and Hayes, Warner and Widney give the honor to one Francisco Lopez and another *vaquero*; Bidwell, who visited the mines in '45, to Jean Rouelle.[331] Alvarado, without naming the discoverer, also speaks[332] of two San Fernando Mission *vaqueros* resting on the ground from their labors. They took their find for particles of copper, but learned from Sonoran experts in town that it was gold.

Whatever the fact as to details and priority, the San Fernando deposits soon proved extensive. "By May the gold region had been found to extend over two leagues, and the dirt, with a scanty supply of water, was paying two dollars per day to each man engaged in mining." Some small nuggets were found with the dust. The "gold rush,"

---

[330] *Primitivo Descub.*, MS, pp. 2,4. He is quite specific about the location of the placers. They were "about 8 leagues from the Mission of San Fernando and 14 leagues from Los Angeles," and "in a northerly direction toward the Sierra Nevada," on the ranch "known today as Baca Billa" -- the property of Don Juan Manuel Baca.

[331] Bancroft, *Calif.*, vol. 2, pp. 630--31, n. 11, "1842."

[332] *Primitivo Descub.*, MS, pp. 1--2.

while proportionate in numbers to the country's small population, became important enough to cause the erection of a mining district under the administration of Ignacio del Valle as *encargado de justicia.* A committee was also appointed to make observations with a view to proper regulation. Valle recommended that no tax be imposed for the present.

At one time as many as one hundred men were at work. Toward the end of the summer, Don Ignacio reported that lack of water, impeding the operations, had reduced the number to fifty; but the miners were expected to return with the rains.[332a]

Nor was this activity a flash in the pan. While most of the workers were unskilled, and gleaned no more than two dollars a day -- even as little as twenty-five cents, in some cases -- Mofras relates that his countryman Baric took out about an ounce of gold daily; and the placer, which came to be known as the "San Feliciano," was more or less continuously worked, chiefly by Sonoreños, down to 1846. At that date, Larkin wrote to the New York *Sun* that a common laborer could pick up two dollars a day in the California goldfields.[333]

[332a] Alvarado, *Prim. Desub.,* MS, pp. 1--3, also made a point of the water shortage, and of the suffering, as well as the handicap to mining operations, which it entailed.

[333] Bancroft, *Calif.,* vol. 4, pp. 296--97; 630--31, n. 11, "1842." Alvarado, *op. cit.,* pp. 2--3, says that the placer became worked out after yielding, by conservative estimation, 2,000 *onzas.*

From the first specimens of the "strike" taken to Monterey, Alvarado had ear pendants made for his wife and a ring for his daughter. (The latter trinket was for a time in Bancroft's possession.) The first California gold known to have been coined was sent by Abel Stearns, in charge of Alfred Robinson, to the Philadelphia mint, and there deposited in July 1843.[334]

A good deal of the output of the placers found its way, in the natural course of things, to the hands of the merchants. Henry Mellus, the Yerba Buena trader, collected soon after the discovery as much as $5,000 in flakes of fine quality, according to Davis who handled some of it. This was but the first of several such accumulations made by Mellus in his trips south. Davis estimated that during the first two years of activity at the mines, "probably eighty to one hundred thousand dollars worth of gold dust was taken from these diggings." He adds that while "the results were small," the "finding of gold continued there for several years, up to the time of what is known as the big gold discovery in the Sacramento valley."[335]

In a letter of 1844, Hartnell declares that "no mines of any description are at present worked in

---

[334] Alvarado, Prim. Descub., MS, p. 5; Bancroft, Calif., pp. 631, n. 11, "1843."; 297, n. 44.

[335] Seventy-five Years, p. 159.

California, but there is no doubt that coal, asphalte and the precious metals do exist and the latter in abundance." He proceeds immediately to qualify his negation of mining activity with the statement that a *placer de oro* has lately been found in the neighborhood of "the Pueblo [Los Angeles], and there are at this moment a quantity of persons employed washing for gold, which is of very good quality, and although generally found in very small pieces, lumps of the weight of half an ounce have been picked up.[336]

---

[336] April (no day), 1844, Hartnell to Willey, in *Pio Pico Doc.*, MS, vol. 1, #87, p. 3; April 20, 1844, same to same, in ibid., #85, p. 1. (Document #87 breaks off abruptly in the middle of the quotation here given, at the phrase "at this moment." The statement is continued in a marginal note across the top of document #85, p. 1. This is undoubtedly a mere error of placement in copying; for context, ink and "mood" of writing all indicate that the marginal note on document #85 continues the incomplete sentence with which document #87 breaks off, and has no relation to document #85.)

Writing in 1876, Hayes, Warner and Widney relate that "the working of these fields has been pursued intermittingly, more or less successfully, from their discovery to the present time." They add : "The small supply of water, available for hydraulic mining over this large field, is the cause why it has not been more thoroughly worked."[336a]

Larkin wrote[337] in 1846 that some gold was being exported at that time, his estimate for January 1 to June 15, 1846 being 200 ounces valued at $17 per ounce -- $3,400 for the 6½ months, therefore.

Meanwhile, territorial authorities were by no means indifferent to the importance of the precious metals. Alvarado's vain efforts to have the supreme government undertake a metallurgical survey of California and otherwise "foment" the mining industry were followed up in Mexico by Congressman Castañares. He sang the abundance and fineness of the ores already discovered, and asserted that California's mines constituted one of her most valuable resources. "Besides the silver mines discovered and tested by the extraction of ore, the gold placer

---

[336a] *Hist. Sketch of L. A.*, p. 10.

[337] *Official Corresp.*, MS, vol. 2, pp. 100, 94.

approximately thirty leagues in extent, discovered in 1843, is particularly worthy of note; and the coal mines and rock quarries."338

In his efforts to arouse the active interest of the Mexican authorities, Castañares sent to the Minister of Relations an original assay certificate issued by the national Mint, establishing the superior fineness of Californian gold. He called attention to the fact that the greater part of the wealth extracted was being sent out of the country to the United States. His estimate

---

338 Castañares, Col. de Doc., pp. 10, 23--24. Apparently these were the fields referred to by Hartnell (ante, p. 617), not to be confused with the finds of the earlier '40s. The congressman alludes, under date of March 2, 1844, to "the gold deposits discovered midway of last year."

The old Spanish league was 2.63 miles long (Webster's New International Dictionary), which would make the southern California placers close to eighty miles in extent according to Castañares. This may have been exaggeration in a worthy cause; or it may indicate that the goldfields had actually been so much enlarged by the discovery of new placeres.

of the amount of this treasure was in excess of "two thousand onzas."[339] This seems to make his calculation of the yield for the past eighteen months $30,000 American, which indicates a production rate for 1842--43 or thereabout tallying perfectly with Alvarado's figure for the original placers before they were worked out, and with Davis's evaluation of $80,000 to $100,000 for the first two years' harvest of the goldfields.[340]

Indeed, were it not that these authorities differ notably on other details, including the location and time of the activity, the guess might be hazarded that their production figures were derived from a single source. The inference does suggest itself that the

---

[339] Castañares, Col. de Doc., pp. 10, 24. The word onza has two meanings. As a measure of weight, it numbers sixteen to the pound avoirdupois, twelve to the pound troy, like our ounce. At a valuation of $16 per ounce, which was the prevailing price of California gold in 1848 and subsequently, two thousand onzas' weight would appraise at $32,000 in American money. Obviously this insignificant sum would not be cited by Castañares in his attempt to interest Mexico in California's gold mining industry; and it is low out of all proportion to other estimates of the richness of "the diggings." Castañares seems here to have in mind the coin onza, equal to eighty pesetas, or $40 American.

[340] See ante, p. 615, n. 333; p. 616.

figures represent a production rate generally accepted in contemporary authoritative quarters as average for the placers all along the vein.

Unfortunately, complained Castañares, and although mining (despite its great importance as one of the department's most valuable sources of wealth) was less worthy of being stressed than agriculture, it was also worse off than agriculture, "being not yet born, so to speak."[341]

Quite probably one of the reasons for the slow development of the industry in California was the ever vexatious scarcity of quicksilver, used in the process of amalgamation. In Spanish times, the supply of that indispensable had been limited (by force of regulation, not of available supply, since Mexico had rich deposits of her own) to Almadén in the mother country. Even then "the problem of providing enough quicksilver . . . . was one of the chief cares of the viceroy," says Fisher. Whenever there was a scarcity of mercury in New Spain mining decreased. Likewise when the price of quicksilver was raised [and it was a highly oppressive government

---

[341] Col. de Doc., p. 24.

monopoly] the miners could not pay expenses."[342]

Quicksilver continued *en estanco* and the handicap continued formidable throughout California's Mexican period, and in the republic itself thereafter. In a United States government trade report published in 1855, it is stated that "the production of gold and silver [in Mexico] . . . has arrived at a state of great prosperity; but the inadequate supply of quicksilver is felt as a considerable obstacle to the still greater development of the mineral wealth of Mexico."[343]

---

[342] Fisher, *Viceregal Admin.*, pp. 115--16. Bancroft states (*Hist. of Mex.*, vol. 3, pp. 302--3) that the quicksilver situation had "well nigh paralyzed the mining industry under Spain." Not only was the price exorbitant. Regulations concerning purchase entailed so much additional expense that "the practical effect was that if the discoverer of a mine happened to be a man without means he was compelled to take others into partnership; and when the mine proved valuable, litigations would follow, and the discoverer would too often lose his interest."

[343] Flagg, "Report," in "U. S. Govt. Doc.," 34th Cong., 1st Sess., *Sen. Exec. Doc.* #107, p. 578.

Here is explanation enough of the failure of an aggressive mining development policy in California in 1822--46.

Yet as early as 1796 what was believed to be quicksilver-bearing mud had been discovered in the Santa Barbara region, and a sample had been taken out at Borica's order; "but nothing further is heard of it," says Bancroft[343a] -- probably because of Spanish Almadén's exclusive privilege.

The cinnabar difficulty was solved eventually for California -- though like so many other problems in her historical evolution just in time to benefit outsiders. In 1845 the Mexican captain Andrés Castillero, who since Chico's time had been prominent in Californian affairs both in the department and in Mexico, discovered and made claim to the since famous New Almadén mine in the San José region.[344]

[343a] *Calif.*, vol. 1, p. 670.

[344] Bancroft, *op. cit.*, vol. 2, p. 749. Having "denounced" the site in accordance with Mexican law, Castillero secured possession from the *alcalde* of the district, his grant extending 3,000 *varas* in all directions from the mine proper. He divided his claim into 24 shares, four of which he gave to José Castro and four to the brothers Secundino and Leodero Robles. He retained ownership of the remaining sixteen shares until the first winter of the war with the United States, when he sold a portion to the English firm of Barron, Forbes and Company of Tepic. Meantime, Castillero had employed an American from New York to open the mine. Bancroft, *op. cit.*, vol. 7, p. 656, n. 20.

The ore yielded from 15% to 60%, according to Larkin, who also related that he had seen Castillero himself "run out about 20% in pure quicksilver from an old gun-barrel in 30 minutes."[345]

Meantime, the mining excitement set afoot by the discoveries of the early '40s did not die out. Newmark speaks of "the placer gold mining carried on in the San Gabriel and San Francisquito cañons" well into the '50s, indicating that the early deposits continued to attract their quota of gleaners even while the Mother Lode boom was at its height. Although this extreme southern activity "was on the whole unimportant," Francisco García, "who used gangs of Indians," took out "in the one year 1855 over sixty thousand dollars' worth of gold — one nugget being nearly two thousand dollars in value."[346]

Nor were the momentous finds of 1848 and later entirely unanticipated by the Mexicans and Californians. Mention has already been made of the belief of Alvarado and others that the department's resources in precious metals were extensive. The record also shows at least one project by a

---

[345] April 3, 1846, Larkin to Sec. of State, in *Official Corresp.*, MS, vol. 1, #91, p. 71.

[346] Newmark, *Sixty Years*, p. 95. There seems room to speculate — or to prospect, if one is so minded — on the chance that these original California placers were resown with golden grains by the flood-waters which devastated the entire Santa Clara Valley when the San Francisquito Dam collapsed in 1928.

Mexican-Californian to seek gold in the northern Mother Lode region before the strike of '48 focussed the world's attention there.

In 1844, Pablo Gutierrez, then in Sutter's employ, and grantee of a rancho in present Yuba County, laid plans with John Bidwell who was that year naturalized and granted the Ulpinos Rancho in present Solano County, for a prospecting trip along the Bear River. According to Bidwell's own account, the enterprise was thwarted by the death of Gutierrez, whom Castro captured and had hanged during the Micheltorena campaign. "Sutter tells a similar story," concludes Bancroft, "but I know nothing further of the matter."[347]

Bidwell, who proceeded to secure the grant of the Colus Rancho in present Colusa County in 1845, did not

---

[347] *Calif.*, vol. 3, p. 772; vol. 2, p. 713. California, of course, is full of Bear rivers and creeks; but in view of the Gutierrez and Bidwell landholdings and interests, there seems no reason to doubt that the Bear River of their plans was that considerable stream rising in present Placer County on the north slope of Ward Peak -- in the near vicinity of the Gutierrez grant -- and flowing in a northeasterly direction to drain into the Truckee River. *Gazeteer of Surface Waters of California, Part III* U. S. Geolog. Survey Water Supply Paper #297, comp. by B. D. Wood, p. 23, 23.

abandon the idea of gold-seeking in the region. During the next year of so, "his travels in the valley and foothills were extensive," says Bancroft, "and he had many narrow escapes from making the grand discovery of gold."[348] Had Gutierrez lived, he would have been a partner in the hunt, and perhaps the two would have succeeded where the one failed. Certainly it seems due rather to providence than to improvidence that a territorial did not at least share in the revelation of the Sierran treasure prodigy.

At least, a good many Californians seized the opportunity of the great discovery when it came. Among those who tapped the great lode were Spanish-born Antonio María Suñol and the Mexicans Antonio Francisco Coronel and Pablo Portilla -- all become good *Californios* between 1818 and 1834; and native sons Inocente García, José Amador, Andrés Pico, Salvador Vallejo and his illustrious brother the general.[349]

---

[348] *Calif.*, vol. 2, p. 719. Bidwell's most famous holdings -- the Arroyo Chico ranches -- were acquired after the conquest.

[349] Bancroft, *Calif.*, vol. 5, p. 738; vol. 2, p. 768; vol. 4, p. 782; vol. 3, pp. 752--53; vol. 4, pp. 776--77; vol. 5, pp. 759, 758; vol. 2, p. 585, n. 3.

Most of these men carried on large-scale operations with Indian labor. An eastern visitor of 1849 wrote of meeting Captain Portilla, then seventy-five years old but "hale and full of enterprise" at the head of thirty <u>Sonorenses,</u> bound for the mines.[350] Captain Pico had a band of laborers at work for him on the Mokelumne, in 1848--49.[351] Salvador Vallejo was reported to have made "a large amount of money . . . by the aid of Indian miners" in the same period;[352] while Don Guadalupe acquired an impressive fortune by similar means.

"When gold was discovered, three thousand tamed natives answered to his call; in the hall of his dwelling at Sonoma, soon after, were stacked jars of the precious metal, as though it had been flour or beans," says Bancroft.[353]

Despite such glittering successes on the part of Californians whose resources enabled them to multiply their energies, it is undoubtedly true that the ranching interests of a great many <u>hijos del país</u> demanded their major attention; that the call to defend their property against squatters and their titles against legal despoilers was imperative; and,

---

[350] Bancroft, <u>Calif.,</u> vol. 4, p. 782.
[351] <u>Ibid.,</u> pp. 776--77.
[352] <u>Ibid.,</u> vol. 5, p. 759.
[353] <u>Idem, Literary Industries,</u> p. 378.

finally, that the scant respect for the rights of "greasers" exhibited by Mother Lode's non-Hispanic hordes left little incentive for the average Mexican-Californian to try his luck at the mines, and little assurance that he would be allowed to retain whatever profits he might accumulate.

That the vanquished gleaned meagrely in the days of '49 no more indicates congenital shiftlessness than did their slight development of mines and mining before chance lay the secret of the Sierras glimmering at Marshall's feet.

64. Making by Hand

Manufacturing in Mexican California meant literally making by hand. The country was still in the early phases of raw goods production, and her chief outlet, the Boston ships, brought superior machine manufactures to her shores for trade. Hence any length explanation of her failure to develop manufacturing industries would be supererogatory. The subject will therefore be dealt with very briefly here.

Under the mercantilist system in effect throughout practically the whole of the Spanish régime, the colonies were of course confined to the production of raw materials for the exclusive benefit of the metropolis; and to the consumption of finished goods fashioned from their own or other products and purveyed by Spain. The enforcement of this system was especially easy and successful in California, due to the peculiar conditions of that remote missionary-military frontier.

In Mexico, where non-clerical entrepreneurs were numerous and in command of gang-labor both native and negro, mercantilism was only partially enforceable. There, for example, Cortes introduced silk manufacture, which was for decades eagerly fostered by Spanish kings in contravention of mercantilist theory, and soon became an extensive and important south Mexican industry. The Andalusian silk growers encompassed the ruin of silk culture and manufacture in the viceroyalty in 1679, by securing royal mandate for the destruction of the worms and mulberry trees. Yet early in the nineteenth century, the priest Hidalgo revived the industry, among his parishioners, teaching them also vine and olive culture.[354]

---

[354] Priestley, *Mex. Nation*, pp. 142, 207.

Meanwhile, also in defiance of mercantilism, weaving and spinning had steadily developed to immense importance in Mexico. Fisher writes[355] that the city of Puebla early became famous for its textiles. In 1794 it had forty-three woolen mills and produced cotton and silk cloth as well. By the early nineteenth century, its weavers of cotton materials numbered more than twelve hundred; while the intendancy of Guadalajara was turning out cottons and woolens to the value of 1,601,200 piastres.

The development of the great textile interests in Mexico did not point the way to similar emancipation from repression for California. Instead, it presently worked great hardship on the younger colony. Although in 1814 the Spanish Cortes declared all industries open to all Spaniards and foreigners in the dominion,[356] California came too soon under Mexican control to be

---

[355] Viceregal Admin., pp. 112, 113. The Spanish piastre is more commonly known as the peso. (Webster's New International Dictionary).

[356] Fisher, Background of Revolution, p. 183.

advantaged by the new freedom. For Mexico undertook to protect her own industries by the same short-sighted colonial policies from which she had suffered as a viceroyalty. To that end she subjected California to most of the traditional disabilities, inflicted by means of exorbitant and multiple import and export duties, outright prohibitions and government monopolies. The medieval gild system which, having prevailed for centuries in Mexican industry, had become very powerful according to Fisher,[357] substituted gild prerogatives, in some cases approximating or attaining to monopoly, for the *imperium* which had been enjoyed by the privileged companies under the crown.

Thus Mexican textile development meant the prohibition of cloth manufacture in California and the imposition of prohibitive customs charges on imported foreign weaves, American cotton of an intrinsic value of 6¢ a yard being subjected to a duty of as much as 20¢.[358]

---

[357] *Viceregal Admin.*, pp. 117--19.

[358] Nov. 22, 1845, Vallejo to Bustamante, in *Vallejo Doc.*, MS, vol. 12, #167, pp. 3--4 (Prudon draft); Larkin to Rogers, in p. 1.

Similar conditions served to protect in Mexico and discourage in California other industries peculiarly suited to both countries, such as glass- and earthenware manufacture and the making of wine and brandy.

Bancroft provides a concise and rather vivid summary of the beginnings of Californian manufacture. The first artificers were presidial soldiers -- smiths, armorers and carpenters -- and the Christianized or gentile Indians who could be induced to become their pupils. From 1773, sailors were enlisted for the California service to supplement this class of labor; while the founding of the pueblos introduced a few men with trades, "on which, however, none seem to have depended for subsistence. This was the condition of mechanical industry down to 1790. Besides the repairs executed on arms, implements and articles of clothing, there were rude attempts at tanning and various other simple and necessary processes suggested by the needs of the soldiers and ingenuity of the friars; but progress was slight and but vaguely recorded . . . ."[359]

Nor were the padres complaisant toward the induction of the Indians into extra-mission craft-activities. They protested that the grain and clothing so earned by

---

[359] *Calif.*, vol. 1, pp. 613--14.

the gentiles removed a chief incentive to their becoming Christianized. An attempt to instruct the Indians through sailor-workmen within the mission preserves ended in friction, a quarrel as to who should pay the instructors, and the deportation of the latter to SanBlas in 1795. The case, like others before and after it, demonstrated the impossibility of maintaining the secular and the missionary systems in harmonious combination or independently side by side.

Nevertheless, manufacture was definitely promoted in the 1790s, and "with considerable success." Skilled artisans were dispatched from Mexico under contract to teach the trades to neophytes and white apprentices. About twenty were sent, chiefly in 1792 and 1795, Bancroft found. A few remained permanently as settlers; but the majority retired before 1800, on termination of their contracts. The question of whether the government or the missions should pay for their services had again provoked controversy; and white apprentices had been scarce.

"The results of all these efforts were that before 1800 rude looms were set up in many of the missions, on which by Indian labor the wool of the country was woven into blankets and coarse fabrics with which the neophytes were clothed; hides were tanned and made into shoes, some of the coarser parts of saddles and other leather goods being also manufactured, though not enough as yet to avoid importation from Mexico. Soap was made of suitable quality and quantity to supply home needs after 1798; coarse pottery produced at San Francisco and several other places; and water-power flouring-mills built at Santa Cruz and San Luís Obispo, possibly also at San Gabriel and San Jose, which with the tahonas worked by horse or man power and the metates of the neophyte women, supplied the province with flour."360

As the mission population grew out of all proportion to the population de razon, bulk manufacture in so far as it developed at all in the later years of Spanish dominance became a mission monopoly. The presidios afforded the sole market for goods beyond the capacity of the mission communities themselves to absorb. Consequently no encouragement or scope was left for private enterprise, "as it was manifestly impossible," comments Bancroft, "to compete with the costless labor in so limited a market requiring only the coarsest articles."361

The first decade or so of Mexican control introduced no factors to alter this situation. Bancroft

---

360 Bancroft, Calif., vol. 1, pp. 614--17, passim.
361 Ibid., vol. 2, p. 175.

surmised that manufacturing declined somewhat, though he found "no items or references of value" on the subject. From occasional sources it is apparent that "as before, coarse woollen fabrics were woven at the missions; hides were tanned for shoes, sacks and rude saddles; soap was made in considerable quantities; and a variety of necessary articles of wood, iron or leather were produced by native or foreign workmen. " Hat-making was another branch of neophyte industry. Missions San Gabriel, Santa Bárbara, San Luis Rey, and in the earlier years of the Mexican régime San Luis Obispo were the most important manufacturing centers.[362]

Not only the Mexican and New England manufacturers now competed with the mission producers for supply of the limited Californian market; the New Mexican traders invaded the textile field. Early in 1834 a caravan arrived from the desert country with 1,645 serapes, 341 blankets, 171 coverlets and 4 tirutas (?) for exchange. Tax exemption was claimed for these goods under a Mexican decree of 1830.[363] The New Mexican traders found ready buyers among the rancheros, who

---

[362] Bancroft, Calif., vol. 2, pp. 665; 574, n. 38.
[363] Depart. St. Pap., Ben., M3, vol. 2, p. 16.

were glad of the opportunity to trade off some of their too rapidly multiplying herds.[364]

Nevertheless, and despite Mexican efforts at monopoly already referred to, Alvarado attempted to eliminate competition and foment cloth manufacture at the missions (then in course of secularization). In his *reglamento* of 1839 for the guidance of the administrators, he declared that "'the traffic of mules and horses for woollen stuffs now practised is absolutely prohibited; and instead, the looms must be started.'"[365] Here was an attempt to fit the ex-neophytes for citizen pursuits with high potentialities of benefit for themselves and the country.

That weaving and other mission industries did not quite die out in these years is evident from a report of 1839, in which the administrator at Santa Barbara declared that that mission had long derived more wealth from weaving and shoemaking, carpentering, blacksmithing, tile manufacture, etc., than from pastoral and agricultural pursuits, for which range and water were lacking.[366]

---

[364] Warner, Hayes and Widney, *Hist. Sketch*, p. 18.

[365] *Reglamento Provisional para Administradores de Misiones, 17 de Enero, 1839*, MS, Art. 8; summarized in Bancroft, *Calif.*, vol. 4, p. 55, n. 21.

[366] Nov. 18, 1839, Manuel Cota in *St. Pap., Miss.*, MS, vol. 9, p. 39.

Had the neophytes, upon their emancipation, assimilated in any considerable numbers with the population de razon, a working and consuming class would have developed. As will be seen, however,[367] apart from the few who remained at the ex-missions, they dispersed, for the most part becoming vagabonds or renegades. The scanty white population therefore continued after secularization much as before -- exchanging their country produce for the imported manufactures offered in trade, and for the rest supplying their needs with home-made articles, after the fashion of small and isolated populations in all times and places.

Territorial manufactures were naturally contrived without machinery, and from such materials as limited market facilities made it worth while for the Californios to produce. Davis contributes an interesting side-light on this phase of economy. "The Californians cut up a great many hides for the use of the ranchos. Strips of the skins were used for reatas and in building corrals, also for covering wagons and for many other purposes. Many of the rancheros tanned their own leather, for corazas [armor], mochilas [knapsacks], anguilas [whips], and tapaderas [stirrup-hoods].

---

[367] Post, chap. VII.

"Some of the sons of the rancheros were shoemakers, and made shoes for home use. The soles of the shoes were made from the leather, and tanned deer skin was used for the uppers. The hides were also used to cover the trees of the saddles and for other purposes. Large quantities of tallow were used by the rancheros for candles and for soap. Large amounts of the latter were made by the rancheros of the valleys of San José, Gilroy, and Pajaro [sic] and sold to the Russians for export to Alaska."[368]

Salvador Vallejo was among the number of the shoemakers; and also quarried and ground mill-stones, not to mention the ranching, military, fishing, hunting and lightering activities which made up his non-manufacturing pursuits.[369]

Richman cites[370] an article in the *Century Magazine* quoting General Vallejo to the effect that "a charming custom of the middle and lower classes was the making of the satin shoes by the groom for the birde" -- indicating a rather general proficiency in shoemaking among the men of the country.

---

[368] Davis, *Seventy-five Years*, p. 257.

[369] S. Vallejo, *Notas Hist.*, MS, pp. 35--36.

[370] *Spain and Mexico*, p. 500.

Of Sonoma, General Vallejo made a considerable manufacturing center, employing both northern mission-trained Indian labor and craftsmen drawn from the older settlements.[371]

Larkin referred, in 1845, to the fact that shingles, staves, spars and timbers were being shipped to the Sandwich Islands. He believed that a million feet of lumber (staves and shingles included) left the country between January and the middle of June 1846.[372]

Saddle-making, as might be supposed, was a Californian manufacturing specialty, although not even this branch was free from foreign competition, as will be shown in a moment. Newmark recalls it as a rather important industry, engaging "quite a number of skilled paisanos. . Among the most expert was Francisco Moreno, who had a little shop on the south side of Aliso Street, not far from Los Angeles. One of these hand-worked saddles often cost two hundred dollars or more, in addition to which expensive bridles, bits and spurs were deemed necessary accessories. Antonio María Lugo had a silver-mounted saddle, bridle and spurs

---

[371] See ante, pp. 122--23, 560.
[372] Official Corresp., MS, vol. 2, pp. 100, 94.

that cost fifteen hundred dollars."[373]

Reverting to the subject of foreign competition, it is notable that the Californians had to contend not only with the sophisticated style and the mass production of American machine-made specialties, but with the underpriced output of European, Asiatic and Pacific island labor still more depressed economically than the local producers. These competitive goods were not only dumped on the very thresholds of the territorials; they were the preferred exchange medium tendered by the sea-traders (who controlled the situation) for the goods of the country.

Russia, by way of example, could furnish "remarkably cheap" boots and shoes in quantity from Finland, at five shillings a pair, Douglas remarked.[374] In contrast with such a ready and low-priced supply, locally manufactured footgear sometimes entailed considerable nuisance to the buyer. Probably because the Californian shoemaker who devoted himself closely enough to his last to become expert could not also produce the materials of his trade; and because the country's small population would not have made a findings branch of the industry profitable, the

---

[373] Newmark, Sixty Years, p. 159.

[374] Journal, MS, p. 17.

customer was, in some cases at least, expected to furnish leather, thread, etc., with his order.

Among the Vallejo papers in the Bancroft Library is preserved a letter -- quaint in writing, spelling, dialect and content -- to the general from his shoemaker. It is dated at Petaluma in 1845; advises that the writer is sending some little shoes for the children; and requests Vallejo to dispatch the materials -- leather, chamois, thread and a bit of silk if he has any -- for his own shoes and those to be made for his soldiers.[375]

Even Figueroa, anxious as he was to promote territorial industry, was not proof against the attraction of foreign goods when they were more readily obtainable, of superior workmanship or -- especially -- cheaper than home-made productions. In 1833, he authorized Vallejo to negotiate at Ross not only for carbines, sabres and lead; but for uniforms, shoes and "200 saddles . . . . if the Russians can make them for less than the prevailing price here . . . ."[376]   The governor

---

[375] Jan. 7, 1845, Miguel Alvarado to Vallejo, in Vallejo Doc., MS, vol. 12, #131.

[376] April 11, 1833, Depart. St. Pap., Ben., Mil., MS, vol. 79, pp. 33--34.

can hardly be blamed, in view of the extreme financial pressure under which he labored, and the immediate need of quantities of articles which the territorials were not equipped to turn out at short notice or expertly. Yet the situation was obviously prejudicial to the development of domestic manufacture.

It is to be noted that shoes and locally woven fabrics were on the suggested list of prohibited imports recommended to the Minister of War by Vallejo in 1841, in the interests of California's industrial development.[377]

Meantime, foreigners skilled in one or another of the manufacturing arts had begun to seep into the country. These early immigrants were neither over-numerous nor of an undesirable sort. Most of them became an integral part of their adopted communities, forming a solid and valuable element. Naturally, they were welcomed as both producers and teachers of their crafts.[378]

In 1845 Larkin wrote: "The Indians who were taught by the Spanish Padres the different Mechanical arts are now dead, and no more of their tribe will

---

[377] See ante, pp. 460--61.
[378] See post, chap. VIII.

ever take their places. Foreigners are now doing all the work of this Class in California."[379]

Thus once more the old order changed, and so rapidly and inevitably that no time was allowed for natural growth in the interval.

65. Who'll Buy?

What has been said elsewhere[380] about markets and access to markets as retarding the development of agriculture in California applies of course to all branches of production. Without outlet, trade fails; without trade, industry languishes.

Figueroa was one of the numerous territorial officials who clearly perceived and reiterated this elementary truth. He attributed to Governor Sola's opening of the ports to foreign trade the beginnings of agricultural and general economic development in California, which from that time, he declared, "began to emerge from the poverty in which the court of Madrid had kept her."[381]

---

[379] *Official Corresp.*, MS, vol. 2, p. 95.

[380] *Ante*, pp. 559--73.

[381] Nov. 28, 1834, Figueroa, "Report on Commerce and Revenues of California," in *Depart. St. Pap.*, MS, vol. 3, pp. 192--93.

Even then, however, the territory's situation was comparable with that which, according to critics of the Matanuska plan today, makes any considerable development or prosperity impossible for the Alaskan colony: she was abundantly fertile and capable of a variety of production; but she was too isolated from the markets of the world to make feasible the distribution of her surplus. Less readily even than the Matanuska settlers could the Californian <u>rancheros</u> command ready and cheap transport facilities; and they had no refrigeration aids for the conservation of their perishables in transit.

From the early days of the pueblos this lack of accessibility to markets had discouraged enterprise. Although Spanish law required the returning Philippine galleons to put in at Monterey, the captains often preferred to pay the penalty of the fine rather than break the homeward voyage. In any case, trade with the galleons — except on the royal account — was strictly and repeatedly forbidden.

Governor Neve attempted to have this prohibition repealed in the interest of progress, in the 1780s. Both his successor, Governor Fages, and <u>Ayudante Inspector</u> Soler disapproved, however. They considered that supply by government transport offered the advantages of regularity, uniformity in prices, and equal service to all. The galleon could not touch at all the presidios, so monopoly and inequality would result from traffic with it. China goods were not adapted to the California market. There was no money with which to pay for them, anyway. Opportunities for trade would distract the soldiers from their duties. Finally, avarice and pride would be engendered.[382]

Forbes thought that "the greatest impulse which the [commercial] intercourse between Mexico and California ever had" occurred when, at the time of the Nootka Sound controversy in 1792--93, the Spanish squadron on its way north from San Blas put in at Monterey and other Californian ports for provisions. Thereafter, he adds, there was a relapse into isolation until after the revolution.[383]

In 1794 the military engineer Miguel Costansó lamented the absence of commercial development on the Pacific coast. "'The Cadiz merchants from mistaken motives stifled the trade in its infancy. A grand commerce might be developed, affording California colonists a market for their products, including fish and salted meats.'"[384]

---

[382] Bancroft, Calif., vol. 1, pp. 443--43.
[383] Alta Calif., pp. 381--82.
[384] Bancroft, op. cit., p. 624.

"Not a trading vessel proper touched on the coast before 1800," says Bancroft. The small business (of a barter character and limited to Spanish-American goods) which had been carried on with the government transports traced back only to 1785. "The methods of conducting this traffic are not clearly indicated, but apparently the officers and even the sailors . . . brought up from San Blas on private speculation such articles as they could barter with the soldiers. In the absence of money this trade could not have assumed large proportions . . . . Within the limits of California trade consisted in the delivery of goods from the presidio warehouse to the soldiers for their pay and rations and to the settlers in payment for grain and other supplies, the habilitados being required to purchase home productions rather than to order from Mexico." In the supply of grain for the troops, however, the settlers had the competition of the missions, with their thousands of unpaid neophyte laborers.[385]

---

[385] Ibid., pp. 624--26, passim.

In 1797 Governor Borica reported to the viceroy that the pobladores had a 2,000-fanega grain surplus, for which there was no market; and at about the same time Fathers Señan and Salazar pointed out and Borica agreed that among the chief deterrents to the success of Spain's colonization of the province was the lack of markets and of trade facilities.[386]

Borica made earnest efforts to secure the needed aids to progress. One of his proposals was for the stimulation of pueblo trade by the sending of special government invoices to free the settlers from the monopoly of the San Blas ships, which supplied inferior goods and charged exorbitant prices.[387] This project was eagerly seconded by Captain Manuel Cárcaba, habilitado general in charge of California business.

In May 1797 Don Manuel reported at length in favor of Borica's recommendation, "explaining," says Bancroft, "that nothing but a market for produce could arouse Californian industries from stagnation to prosperity; enumerating the facilities for a profitable exportation of furs, hides, fish, grain,

---

[386] Bancroft, Calif., vol. 1, pp. 603--5, passim; ante, p. 82.

[387] Calif., vol. 1, p. 626.

flax, oil, and wine, and especially sardines, herring and salmon, and insisting that the government must take the initiative in opening this provincial commerce, since the prospects at the first were not sufficiently flattering to attract private companies. He urged the sending of an experimental invoice of $6,000, and gave many details respecting the management of the business. Here so far as the records show the matter ended without practical benefit . . . ."[388]

In 1805, Carcaba's successor and California's second habilitado general, Captain Goycoechea, in a report on "Medios para el Fomento de California," renewed the appeals for an outlet for Californian produce, and asked for a vessel to be employed in that particular service. "The vessel," Bancroft remarks succinctly, "was not forthcoming."[389]

That such additional transport was needed is indicated by an order of the year before, giving preference for cargo space to the tithes and other royal property.[390]

Meantime, in the 1790s, permission was granted for several three-cornered trading enterprises between

---

[388] Bancroft, Calif., vol. 1, pp. 627--28.
[389] Ibid., vol. 2, p. 186.
[390] Ibid., p. 185, n. 20.

Spain, Mexico and California. There were no practical results. In 1800, Juan Ignacio Mendez, who had come to California in 1798 on a supply ship, bringing with him some goods for sale, and who had remained in the province as a carpenter, sought a license to export products of the country in the transports, on his own account; and Juan Bautista Ovineta requested approval of a contract which he had tentatively closed with San José and Branciforte *pobladores* for a thousand *fanegas* of wheat annually, for which he offered $2.50 a *fanega*. Viceroy *fiscal* were agreed in favoring these enterprises, but referred the matter to Governor ad interim Arrillaga;[391] and once again -- whether because Don José Joaquin's enthusiasm for the country's potentialities was not as robust as had been his predecessor Don Diego de Boricá's or for other reasons -- a rosy promise of the *fomento de California* faded and died.

Thereafter to the close of the period, although contraband trade waxed as Spanish control waned, any spurt of productive activity on the part of the provincials could result only in a saturation of the market. Despite the righteous railing of the padres against urban idleness and vice -- censure common enough in our own hard-working world -- there seems no weight of

---

[391] Bancroft, *Calif.*, vol. 1, pp. 627, 628; vol. 4, p. 737.

evidence
∧that the flesh and the devil were alone responsible nor indeed entirely successful in undermining Californian industry. Los Angeles pueblo, for example, bore a particularly bad reputation. (One territorial official was to propose renaming it "Los Diablos.") Yet Sola reported in 1817 that the Angelinos had excellent lands and supplied the presidio plentifully with food, producing, in fact, all that there was a market for.[392]

The opening of the country to foreign trade in the Mexican period did not, as has been seen, clear unlimited channels to consumers. The over-seas merchants were not altruists. They sought and would accept from California only a very few commercial desiderata more plentiful and available there than elsewhere. The preponderant demand throughout the period was for hides and tallow.

The Begg contract of 1822 specified hides alone as acceptable in unlimited amounts. Wheat would be received in quantity only when the Chilean crop was short. Even so, this demand was hailed by Sola as a much-needed outlet for settlers' produce.[393]

---

[392] Bancroft, Calif., vol. 2, p. 350; vol. 3, pp. 588--89.

[393] July 6, 1822, Sola to Comisionado Luís Peralta, in St. Pap., Sac., MS, vol. 6, p. 49.

In 1828, Bandini complained that the foreign traders were interested only in hides and tallow; so that the hemp, oil and other articles which could be highly profitable were produced only in quantities necessary for home consumption. In any case, most of the trade was with the missions, private individuals, who still lacked land, having an inconsequential part in it.[394]

Again in 1829, Echeandía reported that the country's trade was for the most part in hides and tallow.[395]

The combined voices of the rancheros of the San Francisco Bay region took up this same cry in 1839 and again in 1844.[395a]

Indeed, throughout the period, evidence is ample that the Boston men carried their insistence on these cattle products almost to the point of oppression; beyond all doubt to that of repression of territorial productive enterprise.

By 1839, Bandini was predicting exhaustion of the herds and general economic disaster. Indeed, he declared

---

[394] Nov. (?) 3, 1828, Bandini to Barron, in Bandini Doc., MS, unnumbered document, pp. 12--13; 15--17. (On the location of this letter see ante, p. 292, n. 274.

[395] May 19, 1829, Echeandía to Sec. of State and Rel., in Depart. Rec., MS, vol. 7, p. 16; and see ante, pp. 456--57.

[395a] See post, pp. 656--57; 659--62.

that the past eight years had brought the country to "a state almost of ruin. Stockraising was and is the principal occupation of the Californians, but in the time mentioned it has fallen off inevitably, due to .... the raids of Indians and others, and the sole interest of national and foreign commerce in tallow and hides for exchange." He deplored the corresponding failure to develop agriculture, and submitted the imperishable poser: "What is going to become of the country?"[396]

As has been mentioned, the Boston traders exchanged most of their tallow with Peruvian or Mexican buyers. The direct trade with the Sandwich Islands, opened in 1826,[397] was largely in furs, although horses and some lumber were demanded. The Scotch merchant David Spence, a resident of California from 1824 and of Lima before that, summed up: "The United States

---

[396] Aug. 9, 1839, Bandini to L. A. Ayuntamiento, in Leg. Rec., MS, vol. 3, pp. 44--45.

[397] Bancroft, Calif., vol. 3, p. 118.

was interested chiefly in hides, Peru and Mexico in tallow, and the Sandwich Islands in sea otter skins . . . ."[398]

As we have seen,[398a] this latter commodity was speedily vanishing from Californian waters. So far, therefore, demand conditions were decidedly not to the territorial advantage.

The Russians afforded outlet for some Californian grain and other produce. This market has already been mentioned, as have territorial efforts to promote business in that quarter by making special concessions to the northern buyers -- such as permitting their produce-ships to enter through San Francisco instead of continuing down to the legal port of entry at Monterey.[399] But as Ross had been established largely as a farm colony to supply the more northerly establishments with fresh food, the Russian-American consumer demand was obviously limited.

When the Hudson's Bay Company sought to open trade relations, toward the close of the period, the emphasis

---

[398] *Hist. Notes*, MS p. 3. Honolulu, of course, by virtue of situation and low port and storage charges, was the great clearing-house of the Pacific trade. There foreign traders from all the ports on the ocean's rim met to exchange commodities not wanted in their home ports for others in demand. Most of the goods shipped to the island depôt -- except horses -- were re-exported.

[398a] *Ante*, sec. 62.

[399] See *ante*, pp. 555--56.

was all on fur. Mrs. Harvey relates[400] that wheat was offered and not desired. She mentions that the grain was of bad quality; but in this connection it should be remembered that 1841 was a year of such severe drouth that harvests were ruined, flour had to be imported from Mexico, and even plantings of new crops had to be abandoned.[401] Naturally, whatever harvest was salvaged under such disastrous conditions could not have been choice, and should not be assumed of standard grade. That California grain was not uniformly too bad is indicated by the fact that annually from 1836--40 two British vessels carried wheat and other agricultural products to the Columbia River posts.[402]

Mexico herself offered hardly more promise of absorbing any considerable Californian surplus than did the foreign markets. Her primary concern was

---

[400] Eloise Harvey, Life of McLoughlin, MS, p. 24. Mrs. Harvey was the daughter of the British company's great Chief Factor, and as the young wife of William Glen Rae, whom her father placed in charge of the San Francisco establishment in 1841, became a first-hand witness of events at that time and place. (Bancroft, Calif., vol. 5, p. 687, "Rae").

[401] See ante, p. 576.

[402] Bancroft, Calif., vol. 4, pp. 79--80.

the protection of her own interests, which often conflicted with those of the territory. The wheat of her plateau lands, for instance, was one of her leading crops, and was "equal to the best in the world," reported Flagg in the decade following the conquest. ". . . . when not absolutely forbidden, a heavy duty rests upon the imported article, which, unless in times of scarcity, is equal to prohibition."[403] Other instances of rival productions have been mentioned and might be multiplied.

On Californian goods imported into Mexico, moreover, even though no ordinary import levies were made, municipal duties would be exacted at the port of entry, and a tax would be added "at every remove from state to state,"[404] the interior customs frontiers not having been abolished.

As to the opportunities afforded by the domestic -- which is to say the presidial -- market, those were limited by the two factors of mission competition with its "costless labor" and treasury insufficiency. Of these, the second aggravated the first; for the padres could afford to give credit, whereas the pobladores

---

[403] "Report," in "U. S. Govt.Doc.," 34th Cong., 1st Sess., Sen. Exec. Doc. #107, p. 518.

[404] Ibid.

could not. In 1829, Echeandía reported that although the latter had "little or no industry other than that of agricultural labor for their own maintenance," and were without funds, there was "no money with which to pay them for raising supplies for the garrisons . . . ."[405]

Considerable space has already been devoted to the eagerness with which the *Californios* welcomed the whaler market; the concessions and indulgences granted in the effort to "foment" that traffic; the need to tighten up on regulations from time to time, when abuses became flagrant and the whalers, by their increasing volume of business, threatened to drive away the needed Boston traders; and the emphatic protest of the *rancheros* against interference with their produce market.[406] Bancroft declared[407] that such protests were many. Only one need be cited here: a défi of 1839, signed by Salvador Vallejo on behalf of the principal ranchers of the San Francisco frontier. These growers,

---

[405] May 19, 1839, Echeandía to Sec. of State and Rel., in *Depart. Rec.*, MS, vol. 7, p. 15.

[406] See *ante*, pp. 260--64; 286--87, 559--60.

[407] *Calif.*, vol. 4, p. 429.

ran the printed announcement,[408] would trade with foreign vessels only on the express stipulation that any and all products of the country be accepted in trade.

Whether as a result of a growing resolution of the *hijos del país* to force that issue, or of herd depletion, or both, Bancroft notes[409] that in 1841 hides and tallow were less readily obtained than formerly.

In 1845, Larkin wrote to Buchanan: "The Californians are determined to exchange their produce with whalers for domestics, etc., their own way."[410]

It was their overwhelming need of markets, even more than their desire for the manufactured goods purveyed by the foreign sea-traders, that made the territorials submit to and partially condone foreign business tactics not otherwise to have been endured. Time and

---

[408] Aug. 15, 1839, S. Vallejo, *Alviso al Publico*, in "Earliest Printing," Doc. #54. A product of M. G. Vallejo's hand-press at Sonoma.

[409] *Calif.*, vol. 4, p. 190.

[410] Sept. 29, 1845, Larkin to U. S. Sec. of State, in *Official Corresp.*, MS, vol. 2, #36, p. 28.

again not only the necessity of revenue and lack of enforcing power, but the need for buyers for the country's output defeated high-minded projects for foreign trade reform. To insist on the law, concluded Figueroa in abandoning one such cherished program, "would be to place the people under handicap of . . . . losing their sole market for their produce."[411]

The relationship of foreign consumption and territorial *fomento* was explicitly and generally recognized throughout the period under consideration. The *diputación* of 1824, functioning under the tentative *Plan de Gobierno*, unanimously agreed that "in order to afford provincials opportunity for export of their produce, the *comandantes* of all the ports should take especial care to facilitate in every way possible the sale of crops whenever any interested vessel is in port. It would be an incentive to produce if the growers could know that sales would be facilitated." At about the same time, the *vocales* suspended the tax on exports, effective January 1825.[412]

---

[411] Nov. 28, 1834, "Report on Commerce and Revenues of Calif.," in *Depart. St. Pap.*, MS, vol. 3, p. 199.

[412] *Leg. Rec.*, MS, vol. 1, pp. 37--38; Bancroft, *Calif.*, vol. 2, p. 521.

Characteristic of the current pragmatism were the persevering endeavors of the abajeños to have San Diego constituted a port of entry of the first class; those of General Vallejo, on behalf of the northern communities, to secure the transfer of customs headquarters from Monterey to the potentially greater trade emporium of San Francisco; the general and unremitting demands for customs reforms (removal of prohibitions, reduction of heavy import duties, abolition of export duties and of oppressive sales taxes) all in conformance with the peculiar circumstances of the country; and Decree No. 9 of the Constituent Congress of 1836, abating customs and tonnage charges.[413]

These were not personal projects of a few individuals, but widely -- some unanimously -- urged policies expressive of the average Californian conviction. In the face of such an overwhelming mass of evidence, it is hard to see where the "man in the street" today is more intently or intelligently concerned with problems of public economy than was his counterpart of a hundred years ago, California's "man in the saddle" so to speak.

There is little in spirit or reasoning to differentiate the following farmer-protest from similar outcries of our own time. Except for some variation in the conditions complained of, the document of 1844 --

----

[413] See ante, chap. III, passim; and post, pp. 742--51.

a petition to Mexico, submitted by Californian rancheros — might have been written yesterday. The content is given in paraphrase:

The farming class, everywhere the most necessary, is by an incomprehensible or inexplicable fatality the one everywhere least considered and most burdened. .... It feels most directly and heavily the enormous customs duties. The high tariff, designed to build up and develop most of the departments of the Republic, is ruining California. Mexico has many manufactures, of sufficient excellenceto compete with foreign products, and therefore to be protected by tariff. California has no such industries, and the very articles which she needs most urgently are the ones prohibited or heavily taxed. The cloth that a Mexican farmer can buy for 18 centavos per vara costs in California 6 reales, due to the excessive duty of 16 to 20 centavos per vara. Even Mexican goods shipped in national vessels are sold in California at the same prices as are foreign goods: for example, hats which sell in Mexico at 6 reales up to 1 peso cost 6 pesos 8 reales and up to 10 pesos in California.

This is an infant country (país naciente), in which there has been no time nor opportunity to develop industry. If this is not taken into account, we farmers must continue as heretofore, either going naked or being serfs of the ocean traders, foreign and Mexican. At least the old seignorial dues were recompense for duties rendered; we are worse oppressed.

California has three branches of abundant wealth: otter, beaver, livestock. Foreign adventurers have wiped out the first and are doing the same to the second; and the supercargoes are beginning a similar destruction of the third and last. Besides charging prices so exorbitant as to be fraudulent, they all stand together in accepting only hides and tallow, and no agricultural products. Thus it is that the rancher does not cultivate his fields and the stock is diminishing . . . .

The petitioners therefore request permission for the whale-boats to sell 500 <u>pesos'</u> worth of goods each, subject to current tariff rates; and to remain in port long enough to make repairs, take on provisions, help apprehend deserters, etc. With such guaranties at least 300 whalers would come annually to these coasts, and even though their goods sold at twice their cost, as a result of duty charges, they would still be lower than the goods of the merchant traders, who have heavy expenses . . . . and demand not less than 300% to 400%

profit, which the rancher must pay. The whalers have fewer expenses -- they give no credit, etc., and accept a much more moderate profit; and they come not for hides and tallow, butfor supplies, thus fomenting agriculture. They also leave some money in the country. Three hundred whalers, remaining one month each in the territory, as they certainly would, would buy the amount indicated on the attached note -- a very low estimate.[414]

Unfortunately, the estimate referred to as being attached to the petition is not included with either of the transcripts of this document in the Bancroft Library.

One other example may be cited of the solicitude of the Californians for their commercial interests, namely, their demand for a mercantile tribunal. The purpose was to emancipate business from the blunders and delays incidental to trial of commercial cases before inexpert judges of first instance or remote superior courts. This subject received considerable attention in 1845. Although the diputacion already had it under consideration, merchants of Monterey and of San Diego presented supporting petitions.[415]

---

[414] Sonoma, Oct. 9, 1844, "Petition to Mexico, from Californian ranchers," in Vallejo Doc., vol. 34, #64. There is also a copy, signed S.M.B., in Corresp. Hist., MS, pp. 144--49.

[415] Leg. Rec., MS, vol. 4, pp. 48, 60, 75; and on handicaps in the administration of justice, see post, chap. VI.

The Spanish <u>consulado</u>, which Fisher compares with a modern chamber of commerce, had also maintained its own "judicial tribunal, consisting of a prior with functions as president and two consuls who were judges. Before this court was held practically every civil case arising from the trade of the Indies, such as bankruptcies, and the collection of debts."[416]

California had not benefitted by that institution as operated in Mexico. Monopolistic privileges, shared by the <u>consulado</u> with the great merchants, had gradually impaired its general usefulness, so that by the nineteenth century it had ceased to meet the needs of Hispanic-America.[417]

The territory might well have benefitted, however, from a local court of the kind, which would have had the protection of local interests in view.

---

[416] "Commercial Conditions in Mexico," pp. 148, 146. The expenses of the <u>consulados</u> were defrayed from tonnage dues.

[417] Fisher, <u>op. cit.</u>, pp. 151, 146.

66. Aspirations toward Sea Power

Attention has already been called to efforts of Mexican and Californian leaders to secure naval and coast-guard protection for the territory. It will be remembered that the <u>Junta de Fomento de Californias</u> went so far as to recommend the transfer of the San Blas shipyards to Monterey, and projected the Compania Asiatic-Mexicana whose trade fleet should ply between the Americas and the Orient; and that attempts at naval development were made, though without success, by both national and territorial officials. Incidental references have been made also to aspirations toward the development of a Californian merchant marine.[418] This latter ambition was so vital a feature of the program for territorial <u>fomento</u>, both in fact and in the realization of the promoters, that it cannot be overlooked in any review of territorial economy.

Command of even a small fleet of merchant ships to break the practical embargo maintained by the foreign traders and give access to varied and competitive markets would have changed many aspects -- perhaps the entire outline -- of Mexican-Californian history. That the men

---

418 See <u>ante</u>, pp. 38--51, 64--65; sec. 44.

of the country were keenly alive to their need, and strove to fill it, will become evident in the following pages.

Under Spanish industrial and commercial regimentation, a provincial trading fleet was an impossibility. Nor could such a fleet be conjured into existence immediately on the relaxation of autocratic control. Forbes says of the conditions prevailing in the Spanish-American colonies during the period of liberalization of the 1770s and '80s that one of the hindrances to external enterprise "sprang from the immense field which every one found unoccupied in his immediate neighborhood, and which presented at home more objects than his industry or his capital could embrace, and prevented him from embarking in maritime enterprises to distant parts, with which he had few or no commercial relations, and of which he had little geographical knowledge." Even when broader opportunities came with independence, "the native inhabitants were without knowledge or means to profit by the circumstances, in so far as regarded the navigation and commercial facilities of these coasts."[419] Their creole wardship had prepared them no better for business than for politics.

Nevertheless, as we have seen, Mexico's _Junta de Fomento_ aspired to wrest Pacific commercial supremacy

---

[419] _Alta Calif._, p. 283.

from Britain and the United States, and to shift the center of trading operations from Honolulu to Monterey in Upper California; and Minister of Relations Alaman directed the attention of Congress and the administration to the northern territory's importance for national commerce and the creation of a national marine.

The purpose which failed in the '20s was renewed in the '30s, with the organization of the Compañía Cosmopolitana (in connection with the Hijar and Padres Colony), to the end of building up and operating a territorial trading fleet. General Anaya, who later became president of the Republic, was head of the Cosmopolitan Company; and prominent in it, besides "several respectable Mexican merchants," were Judge Castillo Negrete, territorial finance administrator Herrera, and the energetic Juan Bandini.[420]

Unfortunately, Bancroft tells us, their first vessel, the brig "Natalia," was wrecked, "becoming a liability, since it had been bought with the understanding that it was to be paid for in California tallow" yet unpurchased.[421] For all the impressiveness of its directors' list, the

---

[420] Bandini, Hist. de Calif., MS, pp. 64--66.

[421] Calif., vol. 3, pp. 363--64; 267--68.

company was unable to survive that blow and the failure of the colony project generally.

Mexico's inability to put sails to her dreams and make them float left the development of Californian shipping to the territorials. Even less than the men of the older colony were they prepared to launch a merchant flotilla. The general scarcity of coin, the prevalence of high interest rates, and the tax on exported money have already been mentioned.[422] Here were powerful initial checks to the purchase of vessels from abroad. As to shipbuilding within the territory, that highly specialized industry could not conceivable spring into importance overnight or within a few years. Funds and the expert knowledge were lacking. Yet at both ship purchases and ship construction (with the aid of foreign skill) the Californians made essays, as will shortly be seen.

Indeed, the _hijos del país_ were by no means the land-bound population generally supposed. The _rancheros_ whose grants fronted ocean or bay had their private _embarcaderos_, and launches for local transportation and freighting -- quite in the manner of the southern planters of the Atlantic tidelands. These small craft were either

---

[422] Ante, sec.. 29.

built especially for the use of the dons or bought from whatever source opportunity permitted.

The nearest place of worship for the Castros of San Pablo was San Rafael Mission, across the bay, "in consequance of which a boat has been built, so that the family be not in want of spiritual food," stated Don Francisco in 1823, in his petition to the territorial assembly for confirmation of the grant.[423]

Don Victor Castro, son of Don Francisco, owned both a "schooner-launch" and a whale-boat. " . . . . The latter he had obtained from one of the whale ships in exchange for vegetables. This whale boat of Castro's was the only ferry that connected Yerba Buena and Sausalito; socially and commercially, with the opposite shore of the bay, known . . . as Contra Costa . . . . Cerritos, a part of the San Pablo rancho, was a sort of terminus for travelers coming to or going from the eastern shore until as late as 1850--51 when the steam ferry began making trips from San Francisco up the San Antonio creek or estuary."[424]

Comandante Martinez of San Francisco, and later of the Pinole Rancho on the contra costa, purchased an old

---

[423] Abstract of Title, Rancho San Pablo, p. 7.

[424] Davis, Seventy-five Years, p. 218.

boat from the Russians, in 1823, for 12 <u>fanegas</u> of wheat. Indeed, Bancroft learned from Russian sources that several vessels were built at Ross for sale to the Spaniards.[425] As has been mentioned earlier, the <u>cayucos</u> of the California Fishing Company were rented from the Russians; although Salvador Vallejo obtained his whale-boat from the Scotch traders Wilson and Scott. He shipped a crew of six Indian oarsmen, but records proudly: "I always handled the rudder."[426]

An account-sheet of 1842 shows that Don Salvador was also owner, with J. P. Leese, of the lighter "Rosalía", and that his share of current earnings was 307 <u>pesos.</u>[427]

General Vallejo was also a commodore in his own right, being proprietor of a launch manned by several sailors.[428]

The padres, too, were more nautical-minded than is generally supposed. Says Davis: "The Padres not only

---

[425] <u>Calif.,</u> vol. 2, p. 640, n. 10.
[426] S. Vallejo, <u>Notas,</u> MS, p. 36.
[427] <u>Vallejo Doc.,</u> MS, vol. 11, #275.
[428] April 6, 1844, Juan N. Padilla to M. G. Vallejo, in <u>Vallejo Doc.,</u> MS, vol. 12, #24, p. 1.

taught the Indians to build vessels and boats, but instructed them also in their management, and made sailors of them. They were sometimes employed as such by myself and other merchants at Yerba Buena, upon boats that were attached to the vessels, or that were owned on shore, in the delivery of goods and collecting hides and tallow. . . . . I remember that in 1833, hides and tallow were brought to the vessel in schooners and launches manned and commanded by Indians, from the Mission Dolores and the Missions of San José, Santa Clara and San Rafael, the vessels and boats having been built at the Missions by the Indians, under instructions from the Padres, after designs and models prepared by them of a very ancient pattern. They reminded me of illustrations of old Spanish vessels.

"Richardson owned one of these vessels, built at the Mission of San Rafael . . . . Old Domingo Peralta had another of these peculiar boats, built at one of the Missions. Nathan Spear had control of a boat of this kind in 1839, belonging to the Mission of San José. . . . ."[429]

It would have been strange had the provincials of the great sea-faring nation that Spain had been, failed to inherit and to pass on to their creole sons something of

---

[429] Davis, Seventy-five Years, pp. 252, 253.

that impulse seaward from which so large a share of the motherland's power and glory sprang.

To be sure, launches, of however many oars and even if equipped with sails, were modest aids indeed to marine greatness; but neither padres nor lay Californians stopped at launches. In 1826, San Francisco Mission acquired one of the Russian-built ships, with sails and rigging, for $1,200. A year later, a barge was obtained from the same source for Mission San José, the price being $1,500.[430] Still more enterprising had been the purchase in 1823 for $3,000 in coin of a quarter-share of the English ship "Thomas Nowlan," by Padre Martinez of San Luís Obispo.[431]

The marine-mindedness of the territorial government was given practical demonstration almost immediately following the transfer of allegiance from Spain to Mexico. Without waiting to see what benefits the new régime might eventually confer, ad interim governor Luis Argüello seized an opportunity in 1823 to buy the American 83-ton schooner "Rover" from Captain John R. Cooper, just arrived with a cargo from China.

The transaction seems to have been on His Excellency's personal account, although for territorial service.

---

[430] Bancroft, Calif., vol. 2, p. 640, n. 10.
[431] Guerra Doc., MS, vol. 3, p. 46; Bancroft, op. cit., vol. 4, p. 734.

(In 1824, as owner of the vessel, he secured from the diputación a grant of 5% of the net value of the cargo to be secured by the vessel.)[432] Don Luís was by no means exceptional among native sons in thus combining patriotism with personal enterprise. On the contrary, the identity of private with public prosperity was been generally and with clarity. It is even possible that the governor became shipowner only as an accomodation, with the idea of re-sale to the government when the treasury permitted; for Alvarado, throughout his account of the "Rover," speaks of it as a government vessel, even making the point that Argüello had no authority to buy it, but in doing so broke "the bonds of slavery and of provincial tutelage to guide the ship of state toward progress."[433]

The price paid for the schooner is variously given as $8,000, $9,000 and $11,000. How the amount was raised is a matter of doubt.[434] Alvarado's belief was that "Governor Argüello paid with money which the father

---

[432] Leg. Rec., MS, vol. 1, p. 30.

[433] Hist. de Calif., MS, vol. 2, pp. 14--19.

[434] Bancroft, Calif., vol. 2, pp. 493--94.

president of the missions loaned him."[435] J. J. Vallejo concurred[436] in this opinion. Bancroft, however, concluded[437] that although Señan approved the object and would have approved the loan, he feared that the other missionaries would not agree with him as to the utility of the purchase; and so felt obliged to refuse the governor's appeal for the money.

General Vallejo "heard it said that governor Argüello paid Captain Cooper 8000 pesos in onzas de oro which reverend father Mariano Payeras, anxious to promote the national prosperity of the Californias, had loaned the governor without interest or security; but it has also been said that the Rover was bought with the understanding that its cost was to be deducted from the sale of the skins [taken under the Russian contract and shipped to China on the "Rover" for government account]; but I am of the opinion that it was bought with hard cash . . . ." The general adds, however, his belief that, having paid Cooper, the governor borrowed back several thousand pesos of the purchase price.[438]

---

[435] Alvarado, Hist. de Calif., MS, vol. 2, p. 16.

[436] J. J. Vallejo, Reminiscencias, MS, p. 15.

[437] Calif., vol. 2, p. 493, n. 2.

[438] Vallejo, Hist. de Calif., MS, vol. 1, p. 340. The bill of sale is dated Dec. 29, 1823, and Prefect Payeras had died on April 28th of that year. (Bancroft, Calif., vol.2, pp. 493, n. 32; 489). It therefore seems unlikely that Payeras advanced the money.

This last version seems borne out by the contract of 1824, under which Cooper, sailing the "Rover" for the government, was assigned $10,000 for freighting cargoes to and from China, and the privilege of bringing $10,000 worth of return cargo, on his own account, free of duties.[439] Probably the concessions represented deferred payments, or -- if the governor had borrowed from the missions to pay for the vessel and then borrowed from Cooper toward refunding the original loan -- return of the second loan. In either case, a high interest charge was undoubtedly included -- probably enough to account for the above-mentioned discrepancies in reports of price.

It does seem definitely indicated that the purchase was contrived only by the exercise of some financial ingenuity. Success was therefore the more glorious. Thanks to the resolution which overcame all difficulties, the territory secured the use of a ship at a time when "in the seas of California there was not so much as one brigantine flying the Mexican flag."[440]

It was the governor's intention to use the "Rover" first and foremost to convey Californian produce to market and

---

[439] Bancroft, *Calif.*, vol. 2, p. 520, n. 15.
[440] Alvarado, *Hist. de Calif.*, MS, vol. 2, p. 14.

bring back commodities much needed by the troops especially; and second to carry the mails between Monterey, San Blas and Mazatlan. As the territory naturally lacked navigators of its own, the vessel was bought on the understanding that Cooper should continue as captain and supercargo, and "should make a voyage to China, taking with him for sale there for the account of the government the otter skins in the Monterey warehouse, and such other articles as his excellency might find convenient to send to Canton or some other Chinese port."[441]

Another of the conditions of purchase was that Cooper should take on young men of the territory as apprentice-seamen. Santiago Estrada and Marcelino Escobar seem to have shipped in that capacity for the China voyage of 1824.[442]

Many months had been consumed in effecting the purchase of the "Rover." Promptly on the acquisition, however, the diputación took up the matter of the

---

[441] Vallejo, Hist. de Calif., MS, vol. 1, p. 339; Alvarado, Hist. de Calif., MS, vol. 2, p. 16.

[442] Fernandez, Cosas de Calif., MS, pp. 23—24, 26.

vessel's employment. Within a month, the freight was stowed. It consisted chiefly of 302 otter skins and 1,310 seal skins -- the greater part of the catch made to date under the first contract with the Russians. Orders for the disposal of the cargo and for the purchase of army and other supplies were issued to Captain Cooper, and the "Rover" sailed, probably in February, for China.[443]

The voyage seems to have been considered a great success. The vessel anchored in home waters early in November, with a return cargo valued at $12,781 and including cloth and clothing, blankets, rice and furniture. The welcome tendered the vessel and her captain by the needy territorials was not easy to describe, wrote J. J. Vallejo; and his brother the general added that the benefits derived were substantial, the clothing -- especially the *pantalones* -- being especially useful to the troops, the greater number of whom had been wearing trousers fashioned from blankets.[444]

---

[443] *Leg. Rec.*, MS, vol. 1, pp. 28--31; Alvarado, *Hist. de Calif.*, MS, vol. 2, p. 18; Vallejo, *Hist. de Calif.*, MS, vol. 1, p. 339; Bancroft, *Calif.*, vol. 3, p. 520.

[444] J. J. Vallejo, *Reminiscencias*, MS, pp. 15--16; M. G. Vallejo, *Hist. de Calif.*, MS, vol. 1, p. 341; Bancroft, *Calif.*, vol. 2, p. 520.

Almost before this precious freight could be set ashore, Argüello contracted with Cooper for a second trip, to be made in 1825. Again fur was consigned, bringing $7,000 in the Canton market; and again the proceeds were invested chiefly on behalf of the troops. The "Rover" completed her homeward voyage in April 1826.

Argüello was not as well pleased with the conduct of the 1825--26 trading operations as he had been with those of 1824. He believed that Cooper had sold too low and bought too high. Delay in delivery of the return cargo to the interested Californian authorities, loss of the ship's papers, and disagreements over the personal accounts of governor and skipper aggravated matters. A lawsuit developed, and dragged on for two or three years. Nevertheless, plans went forward for the continued operation of the "Rover" -- to be rechristened the "San Rafael."[445]

At the end of 1826, she sailed for Mexico, according to Fernandez,[446] with a cargo of tallow, fur, wine and samples of all California's principal products, to be exchanged for serapes, blankets, hats and munitions. With her went detailed reports from Argüello of all that he

---

[445] Bancroft, Calif., vol. 3, pp. 119--20.
[446] Cosas de Calif., MS, p. 37.

had done to promote the welfare of the Californias, "including the details of the purchase of the goleta (Rover,) the privileges conceded to Hartnell and Gale, the concessions made to the Russians, and his motives . . . .," Alvarado continues the story.

These dispatches, "delivered by Cooper with all haste and importunity, called forth from the authorities only severe strictures on Argüello for his independence of action, deemed in contempt of Mexican authority; and, eventually, an official note to him to the effect that the federal government was functioning and that when press of current business subsided a little the administration would turn its attention to the territories. . . . . Argüello never again bothered Mexican officials with matters of Californian interest," concludes Don Bautista dryly.[447]

The "Rover" -- or "San Rafael" -- never returned to California. Scarcely had she anchored, says Vallejo, when she was "seized by the federal authorities, who forgot all about her; and in a storm she went on the beach and became a total loss."[448]

Alvarado and Fernandez bear out the story of the

---

[447] Alvarado, Hist. de Califl. MS, vol. 2, pp. 84, 85--86.

[448] Vallejo, Hist. de Calif., MS, vol. 1, p. 341.

internment of vessel and cargo, and the latter -- himself a sailor -- writes feelingly of the sacrifice of the good ship "which had ploughed the turbulent Atlantic, doubled perilous Cape Horn and survived the typhoons of the China Sea. She was left day after day exposed to the burning rays of the tropical sun, with none to keep her in condition. Her sides began to gape, and she shipped water, and finally she foundered."[449]

Sharp as was this blow to territorial maritime endeavor, it by no means staggered enterprise, public or private. Several California-built vessels were the next development in the struggle for a merchant marine. The record is somewhat confused as to the exact dates, names and ownership of these early products of the local shipyards. Apparently, however, the first to slip down the ways was the 33-ton schooner "Santa Barbara," whose keel was laid near the town of the same name, in 1829, for Carlos Carrillo and William G. Dana, for use in the coasting trade and otter hunting. Young José Carrillo, son of Don Carlos, was to be captain.[450] Construction was delayed by Governor Echeandía, pending official permit. This authorization was issued at the end of May 1829;

---

[449] Fernandez, Cosas de Calif., MS, p. 38; Alvarado, Hist. de Calif., MS, vol. 2, p. 84.

[450] Bancroft, Calif., vol. 2, p. 745.

and in August a trading license was granted for one year.[451]

The sailor Michael White tells of working, also in 1829, with eighteen assistants, on the construction of a schooner, at the place now known (in honor of the ship, runs the account) as Goleta. This vessel, according to "Don Miguel," was being built for de la Guerra; but "revolution" interrupted the work. (The allusion must be to the Solís revolt, which reached Santa Bárbara in December 1829.)[452]

On Christmas Eve, continues White, the American brig "Danube" -- "a splendid vessel" -- was wrecked at San Pedro,[453] and Captain de la Guerra bought her. Apparently the intention was to recondition her; but as the salvagers were trying to get her afloat to take her to Santa Bárbara, she was driven ashore and battered to pieces in the gale. From her wreckage White and the others fashioned the -- or a -- "Santa Bárbara."[454] So runs this account of "the first vessel ever built in California." Whether the "Danube's" materials completed the ship already begun, or were used in an entirely new structure, is not made clear --though the

---

[451] Bancroft, Calif., vol. 3, pp. 139--40.
[452] Ibid., p. 77.
[453] Ibid., vol. 2, p. 140: "The Danube appears not to have been wrecked until the spring of 1830, but this is not quite certain." (Possibly she was disabled on Christmas Eve and for caution's sake allowed to lie at anchor until spring, when, after all, a late storm defeated the salvage attempt.)
[454] M. White, Calif. in '28, MS, pp. 11--14.

first possibility seems the more likely on all counts.[455]

Nor is it possible with the tangled threads at hand to weave a perfect web of fact as to the territory's initial venture at ship construction. There is a bare chance that there were two "Santa Barbaras"; but it seems far more likely that there was only one, built and licensed in '29 and launched in '30. Captain Thomas Robbins, who became skipper of the vessel figuring in trade annals as the "Santa Barbara" of California, recorded in his diary that she had been built in 1830, for Carrillo and Dana, at Hill's Rancho or Goleta.[456] Possibly, if this was White's "Santa Barbara" framed for Guerra, she changed hands before completion. More likely Captain Guerra had a financial interest in her along with Carrillo and Dana; or he may merely have supervised the building for them.

Between Guerra and Carlos Carrillo there were strong bonds of friendship, agreement on important political and religious matters and relationship by marriage, Don José's wife being the only sister of Don Carlos.[457]

---

[455] According to papers in the Carrillo collection, Guerra abandoned his idea of building a vessel from the wreckage. Bancroft, *Calif.*, vol. 3, p. 140, n. 57.

[456] Bancroft, *loc. cit.* Robbins had been mate of the "Rover," in 1823--25. *Ibid.*, vol. 5, p. 697.

[457] Bancroft, *op. cit.*, vol. 2, p. 746.

As for Dana and Robbins, the first had married Josefa, and the second soon took to wife Encarnación -- both daughters of Don Carlos.[458]

All these details are of interest here as showing how closely the building and operating of this first home-produced ship centered around a *Californio* element devoted not alone to private commercial interests but to the highest welfare of the territory.

Unfortunately, the records are almost silent on the subsequent history of the "Santa Bárbara." Bancroft found only that in 1833 she was at the port for which she had been named, from Mazatlan, with six passengers. Robbins was still her master. She carried a crew of five.[459]

Having completed the building of the "Santa Bárbara" for Guerra, White says, he and his crew constructed another ship, named the "Guadalupe," for Mission San Gabriel.[460] She was a 60-tonner, says Bancroft, framed

---

[458] Bancroft, vol. 2, pp. 744, 774; vol. 5, p. 697.

[459] *Ibid.*, vol. 3, p. 384.

[460] *Calif. in '38*, MS, pp. 14--15. The José Carrillo documents also contain references to the construction of a schooner, in September 1830, for Father Sánchez of San Gabriel, though "José el Americano" (Joseph Chapman) is named as the builder, says Bancroft (*op. cit.*, vol. 3, p. 140, n. 57). White may have helped.

at San Gabriel and hauled in carts to San Pedro where she was put together and launched. Robinson, who observed the launching, called her the second vessel built in California (south of the Russian establishments, of course). Warner thought that the second vessel was the "Refugio," built in 1831--32 for Wolfskill, Yount and other otter hunters. Possibly two vessels are confused here, says Bancroft; or the "Guadalupe" and the "Refugio" may have been the same.[461]

Figueroa's instructions of 1832 included the promotion of commerce and exportation, and the persuasion

---

[461] *Calif.*, vol. 3, pp. 382, 384, 363, n. 1. The last-named reference gives the burden of the "Guadalupe" as 6 tons -- an obvious typographical error. Michael White called her 99 tons. (*Calif. in '28*, MS, pp. 14--15). Neither the "Guadalupe" nor the "Refugio" appears -- unless renamed -- on the maritime lists of subsequent years.

Wolfskill was a Mexican citizen from New Mexico. Yount, who came to California with the Wolfskill party, had perhaps also been naturalized before entering the territory, as Bancroft does not refer to his taking out papers before receiving his grants in the Napa region, although he was baptized in 1835. Bancroft, *Calif.*, vol. 5, pp. 779, 783.

of the missions to build small vessels to that end.[462] Official Mexico had partially revised her ideas since the impounding of the "Rover."

In 1833, in an attempt to "foment" the national merchant marine, Congress decreed a rebate of one-fifth of the import duties on foreign goods introduced into the Republic in national vessels.[463]

In 1834, Figueroa reported to the supreme government that the territory's lack of ships, as well as of money and land transport, made it impossible to enforce the restrictions on the foreign traders, on whom the people of the country were dependent for both markets and supply.[464]

In that same year, California's first Mexican-built vessel was fashioned -- the "Peor es Nada" or "Better than Nothing," a schooner of 20 tons' burden constructed at Monterey by Joaquín Gomez.[465] The name, from which

---

[462] May 17, 1832, Ortiz Monasterio to Figueroa, in Sup. Govt. St. Pap., Decrees and Despatches, MS, vol. 8, p. 35, Art. 6.

[463] Oct. 24, 1833, Depart. St. Pap., Mont., MS, vol. 7, pp. 3--4.

[464] Nov. 28, 1834, Figueroa on "Commerce and Revenues," in Depart. St. Pap., MS, vol. 3, p. 199.

[465] Bancroft, Calif., vol. 3, p. 383. Gomez was a Mexican trader who settled in the territory in 1830, at once becoming prominent politically and as a man of property and influence. (Ibid., pp. 758--59).

characteristic Mexican humor twinkles out, reveals clearly enough the realization that necessity must not be proud. Whether because Don Joaquín or her navigator lacked skill, or merely because destiny was adverse, the "Peor es Nada" foundered early in 1836, in the Golden Gate, en route from Monterey with a load of lumber.[466]

But projects for the building up of a territorial merchant fleet went marching on. Sea-power was one of the prime concerns of the Alvarado-Vallejo administration. It will be remembered that in 1837 Don Bautista was in the market for ships, to be bought with mission produce, "at the cost of some sacrifice if necessary."[467] Although at the moment the governor, apprehensive over the possibility of centralist aggression, was particularly anxious to acquire a small armada, he had not lost sight of the need of a merchant fleet as well.

So when Captain Henry Paty of Boston and Honolulu proved willing to sell his 80-odd-ton schooner "Clarion"

---

[466] Bancroft, Calif., vol. 4, p. 105.

[467] See ante, pp. 417--19.

(or "Kaniu" as she was known at the Islands), Alvarado made haste to buy. Duties of $6,424 on her cargo were rebated, and a balance to make up $9,000 was paid in hides and tallow.[468] The newly acquired merchant packet was promptly and proudly rechristened the "California."

Her first voyage was under Captain Robbins, to San Blas, whither she carried Andrés Castillero as special commissioner to present the territorial side of the revolution of 1836 to the Mexican authorities and to urge the sending of supplies, armaments and financial aid. In 1838, she brought him back, with the news that the supreme government had recognized and legalized the Alvarado-Vallejo administration. She brought, also, much-needed arms and army stores, for which the territory had long petitioned.

Among the dispatches brought by Don Andrés was one expressing the appreciation of the Mexican authorities for the "gift" of the "paquete mercante California." At about the same time, Virmond wrote to General Vallejo from Mexico: "I understand that the schooner California is to become a mail packet between Mexico and California."

---

[468] Bancroft, Calif., vol. 3, pp. 531--32; vol. 4, p. 101. Davis (Seventy-five Years, p. 102) says that she mounted one or two small guns, although she was not adapted to revenue cutter service.

Bancroft remarks: "There is no other evidence that such a gift had been thought of in California."[469]

For the next several years the vessel had the freedom of the seas, and served the territory well. In 1839 she was entrusted, as had been her predecessor the "Rover--San Rafael," to the command of Captain Cooper, whose general popularity had apparently not suffered through his litigation with Argüello, andfor whom Alvarado had a whole-hearted enthusiasm doubtless augmented by a feeling of kinship, since Cooper had married Encarnación Vallejo, sister of the general and a favorite aunt of the governor.[470]

During the next five years Cooper sailed the "California" many times to Mexico and the Sandwich Islands.[471] Limited as her capacity was, she nevertheless

---

[469] Calif., vol. 4, p. 101; vol. 3, pp. 531, 574; June 20, 1838, Virmond to Vallejo, in Vallejo Doc., MS, vol. 5, #97, pp. 5--8.

[470] Alvarado, Hist. de Calif., MS, vol. 2, p. 17; Bancroft, Calif., vol. 2, pp. 756, 765--66.

[471] Bancroft, op. cit., vol. 2, p. 765. Cooper's original Log of the California is preserved in the Bancroft Library.

performed great service as a carrier of territorial products to favorable markets. She seems to have demonstrated that, given ocean transport, the Californians could even compete with Mexican productions in Mexico's own ports; for her cargo to Mazatlan on a trip of 1843 included 127 casks of brandy, 23 barrels of wine, 6 barrels of pisco, one barrel of olives, a can of dried fruit and sixteen hams, besides (Forbes to the contrary notwithstanding) 112 cheeses.[472]

The "California's" was a stirring though brief history, and the variety of uses to which she was put leaves no question of her recognized value to the territory. Primarily a government trader, carrying government merchandise, dispatches, commissioners, stores -- even, in one instance, government prisoners -- she also took paying passengers and was even chartered out on occasion to private interests. In 1842 she was "captured" by Commodore Jones, at Monterey; but had to endure the humiliation only overnight.[473]

Indeed, it was Mexico, again, not the United States, which was to wrest from the territory this second winged

---

[472] Bancroft, *Calif.*, vol. 4, p. 563, n. 42.
[473] *Ibid.*, pp. 101--2; 308, n. 16; 312; 563--64.

victory over commercial isolation. In 1844 the "California" was detained at Acapulco. Although her owners evidently attempted to keep her in repair, as indicated by expenses running to June 1845,[474] she seems to have suffered a fate similar to that of the "San Rafael."

Congressman Castañares exerted himself earnestly for her rescue. He had reason to hope that he had been successful when, in November 1844, he was given official assurance that the reconditioning of the goleta "California" had been ordered. Don Manuel, however, knew better than to relax his efforts. Early in January he pressed the matter on the attention of the Minister of War and Marine. The "California" had been kept at Acapulco since July 1844, he averred. In a violent storm of October she had broken from her anchorage and been washed ashore. She was in bad shape, and unable to carry her crew.

The Minister of War was therefore urged to afford means of getting the vessel to Mazatlan, where the supreme government could take the necessary measures to put her back into service. The "California" was the only means of communication between the supreme government and "aquel desgraciado país, cuya suerte nos tiene en ansiedad."

---

[474] Bancroft, *Calif.*, vol. 4, pp. 563--64, n. 41, "California."

The Minister of War advised, after two or three weeks, that he had taken up the matter with the comandante militar at Acapulco and with the Treasury Department.

On the same day, Congressman Castañares carried the case to the Minister of Relations. California had made great sacrifices to maintain this sole means of communication with the supreme government, pleaded Don Manuel tactfully; but all would be vain unless the captain was supplied with 400 to 500 pesos to make possible the voyage to Mazatlan. The Minister was supplicated also to see that once arrived in that port, the ship be given the attention deemed essential by the naval commandant of the Department of the South.[475]

Here, abruptly, ends the known career of the schooner. Bancroft found "no evidence that she ever returned to California."[476]

Undoubtedly, she would have had a successor had not the conquest followed so quickly. For the

---

[475] Castañares, Col. de Doc., pp. 6, 54--55.
[476] Calif., vol. 4, pp. 563--64, n. 41, "California."

territorial authorities had become too addicted to their water transport to get along without it. They went so far, in fact, as to commandeer the 24-ton schooner "Rosalía," with her crew, and place her under the command of Captain Cooper in 1843.[477] That this craft was the property of General Vallejo's brother Salvador and his brother-in-law Jacob Leese[478] did not prevent its impressment when public need dictated.

Meantime, and for years past, the beginnings of what promised to develop into a territorial merchant marine had been forming under private auspices -- the empresarios being chiefly Spaniards or Mexicanized Yankees.who had become residents of the department. Unfortunately, Mexico found political reasons for expelling from her dominions several of these valuable aides to empire.

---

[477] May 3, 1843, Victor Prudon to Vallejo, in Vallejo Doc., MS, vol. 11, #369.

[478] Bancroft, Calif., vol. 4, p. 710, "Leese." In Bancroft's marine list for 1841--45, an obvious typographical error identifies the "Rosalía" with the United States man-of-war "Savannah," instead of with the national vessel "Susannah," called the "Rosalía" in Cooper's Log. Ibid., pp. 568, 569.

There was, for example, Don Antonio José Cot, who first visited the territory in 1820, on a trading trip from Lima. Two years later he brought his family and established residence. In the late '20s and early '30s -- crucial years in California's development -- he was banished as a Spaniard of supposedly anti-Mexican leanings. He returned, however, during or before the Alvarado-Vallejo régime, to become a resident of Los Angeles, whence he continued to conduct sea-trade.[479] Davis mentions[480] his chartering of the "Don Quixote" for a California-Lima-Honolulu voyage.

Don Juan Ignacio Mancisidor -- another Spaniard -- was a partner of Cot. He came in 1822 as supercargo of the "Colonel Young," and again in 1825. From that time he remained until expelled in 1830 despite a petition to be allowed to continue his residence in the territory.[481]

Don Miguel de Pedrorena arrived from Peru in

---

[479] Bancroft, *Calif.*, vol. 2, p. 763.

[480] *Seventy-five Years*, p. 202.

[481] Bancroft, *op. cit.*, vol. 4, p. 729.

1837 or '38, as supercargo and part owner of the
"Delmira." Before 1840, he came again as supercargo
of the "Juan José," of which Cot was part owner. He
was along the coast again in 1842--43. The Lima firm
which he represented conducted business with Europe
and California. In 1845 he took up residence at San
Diego. A native of Spain, he settled in California
late enough to escape proscription by the Mexican
authorities, but also too late to aid greatly in the
building of a territorial merchant marine and a territorially conducted overseas trade, though he became a
prominent and influential citizen. Douglas called
him, in 1841, "the most popular and best salesman on
the coast."[482]

In partnership with Pedrorena was the Spanish
Basque José Antonio Aguirre, owner of the 210-ton
Mexican brig "Joven Guipuzcoana" (formerly the American
"Roger Williams"); the 317- or 318-ton Colombian or
Mexican "Juan José"; the 306-ton Mexican "Leonidas" (the
American "Dolphin" rechristened); and perhaps one or
more other vessels. He entered the territorial trade in
1833--34, and from shortly thereafter made his home in
Santa Bárbara, becoming one of the most prominent of

---

[482] Bancroft, Calif., vol. 4, p. 770; Davis, Seventy-five Years, p. 250; Douglas, Journal, MS, p. 83.

California's early merchants.[483]

Davis relates that at the time of Mexico's separation from Spain, Aguirre was in business in the city of Mexico, trading largely in Manila and Canton. "He remained loyal to Spain after the separation, and in consequence was expelled from Mexico, as was the case with many other loyal Spaniards. Coming to California he made his mercantile headquarters at Santa Barbara and San Francisco. .... He was a genuine merchant, thoroughly educated."[484]

Supercargo Eulogio Célis managed the Californian affairs of Henry Virmond of Acapulco and Mexico City. Célis was a Spaniard, but settled in Los Angeles and soon became one of the best-known and wealthiest of the territorial merchants.[485]

As for Virmond, although it does not definitely appear that he renounced his native allegiance, his Mexican marriage and his closeness to political and ecclesiastical powers imply that he did. In any event, he was as deep in Mexican and Californian affairs and confidences, and apparently as

---

[483] Bancroft, Calif., vol. 2, p. 688; vol. 4, pp. 104, 566; Douglas, Journal, MS, p. 83.

[484] Seventy-five Years, p. 248

[485] Bancroft, op. cit., vol. 2, p. 755

much in sympathy, as any native of the republic. Although he maintained residence in Mexico, his Californian business was of such magnitude and his Californian affiliations and associations so important that he might almost be regarded as the territory's Colonel House. Manipulator of extensive trading operations, and owner of the "Leonor," the "María Ester," the "Catalina," the "Clarita," and "many other vessels well-known in the California trade" according to Bancroft,[486] he ~~also~~ loomed for a time as the father of an infant Mexican-Californian merchant marine.

Of 11 vessels trading in Alta California under the flag of the republic in 1842, according to a list compiled by Mofras,[487] 1 was the territorially owned "California," 2 were the property of Aguirre of Santa Barbara, and 1 of José Castaños, a Spaniard of Tepic. The rest were registered to non-Hispanic names; but Virmond owned 2 of them, and brief consideration of the other proprietors reveals that most, if not all, were naturalized Mexican citizens who had transferred their allegiances in good faith and had definitely identified their interests with those of Mexico -- particularly of California. The list, with side-lights from Bancroft's "Pioneer Register," follows:

---

[486] *Calif.*, vol. 5, p. 764.
[487] *Exploration*, vol. 1, p. 506.

Captain Henry D. Fitch -- First came to California in 1826, as master of Virmond's "María Ester"; declared intention to become a citizen, 1827; was baptized, and married Josefa Carrillo, 1829; from 1830, legal resident of San Diego, though much of the time at sea; held many local offices; grantee of lands. ". . . . one of the earliest, most prominent and most popular of the early pioneers; straightforward in his dealings . . . ."[488]

Captain Hugo Reid (Mofras has it "Red") -- Came to California in 1834, when 23 years old, after 6 years spent in Mexico; settled at Los Angeles; naturalized, 1839; grantee of land, 1841. In 1839, he had a Mexican wife.[489]

Captain John Wilson -- Arrived in California about 1826 or 1828; before '36, married Ramona Carrillo de Pacheco, after which he made Santa Bárbara his home; naturalized, 1837; became a grantee of land. "There were few of the old pioneers better known or more respected than Captain John Wilson."[490]

Captain James Scott -- First visited California in

---

[488] Bancroft, *Calif.*, vol. 3, pp. 739--40.
[489] *Ibid.*, vol. 5, p. 691.
[490] *Ibid.*, p. 777.

1826. From 1830, he seems to have considered Santa Barbara his home, though constantly on the move . . . . Supercargo and master of various vessels; grantee of land (hence was in all probability naturalized). "Not friendly to Americans in '46--7 . . . ."[491]

"Capitaine Daze" -- Bancroft's "Pioneer Register" includes no such name, nor any Captain "Dawes," of which "Daze" might be the French equivalent. Undoubtedly Mofras meant "Davis," whose softened Spanish pronunciation would be approximated in French by "Daze" -- not William Heath, Jr., who was not a shipowner in 1842, but John Calvert Davis, the English ship's-carpenter and blacksmith (though Mofras calls him American) who had been five years before Mexican masts and who had probably touched in Californian ports before taking up his residence in the territory. He was naturalized in 1839. In November 1841, he finished building the "Susana," in Napa Creek. Receiving permission to sail her under the Mexican flag, he took her to Mazatlan and back in 1842--43. He lost his naturalization papers on the voyage, and received new ones in 1844. That year he built to "Londresa." In partnership with the English

---

[491] Bancroft, *Calif.*, vol. 5, p. 714.

"chips" William John Reynolds (naturalized 1844) and the Scotch sailor and carpenter John Rose (naturalized 1844) he built houses, as well as ships. Was corporal of San Francisco defensores, 1844.[492]

Here, then, was the promising nucleus of a bona fide Mexican-Californian merchant marine. It is probable, too, that the 11 Mexican vessels recorded by Mofras as trading in the territory in January 1842 made up nearly half the merchant fleet of that year; for although Bancroft lists 38 ships in territorial ports, only 26 or 28 of those were traders.[493] A casual check of Bancroft's data indicates that, while the foreign and particularly the Yankee merchantmen were consistently of greater burden than those flying the Mexican flag, Mexico matched the Americans almost ship for ship in Californian waters in 1842, and outnumbered the British Californian fleet nearly three to one. For the rest, the merchant vessels of the year included only 1 German ship, 1 Chilena, and 1 of uncertain registration, either Colombian or Mexican. As for the twelve months of September 1840 to September 1841, by Mofras's showing[494]

---

[492] Bancroft, Calif., vol. 2, p. 776; vol. 5, pp. 692, 704.

[493] Ibid., vol. 4, pp. 339, 562--70.

[494] Exploration, vol. 1, pp. 504--5.

there were 10 Mexican merchant vessels, as 10 American. Larkin recorded 22 Mexican and 28 American vessels in the port of Monterey in 1844. His shipping list for the same port for 1845 showed 27 American vessels to only 18 Mexican; but 5 of the American ships were men-of-war.[495] Undoubtedly several others were whalers. The imminence of war probably accounts for the slight falling off in Mexican arrivals. As for England, her Californian fleet numbered only 2 in 1844, and 4 in '45.[496]

This growth of a territorial trading fleet had come about in spite of Mexican political intolerance of several leaders in the development. Yet the supreme government had endeavored to rally the men of the republic to maritime pursuits and investments. Her fault, indeed, had probably been too great a jealousy. Said Forbes, about 1835, of the young Spanish-American republics:

" . . . . the native inhabitants were without knowledge or means to profit . . . in as far as regarded

---

[495] *Official Corresp.,* MS, vol. 2, pp. 110, 36.

[496] Bancroft, *Calif.,* vol. 4, pp. 432--33, n. 23; 561, n. 41; 562--70, n. 42, *passim.*

the navigation and commercial facilities of these coasts. The want was at first almost entirely supplied by strangers . . . . This, however, was soon looked on with jealousy by the new republics, although some of the more enlightened saw that the only way to create a marine was to admit foreign vessels, and foreign capital, in order to breed up their own people to a seafaring life, and to give time for native artisans and native capital to grow up . . . . but Mexico, which is the least maritime of all the others, and ought to admit foreign seamen with the most freedom, has adopted the old-fashioned and exclusive measures . . . . decreeing that all Mexican vessels shall be commanded and officered by native seamen. This wise decree was made when there was not one Mexican captain, officer or seaman on the whole Pacific coast of the Mexican republic! Mexico, in this, as well as in all other matters of commercial regulation, has adhered more than any of her sister republics to the old Spanish regimen, and, like her maternal prototype, has suceeded in putting herself almost out of the list of commercial countries . . . . If the laws now in existence on paper were rigidly enforced, there would not at this moment be a single coasting-vessel on all the Mexican coast of the Pacific. There is not a single vessel at this moment commanded by a Mexican, nor are there any officered or manned by natives . . . ."[497]

Whether or not Forbes was strictly accurate in that last statement, it seems to be a fact that Mexico probably overstepped herself in her efforts -- evident throughout her Californian relations -- to call into being a nationally owned and operated trading fleet. Not only was maritime personnel nationalized -- in the statute-books. As early as 1828 an attempt was made to legislate all coast trade into Mexican bottoms.[498] Customs rebates were offered on goods transported in such carriers.

More than legal enactments were necessary, however, to make Mexico over into a Britannia of the South Sea waves. In 1830 Echeandía reported a complaint from the vice-president that many nationalized vessels were failing to comply with the laws requiring captain, pilot and one-third of the crew to be citizens of the republic. Any vessel arriving without her required complement

---

[497] Forbes, *Alta Calif.*, pp. 296--98, *passim*.
[498] Bancroft, *Calif.*, vol. 3, p. 131.

of Mexican officers and men was to be denied reduction in duties, even though she flew the national flag.[499]

Three years later, Congress defined national vessels as those "constructed in some part of the Republic, of Mexican ownership, and carrying a crew of which at least one-half are Mexicans; furthermore, the captain and pilot must be Mexican."[500]

In 1834, naval captain Buenaventura Araujo -- the same who rendered distinguished service against Scott at Vera Cruz in 1847 -- was sent to California, "perhaps with a few subordinates," along with the Hijar and Padrés Colony, "to take command of the Californian fleet -- of the future," says Bancroft.[501]

It does not clearly appear that Mexico herself developed any outstanding mariners in the California trade before 1846. Several Hispanic names in addition to those of Spanish shipowners and supercargoes already mentioned appear in her ocean annals. There are captains Benito Machado, Juan Gomez and Juan Malarin, and perhaps a few others. But Malarin is known to have been a native of Peru, though he became a Mexican naval lieutenant in

---

[499] *Depart. Rec.*, MS, vol. 8, p. 125.
[500] *Depart. St. Pap., Mont.*, MS, vol. 7, pp. 3--4.
[501] *Calif.*, vol. 2, p. 699; vol. 3, p. 378.

in 1825 or so, married a Californian woman and maintained residence in Monterey while continuing to follow the sea for a livelihood.[502] Neither Gomez, master of the "Natalia" in 1834, nor Machado, commanding the "Joven Dorotea" then, could have been Mexican -- by birth or adoption -- if Forbes is to be taken literally as to the republic's total lack of navigators and seamen at about that time; though Gomez may have become naturalized by 1836, when he returned to the territory in command of the "Leonidas."[503]

Meanwhile, the Californians were endeavoring to train their own youth in the arts of the sea and of ships. In contrast with Mexico's exclusory policy, however, the territorials welcomed nautical foreigners for the skills which they could impart. As early as 1823, when the English mate W. A. Richardson of the whaler "Orion" petitioned to be allowed to remain in the country, Governor Sola granted the request on the condition that the applicant teach the hijos del país

---

[502] Bancroft, Calif., vol. 4, p. 728.

[503] Although Forbes's book was not published until 1839, it was written (save for a few additions) and dispatched to England in 1835. Alta Calif., p. 149. Bancroft, op. cit., vol. 3, p. 759; vol. 4, p. 727. Gomez is not to be confused with the Mexican Joaquin Gomez who built the "Peor es Nada." See ante, pp. 684--85.

navigation and carpentry. Davis published[504] a translation of the governor's permit, of which the original, he tells us, was written on the margin of Richardson's petition:

Monterey, October 12, 1822

Being aware that the petitioner, besides being a navigator, is conversant with and engaged in the occupation of a carpenter, I hereby grant the privilege he asks for with the obligation that he shall receive and teach such young men as may be placed in his charge by my successors.

Sola

Bancroft gives[505] a similar version of the conditions on which "Don Guillermo." became a resident of the territory!

When Sola's successor, Argüello, purchased the "Rover" from Captain Cooper in 1823, he stipulated that Don Juan receive aboard the vessel as many as four young Californians to be educated in the arts of navigation.[506]

---

[504] Seventy-five Years, p. 9. Sola was on the point of leaving California to claim his seat in the Mexican Congress.

[505] Calif., vol. 5, p. 694.

[506] Fernandez, Cosas de Calif., MS, p. 24.

Both Richardson and Cooper seem to have justified expectations of them as instructors, and won popularity for a variety of services to the territory. In 1827 or so, Padre Altimira of San Francisco Mission certified to Richardson's great usefulness as a teacher of calking and carpentry.[507] It will be remembered that at least two Californian youths accompanied Cooper as nautical apprentices on the "Rover's" first government voyage;[508] and undoubtedly others acquired training and experience through association with the able capitán in his subsequent California career.

But the local authorities had larger ideas for directing the enthusiasm of their young men oceanwards. In 1827, the diputación discussed petitioning the supreme government for a naval training school and shipyard (a "corchadero," as Bandini had it) with sufficient masters to supply the naval vessels of the nation.[509]

What became of this project is not known; but California's sea-mindedness continued to manifest itself. When the Santa Bárbara was built in 1829, it was planned

---

[507] Bancroft, Calif., vol. 5, p. 694.
[508] See ante, p. 675.
[509] Leg. Rec., MS, vol. 1, p. 54. Don Juan seems to have meant corchadura, a variant of encorchadura. Possibly corchadero was a Peruvian form.

not only that a native son -- young José Carrillo -- should captain her, but that more than half her crew of six should be Mexicans.[510]

Mention has already been made of the efforts of the Alvarado-Vallejo administration to develop a naval service which should include not only a branch of fighting marines, but a nautical training-school; and of Don Bautista's confidence that California could more readily build a fleet than could Mexico, since the territory possessed, if not money, natural resources, and if not native mariners, eager native aspirants along with experienced navigators and seamen of other countries who had become established Californians and taken daughters of the country as wives.[511] When the administration succeeded in acquiring the "California," the trainingschool idea seems to have been followed up.

Bancroft says that in 1837 the vessel carried a crew of 16 men and a boy, "only five being of Spanish-American blood."[512] If those five were already seasoned with sea salt, the territory may well have felt proud to make so strong a showing, under the circumstances. It seems likely, however, that some, possibly all, were

---

[510] Bancroft, Calif., vol. 3, p. 140; vol. 2, p. 745.
[511] See ante, pp. 417--19.
[512] Bancroft, op. cit., vol. 3, p. 532, n. 29.

apprentices. Certain letters of 1839, preserved among the Vallejo Documents, indicate that the "California" was definitely regarded as a school-ship in one of her capacities.

Nor was the opportunity of shipping on her for instruction limited to creole lads. Ex-mission Indians were to be given their chance at livelihood and service in the territorial flotilla. In the spring of 1839 General Vallejo ordered the commandants at San José, Santa Clara and San Francisco, and the administrator at San Rafael, each to assign two of the liveliest and most promising young Indians of his jurisdiction to the "California" to learn seamanship. He requested San Francisco's captain of the port Richardson to list on the marine register the Indian apprentices embarking. Richardson reported nine neophytes recruited and registered; and Vallejo acknowledged receipt of the report.[513]

No sweeping conclusions can be drawn from so fragmentary a record, particularly as Bancroft mentions[514] a crew of fourteen, "all foreigners but two" as manning the "California" in 1842; and refers to smallpox among "the Kanaka crew" in 1844 -- though this does not preclude the presence of apprentices aboard. It is at least clear,

---

[513] Vallejo Doc., MS, vol. 6, #s 360, 361, 451, 483.

[514] Calif., vol. 4, p. 563, n. 42. Mofras (Exploration, vol. 1, p. 506) states that the crew numbered ten, in January of that year, but throws no light on its make-up.

however, that whether or not consistently and successfully followed, the training-ship idea persisted for at least two years after the purchase of the vessel, and was actually given a trial. The relevant communications of 1839, moreover, are allso laconic as to suggest that they were part of a familiar routine, rather than of an expériment.

The records afford no indication of the number of Indian forecastle hands developed. Some fragments of information do remain concerning young men of leading families who were actuated or encouraged to try the sea. Don Antonio Suñol, who (though Spanish-born) had served in the French navy, and Captain Juan Malarin each sent a son for a voyage on the British "Lama," in 1837. With them went a son of Don (José) Mariano Estrada, whose own career had been military, but whose boy Santiago had been one of the youthful adventurers on the "Rover's" first voyage for the territory.[515]

Romualdo Pacheco the second -- he who became so distinguished in public life after the conquest --[516] shipped on the American trader "Sterling" in the early '40s. Davis says that "for a year or more he travelled about in company with Thomas B. Park, supercargo, from whom he received a good deal of instruction in mercantile

---

[515] Richardson, *Salidas de Buques, 1837--8,* MS, p. 1.
Bancroft, *Calif.,* vol. 5, p. 738; vol. 2, pp. 792, 793.
[516] *See post,* chap. XI.

matters . . . ."[517] Bancroft states that he "spent some years on the "Sterling" and other vessels as supercargo's clerk, but in '48 settled on his mother's land in San Luis Obispo."[518] Pacheco's mother, incidentally, after several years of widowhood, had become the wife of the Scotch sea-captain and trader John Wilson, in 1836 or earlier.[519]

Thus, in one guise or another and for good or ill, the foreign influence continued strong in California's maritime history. Nor did the territorials resent this influence, in so far as it was legitimately exercised. Instead, to the end of the period, they welcomed foreign enterprise, capital and experience whenever those seemed likley to conduce to the upbuilding of the country. Thus, in 1841, Osio was gratified to write to General Vallejo that among the prospective immigrant settlers of the northern frontier was "an American with a Californian family, who is a good blacksmith and carpenter, has a boat and a capital of 14,000 pesos. His voyages just to Mazatlan return him 300%."[520]

---

[517] Seventy-five Years, p. 255.

[518] Calif., vol. 4, p. 764. Park was another foreign sea-trader who became a naturalized Mexican before the conquest, although he did not marry in the country. Ibid., p. 767.

[519] Ibid., vol. 5, p. 777.

[520] Jan. 27, 1841, Osio to Vallejo, in Vallejo Doc., MS, vol. 10, #53, p. 2.

The Californians did not, however, voluntarily yield undue scope to foreign settlers and concessionaires. The promotion of territorial interests was the unremitting purpose of the native leaders and the best of the Mexican. Their policies constituted an attempt at an integrated program to that end.

Maritime development was to be supplemented by locally owned and controlled port facilities. "I plan to build next year at whatever cost some public warehouses at Yerba Buena, so that the Russians cannot claim the need to build them," Alvarado wrote to Vallejo in 1839. He asked the general's advice and cooperation, and his recommendation of a suitable person to handle the enterprise, which would "be very useful to the nation and to the commerce of the port."[521] Inland navigation was likewise to be fomented; and efficient land transport was to tie the whole great system together.

---

[521] May 10, 1839, Alvarado to Vallejo, in *Vallejo Doc.*, Ms, vol. 7, #32, p. 1.

Bay, river and local coasting traffic were then very recent developments. "In 1823, the Sacramento and San Joaquín Rivers could not be navigated, due to hostility of the many Indians of the region," wrote Fernandez.[522] With the occupation of the northern frontier, and the partial pacification of the valley tribes, the territory's inland waters became important channels of travel and freighting, while the growth of Yerba Buena and Santa Cruz made lightering along the coast profitable. By 1836, this last form of enterprise had become important enough to call for regulation; and Governor Chico ruled that Nathan Spear, who was operating a schooner between Monterey and Santa Cruz, must prove himself naturalized or regularly enrolled on the territory's marine register, or sell his lighter.[523]

It will be remembered that by Decree No. 9 of the Constituent Congress of December 1836, the creeks of the state were opened to foreign trade. This was but a temporary measure, for specific purposes, as has been mentioned elsewhere.[524] An order of 1839 from General

---

[522] *Cosas de Calif.* MS, p. 25.
[523] Bancroft, *Calif.*, vol. 4, p. 83; vol. 5, p. 730.
[524] See *ante*, pp. 243--44.

Vallejo to the captain of the port of San Francisco emphatically prohibited local freighting (as well as coast trading) by foreign craft. Instead, "preference must be given to owners and masters of national vessels to carry on all sorts of business."[525]

In the promotion of the northern frontier, one of the attractions held out to prospective colonists was that they could run launches as well as farm.[526] By the early 1840s, 7 lighters were kept busy in the territory's inland waters,[527] and Castañares was expounding to the Mexican Congress the importance of the navigable rivers of California, "the only department of the republic abounding in that great resource."[528]

The dreams and endeavors of the native sons were beginning to come true. The limits of occupation had been pushed back. California's great "inland sea" had become a pool for world commerce. San Francisco was a clearinghouse for Pacific cargoes and the freight of the "brimful rivers" of the interior. The development of a lively

---

[525] Oct. 23, 1839, Vallejo to Captain of Port of S.F., in *Vallejo Doc.*, MS, vol. 8, #231.

[526] Jan. 27, 1841, Osio to Vallejo, in *Vallejo Doc.*, MS, vol. 10, #53, p. 3.

[527] Bancroft, *Calif.*, vol. 4, pp. 569--70.

[528] *Col. de Doc.*, p. 25.

overland transport was at least foreshadowed by so great a concourse of ships, and by the express ambitions of the territorials to develop such a branch.

Most important, in contrast to their role of a score of years earlier, the *Californios* were participants in all this progress -- in a small way, still; but steadily and purposefully shouldering forward.[529]

67. Purchasing Power and Volume of Trade

Meanwhile, as widened commercial opportunities enabled them to exchange home productions for their share of the world's goods, their consumer-demand became correspondingly larger and more sophisticated. Along with medicines, sugar, chocolate and coffee, they required fine shirts, stockings, hats, porcelain, -- "a multitude of articles necessary for daily use in comfortable living."[530] Indeed, Don Juan Bandini was moved to denounce with the sternness of a Cato the "urban elegance" which prompted decimation of the herds that fine textiles might be bought. "What will become of the country within a few years?" he demanded, with an alarm as sharp as if crisis had been peculiar to his own times.[531]

---

[529] See *ante*, pp.251, 458--61 for efforts and predictions of Alvarado and Vallejo to this end; also *post*, pp. 744--50.

[530] Alvarado, *Hist. de Calif.*, vol. 2, p.

[531] Aug. 9, 1839, Bandini to L. A. *Ayuntamiento*, in *Leg. Rec.*, MS, vol. 3, p. 44.

Compared with the buying frenzy of the motor and radio era in its pre-1929 phase, the Californian urge to possess which called down Bandini's censure seems moderate enough. Yet by contrast with the years of deprivation which had preceded, it did certainly represent a heightened standard of living. It must be remembered, too, that common as many of the imports were, high prices made their purchase an extravagance; especially when coarser goods of the country might have been had cheaply enough.

Hartnell has left[532] a list of the principal English manufactures imported for the Californian market: brown and white cottons, coarse and fine, for shirting, sheeting, etc.; prints of good quality and fast, handsome colors; cotton and silk handkerchiefs of all descriptions; good, strong velveteen; fustian; muslin, cambric and bishop's lawn; cotton lace; cloth of all kinds, in fact, principally blue and black "casimeri"; flannel; a very small assortment of linen goods including some of the finest Irish linen and cambric; cotton, woollen and silk

---

[532] Pio Pico Doc., MS, vol. 1, #85, pp. 1--2.

stockings; handsome gown patterns; "casimeri" shawls; all kinds of hardware, tinware, earthenware, glassware; Scotch griddles; iron pots and kettles; candlesticks; needles, mostly very fine; cotton and linen thread, sewing silk; hats, boots and shoes; butcher's knives, knives and forks; scissors, silver and brass thimbles; stout hoes, spades, shovels; sickles; window glass; nails of all kinds, particularly cut nails; furniture of all kinds -- a small assortment very elegant and the rest of middling quality; teatrays; carpeting in small quantity; oilcloth; gold and silver lace; perfumery; a few good common silver hunting watches.

It will be seen that the luxury articles were chiefly textiles and wearing apparel, with home furnishings next in importance; though possibly the importation of a four-wheeled carriage on the "California" in 1840[533] presaged a vogue which would soon have culminated in the decadent recklessness of a horse-and-buggy age, with its attendant luxury trade, even though the country had not been taken over by Yankee progressives.

Wood made interesting comment on the women's wear of the time. He observed that the coarse quality of their ordinary dress resulted from "the high price of

---

[533] Bancroft, *Calif.*, vol. 4, p. 102.

manufactured articles; the common checked calico of their dresses probably cost the wearers more than the tasteful and finer articles worn by females in the United States, materials worth ten or twelve cents with us, being in Monterey worth fifty or seventy-five." A window-shopping tour gave him wholesome respect for the purchasing power of the Californian ladies. "Their evening attire is very expensive . . . . A reboso . . . . cost, in Monterey, from fifty-five to sixty dollars; and in one store I saw some embroidered silk cloaks, for which four hundred and thirty dollars each, were asked."[534]

Says Davis: "Silk was largely used by the California ladies, the wealthier class dressing in that material. The rich men of the department were generous to their wives and daughters, never refusing them what they required in dry goods and other materials."[535]

On a trading voyage up the California coast in 1841, Fitch wrote to General Vallejo[536] that he had been unable to take his family along, having such a large cargo that there was no room for them.

---

[534] Wandering Sketches, pp. 237--38.

[535] Seventy-five Years, p. 145.

[536] July 28, 1841, in Vallejo Doc., MS, vol. 10, #233.

Davis uniformly reported excellent business and collections, both as his own experience and as that of his father before him. Refugio, on the Santa Bárbara coast, was a favorite rendezvous for the sea-traders and "many of the wealthier Californians . . . . [who] purchased from the vessel choice articles of merchandise . . . . " The elder Davis "did not take hides and tallow in payment, but the rancheros and the priests brought with them bags of Spanish doubloons, and paid for their purchases in coin, or in sea-otter skins . . . . "

Mrs. Davis, Senior, describing one such trip, declared according to her son that she had never seen "so many piles of gold (Spanish doubloons) as were collected on board the vessel — the result of sales of goods . . . ."

"My father's voyages . . . were very successful; . . on each voyage he realized about twenty-five thousand dollars' profit, in Spanish doubloons and sea otter skins . . . ." asserted Davis, Junior,[537] on the authority of Captain John Meek, first officer of a vessel belonging to the elder Davis in late Spanish times. Obviously, despite prevalent economic depression,

---

[537] *Seventy-five Years,* pp. 200, 201.

there was some wealth in the country in the early nineteenth century, as today.

The growth in Californian purchasing power during the developmental period of the '30s and '40s was of course reflected in augmented profits to the traders. Not even their far greater numbers and the concessions which competition wrung from them prevented their individual gains from mounting. In this later period, the vessel "Euphemia," owned by Davis, Junior and Hiram Grimes, made numerous voyages between Honolulu and San Francisco, all "very prosperous financially."

At Monterey in 1841, Davis declared,[538] he cleared $30,000 on the day he secured his customs receipt and license to trade along the coast.

In May of that year, he disposed of $25,000 worth of goods at San Pedro — between $2,000 and $3,000 of it going to the widow of Don Tomás Yorba; made large sales in Los Angeles; and unloaded $8,000 to $10,000 worth more at Santa Bárbara.[539]

Again at Monterey, he sold $15,000 worth of goods and collected $5,000 in cash payments, all within one week. Sailing on to Santa Cruz, he exchanged much

---

[538] *Seventy-five Years*, p. 306; Bancroft, *Calif.*, vol. 2, p. 777.

[539] Davis, *op. cit.*, pp. 266, 286, 288.

merchandise for lumber, hides and tallow. "I then sent the vessel to Yerba Buena, and came up by land, making sales at San José, Santa Clara and other places, . . to the rancheros and merchants -- doing well." Yerba Buena's buying public emptied his ship of her remaining cargo.[540]

At trade's end, in 1847, he "had on board over $20,000 in coin (Mexican dollars and doubloons) and purser's bills, ... besides what was trusted out."[541]

Oddly enough, California's capacity to buy over the world's counter has been interpreted as an indication not of prosperity but of shiftlessness. She should have produced, not purchased, is the stricture. The fact seems to be that she did produce; and that the actual balance of trade -- though, as a result of foreign exploitation, not the financial advantage -- was overwhelmingly in her favor well before the end of the period.

Export trade statistics, except for a few random items, are not available, unfortunately. However, enough is positively known of the territory's foreign

---

[540] Davis, *Seventy-five Years*, pp. 264--65.
[541] Ibid., p. 293.

trade conditions to make inescapable certain conclusions regarding the volume of export business.

Facts are not unilateral abstractions, incapable of manipulation. Like coins, they have their reverse sides. Like coins, too, they can be spent cavalierly or, by thoughtful application, can be made to yield far more than their face value. The employment of accumulated factual capital to yield the highest interest compatible with safety makes all the difference between informational poverty and competence. That is the economics of historical investigation.

Nevertheless, the productive value of long familiar facts of Californian history continues to be overlooked. The importation of hundreds of thousand of dollars' worth of manufactured goods, in the '30s and '40s, for instance, is still regarded as evidence merely of territorial indolence and ineptitude. Here is a strikingly unthrifty use of data. For it should be obvious that all importations had to be paid for -- partly in cash, but, since cash was so scarce, preponderantly in productions of the country. Therefore the rapid rise of the consumption curve must have been accompanied by a sharp upward swing of the production curve.

Nor were these trend-lines parallel. Tariff charges, alone, would have made the selling price of imports about double their cost.[542] So the importation of a $50,000 cargo would have necessitated the exportation of $100,000 worth of territorial goods and coin.

But the Californians paid added premiums. As has been pointed out,[543] voyage expenses and maintenance of vessels, the commissions of supercargoes, the long credit allowed purchasers, and the total capital invested made costs very heavy for the traders. Naturally they had to sell at figures which would compensate for those factors as well as for the heavy customs toll.

In addition, they demanded liberal returns. Salvador Vallejo complained to the supreme government of prices running 300% to 400% of value; and Douglas wrote of Aguirre's business practice: " . . . . he deals largely on credit, and sells high about 300 per cent on cost, calculating that if he collects only one half of these outstanding amounts still to make handsome profits."[544] If the Californians had habitually defaulted on their bills, exports would have totalled sensibly less than

---

542 See ante, p. 178.
543 Ante, pp. 521--27.
544 Ante, pp. 661; Douglas, Journal MS, pp. 83--84.
--62

import values plus extra charges; but, leaving aside the suspiciousness of Douglas the Scot, and Aguirre's canny justification of exorbitant prices, imputations against territorial credit-worthiness seem strikingly absent.

The spread between cost and selling price -- that is, between import and export business -- in 1845 was $177,500 according to the following figures supplied by Larkin:[545]

Value of Imported Cargoes in California...$367,000
Cost of Cargoes............................189,500
$177,500

In the same context, the American Consul gives the year's customs total variously as $138,360 and $142,309 -- considerably less than 100% of invoice value. Bancroft[546] found a total of $144,913 given in one customhouse source. It seems probably that some falling off in port receipts followed, that year, on Pico's letting down of the bars to foreign goods nationalized in Mexico. Such goods, it will be remembered, were frequently entered duty-free on the specious plea that all customs charges had been paid in Mexico.[547] Even with this apparent reduction of duty costs, however, the imports of 1845 must have

---

545 Official Corresp., MS, vol. 2, p. 111.
546 Calif., vol. 4, p. 561, n. 41.
547 See ante, pp. 258, 256--57.

sold, according to Larkin's figures, for almost 200% of their purchase price. In other words, imports and exports, figured on the basis of value, must that year have been in the ratio of 1 to 2.

Statistical fragments for other years make a still stronger case for the territory. Bancroft found, for example, that for three years of 1836--40 San Francisco alone exported an average of $83,000 worth of produce annually.[548] Known customs receipts for the same period for the entire country averaged less than $69,500.[549]

In 1839 customs collections totalled something over $85,000.[550] A check by Captain of the Port Richardson showed $87,529 in produce shipped out of San Francisco alone in that year.[551]

The fact that the customs totals include export with import taxes makes the preponderance of exports over imports even greater than appears at first glance at the figures. Douglas estimated the territory's annual exports as averaging $241,000 at about this time.[552]

---

[548] *Calif.*, vol. 4, p. 80.

[549] See *ante*, p. 298, Table VIII.

[550] *Ibid.*

[551] Bancroft, *Calif.*, vol. 4, p. 93, n. 31.

[552] *Ibid.*, pp. 80, 310.

Duflot de Mofras has supplied[553] some data for the twelvemonth September 1840 -- September 1841 which indicates better than a 1 to 2 import-export ratio in foreign trade, and a 1 to 1.3 ratio in trade with Mexico:

TABLE XV

Import-Export Values and Ratio, 1840--41

(after Duflot de Mofras)

Nation	Imports from*	Exports to*	Import-Export Ratio
United States	$ 70,000	$150,000	1 to 2.15
England	20,000	45,000	1 " 2.25
Miscellaneous	10,000	20,000	1 " 2.00
Totals	$100,000	$215,000	1 " 2.15
Mexico	50,000	65,000	1 " 1.30
Grand Totals	$150,000	$280,000	1 " 1.72

* All figures relate to business with the merchant vessels only, exclusive of trade with the whalers, and of contraband trade.

With reference to the Mexican-Californian trade, it is to be remembered that Mexico was a rival grower of many of the territory's important products, such as grain, grapes and olives. By certain restrictions, moreover -- such as the prohibition of textile manufacturing -- the metropolis

---

[553] Exploration, vol. 1, pp. 499--500.

was able to command a considerable amount of Californian buying which would not have been given voluntarily.

Mofras analyzed[554] territorial export values for the year of his estimate as:

        Hides $210,000
        Tallow   55,000
        Miscellaneous . 15,000
                        $280,000

These figures are conservative enough. Indeed, that for miscellaneous exports can be regarded only as a glaring underestimate, in view of the tens of thousands of dollars' worth of agricultural produce known to have been exported annually, even in the '30s.[555]

---

[554] *Exploration,* vol. 1, p. 500.

[555] The Frenchman had ample opportunity to collect reliable data, but Bancroft describes him as "bent on amusing himself, fonder of personal comforts than of study; not disposed to go far out of his way for historical information" though "using intelligently such material as came into his hands . . . ." His "researches and observations were not so extensive and careful as was desirable. Had he been a harder student and more diligent investigator, he might have avoided many petty errors . . . ." *Calif.,* vol. 4, pp. 254--55.

Customs receipts of course suggest themselves as a basis for arriving at some idea of the territory's year by year export trade volume. There are complications, however. Without careful check of the accounts extant, it would be impossible to say what portion of such collections derived from imports and what portion from exports. However, export charges bulked comparatively small. For example, in 1843, the coin tax combined with excise tax income is recorded as less than $1,200, as against total duties of more than $52,000.[556] At times, even export dues were entirely remitted, as in 1825 in accordance with the resolution of the diputación.[557] Records indicate that in 1841 legal imports and customs receipts both approximated $100,000.[558]

Another factor must be taken into account -- this time one which for the most part does not show in the customs figures: the volume of trade with the whalers. It will be recalled that before 1841 these vessels had been allowed to exchange merchandise duty-free for supplies, and that after 1841 their anchorage and tonnage charges were abated; that all attempts at limiting their cargoes failed; and

---

[556] Bancroft, Calif., vol. 4, p. 377, n. 16, "Financial Items."

[557] Ibid., vol. 3, p. 29.

[558] Ibid., vol. 4, pp. 209-10.

that finally (along with contraband trade and the introduction of cut-rate "nationalized" goods from Mexico) the whaler traffic made such inroads into the profits of the merchants that the Boston men threatened to abandon the California trade altogether. The whalers "play the deuce" with business, complained the San Francisco storekeeper Nathan Spear, in 1841.[559]

Nearly all this trade is off the record. Yet as early as 1833, Customs Administrator Gonzalez thought it "safe to say that they [the whalers] left not less than 35,000 to 40,000 pesos" in the country in some years.[560] Certainly it is justifiable to disregard the inclusion of export taxes with customs receipts, in an attempt to hypothecate a territorial export trade volume, if the whaler market is also left out of the picture.

The contraband trade complication, however, is too enormous to omit from the reckoning. Speaking generally, Davis surmised[561] that probably half the

---

[559] See ante, pp. 260--64; Larkin Doc., MS, vol. 1, p. 193.

[560] Feb. 15, 1833, Gonzalez to Director General of Revenues, in Depart. St. Pap., Ben., C.-House, MS, vol. 2, p. 8.

[561] Seventy-five Years, p. 107.

customs dues were evaded. Bancroft thought that
double the $13,000 collected in 1826 would have
been but "a small part of the percentage due on
imports." Vallejo called the collections of 1836--38
"nothing of any account" due to an access in smuggling.
Bancroft concluded that during 1836--40 illegal imports
must have been at least equal to the average of $70,000
worth a year introduced legally; that in 1841 contraband
was "certainly not less than half" the amounts entered
at the custom-house; and that "there can be no doubt"
that in 1843 three-fourths of the year's importations
(that is, $156,000 worth as against $52,000 worth duly
entered) paid no duties.[562] Certainly it is safe to
assume that over the entire Mexican period the territory
bought and paid for half as much merchandise again as
the customs records indicate.

With all these factors in mind, an average export-
import ratio can be worked out, conservative enough to
form the basis for a probable minimum year by year average
export volume. Customs receipts will be considered as
equal to invoice value, though at times they may actually

----

[562] See ante, pp. 288--89; 276--79.

have been as low as 80% of value. Contraband trade will be estimated at 50% of licit business -- a reasonably (if not unreasonably!) small proportion. Selling price will be assumed as equal to value and a half, though it probably generally ran to 200% of value, at least.

From these equations, it appears that for every $100,000 collected in duties, $100,000 worth of goods was legally imported, along with $50,000 worth of contraband -- a total of $150,000. Buying at a 50% increase over value, the territorials must have paid for their imports with exports of the country's goods worth $225,000. In other words, the average import-export ratio seems safely computable as 1 to 2.25 -- tallying fairly closely with the result from the Mofras figures for 1840--41 for licit trade only.[563]

From the table of customs receipts already compiled,[564] it is now possible to calculate the territory's minimum annual export trade for each year of known customs receipts, and the average per year for the period.

---

[563] See ante, p. 724, Table XV.

[564] Ante, p. 298, Table VIII.

That the estimates are not inflated follows from the incompleteness of the customs figures, the very moderate price level assumed and, most consequently, the extremely cautious evaluation of the trade under the stars. That they are perhaps ridiculously low looms as a possibility when they are measured by the standards of the Mofras computation of licit merchant-trade only, and the Davis ultra-conservative appraisal of hide-tallow exportation on the basis of known sailings and capacities of trading vessels only.[564a] Understatement, however, is always preferable to overstatement; and the following tabulation is offered as a mere broad indication of the relative volumes of the territory's import and export business.

[564a] See ante, p. 535, Table XIV. See also pp. 535--36 for the Pierce-Larkin estimate.

TABLE XVI

Estimated Import-Export Business, 1823--45

Year	Estimated Minimum Import Business	Estimated Minimum Export Business
1823	$18,000	$40,500
1824	8,000	18,000
1825	11,000	24,750
1826	13,500	30,375
1827	14,000	31,500
1828	24,500	55,125
1831	32,000	72,000
Je. '33--Je. '34	50,000	112,500
1835	50,000	112,500
1836	50,000	112,500
1839	85,600	192,600
1840	72,300	162,675
1841	100,000	225,000
1842	73,700	165,825
1843	52,000	117,000
1844	76,600	172,350
1845	140,000	315,000
Totals	$871,200	$1,960,200
Average Annual Business	$51,247	$115,305

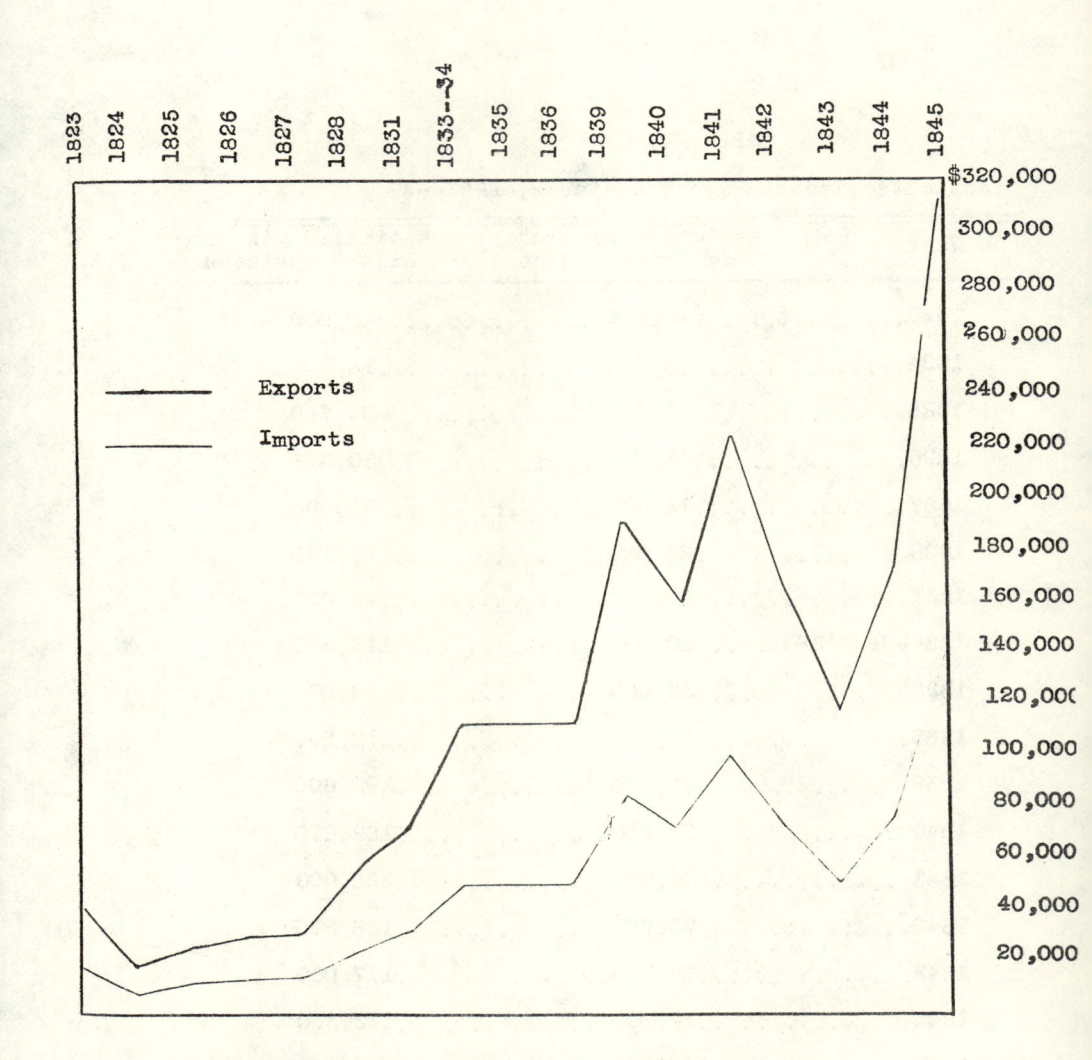

Estimated Import-Export Trade, 1823--1845

Here is a creditable enough trade record -- a record showing that with all her handicaps the country was steadily and rapidly working her way out of that economic impasse to which the Spanish régime had condemned her. What might have been, in the score of years that followed, had not the conquest intervened, offers solid food for thought.

68. <u>Dons</u> of the Counter and Counting-house

The same conditions which had limited the Spanish Californians to the government transports for merchandise supply and produce outlet had precluded the development of any considerable retail trade within the province.[565]

Although against naval regulations, officers and crews of the transports had been allowed to sell privately in Californian ports such small stocks of commodities as they had been able to stow along with their personal effects. For these desiderata, the transport speculators commanded handsome prices! Their conversion of privilege into monopoly was a foregone conclusion. This traffic, therefore, resulted in further restriction, rather than in expansion of trade opportunities for the

---

[565] General trade limitations have been touched on <u>ante</u>, pp. 569--73 and sec. 65.

provincials. By 1803, the abuse had become so flagrant that the viceroy strictly prohibited trading by supply-ship personnel, and made it obligatory for the transports to carry goods of traders and private individuals to and from the province (at regular freight rates) whenever space remained after the royal cargoes had been stowed.[566]

With so small an opportunity for importing stocks of merchandise (supplemented only by contraband supply) it is little wonder that no retail trade of proportions was developed in Spanish times. A few petty *empresarios* there were -- "'Tia' Boronda and 'tíos' Armenta and Cayuelos, who in their extra-mural cots at Monterey are said to have kept a variety of small articles for sale, some of which there is much reason to fear never paid duties. Tio Armenta was a great man in this little band, ... and he sometimes engaged in grand affairs, such as raffling a dozen China handkerchiefs, or getting a bushel of salt from the *salinas* in spite of the Spanish *estanco*."[567]

Better stocked were the stores run at the missions. They probably corresponded to our own Indian reservation

---

[566] Bancroft *Calif.*, vol. 1, p. 626; vol. 2, p. 185.
[567] *Ibid.*, vol. 2, p. 420.

trading posts, but catered as well to the population
de razon. "Their stock was necessarily large. .....
The Padres bought goods cheaper than the rancheros;
their purchases being always larger, a reduction was
made in prices . . . ."[568] Here was formidable competition with private enterprise.

In any case, there was little scope for the small
business man in a society where each household was self-
maintaining save for such needs as could be supplied
only from abroad; and where lack of currency kept trade
on a barter basis.

Few, moreover, were the colonists of Spanish California who had found it possible to save out a nest-egg
with which to coax fortune. As for borrowing for investment, high interest rates made that course prohibitive
for most. The favored few who did possess capital for
buying retail stocks abroad were confronted at the outset
by the export tax on coin and the shortage of shipping
facilities.

Then suddenly, with the Mexican liberalization,
the floating bazaars of the foreign merchants sailed
into every port and embarcadero. Amphibious supercargoes
penetrated, with their sample-books, to the most isolated

---

[568] Davis, Seventy-five Years, p. 204,

hacienda. Not only supply, but credit was urgently tendered. Almost overnight the hide-buyers, working the magic of demand, turned every troublesomely prolific herd into a bonanza. Corral and range became all at once rainbow's end for the men of California, while the Yankee wizards, reiterating their "credit-is-good" incantation, tightened the spell of their combined wholesale and retail hold on the country. Even the resourceful British deemed challenge of that monopoly too hazardous.[569]

Of such infant retail trade projects as the territory could bring forth under those conditions, only a small number could possibly have been viable. Yet a few did survive to match their puny strength with the interlopers' power. Probably the majority lived furtively, fattening -- if they did fatten -- on contraband. Several, however, occupied their places in the sun beside modest shop-fronts.

In the latter group belonged San Gabriel--born Pio Pico, who kept store in San Diego before entering public life; and the native Angelino Inocente García.[570]

---

[569] On the costs and conduct of the hide-tallow trade which favored American monopoly, see *ante*, pp. 521--27, *passim*.

[570] Bancroft, *Calif.*, vol. 4, p. 778; vol. 3, pp. 752--53.

Ignacio Coronel, too, set up in a small way in Los Angeles in the late '30s. Don Ignacio had come with the Hijar and Padres colony. When, with the failure of that project, his salaried teaching appointment fell through, he entered new lines of gainful effort.[571]

Antonio Suñol, a native of Spain and for a time a sailor in the French service, but a Californian resident from 1818, became a shopkeeper in the land of his final allegiance, setting up his counter in San José.[572]

Another grand old Spaniard, José de la Guerra y Noriega of Santa Barbara, whose fame rests on distinguished military and civil service, was also a prosperous retail merchant -- probably the most successful of the Hispano-Californians in that field. He had, indeed, been shopkeeper before he became soldier or statesman. It was to clerk in his uncle's store in Mexico that he had left Spain as a boy. When, at the age of twenty or so, he sought a career in the army and public life, he did not forswear commercial pursuits. Preserved in the Bancroft Library is a small

---

[571] Bancroft, *Calif.*, vol. 2, p. 768.

[572] *Ibid.*, vol. 5, p. 738.

sheaf of documents dating from 1808 to 1820 and showing that after settling in California Don José imported considerable stocks of goods from Mexico City and Tepic, for resale.

The accounts and invoices extant indicate a business running into many thousands of pesos, and show that Guerra bought from several wholesalers. Apparently he conducted a brokerage business, too, for in 1817 he recorded several thousand dollars' worth of merchandise on hand for sale on account of José Bavenencia of Lima.[573]

Just when Guerra retired from trade does not appear. Perhaps it was about 1827, when he regretted that the few merchants of the territory would probably have to abandon the field to the foreigners, "with whom it is impossible to compete."[574]

That his adventures as a tradesman had been profitable seems certain. Davis, who came to know him well in the '40s, and sold him large bills of

---

[573] _Guerra Doc., MS_, vol. 3, pp. 30--34, 36--40; Bancroft, _Calif._, vol. 3, p. 769; vol. 2, p. 186. Bancroft suggests that Guerra's uncle may have been a partner in this business.

[574] _Guerra Doc., MS_, vol. 1, p. 2.

goods for household and ranch use, relates: "He was a close buyer, generally paying cash (Mexican and Spanish doubloons) . . . . While supercargo of the 'Don Quixote' in 1842 and '43 I made four or five sales to him, ranging from $2,000 to $4,000 each. On these occasions Noriega took me to the attic of his house, where he kept his treasure, the room being used exclusively for that purpose. . . . . ranged round about were twelve or fifteen <u>coras</u> -- strong, compactly woven baskets . . . . the largest holding, perhaps, half a bushel -- all of which contained gold, some nearly full . . . . I asked him how he managed to collect so much gold, and he replied that it was the accumulations of all the years he had been on the coast. The Spanish soldiers, when they were paid off, spent their money freely, and he had supplied them with what they wanted, having carried on a store of his own." He had of course built up several other sources of income as well; and, concludes Davis: "Being a good merchant and shrewd manager, he knew how to take care of money."[575]

In California's circumstances, however, no mere private initiative and shrewdness could stand against

---

[575] <u>Seventy-five Years</u>, pp. 239--40.

the commercial aggression of the foreigners. Recognition of that fact was implicit in the comprehensive Plan Politico-Mercantil of the Junta de Fomento de Californias. That prompt attempt to meet the issue failed, for reasons already discussed.[576] So did plans for the Compañia Cosmopolitana, projected in connection with the Hijar and Padres colony.[577]

Similarly dismal was the outcome of the various efforts of Mexican and territorial administrations to legislate the foreign argosies out of the retail trade. Those endeavors were of course interrupted from time to time by the retail concession to foreigners, forced by territorial need of the customs revenue involved, and, more especially, of markets for produce.[578]

Perfect consistency -- rarely possible in political economy -- was here out of the question, due to the conflicting urgencies of California's situation. Moreover, any continuous and effective injunction against retailing by foreigners would have had to

---

[576] Ante, pp. 40--51.
[577] See ante, 108, 666--67.
[578] See ante, pp. 232--64, passim.

withstand the official resentment of the United States. The Thompson-Bocanegra diplomatic exchanges of 1843--44[579] afford documentary evidence of the disposition of the neighboring power to go far on this point, despite positive treaty stipulations as to the southern republic's freedom to regulate her own trade.

So Mexican and Californian leaders might strain to make real their visions of a territorial retail trade supplementing a territorially dominated Pacific trade, the whole freighted in territorial ships and by territorial overland carriers; but those were proposals toward which the gods were not disposed.

69. Promotion of the Northern Frontier

Direction of affairs on the northern frontier were from the first confided to M. G. Vallejo. Such were his peculiar fitness and devotion that the early history of the region which he may be said to have fathered is largely the history of his efforts and ambitions for it.

Some mention has been made of the spread of occupation in the '30s and early '40s.[580] Various incidental references to development have occurred in connection with custom-house administration, the whaler trade and

---

[579] See ante, pp. 252--54.

[580] Ante, pp. 121--24.

produce exportation generally. It remains to indicate by a few random cullings from the documents the comprehensiveness, persistence and ardor with which the program for promotion of the northern frontier was carried forward. The writings of Vallejo are the natural place to look for such indications, although it is not therefore to be inferred that this project was a one-man affair. Examples of the interest and the co-operation of other Californian leaders are numerous enough, both in the documents and in the rapidity of actual development.

Years before he was entrusted with opening up the bay region and its hinterlands, Vallejo must have been inspired by its tremendous potentialities. The thrill with which he noted Echeandía's response to his first revelation of the inland sea with its majestic perspectives of rimming heights and tidelands, vibrates in the words which he set down nearly half a century later. The governor was "electrified" by the bay, wrote the general then. He had exclaimed: "Mexico doesn't know what she has here!"[581]

From the time when he assumed directorship of colonization and military command of the northern

---

[581] Vallejo, Hist. de Calif., MS, vol. 2, pp. 69--70.

districts, Vallejo kept up a promotive and directive correspondence nothing less than amazing in its volume and painstaking thoroughness of presentation. Letter after closely written letter went out from Sonoma, to officials and private individuals in Mexico and California ranging in importance from the President of the Republic to the humble and barely literate corporal keeping the ruined San Francisco presidio with his half dozen ragged soldiers.

Sometimes a few needs and precautions of utmost urgency at the moment made up the subject of these communications. More often, and even though he wrote for some important specific purpose, the anxious guardian of the north would cram into his message a rush of argument and appeal running to several pages and broadly resuming the whole case of the frontier and indeed of the territory.

Several times he prepared comprehensive briefs for one or another phase of the causes which he pleaded, and gave them titles calculated to add to their impressiveness. Such were his "Males de California y Sus Remedios," addressed in 1841 to the Minister of War;[582] and his Exposición que hace el comdanante [sic] general interno de la Alta California

---

[582] In Vallejo Doc., MS, vol. 10, #385.

al Gobernador de la misma, of 1837. The latter document he took the pains to have printed on the little hand-press whose extant productions are so highly valued as examples of California's earliest printing.

Vallejo always recognized that the fortunes of the frontier were bound inextricably with those of the department as a whole, and his policies were shaped accordingly. Therefore it is hard to isolate his frontier program from his general platform. Exclusion of contraband, and absolute prohibition of the foreign floating retail trade in accordance with the law of 1827, would become practicable only with the transfer of the custom-house to San Francisco, and the erection at that port of effective defenses, particularly on strategic Angel Island, he argued consistently through the years. Free trade in most commodities -- for the whole department, or at least for the "infant" northern frontier and at least for a few years -- along with a few import prohibitions and a limited protective tariff in the interests of Californian industry, alone could release the country from the economic paralysis to wich it was condemned by the injustices and ineptitude of the high tariff system maintained for

Mexico's advantage. But customs abatement would be possible only if territorial revenue needs could be met for a period of adjustment by prompt and regular subsidies from the supreme government, and thereafter (or, if subsidies could not be managed) by taxes on productive property. Such were some of the general reforms which he advocated.

Duflot de Mofras declared that Vallejo's object in promoting the custom-house transfer was to secure the handling of the revenues to himself. This allegation was as ill-founded as it was unjust, in no way fitting in with the facts of Vallejo's statesmanship. Bancroft, while observing that, sound as the general's motives were for the most part, they were "not quite disinterested," adds that "Mofras was an enemy of Vallejo, whose only interested motive was probably to increase the value of Sonoma property."[583]

Vallejo himself anticipated any charges against his integrity of purpose with the dignified and reasonable statement in 1837: " . . . . it does not seem untimely that those of us who feel most nearly these evils devote themselves to their remedy, being animated by a lively desire for the national prosperity

---

[583] Bancroft, *Calif.*, vol. 4, p. 88

and at the same time by consideration of our private interests . . . ."[584] Elsewhere he pointed out[585] that he had not established himself on the department's most exposed frontier for his own sake, but to defend the region.

In the Exposición he dilated on the superiority of San Francisco over Monterey as a port of entry, expatiating on its land-locked security; its enormous extent and unlimited capacity for vessels; its continuity with the great system of navigable rivers threading the interior; its abundance and variety of timber suited to shipbuilding; its temperate climate, more benign than that of Monterey; the greater fertility of its adjacent lands, the variety of their productive capacity and the surpassing excellence of their stock ranges; the strategical advantages which could be made to render the location impregnable; its various islands, especially that of "Los Angeles," wooded and watered, suitable for fortification and affording adequate anchorages, landing coves and building sites; the commanding eminence of the presidial site, with its wood, water, pastureland and other natural assets

---

[584] Exposición, p. 2.
[585] May 18, 1843, Vallejo to Micheltorena, in Vallejo Doc., MS, vol. 2, #376, p. 2, Prudon original.

capable of rendering it invincible; its surrounding settlements -- San Francisco, Dolores, Albarado or San José Guadalupe; its neighboring seventeen haciendas and more than five and twenty ranchos; and the abundance of its meat and grain and produce supply.

Each settlement around the bay, moreover, had its own little landing, and many had their own little piers. All navigators, foreign and Mexican, familiar with the various ports of the globe declared consistently that there was no other harbor with so many natural advantages for a port of entry. Monterey lacked many of those advantages, especially the strategical features for necessary defense. And Monterey had nothing like the population of the San Francisco region.

San Francisco communicated by wagon-road, as well as by navigable streams, with all the settlements of the country, being therefore a natural distributing point as well as a natural port of entry. If all imports were entered through it and distributed from it Californians could take into their own hands coast and river transport and the overland carrying trade.

Incidentally, the frontier of the Republic would

be developed along the line of contact with the
United States, the Russian and British establishments and the gentile hordes of the interior. In
recent years damages perhaps irreparable had been
suffered in Sonora and Durango and other parts of
the Republic contiguous with Indian lands. The
San Francisco port project would advantage civilian
populations which would gladly, in their own interests, aid in resisting savage raids. A presidial
force would necessarily be maintained in the region
permanently; and would not need to remain unpaid.[586]

So cogently did the general, in 1837, champion
for the port of entry the incomparably superior San
Francisco Bay site as against lovely but less defensible
and otherwise less suitable Monterey.

Free entry of goods for northern consumption was
a part of Vallejo's program for the stimulation of settlement and the subsidization of frontier families.
All foreigners cast ambitious eyes on mighty San Francisco Bay. No step should be neglected in its protection. Its shores and environs should be occupied, as
a checkmate to penetrating English and Americans. If

---

[586] Exposición, passim.

the supreme government would suspend duties in the port of San Francisco, it would very soon succeed in that matter of such long and close concern, the population of the frontier.[587]

Following up the Russian withdrawal, Vallejo pushed with renewed spirit his plans for the northward extension of occupation, including Bodega in his pleas for free port privileges. Pioneer families had to endure many privations. To exempt them for a decade from duties on goods brought by ships putting in only at northern points would encourage settlement . . . . "[588]

In 1841 he renewed his plea to the Minister of War: "I have the honor to reiterate my petition of May 10, 1839, for the rehabilitation of the Port of San Francisco and exemption from duties for that of Bodega. In your communication of August of that year, Your Excellency was good enough to advise me that my solicitation had been acted on favorably and recommended to the legislature by His Excellency the

---

[587] April 10, 1839, Vallejo to Pres. Bustamante, in Vallejo Doc., MS, vol. 7, #37, pp. 2--3.

[588] May 10, 1839, Vallejo to Min. of War, in Vallejo Doc., MS, vol. 7, #28, p. 4.

President of the Republic. I beg you to be so kind as to advise me of the disposition of this important matter by the Congress. If that honorable body has not yet come to a decision, I renew my plea that His Excellency the President lend his support to the project, which would conduce greatly to the prosperity of California, ... very actively stimulating settlement and so aiding in the defense of this region so generally appreciated and coveted and so much more in danger because so scantily populated."[589]

Vallejo's perception was perfectly clear both as to the foreign menace and the almost illimitable developmental possibilities of the bay area. His foresight envisioned indeed a picture of progress which is still only in the initial phases of realization. Calling the region to Micheltorena's attention as "a rare and incalculable treasure of the Republic" which was attracting the envious and ambitious attention of enemies, he predicted that settlement around the imposing and picturesque bay -- "a sea in size, a lake in its pacific aspect" -- would one day resemble the multitudes in an amphitheater. Fortified and declared

---

[589] Dec. 11, 1841, Vallejo to Min. of War, in Vallejo Doc., MS, vol. 10, #386.

an open port, the precious region might be saved from desirous foreigners; otherwise, its preservation was doubtful. For it was "the cynosure of all enemy eyes and ambitions."[590]

Vallejo was as prescient of the industrial potentialities of the vast aggregation of workers with which his anticipation peopled the region. Only the misfortunes of revolution, dominating Mexico and therefore California during the twenty-odd years of her Mexican adherence, prevented the territory from taking first rank, from 1836, among Pacific centers of commerce, was his conviction.[591]

Despite all handicaps, however, commercial progress was remarkable. According to such scraps of data as Bancroft could find, in the five years 1837--41 shipments to Ross alone totalled $71,300 -- an average in excess of $14,000 annually.[592] (Ross was chiefly a San Francisco customer.)

---

[590] May 18, 1843, Vallejo to Micheltorena, in Vallejo Doc., MS, vol. 11, #376, Prudon original.
[591] Vallejo, Hist. de Calif., MS, vol. 1, p. 317.
[592] Bancroft, Calif., vol. 2, p. 636, n. 7. Bancroft states that he attaches very little value to these statistical fragments -- apparently because of their incompleteness rather than because of any unreliability.

As 1841 was the year of the abandonment of the Russian colonies, moreover, it was a very short trade year, bringing down the average for the period.

Richardson recorded $75,711 in produce shipped out of San Francisco in 1837; $81,700 or $86,000 in 1838; and $87,529 in 1839. Bancroft's average for 1836--40 was $83,000 a year.[593] The amounts include the output of the Contra Costa, of course, and of bay communities as far south as San José. They fail, however, to account for contraband and possibly for some of the whaler trade.

70. Conclusions: Arcadians at Work

The facts heretofore presented were overlooked by writers like Beechey and Morrell, who attributed all California's "desolation" and poverty to "the indolence of the people." Irresponsibles of the Hastings and Farnham type were still further from the faintest appreciation of or regard for the truth. Even Lieutenant Wilkes, commander of a United States exploring expedition numbering six hundred officers and men whose scientific findings filled eight handsome and impressive tomes, produced, for his descriptive *Narrative* of the country and its people an account remarkable only for its careless misrepresentation. Yet the tradition

---

[593] Bancroft, *Calif.*, vol. 4, pp. 88, n. 19; 89, n. 21. Ante, p. 723. On Vallejo's attempt to create a Pacific metropolis on his Soscol Rancho beside Carquines Strait, in cooperation with Robert Semple, see post. p. 784.

of Arcadian California has been reared on the foundations of this and similar literature.

There is irony in the fact that some of the most scathing critics of the *hijos del país* failed, themselves, to perceive the territory's possibilities. Wilkes thought badly of the climate; posited that a large part of the Sacramento Valley was "undoubtedly barren and unproductive, and must forever remain so"; and found the region between Santa Clara and San Francisco "to all appearance entirely unfit for cultivation."[594]

It was not of the country's sterility that the territorials complained, but of her "nascent" condition. Everything was to be done. But everything _could be done_, would Mexico -- and the foreigners -- only permit.

Historians, however, have tended to ignore Mexican California's "nascency," rather assuming that she should have flourished spontaneously and promptly on emerging from her Spanish tutelage. Even Bancroft, amazingly full and fair as was his presentation of the facts, did not always emphasize the difference between lack of accomplishment and lack of opportunity. His _History of California_, moreover, appeared at a time

---

[594] *Narrative*, vol. 5, pp. 163--64, 206, 226.

when the miracles of technology and big business, climaxing Mother Lode and Comstock magic, were filling the dinner-pails of the country generally with such lavishness that only the indolent need hunger and the perverse be poor,

It would have been strange if Americans had not carried over something of the individualistic bias of their time into their appraisal of California's past, when Bancroft called that subject to their attention. For the philosophy of the self-made man was then dominant, and that unconscious Pharisaism shared few laurels with Providence, cherished little humility to remind, in the presence of failure: "There, but for the grace of God, go I!" The great history of California, in fact, appeared at a psychological juncture most unfavorable for its just interpretation.

So the light which Bancroft shed was refracted through the prism of subjectivity, whose deflecting surfaces were ill-founded tradition and false doctrines of success on a base of assumed racial superiority. So the Hispano-Californians continued to be regarded as having lived for generations of wasted opportunity on their ancestral leagues; their poverty continued to be attributed to sloth, and their "nascent" progress to Arcadian apathy.

That is why it has been deemed worth while to make careful re-examination of available data on the economic and social history of Mexican California, and to offer the results in monograph form.

Those results establish beyond question the ambition and well-directed diligence of the territorials. That so much of their endeavor was wasted was not all their fault. Despite the tendency of "rugged individualists" to regard themselves as creators of success, rather than as favored opportunists, man has not yet mastered all the forces of destiny. If those forces are uncompromisingly adverse, the most valiant onslaughts upon them must fail. It was against a conjunction of unpropitious circumstances that the Californians struggled helplessly in 1822--46. Given time, with its changes, they might presently have been favored with opportunities and grasped them. But they were not given time.

The territory was too weak numerically to allow of any rapid internal development, even had there been no complication of savage tribes to be fended off.

Says Lippincott: "Men both demand and supply goods. .... The growth of population, therefore, is related to all departments of industry. If the United States has the largest domestic market of any country in the world, it is because our numbers are so large and the productivity of our people so great."[595]

The Californians, when relieved from dependence on the transports of Spain and permitted to fend for themselves, were confronted at once by our own great problem of overproduction, actual or imminent. Only the army suffered from supply shortages, from the middle '20s on, and that not through inability of the land or the people to produce, but of the government to pay.

Distant markets were accessible for less than a generation's span, and then chiefly by foreign ships. Land was held in private ownership for little more than a decade before the conquest, and then without guaranty of title. Every sort of enterprise suffered heavily at the start from adverse commercial regulations and foreign exploitation impossible to curb. Men ventured into new fields of endeavor without capital or credit, without expertness or theoretical

---

[595] Econ. Develop. of U. S., p. 307.

knowledge. "Experience will gradually dictate the requirements of commercial prosperity," observed the Junta de Fomento sagely. And so it did.

It is a curious bias which ascribes great commercial talents to the Yankees in California, and to the men of the country none. If the territorials had had nothing of value to exchange, the Yankees would have been poor traders indeed! That the products of the country were so largely pastoral and agricultural was in the natural order, as well as a result of market limitations. It would have been neither good logic nor good economy for industrial development to precede large-scale production of raw materials. Probably more than 95% of the population of the United States were still agriculturists as late as 1790,[597] more than two centuries after the first tentatives at English colonization of the Atlantic coast and more than a hundred and eighty years after the founding of Jamestown.

In a score or so of years, California's population of soldiers and subsistence farmers had developed a class of wealthy rancheros, merchants and even ship-owners. Surely it was unreasonable to expect that concurrently they should become manufacturers as well,

---

[596] Coleccion, Item 5 (Iniciativa de ley), p. 26.
[597] Lippincott, Econ. Develop. of U. S., p. 131.

competing with the capital, machinery and techniques of the industrially revolutionized outer world whose highly specialized products were the proffered medium of exchange for their own surplus production!

If their successes were less spectacular than those of the self-made men of Bancroft's era, they were well earned and substantial. Even San Diego, "the least bustling of the California towns" and always much harried by Indians, emerged from the "ever-increasing destitution" of the early '20s to a half-decade of "tranquil prosperity" immediately preceding the conquest.[598]

It is true that the Californians still had far to go politically. Recently freed from the suppression of the Spanish system, inexperienced in government yet fired by republican idealism and by resentment of Mexico's failures, some of them loved politics not wisely but too well, and most of them had yet to acquire the aptitudes for public life. Their situation was moreover peculiarly complicated by the youth of those whom circumstances made their leaders, and by the endless ramifications of blood and marriage ties which

---

[598] Bancroft, *Calif;*, vol. 4, p. 618; vol. 2, p. 343.

rendered their political courses as unpredictable as family quarrels.[599] There is no reason to doubt however, that their sons, profiting by their experience and by wider social horizons, would have done better, particularly if disinterested foreign counsel had been available.

There is even reason to surmise that that first generation of native Californians, left to themselves, would have struggled through to something like political stability.[600] Several of them, along with many of their sons, lived to pursue distinguished careers as American citizens.[601] The most active of them -- Vallejo, Alvarado, Castro, Andrés Pico -- were all well within their thirties in 1846.[602]

Those matters, however, are the stuff of other chapters of the territory's story, to be discussed elsewhere. They are relevant here only as rounding

---

[599] See post, chap. X.

[600] See post, chap. VI.

[601] See post, chap. XI.

[602] Bancroft, Calif., vol. 5, p. 757; vol. 2, pp. 693, 751; vol. 4, p. 776.

out the variety and extent of the problems challenging the men of Mexican California. With only a few hundred adult males in all,[603] and with a low literacy rate, it was incumbent on the few qualified to perform each his share of public service. In many cases, such activities seriously interfered with the conduct of private business. Requests for release and refusals to accept office, on that account, are common in the records.

Distracted as they were between public and private affairs, the men of the country nevertheless raised California from commercial nonentity to importance in the trade of four continents; built up an export-import balance in her favor; and were on the verge of balancing her budget -- if indeed they had not actually done so -- by spring of 1846. Prosperity seemed "just around the corner" when Mars blocked the turn.

Those truths seem more significant today than does the fact that a score of years were insufficient to bring a totally undeveloped, unsubsidized and maladministered countryside to order and opulence. The world has

---

[603] It will be remembered that the total Hispano-Californian population in 1845 was only 6,620. (Ante, p. 153, Table I.) Of these, the majority would of course be minors and women.

been learning, since 1918 and particularly since 1929, that economic depression is not to be sloughed off with such neat dispatch and political inconsequence, even when physical resources, practical experience and theory all abound.

BIBLIOGRAPHY

With Annotations on the Unpublished Sources and

on Papers in Periodicals*

Guides to Sources

Bolton, Herbert Eugene

    Guide to materials for the history of the United States in the principal archives of Mexico (Washington, D. C., 1913).

Chapman, Charles Edward

    "The literature of California history," Southwestern historical quarterly, vol. 22 (April, 1919), pp. 318--52. This concise survey is given also in the bibliographical section of Idem, A history of California: the Spanish period (cited post, p. 797).

Cowan, Robert Ernest

    A bibliography of the history of California and the Pacific West (San Francisco, 1914).

---

    * Save for particular cases and purposes, it has been deemed unnecessary to devote space here to comment on bibliographical items in print other than papers in periodicals. Bancroft's evaluations of the older published materials are admirable. Authoritative reviews of the newer publications are ready of access. Incidental bibliographical comment is scattered freely through the foregoing pages.

Wagner, Henry Raup

The Spanish Southwest, 1542--1794: an annotated bibliography (Berkeley, California, 1924).

Manuscript Materials

Public Archives:

Archivo de California

63 volumes of Bancroft transcripts representing 273 original volumes of official archives; and 1 volume of copies of loose official papers. Most of the originals were housed in the office of the United States Surveyor-General in San Francisco, and were destroyed in the fire of 1906.

Departmental records. 14 vols. in 4.

Departmental state papers. 20 vols. in 7.

Departmental state papers, Angeles. 12 vols. in 4.

Departmental state papers, Benicia. 5 vols. in 2.

Departmental state papers, Benicia, commissary and treasury. 5 vols. in 1.

Departmental state papers, Benicia, custom-house. 8 vols. in 1.

Departmental state papers, Benicia, military. 36 vols. in 3.

Departmental state papers, Benicia, prefecturas y juzgados. 6 vols. in 1.

764

<u>Departmental state papers, Monterey.</u> 8 vols. in 1.
<u>Departmental state papers, San José.</u> 7 vols. in 2.
<u>Legislative records.</u> 4 vols. in 3.
<u>State papers, missions.</u> 11 vols. in 2.
<u>State papers, missions and colonization.</u> 2 vols. in 2.
<u>State papers, Sacramento.</u> 19 vols. in 3.
<u>Superior government state papers.</u> 21 vols. in 2.
<u>Superior government state papers, decrees and despatches.</u> 18 vols. in 1. (This is vol. 1 of the <u>Superior government state papers.</u>)

<u>Archivo de Los Angeles.</u> 5 vols.
More Bancroft transcripts and excerpts, made by and under the direction of Benjamin Hayes. (<u>See infra.</u>)

<u>Archivo de San Diego.</u> 1 vol.
Originals and copies compiled by Hayes and turned over by him to Bancroft. For nearly a quarter of a century before the inception of Bancroft's great work, Judge Hayes collected Californian data and documents, with a view to writing a history worthy of the subject. Official and personal responsibilities frustrated this dearest ambition; but in 1874 he placed in Bancroft's hands his inestimably valuable collection of original materials, abstracts, indices to mission and pueblo archives, annotated newspaper items and photographs — all bearing chiefly on San Diego. As well, he engaged

himself to assist in further collecting and abstracting, on Bancroft's behalf.

As executor of several Hispano-Californian estates, and legal adviser to the heirs, he was able to obtain some original documents; and, with the assistance of two copyists, he indexed, copied and abstracted from the 12 volumes of archives preserved by Los Angeles County. Nor did his activities cease there. Despite advanced years and realization of approaching death, he spent his last months in diligent and successful endeavors to increase Bancroft's stock of historical materials.

Archivo de San José. 6 vols. in 1.

Copies and extracts. Besides 5 vols. of copies of bound documents, the collection includes a volume of copies of loose papers found in the office of the City Clerk.

Larkin, Thomas Oliver

Official correspondence as United States Consul and Navy Agent, 1844--49. 2 vols. in 1.

A complete file of copies of his communications in his official capacity. On the importance of these and the other Larkin documents, see post, pp. 772--73.

Richardson, William A.

Salidas de buques del puerto de San Francisco, 1837--8.

These records of the Captain of the Port of San Francisco

contain valuable data on export trade, though the document is brief.

Private Archives, Manuscript Histories, Memoirs, etc.:
Much of this material is of similar nature to that contained in the public archives, and is composed of original documents as well as of copies -- official papers of all sorts, and remarkably complete files of correspondence official and private. In large part it should have been turned over to the United States Government or to the Catholic Church, but was withheld when other public and mission records were so delivered up. The histories and memoirs were in a few cases written down before Bancroft undertook his researches; but the majority were compiled or dictated specifically at his request for use in the preparation of his History of California.

Alvarado, Juan Bautista
> Historia de California (San Pablo and San Francisco, 1874--76). 5 vols.
>
> Alvarado was secretary of the diputación from 1827--34; revolutionary governor from December 7, 1836 to July 9, 1837, and thereafter governor ad interim or by appointment from Mexico until December 31, 1842. In 1843 he was commissioned a colonel of the Mexican army, and from 1847 was colonel of defensores, although his early arrest and parole prevented any protracted or notable participation in the Mexican War. One of the

most prominent of the native sons, he possessed a brilliance and energy far above average in any setting. Said Bancroft: "Alvarado might have taken his place beside eminent statesmen in a world's congress."

He proved as well an enthusiastic and generally competent historian, with definite literary gifts, once he had finally been prevailed on to cooperate with Bancroft. While his history -- unreliable in spots -- does not compare in importance with his original letters, especially those of 1836--43, it is on the whole a valuable contribution.

<u>Primitivo descubrimiento de placeres de oro en California, 1841</u> (San Francisco, 1876).

Don Bautista's statement of the discovery of the San Fernando placers during his governorship in 1841; of their development; and of his own futile efforts to secure a metallurgical survey of California by Mexican experts.

Amador, José María

<u>Memorias sobre la historia de California</u> (Watsonville, 1877).

Amador was born at San Francisco in 1794. He served both Spain and Mexico during a seventeen-year army career marked by frequent Indian engagements. In 1827 he became majordomo of San José Mission. He secured his grant in the San Ramon Valley in 1834, and thereafter for many years devoted himself to ranching; though he took time out for a profitable sojourn along the Mother Lode in the '40s.

Don José was 83 years old when he dictated his recollections for Bancroft's use. His long and varied experience enhances the interest of his narrative. Thomas Savage, who took down the memoirs, declared: "Amador's memory was quite fresh, and . . . . his contribution may be called a substantial one." Bancroft also considered the Amador dictation a valuable one, "though . . . . the old soldier 'draws the long bow' in relating adventures of Indian warfare, and is very inaccurate in his dates."

Ashley, D. R., compiler

Documents for the history of California, 1827--1860.
Copies of records and correspondence of the Monterey ayuntamiento, with miscellaneous papers, assembled by a pioneer of the American period.

Bandini, Juan

Documentos para la historia de California, 1776--1864.
A valuable collection, though comparatively small.

Historia de la Alta California, 1769--1845.
A copy, made in 1874 for Bancroft, of Bandini's Apuntes para la historia de la Alta California, 1769--1845. MS, apparently compiled in 1847--50.

Bandini was a native of Lima, born in 1800. He seems
to have come to California at about the age of twenty.
A member of the diputación from 1827--28, he was thereafter continually in public life, serving as member of
Congress in 1833 and returning the next year as vice-
president of the Híjar and Padrés company, supercargo
of the company's vessel (the "Natalia"), and customs
inspector for California. Although the colony project
failed in all its phases, Don Juan continued to figure
largely in office, holding a great variety of posts,
territorial and municipal, taking in practically every
branch of public service from mission administration
to a fiscalship in the tribunal superior.

Less brilliant than Alvarado, lacking Vallejo's stability,
and greatly given to sectional and personal partisanship,
Don Juan was nevertheless one of the best informed men
of the territory. Bancroft considered his Historia,
despite its brevity, "important, especially when supplemented and explained by the author's private correspondence."

Coronel, Antonio Francisco

Documentos para la historia de California.

A valuable collection deposited by Don Antonio in the
Bancroft Library in 1878. Many of these papers are
in a very poor state of preservation and should be
copied.

Coronel came to California when seventeen years old,
with the Hijar and Padrés colony. His principal participation in affairs dated from the '40s, and extended far into the American period, although his interest lay in agriculture rather than in public life. He performed local and special territorial duties, and served as captain in all the southern military operations against the United States in 1846--47. He mined successfully in 1848.

Douglas, Sir James

Journal, 1840--41 (including "Voyage from the Columbia").
Unfortunately, this document is fragmentary. It partially covers the dates April 22, 1840 to September 26, 1841, and includes (pp. 65--108) an account of the voyage from the Columbia to California.

Chief Factor Douglas visited the territory on business for the Hudson's Bay Company. He brought a party of hunters, a cargo of merchandise for sale, plans to purchase a drove of cattle, and propositions regarding fur-hunting in the interior and the establishment of a permanent trading post at San Francisco, with others to be located at other ports if business should warrant. His chief interest was therefore in commercial matters; but his general observations of the country and the people are keen and fair, as well as animated.

Fernandez, Captain José

  Cosas de California (Santa Clara, 1874).

    A Spanish sailor who came to California in 1817, Captain Fernandez soon showed his versatility by serving in the colonial and territorial armies, and in various municipal and district capacities -- as secretary of the San José ayuntamiento, partido elector, juez de paz, síndico, and council member after the conquest. A man whom Bancroft found always to have "merited the respect and esteem of those who knew him," Don José contributed documents as well as his important narrative to the great history enterprise.

Guerra y Noriega, José de la

  Documentos para la historia de California. 7 vols.

    Copies of the Guerra archives, made for Bancroft by Edward F. Murray and Thomas Savage, in 1878. This is the most extensive and important private collection of a Hispano-Californian, next to M. G. Vallejo's, secured by Bancroft. The explanation lies in Don José's career.

    A native Spaniard, he divided his boyhood in Mexico between clerking in his uncle's store and assisting in the office of the habilitado general. Enrolled as a cadet in the provincial army, he came to California in 1801, at the age of twenty-two. Thereafter his public service lay primarily in the presidial sphere -- at Monterey, San Diego and especially Santa Bárbara, where he was commandant from 1815 until his retirement, after more than forty years' service, in 1842. Meantime, however, he also exerted wide political and personal influence in his district and through his brother-in-law, Congressman Carlos Carrillo; and served for many years as síndico apostólico -- "a kind of treasurer and confidential agent" of the friars. Finally, he had extensive commercial and ranching interests of his own.

Harvey, Eloise McLoughlin Rae (Mrs. Daniel Harvey)
   Life of John McLoughlin (Portland, Oregon, 1878).
   This dictation was contributed by the great Chief Factor's daughter, and includes interesting observations on conditions in and around San Francisco as Mrs. Harvey (then Mrs. William Glen Rae) saw them in the early '40s, during which her husband had charge of the Californian post.

Larkin, Thomas Oliver
   Documents for the history of California, 1839--56. 9 vols.
   Presented to Bancroft in 1875 by Larkin's son-in-law, Sampson Tams. The collection contains more than 3,400 documents.
   Bancroft says of these materials: "Nothing could be more important in the history of that epoch," and again that they were "beyond all comparison the best source of information on the history of 1845--6, which in fact could

not be correctly written" without them. . . . .

"Indeed it is difficult to overestimate the historical value of these precious papers."

Larkin came to California in 1832, and engaged in trade, building up extensive interests in the territory and affiliations with leading merchants of Mexico, Honolulu and the United States. In addition, he was United States Consul from 1843; confidential agent of the Polk administration in 1845--48, entrusted especially with furthering the peaceful acquisition policy; and United States Naval agent in 1846--49. The range and importance of his official and private papers was therefore enormous.

Lorenzana, Apolinaria

Memorias de Doña Apolinaria Lorenzana, "La Beata" (Santa Bárbara, 1878).

One of the foundlings sent to California under Spanish auspices in 1800, "La Beata," as she earned the right to be called, spent her life in good and useful works as hand-maid, sick-nurse and nurse and teacher of children. She spent many years in the employ of the Carrillo family at Monterey, Santa Bárbara and San Diego; and for long periods served the padres of San Diego and San Luís Rey missions. Her dictation is a humble, rather touching document, supplementing on the human side more pretentious manuscripts concerned with political and economic themes.

Olvera, Agustín

> Documentos para la historia de California.
>> Copies and extracts made in 1878 by Thomas Savage for Bancroft, from the originals loaned by Don Agustín's son, Don Carlos Olvera.
>> Don Agustín came to California as a boy, with the Híjar and Padrés colony. He was commissioner in charge of the distribution of lands at San Juan Capistrano in 1841, and juez in 1842--43. In 1845 and '46 he was secretary as well as alternate vocal of the territorial legislature, and in 1847 was one of the commissioners to sign the Cahuenga treaty. He reached his greatest prominence in public affairs after the conquest. Like several other of the Californios, he long aspired to write his own history of the territory.

Ord, María de las Angustias de la Guerra (Mrs. James L. Ord)
> Ocurrencias en California (Santa Bárbara, 1878).
>> Recounted to Thomas Savage for Bancroft's use.
>> A native Californian, daughter of José de la Guerra y Noriega, Doña Angustias became in 1833 the wife of the Mexican official Manuel Jimeno Casarín, prominent from 1828 in the customs service, Monterey ayuntamiento, diputación, as comisionado of secularization at San Luis Obispo, and as secretary of state and frequently acting governor under Alvarado. After Don Manuel's death in

the early '50s, Doña Angustias married Dr. James L. Ord, who had come to California as a civilian surgeon attached to an American army unit in '47.

Obviously, she had unusual opportunities for keeping abreast of her times, rapidly and continuously as they changed. That she utilized her advantages is evident in the interest and accuracy of her narration, which Bancroft rated among the best of his collection.

Osio, Antonio María

<u>Historia de California, 1815--48</u> (1851, <u>ca.</u>).

A copy made from a copy, in 1878, for the Bancroft Library. It does not appear when Don Antonio, a native of Lower California, came to the upper territory; but in 1827 he was candidate for the treasurership, and thereafter figured almost continuously in office, particularly in the revenue and customs branches, although he served as well as member of the <u>diputación</u> and of the Los Angeles <u>ayuntamiento,</u> and as a justice of the superior court from 1840--45. He was also congressional alternate in 1839 and 1843, and in 1844 one of the <u>quinterna</u> for governor.

His <u>Historia</u> is particularly useful for its data and observations on customs administration, revenue matters generally and the contraband evil. As Bancroft remarks, "like all writings of this class, it is of very uneven quality as a record of facts," but "valuable as a supplement to those of Vallejo, Alvarado and Bandini . . . . None of them, nor all combined, would be a safe guide in the absence of the original records; but with these records they all have a decided value."

Pico, Pio

<u>Documentos para la historia de California, 1831--50.</u> 2 vols.

This collection contains something under 400 documents. (In volume 1, the documents are numbered; in volume 2, the pages are numbered.)

Native son Pio Pico was a member of the territorial legislature in 1828 and repeatedly thereafter. A leader of the southern opposition to General Victoria in 1831, he narrowly missed being governor ad interim, by virtue of being senior <u>vocal</u> and president of the <u>diputación</u>. A few years later he was one of the <u>terna</u> for governor. In 1845, being again president of the junta, he became temporary governor on Micheltorena's downfall; then constitutional <u>gefe político,</u> by confirmation from Mexico, the next year. Though lacking brilliance, Pico was a much more able man than he has generally been represented as being. His collection naturally includes important papers.

Pinto, Rafael

<u>Documentos para la historia de California.</u> 2 vols.

About 650 documents, manuscript and printed.

Pinto was a native of Branciforte (Santa Cruz) who won a
lieutenancy of volunteers in the Alvarado forces at the
age of eighteen, and a regular commission from Mexico as
alférez shortly afterward. He was one of the military
escort of the Graham exiles in 1840; an aide to Micheltorena in 1843, and thereafter in the customs service
until the war, being collector of the Port of San Francisco
at the time of the American occupation. The papers which
he furnished are of special importance for commercial
topics.

Savage, Thomas

Documentos para la historia de California. 4 vols.
About 1,800 documents compiled in 1874 for Bancroft by
Savage, from original papers in various personal archives.
Thomas Savage was such a character as would have supplied
O. Henry with inexhaustible inspiration. Of Bostonian
derivation, he was born in Habana, Cuba, where many years
of his life were passed. At nine years of age his Spanish
was better than his English, though his French was still
more fluent. Twenty-one years in the United States con-
sulate at Habana took in the California gold rush and the
Civil War periods, and provided him with many absorbingly
interesting experiences and opportunities for very signal
service to his country and his countrymen. A similar
though brief service in Panamá and San Salvador followed.

When, in 1873, Mr. Savage entered Bancroft's employ in San Francisco, he came with "good scholarship, ripe experience, and a remarkable knowledge of general history," besides "strong literary tastes, a clear head, and methodical habits." He became Bancroft's "main reliance on Spanish-American affairs." His services as collector, translator, and supervisor of the work of other copyists and abstracters were devoted and marked by initiative, sound judgment and an instinct for the running down and securing of important historical materials.

Spence, David

Historical notes, 1824--49 (Monterey, 1872).

The Scotchman Spence came to California in 1824 on business of Begg and Company, after a residence of several years in Lima. In 1827 he opened his own merchandising business. He became a naturalized Californian, married in the country, secured land and served in the diputación in 1836 and again in 1843--45. His contribution to Bancroft is brief, but interesting.

Sutter, John Augustus

Personal Reminiscences (Litiz, Pa., 1876).

The German-Swiss or German adventurer Sutter arrived in California in 1839, by way of New Mexico (where he had lived for several years), Vancouver, Honolulu and Alaska. He visited Ross shortly afterward, perhaps deriving from the fort there the inspiration for his own Californian establishment. From his ambition to secure a grant of land as an *empresario* of colonization he was dissuaded by Alvarado, on whose advice he contented himself with an individual grant after having established a year's residence and become a citizen. His selection of the Sacramento site was motivated very largely by his desire to place himself as far as possible beyond supervision by the territorial authorities.

The history of his erection and lordship of Fort Sutter, development of various ambitious enterprises and acquirement of the Fort Ross chattels including armament -- all effected by his recklessly optimistic use of credit -- is too well known to need recapitulation here. As common knowledge are his various political and speculative intrigues, and the importance of his establishment as a rendezvous for immigrants and as the nucleus about which swirled the gold discovery and excitement of 1848 and following.

Sutter's was one of those curiously well-intentioned but warped egos incapable of disinterest or of clear and objective perception. There can be no question that he was self-deceived, as well as deceiver. His memoirs must

therefore be liberally seasoned with salt to help
digestion. Yet, though reliable in point of fact
only when borne out by other evidence, these "Recollections" of a key figure in the crucial and stirring
drama of the '40s deserve thoughtful reading, if only
because of the light which they shed on the devious
personality that was Sutter.

Valle, Ignacio del

　Lo pasado de California　(Camulos, 1878).

　　A native of Jalisco, Ignacio del Valle came to California
　　in 1825 with Echeandía. He saw military service at
　　Santa Bárbara, San Diego and Monterey, and is named as
　　habilitado in 1839; was comisionado of secularization
　　for San Gabriel, Santa Cruz and San Francisco missions;
　　was at various times alternate, vocal and secretary of
　　the legislature, and was treasurer of the civil govern-
　　ment under Pico. During the gold excitement of the
　　early '40s he became juez of the mining district set up
　　at the placers. He continued in public life after the
　　conquest, as alcalde at Los Angeles, recorder, council-
　　man and legislator. "His record throughout his career
　　is that of a faithful officer and excellent citizen,"
　　summarized Bancroft. Don Ignacio gladly placed at Ban-
　　croft's disposal the documents and recollections amassed
　　during his busy and useful years.

Vallejo, José de Jesús

Reminiscencias históricas de California (Mission San José, 1875).

This important dictation was made to Enrico Cerruti for Bancroft during a serious illness of Don José's. General Vallejo, in fact, then wholeheartedly lending every support to Bancroft's human researches, had been summoned to what was expected to be his brother's deathbed. Don José survived for half a dozen years longer, although Henry Oak wrote to Bancroft at the time of the supposed "last words" of the Reminiscencias: "'The chief difficulty seems to be to keep the general from killing his brother with historical questions. He fears his brother may die without telling him all he knows.'"

That Don José knew enough to make valuable copy for Bancroft is evident in his dictation and in the facts of his life. Born in San José in 1798, he seems to have commanded a battery at the time of the Bouchard invasion; served as captain of militia artillery under Alvarado; and was military commandant at San José from 1841--42. In civil capacities he acted as regidor at Monterey, comisionado and administrator of San José Mission from 1836, and in 1833 and 1839 was an alternate member of the legislature.

Vallejo, Mariano Guadalupe

Correspondencia histórica.

A small miscellany of copies by Enrico Cerruti of some of the Vallejo documents -- a sort of sample-book compiled at Sonoma in 1874 for Bancroft's enlightenment as to the nature and range of the Vallejo papers. It was the revelation here made that determined Bancroft to win Vallejo's full coöperation; and the confidence gradually built up through the daily association of "the two generals" (Vallejo and Cerruti) that won Vallejo's friendship and his inestimably valuable and devoted coöperation.

Documentos para la historia de California, 1769--1850.

37 vols.

"Vallejo," says Bancroft somewhere, paraphrasing his gifted though eccentric Italian assistant Cerruti, "was California on legs." Not even Alvarado's destinies were so intimately and continuously identified with the history of the country throughout the first half of the nineteenth century.

Born at Monterey in 1808, of pure Spanish extraction and of a family numbering many persons of education and prominence in Spain and Mexico, Don Guadalupe enlisted as a cadet in the Monterey Company in 1823. His subsequent career was marked by steadily mounting rank and responsibilities which, though laid on him in his military capacities, partook of every phase of civil and promotive, as well as martial, enterprise. He was a member of the diputación in 1831 and 1832, besides being commandant of the San Francisco presidial company. But from 1834--35, when, commissioned a lieutenant, he was established by Figueroa as commander of the northern line (extending south to Santa Inés!), comisionado of secularization for Solano Mission, and colonization director of the northern frontier, the demands on his initiative, courage, energy, liberality and developmental prowess were enormous. So were his grasp of affairs, and his accomplishments. Yet his aspirations were still more impressive.

From 1836, as gefe militar, he shared with the revolutionary governor Alvarado the administration of the provisionally "free and sovereign state of California"; and continued in the capacity of comandante militar under Mexican authority from 1839 through most of 1842. Through all these years he consecrated himself to the reorganization and recruitment of the presidial forces, the rehabilitation of the territorial defense-works, Indian pacification, the staving off of foreign aggression and aggressiveness, and the civil, agricultural, commercial and industrial interests of the northern frontier and of the territory generally.

Following the conquest, he served as legislative councillor and Indian agent; and as a member of the first constitutional convention and of the state's first Senate. In 1846, in an effort to create a Pacific metropolis, he deeded to Robert Semple for promotive purposes half of a five-mile-square tract of his Soscol Rancho, bordering Carquinez Strait; and after the conquest tendered to the state the present site of Benicia with a promise to erect the buildings for a permanent state capital. This was one more case in which his ambition to accomplish was foiled by circumstances.

The more than 11,000 documents preserved in the course of his remarkable career constitute priceless historical materials. Their gift to Bancroft was the princely gesture with which General Vallejo -- his suspicions of the Yankee book-man's motives and abilities finally allayed -- intimated his complete capitulation and dedication to Bancroft's great historical project for California.

<u>Historia de California</u> (Sonoma, 1874--76). 5 vols.

Long before Bancroft's historical enterprise was conceived -- before the conquest, even -- General Vallejo wrote, from the documents at his command, a history of California totalling between 700 and 800 manuscript pages. This work, together with the larger portion of the papers till then preserved by his father (prominent

in Spanish California) and himself, was consumed
in a few moments' time by the fire that destroyed
his Sonoma home in 1867. Tragic as this loss was,
it did not kill Don Guadalupe's hope of some day
giving to the world a just and adequate history of
California.

When, through Cerruti's inspired diplomacy, he was
gradually inducted into a realization of the magnificent scope and disinterestedness of Bancroft's
project, he freely offered to dictate this second and
more extensive *Historia* for Bancroft's sole reference
-- "not to be printed," says Bancroft, "unless I
should so elect, and this was not at all probable.
. . . . The two years of labor . . . . was cheerfully
borne by the author for the benefit it would confer
upon his country, and that without even the hope of
some time seeing it in print. Undoubtedly there was
personal and family pride connected with it; yet it
was a piece of as pure patriotism as it has ever been
my lot to encounter."

Yet the Vallejo history was written in no spirit of narrow nationalism or partisanship. In addition to unusual literary fluency and cogency, Don Guadalupe was
endowed with mental breadth and an ample appreciation
of the obligations of the historian. His contribution
is no shallow compilation of reminiscence and prejudice.

It was written from the documents. Where those failed, the general tested his own memory by comparison with the remembrance of others best qualified to speak on the particular points.

The results are, naturally, far from proof against criticism. Yet the talents expended were far out of the ordinary; the competence of the author superlative; and the intent wholly conscientious. Nor was Don Guadalupe to be hastened into carelessness. Rebuking impetuous Cerruti, whom delays irked, he intimated in neat epigram his realization of the responsibility undertaken: "Do you expect me to write history on horseback?"

Vallejo, Salvador

Notas históricas sobre California (Sonoma, 1874).

(The first 29 pages of these notes are devoted to a true copy of the attestation to the legitimacy and purity of blood of Don Ygnacio Vicente Ferrer Vallejo, founder of the Vallejo family in California, which has always taken pride in its unmixed Spanish lineage.)

Salvador Vallejo's is a brief and not entirely reliable dictation, being heavily, even bitterly, tinged with prejudice. Don Salvador did not share his brother the general's great qualities. He did, however, possess his quota of the Vallejo energy and versatility. Born in 1814, he became captain of militia at Sonoma when twenty-two years old; was frequently commanding officer of the garrison; and participated in many Indian campaigns. He was a captain of <u>defensores</u> in 1844. Meantime, he had served as <u>juez de paz</u> and as administrator of Solano Mission. His private interests were divided between ranching, otter-fishing, manufacture in a small way and commerce.

White, Michael

<u>California</u> <u>all</u> <u>the</u> <u>way</u> <u>back</u> <u>to</u> <u>1828</u> (San Isidro Rancho, 1877).

The English or Irish sailor Michael White -- better known in California as Don Miguel Blanco -- settled at Santa Barbara in 1829, after a dozen years on Mexican and Hawaiian vessels as mate and master. His part in the building of a Californian merchant marine has been touched on (<u>ante</u>, pp. 680--83). He married in the country, obtained lands, and divided his time between shopkeeping, ranching and occasional voyages, besides making a trip to New Mexico, serving in the foreign company against Micheltorena, and being taken prisoner at Chino. His narrative is brief but interesting. Savage, who took down the dictation, remarked that White's memory seemed "quite fresh," and that he appeared like a man who "means always to speak the truth."

Published Materials

Public Records and Official Documents:

Arrillaga, Basilio José
 <u>Recopilación de leyes, decretos, bandos, reglamentos, circulares y providencias de los supremos poderes y otras autoridades de la República mexicana, formada de órden del supremo gobierno</u> (México, D. F., 1838--66).

 The compilation begins with the year 1828. The Bancroft Library has 17 vols. in 20.

Ayala, Tadeo Ortiz de
 <u>See post,</u> Ortiz de Ayala

Beechey, Frederick William
 <u>Narrative of a voyage to the Pacific and Beering's</u> [sic] <u>Strait, to co-operate with the polar expeditions: performed in His Majesty's Ship "Blossom," under the command of Captain F. W. Beechey, R. N., F. R. S., etc., in the years 1825, 1826, 1827, 1828</u> (London, 1831). 2 vols.

California. Comandancia General
 <u>Ecspoción que hace el comdanante</u> [sic] <u>general interino de la Alta California al gobernador de la misma</u> (Sonoma, 1837, <u>ca.</u>).

Órdenes de la Comandancia general, 1837--9 (Sonoma, 1837--39).

Carrillo, Carlos Antonio
Exposición dedicada a la cámara de diputados del Congreso de la Unión por el Señor Don Carlos Antonio Carrillo, diputado por la Alta California, sobre arreglo y administración del fondo piadoso (México, D. F., 1831).

Castañares, Manuel
Colección de documentos relativos al departamento de Californias (Mexico, D. F., 1845).

Dublan, Manuel, y Lozano, José María, compilers
Legislación mexicana o colección completa de las disposiciones legislativas expedidas desde la independencia de la República (Edición oficial; México, D. F., 1876--78). 11 vols.

The compilation begins with the year 1687.

Duflot de Mofras, Eugène
Exploration du territoire de l'Oregon, des Californies et de la Mer Vermeille, executée pendant les années 1840, 1841 et 1842 (Paris, 1844). 2 vols.

Dwinelle, John W.
The colonial history of the city of San Francisco: being a narrative argument in the Circuit Court of the United States for the State of California, for four square

leagues of land, claimed by that city under the laws of Spain, and confirmed to it by that court, and by the Supreme Court of the United States (4th edition; San Francisco, 1867).

"Earliest Printing Collection"
  A collection of Bancroft Library examples of early Californian Spanish imprints listed in George L. Harding, "Checklist and Census of California Spanish imprints, 1833--1845," California Historical Society Quarterly, vol. 12 (June, 1933), pp. 125--36.
  Of the 74 examples listed, the Bancroft Library catalogs 54, and the University of California Library, 1. The documents are bandos, decretos, reglamentos, etc.

Flagg, Edmund
  "Report on the commercial relations of the United States with all foreign nations" (Washington, D. C., 1855) in "United States Congressional Documents," 34th Cong., 1st Sess., Senate Executive Document #107 (ser. no. 828).

Halleck, Henry Wager
  "Report on land titles in California" (Washington, D. C., 1849), in "United States Congressional Documents," 31st Cong., 1st Sess., House Executive Document #17 (ser. no. 573).

Kotzebue, Otto von

  A new voyage round the world in the years 1823, 1824, 1825 and 1826 (London, 1830). 2 vols.

Lozano, José María, compiler

  See ante, Dublan, Manuel, y Lozano, José María

Malloy, William M., compiler

  Treaties, conventions, between the United States of America and other powers, 1776--1909 (Washington, D. C., 1910). 2 vols.

Mexico

  Junta de Fomento de Californias

    Colleción de los principales trabajos en que se ha ocupado la Junta nombrada para meditar y proponer al Supremo Gobierno los medios mas necesarios para promover el progreso de la cultura y civilización de los territorios de la Alta y de la Baja California (México, D. F., 1827).

  Laws, etc.

    See ante, Arrillaga, and Dublan y Lozano.

  Ministerio de Justicia

    Memoria que leyó el secretario de estado y del despacho universal de justicia y negocios eclesiásticos (México, D. F., 1830).

Ministerio de Relaciones Interiores y Exteriores

Memoria que el secretario de estado y del despacho de relaciones esteriores e interiores presenta al soberano Congreso Constituyente sobre los negocios de la secretaría de su cargo leida en la sesión de 8 de Noviembre de 1823 (México, D. F., 1823).

Memoria del ministerio de relaciones interiores y exteriores de la República mexicana leida en la cámara de diputados el 10, y en la de senadores el 12 de Enero de 1827 (México, D. F., 1827).

Mofras, Eugène Duflot de

See ante, Duflot de Mofras.

Ortiz de Ayala

Resumen de la estadística del imperio mexicano (México, D. F., 1822).

San Pablo, Rancho de

See post, Wittenmyer, L. C.

Schmidt, Gustavus

The civil law of Spain and Mexico, arranged on the principles of the modern codes, with notes and references; preceded by a historical introduction to the Spanish and Mexican law; and embodying in the appendix some of the most important acts of the Mexican Congress (New Orleans, 1851).

Tamariz, Francisco de Paula

"Memoria que presenta al Rey sobre mejorar el sistema de gobierno de la Alta California," "Archivo y Biblioteca de la Secretaría de Hacienda, Colección de documentos históricos," vol. 2: Las Misiones de California (México, D. F., 1914), pp. 88--111. Relevant correspondence, pp. 111--17.

Trask, John W.

Vital statistics: a discussion of what they are and their uses in public health administration, "United States Government Public Health Reports," Supplement No. 12 (Washington, D. C., 1914).

United States

Bureau of Census (Department of Commerce)

Fifteenth census of the United States: 1930. Volume 1: Population (Washington, D. C., 1931).
(Over)

Congressional Documents

28th Cong., 1st Sess., Senate Doc. #390 (ser. no. 436): "Copies of the correspondence with the government of Mexico, in relation to the expulsion of citizens of the United States from Upper California," Dec. 23, 1843 --February 8, 1844.

30th Cong., 1st Sess., Senate Report #75 (ser. no. 512): "Report of the committee on military affairs on the memorial of John Charles Frémont, praying an investigation

of the claims of citizens of California against the
United States, for money and supplies furnished by
them for the use of the United States" (Washington, D. C.,
1847).

31st Cong., 1st Sess., House Executive Document #17
(ser. no. 573): California and New Mexico, "Halleck's
Report" (Washington, D. C., 1849).

See ante, Halleck, Henry Wager.

34th Cong., 1st Sess., Senate Executive Document #107
(ser. no. 828): "Flagg's Report" (Washington, D. C.,
1855).

See ante, Flagg, Edmund.

Congressional Globe (Washington, D. C., 1834--73).
28th Cong., 1st Sess., Appendix (Washington, D. C.,
1843--44).

The Globe covers the period December 2, 1833--March 3, 1873
(23rd to 42nd Congress). The Congressional Record
continues the series.

Geological Survey
Department of the Interior, Water Supply Paper #297
("Gazeteer of Surface Waters of California, Part III"):
Pacific Coast and Great Basin Streams, B. D. Wood,
compiler (Washington, D. C., 1913).

"Public Health Reports," Supplement No. 12 (Washington, D. C., 1914).

See ante, Trask, John W.

Vallejo, Mariano Guadalupe

See ante, California, Comandancia General.

Wheeler, Alfred

Land titles in San Francisco, and the laws affecting the same, with a synopsis of all grants and sales of land within the limits claimed by the city (San Francisco, 1852).

Wilkes, Charles

Narrative of the United States Exploring Expedition during the years 1838, 1839, 1840, 1841, 1842 (Philadelphia, 1844). 5 vols.

Willcox, Walter F.

See ante, United States, Bureau of Census (Department of Commerce).

Wittenmyer, L. C., compiler

Complete search and abstract of the title to the Rancho de San Pablo, in Contra Costa County, California, down to the commencement of the action for the partition thereof (San Francisco, 1867).

Wood, B. D., compiler
   See ante, United States, Geological Survey.

Other Publications:

Alaman, Lúcas
   Historia de Méjico desde los primeros movimientos que prepararon su independencia en el año de 1803, hasta la época presente (México, D. F., 1849--52). 5 vols.

Bancroft, Hubert Howe
   History of California (San Francisco, 1884--90). 7 vols.
   History of Mexico (San Francisco, 1883--87). 6 vols.
   Literary Industries (San Francisco, 1890).

Bernard du Hautcilly, Auguste
   Viaggio intorno al globo principalmente alla California ed alle isole Sandwich negli anni 1826, 1827, 1828 e 1829, con l'aggiunta delle osservazioni sugli abitanti de quei paesi di Paolo Emilio Botta (Traduzione dal francesa nell' italiano de Carlo Botta; Torino, 1841). 2 vols.

Bishop, William Henry
   Old Mexico and her lost provinces (New York, 1883).

Bustamante, Cárlos María

    Medidas para la pacificación de la America mexicana
       (México, D. F., 1820). 2 vols. in 1.

    El nuevo Bernal Diaz del Castillo, o' sea historia de
       la invasión de los Anglo-Americanos en México
       (México, D. F., 1847). 2 vols. in 1.

Chapman, Charles Edward

    A history of California: the Spanish period (New York,
       1921).

Davis, William Heath

    Seventy-five years in California -- a history of events
       and life in California: personal, political and mili-
       tary; under the Mexican régime; during the quasi-
       military government of the territory by the United
       States, and after the admission of the state to the
       Union (Douglas S. Watson, editor; San Francisco,
       1929).

Duhaut-Cilly, Auguste Bernard

    See ante, Bernard du Hautcilly, Auguste.

Fisher, Lillian Estelle

    The background of the revolution for Mexican independence
       (Boston, 1934).

    Viceregal administration in the Spanish-American colonies,
       "University of California publications in history,"
         vol. 15 (Berkeley, California, 1926).

Flett, John Smith
"Limestone," *Encyclopedia Britannica* (11th edition; Cambridge, England, 1911), vol. 16, pp. 697--98.

Forbes, Alexander
California, a history of Upper and Lower California from their first discovery to the present time comprising an account of the climate, soil, natural productions, agriculture, commerce, etc., a full view of the missionary establishments and condition of the free and domesticated Indians with an appendix relating to steam-navigation in the Pacific (San Francisco, 1919).

García Cubas, Antonio
Atlas pintoresco e histórico de los Estados Unidos Mexicanos (México, D. F., 1885)

Hayes, Benjamin; with Warner, J. J., and Widney, J. P.
An historical sketch of Los Angeles County, California, from the Spanish occupancy by the founding of the Mission San Gabriel Archangel [sic]*, September 8, 1771, to July 4, 1876* (Los Angeles, 1876).

Lippincott, Isaac
Economic development of the United States (New York and London, 1923).

McCormac, Eugene Irving
 <u>James K. Polk, a political biography</u> (Berkeley, California, 1922).

Newmark, Harris
 <u>Sixty years in Southern California, 1853--1913</u> (New York, 1916).

<u>Niles' Weekly Register, containing political, historical, geographical, scientific, statistical, economical, and biographical documents, essays and facts; together with notices of the arts and manufactures, and a record of the events of the times</u> (Baltimore, etc., 1811--49). 76 vols.

Priestley, Herbert Ingram
 <u>The Mexican nation; a history</u> (New York, 1923).

Richman, Irving Berdine
 <u>California under Spain and Mexico, 1535--1847</u> (Boston and New York, 1911).

Riva Palacio, Vicente, editor
 <u>México a través de los siglos: historia general y completa del desenvolvimiento social, político, religioso, militar, artístico, científico y literario de México desde la antigüedad más remota hasta la época actual</u> (México, D. F., y Barcelona, 1888--89). 5 vols.

San Francisco [California] Chronicle (daily) (1865—   ).

Warner, J. J.
   See ante, Hayes, Benjamin.

Whitaker, Joseph, compiler and editor
   Whitaker's Almanac (London, 1935).

Widney, J. P.
   See ante, Hayes, Benjamin.

Wood, William M.
   Wandering Sketches (Philadelphia, 1849).

World Almanac and Book of Facts for 1935 (Robert Hunt Lyman, editor; New York, 1935).

Articles in Periodicals:

Fisher, Lillian Estelle
   "Commercial conditions in Mexico at the end of the colonial period," New Mexico historical review, vol. 7 (April, 1932), pp. 143—64.
   Like Dr. Fisher's books cited elsewhere, this article is the fruit of intimate and extensive research in the documents, affording valuable insight into matters to which, despite their profound human appeal and significance, far too scanty attention has been given. The

emphasis is on the many-sided benefits to Mexico of Spain's restricted free trade regulation of 1778, following the general breakdown of the mercantilistic system; and the growing spirit of independence, stimulated by a taste of commercial liberalism and a realization of what true emancipation would mean, and by the republicanism at the time spreading over the world, is suggested. This article thus provides a natural transition to Dr. Fisher's Background of the revolution for Mexican independence, cited ante, p. 797.

Francis, Jessie Davies

"Los Angeles, area 4 square leagues, population 44," California history nugget, vol. 3 (April--May, 1930), pp. 65--71. (Map by Owen C. Coy).

An account of the founding and early years of California's first officially authorized pueblo.

"San Jose was modern 150 years ago," California history nugget, vol. 3 (December, 1930--January, 1931), pp. 114--20. (Map by Owen C. Coy).

The first of all the California pueblos was a sort of extra-official experiment, founded by Governor Neve in anticipation of enabling authority from Spain. The article here cited reviews briefly the circumstances of founding and conditions of life in Spanish and Mexican San José.

Despite its humble format, which to the casual eye suggests elementary contents, the *Nugget* is almost in its entirety made up of staff-written articles which are not only soundly based and conceived in relation to the general historical field, but represent in the majority of cases considerable original research, some of it not elsewhere summarized in print.

Harding, George L.
   See *ante*, p. 790, "Earliest Printing Collection."

Howren, Alleine
   "Causes and origin of the Decree of April 6, 1830," *Southwestern historical quarterly*, vol. 16 (April, 1913), pp. 378--422.
   An exceptionally comprehensive and able discussion based on manuscript materials in the Austin Papers at the University of Texas and transcripts from the Mexican Archives made under University of Texas auspices. Used freely, *ante*, pp. 60--63.

Paxson, Frederic Logan
   "England and Mexico, 1824--25," "University of Colorado Studies," vol. 3, #3 (June, 1906). Reprinted from the *Quarterly* of the Texas State Historical Association, vol. 9 (October, 1905), pp. 138--41.

A very concise statement, based on British Foreign Office correspondence, of the motivation of Britain's interest in Mexico in the first years of the Republic, namely: the desire to obtain precise information, looking to ultimate recognition; and apprehension lest the United States press her advantages in Mexico to create an unduly powerful sphere of influence. As early as 1325 British attaché Ward pointed out to then Foreign Minister Canning the strong probability of the annexation of Texas by the American power.

THE CHICANO HERITAGE

An Arno Press Collection

Adams, Emma H. **To and Fro in Southern California.** 1887

Anderson, Henry P. **The Bracero Program in California.** 1961

Aviña, Rose Hollenbaugh. **Spanish and Mexican Land Grants in California.** 1976

Barker, Ruth Laughlin. **Caballeros.** 1932

Bell, Horace. **On the Old West Coast.** 1930

Biberman, Herbert. **Salt of the Earth.** 1965

Casteñeda, Carlos E., trans. **The Mexican Side of the Texas Revolution (1836).** 1928

Casteñeda, Carlos E. **Our Catholic Heritage in Texas, 1519-1936.** Seven volumes. 1936-1958

Colton, Walter. **Three Years in California.** 1850

Cooke, Philip St. George. **The Conquest of New Mexico and California.** 1878

Cue Canovas, Agustin. **Los Estados Unidos Y El Mexico Olvidado.** 1970

Curtin, L. S. M. **Healing Herbs of the Upper Rio Grande.** 1947

Fergusson, Harvey. **The Blood of the Conquerors.** 1921

Fernandez, Jose. **Cuarenta Años de Legislador:** Biografia del Senador Casimiro Barela. 1911

Francis, Jessie Davies. **An Economic and Social History of Mexican California** (1822-1846). Volume I: Chiefly Economic. Two vols. in one. 1976

Getty, Harry T. **Interethnic Relationships in the Community of Tucson.** 1976

Guzman, Ralph C. **The Political Socialization of the Mexican American People.** 1976

Harding, George L. **Don Agustin V. Zamorano.** 1934

Hayes, Benjamin. **Pioneer Notes from the Diaries of Judge Benjamin Hayes, 1849-1875.** 1929

Herrick, Robert. **Waste.** 1924

Jamieson, Stuart. **Labor Unionism in American Agriculture.** 1945

Landolt, Robert Garland. **The Mexican-American Workers of San Antonio, Texas.** 1976

Lane, Jr., John Hart. **Voluntary Associations Among Mexican Americans in San Antonio, Texas.** 1976

Livermore, Abiel Abbot. **The War with Mexico Reviewed.** 1850

Loyola, Mary. **The American Occupation of New Mexico, 1821-1852.** 1939

Macklin, Barbara June. **Structural Stability and Culture Change in a Mexican-American Community.** 1976

McWilliams, Carey. **Ill Fares the Land:** Migrants and Migratory Labor in the United States. 1942

Murray, Winifred. **A Socio-Cultural Study of 118 Mexican Families Living in a Low-Rent Public Housing Project in San Antonio, Texas.** 1954

Niggli, Josephina. **Mexican Folk Plays.** 1938

Parigi, Sam Frank. **A Case Study of Latin American Unionization in Austin, Texas.** 1976

Poldervaart, Arie W. **Black-Robed Justice.** 1948

Rayburn, John C. and Virginia Kemp Rayburn, eds. **Century of Conflict, 1821-1913.** Incidents in the Lives of William Neale and William A. Neale, Early Settlers in South Texas. 1966

Read, Benjamin. **Illustrated History of New Mexico.** 1912

Rodriguez, Jr., Eugene. **Henry B. Gonzalez.** 1976

Sanchez, Nellie Van de Grift. **Spanish and Indian Place Names of California.** 1930

Sanchez, Nellie Van de Grift. **Spanish Arcadia.** 1929

Shulman, Irving. **The Square Trap.** 1953

Tireman, L. S. **Teaching Spanish-Speaking Children.** 1948

Tireman, L. S. and Mary Watson. **A Community School in a Spanish-Speaking Village.** 1948

Twitchell, Ralph Emerson. **The History of the Military Occupation of the Territory of New Mexico.** 1909

Twitchell, Ralph Emerson. **The Spanish Archives of New Mexico.** Two vols. 1914

U. S. House of Representatives. **California and New Mexico:** Message from the President of the United States, January 21, 1850. 1850

Valdes y Tapia, Daniel. **Hispanos and American Politics.** 1976

West, Stanley A. **The Mexican Aztec Society.** 1976

Woods, Frances Jerome. **Mexican Ethnic Leadership in San Antonio, Texas.** 1949

Aspects of the Mexican American Experience. 1976
Mexicans in California After the U. S. Conquest. 1976
Hispanic Folklore Studies of Arthur L. Campa. 1976
Hispano Culture of New Mexico. 1976
Mexican California. 1976
The Mexican Experience in Arizona. 1976
The Mexican Experience in Texas. 1976
Mexican Migration to the United States. 1976
The United States Conquest of California. 1976
Northern Mexico On the Eve of the United States Invasion:
    Rare Imprints Concerning California, Arizona, New Mexico, and Texas, 1821-1846. Edited by David J. Weber. 1976